# BERTHOLD FOTOTYPES E3

*Edition 3*

# BERTHOLD HEADLINES E3

1400 Titelsatzschriften nach ihrer Ähnlichkeit geordnet
1400 Headline faces arranged according to similarity
1400 caractères pour titres classés en fonction de leur similitude

Erläutert
und zusammengestellt von
Götz Gorissen
1982

BERTHOLD BERLIN *&* CALLWEY MÜNCHEN

© 1982, Juni
H. Berthold AG, 1000–Berlin 46, Teltowkanalstraße 1–4
Typographie: Götz Gorissen
Printed in Germany
Alle Rechte vorbehalten
Gesetzt mit den Fotosetzmaschinen der H. Berthold AG
«staromat», «berthold ads 3000» und «berthold apu 3608»
im Fotosatzatelier der H. Berthold AG
Grundschrift: Baskerville Book normal und
Akzidenz-Grotesk Buch mager
Druck: Kupijai & Prochnow, Berlin
Bindearbeiten: Lüderitz & Bauer Buchgewerbe GmbH, Berlin
Papier: Sprint-Offset, matt gestrichen fein holzhaltig, 90 g/qm

CIP-Kurztitelaufnahme der Deutschen Bibliothek
H.-Berthold-AG (Berlin, West):
Berthold Fototypes / erl. u. zgest. von Götz Gorissen –
Berlin: Berthold; München: Callwey.
NE: Gorissen, Götz [Hrsg.]; HST
E 3.
Berthold Headlines: 1400 Titelsatzschr. nach ihrer
Ähnlichkeit geordnet. – 1982.
ISBN 3-7667-0538-5

# *Inhalt, Contents, Sommaire*

| ERLÄUTERUNGEN | EXPLANATORY TEXTS | EXPLICATIONS |
|---|---|---|
| Einführung ................... VII | Introduction .................. VIII | Introduction ..................... IX |
| Übersichtstafel<br>　mit Klassifikationsbeispielen ..... X | Survey table with<br>　examples of classification ........ X | Tableau synoptique avec exemples<br>　de classification ................ X |
| Klassifikation der<br>　Druckschriften ............... XIII | Classification<br>　of printing typefaces .......... XII | Classification<br>　de caractères .................. XII |
| Verzeichnis der Schriftgestalter ... XIX | List of type designers .......... XVIII | Liste de créateurs ............. XVIII |
| Informationen<br>　zu den Schriftproben ...... XXXVII | Information on typeface<br>　specimens ............... XXXVIII | Informations concernant les formes<br>　de présentation ............... IXL |

| KATALOG | CATALOGUE | CATALOGUE |
|---|---|---|
| Schriftenverzeichnis ............... 1 | List of typefaces ................... 1 | Liste de caractères ................. 1 |
| Gebrochene Schriften ............. 63<br>　Gruppe I | Black Letters .................... 63<br>　Group I | Gothiques ....................... 63<br>　Groupe I |
| Renaissance-Antiqua .............. 71<br>　Gruppe II | Old Style ........................ 71<br>　Group II | Garaldes, Humanes .............. 71<br>　Groupe II |
| Barock-Antiqua ................. 107<br>　Gruppe III | Transitionals ................... 107<br>　Group III | Latines ......................... 107<br>　Groupe III |
| Klassizistische Antiqua ........... 185<br>　Gruppe IV | Modern ........................ 185<br>　Group IV | Didones ........................ 185<br>　Groupe IV |
| Serifenbetonte Linear-Antiqua .... 215<br>　Gruppe V | Slab Serifs (Square Serifs) ........ 215<br>　Group V | Mécanes ........................ 215<br>　Groupe V |
| Serifenlose Linear-Antiqua ....... 251<br>　Gruppe VI | Sans Serifs (Grotesques) ......... 251<br>　Group VI | Linéales ........................ 251<br>　Groupe VI |
| Antiqua-Varianten ............... 371<br>　Gruppe VII | Decoratives .................... 371<br>　Group VII | Variantes ....................... 371<br>　Groupe VII |
| Schreibschriften ................. 435<br>　Gruppe VIII | Scripts ......................... 435<br>　Group VIII | Scriptes, Manuaires .............. 435<br>　Groupe VIII |
| Nicht-lateinische Schriften ....... 455<br>　Gruppe IX | Non Latins ..................... 455<br>　Group IX | Caractères non-romains .......... 455<br>　Groupe IX |
| Sonderbelegungen<br>　und Layouts .................. 463 | Specials<br>　and Layouts .................. 463 | Plaquettes spéciales et<br>　schémas de disposition ......... 463 |
| Zierbuchstaben .................. 477 | Swash Letters ................... 477 | Lettres ornées ................... 477 |
| Sonderbelegungen für slawische<br>　Länder, Island, Türkei, USA ... 496 | Special layouts for slavic countries,<br>　Iceland, Turkey, USA .......... 496 | Schémas spéciaux pour pays slaves,<br>　Islande, Turquie, Etats-Unis .... 496 |

| NACHTRAGSDIENST | UP-DATING SERVICE | SERVICE DE MISE À JOUR |
|---|---|---|
| Bestellkarte ..................... 501 | Order card ...................... 501 | Carte de commande ............. 501 |

Wir danken allen, die am Zustandekommen dieses
Kompendiums beteiligt waren:
We would like to thank all those who were involved in the
compilation of this compendium:
Nous remercion tous ceux qui ont contribué à la réalisation
du présent catalogue:

Brusoni, Gianni A. – Übersetzung ins Französische
Buddée, Barbara – ads-Satz und Korrektur
Cornils, Corinna – Titelsatz und Montage
Dreyer, Bertel – Titelsatz und Montage
Gembitzki, Jörg – Titelsatz
Hirsinger, Pamela – Übersetzung ins Englische
Irmsch, Renate – ads-Satz
Marlow, Wolfgang – Organisation und Endkontrolle
Matthes, Günther – ads-Satz
Mokelke, Bruno – Korrektur
Ohse, Hartmut – Titelsatz
Prill, Christa – Datenorganisation
Schmidt-Przybylska, Alina-Jolanta, ads-Satz und Montage


Zu ganz besonderem Dank sind wir verpflichtet
Herrn Prof. Hermann Zapf, der uns wertvolle Ratschläge bei
der Unterteilung der Klassifikations-Gruppen gegeben hat,
und Herrn Hans W. Reichardt, der zahlreiche Daten über
Schriftkünstler und Entstehungsjahr der Schriften
beigesteuert hat.
Our special thanks go to Herr Prof. Hermann Zapf who gave
us valuable advice on the subdividing of the classification
groups, and to Herr Hans W. Reichardt who provided us
with a great deal of information on the designers and on the
year of origin of the typefaces.
Nous désirons en particulier exprimer notre reconnaissance
à M. le Professeur Hermann Zapf qui nous a donné de
précieux conseils sur la subdivision des groupes dans le
classements, ainsi qu'à M. Hans W. Reichardt qui nous a fourni
un grand nombre de renseignements sur les auteurs et les
années de parution des différents caractères.

# *Einführung*

Dieses Schriftenbuch lädt ein zu einer Entdeckungsreise durch den Dschungel der Schriftenvielfalt. Es versteht sich gleichzeitig als Schriftenbestimmungsbuch wie als Schriftenkompaß, mit dessen Hilfe man schnell und sicher in den Hafen der »Einzig Richtigen« findet.

Dieses Buch wendet sich zuallererst an den typographischen Gestalter, der mit einer konkret noch undeutlichen, aber gefühlsmäßig sicheren Vorstellung eine Schrift sucht, die in Klang, Anmutung und Ausdruck in vollendeter Kongruenz zur Botschaft, die es zu übermitteln gilt, steht. »E 3« ist in keiner Weise Schmalspurtypographen vonnutzen, die alles Gedruckte mit der Einheitssauce einer grauwertneutralen mittellängenhohen Grotesk (grundsätzlich minus eins) begießen.

Das Schriftenkompendium ordnet die Vielfalt, um sie zugänglich zu machen. Ähnliches ist Ähnlichem zugesellt. Mit einem Blick zeigt jede aufgeschlagene Doppelseite faszinierende Alternativen auf. Man kann präziser werden, den Ton besser treffen, ohne sich dem zeitraubenden Aufwand zu beugen, endlose Katalogreihen nach geeigneten Schriften durchforsten zu müssen.

Alle im »E 3« vorgestellten Schriften werden als »staromat«-Typenplatten für den Titelsatz angeboten. Damit präsentiert sich eine Schriftenbibliothek, die in Vielfalt und Qualität weltweit ihresgleichen sucht. Alle Schriften werden mit »the quick brown fox jumps over the lazy dog« vorgestellt. Dieser Satz enthält das komplette Alphabet. Die Schrift wird als Minuskel- und Versalzeile gezeigt, die letztere zusätzlich mit dem Ziffernsatz.

»E 3« ist mehr als ein bloßes Arbeitsbuch. Es verlockt dazu, Schriften zu vergleichen, ihre Einzelformen zu studieren, genauer und detailreicher sehen zu lernen. Man erfährt, wer die Schrift entworfen hat und wann sie erstmals vorgestellt wurde. Das unmittelbare Nebeneinander ähnlicher Schriften schärft das Auge für die Wahrnehmung von Unterschieden und sensibilisiert das Gefühl für ihren Ausdruckswert. »E 3« kann dazu beitragen, die Qualität der gedruckten Information zu verbessern. Wenn Text, Typographie und Bild die Stimmungslage des Empfängers richtig treffen, dann bringt die gelungene Schriftwahl die Nachricht unverfälscht an den Adressaten. Schrift ist zu Zeichen geronnene Sprache. Wer alles mit dem Leierton der »Ewig Gleichen« dahinnuschelt, braucht sich nicht zu wundern, daß ihm niemand mehr zuhören will.

»E 3« hebt jede Schrift aus dem Niemandsland der anonymen Masse heraus. Jeder Buchstabe, jedes Zeichen, jedes Wort der vorgestellten Schriften hat Form gefunden durch die schöpferische Leistung eines Schriftgestalters. Ohne ihn gäbe es keine Lesefreude, keinen Lesegenuß. – Was herauskommt, wenn man Technikern und Theoretikern das Handwerk überläßt, machen die auch in diesem Buch gezeigten DIN-Schriften erschreckend deutlich. Das »Verzeichnis der Schriftgestalter« zählt alle für Berthold tätigen Designer in alphabetischer Folge auf. Ihr Œuvre ist chronologisch aufgelistet.

Die Schriften sind im Hauptteil nach Ähnlichkeit geordnet. Nicht nach abstrakten, theoretischen Gesichtspunkten, sondern nach einer Methode, die sich auf das Auge als letzte gültige Instanz verläßt: die verwandte Stimmlage war beim Zusammenfügen wichtiger als das DIN-beschriebene Detail. Der Schriftgestalter kümmert sich – dem Himmel sei Dank – herzlich wenig um die Nöte, die den Klassifikateur befallen, wenn er eine aus der Art geschlagene Schrift, einen wohlgelungenen Bastard, in die rechte Rubrik einordnen muß. Herausgekommen ist für »E 3« eine Ordnung, die sich in den großen Zügen an DIN orientiert. Hundert Untergruppen gliedern die Hauptgruppen in optisch faßbare Untergruppen. Die lineare, eindimensionale Folge verdeckt natürlich Berührungspunkte und Übergänge. Ein sphärisches Modell wäre am ehesten geeignet, das Zusammenströmen und Auseinanderfließen der Stilrichtungen darzustellen. Doch unser Medium ist zweidimensional. Mit dem »E 3« ist der Versuch gewagt worden, die Gesamtheit der Druckschriften in einer praktikablen, überschaubaren Ordnung zu präsentieren.

Dieses Schriftenbuch ist eine nachdrückliche Aufforderung, sich des Reichtums der typographischen Ausdrucksmittel zu bedienen, um der gestalterischen Verödung und Gleichschaltung entgegenzuwirken. Berthold stellt das Rüstzeug zur Verfügung. Arbeiten Sie damit!

Nahezu alle Layoutsetzereien produzieren mit dem »staromat« oder anderen Berthold-Titelsetzgeräten. Dort bekommen Sie Ihre Titelsatzschriften. Falls eine Schrift mal nicht vorhanden sein sollte, kann sie von Berthold kurzfristig geliefert werden. Die meisten Titelsetzgeräte sind mit Verzerrungseinrichtungen ausgerüstet, mit denen Schriften beliebig modifiziert werden können. Die Berthold-Titelsatzschriften überzeugen durch formale Qualität, durch Konturenschärfe und tiefsatte Schwärzung. Die Schriftenbibliothek führt alles, was Rang und Namen hat in der internationalen Typographie. Das Programm lebt. Es wird ständig erweitert. Halten Sie Ihr »E 3« auf dem laufenden. Sie brauchen nichts anderes zu tun, als uns die Antwortkarte am Schluß des Buches zuzusenden. Diese Karte berechtigt den Einsender, den Nachtragsdienst kostenlos in Anspruch zu nehmen. In den Nachträgen wird jede Schrift in gleicher Weise wie in diesem Band dargestellt.

# Introduction

This typeface book invites the reader to join in on a voyage of discovery through the jungle of typeface variety. It should be regarded as both a typeface definition book and as a typeface compass with the aid of which the traveller arrives safely and speedily in the harbour of the "one and only right typeface".

This book addresses first and foremost the typographical artist who is looking for a certain typeface, and although his notion of this typeface is not yet tangibly clear, his feelings tell him with certainty of what he is looking for – a typeface which is in complete congruity with the message it is meant to convey. »E3« is of no use at all to typographers looking for short cuts and who pour a standard gravy of grey-value neutral, x-height Sans Serif (always with minus 1) over all printed matter.

This typeface compendium presumes to arrange this abundance in order to make it accessible. Similar typefaces are grouped together. Every double page opened shows, at a glance, fascinating alternatives. One can be more precise, find the right note more easily without having to submit to the time-consuming task of wading through endless catalogues looking for suitable faces.

All the typefaces presented in »E3« are available as »staromat« type plates for headline setting. Thus we obtain a typeface library which is without comparison throughout the world. All the faces are presented in the form of the sentence: "the quick brown fox jumps over the lazy dog". This sentence contains every letter of the alphabet. The typeface is shown in both lower- and upper case characters, the latter along with a set of numerals.

»E3« is more than merely a work aid. It tempts one to compare typefaces, to study their individual form, to look more closely and observe more detail. The reader discovers who has designed the face and when it was first presented. By placing similar faces directly next to each other, the reader's eye is made keener in the perception of differences and he develops more sensitivity in his feeling for their expressional value. »E3« can contribute to improving the quality of the printed information. When text, typography and images strike the right mood of the recipient, then the correct typeface has been selected successfully and the message brought unadulterated to the addressee. Type is language consolidated into characters. Someone who harps on in the same tone and says the same thing over and over again should not be surprised if no-one wants to listen any more.

»E3« throws every typeface into relief against the no-man's-land of the anonymous mass. Every character, every symbol, every word of the typefaces presented has found form thanks to the creative achievement of a typeface designer. Without him, there would be no pleasure, no enjoyment in reading. The DIN typefaces which are also shown in this book make it horrifyingly clear what comes out when this craft is left to technologists and theoreticians. The "List of Typeface Designers" presents, in alphabetical order, the names of all the designers who work with or for Berthold. Their works are listed chronologically.

In the main section, the typefaces are listed according to similarity. Not according to abstract, theoretical aspects, but according to a method which relies on the eye as the ultimate valid judge; the related pitch was more important in the composition than the details described in the DIN standards. The typeface designer shows very little concern – thank goodness – for the needs of the classification pedant who has to classify a typeface which has been isolated from its kin, a successful bastard, under the correct heading. As a result, »E3« has acquired a classification system which by and large is based on the DIN standards. A hundred sub-divisions serve to arrange the main groups in optically tangible sub-groups. The linear, one-dimensional sequence conceals points of contact and transitions of course. A spherical model would be best suited in illustrating the converging and diverging of stylistic trends. With »E3«, we have dared to make an attempt to present the whole complex of printing typefaces in a practical, easy-to-follow arrangement.

This book of typefaces is a definite challenge to make use of the rich variety of the expressive means available in typography in order to counteract the creative desolation and trend to uniformity of form. Berthold provides the tools. It is up to you to make use of them.

Nearly all layout shops work with the »staromat« or other Berthold headline-setting machines. It is there that you can obtain your headline faces. If a specific face is not available from time to time, then this can be obtained from Berthold at short notice. Most headline-setting machines are equipped with distortion devices, by means of which typefaces can be modified as desired. The Berthold headline faces convince the customer by their formal quality, by their sharpness of contours and by their rich density. The typeface library includes everything of importance and reputation in international typography. The program is alive. It is constantly growing.

Keep your »E3« up to date. All you need to do is to send in the reply card at the back of this book. This card entitles the sender to take advantage of our up-dating service free of charge. In the supplements, each typeface is presented in the same way as in this main volume.

# *Introduction*

Ce catalogue veut inviter le lecteur à explorer le foisonnement des caractères typographiques. D'autre part, ce livre devrait être un guide, voire une boussole, pour diriger l'utilisateur vers le choix du «juste caractère au juste endroit».

«E 3» s'adresse en tout premier lieu aux spécialistes d'une certaine recherche typographique, qui désirent trouver un type de caractère dont l'aspect et la signification correspondent pleinement au message qu'il est appelé à transmettre. «E 3» n'est, par exemple, pas du tout conçu pour être utilisé par des typographes «bas de gamme» prêts à présenter n'importe quel imprimé par un caractère neutre et fade, bon à tout faire.

Dans notre catalogue, la matière évidemment complexe est présentée de telle manière qu'elle en devienne plus accessible. Les caractères sont groupés en fonction de leur similitude. Il suffit de jeter un coup d'œil sur l'une des pages doubles pour se rendre compte des choix intéressants qui y figurent. Ce système permet à l'utilisateur de sélectionner ses caractères avec rapidité et précision, sans devoir feuilleter de fastidieux catalogues, ce qui fait perdre un temps précieux et, en plus, complique la recherche.

Tous les caractères figurant dans le manuel «E 3» sont présentés comme plaquettes de caractères «staromat» pour la composition des titres. Le résultat équivaut, pour ainsi dire, à une «bibliothèque» de caractères, sans égale dans le monde de l'impression par sa multiplicité et sa qualité. Pour la présentation de tous les caractères est utilisée la phrase anglaise "the quick brown fox jumps over the lazy dog", qui contient toutes les lettres de l'alphabet. Le caractère figure en lettres minuscules et majuscules ainsi qu'en chiffres.

«E 3» est bien plus qu'un simple instrument de travail. Il encourage le lecteur à comparer les caractères, à étudier leur formes spécifiques, à prendre conscience des détails. On apprend à connaître l'auteur des caractères, ainsi que l'année ou la période de leur parution. La juxtaposition immédiate de caractères similaires habitue l'œil à percevoir les différences et affine le sentiment de leur valeur expressive. «E 3» peut donc contribuer à améliorer la qualité des messages imprimés. Si tel texte, telle présentation typographique et telles images ont pour résultat d'éveiller l'intérêt et l'attention du destinataire, le choix du caractère équivaut, quant à lui, à une signification et à une correspondance de même nature. Le caractère personnalise la langue en la revêtant de signes expressifs. Qui se limite à un seul caractère, toujours le même, ne peut s'étonner de ne trouver guère d'audience.

«E 3» fait sortir chaque caractère d'une masse par définition anonyme. Chaque lettre, chaque signe, chaque mot, formulés par les caractères ainsi présentés, trouvent leur forme par le pouvoir de l'esprit créatif d'un expert en la matière. Sans cette créativité, la lecture ne susciterait aucune joie, aucun plaisir. Laisser le travail manuel à des spécialistes s'est assurer la clarté des caractères DIN qui figurent dans ce catalogue. La «liste des auteurs de caractères» énumère, par ordre alphabétique, l'ensemble des graphistes qui travaillent pour Berthold. Leurs réalisations sont présentées de manière chronologique.

Comme nous l'avons dit, les caractères sont classés, dans la section principale, en fonction de leur similitude, et non pas selon des critères abstraits et théoriques, mais bien en laissant à l'œil le jugement définitif: la parenté d'ordre esthétique a joué, dans la juxtaposition des caractères, un rôle plus important que les détails décrits dans les normes DIN. L'auteur de caractères n'est pas entravé – on s'en félicite – par les contraintes qui conditionnent le travail du classificateur, quand il doit précisément classer les caractères dans les rubriques correspondantes. Dans l'ensemble, la disposition de la matière, dans le catalogue «E 3», s'inspire des normes DIN. Les groupes principaux sont subdivisés en sous-groupes au nombre de 100, le tout constituant un tableau synoptique clair. La succession des caractères, linéaire et unidimensionnelle, comprend naturellement des points de contact et des transferts ou passages entre un sous-groupe et tel autre. Certes, la façon la plus appropriée de présenter la matière, la mise en évidence des confluances et des ramifications entre les divers styles d'écriture, aurait été un modèle sphérique. Mais notre «medium» étant bidimensionnel, nous nous sommes efforcés de présenter la totalité des caractères d'imprimerie dans un classement synoptique et facilement utilisable dans l'activité pratique de tous les jours.

Notre catalogue a donc été réalisé dans le but de présenter une grande variété de caractères, de façon à stimuler l'imagination des graphistes et à combattre la monotonie d'une présentation typographique uniforme et dénuée de toute expressivité. Berthold a créé l'outil. A vous maintenant de vous en servir!

La plupart des titreuses sont équipées de dispositifs spéciaux qui permettent de modifier les caractères à volonté. Les phototitreuses Berthold se distinguent par la qualité formelle, la netteté des contours et le noircissement complet des caractères. La «bibliothèque» de caractères que nous vous présentons constitue, pour ainsi dire, la bible de l'art typographique international. C'est un programme vivant qui s'élargit constamment. Pour tenir à jour votre «E 3», vous n'avez qu'à remplir et nous retourner la carte-réponse figurant à la fin du catalogue. Sans frais de votre part, vous pourrez ainsi profiter de nos services pour tout ce qui est prévu dans les suppléments du présent catalogue. Dans ces suppléments, les caractères sont présentés de la même façon que dans le catalogue principal.

| Leitschrift | Seite | Leitschrift | Seite |
|---|---|---|---|
| **Gebrochene Schriften, Gruppe I**  Black Letters – Caractères «allemands» (Gothiques) | | [22] LSC Caslon No. 223 | 139 |
| [1] Breda-Gotisch | 65 | [23] Century Schoolbook | 143 |
| [2] Alte Schwabacher | 65 | [24] *Century Schoolbook* | 145 |
| [3] Weiß-Rundgotisch | 65 | [25] Cheltenham | 149 |
| [4] Walbaum-Fraktur | 67 | [26] *Cheltenham* | 155 |
| [5] Breite Kanzlei | 67 | [27] Promotor | 157 |
| [6] Tannenberg | 69 | [28] Souvenir | 159 |
| **Renaissance-Antiqua, Gruppe II**  Old Style – Garaldes, Humanes | | [29] *Souvenir* | 173 |
| | | **Klassizistische Antiqua, Gruppe IV**  Modern – Antiqua classique (Didones) | |
| [7] Horley Old Style | 73 | [30] Augustea | 187 |
| [8] *Horley Old Style* | 75 | [31] *Augustea* | 189 |
| [9] Garamond | 77 | [32] Bodoni-Antiqua | 193 |
| [10] *Garamond* | 85 | [33] *Bodoni* | 199 |
| [11] Trump-Mediäval | 91 | [34] Bodoni-Antiqua | 205 |
| [12] *Trump-Mediäval* | 95 | [35] *Bodoni* | 207 |
| [13] Garamond | 97 | [36] Firenze | 209 |
| [14] *Garamond* | 101 | [37] Britannic | 211 |
| [15] Zapf Chancery | 103 | **Serifenbetonte Linear-Antiqua, Gruppe V**  Slab Serifs (Square Serifs) – Mécanes | |
| [16] *Zapf Chancery* | 105 | [38] Melior | 217 |
| **Barock-Antiqua, Gruppe III**  Transitionals – Latines | | [39] *Melior* | 221 |
| [17] Caslon Buch | 109 | [40] Clarendon | 223 |
| [18] *Caslon Buch* | 117 | [41] Rockwell | 225 |
| [19] Baskerville | 125 | [42] *Rockwell* | 237 |
| [20] *Baskerville* | 129 | [43] **Rockwell** | 239 |
| [21] LSC Caslon No. 223 | 133 | | |

| Leitschrift | Seite | Leitschrift | Seite |
|---|---|---|---|
| [44] Clarendon | 243 | [67] AG Buch Rounded | 357 |
| [45] Old Towne No. 536 | 243 | [68] Benguiat Gothic | 361 |
| [46] Thunderbird | 247 | [69] Poppl Leporello | 363 |
| [47] Latin | 247 | [70] Plural | 367 |
| [48] Italia | 249 | | |

Serifenlose Linear-Antiqua, Gruppe VI
Sans Serifs (Grotesques) – Linéales

Antiqua-Varianten, Gruppe VII
Decoratives – Variantes

| Leitschrift | Seite | Leitschrift | Seite |
|---|---|---|---|
| [49] Newtext | 253 | [71] Eckmann | 373 |
| [50] Newtext | 259 | [72] Mark Twain | 377 |
| [51] Optima | 261 | [73] Calligraphia | 383 |
| [52] Optima | 273 | [74] Santana | 385 |
| [53] Gill Sans | 275 | [75] Gesh Export 233 | 389 |
| [54] Futura | 275 | [76] Westminster | 391 |
| [55] Futura | 283 | [77] AG Buch Outline | 393 |
| [56] Futura | 285 | [78] AG Buch White | 405 |
| [57] Univers 45 | 289 | [79] AG Buch Inline | 413 |
| [58] Univers 46 | 307 | [80] Bodoni-Antiqua | 417 |
| [59] Univers 49 | 315 | [81] Churchward Design 70 | 421 |
| [60] Univers 59 | 319 | [82] Churchward Design 70 | 425 |

Schreibschriften, Gruppe VIII
Scripts – Scriptes, Manuaires

| Leitschrift | Seite | Leitschrift | Seite |
|---|---|---|---|
| [61] Univers 57 | 325 | [83] Churchward Brush | 437 |
| [62] Univers 58 | 333 | [84] Churchward Brush | 439 |
| [63] Univers 53 | 337 | [85] Choc | 441 |
| [64] Grotesk | 345 | [86] El Greco | 443 |
| [65] Churchward Design 70 | 347 | [87] Poppl Residenz | 445 |
| [66] Churchward Design 70 | 355 | [88] Piccadilly-Script | 451 |

# Classification of Printing Typefaces
# Classification de Caractères

The typefaces presented in this compendium are arranged according to their similarity. Upon looking up any random typeface, the reader finds in immediate proximity – on the same double page – a selection of other typefaces which are either formally or stylistically similar. Similar faces are all grouped together. By placing similar faces next to each other, the differences between them become more apparent, the eye is made more keen.

The block letter types are arranged according to the DIN-classification in a modified form. The order of the main groups was largely taken over unchanged. As opposed to the DIN arrangement, we have placed the broken types at the beginning – the first printed book was set in a broken type. We have combined DIN groups I and II "Humanists" and "Garaldes" (Old Style) to form group II. The DIN group IX "Graphics" was omitted altogether. Where any typeface from this group shows any "handwriting" characteristics, it can be found in group VIII "Scripts".

The nine main groups have been divided into a hundred subsidiary groups – these being orientated on the present Berthold typeface library. It was only possible to offer a direct critical comparison of related typefaces by means of this fine differentiation. The number of the sub-groups necessary for this is determined by the variety, the range and the volume of the typeface material to be classified. Activity in the creation of new typefaces is as lively and even more so than it has ever been in the past. Certainly some of the material awaiting us in the next few years will not fit into the classification scheme draughted for this book. We shall have to be flexible and extend and modify the subsidiary groups to accomodate the typefaces available.

We would ask you to regard the names given to the subsidiary groups as a suggestion; in some cases alternative designations were discussed. It would be desirable if the names for the subsidiary groups could find widespread approval on the basis of competent and expert discussion.

As a mental signpost and crib, the name of one typeface belonging to each sub-group is given in italics.

C'est en fonction de leur similitude que sont classés les caractères figurant dans ce catalogue. A tel caractère précis correspond sur la même double page un grand nombre de caractères semblables de par leur forme et leur style. C'est donc selon une parenté d'ordre esthétique que sont groupés les caractères en question. Une telle disposition présente l'avantage de rendre plus visibles les différences qui existent entre eux.

La structure de ce catalogue obéit au classement DIN modifié. La nomenclature des groupes principaux a été en grande partie acceptée. Mais, ce qui n'est pas le cas dans le classement DIN, les caractères «allemands» ont été placés en tête (le premier livre imprimé le fut d'ailleurs de cette manière). Le groupe I («Renaissance vénitienne Antiqua» et «Renaissance Française Antiqua») a été, quant à lui, inclus dans le groupe principal II («Renaissance Antiqua»). Le groupe DIN «Caractères à la main Antiqua» a été supprimé. Nous retrouverons toutefois ces caractères dans le groupe VIII «Caractères d'écriture», dans la mesure où ils correspondent à un type d'écriture manuscrite.

Les groupes principaux sont l'objet de cent subdivisions ou sous-groupes, selon le nombre actuel des caractères Berthold. Seule cette subdivision, précise et détaillée, permet, pour mieux les présenter, la juxtaposition des caractères apparentés: leur comparaison en est ainsi facilitée. Ce sont la diversité des caractères, leur largeur et leur grosseur qui déterminent le nombre des sous-groupes jugés nécessaires. Mais il ne faut pas cacher que l'apparition de nouveaux caractères d'imprimerie est aujourd'hui fréquente – comme il en fut rarement dans le passé – et que toutes les nouveautés qui verront le jour ces prochaines années ne pourront trouver toujours place dans le classement proposé dans ce catalogue. Il nous faut donc prévoir la possibilité d'élargir et de modifier les sous-groupes en fonction du nombre de caractères qui apparaîtront sur le marché un proche avenir.

Les dénominations des sous-groupes ne sont nullement définitives. Dans nombre de cas, d'autres noms pourront être pris en considération. Quoi qu'il en soit, il serait souhaitable que lors de discussions entre spécialistes on pût arriver, à ce sujet, à un accord aussi large que possible.

Chaque sous-groupe qui figure dans la liste suivante comprend un caractère-guide en italique, qui tient lieu d'indicateur théorique et facilite ainsi la compréhension de l'ouvrage.

# Klassifikation der Druckschriften

Die in diesem Kompendium vorgestellten Schriften sind nach Ähnlichkeit geordnet. Wer eine x-beliebige Schrift aufschlägt, findet in ihrem direkten Umfeld – auf der gleichen Doppelseite – eine Vielzahl formal und stilistisch ähnlicher Schriften. Ähnliches wird zu Verwandtem gesellt. In diesem Nebeneinander werden Unterschiede deutlicher, wird das Auge geschärft.

Die Gliederung der Druckschriften erfolgt nach modifizierter DIN-Klassifikation. Die Folge der Hauptgruppen wurde weitgehend übernommen. Anders als bei DIN werden die Gebrochenen Schriften an den Anfang gestellt – das erste gedruckte Buch wurde aus einer gebrochenen Schrift gesetzt. Die Gruppe I »Venezianische Renaissance-Antiqua« und »Französische Renaissance-Antiqua« haben wir in einer Hauptgruppe II »Renaissance-Antiqua« zusammengefaßt. Die DIN-Gruppe »Handschriftliche Antiqua« wurde aufgelöst. Soweit die dort versammelten Schriften tatsächlich Handschriftcharakter aufweisen, finden wir diese in der Gruppe VIII »Schreibschriften« wieder.

Die Hauptgruppen wurden – orientiert an dem aktuellen Berthold-Schriftenbestand – in hundert Untergruppen gegliedert. Erst diese feine Differenzierung erlaubte es, verwandte Schriften in direktem Nebeneinander zum beurteilenden Vergleich anzubieten. Die Zahl der dazu notwendigen Untergruppen wird von der Mannigfaltigkeit, der Spannweite und dem Umfang des zu ordnenden Schriftenangebots diktiert. Das Schriftschaffen ist lebendig wie selten zuvor. Sicherlich wird so manches, was uns in den nächsten Jahren erwartet, nicht in die für dieses Buch entwickelte Gliederung passen. Wir werden die Untergruppen dem Schriftenangebot entsprechend flexibel erweitern und modifizieren müssen.

Die Bezeichnungen der Untergruppen bitten wir als Vorschlag zu werten: in dem einen oder anderen Fall standen alternative Bezeichnungen zur Debatte. Es wäre zu wünschen, wenn in fachlich kompetenter Auseinandersetzung auch für die Namensgebung der Untergruppen ein breiter Konsens gefunden werden könnte.

Jeder Untergruppe haben wir in dieser Übersicht als gedanklichen Wegweiser und Eselsbrücke in *Kursiv* eine Leitschrift zugeordnet. (Siehe auch Seite 10 und 11.)

**Gebrochene Schriften, Gruppe I**
**Black Letters**
**Caractères «allemands» (Gothiques)**

1 Gotisch
  Textura
  Gothique
  *Breda-Gotisch*
2 Schwabacher
  Schwabacher
  Caractère dit de Schwabach
  *Alte Schwabacher*
3 Rundgotisch
  Rotunda
  Gothic rond
  *Weiß-Rundgotisch*
4 Fraktur
  Fraktur
  Caractère allemand «Fraktur»
  *Walbaum-Fraktur*
5 Kanzlei
  Chancery
  Caractère allemand «Kanzlei»
  *Breite Kanzlei*
6 Sonstige
  Others
  Autres
  *Tannenberg*

**Renaissance-Antiqua, Gruppe II**
**Old Style**
**Renaissance-Antiqua (Garaldes, Humanes)**

7 Venezianische Renaissance-Antiqua
  Venetian Old Style
  Renaissance vénitienne Antiqua
  *Horley Old Style normal*
8 Venezianische Renaissance-Antiqua, kursive
  Venetian Old Style, italic
  Renaissance vénitienne Antiqua, italique
  *Horley Old Style kursiv*
9 Französische Renaissance-Antiqua
  French Old Style
  Renaissance française Antiqua
  *Garamond normal*

10 Französische Renaissance-Antiqua, kursive
French Old Style, italic
Renaissance française Antiqua, italique
*Garamond kursiv*

11 Jüngere Renaissance-Antiqua
Old Style (Early Renaissance)
Renaissance Antiqua récente
*Trump-Mediäval normal*

12 Jüngere Renaissance-Antiqua, kursive
Old Style, italic (Early Renaissance)
Renaissance Antiqua récente, italique
*Trump-Mediäval kursiv*

13 Renaissance-Antiqua, schmale
Old Style, condensed
Renaissance Antiqua, étroit
*Garamond schmalmager*

14 Renaissance-Antiqua, kursiv schmale
Old Style, italic condensed
Renaissance Antiqua, étroit
*Garamond kursiv schmalmager*

15 Kalligraphische Schriften
Calligraphic
Caractères calligraphiques
*Zapf Chancery normal*

16 Kalligraphische Schriften, kursive
Calligraphic, italic
Caractères calligraphique, italique
*Zapf Chancery kursiv*

**Barock-Antiqua, Gruppe III**
**Transitionals**
**Latines**

17 Englische Antiqua
English Transitional
Anglais Antiqua
*Caslon Buch normal*

18 Englische Antiqua, kursive
English Transitional, italic
Anglais Antiqua, italic
*Caslon Buch kursiv*

19 Barock-Antiqua
Transitional
Baroque Antiqua
*Baskerville normal*

20 Barock-Antiqua, kursive
Transitional, italic
Baroque Antiqua, italique
*Baskerville kursiv*

21 Holländische Antiqua
Dutch Transitional
Hollandais Antiqua
*LSC Caslon No. 223 mager*

22 Holländische Antiqua, kursive
Dutch Transitional, italic
Hollandais Antiqua, italique
*LSC Caslon No. 223 kursiv mager*

23 Jüngere Barock-Antiqua
Early Transitional
Baroque Antiqua récent
*Century Schoolbook normal*

24 Jüngere Barock-Antiqua, kursive
Early Transitional, italic
Baroque Antiqua, italique
*Century Schoolbook kursiv*

25 Barock-Antiqua, schmale
Transitional, condensed
Baroque Antiqua, étroit
*Cheltenham schmalmager*

26 Barock-Antiqua, kursiv schmale
Transitional, condensed italic
Baroque Antiqua, italique étroit
*Cheltenham kursiv schmal*

27 Barock-Antiqua, breite
Transitional, extended
Baroque Antiqua, large
*Promotor*

28 Sonstige
Others
Autres
*Souvenir mager*

29 Sonstige, kursive
Others, italic
Autres, italique
*Souvenir kursiv mager*

**Klassizistische Antiqua, Gruppe IV**
**Modern**
**Antiqua classique (Didones)**

30 Neoklassizistische Antiqua
Neo-Classicist
Antiqua néo-classique
*Augustea normal*

31 Neoklassizistische Antiqua, kursive
Neo-Classicist, italic
Antiqua néo-classique, italique
*Augustea kursiv*

32 Klassizistische Antiqua
Modern Face
Antiqua classique
*Bodoni-Antiqua normal*

33 Klassizistische Antiqua, kursive
Modern Face, italic
Antiqua classique, italique
*Bodoni kursiv*

34 Klassizistische Antiqua, schmale
Modern Face, condensed
Antiqua classique, étroit
*Bodoni-Antiqua schmal*

35 Klassizistische Antiqua, kursiv schmale
Modern Face, condensed italic
Antiqua classique, italique étroit
*Bodoni kursiv schmal*

36 Sonstige
   Others
   Autres
   *Firenze*
37 Sonstige, kursive
   Others
   Autres
   *Britannic kursiv fett*

**Serifenbetonte Linear-Antiqua, Gruppe V**
**Slab Serifs (Square Serifs)**
**Linéar Antiqua avec empattements (Mécanes)**

38 Serifenbetonte Antiqua
   Legibility Faces
   Antiqua de transition
   *Melior normal*
39 Serifenbetonte Antiqua, kursive
   Legibility Faces, italic
   Antiqua de transition, italique
   *Melior kursiv*
40 Clarendon
   Clarendon
   Clarendon
   *Clarendon mager*
41 Egyptienne
   Egyptian
   Egyptienne
   *Rockwell mager*
42 Egyptienne, kursive
   Egyptian, italic
   Egyptienne, italique
   *Rockwell kursiv mager*
43 Serifenbetonte Linear-Antiqua, schmale
   Slab Serifs, condensed
   Linéar Antique avec empattements, étroit
   *Rockwell schmal*
44 Serifenbetonte Linear-Antiqua, breite
   Slab Serifs, extended
   Linéar Antique avec empattements, large
   *Clarendon breitfett*
45 Italienne
   Italienne
   Italienne
   *Old Towne No. 536*
46 Tuscan
   Tuscan
   Tuscan
   *Thunderbird extraschmal*
47 Latin
   Latin
   Latin
   *Latin fett*
48 Sonstige
   Others
   Autres
   *Italia normal*

**Serifenlose Linear-Antiqua, Gruppe VI**
**Sans Serifs (Grotesques)**
**Linéar Antiqua sans empattements (Linéales)**

49 Serifs
   Serifs
   Serifs
   *Newtext Buch*
50 Serifs, kursive
   Serifs, italic
   Serifs, italique
   *Newtext Buch kursiv*
51 Lapidar
   Lapidar
   Lapidaire
   *Optima normal*
52 Lapidar, kursive
   Lapidar, italic
   Lapidaire, italique
   *Optima kursiv*
53 Lapidar, schmale
   Lapidar, condensed
   Lapidaire, étroit
   *Gill Sans extra schmalfett*
54 Ältere Grotesk
   Grotesque
   Grotesque ancien
   *Futura Buchschrift*
55 Ältere Grotesk, kursive
   Grotesque, italic
   Grotesque ancien, italique
   *Futura Buchschrift schräg*
56 Ältere Grotesk, schmale
   Grotesque, condensed
   Grotesque ancien, étroit
   *Futura schmalmager*
57 Jüngere Grotesk
   Late Grotesque
   Grotesque moderne
   *Univers 45*
58 Jüngere Grotesk, kursive
   Late Grotesque, italic
   Grotesque moderne, italique
   *Univers 46*
59 Jüngere Grotesk, enge
   Late Grotesque, narrow
   Grotesque moderne, très étroit
   *Univers 49*
60 Jüngere Grotesk, engschmale
   Late Grotesque, narrow condensed
   Grotesque moderne, étroit
   *Univers 59*
61 Jüngere Grotesk, schmale
   Late Grotesque, medium condensed
   Grotesque moderne, demi-étroit
   *Univers 57*

62 Jüngere Grotesk, kursiv schmale
   Late Grotesque, condensed italic
   Grotesque moderne, italique étroit
   *Univers 58*
63 Jüngere Grotesk, breite
   Late Grotesque, extended
   Grotesque moderne, large
   *Univers 53*
64 Jüngere Grotesk, kursiv breite
   Late Grotesque, extended italic
   Grotesque moderne, italique large
   *Akzidenz-Grotesk kursiv breitfett*
65 Circle
   Geometric Sans Serif
   Circle
   *Churchward Design 70 normal*
66 Circle, kursive
   Geometric Sans Serif, italic
   Circle, italique
   *Churchward Design 70 kursiv*
67 Gerundete Grotesk
   Rounded
   Rounded
   *AG Buch Rounded halbfett*
68 Gerundete Grotesk, kursive
   Rounded, italic
   Rounded, italique
   *Benguiat Gothic kursiv*
69 Sonstige
   Others
   Autres
   *Poppl Leporello*
70 Sonstige, kursive
   Others, italic
   Autres, italique
   *Plural*

**Antiqua-Varianten, Gruppe VII**
**Decoratives**
**Variantes**

71 Jugendstil
   Art Nouveau
   Art Nouveau
   *Eckmann*
72 Fancy
   Fancy
   Fancy
   *Mark Twain*
73 Fancy, kursive
   Fancy, italic
   Fancy, italique
   *Calligraphia*
74 Pop
   Pop
   Pop
   *Santana*

76 Stencil
   Stencil
   Stencil
   *Gesh Export 233*
76 Computer
   Computer
   Computer
   *Westminster*
77 Outline
   Outline
   Outline
   *AG Buch Outline halbfett*
78 Shaded
   Shaded
   Shaded
   *AG Buch White halbfett*
79 Kontur
   Contour
   Contour
   *AG Buch Inline halbfett*
80 Gravur
   Engraved
   Gravure
   *Bodoni-Antiqua licht*
81 Double- und Multilines
   Double and Multilines
   Double-lines et multilines
   *Churchward Design 70 No-End*
82 Ornamented und 3 D
   Ornamented and 3 D
   Ornamented et 3 D
   *Churchward Design 70 Chisel*

**Schreibschriften, Gruppe VIII**
**Scripts**
**Scriptes, Manuaires**

83 Handschriftliche Antiqua
   Informal
   Caractère d'écriture à la main Antiqua
   *Churchward Brush normal*
84 Handschriftliche Antiqua, kursive
   Informal, italic
   Caractère d'écriture à la main Antiqua, italique
   *Churchward Brush kursiv*
85 Pinselschriften
   Brush Scripts
   Caractères à pinceau
   *Choc*
86 Federschriften
   Formal Pen
   Caractères à plume
   *el Greco*
87 Kurrent
   Current
   Kurrent
   *Poppl-Residenz*

88 Handschriften
Free Style
Caractères d'écriture à la main
*Picadilly-Script*

**Nichtlateinische Schriften, Gruppe IX**
**Non Latins**
**Caractères non-romains**

89 Griechisch
Greek
Grec
90 Kyrillisch
Cyrillic
Cyrillique
91 Arabisch
Arabic
Arabe
92 Hebräisch
Hebrew
Hébreux
93 Indische Schriften
India Typefaces
Ecritures indiennes

94 Burmesisch
Burmese
Birman
95 Siamesisch
Siamese
Siamois
96 Chinesisch
Chinese
Chinois
97 Japanisch
Japanese
Japonais
98 Koreanisch
Korean
Coréen
99 Armenisch
Armenian
Arménien
100 Koptisch
Coptic
Copte

# *List of Typeface Designers*
# *Liste des auteurs de caractères*

Included in this list are all Berthold body types (»E 2« up to and including supplement VI–81) and all the headline faces presented here in »E 3«. The first column tells us where the typeface first appeared, or, alternatively, who holds or held the last copyright. The second column states the year of original publication, the third gives the typeface name. The typefaces are arranged chronologically beneath the name of the designer. If the year of original publication is not known to the author, this is indicated by the abbreviation o.J. (no date). Where a year is given in brackets, this indicates that the typeface first appeared in the year stated, and that then a new design cut orientated on the original was made later by another designer – this new design cut is then given, along with the year of origin, after the typeface name. The names given in the first column are abbreviations for the following companies, which are listed next page in full.

Dans cette liste figurent tous les caractères pour textes Berthold («E 2» jusqu'au supplément VI–81 compris) ainsi que tous les caractères pour titres Berthold contenus dans le présent catalogue «E 3». La première colonne indique où le caractère est apparu, ou bien où se situent ou se situaient en dernier lieu les droits d'utilisation. Dans la deuxième colonne figure l'année de la première parution tandis que la troisième colonne contient les noms des caractères. Ces derniers sont classées par ordre chronologique selon le noms des graphistes qui les ont crées. Si l'année de la première parution est inconnu, au lieu de l'année figure l'abréviation «o.J.» (=s.a., c'est-à-dire: «sans année»). Les chiffres des années entre parenthèses signifient que le caractère a paru pour la première fois dans l'année indiquée. A cet égard, des modifications peuvent avoir été introduites, dans la suite, par un autre graphiste; ces modifications sont alors indiquées par le chiffre de l'année figurant après le nom du caractère. Les initiales de la première colonne désignent les noms en abrégé des entreprises, mais suivent leur nom complet et l'indication de leur siège.

# Verzeichnis der Schriftgestalter

In dieser Aufstellung sind alle Berthold-Textschriften (»E 2« bis einschließlich Nachtrag VI–81) und alle in diesem »E 3« vorgestellten Headline-Schriften aufgeführt. Die erste Spalte sagt aus, wo die Schrift erschienen ist bzw. wo die letzten Rechte liegen oder lagen. Die zweite Spalte informiert über das Jahr der ersten Veröffentlichung, die dritte bringt den Schriftennamen. Die Schriften sind jeweils unter den entsprechenden Schriftkünstlernamen chronologisch geordnet; wenn das Jahr der Erstveröffentlichung dem Verfasser unbekannt war, wurde die Schrift mit dem Kürzel o. J. (ohne Jahr) hinten angehängt. Jahreszahlen in Klammern bedeuten: die Schrift erschien erstmals in dem aufgeführten Jahr, daran orientiert entstand später ein Neuschnitt von einem anderen Schriftkünstler – dieser Neuschnitt ist mit Jahreszahl hinter dem Schriftnamen aufgeführt.

Die in der ersten Spalte genannten Namen sind Kürzel der Firmen, die nachfolgend voll ausgeschrieben sind:

| | |
|---|---|
| ATF | American Typefounders, Elizabeth, New Jersey |
| Berlingska | Berlingska Boktryckeri & Stilgjuteri AB, Lund |
| Berthold | H. Berthold AG, Berlin |
| Czech Art | Czech Art, Prag |
| Designers | Type Designers International, Los Angeles |
| Facsimile | Facsimile Fonts, Los Angeles |
| Graphic | Graphic Systems, London |
| Haas | Haas'sche Schriftgießerei AG, Münchenstein |
| Hell | Dr.-Ing. Rudolf Hell GmbH, Kiel |
| ITC | International Typeface Corp., New York |
| Lettergieterij | Lettergieterij Amsterdam, Amsterdam |
| Ludlow | Ludlow Typograph Co., Chicago |
| L & M | Ludwig & Mayer, Frankfurt am Main |
| Monotype | Monotype Corporation Ltd., Salfords, GB |
| Nebiolo | Societa Nebiolo S. p. A., Torino |
| Neufville | Fundición Tipográfica Neufville, S.A., Barcelona |
| Olive | Marcel Olive, Marseille |
| Photoscript | Photoscript Ltd., London |
| Stempel | D. Stempel AG, Frankfurt am Main |
| Stephenson | Stephenson Blake & Company Ltd., Sheffield |
| TSI | Typographic Systems Intern. Ltd., London |
| Typoart | VEB Typoart, Dresden |
| Typsettra | Typsettra Foto-Comp Ltd., Toronto |
| TypeSpectra | TypeSpectra, Inc., Dallas |
| Visual | Visual Graphics Corporation, New York |
| Wagner | Johannes Wagner, Ingolstadt |

ABOLD, THOMAS
Berthold   1972   Abold kursiv

ADLER, OTMAR F.
Berthold   1976   Black Wings

AMERICAN TYPEFOUNDERS, HAUSSCHNITTE
ATF   1885   Gold Rush
ATF   1903   Copperplate Gothic normal
ATF   1904   Copperplate Gothic schmalmager
ATF   1904   Copperplate Gothic schmal
ATF   1921   Goudy Catalogue kursiv
ATF   1925   Caslon Old Face fett
ATF   o. J.   Caslon halbfett
ATF   o. J.   Caslon schmalhalbfett
ATF   o. J.   Caslon 540 kursiv
ATF   o. J.   Engravers Roman normal
ATF   o. J.   Engravers Roman halbfett
ATF   o. J.   Franklin Gothic schmal licht
ATF   o. J.   Goudy schmal extrafett
ATF   o. J.   Goudy Mediäval
ATF   o. J.   New Caslon normal
ATF   o. J.   New Caslon kursiv
ATF   o. J.   Old Towne No. 536
ATF   o. J.   Thunderbird normal
ATF   o. J.   Thunderbird extraschmal

AUSPURG, ALBERT
Haas   1924   Castor
L & M   1930   Mona Lisa

AUSTIN, RICHARD
Monotype   1788   Bell normal
Monotype   1788   Bell kursiv

BAKER, RAY
ITC   1974   Newtext mager
ITC   1974   Newtext kursiv mager
ITC   1974   Newtext Buch
ITC   1974   Newtext Buch kursiv
ITC   1974   Newtext normal
ITC   1974   Newtext kursiv
ITC   1974   Newtext halbfett
ITC   1974   Newtext kursiv halbfett
ITC   1977   Quorum mager
ITC   1977   Quorum Buch
ITC   1977   Quorum normal
ITC   1977   Quorum halbfett
ITC   1977   Quorum Black

BARTH, A. M.; REICHEL, H.
Berthold     1972     Santana

BARZ, MANFRED
Berthold     1979     Quadriga-Antiqua normal
Berthold     1979     Quadriga-Antiqua Kapitälchen
Berthold     1979     Quadriga-Antiqua kursiv
Berthold     1979     Quadriga-Antiqua halbfett
Berthold     1979     Quadriga-Antiqua fett
Berthold     1979     Quadriga-Antiqua extrafett

BAUER, KONRAD F.; BAUM, WALTER
Neufville    1952     Imprimatur normal
Neufville    1952     Imprimatur halbfett
Neufville    1954     Imprimatur kursiv
Neufville    1954     Imprimatur fett
Neufville    1955     Imprimatur schmalfett
Neufville    1956     Volta normal
Neufville    1956     Volta halbfett
Neufville    1956     Volta fett
Neufville    1956     Folio schmalfett
Neufville    1957     Volta kursiv halbfett
Neufville    1957     Folio mager
Neufville    1957     Folio halbfett
Neufville    1959     Folio kursiv mager
Neufville    1959     Folio fett
Neufville    1959     Folio extrafett
Neufville    1959     Folio breithalbfett
Neufville    1959     Folio kursiv breithalbfett
Neufville    1962     Folio schmalmager
Neufville    1962     Folio schmalhalbfett
Neufville    1963     Folio breitfett
Neufville    1963     Impressum mager
Neufville    1964     Folio kursiv schmalfett
Neufville    1964     Impressum kursiv mager
Neufville    1964     Impressum halbfett
Neufville    1964     Impressum kursiv halbfett
Neufville    1965     Folio Buch
Neufville    1966     Folio engfett

BAUERSCHE GIESSEREI, HAUSSCHNITTE
Neufville    1880     Comstock
Neufville    1900     Manuskript-Gotisch
Neufville    1907     Venus mager
Neufville    1907     Venus halbfett
Neufville    1911     Venus dreiviertelfett
Neufville    1911     Venus breithalbfett
Neufville    1912     Venus schmalmager
Neufville    1913     Venus schmalhalbfett
Neufville    1925     Lucian halbfett
Neufville    1926     Bodoni Versal
Neufville    1927     Venus breitfett
Neufville    1948     Weiß-Antiqua fett
Neufville    1950     Futura schmalmager
Neufville    o. J.    Venus linkskursiv
Neufville    o. J.    Venus-Egyptienne halbfett
Neufville    o. J.    – kursiv halbfett

BAYER, HERBERT
ITC          (1925)   Universal (Bauhaus)

BAYERISCHES LANDESVERMESSUNGSAMT
Berthold     1967     Kursivschrift liegend Haar

BEAN, RUSSELL
Designers    1970     Washington extramager
Designers    1970     Washington mager
Designers    1970     Washington normal
Designers    1970     Washington halbfett
Designers    1970     Washington Black

BELSER, EBERHARD
Berthold     1975     Jalousette
Berthold     1975     Paperline

BENGUIAT, ED
ITC          1970     Souvenir mager
ITC          1970     Souvenir kursiv mager
ITC          1970     Souvenir normal
ITC          1970     Souvenir kursiv
ITC          1970     Souvenir halbfett
ITC          1970     Souvenir kursiv halbfett
ITC          1970     Souvenir fett
ITC          1970     Souvenir kursiv fett
ITC          1970     Souvenir fett licht
ITC          1974     Tiffany mager
ITC          1974     Tiffany normal
ITC          1974     Tiffany halbfett
ITC          1974     Tiffany fett
ITC          1974     Avant Garde Gothic Buch schmal
ITC          1974     Avant Garde Gothic schmal
ITC          1974     Avant Garde Gothic schmalhalbfett
ITC          1974     Avant Garde Gothic schmalfett
ITC          1975     Bookman mager
ITC          1975     Bookman kursiv mager
ITC          1975     Bookman normal
ITC          1975     Bookman kursiv
ITC          1975     Bookman halbfett
ITC          1975     Bookman kursiv halbfett
ITC          1975     Bookman fett
ITC          1975     Bookman kursiv fett
ITC          1975     Bookman licht
ITC          1975     Bookman Kontur
ITC          1977     Korinna kursiv
ITC          1977     Korinna kursiv halbfett
ITC          1977     Korinna kursiv fett
ITC          1977     Korinna kursiv extrafett
ITC          1978     Benguiat Buch
ITC          1978     Benguiat Buch kursiv
ITC          1978     Benguiat normal
ITC          1978     Benguiat kursiv
ITC          1978     Benguiat halbfett
ITC          1978     Benguiat kursiv halbfett
ITC          1979     Benguiat Buch schmal
ITC          1979     Benguiat Buch kursiv schmal
ITC          1979     Benguiat schmal

| | | | | | |
|---|---|---|---|---|---|
| ITC | 1979 | Benguiat kursiv schmal | ATF | 1911 | Clearface fett |
| ITC | 1979 | Benguiat schmal halbfett | ATF | 1911 | Clearface kursiv fett |
| ITC | 1979 | Benguiat kursiv schmalhalbfett | ATF | 1912 | Goudy Handtooled |
| ITC | 1979 | Benguiat Gothic Buch | ATF | 1913 | Franklin Gothic kursiv |
| ITC | 1979 | Benguiat Gothic Buch Kapitälchen | ATF | 1915 | Century Schoolbook normal |
| ITC | 1979 | Benguiat Gothic Buch kursiv | ATF | 1919 | Century Schoolbook kursiv |
| ITC | 1979 | Benguiat Gothic normal | ATF | 1923 | Century Schoolbook halbfett |
| ITC | 1979 | Benguiat Gothic normal Kapitälchen | ATF | 1928 | Bodoni-Antiqua licht |
| ITC | 1979 | Benguiat Gothic kursiv | ATF | 1928 | Bulmer normal |
| ITC | 1979 | Benguiat Gothic halbfett | ATF | 1928 | Bulmer kursiv |
| ITC | 1979 | Benguiat Gothic kursiv halbfett | ATF | 1928 | Ultra Bodoni normal |
| ITC | 1979 | Benguiat Gothic fett | ATF | 1929 | Broadway normal |
| ITC | 1979 | Benguiat Gothic kursiv fett | ATF | 1930 | Ultra Bodoni kursiv |
| | | | ATF | 1931 | Stymie mager |

BENGUIAT, ED; CARUSO, VIC

| | | | | | |
|---|---|---|---|---|---|
| ITC | 1975 | Bauhaus mager | ATF | 1931 | Stymie kursiv mager |
| ITC | 1975 | Bauhaus normal | ATF | 1931 | Stymie normal |
| ITC | 1975 | Bauhaus halbfett | ATF | 1931 | Stymie kursiv |
| ITC | 1975 | Bauhaus fett | ATF | 1931 | Stymie halbfett |
| ITC | 1975 | Bauhaus extrafett | ATF | 1931 | Stymie kursiv halbfett |
| ITC | 1975 | Bauhaus extrafett licht | ATF | 1931 | Stymie Black |
| ITC | 1974 | Korinna normal | ATF | o.J. | Cheltenham Old Style schmal |
| ITC | 1974 | Korinna halbfett | ATF | o.J. | Clearface schmalfett |
| ITC | 1974 | Korinna fett | ATF | o.J. | Franklin Gothic kursiv schmal |
| ITC | 1974 | Korinna extrafett | ATF | o.J. | Franklin Gothic Wide |
| ITC | 1974 | Korinna licht | ATF | o.J. | Typo-Script |

BENTON, MORRIS F; CLELAND, T. M.

| | | | | | |
|---|---|---|---|---|---|
| | | | Lettergieterij | 1914 | Garamont normal |

BENTON, MORRIS F.

| | | | | | |
|---|---|---|---|---|---|
| ATF | 1900 | Century normal | Lettergieterij | 1917 | Garamont Kapitälchen |
| ATF | 1900 | Century kursiv | Lettergieterij | 1918 | Garamont kursiv |
| ATF | 1902 | Engravers Old English normal | Lettergieterij | 1931 | Garamont halbfett |
| ATF | 1903 | Alternate Gothic No. 3 normal | Lettergieterij | 1931 | Garamont kursiv halbfett |
| ATF | 1904 | Franklin Gothic normal | | | |
| ATF | 1904 | Whitin Black normal | BENTON, MORRIS F.; GOODHUE, B. | | |
| ATF | 1904 | Whitin Black schmal | ATF | 1904 | Cheltenham halbfett |
| ATF | 1904/11 | Cheltenham schmal halbfett | ATF | 1905 | Cheltenham kursiv halbfett |
| ATF | 1904/11 | Cheltenham eng halbfett | ATF | 1906 | Cheltenham breithalbfett |
| ATF | 1905 | Century halbfett | ATF | 1908 | Cheltenham licht halbfett |
| ATF | 1905 | Century kursiv halbfett | ATF | o.J. | Cheltenham Old Style schmal |
| ATF | 1905 | Cheltenham kursiv fett | | | |
| ATF | 1906 | Century Old Style normal | BENTON, MORRIS F.; GOUDY, FREDERIC W. | | |
| ATF | 1906 | Century Old Style kursiv | ATF | 1921 | Goudy Catalogue normal |
| ATF | 1906 | Franklin Gothic schmal | | | |
| ATF | 1906 | Franklin Gothic extraschmal | BERNHARD, LUCIAN | | |
| ATF | 1907 | Clearface halbfett | Neufville | 1912 | Bernhard fett |
| ATF | 1907 | Clearface schmal | Neufville | 1912 | Bernhard schmalfett |
| ATF | 1907 | Engravers Old English fett | Neufville | 1925 | Bernhard Schönschrift zart |
| ITC | (1907/11) | Clearface-Serie 1979 | Neufville | 1925 | Lucian normal |
| ATF | 1908 | Clearface Gothic normal | Neufville | 1928 | Bernhard Schönschrift kräftig |
| ATF | 1908 | Clearface Gothic fett | ATF | 1929 | Bernhard Gothic halbfett |
| ATF | 1908 | Clearface Gothic extrafett | ATF | 1930 | Bernhard Gothic mager |
| ATF | 1908 | Commercial Script | ATF | 1930 | Bernhard Gothic fett |
| ATF | 1908 | Lightline Gothic | ATF | 1930 | Bernhard Modern fett |
| ATF | 1908 | Monotone Gothic | ATF | 1931 | Bernhard Gothic extrafett |
| ATF | 1909 | Century schmalhalbfett | ATF | 1937 | Bernhard Modern normal |
| ATF | 1909 | News Gothic normal | ATF | 1938 | Bernhard Modern kursiv fett |
| ATF | 1909 | News Gothic schmal | ATF | o.J. | Bernhard Modern kursiv |
| ATF | 1910 | Hobo | | | |

Berthelmann, Klaus
Berthold      1975      Bulk

Berthold, Friedrich
Berthold      1962      Primus

H. Berthold AG; Hausschnitte
Berthold      1804      Walbaum-Antiqua normal
Berthold      1804      Walbaum-Antiqua kursiv
Berthold      1860      Normande normal
Berthold      1860      Normande kursiv
Berthold      1896      Akzidenz-Grotesk schmalhalbfett
Berthold      1896      Akzidenz-Grotesk schmalfett
Berthold      1898      Akzidenz-Grotesk normal
Berthold      1902      Akzidenz-Grotesk mager
Berthold      1904      Herold Reklameschrift licht
ITC           (1904)    Korinna-Serie 1974
Berthold      1905      Sorbonne normal
Berthold      1905      Augustea normal
Berthold      1906      Augustea kursiv
Berthold      1906      Augustea halbfett
Berthold      1906      Sorbonne kursiv
Berthold      1906      Sorbonne halbfett
Berthold      1908      Sorbonne fett
Berthold      1908      Sorbonne schmalhalbfett
Berthold      1909      Akzidenz-Grotesk halbfett
Berthold      1909      Akzidenz-Grotesk fett
Berthold      1909      Akzidenz-Grotesk breit
Berthold      1911      Akzidenz-Grotesk breitmager
Berthold      1912      Akzidenz-Grotesk eng
Berthold      1912      Augustea fett
Berthold      (1913)    Berliner Grotesk mager
Berthold      (1913)    Berliner Grotesk halbfett
Berthold      1926      Augustea kursiv fett
Berthold      1926      Hochblock
Berthold      1926      Plastica
Berthold      1928      Berthold-Grotesk normal
Berthold      1929      Berthold-Grotesk fett
Berthold      1930      Bodoni-Antiqua normal
Berthold      1930      Bodoni kursiv
Berthold      1930      Bodoni-Antiqua halbfett
Berthold      1930      Bodoni kursiv halbfett
Berthold      1930      Bodoni-Antiqua fett
Berthold      1930      Bodoni kursiv fett
Berthold      1930      Bodoni-Antiqua schmalfett
Berthold      1933      Walbaum-Antiqua halbfett
Berthold      1935      Berthold-Grotesk schmal
Berthold      1935      Berthold-Grotesk schmalfett
Berthold      1952      Normande schmal
Berthold      1953      Akzidenz-Grotesk schmalmager
Berthold      1954      Regina
Berthold      1957      Akzidenz-Grotesk breitfett
Berthold      1961      Akzidenz-Grotesk breithalbfett
Berthold      1961      Baskerville normal
Berthold      1961      Baskerville Kapitälchen
Berthold      1961      Baskerville kursiv
Berthold      1961      Baskerville fett
Berthold      1965      Baskerville halbfett

Berthold      1969      Schreibmaschinenschrift
Berthold      1970      Englische Schreibschrift normal
Berthold      1972      Englische Schreibschrift halbfett
Berthold      1972      Englische Schreibschrift fett
Berthold      1972      Bodoni kursiv schmalfett
Berthold      1975      Bodoni-Antiqua schmal
Berthold      1975      Bodoni kursiv schmal
Berthold      1976      Bodoni-Antiqua schmalhalbfett
Berthold      1976      Bodoni kursiv schmalhalbfett

Berthold-Schriftenatelier
Neufville     1976      Futura fett licht
Neufville     1976      Futura extrafett schmal licht
Neufville     1976      Futura Black Art Deco Flipper
Neufville     1976      Futura Black Art Deco Flipper Outl.
Neufville     1976      Futura Black Art Deco Gravur
Neufville     1976      Futura Black Art Deco Horizont
Neufville     1976      Futura Black Art Deco Light Inline
Neufville     1976      Futura Black Art Deco Original
Neufville     1976      Futura Black Art Deco Outline
Neufville     1976      Futura Black Art Deco Point
Neufville     1976      Futura Black Art Deco Reflex Duo
Neufville     1976      Futura Black Art Deco Stripes
Neufville     1976      Futura Black Art Deco Stripes Diag.
Neufville     1976      Futura Black Art Deco Textil
Neufville     1976      Weiß-Antiqua extrafett
Neufville     1976      Weiß-Antiqua ultrafett
Neufville     1976      Weiß-Antiqua schmalfett
Neufville     1976      Weiß-Antiqua schmal extrafett
Neufville     1980      Futura extrafett licht
Neufville     1980      Futura extrafett schattiert
Neufville     o.J.      Beton Hairline
Neufville     o.J.      Futura extrafett
Neufville     o.J.      Futura schräg extrafett
Neufville     o.J.      Futura schräg schmalfett
Neufville     o.J.      Futura extrafett schmal
Neufville     o.J.      Futura schräg extrafett schmal

Bilz, W.; Simoncini, F.
L&M           1965      Life mager
L&M           1965      Life kursiv
L&M           1965      Life fett

Blass, Ernst
Berthold      1979      Schwabing Day
Berthold      1979      Schwabing Night

Bohn, Hans
Stempel       1958      Künstlerschreibschrift fett
Berthold      1974      Bohn-Script

Boldizar, Ivan
Berthold      1975      Boldiz
Berthold      1975      Janus
Berthold      1975      Triton

Bonder, Ronne; Carnase Tom
ITC           1970      Bernase Roman

XXII

| | | |
|---|---|---|
| ITC | 1970 | Bolt fett |
| ITC | 1970 | Caslon Headline |
| ITC | 1970 | Didi |
| ITC | 1970 | Gorilla |
| ITC | 1970 | Grizzly |
| ITC | 1970 | Grouch |
| ITC | 1970 | Honda Display |
| ITC | 1970 | LSC Condensed normal |
| ITC | 1970 | LSC Condensed kursiv |
| ITC | 1970 | Machine normal |
| ITC | 1970 | Machine fett |
| ITC | 1970 | Milano Roman |
| ITC | 1970 | Pioneer |
| ITC | 1970 | Stymie Hairline |
| ITC | 1970 | Tom's Roman |

Boton, Albert

| | | |
|---|---|---|
| ITC | 1976 | Eras mager |
| ITC | 1976 | Eras Buch |
| ITC | 1976 | Eras normal |
| ITC | 1976 | Eras halbfett |
| ITC | 1976 | Eras fett |
| ITC | 1976 | Eras licht |
| ITC | 1976 | Eras Kontur |

Boton, Albert; Hollenstein, Albert

| | | |
|---|---|---|
| Berthold | 1968 | Eras mager |

Brian, George

| | | |
|---|---|---|
| TypeSpectra | 1977 | Souvenir Gothic mager |
| TypeSpectra | 1977 | Souvenir Gothic kursiv mager |
| TypeSpectra | 1977 | Souvenir Gothic normal |
| TypeSpectra | 1977 | Souvenir Gothic kursiv |
| TypeSpectra | 1977 | Souvenir Gothic halbfett |
| TypeSpectra | 1977 | Souvenir Gothic kursiv halbfett |

Brignall, Colin

| | | |
|---|---|---|
| ITC | 1977 | Italia Buch |
| ITC | 1977 | Italia normal |
| ITC | 1977 | Italia halbfett |
| TSI | 1979 | Romic mager |
| TSI | 1979 | Romic normal |
| TSI | 1979 | Romic halbfett |
| TSI | 1979 | Romic fett |

Butti, A.; Novarese Aldo

| | | |
|---|---|---|
| Nebiolo | 1951 | Augustea licht |

Caflisch, Max

| | | |
|---|---|---|
| Neufville | 1952 | Columna open |

Campbell, Jerry; Isbell, Richard

| | | |
|---|---|---|
| ITC | 1981 | Isbell Buch |
| ITC | 1981 | Isbell Buch Kapitälchen |
| ITC | 1981 | Isbell Buch kursiv |
| ITC | 1981 | Isbell normal |
| ITC | 1981 | Isbell normal Kapitälchen |
| ITC | 1981 | Isbell kursiv |
| ITC | 1981 | Isbell halbfett |
| ITC | 1981 | Isbell kursiv halbfett |
| ITC | 1981 | Isbell fett |
| ITC | 1981 | Isbell kursiv fett |

Carnase, Tom; Bonder, Ronne

| | | |
|---|---|---|
| ITC | 1970 | Bernase Roman |
| ITC | 1970 | Bolt fett |
| ITC | 1970 | Caslon Headline |
| ITC | 1970 | Didi |
| ITC | 1970 | Gorilla |
| ITC | 1970 | Grizzly |
| ITC | 1970 | Grouch |
| ITC | 1970 | Honda Display |
| ITC | 1970 | LSC Condensed normal |
| ITC | 1970 | LSC Condensed kursiv |
| ITC | 1970 | Machine normal |
| ITC | 1970 | Machine fett |
| ITC | 1970 | Milano Roman |
| ITC | 1970 | Pioneer |
| ITC | 1970 | Stymie Hairline |
| ITC | 1970 | Tom's Roman |

Carnase, Tom; Lubalin, Herb

| | | |
|---|---|---|
| ITC | 1970 | Avant Garde Gothic mager |
| ITC | 1970 | Avant Garde Gothic Buch |
| ITC | 1970 | Avant Garde Gothic normal |
| ITC | 1970 | Avant Garde Gothic halbfett |
| ITC | 1970 | Avant Garde Gothic fett |

Caruso, Vic

| | | |
|---|---|---|
| ITC | 1973 | Friz Quadrata fett |
| ITC | 1979 | Clearface normal |
| ITC | 1979 | Clearface kursiv |
| ITC | 1979 | Clearface halbfett |
| ITC | 1979 | Clearface kursiv halbfett |
| ITC | 1979 | Clearface fett |
| ITC | 1979 | Clearface kursiv fett |
| ITC | 1979 | Clearface extrafett |
| ITC | 1979 | Clearface kursiv extrafett |
| ITC | 1979 | Clearface licht |
| ITC | 1979 | Clearface licht schattiert |
| ITC | 1979 | Clearface Kontur |
| ITC | 1980 | Franklin Gothic Buch |
| ITC | 1980 | Franklin Gothic Buch Kapitälchen |
| ITC | 1980 | Franklin Gothic Buch kursiv |
| ITC | 1980 | Franklin Gothic normal |
| ITC | 1980 | Franklin Gothic normal Kapitälchen |
| ITC | 1980 | Franklin Gothic kursiv |
| ITC | 1980 | Franklin Gothic halbfett |
| ITC | 1980 | Franklin Gothic kursiv halbfett |
| ITC | 1980 | Franklin Gothic fett |
| ITC | 1980 | Franklin Gothic kursiv fett |
| ITC | 1980 | Franklin Gothic licht |
| ITC | 1980 | Franklin Gothic Kontur |

Caruso, Vic; Benguiat, Ed

| | | |
|---|---|---|
| ITC | 1975 | Bauhaus mager |

| | | | | | | |
|---|---|---|---|---|---|---|
| ITC | 1975 | Bauhaus normal | | Berthold | 1970 | Churchward Brush kursiv |
| ITC | 1975 | Bauhaus halbfett | | Berthold | 1970 | Churchward Marianna normal |
| ITC | 1975 | Bauhaus fett | | Berthold | 1970 | – kursiv |
| ITC | 1975 | Bauhaus extrafett | | Berthold | 1970 | – schattiert |
| ITC | 1975 | Bauhaus extrafett licht | | Berthold | 1970 | – kursiv schattiert |
| ITC | 1974 | Korinna normal | | Berthold | 1972 | Churchward Blackbeauty normal |
| ITC | 1974 | Korinna halbfett | | Berthold | 1972 | – licht |
| ITC | 1974 | Korinna fett | | Berthold | 1972 | – schattiert |
| ITC | 1974 | Korinna extrafett | | Berthold | 1972 | Churchward Maricia normal |
| ITC | 1974 | Korinna licht | | Berthold | 1972 | – kursiv |
| | | | | Berthold | 1972 | – schattiert |

CASLON, WILLIAM
Stempel 1919 Caslon-Gotisch

Berthold 1972 – kursiv schattiert
Berthold 1972 Churchward Tua normal
Berthold 1972 Churchward Tua kursiv

CASSANDRE, A. M.
Haas 1937 Peignot mager
Haas 1937 Peignot halbfett
Haas 1937 Peignot fett

Berthold 1972 Churchward Tranquillity
Berthold 1972 – normal
Berthold 1972 – kursiv
Berthold 1972 – halbfett
Berthold 1972 – kursiv halbfett

CHAPPELL, WARREN
ATF 1938 Lydian normal

CLELAND, T. M.; BENTON, MORRIS F.
Lettergieterij 1917 Garamont normal
Lettergieterij 1917 Garamont Kapitälchen

CHURCHWARD, JOSEPH
Berthold 1969 Churchward 69 extrafett
Berthold 1969 Churchward 69 kursiv extrafett
Berthold 1969 Churchward 69 ultrafett
Berthold 1969 Churchward 69 kursiv ultrafett
Berthold 1969 Churchward 69 schmalhalbfett
Berthold 1969 Churchward 69 kursiv schmalhalbfett
Berthold 1969 Churchward 69 schmalfett
Berthold 1969 Churchward 69 kursiv schmalfett
Berthold 1970 Churchward Design 70 ultraleicht
Berthold 1970 – kursiv ultraleicht
Berthold 1970 – leicht
Berthold 1970 – kursiv leicht
Berthold 1970 – mager
Berthold 1970 – normal
Berthold 1970 – kursiv
Berthold 1970 – halbfett
Berthold 1970 – kursiv halbfett
Berthold 1970 – fett
Berthold 1970 – kursiv fett
Berthold 1970 – extrafett
Berthold 1970 – kursiv extrafett
Berthold 1970 – Chisel
Berthold 1970 – Deep Shadow normal
Berthold 1970 – Deep Shadow kursiv
Berthold 1970 – Double
Berthold 1970 – Lines
Berthold 1970 – Lines Deep Shadow normal
Berthold 1970 – Lines Deep Shadow kursiv
Berthold 1970 – Metalic
Berthold 1970 – Modern normal
Berthold 1970 – Modern kursiv
Berthold 1970 – No-End
Berthold 1970 – Sparkly normal
Berthold 1970 – Sparkly kursiv
Berthold 1970 Churchward Brush normal

Lettergieterij 1917 Garamont kursiv
Lettergieterij 1917 Garamont halbfett
Lettergieterij 1917 Garamont kursiv halbfett

COOPER, OSWALD B.
ATF 1919/24 Cooper Old Style normal
ATF 1919/24 Cooper Old Style kursiv
ATF 1921 Cooper Black normal
ATF 1921 Cooper Black kursiv
ATF 1921 Cooper Black schmal
ATF 1924 Cooper Black licht

CRAW, FREEMAN
ATF 1957 Craw Clarendon Buch
ATF 1961 Ad Lib
ATF 1966 Craw Modern normal
ATF 1966 Craw Modern kursiv
ATF o.J. Craw Clarendon licht

CROSBY, FLETCHER, FORBES
Crosby o.J. Airport

CZECH ART; HAUSSCHNITT
Czech Art 1965 Vega-Grotesk

DAVIS, WHEDON
ATF 1965 Gothic Outline Title

DESKIN, JACK
ITC 1970 Uptight normal
ITC 1970 Uptight Neon

DIETHELM, WALTER
Haas 1948 Diethelm-Antiqua normal
Haas 1948 Diethelm-Antiqua kursiv

| | | |
|---|---|---|
| Haas | 1948 | Diethelm-Antiqua halbfett |
| Haas | 1957 | Sculptura |

DISPIGNA, ANTONIO; LUBALIN, HERB
| | | |
|---|---|---|
| ITC | 1974 | Serif Gothic mager |
| ITC | 1974 | Serif Gothic normal |
| ITC | 1974 | Serif Gothic fett |
| ITC | 1974 | Serif Gothic extrafett |
| ITC | 1974 | Serif Gothic ultrafett |
| ITC | 1974 | Serif Gothic Black |
| ITC | 1974 | Serif Gothic licht |

DISPIGNA, LUBALIN, SUNDWALL
| | | |
|---|---|---|
| ITC | 1974 | Lubalin Graph mager |
| ITC | 1974 | Lubalin Graph Buch |
| ITC | 1974 | Lubalin Graph normal |
| ITC | 1974 | Lubalin Graph halbfett |
| ITC | 1974 | Lubalin Graph fett |

DOM, PETER
| | | |
|---|---|---|
| ATF | 1950 | Polka normal |
| ATF | 1950 | Polka halbfett |

DOMNING, KARL-HEINZ
| | | |
|---|---|---|
| Berthold | 1971 | Diador |
| Berthold | 1971 | Telegraph |
| Berthold | 1972 | Beat Star |
| Berthold | 1972 | Milanor |
| Berthold | 1972 | Ocean Current |
| Berthold | 1972 | Umbra 27 |
| Berthold | 1973 | Viola |
| Berthold | 1974 | Couture Antiqua |
| Berthold | 1974 | Datonga |
| Berthold | 1974 | Quadra 57 |
| Berthold | 1974 | Simone |

DOOIJES, DICK
| | | |
|---|---|---|
| Lettergieterij | 1958 | Mercator normal |
| Lettergieterij | 1958 | Mercator fett |
| Lettergieterij | 1966 | Contura |
| Lettergieterij | 1969 | Lectura normal |
| Lettergieterij | 1969 | Lectura kursiv |
| Lettergieterij | 1969 | Lectura halbfett |
| Lettergieterij | 1969 | Lectura schmalfett |

DRESCHER, ARNO
| | | |
|---|---|---|
| Wagner | 1936 | Arabella |
| Wagner | 1939 | Arabella Favorit |
| Wagner | 1955 | Antiqua 505 normal |
| Wagner | 1956 | Antiqua 505 fett |

ECKMANN, OTTO
| | | |
|---|---|---|
| Stempel | 1900 | Eckmann |

EIDENBENZ, HERMANN
| | | |
|---|---|---|
| Haas | 1945 | Graphique |
| Haas | 1953 | Clarendon kräftig |
| Haas | 1953 | Clarendon fett |

ERBAR, JACOB
| | | |
|---|---|---|
| L&M | 1926 | Erbar-Grotesk fett |
| L&M | 1929 | Erbar-Grotesk halbfett |
| L&M | 1929 | Erbar-Grotesk schmalhalbfett |
| L&M | 1936 | Candida normal |
| L&M | 1936 | Candida schmalmager |
| L&M | 1936 | Candida schmalhalbfett |
| L&M | 1937 | Candida kursiv |
| L&M | 1937 | Candida halbfett |
| L&M | 1960 | Erbar-Werkschrift |

EXCOFFON, ROGER
| | | |
|---|---|---|
| Olive | 1953 | Mistral |
| Olive | 1955 | Choc |
| Olive | 1960 | Antique Olive Nord normal |
| Olive | 1961 | Antique Olive Nord kursiv |
| Olive | 1962 | Antique Olive kompakt |
| Olive | 1963 | Antique Olive normal |
| Olive | 1964 | Antique Olive halbfett |
| Olive | 1965 | Antique Olive fett |
| Olive | 1966 | Antique Olive kursiv |
| Olive | 1967 | Antique Olive schmal |
| Olive | 1968 | Antique Olive schmalfett |
| Olive | 1968 | Antique Olive breit |
| Olive | 1969 | Antique Olive mager |

FACSIMILE FONTS; HAUSSCHNITTE
| | | |
|---|---|---|
| Facsimile | o.J. | Blippo halbfett |
| Facsimile | o.J. | Blippo Black |
| Facsimile | o.J. | Blippo Black licht |
| Facsimile | o.J. | Bookman Meola |
| Facsimile | o.J. | Buxom |
| Facsimile | o.J. | Handel Gothic normal |
| Facsimile | o.J. | Roberta |
| Facsimile | o.J. | Roberta Raised schattiert |
| Facsimile | o.J. | Uncle Bill |

FAIRBANK, ALFRED
| | | |
|---|---|---|
| Monotype | 1930 | Bembo kursiv |

FELDSTEIN, ILJA
| | | |
|---|---|---|
| Graphic | 1972 | Embrionic |

FORSBERG, KARL ERIK
| | | |
|---|---|---|
| Berlingska | 1951 | Berlin-Antiqua normal |
| Berlingska | 1954 | Carolus |

FREY, HACE
| | | |
|---|---|---|
| L&M | 1967 | Charleston |

FRIZ, ERNST
| | | |
|---|---|---|
| ITC | 1973 | Friz Quadrata normal |
| Visual | (1965) | Friz Quadrata normal |

FRUTIGER, ADRIAN
| | | |
|---|---|---|
| Haas | 1954 | Ondine |
| Haas | 1957 | Méridien normal |
| Haas | 1957 | Méridien halbfett |

| | | | | | | |
|---|---|---|---|---|---|---|
| Haas | 1957 | Méridien fett | | GOODHUE, B.; BENTON, MORRIS F. | | |
| Haas | 1957 | Univers 45 | | ATF | 1904 | Cheltenham halbfett |
| Haas | 1957 | Univers 46 | | ATF | 1905 | Cheltenham kursiv halbfett |
| Haas | 1957 | Univers 55 | | ATF | 1906 | Cheltenham breithalbfett |
| Haas | 1957 | Univers 56 | | ATF | o.J. | Cheltenham Old Style schmal |
| Haas | 1957 | Univers 65 | | GOUDY, FREDERIC W. | | |
| Haas | 1957 | Univers 66 | | ATF | 1901 | Copperplate Gothic mager |
| Haas | 1957 | Univers 75 | | ATF | 1915 | Goudy Old Style normal |
| Haas | 1957 | Univers 76 | | ATF | 1915 | Goudy Old Style kursiv |
| Haas | 1957 | Univers 85 | | Monotype | 1924 | Italian Old Style normal |
| Haas | 1957 | Univers 39 | | Monotype | 1924 | Italian Old Style kursiv |
| Haas | 1957 | Univers 49 | | Monotype | 1924 | Italian Old Style halbfett |
| Haas | 1957 | Univers 59 | | ATF | 1926 | Goudy halbfett |
| Haas | 1957 | Univers 47 | | ATF | 1926 | Goudy fett |
| Haas | 1957 | Univers 48 | | ATF | 1926 | Goudy extrafett |
| Haas | 1957 | Univers 57 | | ATF | 1926 | Goudy Heavyface |
| Haas | 1957 | Univers 58 | | GOUDY, F.W.; BENTON, M.F. | | |
| Haas | 1957 | Univers 67 | | ATF | 1921 | Goudy Catalogue normal |
| Haas | 1957 | Univers 68 | | GSCHWIND, GÜRTLER, MENGELT | | |
| Haas | 1957 | Univers 53 | | ITC | 1977 | Avant Garde Gothic schräg mager |
| Haas | 1957 | Univers 63 | | ITC | 1977 | Avant Garde Gothic Buch schräg |
| Haas | 1957 | Univers 73 | | ITC | 1977 | Avant Garde Gothic schräg normal |
| Haas | 1957 | Univers 83 | | ITC | 1977 | Avant Garde Gothic schräg halbfett |
| Haas | o.J. | Univers 65 halbfett licht | | ITC | 1977 | Avant Garde Gothic schräg fett |

FURRER, F.
Berthold 1975 Furrer Fono

HAAS'SCHE SCHRIFTGIESSEREI AG; HAUSSCHNITTE
| | | |
|---|---|---|
| Haas | 1900 | Elzévir halbfett |
| Haas | 1908 | Titania |
| Haas | 1940 | Caslon 471 normal |
| Haas | 1940 | Caslon 471 kursiv |
| Haas | 1940 | Helvetica schmalhalbfett |
| Haas | 1946 | Helvetica schmalfett |
| Haas | 1955 | Vertikal |
| Haas | 1967 | Helvetica kursiv fett |
| Haas | 1969 | Helvetica kursiv halbfett |
| Haas | 1970 | Helvetica ultraleicht |
| Haas | o.J. | Alexandria |
| Haas | o.J. | Anzeigen-Grotesk |
| Haas | o.J. | Bodoni-Antiqua halbfett |
| Haas | o.J. | Bodoni kursiv halbfett |
| Haas | o.J. | Boutique |
| Haas | o.J. | Breite Kanzlei |
| Haas | o.J. | Chrystal |
| Haas | o.J. | Clarendon schmalfett |
| Haas | o.J. | Egyptienne Filetée |
| Haas | o.J. | Etienne Modern normal |
| Haas | o.J. | Etienne schmalfett |
| Haas | o.J. | Fette Kanzlei |
| Haas | o.J. | Helvetica kursiv ultraleicht |
| Haas | o.J. | Helvetica breitfett |
| Haas | o.J. | Helvetica Diagonal |
| Haas | o.J. | Herkules |
| Haas | o.J. | Kompakte Grotesk |
| Haas | o.J. | Renaissance kursiv fett |

GANEAU, FRANÇOIS
| | | |
|---|---|---|
| Olive | 1952 | Vendôme normal |
| Olive | 1952 | Vendôme kursiv |
| Olive | 1952 | Vendôme halbfett |
| Olive | 1952 | Vendôme kursiv halbfett |
| Olive | 1952 | Vendôme fett |
| Olive | 1952 | Vendôme schmal |

GASSNER, CHRISTOF
| | | |
|---|---|---|
| Berthold | 1976 | Knirsch |
| Berthold | 1976 | Leopard |

GEARD, M.N.
Berthold 1974 Geard Graphic

GILL, ERIC
| | | |
|---|---|---|
| Monotype | 1927 | Perpetua normal |
| Monotype | 1928/30 | Gill Sans mager |
| Monotype | 1928/30 | Gill Sans kursiv mager |
| Monotype | 1928/30 | Gill Sans normal |
| Monotype | 1928/30 | Gill Sans kursiv |
| Monotype | 1928/30 | Gill Sans halbfett |
| Monotype | 1928/30 | Gill Sans kursiv halbfett |
| Monotype | 1928/30 | Gill Sans fett |
| Monotype | 1928/30 | Gill Sans schmalhalbfett |
| Monotype | 1928/30 | Gill Sans eng halbfett |

GILLÉ
Haas 1820 Lettres Ornées

| | | |
|---|---|---|
| Haas | o.J. | Renaissance schmal |
| Haas | o.J. | Römische Zirkular |
| Haas | o.J. | Titania |

**Harling, Robert**
| | | |
|---|---|---|
| Stephenson | 1939 | Chisel |

**Dr.-Ing. Rudolf Hell GmbH; Hausschnitte**
| | | |
|---|---|---|
| Hell | 1968 | Digi-Grotesk Serie S schmal |
| Hell | 1968 | – schmal kräftig |

**Hofelich, Ursula**
| | | |
|---|---|---|
| Berthold | 1972 | Klio |

**Hoffmann, H.**
| | | |
|---|---|---|
| Berthold | 1901 | Herold Reklameschrift |
| Berthold | 1904 | Herold schmal |
| Berthold | 1908 | Block normal |
| Berthold | 1919 | Block schwer |
| Berthold | 1922 | Block schmal |
| Berthold | 1926 | Block eng |
| Berthold | 1927 | Block kursiv |

**Hoefer, Karlgeorg**
| | | |
|---|---|---|
| L&M | 1962 | Permanent halbfett |
| L&M | 1963 | Permanent breithalbfett |

**Hoffmeister, Heinrich**
| | | |
|---|---|---|
| Stempel | 1909 | Madison mager |
| Stempel | 1909 | Madison halbfett |
| Stempel | 1919 | Madison fett |
| Stempel | 1919 | Madison schmalmager |
| Stempel | 1922 | Madison schmalhalbfett |

**Höhnisch, Walter**
| | | |
|---|---|---|
| L&M | 1935 | Skizze |
| L&M | 1939 | Stop 2 |
| L&M | 1957 | Express |

**Hollenstein, Albert**
| | | |
|---|---|---|
| Berthold | o.J. | Brasilia normal |
| Berthold | o.J. | Brasilia halbfett |
| Berthold | o.J. | Roc mager |
| Berthold | o.J. | Roc normal |

**Hollenstein, Albert; Boton, Albert**
| | | |
|---|---|---|
| Berthold | 1968 | Eras mager |
| ITC | 1976 | Eras mager |

**Hughes, Charles E.**
| | | |
|---|---|---|
| ATF | 1966 | Century Nova |

**Isbell, Richard**
| | | |
|---|---|---|
| ATF | 1965 | Americana normal |
| ATF | 1965 | Americana halbfett |

**Isbell, Richard; Campbell, Jerry**
| | | |
|---|---|---|
| ITC | 1981 | Isbell Buch |
| ITC | 1981 | Isbell Buch Kapitälchen |
| ITC | 1981 | Isbell Buch kursiv |
| ITC | 1981 | Isbell normal |
| ITC | 1981 | Isbell normal Kapitälchen |
| ITC | 1981 | Isbell kursiv |
| ITC | 1981 | Isbell halbfett |
| ITC | 1981 | Isbell kursiv halbfett |
| ITC | 1981 | Isbell fett |
| ITC | 1981 | Isbell kursiv fett |

**Jackson, Johnstone, Mason, Meynell**
| | | |
|---|---|---|
| Monotype | 1912 | Imprint normal |
| Monotype | 1912 | Imprint kursiv |
| Monotype | 1912 | Imprint halbfett |
| Monotype | 1912 | Imprint kursiv halbfett |

**Jaeger, Gustav**
| | | |
|---|---|---|
| Berthold | 1973 | Jumbo normal |
| Berthold | 1973 | Jumbo kursiv |
| Berthold | 1973 | Mark Twain |
| Berthold | 1973 | Pinocchio |
| Berthold | 1973 | Sacher |
| Berthold | 1976 | Komet |
| Berthold | 1976 | Semin-Antiqua |
| Berthold | 1977 | Seneca normal |
| Berthold | 1977 | Seneca kursiv |
| Berthold | 1977 | Seneca halbfett |
| Berthold | 1977 | Seneca fett |
| Berthold | 1977 | Seneca extrafett |
| Berthold | 1979 | Seneca mager |
| Berthold | 1980 | Aja |

**Jäntsch, Günter**
| | | |
|---|---|---|
| Berthold | 1973 | Pierrot |
| Berthold | 1975 | Persona Black |
| Berthold | 1981 | Plural |

**Jannon**
| | | |
|---|---|---|
| Haas | (1621) | Garamont normal |
| Haas | (1621) | Garamont kursiv |

**Johnstone, Jackson, Mason, Meynell**
| | | |
|---|---|---|
| Monotype | 1912 | Imprint normal |
| Monotype | 1912 | Imprint kursiv |
| Monotype | 1912 | Imprint halbfett |
| Monotype | 1912 | Imprint kursiv halbfett |

**Jost, Heinrich**
| | | |
|---|---|---|
| Neufville | 1930 | Beton Open |
| Neufville | 1930 | Beton extrafett |
| Neufville | 1931 | Beton mager |
| Neufville | 1931 | Beton halbfett |
| Neufville | 1931 | Beton fett |
| Neufville | 1936 | Beton schmalfett |

**Kaden, Joel; Stan, Tony**
| | | |
|---|---|---|
| ITC | 1974 | American Typewriter mager |
| ITC | 1974 | American Typewriter normal |

| | | | | | |
|---|---|---|---|---|---|
| ITC | 1974 | American Typewriter fett | Berthold | 1972 | Akzidenz-Grotesk Buch schmalfett |
| ITC | 1974 | American Typewriter schmalmager | Berthold | 1972 | – schmalhalbfett |
| ITC | 1974 | American Typewriter schmal | Berthold | 1972 | – breitmager |
| ITC | 1974 | American Typewriter schmalfett | Berthold | 1972 | – breit |
| ITC | 1974 | American Typewriter fett licht | Berthold | 1972 | – breithalbfett |
| | | | Berthold | 1972 | – breitfett |

KIRN, JULIUS
Stempel 1938 Bison

KIS, NICHOLAS
Stempel (1690) Janson-Antiqua normal

KLAUSS, KARL
Berthold 1935 Arkona normal
Berthold 1935 Arkona halbfett

KLUMPP, E. J.
ATF 1956 Murray Hill

KOCH, RUDOLF
Stempel 1927 Kabel leicht
Stempel 1928 Kabel grob
Stempel 1928 Kabel schmalhalbfett
Stempel 1930 Kabel fett
ITC (1927/30) Kabel-Serie 1976

G. K. W. G. KUHLE WERBUNG
Berthold 1974 G.K.W. Computer

LAICH, REINER
Berthold 1971 Oriente

LANGE, GÜNTER GERHARD
Berthold 1957 Champion
Berthold 1958 Akzidenz-Grotesk extra
Berthold 1963 Akzidenz-Grotesk kursiv halbfett
Berthold 1964 El Greco
Berthold 1966 Akzidenz-Grotesk extrafett
Berthold 1967 Akzidenz-Grotesk kursiv
Berthold 1968 Akzidenz-Grotesk kursiv fett
Berthold 1968 Akzidenz-Grotesk super
Berthold 1968 Akzidenz-Grotesk kursiv extra
Berthold 1968 Akzidenz-Grotesk kursiv breitfett
Berthold 1969 Akzidenz-Grotesk Buch mager
Berthold 1969 Akzidenz-Grotesk Buch normal
Berthold 1969 Akzidenz-Grotesk Buch kursiv
Berthold 1969 Akzidenz-Grotesk Buch halbfett
Berthold 1969 Concorde normal
Berthold 1969 Concorde kursiv
Berthold 1969 Concorde halbfett
Berthold 1969 Concorde schmalhalbfett
Berthold 1972 Akzidenz-Grotesk Buch ultraleicht
Berthold 1972 – kursiv ultraleicht
Berthold 1972 – kursiv mager
Berthold 1972 – kursiv halbfett
Berthold 1972 – fett
Berthold 1972 – schmalmager
Berthold 1972 – schmal

Berthold 1972 Concorde schmalfett
Berthold 1972 Garamond normal
Berthold 1972 Garamond Kapitälchen
Berthold 1972 Garamond kursiv
Berthold 1972 Garamond halbfett
Berthold 1972 Garamond kursiv halbfett
Berthold 1973 AGB kursiv schmalmager
Berthold 1973 Concorde schmal
Berthold 1975 Concorde Nova normal
Berthold 1975 Concorde Nova Kapitälchen
Berthold 1975 Concorde Nova kursiv
Berthold 1975 Concorde Nova halbfett
Berthold 1975 Garamond fett
Berthold 1975 Garamond schmal
Berthold 1975 Garamond schmalhalbfett
Berthold 1975 Walbaum Buch normal
Berthold 1975 Walbaum Buch Kapitälchen
Berthold 1975 Walbaum Buch halbfett
Berthold 1976 AGB Rounded halbfett
Berthold 1976 AGB Rounded fett
Berthold 1976 AGB Rounded schmalfett
Berthold 1976 Concorde schmalfett licht
Berthold 1976 Franklin-Antiqua normal
Berthold 1976 Franklin-Antiqua Kapitälchen
Berthold 1976 Franklin-Antiqua kursiv
Berthold 1976 Franklin-Antiqua halbfett
Berthold 1976 Franklin-Antiqua kursiv halbfett
Berthold 1976 Franklin-Antiqua fett
Berthold 1976 Walbaum Buch kursiv
Berthold 1976 Walbaum Buch kursiv halbfett
Berthold 1976 Walbaum Buch fett
Berthold 1976 Walbaum Buch kursiv fett
Berthold 1976 Walbaum Standard normal
Berthold 1976 Walbaum Standard kursiv
Berthold 1977 AGB Inline halbfett schattiert
Berthold 1977 AGB Outline halbfett
Berthold 1977 AGB Outline fett
Berthold 1977 AGB Rounded fett licht
Berthold 1977 AGB White halbfett schattiert
Berthold 1977 Berthold Script normal
Berthold 1977 Berthold Script halbfett
Berthold 1977 Caslon Buch normal
Berthold 1977 Caslon Buch Kapitälchen
Berthold 1977 Caslon Buch kursiv
Berthold 1977 Caslon Buch halbfett
Berthold 1978 Concorde kursiv halbfett
Berthold 1978 Walbaum Standard Kapitälchen
Berthold 1979 AGB Rounded schmalfett licht
Berthold 1979 Walbaum Standard halbfett
Berthold 1980 AGB Rounded halbfett licht
Berthold 1980 Baskerville Book normal
Berthold 1980 Baskerville Book Kapitälchen

| | | | | | | |
|---|---|---|---|---|---|---|
| Berthold | 1980 | Baskerville Book kursiv | | | | |
| Berthold | 1980 | Baskerville Book halbfett | | | | |

LANGER, HELMUT
Berthold   1975   Logotype schattiert

LEE, GEOFFREY
Lettergieterij 1965   Impact

LENZ, EUGEN; LENZ, MAX
Haas   1947   Profil

LETTERGIETERIJ AMSTERDAM; HAUSSCHNITTE
Lettergieterij 19.Jh.   Egyptienne schmalfett
Lettergieterij o.J.   Amsterdam 698
Lettergieterij o.J.   Annonce fett
Lettergieterij o.J.   Bodoni-Antiqua normal
Lettergieterij o.J.   Bodoni kursiv
Lettergieterij o.J.   Bodoni-Antiqua fett
Lettergieterij o.J.   Bodoni kursiv fett
Lettergieterij o.J.   Egyptienne schmalhalbfett
Lettergieterij o.J.   Egyptienne breithalbfett
Lettergieterij o.J.   breitfett
Lettergieterij o.J.   Grotesk kursiv fett
Lettergieterij o.J.   Grotesk schmal
Lettergieterij o.J.   Grotesk schmalfett
Lettergieterij o.J.   Grotesk breitfett

LUDLOW TYPOGRAPH CO.; HAUSSCHNITTE
Ludlow   o.J.   Bookman normal
Ludlow   o.J.   Bookman kursiv
Ludlow   o.J.   Bookman fett

LUBALIN, HERB
ITC   1970   Busorama mager
ITC   1970   Busorama halbfett
ITC   1970   Busorama fett
ITC   1970   Firenze
ITC   1970   Ronda mager
ITC   1970   Ronda normal
ITC   1970   Ronda fett
ITC   1970   LSC Book Roman normal
ITC   1970   LSC Book kursiv
ITC   1970   LSC Book Roman halbfett
ITC   1970   LSC Book kursiv halbfett
ITC   1970   LSC Book Roman fett
ITC   1970   LSC Book kursiv fett
ITC   1970   LSC Caslon No. 233 mager
ITC   1970   LSC Caslon No. 233 kursiv mager
ITC   1970   LSC Caslon No. 233 normal
ITC   1970   LSC Caslon No. 233 kursiv
ITC   1970   LSC Caslon No. 233 fett
ITC   1970   LSC Caslon No. 233 kursiv fett
ITC   1970   LSC Caslon No. 233 extrafett
ITC   1970   LSC Caslon No. 233 kursiv extrafett
ITC   1970   LSC Manhattan

LUBALIN, HERB; CARNASE, TOM
ITC   1970   Avant Garde Gothic mager
ITC   1970   Avant Garde Gothic Buch
ITC   1970   Avant Garde Gothic normal
ITC   1970   Avant Garde Gothic halbfett
ITC   1970   Avant Garde Gothic fett

LUBALIN, HERB; DISPIGNA, ANTONIO
ITC   1974   Serif Gothic mager
ITC   1974   Serif Gothic normal
ITC   1974   Serif Gothic fett
ITC   1974   Serif Gothic extrafett
ITC   1974   Serif Gothic ultrafett
ITC   1974   Serif Gothic Black
ITC   1974   Serif Gothic licht

LUBALIN, DISPIGNA, SUNDWALL
ITC   1974   Lubalin Graph mager
ITC   1974   Lubalin Graph Buch
ITC   1974   Lubalin Graph normal
ITC   1974   Lubalin Graph halbfett
ITC   1974   Lubalin Graph fett

LUDWIG & MAYER; HAUSSCHNITTE
L&M   1925   Lichte Fette Grotesk
L&M   1927   Firmin Didot normal
L&M   1927   Firmin Didot fett
L&M   1929   Nicolas Cochin normal
L&M   1929   Nicolas Cochin kursiv
L&M   1929   Nicolas Cochin fett
L&M   1932   Le Cochin normal
L&M   1932   Le Cochin kursiv
L&M   1967   Permanent Headline normal
L&M   1968   Permanent Headline licht
L&M   1969   Permanent Headline kursiv

MAGGS, LEO
Berthold   1973   Westminster

MAGIN, WOLF
Berthold   1976   Black Line

MASON, JACKSON, JOHNSTONE, MEYNELL
Monotype   1912   Imprint normal
Monotype   1912   Imprint kursiv
Monotype   1912   Imprint halbfett
Monotype   1912   Imprint kursiv halbfett

MATHEIS, HELMUT
L&M   1959   Slogan
L&M   1963   Contact

MCKAY, WALTER H.
Lettergieterij 1955   Columbia

MEEKS, ALAN
TSI   1979   Bramley mager

Mendoza y Almeida, José
Lettergieterij  1960  Pascal

Meier, Klaus
Berthold  1974  Harlekin

Mengelt, Gschwind, Gürtler
ITC  1977  Avant Garde Gothic schräg mager
ITC  1977  Avant Garde Gothic Buch schräg
ITC  1977  Avant Garde Gothic schräg normal
ITC  1977  Avant Garde Gothic schräg halbfett
ITC  1977  Avant Garde Gothic schräg fett

Meyer, Hans Eduard
Stempel  1968  Syntax normal
Stempel  1969  Syntax halbfett
Stempel  1970  Syntax extrafett
Stempel  1972  Syntax kursiv

Meyer, Erich
Stempel  1934  Tannenberg

Meynell, Jackson, Johnstone, Mason
Monotype  1912  Imprint normal
Monotype  1912  Imprint kursiv
Monotype  1912  Imprint halbfett
Monotype  1912  Imprint kursiv halbfett

Middleton, R. H.
Ludlow  1930  Tempo Black normal
Ludlow  1930  Tempo Black schmal
Ludlow  1937  Coronet

Middleton, R. H.; Powell, Gerry
ATF  1938  Stencil

Miedinger, Max
Haas  1954  Pro Arte
Haas  1957  Helvetica halbfett
Haas  1958  Helvetica normal
Haas  1959  Helvetica fett
Haas  1961  Helvetica kursiv

Mollowitz, Erich
Wagner  1936  Forelle Auszeichnung

Monotype Corporation Ltd.; Hausschnitte
Monotype  1925  Horley Old Style normal
Monotype  1925  Horley Old Style kursiv
Monotype  1925  Horley Old Style halbfett
Monotype  1930  Bembo normal
Monotype  1930  Bembo Kapitälchen
Monotype  1930  Perpetua kursiv
Monotype  1933  Walbaum-Antiqua halbfett
Monotype  1934  Rockwell mager
Monotype  1934  Rockwell kursiv mager
Monotype  1934  Rockwell normal
Monotype  1934  Rockwell kursiv
Monotype  1934  Rockwell halbfett
Monotype  1934  Rockwell kursiv halbfett
Monotype  1934  Rockwell fett
Monotype  1934  Rockwell schmal
Monotype  1934  Rockwell schmalhalbfett
Monotype  1935  Bembo halbfett
Monotype  1935  Bembo kursiv halbfett
Monotype  1938  Ehrhardt normal
Monotype  1938  Ehrhardt kursiv
Monotype  1938  Ehrhardt halbfett
Monotype  1938  Ehrhardt kursiv halbfett
Monotype  1958  Placard halbfett
Monotype  1958  Placard fett
Monotype  1959  Perpetua halbfett
Monotype  1959  Perpetua kursiv halbfett
Monotype  o.J.  Bell Kapitälchen
Monotype  o.J.  Caslon Open Face
Monotype  o.J.  Gill Sans kursiv ultrafett
Monotype  o.J.  Gill Kayo
Monotype  o.J.  Gill Sans ultra schmalfett
Monotype  o.J.  Gill Sans ultrafett licht
Monotype  o.J.  Gill Sans extrafett licht
Monotype  o.J.  Grotesque No. 9 kursiv schmalfett
Monotype  o.J.  Grotesque No. 9a schmalfett
Monotype  o.J.  Grotesque No. 9b schmalfett
Monotype  o.J.  Grotesque No. 215 normal
Monotype  o.J.  Grotesque No. 216 halbfett
Monotype  o.J.  Modern normal
Monotype  o.J.  Modern Kapitälchen
Monotype  o.J.  Modern kursiv
Monotype  o.J.  Modern halbfett
Monotype  o.J.  Perpetua Black
Monotype  o.J.  Perpetua schattiert
Monotype  o.J.  Plantin mager
Monotype  o.J.  Plantin kursiv mager
Monotype  o.J.  Plantin kursiv
Monotype  o.J.  Plantin halbfett
Monotype  o.J.  Plantin kursiv halbfett
Monotype  o.J.  Plantin schmalfett
Monotype  o.J.  Times kursiv fett
Monotype  o.J.  Times extrafett
Monotype  o.J.  Times Modern normal

Moore, I.
Stephenson  1768  Baskerville Old Face

Morison, Stanley
Monotype  1932  Times New Roman
Monotype  1932  Times New Roman Kapitälchen
Monotype  1932  Times kursiv
Monotype  1932  Times fett
Monotype  1932  Times New Roman 327
Monotype  1932  Times New Roman 327 Kapitälchen
Monotype  1941  Times 421 halbfett

Murr, Günther
Berthold  1975  Murrpoint fett
Berthold  1975  Murrpoint Swing

SOCIETA NEBIOLO S.P.A.; HAUSSCHNITTE
Nebiolo 1908 Torino normal
Nebiolo 1908 Torino kursiv
Nebiolo vor 1920 Etrusco 403–30 fett
Nebiolo vor 1920 Etrusco 403–35 kursiv fett

NEUBAUER, KLAUS
Berthold 1977 Neubauer Black Chips
Berthold 1977 Neubauer White Chips

NEUGEBAUER, MICHAEL
Berthold 1972 Circulus
Berthold 1972 Twice

NOVARESE, ALDO
Nebiolo 1955/58 Egizio normal
Nebiolo 1955/58 Egizio kursiv
Nebiolo 1955/58 Egizio fett
Nebiolo 1955/58 Egizio kursiv fett
Nebiolo 1955/58 Egizio schmal
Nebiolo 1962 Eurostile normal
Nebiolo 1962 Eurostile fett
Nebiolo 1962 Eurostile schmal
Nebiolo 1962 Eurostile schmalfett
Nebiolo 1962 Eurostile breit
Nebiolo 1962 Eurostile breitfett
Nebiolo 1971 Stop 1
Berthold 1972 Editorial Tondo
Berthold 1972 Editorial kursiv
Berthold 1972 Primate
Nebiolo 1974 Eurostile kursiv
Berthold 1977 Fenice normal
Berthold 1977 Fenice kursiv
Berthold 1977 Fenice fett
Berthold 1977 Lapidar
ITC 1980 Novarese Buch
ITC 1980 Novarese Buch Kapitälchen
ITC 1980 Novarese Buch kursiv
ITC 1980 Novarese normal
ITC 1980 Novarese normal Kapitälchen
ITC 1980 Novarese kursiv
ITC 1980 Novarese halbfett
ITC 1980 Novarese kursiv halbfett
ITC 1980 Novarese fett
ITC 1980 Fenice mager
ITC 1980 Fenice kursiv mager
ITC 1980 Fenice normal
ITC 1980 Fenice kursiv
ITC 1980 Fenice fett
ITC 1980 Fenice kursiv fett
ITC 1980 Fenice ultra
ITC 1980 Fenice kursiv ultra

NOVARESE, ALDO; BUTTI, A.
Nebiolo 1951 Augustea licht

OPPENHEIM, LOUIS
Berthold (1913/14) Lo-Type kursiv halbfett
Berthold (1913/14) Lo-Type schmalhalbfett
Berthold (1914) Lo-Type normal
Berthold (1914) Lo-Type fett
Berthold (1924) Lo-Type mager
Berthold (1924) Lo-Type halbfett
Berthold 1927 Fanfare schmal

PARKER, W. A.
ATF 1927 Gallia

PECHEY, ELEISHA
Photoscript 1886 Charlemagne
Stephenson 1910 Windsor licht

PEIGNOT, C.; PEIGNOT, G.
Haas 1928 Garamont normal
Haas 1928 Garamont kursiv

PFEIL, JOH.
Berthold 1973 Touring
Berthold 1973 Vienna

PHOTO-LETTERING INC.
ITC 1976 Kabel Buch
ITC 1976 Kabel normal
ITC 1976 Kabel halbfett
ITC 1976 Kabel fett
ITC 1976 Kabel ultra
ITC 1976 Kabel licht
ITC 1976 Kabel Kontur

PHOTOSCRIPT LTD., HAUSSCHNITTE
Photoscript o.J. Blackfriars normal
Photoscript o.J. Blackfriars kursiv
Photoscript o.J. Chin Century 2000 Nr. 1 normal
Photoscript o.J. – Nr. 2 halbfett
Photoscript o.J. – Nr. 3 kursiv halbfett
Photoscript o.J. De Vinne Ornamented
Photoscript o.J. De Vinne Ornamented kursiv
Photoscript o.J. Granby Elephant
Photoscript o.J. Mexico Olympic
Photoscript o.J. Nova

PIERPONT, F. H.
Monotype 1913 Plantin normal

PISCHNER, WILHELM
Stempel 1928 Neuzeit-Grotesk mager
Stempel 1928 Neuzeit-Grotesk fett
Stempel 1928/30 Neuzeit-Grotesk halbfett
Stempel 1932 Neuzeit-Grotesk leicht
Stempel 1938/39 Neuzeit-Grotesk schmalhalbfett
Stempel 1939 Neuzeit-Grotesk schmalfett

POELL, ERWIN
Berthold 1972 Poell Black
Berthold 1972 Poell Medium Outline
Berthold 1972 Poell Outline

Berthold 1972 Poell Shaded

POPIELATY, GERD-DIETER
Berthold 1976 Dalmock

POPPL, FRIEDRICH
Berthold 1967 Poppl-Antiqua normal
Berthold 1967 Poppl-Antiqua halbfett
Berthold 1968 Poppl-Antiqua fett
Berthold 1969 Poppl Stretto
Berthold 1970 Poppl-Antiqua schmalfett
Berthold 1970 Poppl Exquisit
Berthold 1971 Poppl-Antiqua kursiv schmalfett
Berthold 1971 Poppl Heavy
Berthold 1976 Poppl-Pontifex normal
Berthold 1976 Poppl-Pontifex kursiv
Berthold 1976 Poppl-Pontifex halbfett
Berthold 1977 Poppl Leporello
Berthold 1977 Poppl Residenz mager
Berthold 1977 Poppl Residenz normal
Berthold 1979 Poppl Saladin normal
Berthold 1979 Poppl Saladin licht
Berthold 1980 Poppl-Pontifex fett
Berthold 1981 Poppl-College 1, normal
Berthold 1981 Poppl-College 2, normal
Berthold 1981 Poppl-College 1, halbfett
Berthold 1981 Poppl-College 2, halbfett
Berthold 1981 Poppl-College 1, fett
Berthold 1981 Poppl-College 2, fett
Berthold 1981 Poppl-Pontifex Kapitälchen
Berthold 1981 Poppl-Pontifex schmalhalbfett
Berthold o.J. Poppl-Antiqua kursiv schmalfett
Berthold o.J. Poppl Heavy

POST, HERBERT
Berthold 1939 Post-Antiqua normal
Berthold 1941 Post-Antiqua halbfett
Berthold 1959 Post-Marcato extrafett

POWELL, GERRY
Lettergieterij o.J. Arsis normal
Lettergieterij o.J. Arsis kursiv
Lettergieterij o.J. Stymie Open

POWELL, GERRY; MIDDLETON, R. H.
ATF 1938 Stencil

REICHEL, H.; BARTH, A. M.
Berthold 1972 Santana

REINER, IMRE
Neufville 1934 Corvinus mager
Neufville 1934 Corvinus kursiv mager
Neufville 1934 Corvinus halbfett
Neufville 1934 Corvinus fett

PAUL RENNER
Neufville 1928 Futura mager
Neufville 1928 Futura halbfett
Neufville 1928 Futura fett
Neufville 1928 Futura schmalhalbfett
Neufville 1929 Futura Black
Neufville 1930 Futura schräg mager
Neufville 1930 Futura schräg halbfett
Neufville 1930 Futura dreiviertelfett
Neufville 1930 Futura schräg dreiviertelfett
Neufville 1930 Futura schmalfett
Neufville 1932 Futura Buchschrift
Neufville 1932 Futura licht
Neufville 1932 Futura Display
Neufville 1937 Futura schräg fett
Neufville 1939 Futura Buchschrift schräg
Neufville 1953 Steile Futura fett
Neufville 1954 Steile Futura schrägfett
Neufville 1954 Futura kräftig

RENSHAW, JOHN L.
ATF 1958 News Gothic fett

RIEBLING, JÜRGEN
Berthold 1972 Mr. Big
Berthold 1976 Media normal
Berthold 1976 Media fett
Berthold 1976 Media Inline fett
Berthold 1976 Media Kontur fett
Berthold 1976 Media Outline fett
Berthold 1976 Media Relief fett
Berthold 1978 Media mager
Berthold 1978 Media halbfett
Berthold 1978 Media Triline fett

RIEDEL, ALFRED
L&M 1954 Domino

DE ROOS, S. H.
Lettergieterij 1929/31 Nobel normal
Lettergieterij 1929/31 Nobel fett
Lettergieterij 1929/31 Nobel schmal

ROSENBLUM, STAN
Berthold 1971 Sar Modern

RUBENS
Photoscript 1890 Whelan Antique

SALDEN, GEORG
Berthold 1970 Daphne
Berthold 1973 Transit

SALLWEY, FRIEDRICH KARL
Stempel 1958 Information breitfett

SCHILLING, MARGOT
Berthold 1980 Batik

SCHLESINGER, STEFAN
Lettergieterij 1939  Hidalgo

SCHNEIDLER, F. H. ERNST
Neufville  1930  Ganz Grobe Gotisch
Neufville  1937  Schneidler-Initialen
Neufville  1937  Zentenar-Fraktur normal
Neufville  1937  Zentenar-Fraktur halbfett

SCHÜLE, ILSE
L&M  1951  Rhapsodie

SCHWEITZER, JOHANNES
L&M  1959  Dominante normal
L&M  1959  Dominante kursiv
L&M  1959  Dominante fett

SCHWEKENDICK, GERHARD
Berthold  1972  Gesh Export 233
Berthold  1972  Gesh Introduction
Berthold  1972  Gesh Ortega Roman 275

SCHWERDTNER, W.
Stempel  1928  Metropolis

SEKI, AKIHIKO
ITC  1970  Aki Lines

SEIFERT, J.; WEGNER, K.
Berthold  1973  Trixi

SIMONCINI, F.; BILZ, W.
L&M  1965  Life mager
L&M  1965  Life kursiv mager
L&M  1965  Life fett

SMIT, JOHAN MICHAEL
Berthold  (1750)  Quadriga-Serie 1979

SMIT, LEONARD H. D.
Lettergieterij 1960  Promotor
Lettergieterij 1962  Orator

SMITH, ROBERT E.
ATF  1942  Brush

SOLPERA, JAN
Berthold  1971  Circo

SPIEKERMANN, ERIK
Berthold  1979  Berliner Grotesk mager
Berthold  1979  Berliner Grotesk halbfett
Berthold  1980  Lo-Type mager
Berthold  1980  Lo-Type normal
Berthold  1980  Lo-Type halbfett
Berthold  1980  Lo-Type kursiv halbfett
Berthold  1980  Lo-Type fett
Berthold  1980  Lo-Type schmalhalbfett

STAN, TONY
ITC  1975  Century Buch
ITC  1975  Century Buch kursiv
ITC  1975  Century ultra
ITC  1975  Century kursiv ultra
ITC  1975  Cheltenham Buch
ITC  1975  Cheltenham Buch kursiv
ITC  1975  Cheltenham ultra
ITC  1975  Cheltenham kursiv ultra
ITC  1975  Garamond Buch
ITC  1975  Garamond Buch kursiv
ITC  1975  Garamond ultra
ITC  1975  Garamond kursiv ultra
ITC  1977  Garamond mager
ITC  1977  Garamond kursiv mager
ITC  1977  Garamond fett
ITC  1977  Garamond kursiv fett
ITC  1977  Garamond schmalmager
ITC  1977  Garamond kursiv schmalmager
ITC  1977  Garamond Buch schmal
ITC  1977  Garamond Buch kursiv schmal
ITC  1977  Garamond schmalfett
ITC  1977  Garamond kursiv schmalfett
ITC  1977  Garamond ultra schmal
ITC  1977  Garamond ultra schmal kursiv
ITC  1978  Cheltenham mager
ITC  1978  Cheltenham kursiv mager
ITC  1978  Cheltenham halbfett
ITC  1978  Cheltenham kursiv halbfett
ITC  1978  Cheltenham schmalmager
ITC  1978  Cheltenham kursiv schmalmager
ITC  1978  Cheltenham Buch schmal
ITC  1978  Cheltenham Buch kursiv schmal
ITC  1978  Cheltenham schmalhalbfett
ITC  1978  Cheltenham kursiv schmalhalbfett
ITC  1978  Cheltenham ultra schmal
ITC  1978  Cheltenham ultra schmal kursiv
ITC  1978  Cheltenham licht
ITC  1978  Cheltenham licht schattiert
ITC  1978  Cheltenham Kontur
ITC  1980  Century mager
ITC  1980  Century kursiv halbfett

STAN, TONY; KADEN, JOEL
ITC  1974  American Typewriter mager
ITC  1974  American Typewriter normal
ITC  1974  American Typewriter fett
ITC  1974  American Typewriter schmalmager
ITC  1974  American Typewriter schmal
ITC  1974  American Typewriter schmalfett
ITC  1974  American Typewriter fett licht

STEINER, PETER
Berthold  1972  Alpine
Berthold  1973  Black Body
Berthold  1974  Swing
Berthold  1975  Dektiv Double
Berthold  1975  Jockey

D. Stempel AG, Frankfurt a. M.; Hausschnitte
Stempel     1903        Künstlerschreibschrift halbfett
Stempel     1909/19     Reform-Grotesk
Stempel     1919        Information engfett
Stempel     1919        Information schmalfett
Stempel     1919        Janson-Antiqua normal
Stempel     1919        Janson kursiv
Stempel     1924        Baskerville normal
Stempel     1924        Garamond normal
Stempel     1925        Garamond Kapitälchen
Stempel     1926        Garamond kursiv
Stempel     1926        Baskerville kursiv
Stempel     1927        Garamond halbfett
Stempel     1928        Baskerville halbfett
Stempel     1929        Kabel fett licht
Stempel     1930        Kabel schattiert
Stempel     1932        Garamond kursiv halbfett
Stempel     1960        IBM Dokument
Stempel     1961        Helvetica breithalbfett
Stempel     1962        Clarendon mager
Stempel     1962/63     Clarendon halbfett
Stempel     1963        Helvetica schmalmager
Stempel     1963        Helvetica breitmager
Stempel     1964        Clarendon breitfett
Stempel     1965        Madison kursiv mager
Stempel     1965/66     Neuzeit S Buch
Stempel     1965/66     Neuzeit S kräftig
Stempel     1966        Clarendon schmalmager
Stempel     1966/67     Helvetica leicht
Stempel     1967/68     Helvetica kursiv leicht
Stempel     1969        Helvetica Inserat
Stempel     o.J.        Clarendon schmalfett

Stephenson Blake & Company Ltd.; Hausschnitte
Stephenson  1836        Thorowgood normal
Stephenson  1836        Thorowgood kursiv
Stephenson  1901        Britannic fett
Stephenson  1905        Britannic kursiv fett
Stephenson  1905        Modern No. 20 normal
Stephenson  1905        Windsor mager
Stephenson  1905        Windsor fett
Stephenson  1905        Windsor schmalfett
Stephenson  1940        Elongated Roman schattiert
Stephenson  o.J.        Britannic normal
Stephenson  o.J.        Egyptienne breit schattiert
Stephenson  o.J.        Elongated Roman
Stephenson  o.J.        Grotesque No. 7 eng
Stephenson  o.J.        Latin fett
Stephenson  o.J.        Latin schmalfett
Stephenson  o.J.        Latin Wide
Stephenson  o.J.        Modern No. 20 kursiv
Stephenson  o.J.        Sans Serif schattiert

Stern, Claude-Eric
Berthold    1980        Splash

Sundwall, Dispigna, Lubalin
ITC         1974        Lubalin Graph mager

ITC         1974        Lubalin Graph Buch
ITC         1974        Lubalin Graph normal
ITC         1974        Lubalin Graph halbfett
ITC         1974        Lubalin Graph fett

Tagliente, Giovanni
Monotype    (1524)      Bembo kursiv

Thorowgood
Stephenson  1839        Sans Serif schmal

Trump, Georg
Berthold    1930        City halbfett
Berthold    1930        City fett
Berthold    1937        City mager
Wagner      1937        Schadow-Antiqua mager
Wagner      1938        Schadow-Antiqua halbfett
Wagner      1942        Schadow-Antiqua kursiv
Wagner      1942        Schadow-Antiqua Werk
Wagner      1945        Schadow-Antiqua schmalfett
Wagner      1948        Forum I
Wagner      1952        Schadow-Antiqua fett
Wagner      1952        Amati
Wagner      1952        Forum II
Stempel     1954        Trump-Mediäval normal
Stempel     1954        Trump-Mediäval kursiv
Wagner      1955        Signum
Stempel     1956        Time-Script mager
Stempel     1957        Time-Script halbfett
Wagner      1957        Time-Script fett
Stempel     1958        Trump-Mediäval halbfett
Stempel     1958        Trump-Mediäval fett
Stempel     1960        Trump-Gravur
Stempel     1962        Trump-Mediäval kursiv fett
Stempel     1965        Jaguar

Tschichold, Jan
Stempel     1965/67     Sabon-Antiqua normal
Stempel     1968        Sabon-Antiqua kursiv
Stempel     1968        Sabon-Antiqua halbfett

Tyfa, Josef
Czech Art   1959        Tyfa-Antiqua normal
Czech Art   1959        Tyfa-Antiqua kursiv

Usherwood, Leslie
Typsettra   1971        Graphis extrafett
Typsettra   1973        Oktavia halbfett
Typsettra   1973        Statesman
Typsettra   1980        Flange mager
Typsettra   1980        Lynton mager
Typsettra   1980        Lynton kursiv mager
Typsettra   1981        Flange kursiv mager
Typsettra   1981        Flange normal
Typsettra   1981        Flange halbfett
Typsettra   1981        Lynton normal
Typsettra   1981        Lynton fett
Typsettra   o.J.        Flange fett

VEB Typoart; Hausschnitte
Typoart    1950    Primus-Antiqua mager
Typoart    1950    Primus-Antiqua kursiv mager
Typoart    1950    Primus-Antiqua halbfett

Verkaart, B. Th. P.
Berthold        1967    Annonce fett licht
Lettergieterij  o.J.    Annonce fett

Visual Graphics Corporation; Hausschnitt
Visual     1967    Amalia

Völker, Ernst
Berthold   1978    Voel Beat
Berthold   1978    Voel Bianca
Berthold   1978    Voel Kars

Volkswagenwerk
Berthold   1979    V.A.G.-Rundschrift

Vorarlberger Grafik
Berthold   1972    Motter Alustyle
Berthold   1972    Motter Ombra
Berthold   1975    Motter Tektura halbfett

Wagner, H.
L&M        1950    Largo licht

Wagner, Karlo
Berthold   1971    Fortunata

Johannes Wagner; Hausschnitte
Wagner     1875    Fette Fraktur
Wagner     1911    Fette Gotisch
Wagner     1912    Aurora-Grotesk mager
Wagner     1912    Aurora-Grotesk kursiv mager
Wagner     1912    Aurora-Grotesk dreiviertelfett
Wagner     1912    Aurora-Grotesk fett
Wagner     1912    Aurora-Grotesk kursiv fett
Wagner     1912    Aurora-Grotesk schmalhalbfett
Wagner     1912    Aurora-Grotesk schmalfett
Wagner     1912    Aurora-Grotesk breitmager
Wagner     1912    Aurora-Grotesk breithalbfett
Wagner     1912    Aurora-Grotesk breitfett
Wagner     1912    Steinschrift
Wagner     1913    Fette Antiqua
Wagner     1919    Druckhaus-Antiqua normal
Wagner     1919    Druckhaus kursiv
Wagner     1919    Druckhaus-Antiqua halbfett
Wagner     1926    Elvira kursiv fett
Wagner     1930    Romana mager
Wagner     1930    Romana halbfett
Wagner     1930    Romana ultra
Wagner     1964    Neue Aurora-Grotesk schmalhalbfett
Wagner     1964    Neue Aurora-Grotesk schmalfett

Walbaum, Justus Erich
Berthold   1800    Walbaum-Fraktur

Berthold   (1804)  Walbaum Standard normal
Berthold   (1804)  Walbaum Standard kursiv

Watzl, Peter
Berthold   1976    Austrian Watzlline
Berthold   1976    Fat Watzlline
Berthold   1976    Watzlcross
Berthold   1976    Watzlsnap
Berthold   1977    Watzlform full
Berthold   1977    Watzlform open

Wege, Walter
Berthold   1931    Signal

Wegner, K.; Seifert, T.
Berthold   1973    Trixi

Weiss, Emil Rudolf
Neufville  1928    Weiß-Antiqua normal
Neufville  1928    Weiß-Antiqua kursiv
Neufville  1931    Weiß-Antiqua halbfett
Neufville  1931    Weiß-Kapitale normal
Neufville  1931    Weiß-Kapitale kräftig
Neufville  1937    Weiß-Rundgotisch

West, James
ATF        o.J.    Bank Script

Wiegand, Jürgen
Berthold   1974    Wiegands Adbold
Berthold   1974    Wiegands Roundhead
Berthold   1977    Wiegands Baroque normal
Berthold   1977    Wiegands Baroque kursiv
Berthold   1978    Wiegands Renaissance kursiv

Wilke, Martin
Berthold   1932    Ariston normal
Berthold   1933    Ariston fett
Berthold   1936    Ariston extra
Berthold   1938    Caprice
Stempel    1938    Diskus mager
Stempel    1940    Diskus halbfett
Berthold   1950    Palette
Berthold   1968    Picadilly Script

Wilkens, Georg
Berthold   1971    Manessa
Berthold   1976    Tri-Star

Wirtz, Willy
Berthold   1975    Latus

Wolf, Rudolf
Stempel    1929    Memphis halbfett
Stempel    1930    Memphis zart
Stempel    1932    Memphis mager
Stempel    1933    Memphis fett

ZAPF, HERMANN
| Stempel | 1950 | Palatino normal |
| Stempel | 1950 | Palatino Kapitälchen |
| Stempel | 1951 | Palatino kursiv |
| Stempel | 1951 | Palatino halbfett |
| Stempel | 1952 | Melior normal |
| Stempel | 1952 | Melior kursiv |
| Stempel | 1952 | Melior halbfett |
| Stempel | 1953 | Melior schmalfett |
| Stempel | 1954 | Aldus-Buchschrift |
| Stempel | 1954 | Aldus-Buchschrift Kapitälchen |
| Stempel | 1954 | Aldus-Buchschrift kursiv |
| Stempel | 1958 | Optima normal |
| Stempel | 1958 | Optima kursiv |
| Stempel | 1958 | Optima halbfett |
| Stempel | 1967 | Optima fett |
| Stempel | 1968 | Optima kräftig |
| Stempel | 1969 | Optima kursiv kräftig |
| Berthold | 1976 | Comenius-Antiqua normal |
| Berthold | 1976 | Comenius-Antiqua kursiv |
| ITC | 1976 | Zapf Book mager |
| ITC | 1976 | Zapf Book kursiv mager |
| ITC | 1976 | Zapf Book normal |
| ITC | 1976 | Zapf Book kursiv |
| ITC | 1976 | Zapf Book halbfett |
| ITC | 1976 | Zapf Book kursiv halbfett |
| ITC | 1976 | Zapf Book fett |
| ITC | 1976 | Zapf Book kursiv fett |
| Berthold | 1977 | Comenius-Antiqua halbfett |
| Berthold | 1977 | Comenius-Antiqua fett |
| ITC | 1977 | Zapf International mager |
| ITC | 1977 | Zapf International kursiv mager |
| ITC | 1977 | Zapf International normal |
| ITC | 1977 | Zapf International kursiv |
| ITC | 1977 | Zapf International halbfett |
| ITC | 1977 | Zapf International kursiv halbfett |
| ITC | 1977 | Zapf International fett |
| ITC | 1977 | Zapf International kursiv fett |
| ITC | 1979 | Zapf Chancery mager |
| ITC | 1979 | Zapf Chancery mager Kapitälchen |
| ITC | 1979 | Zapf Chancery kursiv mager |
| ITC | 1979 | Zapf Chancery normal |
| ITC | 1979 | Zapf Chancery normal Kapitälchen |
| ITC | 1979 | Zapf Chancery kursiv |
| ITC | 1979 | Zapf Chancery halbfett |
| ITC | 1979 | Zapf Chancery fett |

ZAPF-VON HESSE, GUDRUN
| Stempel | 1953 | Diotima |

ZIMMERMANN, PAUL
| Wagner | 1945 | Impuls |

ZOCHOWSKI, BOGDAN
| Berthold | 1979 | Globe 6 |

OHNE LIZENZGEBER, DESIGNER NICHT BEKANNT
| NN | o.J. | Alexandra |
| NN | o.J. | Alte Schwabacher |
| NN | o.J. | Antiqua halbfett |
| NN | o.J. | Arnold Böcklin |
| NN | o.J. | Breda-Gotisch |
| NN | o.J. | Calligraphia |
| NN | o.J. | Caslon Adbold |
| NN | o.J. | Clyde |
| NN | o.J. | DIN 16 |
| NN | o.J. | DIN 17 |
| NN | o.J. | DIN 1451 |
| NN | o.J. | DIN Mittelschrift |
| NN | o.J. | DIN Breitschrift |
| NN | o.J. | Flyer fett |
| NN | o.J. | Flyer schmalfett |
| NN | o.J. | Genny |
| NN | o.J. | Georges Lemon |
| NN | o.J. | Girder Heavy |
| NN | o.J. | Haenel-Antiqua schmalfett |
| NN | o.J. | Houston |
| NN | o.J. | ISO 3098 (DIN 6771) |
| NN | o.J. | Italienne breit |
| NN | o.J. | Italique de Giraldon |
| NN | o.J. | Kabel Hairline |
| NN | o.J. | London Text |
| NN | o.J. | Madame |
| NN | o.J. | Neptun |
| NN | o.J. | Nubian |
| NN | o.J. | Okay |
| NN | o.J. | Old Bowery |
| NN | o.J. | Planschrift normal |
| NN | o.J. | Planschrift kursiv |
| NN | o.J. | Planschrift linkskursiv |
| NN | o.J. | Poema |
| NN | o.J. | Thalia |
| NN | o.J. | Tip Top |

# *Informationen zu den Schriftproben*

## SYNOPSIS

Die Synopsis bringt das Verzeichnis von 1400 Berthold-Titelsatzschriften in Normalbelegung. Hinzu kommen einige Hundert nichtlateinische Schriften, Spezialschriften und Sonderbelegungen für Osteuropa, für die USA, die Türkei und Island. Die erste Spalte (1) nennt die Seite, auf der die Schrift im »E 3« in kompletten Alphabeten gezeigt wird. Dann folgt der Schriftenname im Originalcharakter (2), die dritte Spalte (3) informiert in drei Sprachen über die Schnittbezeichnungen (deutsch, englisch, französisch). Die letzte Spalte (4) schließlich gibt über die Art der Belegung und über die Bestellnummer Aufschluß. Darunter ist für interne Belange die laufende Nummer aufgeführt.

N     Normalbelegung nach den Layouts 010, 020, 100 und 101

N 000   bedeutet, daß diese Belegungen in einem oder in wenigen Punkten von der Normalbelegung abweichen

F 006   Fraktur-Belegung (gebrochene Schriften)

V     Versalbelegung nach den Layouts 009 oder 018. Typenplatten nach Belegung V 018 (wie z. B. die Schnitte der Futura Art Deco) tragen jeweils zwei Schriftschnitte

Z 000   Belegung Zierbuchstaben. In vielen Fällen sind Zierbuchstaben verschiedener Schnitte einer Schriftfamilie auf einer Typenplatte zusammengefaßt. Sie erkennen dies an der gleichlautenden Bestellnummer. Außerdem sind Typenplatten mit zwei oder mehr Schriftschnitten durch einen Stern kenntlich gemacht

Sp    Spezialbelegungen. Komplette Figurenverzeichnisse sind auf den Seiten 463 bis 476 abgedruckt.

x 016   Minuskel-Belegung für versallose Schriften

## KATALOG

Der Katalog bringt folgende Informationen:
Schriftfamilie (5)
Schriftschnitt in deutsch, englisch und französisch (6)
Belegung, Layout (7). Mit der aufgeführten Belegung (in der Regel die europäische Standardbelegung) ist die Schriftprobe gesetzt worden. Die Seiten 496 bis 500 informieren über osteuropäische, türkische und isländische Belegungen.
Schriftkünstler und Jahr der ersten Verfügbarkeit (8). Falls kein Schriftkünstler genannt wird, ist die Schrift in aller Regel von einem anonym gebliebenen Schriftkünstler entworfen und von ihm oder anderen Mitarbeitern anonym ausgeführt worden. Die Angaben zu »Schriftgestalter« und »Jahr der ersten Verfügbarkeit« stützen sich auf zum Teil widersprüchliche Literatur. Bei Vorlage abweichender, verläßlicher Daten bitten wir um Mitteilung. Vor Drucklegung des »E 3« haben wir die wichtigsten Lizenzgeber um Prüfung der Daten gebeten. Ihre Korrekturen sind berücksichtigt worden.
Lizenzgeber (9). Inhaber der letzten Rechte an der vorgestellten Schrift bzw. Lizenzgeber der Schrift
Abmessungen der Schrift (10). Angaben zu den Proportionen und Höhenlinien der Schrift:
H = Versalhöhe. Als Bezugsgröße immer 1.
x = Mittellängenhöhe im Verhältnis zur Versalhöhe
k = k-Höhe. Höhe der Minuskeln mit Oberlängen (b d f h k l)
p = Unterlängenbereich im Verhältnis zur Versalhöhe
Damit können die Proportionen für alle Schiften auf einfache Weise errechnet werden. Zum Beispiel für die Ermittlung der Hilfslinien von Skizzen und Entwürfen. Dabei werden die einzelnen Werte mit der gewünschten Versalhöhe multipliziert.

---

① 109   **Baskerville Book** ②                   normal ③   N 020: 081 2474 ④
                                                                                regular
                                                                                 normal            1304

# the quick brown fox jumps over the lazy dog

**Baskerville Book** ⑤
1304
normal ⑥
regular
normal
N 020: 081 2474 ⑦
Günter Gerhard Lange 1980 ⑧
H. Berthold AG ⑨
H 1 – x 0,61 – k 1,01 – p 0,38 ⑩

XXXVII

## Information on the typeface specimens

SYNOPSIS

The synopsis gives a list of the 1400 Berthold headline faces which are available in standard layout. In addition to this, there are several non-Roman typefaces, special typefaces and special layouts for Eastern Europe, for the USA, for Turkey and for Iceland. The first column (1) states the page of »E 3« on which the typeface is shown as a complete alphabet. Following this, the typeface name appears in its original form (2), the third column (3) gives the typeface cut designation in three languages (German, English, French). The final column (4) states the layout and the order number. Below this, the serial number is given for internal purposes .

N  Standard (Normal) layout according to layouts 010, 020, 100 and 101
N 000  means that these layouts differ in only one or in very few points from the standard
F 006  Gothic (Fraktur) layout (broken types)
V  Capital (Versal) layout according to layouts 009 or 018. Type plates according to layout V 018 (such as the designs of Futura Art Deco, for example) each contain two typeface designs
Z 000  Swash letters (Zierbuchstaben) layout. In many cases, swash letters of various designs but belonging to the same typeface family are combined on one type plate. This can be recognized from the fact that two designs have the same order number. In addition, type plates containing two or more designs are indicated by an asterisk
Sp  Special layouts. The complete lists of symbols are given on pages 463–476
x 016  Lower-case layout for typefaces with no upper-case characters

CATALOGUE

The catalogue gives the following information:
Typeface family (5)
Typeface design (cut) in German, English and French (6)
Layout (7). The typeface is set using the layout stated (usually European standard layout). Information on Eastern European, Turkish and Icelandic layouts is given on pages 496–500.
Typeface designer and the year when the typeface first became available (8). Where no designer is named, the typeface has usually been designed by a designer who has remained anonymously either by himself or others. The data on "typeface designer" and "first year of availability" are based on diverse literature which often gives conflicting information. If any reader has reliable information which differs from that given in this book, we would be grateful if he or she would inform us. Before going to print, we asked the most important licensers to check the data given. Their corrections have been respected.
Licenser (9). Person or body in possession of the rights to the typeface shown, or, where appropriate, the typeface licenser.
Dimensions of the typeface (10): Data on the proportions and heights of the typeface.
H = capital letter height with reference value always 1
x = x-height with relation to the capital letter height
k = k-height. Height of lower-case characters with ascenders (b d f h k l)
p = descender range with relation to the capital letter height. Using these values, the proportions for all typefaces can be calculated easily. For example, in determining auxiliary rules in sketches and drafts. The individual values merely have to be multiplied by the desired capital letter height.

① 109  **Baskerville Book** ②          normal ③      N 020: 081 2474 ④
                                       regular
                                       normal              1304

**the quick brown fox jumps over the lazy dog**

Baskerville Book ⑤
1304
normal ⑥
regular
normal
N 020: 081 2474 ⑦
Günter Gerhard Lange 1980 ⑧
H. Berthold AG ⑨
H 1 – x 0,61 – k 1,01 – p 0,38 ⑩

## *Renseignements sur les modèles de caractères*

TABLEAU SYNOPTIQUE

Le tableau synoptique contient, d'une part, la liste des 1400 caractères pour titres Berthold dans leur configuration normale et, d'autre part, quelques centaines de caractères autres que les caractères latins, ainsi que des caractères spéciaux, y compris ceux réservés à l'Europe de l'Est, aux Etats-Unis, à la Turquie et à l'Islande. Dans la première colonne (1) est indiquée la page où figure le caractère dans les alphabets complets. La deuxième colonne (2) indique le nom du caractère, écrit lui-même avec ses caractéristiques propres, tandis que dans la troisième colonne (3) figurent en trois langues (allemand, anglais, français) les désignations des formes. La dernière colonne (4) fournit des renseignements sur le mode de configuration et sur le numéro de commande. En-dessous est indiqué le numéro progressif, pour usage interne.

N      configuration normale selon layouts 010, 020, 100 et 101
N 000   signifie que ces configurations s'écartent en un ou quelques éléments de la configuration normale
F 006   caractères «allemands» (gothiques)
V      lettres capitales selon layouts 009 ou 018. Les plaquettes de caractères selon configuration V 018 (comme, par exemple, les formes de Futura Art Déco) portent deux formes de caractères
Z 000   lettres ornées. Dans plusieurs cas, des lettres ornées sous différentes formes appartenant à une famille de caractères sont regroupées sur une plaquette. Vous pouvez les reconnaître par le numéro de commande similaire. En plus, les plaquettes portant deux ou plusieurs formes de caractères sont identifiables par un astérisque.
Sp      configurations spéciales. Aux pages de 463 à 476 figure la liste complète des configurations
x 016   configuration minuscule pour les caractères n'ayant pas de capitales

CATALOGUE

Le catalogue contient les renseignements suivants:
Famille de caractères (5)
Forme du caractère en allemand, anglais et français (6)
Configuration, layout (7). Le modèle de caractère a été composé dans la configuration indiquée (normalement, la configuration standard européenne). Aux pages de 496 à 500 sont illustrées les configurations de l'Europe de l'Est et islandaise.
Graphiste auteur du caractère et année de la première parution (8). Si aucun auteur n'est mentionné, il est tout à fait concevable que le caractère a été dessiné par un graphiste resté inconnu et réalisé par lui-même ou par des collaborateurs anonymes. Les informations concernant l'«auteur» et l'«année de la première parution» se fondent partiellement sur des documents contradictoires. Nous remercions à l'avance tous ceux qui pourraient nous communiquer des données complémentaires sûres. Avant de passer à l'impression du catalogue «E3» nous avons demandé aux pourvoyeurs de licence principaux de vérifier les données. On a naturellement tenu compte de leurs corrections.
Pourvoyeurs de licence (9): mention du titulaire des droits les plus récents sur le caractère présenté ou indication du pourvoyeur de licence pour le caractère en question.
Dimensions du caractère (10). Données concernant les proportions et les lignes de la hauteur du caractère.
H = hauteur des capitales. Le chiffre 1 vaut toujours comme hauteur de référence
x = hauteur de l'œil de la lettre par rapport à la hauteur des capitales
k = hauteur de la lettre k. Hauteur des minuscules avec jambage supérieur (b d f h k l)
p = fourchette du jambage inférieur par rapport à la hauteur des capitales
On peut ainsi calculer facilement les proportions pour tous les caractères. Par exemple, pour trouver les lignes auxiliaires d'ébauches et de maquettes. Dans ces cas, on multiplie les valeurs individuelles par la hauteur voulue des capitales.

① 109   **Baskerville Book** ②     normal ③   N 020: 081 2474 ④
                                                              regular
                                                              normal               1304

## the quick brown fox jumps over the lazy dog

**Baskerville Book** ⑤
1304 ⑥
normal
regular
normal
N 020: 081 2474 ⑦
Günter Gerhard Lange 1980 ⑧
H. Berthold AG ⑨
H 1 – x 0,61 – k 1,01 – p 0,38 ⑩

IXL

# BERTHOLD HEADLINES

XL

**BERTHOLD HEADLINES**

*Schriftenverzeichnis*
*List of Type Faces*
*Catalogue de Caractères*

# BERTHOLD HEADLINES

# SYNOPSIS

## BERTHOLD HEADLINES

| Page | Typeface | Style (DE / EN / FR) | Code / No. |
|---|---|---|---|
| 211 | *Abold* | kursiv / italic / italique | N 100: 081 1453 / 1 |
| 363 | **Ad Lib** | | N 100: 081 0000 / 2 |
| 299 | **Airport** | | N 100: 081 1470 / 3 |
| 445 | *Aja* | | N 020: 081 0767 / 1258 |
| 423 | AKI LINES ITC | | V 009: 081 1797 / 4 |
| 291 | Akzidenz-Grotesk | mager / light / maigre | N 100: 081 0004 / 5 |
| 293 | Akzidenz-Grotesk | normal / regular / normal | N 100: 081 0001 / 6 |
| 309 | *Akzidenz-Grotesk* | kursiv / italic / italique | N 100: 081 0007 / 7 |
| 299 | **Akzidenz-Grotesk** | halbfett / medium / demi-gras | N 100: 081 1553 / 8 |
| 311 | *Akzidenz-Grotesk* | kursiv halbfett / medium italic / italique demi-gras | N 100: 081 0014 / 9 |
| 301 | **Akzidenz-Grotesk** | fett / bold / gras | N 100: 081 0015 / 10 |
| 311 | ***Akzidenz-Grotesk*** | kursiv fett / bold italic / italique gras | N 100: 081 0017 / 11 |
| 303 | **Akzidenz-Grotesk** | super / super / super | N 100: 081 0018 / 12 |
| 319 | Akzidenz-Grotesk | schmalmager / light condensed / étroit maigre | N 100: 081 0023 / 13 |
| 321 | Akzidenz-Grotesk | eng / condensed / étroit | N 100: 081 0022 / 14 |
| 321 | Akzidenz-Grotesk | schmalhalbfett / medium condensed / étroit demi-gras | N 100: 081 0024 / 15 |
| 329 | **Akzidenz-Grotesk** | schmalfett / bold condensed / étroit gras | N 100: 081 1556 / 16 |
| 333 | **Akzidenz-Grotesk** | extra / extra bold condensed / étroit extra gras | N 100: 081 0029 / 17 |
| 337 | ***Akzidenz-Grotesk*** | kursiv extra / extra bold condensed italic / italique étroit extra gras | N 100: 081 1557 / 18 |
| 333 | **Akzidenz-Grotesk** | extrafett / extra bold / extra gras | N 100: 081 0031 / 19 |
| 339 | Akzidenz-Grotesk | breitmager / light extended / large maigre | N 100: 081 0037 / 20 |
| 339 | Akzidenz-Grotesk | breit / extended / large | N 100: 081 0038 / 21 |
| 341 | **Akzidenz-Grotesk** | breithalbfett / medium extended / large demi-gras | N 100: 081 1559 / 22 |
| 343 | **Akzidenz-Grotesk** | breitfett / bold extended / large gras | N 100: 081 0043 / 23 |

# SYNOPSIS

## BERTHOLD HEADLINES

| Page | Typeface | Style (de/en/fr) | Reference |
|---|---|---|---|
| 345 | *Akzidenz-Grotesk* | kursiv breitfett / bold extended italic / italique large gras | N 100: 081 0048 / 24 |
| 295 | Akzidenz-Grotesk Buch | normal / regular / normal | N 100: 081 0052 / 25 |
| 309 | *Akzidenz-Grotesk Buch* | kursiv / italic / italique | N 100: 081 0053 / 26 |
| 299 | **Akzidenz-Grotesk Buch** | halbfett / medium / demi-gras | N 100: 081 0054 / 27 |
| 415 | AG Buch Inline | halbfett schattiert / medium shaded / demi-gras ombré | N 020: 081 1813 / 28 |
| 399 | AG Buch Outline | halbfett / medium / demi-gras | N 020: 081 1811 / 29 |
| 399 | AG Buch Outline | fett licht / bold outline / gras éclairé | N 020: 081 2230 / 1260 |
| 359 | AG Buch Rounded | halbfett / medium / demi-gras | N 020: 081 1973 / 30 |
| 359 | AG Buch Rounded | fett / bold / gras | N 020: 081 0484 / 31 |
| 359 | AG Buch Rounded | schmalfett / bold condensed / étroit gras | N 020: 081 1974 / 32 |
| 401 | AG Buch Rounded | halbfett licht / medium outline / demi gras éclairé | N 020: 081 2232 / 1259 |
| 401 | AG Buch Rounded | fett licht / bold outline / gras éclairé | N 020: 081 2378 / 33 |
| 401 | AG Buch Rounded | schmalfett licht / bold condensed outline / étroit gras éclairé | N 020: 081 2379 / 34 |
| 409 | AG Buch White | halbfett schattiert / medium shaded / demi-gras ombré | N 020: 081 1812 / 35 |
| 79 | Aldus-Buchschrift | normal / regular / normal | N 020: 081 0204 / 1303 |
| 87 | *Aldus-Buchschrift* | kursiv / italic / italique | N 020: 081 2018 / 1261 |
| 405 | ALEXANDRA | | N 000: 081 1483 / 38 |
| 239 | Alexandria | | N 100: 081 0058 / 39 |
| 363 | Alpine | | N 100: 081 1463 / 40 |
| 329 | Alternate Gothic No. 3 | normal / regular / normal | N 100: 081 0059 / 41 |
| 65 | Alte Schwabacher | | N 100: 081 0060 / 42 |
| 205 | Amati | | N 000: 081 0061 / 43 |
| 391 | Amelia | | N 100: 081 1464 / 44 |
| 157 | Americana | normal / regular / normal | N 100: 081 0063 / 45 |

# SYNOPSIS

## BERTHOLD HEADLINES

| Page | Typeface | Weight | Code |
|---|---|---|---|
| 159 | Americana | halbfett / bold / demi-gras | N 100: 081 1564 / 46 |
| 227 | American Typewriter ITC | mager / light / maigre | N 020: 081 2305 / 47 |
| 231 | American Typewriter ITC | normal / medium / normal | N 020: 081 1151 / 48 |
| 233 | **American Typewriter** ITC | halbfett / bold / demi-gras | N 020: 081 1157 / 49 |
| 239 | American Typewriter ITC | schmalmager / light condensed / étroit maigre | N 020: 081 2231 / 50 |
| 239 | American Typewriter ITC | schmal / medium condensed / étroit | N 020: 081 2234 / 51 |
| 241 | **American Typewriter** ITC | schmalfett / bold condensed / étroit gras | N 020: 081 2237 / 52 |
| 397 | American Typewriter ITC | fett licht / bold outline / éclairé gras | N 020: 081 1846 / 53 |
| 201 | Amsterdam 698 | | N 100: 081 0065 / 54 |
| 343 | **Annonce** | fett / bold / gras | N 100: 081 0068 / 55 |
| 403 | Annonce | licht fett / bold outline / éclairé gras | N 000: 081 0070 / 56 |
| 197 | Antiqua | halbfett / medium / demi-gras | N 100: 081 0710 / 57 |
| 231 | Antiqua 505 | normal / regular / normal | N 100: 081 0074 / 58 |
| 221 | **Antiqua 505** | fett / bold / gras | N 100: 081 0076 / 59 |
| 291 | Antique Olive | mager / light / maigre | N 010: 081 2121 / 60 |
| 295 | Antique Olive | normal / regular / normale | N 100: 081 0080 / 61 |
| 311 | *Antique Olive* | kursiv / italic / italique | N 100: 081 1567 / 62 |
| 299 | **Antique Olive** | halbfett / medium / demi-grasse | N 100: 081 0082 / 63 |
| 303 | **Antique Olive** | fett / bold / grasse | N 100: 081 0083 / 64 |
| 305 | **Antique Olive** | kompakt / compact / compacte | N 100: 081 0092 / 65 |
| 329 | Antique Olive | schmal / condensed / étroite | N 100: 081 1569 / 66 |
| 333 | **Antique Olive** | schmalfett / bold condensed / étroite grasse | N 100: 081 0085 / 67 |
| 341 | Antique Olive | breit / extended / large | N 100: 081 0088 / 68 |
| 345 | **Antique Olive Nord** | normal / regular / normale | N 100: 081 0089 / 69 |

# SYNOPSIS

## BERTHOLD HEADLINES

| Page | Typeface | Style (de/en/fr) | Code |
|---|---|---|---|
| 347 | *Antique Olive Nord* | kursiv / italic / italique | N 100: 081 1570 / 70 |
| 323 | **Anzeigen-Grotesk** | | N 100: 081 0093 / 71 |
| 445 | *Arabella* | | N 100: 081 0094 / 72 |
| 445 | *Arabella-Favorit* | | N 100: 081 1572 / 73 |
| 447 | *Ariston* | normal / regular / normal | N 100: 081 0096 / 74 |
| 373 | Arnold Böcklin | | N 100: 081 1031 / 75 |
| 205 | Arsis | normal / regular / normal | N 100: 081 0097 / 76 |
| 207 | *Arsis* | kursiv / italic / italique | N 100: 081 0098 / 77 |
| 187 | Augustea | normal / regular / normal | N 100: 081 0099 / 78 |
| 189 | *Augustea* | kursiv / italic / italique | N 100: 081 1573 / 79 |
| 187 | **Augustea** | halbfett / medium / demi-gras | N 100: 081 0101 / 80 |
| 189 | **Augustea** | fett / bold / gras | N 100: 081 0102 / 81 |
| 191 | ***Augustea*** | kursiv fett / bold italic / italique gras | N 100: 081 0103 / 82 |
| 417 | AUGUSTEA | licht / outline / éclairé | V 000: 081 0105 / 83 |
| 277 | Aurora-Grotesk | mager / light / maigre | N 100: 081 1574 / 84 |
| 283 | *Aurora-Grotesk* | kursiv mager / light italic / italique maigre | N 100: 081 0109 / 85 |
| 295 | Aurora-Grotesk | halbfett / medium / demi-gras | N 100: 081 0110 / 86 |
| 279 | Aurora-Grotesk | dreiviertelfett / demi-bold / trois quarts de gras | N 000: 081 0113 / 87 |
| 281 | **Aurora-Grotesk** | fett / bold / gras | N 000: 081 0115 / 88 |
| 283 | ***Aurora-Grotesk*** | kursiv fett / bold italic / italique gras | N 100: 081 0118 / 89 |
| 317 | **Aurora-Grotesk** | schmalhalbfett / medium condensed / étroit demi-gras | N 000: 081 0120 / 90 |
| 325 | **Aurora-Grotesk** | schmalfett / bold condensed / étroit gras | N 000: 081 0121 / 91 |
| 337 | Aurora-Grotesk | breitmager / light extended / large maigre | N 000: 081 0122 / 92 |
| 339 | Aurora-Grotesk | breithalbfett / medium extended / large demi-gras | N 100: 081 0124 / 93 |

# SYNOPSIS

## BERTHOLD HEADLINES

| Page | Typeface | Style | Code |
|---|---|---|---|
| 345 | **Aurora-Grotesk** | breitfett / bold extended / large gras | N 100: 081 0126 / 94 |
| 421 | austrian watzlline | | X 016: 081 2226 / 95 |
| 289 | Avant Garde Gothic ITC | mager / extra light / maigre | N 100: 081 1578 / 96 |
| 289 | Avant Garde Gothic ITC | mager Zierbuchstaben / extra light swash letters / maigre lettres ornées | Z 000: 081 1579 / 97 |
| 307 | Avant Garde Gothic ITC | schräg mager / extra light oblique / oblique maigre | N 020: 081 2386 / 98 |
| 291 | Avant Garde Gothic ITC | Buch / book / romain labeur | N 010: 081 2118 / 99 |
| 291 | Avant Garde Gothic ITC | Buch Zierbuchstaben / book swash letters / romain labeur lettres ornées | Z 000: 081 0503 / 100 |
| 307 | Avant Garde Gothic ITC | Buch schräg / book oblique / romain labeur oblique | N 020: 081 2387 / 101 |
| 295 | Avant Garde Gothic ITC | normal / medium / normal | N 100: 081 1581 / 102 |
| 295 | Avant Garde Gothic ITC | normal Zierbuchstaben / medium swash letters / normal lettres ornées | Z 000: 081 1582 / 103 |
| 309 | Avant Garde Gothic ITC | schräg normal / medium oblique / oblique normal | N 020: 081 2388 / 104 |
| 299 | Avant Garde Gothic ITC | halbfett / demi-bold / demi-gras | N 100: 081 1610 / 105 |
| 299 | Avant Garde Gothic ITC | halbfett Zierbuchstaben / demi-bold swash letters / demi-gras lettres ornées | Z 000: 081 1611 / 106 |
| 311 | Avant Garde Gothic ITC | schräg halbfett / demi oblique / oblique demi-gras | N 020: 081 2389 / 107 |
| 303 | **Avant Garde Gothic** ITC | fett / bold / gras | N 100: 081 0132 / 108 |
| 303 | **Avant Garde Gothic** ITC | fett Zierbuchstaben / bold swash letters / gras lettres ornées | Z 000: 081 0133 / 109 |
| 313 | **Avant Garde Gothic** ITC | schräg fett / bold oblique / oblique gras | N 020: 081 2390 / 110 |
| 327 | Avant Garde Gothic ITC | Buch schmal / book condensed / étroit romain labeur | N 100: 081 1606 / 111 |
| 327 | Avant Garde Gothic ITC | Buch schmal Zierbuchstaben / book condensed swash letters / étroit romain labeur lettres ornées | Z 000: 081 1607 / 112 |
| 327 | Avant Garde Gothic ITC | schmal / medium condensed / étroit | N 100: 081 1608 / 113 |
| 329 | Avant Garde Gothic ITC | schmal Zierbuchstaben / medium condensed swash letters / étroit lettres ornées | Z 000: 081 1609 / 114 |
| 329 | Avant Garde Gothic ITC | schmalhalbfett / demi-bold condensed / étroit demi-gras | N 010: 081 2053 / 115 |
| 329 | Avant Garde Gothic ITC | schmalhalbfett Zierbuchstaben / demi-bold condensed swash letters / étroit demi-gras lettres ornées | Z 000: 081 2056 / 116 |
| 331 | **Avant Garde Gothic** ITC | schmalfett / bold condensed / étroit gras | N 010: 081 2059 / 117 |

# SYNOPSIS

## BERTHOLD HEADLINES

| Page | Typeface | | Description | Code |
|---|---|---|---|---|
| 331 | Avant Garde Gothic ITC | | schmalfett Zierbuchstaben / bold condensed swash letters / étroit gras lettres ornées | Z 000: 081 2062 / 118 |
| 449 | Bank Script | | | N 100: 081 1492 / 119 |
| 109 | Baskerville | BERTHOLD | normal / regular / normal | N 100: 081 0139 / 120 |
| 129 | Baskerville | BERTHOLD | kursiv / italic / italique | N 100: 081 0141 / 121 |
| 113 | Baskerville | BERTHOLD | halbfett / medium / demi-gras | N 100: 081 0143 / 122 |
| 117 | Baskerville | BERTHOLD | fett / bold / gras | N 100: 081 0144 / 123 |
| 125 | Baskerville | STEMPEL | normal / regular / normal | N 100: 081 0134 / 124 |
| 129 | Baskerville | STEMPEL | kursiv / italic / italique | N 000: 081 0136 / 125 |
| 113 | Baskerville | STEMPEL | halbfett / medium / demi-gras | N 100: 081 0138 / 126 |
| 109 | Baskerville Book | | normal / regular / normal | N 020: 081 2474 / 1304 |
| 119 | Baskerville Book | | kursiv / italic / italique | N 020: 081 2476 / 1305 |
| 113 | Baskerville Book | | halbfett / medium / demi gras | N 020 081 2475 / 1306 |
| 127 | Baskerville Old Face | | | N 100: 081 1583 / 127 |
| 443 | Batik | | | N 020: 081 0770 / 1262 |
| 347 | Bauhaus ITC | | mager / light / maigre | N 020: 081 1830 / 128 |
| 349 | Bauhaus ITC | | mager Zierbuchstaben / light swash letters / maigre lettres ornées | Z 000: 081 1913 * / 129 |
| 349 | Bauhaus ITC | | normal / regular / normal | N 020: 081 1831 / 130 |
| 349 | Bauhaus ITC | | normal Zierbuchstaben / regular swash letters / normal lettres ornées | Z 000: 081 1913 * / 129 |
| 351 | Bauhaus ITC | | halbfett / medium / demi-gras | N 020: 081 1833 / 132 |
| 353 | Bauhaus ITC | | halbfett Zierbuchstaben / medium swash lettres / demi-gras lettres ornées | Z 000: 081 1913 * / 129 |
| 353 | Bauhaus ITC | | fett / bold / gras | N 020: 081 1837 / 134 |
| 353 | Bauhaus ITC | | fett Zierbuchstaben / bold swash letters / gras lettres ornées | Z 000: 081 1913 * / 129 |
| 355 | Bauhaus ITC | | extrafett / extra bold / extra gras | N 020: 081 1826 / 136 |
| 355 | Bauhaus ITC | | extrafett Zierbuchstaben / extra bold swash letters / extra gras lettres ornées | Z 000: 081 1913 * / 129 |

# SYNOPSIS

## BERTHOLD HEADLINES

| Page | Typeface | Style | Code |
|---|---|---|---|
| 401 | Bauhaus ITC | extrafett licht / extra bold outline / extra gras éclairé | N 020: 081 1827 / 138 |
| 403 | Bauhaus ITC | extrafett licht Zierbuchstaben / extra bold outline swash letters / extra gras éclairé lettres ornées | Z 000: 081 1913 * / 129 |
| 385 | Beat Star | | N 100: 081 1540 / 140 |
| 125 | Bell | normal / medium / normal | N 020: 081 2202 / 141 |
| 129 | Bell | kursiv / medium italic / italique | N 020: 081 2203 / 142 |
| 79 | Bembo | normal / regular / normal | N 100: 081 0147 / 143 |
| 87 | Bembo | kursiv / italic / italique | N 100: 081 0148 / 144 |
| 83 | Bembo | halbfett / bold / demi gras | N 100: 081 0149 / 145 |
| 89 | Bembo | kursiv halbfett / bold italic / italique demi-gras | N 100: 081 0150 / 146 |
| 165 | Benguiat ITC | Buch / book / romain labeur | N 020: 081 2392 / 147 |
| 177 | Benguiat ITC | Buch kursiv / book italic / romain labeur italique | N 020: 081 2395 / 148 |
| 167 | Benguiat ITC | normal / medium / normal | N 020: 081 2393 / 149 |
| 179 | Benguiat ITC | kursiv / italic / italique | N 020: 081 2396 / 150 |
| 171 | Benguiat ITC | halbfett / bold / demi-gras | N 020: 081 2394 / 151 |
| 181 | Benguiat ITC | kursiv halbfett / bold italic / italique demi-gras | N 020: 081 2397 / 152 |
| 149 | Benguiat ITC | Buch schmal / book condensed / étroit romain labeur | N 020: 081 1951 / 153 |
| 155 | Benguiat ITC | Buch kursiv schmal / book condensed italic / italique romain labeur étroit | N 020: 081 1955 / 154 |
| 149 | Benguiat ITC | schmal / medium condensed / étroit | N 020: 081 1953 / 155 |
| 155 | Benguiat ITC | kursiv schmal / medium condensed italic / italique étroit | N 020: 081 1957 / 156 |
| 153 | Benguiat ITC | schmalhalbfett / bold condensed / étroit demi-gras | N 020: 081 1954 / 157 |
| 157 | Benguiat ITC | kursiv schmalhalbfett / bold condensed italic / italique étroit demi-gras | N 020: 081 1958 / 158 |
| 481 | Benguiat-Serie ITC | | Z 000: 081 1577 / 1307 |
| 357 | Benguiat Gothic ITC | Buch / book / romain labeur | N 020: 081 0333 / 1263 |
| 361 | Benguiat Gothic ITC | Buch kursiv / book italic / romain labeur italique | N 020: 081 0369 / 1264 |

9

# SYNOPSIS

## BERTHOLD HEADLINES

| Page | Typeface | Weight (de/en/fr) | Code |
|---|---|---|---|
| 357 | Benguiat Gothic ITC | normal / medium / normal | N 020: 081 0347 — 1265 |
| 361 | *Benguiat Gothic* ITC | kursiv / medium italic / italique | N 020: 081 0372 — 1266 |
| 359 | **Benguiat Gothic** ITC | halbfett / bold / demi-gras | N 020: 081 0350 — 1267 |
| 361 | ***Benguiat Gothic*** ITC | kursiv halbfett / bold italic / italique demi-gras | N 020: 081 0378 — 1268 |
| 359 | **Benguiat Gothic** ITC | fett / heavy / gras | N 020: 081 0364 — 1269 |
| 363 | ***Benguiat Gothic*** ITC | kursiv fett / heavy italic / italique gras | N 020: 081 0381 — 1363 |
| 357 | Berliner Grotesk | mager / light / maigre | N 020: 081 2420 — 1270 |
| 279 | **Berliner Grotesk** | halbfett / medium / demi-gras | N 020: 081 2419 — 159 |
| 77 | Berling-Antiqua | normal / regular / normal | N 100: 081 0151 — 160 |
| 153 | **Bernase Roman** ITC | | N 100: 081 0152 — 161 |
| 169 | **Bernhard** | fett / bold / gras | N 100: 081 1584 — 162 |
| 377 | **Bernhard** | schmalfett / bold condensed / étroit gras | N 100: 081 0153 — 163 |
| 263 | Bernhard Gothic | mager / light / maigre | N 100: 081 1794 — 164 |
| 265 | Bernhard Gothic | halbfett / medium / demi-gras | N 100: 081 1520 — 165 |
| 267 | **Bernhard Gothic** | fett / heavy / gras | N 100: 081 1795 — 166 |
| 269 | **Bernhard Gothic** | extrafett / extra heavy / extra gras | N 100: 081 0155 — 167 |
| 159 | Bernhard Modern | normal / regular / normal | N 020: 081 1832 — 168 |
| 173 | *Bernhard Modern* | kursiv / italic / italique | N 020: 081 1915 — 169 |
| 163 | **Bernhard Modern** | fett / bold / gras | N 020: 081 1838 — 170 |
| 177 | ***Bernhard Modern*** | kursiv fett / bold italic / italique gras | N 020: 081 1844 — 171 |
| 443 | *Bernhard-Schönschrift* | zart / light / maigre | N 020: 081 2182 — 172 |
| 443 | *Bernhard-Schönschrift* | kräftig / regular / normal | N 020: 081 2185 — 173 |
| 279 | Berthold-Grotesk | normal / regular / normal | N 100: 081 0156 — 174 |
| 279 | **Berthold-Grotesk** | fett / bold / gras | N 100: 081 1586 — 175 |

# SYNOPSIS

## BERTHOLD HEADLINES

| Page | Typeface | Weight (de) | Weight (en) | Weight (fr) | Code |
|---|---|---|---|---|---|
| 285 | Berthold-Grotesk | schmal | condensed | étroit | N 100: 081 0157 / 176 |
| 287 | Berthold-Grotesk | schmalfett | bold condensed | étroit gras | N 100: 081 0158 / 177 |
| 447 | Berthold-Script | normal | regular | normal | N 020: 081 1940 / 178 |
| 447 | Berthold-Script | normal Zierbuchstaben | regular swash letters | normal lettres ornées | Z 000: 081 2391 / 179 |
| 447 | Berthold-Script | halbfett | medium | demi-gras | N 020: 081 1941 / 180 |
| 449 | Berthold-Script | halbfett Zierbuchstaben | medium swash letters | demi-gras lettres ornées | Z 000: 081 2399 / 181 |
| 225 | Beton Hairline | | | | N 100: 081 1511 / 182 |
| 227 | Beton | mager | light | maigre | N 100: 081 0160 / 183 |
| 229 | Beton | halbfett | demi-bold | demi-gras | N 100: 081 1793 / 184 |
| 233 | Beton | fett | bold | gras | N 100: 081 0161 / 185 |
| 235 | Beton | extrafett | extra bold | extra gras | N 100: 081 0163 / 186 |
| 243 | Beton | schmalfett | bold condensed | étroit gras | N 100: 081 1587 / 187 |
| 407 | BETON OPEN | | | | V 100: 081 1500 / 188 |
| 441 | Bison | | | | N 100: 081 0164 / 189 |
| 271 | Black Body | | | | N 100: 081 0166 / 190 |
| 273 | Black Body | Zierbuchstaben | swash letters | lettres ornées | Z 000: 081 0167 / 191 |
| 163 | Blackfriars | normal | regular | normal | N 100: 081 1466 / 192 |
| 177 | Blackfriars | kursiv | italic | italique | N 100: 081 1467 / 193 |
| 425 | BLACK LINE | | | | V 000: 081 1588 / 194 |
| 381 | Black Wings | | | | N 020: 081 2283 / 195 |
| 351 | Blippo | halbfett | bold | demi-gras | N 100: 081 1432 / 196 |
| 351 | Blippo | halbfett Zierbuchstaben | bold swash letters | demi-gras lettres ornées | Z 000: 081 2036 / 197 |
| 353 | Blippo Black | | | | N 100: 081 1435 / 198 |
| 353 | Blippo Black | Zierbuchstaben | swash letters | lettres ornées | Z 000: 081 1920 / 199 |

# SYNOPSIS

## BERTHOLD HEADLINES

| Page | Typeface | Style | Code |
|---|---|---|---|
| 403 | Blippo Black | licht / outline / éclairé | N 100: 081 1433 / 200 |
| 403 | Blippo Black | licht Zierbuchstaben / outline swash letters / éclairé lettres ornées | Z 000: 081 1922 / 201 |
| 301 | Block | normal / regular / normal | N 100: 081 0169 / 202 |
| 285 | Block | kursiv / italic / italique | N 020: 081 2418 / 1308 |
| 305 | Block | schwer / heavy / lourd | N 100: 081 1444 / 203 |
| 325 | Block | eng / extra condensed / extra étroit | N 100: 081 0170 / 204 |
| 333 | Block | schmal / condensed / étroit | N 100: 081 0174 / 205 |
| 419 | Bodoni-Antiqua ATF | licht / outline / éclairé | N 100: 081 0210 / 206 |
| 195 | Bodoni-Antiqua BERTHOLD | normal / regular / normal | N 100: 081 0175 / 207 |
| 201 | Bodoni BERTHOLD | kursiv / italic / italique | N 100: 081 0178 / 208 |
| 195 | Bodoni-Antiqua BERTHOLD | halbfett / medium / demi-gras | N 100: 081 0182 / 209 |
| 203 | Bodoni BERTHOLD | kursiv halbfett / medium italic / italique demi-gras | N 100: 081 1591 / 210 |
| 207 | Bodoni-Antiqua BERTHOLD | schmalfett / bold condensed / étroit gras | N 100: 081 0187 / 211 |
| 195 | Bodoni-Antiqua HAAS | halbfett / medium / demi-gras | N 100: 081 0200 / 212 |
| 201 | Bodoni HAAS | kursiv halbfett / medium italic / italique demi-gras | N 000: 081 1595 / 213 |
| 193 | Bodoni-Antiqua AMSTERDAM | normal / regular / normal | N 100: 081 0191 / 214 |
| 201 | Bodoni AMSTERDAM | kursiv / italic / italique | N 100: 081 0194 / 215 |
| 197 | Bodoni-Antiqua AMSTERDAM | fett / bold / gras | N 100: 081 0197 / 216 |
| 203 | Bodoni AMSTERDAM | kursiv fett / bold italic / italique gras | N 100: 081 0193 / 217 |
| 193 | BODONI-VERSAL NEUFVILLE | Versal / title / initiales | V 000: 081 0207 / 218 |
| 383 | Bobn-Script | | N 100: 081 0211 / 219 |
| 381 | Boldiz | | N 100: 081 1852 / 220 |
| 365 | Bolt ITC | fett / bold / gras | N 100: 081 0220 / 221 |
| 111 | Bookman ITC | mager / light / maigre | N 020: 081 2306 / 222 |

# SYNOPSIS

## BERTHOLD HEADLINES

| Page | Sample | Style | Code | No. |
|---|---|---|---|---|
| 111 | Bookman ITC | mager Zierbuchstaben / light swash letters / maigre lettres ornées | Z 000: 081 2317 | 223 |
| 121 | Bookman ITC | kursiv mager / light italic / italique maigre | N 020: 081 2310 | 224 |
| 121 | Bookman ITC | kursiv mager Zierbuchstaben / light italic swash letters / italique maigre lettres ornées | Z 000: 081 2151 | 225 |
| 113 | Bookman ITC | normal / medium / normal | N 020: 081 2330 | 226 |
| 113 | Bookman ITC | normal Zierbuchstaben / medium swash letters / normal lettres ornées | Z 000: 081 2328 | 227 |
| 121 | Bookman ITC | kursiv / medium italic / italique | N 020: 081 2331 | 228 |
| 121 | Bookman ITC | kursiv Zierbuchstaben / medium italic swash letters / italique lettres ornées | Z 000: 081 2329 | 229 |
| 115 | Bookman ITC | halbfett / demi-bold / demi-gras | N 020: 081 2332 | 230 |
| 115 | Bookman ITC | halbfett Zierbuchstaben / demi bold swash letters / demi-gras lettres ornées | Z 000: 081 2334 | 231 |
| 123 | Bookman ITC | kursiv halbfett / demi-bold italic / italique demi-gras | N 020: 081 2333 | 232 |
| 123 | Bookman ITC | kursiv halbfett Zierbuchstaben / demi-bold italic swash letters / italique demi-gras lettres ornées | Z 000: 081 2335 | 233 |
| 117 | Bookman ITC | fett / bold / gras | N 020: 081 2308 | 234 |
| 117 | Bookman ITC | fett Zierbuchstaben / bold swash letters / gras lettres ornées | Z 000: 081 2150 | 235 |
| 123 | Bookman ITC | kursiv fett / bold italic / italique gras | N 020: 081 2309 | 236 |
| 123 | Bookman ITC | kursiv fett Zierbuchstaben / bold italic swash letters / italique gras lettres ornées | Z 000: 081 2153 | 237 |
| 395 | Bookman ITC | licht / outline / éclairé | N 020: 081 2340 | 238 |
| 395 | Bookman ITC | licht Zierbuchstaben / outline swash letters / éclairé lettres ornées | Z 000: 081 2157 | 239 |
| 413 | Bookman ITC | Kontur / contour / contour | N 020: 081 2339 | 240 |
| 413 | Bookman ITC | Kontur Zierbuchstaben / contour swash letters / contour lettres ornées | Z 000: 081 2156 | 241 |
| 109 | Bookman LUDLOW | normal / regular / normal | N 100: 081 1597 | 242 |
| 119 | Bookman LUDLOW | kursiv / italic / italique | N 100: 081 0213 | 243 |
| 119 | Bookman LUDLOW | kursiv Zierbuchstaben / italic swash letters / italique lettres ornées | Z 000: 081 0214 | 244 |
| 111 | Bookman LUDLOW | fett / bold / gras | N 100: 081 0215 | 245 |
| 111 | Bookman LUDLOW | fett Zierbuchstaben / bold swash letters / gras lettres ornées | Z 000: 081 0217 | 246 |

# SYNOPSIS

## BERTHOLD HEADLINES

| Page | Typeface | Style | Code |
|---|---|---|---|
| 109 | Bookman Meola I | Zierbuchstaben / swash letters / lettres ornées | Z 000: 081 1598 — 247 |
| 109 | Bookman Meola II | Zierbuchstaben / swash letters / lettres ornées | Z 000: 081 0219 — 248 |
| 379 | Boutique | | N 100: 081 1600 — 249 |
| 339 | Brasilia | normal / medium / demi-gras | N 100: 081 0225 — 250 |
| 341 | Brasilia | halbfett / bold / demi-gras | N 100: 081 0228 — 251 |
| 65 | Breda-Gotisch | | F 006: 081 2142 — 252 |
| 67 | Breite Kanzlei | | N 100: 081 0229 — 253 |
| 211 | Britannic | normal / regular / normal | N 100: 081 0230 — 254 |
| 209 | Britannic | fett / bold / gras | N 100: 081 0231 — 255 |
| 213 | Britannic | kursiv fett / bold italic / italique gras | N 100: 081 0232 — 256 |
| 209 | Broadway | normal / regular / normal | N 100: 081 0233 — 257 |
| 453 | Brush | | N 100: 081 0234 — 258 |
| 387 | Bulk | | N 100: 081 1863 — 259 |
| 125 | Bulmer | normal / regular / normal | N 100: 081 1602 — 260 |
| 139 | Bulmer | kursiv / italic / italique | N 100: 081 0236 — 261 |
| 347 | BUSORAMA ITC | mager / light / maigre | V 000: 081 1497 — 262 |
| 349 | BUSORAMA ITC | halbfett / medium / demi-gras | V 000: 081 1498 — 263 |
| 349 | BUSORAMA ITC | fett / bold / gras | V 000: 081 1499 — 264 |
| 431 | BUXOM | | V 000: 081 0237 — 265 |
| 383 | Calligraphia | | N 100: 081 1524 — 266 |
| 217 | Candida | normal / regular / normal | N 100: 081 0238 — 267 |
| 221 | Candida | kursiv / italic / italique | N 100: 081 0239 — 268 |
| 219 | Candida | halbfett / medium / demi-gras | N 100: 081 0240 — 269 |
| 437 | CAROLUS | | V 000: 081 0241 — 270 |

# SYNOPSIS

## BERTHOLD HEADLINES

| Page | Typeface | Style | Code |
|---|---|---|---|
| 111 | Caslon Buch  BERTHOLD | normal / regular / normal | N 020: 081 2481  1309 |
| 119 | *Caslon Buch*  BERTHOLD | kursiv / italic / italique | N 020: 081 2484  1305 |
| 115 | **Caslon Buch**  BERTHOLD | halbfett / medium / demi-gras | N 020: 081 2482  1311 |
| 133 | Caslon 471  HAAS | normal / regular / normal | N 100: 081 0242  271 |
| 139 | *Caslon 471*  HAAS | kursiv / italic / italique | N 100: 081 0244  272 |
| 139 | *Caslon 540*  ATF | kursiv / italic / italique | N 000: 081 0246  273 |
| 139 | *Caslon 540*  ATF | kursiv Zierbuchstaben / italic swash letters / italique lettres ornées | Z 000: 081 0248  274 |
| 127 | **Caslon**  ATF | halbfett / bold / demi-gras | N 100: 081 1605  275 |
| 113 | **Caslon Adbold** | | N 100: 081 1505  276 |
| 145 | **Caslon Headline** ITC | | N 100: 081 1791  277 |
| 135 | **Caslon Old Face** | fett / heavy / gras | N 100: 081 0253  278 |
| 151 | **Caslon**  ATF | schmalhalbfett / bold condensed / étroit demi-gras | N 100: 081 0250  279 |
| 417 | Caslon Open Face | | N 100: 081 0251  280 |
| 419 | CASTOR | | V 100: 081 0254  281 |
| 143 | Century  ATF | normal expanded / normal | N 100: 081 0270  282 |
| 147 | *Century*  ATF | kursiv expanded italic / italique | N 100: 081 0272  283 |
| 143 | **Century**  ATF | halbfett / bold / demi-gras | N 100: 081 0258  284 |
| 147 | ***Century***  ATF | kursiv halbfett / bold italic / italique demi-gras | N 100: 081 0259  285 |
| 151 | **Century**  ATF | schmalhalbfett / bold condensed / étroit demi-gras | N 100: 081 0264  286 |
| 143 | Century ITC | Buch / book / romain labeur | N 020: 081 2007  287 |
| 145 | *Century* ITC | Buch kursiv / book italic / italique romain labeur | N 020: 081 2008  288 |
| 145 | **Century** ITC | ultra / ultra / ultra | N 020: 081 2242  289 |
| 147 | ***Century*** ITC | kursiv ultra / ultra italic / itlalique ultra | N 020: 081 2243  290 |
| 149 | Century Nova | | N 100: 081 0269  291 |

# SYNOPSIS

## BERTHOLD HEADLINES

| Page | Typeface | | Style | Code |
|---|---|---|---|---|
| 109 | Century Old Style | | normal / regular / normal | N 020: 081 2336 / 292 |
| 131 | *Century Old Style* | | kursiv / italic / italique | N 020: 081 2296 / 293 |
| 143 | Century Schoolbook | | normal / regular / normal | N 100: 081 0277 / 294 |
| 145 | *Century Schoolbook* | | kursiv / italic / italique | N 100: 081 0278 / 295 |
| 143 | **Century Schoolbook** | | halbfett / bold / demi-gras | N 100: 081 0279 / 296 |
| 441 | *Champion* | | | N 100: 081 0280 / 297 |
| 373 | CHARLEMAGNE | | | V 000: 081 0285 / 298 |
| 373 | Charleston | | | N 100: 081 0286 / 299 |
| 113 | Cheltenham | ATF | halbfett / medium / demi-gras | N 100: 081 0292 / 300 |
| 121 | *Cheltenham* | ATF | kursiv halbfett / bold italic / italique demi-gras | N 100: 081 0296 / 301 |
| 151 | Cheltenham | ATF | eng halbfett / bold extra condensed / extra étroit demi-gras | N 100: 081 0308 / 302 |
| 151 | Cheltenham | ATF | schmalhalbfett / bold condensed / étroit demi-gras | N 100: 081 0303 / 303 |
| 115 | **Cheltenham** | ATF | breithalbfett / bold extended / large demi-gras | N 100: 081 0313 / 304 |
| 395 | Cheltenham | ATF | licht halbfett / bold open / demi-gras éclairé | N 100: 081 0298 / 305 |
| 109 | Cheltenham | ITC | mager / light / maigre | N 020: 081 2429 / 306 |
| 117 | *Cheltenham* | ITC | kursiv mager / light italic / italique maigre | N 020: 081 2430 / 307 |
| 111 | Cheltenham | ITC | Buch / book / romain labeur | N 020: 081 1960 / 308 |
| 119 | *Cheltenham* | ITC | Buch kursiv / book italic / italique romain labeur | N 020: 081 1962 / 309 |
| 115 | **Cheltenham** | ITC | halbfett / bold / demi-gras | N 020: 081 2431 / 310 |
| 123 | ***Cheltenham*** | ITC | kursiv halbfett / bold italic / italique demi-gras | N 020: 081 2432 / 311 |
| 117 | **Cheltenham** | ITC | ultra / ultra / ultra | N 020: 081 1963 / 312 |
| 125 | ***Cheltenham*** | ITC | kursiv ultra / ultra italic / italique ultra | N 020: 081 1965 / 313 |
| 149 | Cheltenham | ITC | schmalmager / light condensed / étroit maigre | N 020: 081 2433 / 314 |
| 155 | *Cheltenham* | ITC | kursiv schmalmager / light condensed italic / italique étroit maigre | N 020: 081 2434 / 315 |

# SYNOPSIS

## BERTHOLD HEADLINES

| Page | Typeface | Weight/Style | Code |
|------|----------|--------------|------|
| 149 | Cheltenham ITC | Buch schmal / book condensed / romain labeur étroit | N 020: 081 2435 / 316 |
| 155 | Cheltenham ITC | Buch kursiv schmal / book condensed italic / italique romain labeur étroit | N 020: 081 2436 / 317 |
| 153 | Cheltenham ITC | schmalhalbfett / bold condensed / étroit demi-gras | N 020: 081 2439 / 318 |
| 157 | Cheltenham ITC | kursiv schmalhalbfett / bold condensed italic / italique étroit demi-gras | N 020: 081 2440 / 319 |
| 155 | Cheltenham ITC | ultra schmal / ultra condensed / ultra étroit | N 020: 081 2437 / 320 |
| 157 | Cheltenham ITC | ultra schmal kursiv / ultra condensed italic / ultra italique étroit | N 020: 081 2438 / 321 |
| 393 | Cheltenham ITC | licht / outline / éclairé | N 020: 081 1994 / 322 |
| 407 | Cheltenham ITC | licht schattiert / outline shaded / éclairé ombré | N 020: 081 1995 / 323 |
| 413 | Cheltenham ITC | Kontur / contour / contour | N 020: 081 1996 / 324 |
| 149 | Cheltenham Old Style | schmal / condensed / étroit | N 100: 081 0318 / 325 |
| 391 | Chin Century 2000 Nr. 1 | normal / regular / normal | N 100: 081 1536 / 326 |
| 391 | Chin Century 2000 Nr. 2 | halbfett / medium / demi-gras | N 100: 081 1538 / 327 |
| 391 | Chin Century 2000 Nr. 3 | kursiv halbfett / medium italic / italique demi-gras | N 100: 081 1539 / 328 |
| 419 | Chisel | | N 100: 081 0319 / 329 |
| 443 | Choc | | N 100: 081 0320 / 330 |
| 419 | CHRYSTAL | | V 000: 081 0322 / 331 |
| 305 | Churchward 69 | extrafett / extra bold / extra gras | N 100: 081 0329 / 332 |
| 315 | Churchward 69 | kursiv extrafett / extra bold italic / italique extra gras | N 100: 081 1446 / 333 |
| 307 | Churchward 69 | ultrafett / ultra bold / ultra gras | N 100: 081 1437 / 334 |
| 315 | Churchward 69 | kursiv ultrafett / ultra bold italic / italique ultra gras | N 100: 081 1438 / 335 |
| 319 | Churchward 69 | schmalhalbfett / elongated / étroit demi-gras | N 100: 081 0330 / 336 |
| 337 | Churchward 69 | kursiv schmalhalbfett / elongated italic / italique étroit demi-gras | N 100: 081 0331 / 337 |
| 325 | Churchward 69 | schmalfett / bold condensed / étroit demi-gras | N 100: 081 0327 / 338 |
| 337 | Churchward 69 | kursiv schmalfett / bold condensed italic / italique étroit gras | N 100: 081 0328 / 339 |

# SYNOPSIS

## BERTHOLD HEADLINES

| Page | Sample | Style | Code |
|---|---|---|---|
| 347 | Churchward Design 70 | ultraleicht / hairline / ultra maigre | N 100: 081 0337 / 340 |
| 355 | Churchward Design 70 | kursiv ultraleicht / hairline italic / italique ultra maigre | N 100: 081 1516 / 341 |
| 347 | Churchward Design 70 | leicht / light / extra maigre | N 100: 081 0338 / 342 |
| 355 | Churchward Design 70 | kursiv leicht / light italic / italique maigre | N 100: 081 1441 / 343 |
| 349 | Churchward Design 70 | mager / regular / maigre | N 100: 081 1458 / 344 |
| 351 | Churchward Design 70 | normal / medium / normal | N 100: 081 0339 / 345 |
| 357 | Churchward Design 70 | kursiv / medium italic / italique | N 100: 081 1440 / 346 |
| 351 | Churchward Design 70 | halbfett / demi-bold / demi-gras | N 100: 081 0340 / 347 |
| 357 | Churchward Design 70 | kursiv halbfett / demi-bold italic / italique demi-gras | N 100: 081 1459 / 348 |
| 353 | Churchward Design 70 | fett / bold / gras | N 100: 081 0342 / 349 |
| 357 | Churchward Design 70 | kursiv fett / bold italic / italique gras | N 100: 081 1460 / 350 |
| 355 | Churchward Design 70 | extrafett / ultra bold / extra gras | N 100: 081 0343 / 351 |
| 357 | Churchward Design 70 | kursiv extrafett / ultra bold italic / italique extra gras | N 100: 081 0344 / 352 |
| 425 | Churchward Design 70 | Chisel / Chisel / Chisel | N 100: 081 0345 / 353 |
| 409 | Churchward Design 70 | Deep Shadow normal / Deep Shadow regular / Deep Shadow normal | N 100: 081 1716 / 354 |
| 409 | Churchward Design 70 | Deep Shadow kursiv / Deep Shadow italic / Deep Shadow italique | N 100: 081 1721 / 355 |
| 425 | Churchward Design 70 | Double / Double / Double | N 100: 081 1542 / 356 |
| 423 | Churchward Design 70 | Lines / Lines / Lines | N 100: 081 1784 / 357 |
| 423 | Churchward Design 70 | Lines Deep Shadow normal / Lines Deep Shadow regular / Lines Deep Shadow normal | N 100: 081 2016 / 358 |
| 423 | Churchward Design 70 | Lines Deep Shadow kursiv / Lines Deep Shadow italic / Lines Deep Shadow italique | N 100: 081 2023 / 359 |
| 425 | Churchward Design 70 | Metalic / Metalic / Metalic | N 100: 081 1036 / 360 |
| 425 | Churchward Design 70 | Modern normal / Modern regular / Modern normal | N 100: 081 0968 / 361 |
| 425 | Churchward Design 70 | Modern kursiv / Modern italic / Modern italique | N 100: 081 0906 / 362 |
| 421 | Churchward Design 70 | No-End / No-End / No-End | N 100: 081 1445 / 363 |

# SYNOPSIS

## BERTHOLD HEADLINES

| Page | Typeface | Style | Code / No. |
|---|---|---|---|
| 425 | Churchward Design 70 | Sparkly normal / Sparkly regular / Sparkly normal | N 100: 081 0954 / 364 |
| 425 | Churchward Design 70 | Sparkly kursiv / Sparkly italic / Sparkly italique | N 100: 081 0923 / 365 |
| 381 | Churchward Blackbeauty 72 | normal / regular / normal | N 100: 081 1472 / 366 |
| 405 | Churchward Blackbeauty 72 | licht / outline / éclairé | N 100: 081 1474 / 367 |
| 411 | Churchward Blackbeauty 72 | schattiert / shaded / ombré | N 100: 081 1475 / 368 |
| 437 | Churchward Brush | normal / regular / normal | N 100: 081 0335 / 369 |
| 439 | Churchward Brush | kursiv / italic / italique | N 100: 081 0336 / 370 |
| 361 | Churchward Marianna | normal / regular / normal | N 100: 081 0323 / 371 |
| 363 | Churchward Marianna | kursiv / italic / italique | N 100: 081 0325 / 372 |
| 411 | Churchward Marianna | schattiert / shaded / ombré | N 100: 081 1461 / 373 |
| 411 | Churchward Marianna | kursiv schattiert / italic shaded / italique ombré | N 100: 081 0326 / 374 |
| 245 | Churchward Maricia | normal / regular / normal | N 100: 081 0334 / 375 |
| 245 | Churchward Maricia | kursiv / italic / italique | N 100: 081 1447 / 376 |
| 409 | Churchward Maricia | schattiert / shaded / ombré | N 100: 081 1534 / 377 |
| 409 | Churchward Maricia | kursiv schattiert / shaded italic / italique ombré | N 100: 081 1535 / 378 |
| 293 | Churchward Tranquillity | normal / medium / normal | N 100: 081 1468 / 379 |
| 309 | Churchward Tranquillity | kursiv / medium italic / italique | N 100: 081 0346 / 380 |
| 297 | Churchward Tranquillity | halbfett / demi-bold / demi-gras | N 100: 081 0348 / 381 |
| 311 | Churchward Tranquillity | kursiv halbfett / demi-bold italic / italique demi-gras | N 100: 081 0349 / 382 |
| 247 | Churchward Tua | normal / regular / normal | N 100: 081 0332 / 383 |
| 247 | Churchward Tua | kursiv / italic / italique | N 000: 081 1469 / 384 |
| 243 | Circo |  | N 100: 081 0351 / 385 |
| 347 | Circulus |  | N 100: 081 1462 / 386 |
| 229 | City | mager / light / maigre | N 100: 081 0356 / 387 |

19

# SYNOPSIS

## BERTHOLD HEADLINES

| | | | |
|---|---|---|---|
| 231 | City | halbfett / medium / demi-gras | N 100: 081 0357 / 388 |
| 235 | **City** | fett / bold / gras | N 100: 081 0358 / 389 |
| 223 | Clarendon | mager / light / maigre | N 100: 081 0359 / 390 |
| 223 | Clarendon | kräftig / medium / normal | N 100: 081 0363 / 391 |
| 225 | **Clarendon** | halbfett / medium / demi-gras | N 100: 081 0362 / 392 |
| 225 | **Clarendon** | fett / bold / gras | N 100: 081 0366 / 393 |
| 239 | Clarendon | schmalmager / light condensed / étroit maigre | N 100: 081 0368 / 394 |
| 241 | **Clarendon** | schmalfett / bold condensed / étroit gras | N 100: 081 0370 / 395 |
| 243 | **Clarendon** | breitfett / bold extended / large gras | N 100: 081 1737 / 396 |
| 163 | Clearface ATF | halbfett / bold / demi-gras | N 100: 081 0371 / 397 |
| 167 | **Clearface** ATF | fett / heavy / gras | N 100: 081 0376 / 398 |
| 179 | *Clearface* ATF | kursiv fett / heavy italic / italique gras | N 100: 081 0377 / 399 |
| 151 | **Clearface** ATF | schmalfett / heavy condensed / étroit gras | N 100: 081 0379 / 400 |
| 161 | Clearface ITC | normal / regular / normal | N 020: 081 2210 / 401 |
| 177 | *Clearface* ITC | kursiv / italic / italique | N 020: 081 2214 / 1271 |
| 163 | **Clearface** ITC | halbfett / bold / demi-gras | N 020: 081 2211 / 402 |
| 177 | ***Clearface*** ITC | kursiv halbfett / bold italic / italique demi-gras | N 020: 081 2215 / 403 |
| 169 | **Clearface** ITC | fett / heavy / gras | N 020: 081 2212 / 404 |
| 179 | ***Clearface*** ITC | kursiv fett / heavy italic / italique gras | N 020: 081 2219 / 1272 |
| 171 | **Clearface** ITC | extrafett / black / extra gras | N 020: 081 2213 / 1273 |
| 181 | ***Clearface*** ITC | kursiv extrafett / black italic / italique extra-gras | N 020: 081 2220 / 1274 |
| 393 | Clearface ITC | licht / outline / éclairé | N 020: 081 2221 / 1312 |
| 407 | Clearface ITC | licht schattiert / outline shadow / éclairé ombré | N 020: 081 2223 / 405 |
| 413 | Clearface ITC | Kontur / contour / contour | N 020: 081 2224 / 1275 |

## BERTHOLD HEADLINES

| Page | Typeface | Weight (DE / EN / FR) | Code |
|---|---|---|---|
| 265 | **Clearface Gothic** | normal / regular / normal | N 020: 081 2281 — 406 |
| 269 | **Clearface Gothic** | fett / heavy / gras | N 020: 081 2282 — 407 |
| 269 | **Clearface Gothic** | extrafett / ultra bold / extra gras | N 020: 081 2255 — 408 |
| 209 | CLYDE | | V 000: 081 1491 — 409 |
| 109 | Columbia | | N 100: 081 0380 — 410 |
| 393 | COLUMNA OPEN | | V 000: 081 0384 — 411 |
| 93 | Comenius-Antiqua | normal / regular / normal | N 020: 081 2490 — 1313 |
| 105 | *Comenius* | kursiv / italic / italique | N 020: 081 2491 — 1314 |
| 93 | **Comenius-Antiqua** | halbfett / medium / demi-gras | N 020: 081 2492 — 1315 |
| 95 | **Comenius-Antiqua** | fett / bold / gras | N 020: 081 2493 — 1316 |
| 449 | *Commercial Script* | | N 100: 081 1503 — 412 |
| 417 | **Comstock** | | N 100: 081 0387 — 413 |
| 111 | Concorde | normal / regular / normal | N 100: 081 0388 — 414 |
| 131 | *Concorde* | kursiv / italic / italique | N 100: 081 0389 — 415 |
| 115 | **Concorde** | halbfett / medium / demi-gras | N 100: 081 0390 — 416 |
| 123 | ***Concorde*** | kursiv halbfett / medium italic / italique demi-gras | N 020: 081 0470 — 1317 |
| 149 | Concorde | schmal / condensed / étroit | N 020: 081 1126 — 1318 |
| 153 | Concorde | schmalhalbfett / medium condensed / étroit demi-gras | N 020: 081 0543 — 1319 |
| 153 | **Concorde** | schmalfett / bold condensed / étroit gras | N 020: 081 1739 — 1320 |
| 149 | Concorde Nova | normal / regular / normal | N 020: 081 1708 — 1321 |
| 131, 155 | *Concorde Nova* | kursiv / italic / italique | N 020: 081 1725 — 1322 |
| 153 | **Concorde Nova** | halbfett / medium / demi-gras | N 020: 081 1711 — 1323 |
| 443 | *Contact* | | N 100: 081 0391 — 417 |
| 393 | Contura | | N 100: 081 0392 — 418 |

SYNOPSIS

# SYNOPSIS

## BERTHOLD HEADLINES

| Page | Typeface | Style | Code |
|---|---|---|---|
| 173 | **Cooper Black** | normal / regular / normal | N 010: 081 2304 / 419 |
| 183 | *Cooper Black* | kursiv / italic / italique | N 100: 081 0398 / 420 |
| 173 | **Cooper Black** | schmal / condensed / étroit | N 100: 081 0403 / 422 |
| 395 | Cooper Black (outline) | licht / outline / éclairé | N 100: 081 0404 / 423 |
| 161 | Cooper Old Style | normal / regular / normal | N 100: 081 0409 / 424 |
| 175 | Cooper Old Style | kursiv / italic / italique | N 100: 081 0410 / 425 |
| 443 | Coronet | | N 100. 081 0411 / 426 |
| 193 | Couture Antiqua | | N 100: 081 1749 / 427 |
| 223 | Craw Clarendon | Buch / book / romain labeur | N 100: 081 0417 / 428 |
| 397 | Craw Clarendon (outline) | licht / outline / éclairé | N 100: 081 1489 / 429 |
| 157 | Craw Modern | normal / regular / normal | N 100: 081 0412 / 430 |
| 147 | Craw Modern | kursiv / italic / italique | N 100: 081 0416 / 431 |
| 389 | Dalmock | | N 020: 081 0140 / 432 |
| 439 | Daphne | | N 100: 081 0418 / 433 |
| 439 | Daphne | Zierbuchstaben / swash letters / lettres ornées | Z 000: 081 0420 / 434 |
| 243 | Datonga | | N 100: 081 1760 / 435 |
| 421 | Dektiv Double | | N 010: 081 2124 / 436 |
| 381 | De Vinne Ornamented | normal / regular / normal | N 100: 081 0421 / 437 |
| 383 | *De Vinne Ornamented* | kursiv / italic / italique | N 100: 081 0423 / 438 |
| 247 | Diador | | N 100: 081 0424 / 439 |
| 195 | Didi ITC | | N 100: 081 1549 / 440 |
| 91 | Diethelm-Antiqua | normal / regular / normal | N 100: 081 0425 / 441 |
| 87 | *Diethelm* | kursiv / italic / italique | N 100: 081 0427 / 442 |
| 87 | *Diethelm* | kursiv Zierbuchstaben / italic swash letters / italique lettres ornées | Z 000: 081 0429 / 443 |

# SYNOPSIS

## BERTHOLD HEADLINES

| Page | Typeface | Style (de/en/fr) | Code |
|---|---|---|---|
| 93 | Diethelm-Antiqua | halbfett / medium / demi-gras | N 100: 081 0426 / 444 |
| 327 | Digi-Grotesk Serie S | schmal / condensed / étroit | N 100: 081 1450 / 445 |
| 331 | **Digi-Grotesk Serie S** | schmal kräftig / bold condensed / étroit gras | N 100: 081 1452 / 446 |
| 295 | **Fette Mittelschrift** | fett / bold / gras | N 020: 081 2548 / 1369 |
| 329 | **Fette Engschrift** | fett / bold / gras | N 020: 081 2547 / 1370 |
| 341 | **DIN-Breitschrift** | | N 000: 081 0433 / 450 |
| 159 | Diotima | | N 100: 081 0434 / 451 |
| 217 | Dominante | normal / regular / normal | N 020: 081 2448 / 1325 |
| 221 | *Dominante* | kursiv / italic / itaique | N 020: 081 2450 / 1326 |
| 219 | **Dominante** | fett / bold / gras | N 020: 081 2449 / 1327 |
| 137 | **Domino** | | N 100: 081 1744 / 452 |
| 217 | Druckhaus-Antiqua | normal / regular / normal | N 100: 081 0435 / 453 |
| 147 | *Druckhaus* | kursiv / italic / italique | N 000: 081 0437 / 454 |
| 219 | **Druckhaus-Antiqua** | halbfett / medium / demi-gras | N 000: 081 0438 / 455 |
| 373 | Eckmann | | N 000: 081 0441 / 456 |
| 207 | **Editorial Tondo** | | N 100: 081 0444 / 457 |
| 209 | ***Editorial*** | kursiv / italic / italique | N 100: 081 0446 / 458 |
| 223 | Egizio | normal / regular / normal | N 100: 081 0447 / 459 |
| 221 | *Egizio* | kursiv / italic / italique | N 100: 081 0448 / 460 |
| 225 | **Egizio** | fett / bold / gras | N 100: 081 0449 / 461 |
| 223 | ***Egizio*** | kursiv fett / bold italic / italique gras | N 100: 081 0451 / 462 |
| 239 | Egizio | schmal / condensed / étroit | N 100: 081 0456 / 463 |
| 239 | **Egyptienne** | schmalhalbfett / medium condensed / étroite demi-grasse | N 100: 081 1517 / 464 |
| 241 | **Egyptienne** | schmalfett / bold condensed / étroite grasse | N 100: 081 0457 / 465 |

# SYNOPSIS

## BERTHOLD HEADLINES

| Page | Specimen | Weight | Code |
|---|---|---|---|
| 243 | Egyptienne | breithalbfett / medium extended / large demi-grasse | N 100: 081 1518 / 466 |
| 243 | **Egyptienne** | breitfett / bold extended / large grasse | N 100: 081 0461 / 467 |
| 409 | Egyptienne | breit schattiert / expanded shaded / large ombrées | N 100: 081 0465 / 468 |
| 431 | EGYPTIENNE FILETEE | | Sp000: 081 0468 / 469 |
| 445 | El Greco | | N 100: 081 0473 / 470 |
| 205 | ELONGATED ROMAN | | V 000: 081 1525 / 471 |
| 407 | ELONGATED ROMAN | schattiert / shaded / ombré | V 000: 081 1796 / 472 |
| 385 | *Elvira* | kursiv fett / bold italic / italique gras | N 000: 081 0474 / 473 |
| 135 | Elzévir | halbfett / medium / demi-gras | N 100: 081 0475 / 474 |
| 355 | **Embrionic** | | N 100: 081 0477 / 475 |
| 355 | **Embrionic** | Zierbuchstaben / swash letters / lettres ornées | Z 000: 081 0478 / 476 |
| 447 | Englische Schreibschrift | normal / regular / normal | N 020: 081 1686 / 1276 |
| 449 | Englische Schreibschrift | halbfett / medium / demi-gras | N 020: 081 1689 / 1328 |
| 451 | Englische Schreibschrift | fett / bold / gras | N 020: 081 1692 / 1277 |
| 157 | ENGRAVERS ROMAN | normal / regular / normal | V 000: 081 0479 / 477 |
| 263 | Eras ORIGINAL HOLLENSTEIN | | N 100: 081 0482 / 478 |
| 261 | Eras ITC | mager / light / maigre | N 020: 081 1930 / 479 |
| 263 | Eras ITC | Buch / book / romain labeur | N 020: 081 1931 / 480 |
| 265 | Eras ITC | normal / medium / normal | N 020: 081 1932 / 481 |
| 267 | **Eras** ITC | halbfett / demi-bold / demi-gras | N 020: 081 1934 / 482 |
| 269 | **Eras** ITC | fett / bold / gras | N 020: 081 1935 / 483 |
| 271 | **Eras** ITC | ultra / ultra / ultra | N 020: 081 1936 / 484 |
| 399 | Eras ITC | licht / outline / éclairé | N 020: 081 2400 / 485 |
| 415 | Eras ITC | Kontur / contour / contour | N 020: 081 2401 / 486 |

# SYNOPSIS

## BERTHOLD HEADLINES

| Page | Typeface | Weight | Code |
|---|---|---|---|
| 277 | Erbar-Werkschrift | | N 100: 081 0483 / 487 |
| 279 | **Erbar-Grotesk** | halbfett / medium / demi-gras | N 100: 081 0488 / 488 |
| 281 | **Erbar-Grotesk** | fett / bold / gras | N 100: 081 0491 / 489 |
| 287 | **Erbar-Grotesk** | schmalhalbfett / medium condensed / étroit demi-gras | N 100: 081 0492 / 490 |
| 373 | Etienne Modern | normal / regular / normal | N 100: 081 0494 / 491 |
| 375 | **Etienne** | schmalfett / bold condensed / étroit gras | N 100: 081 0495 / 492 |
| 305 | **Etrusco 403-30** | fett / extra bold / gras | N 100: 081 1430 / 493 |
| 315 | ***Etrusco 403-35*** | kursiv fett / extra bold italic / italique gras | N 100: 081 1431 / 494 |
| 293 | Eurostile | normal / regular / normal | N 100: 081 0496 / 495 |
| 301 | **Eurostile** | fett / bold / gras | N 100: 081 0501 / 496 |
| 333 | **Eurostile** | schmalfett / bold condensed / étroit gras | N 100: 081 0513 / 497 |
| 339 | Eurostile | breit / extended / large | N 100: 081 0505 / 498 |
| 343 | **Eurostile** | breitfett / bold extended / large gras | N 100: 081 0508 / 499 |
| 441 | *Express* | | N 100: 081 0514 / 500 |
| 387 | **Fanfare** | schmal / condensed / étroit | N 100: 081 1436 / 501 |
| 389 | fat watzline | | X 016: 081 2225 / 502 |
| 193 | Fenice ITC | mager / light / maigre | N 020: 081 2530 / 1364 |
| 199 | *Fenice* ITC | kursiv mager / light italic / italique maigre | N 020: 081 2531 / 1365 |
| 193 | Fenice ITC | normal / regular / normal | N 020: 081 2251 / 503 |
| 199 | *Fenice* ITC | kursiv / italic / italique | N 020: 081 2258 / 504 |
| 197 | **Fenice** ITC | fett / bold / gras | N 020: 081 2252 / 505 |
| 203 | ***Fenice*** ITC | kursiv fett / bold italic / italique gras | N 020: 081 2532 / 1366 |
| 199 | **Fenice** ITC | ultra / ultra / ultra | N 020: 081 2533 / 1367 |
| 203 | ***Fenice*** ITC | kursiv ultra / ultra italic / italique ultra | N 020: 081 2534 / 1368 |

# SYNOPSIS

## BERTHOLD HEADLINES

| Page | Typeface | Style | Code |
|---|---|---|---|
| 199 | Fette Antiqua | | N 100: 081 0519 / 506 |
| 67 | Fette Fraktur | | N 000: 081 0523 / 507 |
| 65 | Fette Gotisch | | N 000: 081 0524 / 508 |
| 67 | Fette Kanzlei | | N 000: 081 0527 / 509 |
| 211 | Firenze ITC | | N 020: 081 1961 / 510 |
| 193 | Firmin Didot | normal / regular / normal | N 100: 081 0528 / 511 |
| 197 | Firmin Didot | fett / bold / gras | N 100: 081 0529 / 512 |
| 259 | Flange | fett / bold / gras | N 020: 081 0025 / 513 |
| 281 | Flyer | fett / bold / gras | N 020: 081 0324 / 514 |
| 287 | Flyer | schmalfett / bold condensed / étroit gras | N 020: 081 2009 / 515 |
| 291 | Folio | mager / light / maigre | N 100: 081 0530 / 516 |
| 309 | Folio | kursiv mager / light italic / italique maigre | N 100: 081 0533 / 517 |
| 297 | Folio | halbfett / medium / demi-gras | N 100: 081 0537 / 518 |
| 303 | Folio | fett / bold / gras | N 100: 081 0540 / 519 |
| 305 | Folio | extrafett / extra bold / extra gras | N 100: 081 0568 / 520 |
| 319 | Folio | engfett / bold extra condensed / extra étroit gras | N 100: 081 0558 / 521 |
| 327 | Folio | schmalmager / light condensed / étroit maigre | N 100: 081 0544 / 522 |
| 329 | Folio | schmalhalbfett / medium condensed / étroit demi-gras | N 100: 081 0549 / 523 |
| 323 | Folio | schmalfett / bold condensed / étroit gras | N 100: 081 0552 / 524 |
| 335 | Folio | kursiv schmalfett / bold condensed italic / italique étroit gras | N 100: 081 0555 / 525 |
| 341 | Folio | breithalbfett / medium extended / large demi-gras | N 100: 081 0559 / 526 |
| 345 | Folio | kursiv breithalbfett / medium extended italic / italique large demi-gras | N 100: 081 0562 / 527 |
| 343 | Folio | breitfett / bold extended / large gras | N 100: 081 0564 / 528 |
| 445 | Forelle Auszeichnung | | N 100: 081 0571 / 529 |

# SYNOPSIS

## BERTHOLD HEADLINES

| Page | Font | Style (de/en/fr) | Code / No. |
|---|---|---|---|
| 381 | Fortunata | | N 100: 081 0573 / 530 |
| 407 | FORUM I | mit Griechisch / with greek / avec grecque | Sp000: 081 0575 / 531 |
| 407 | FORUM II | | Sp000: 081 0577 / 532 |
| 301 | Franklin Gothic ATF | normal / regular / normal | N 100: 081 0580 / 533 |
| 313 | Franklin Gothic ATF | kursiv / italic / italique | N 100: 081 0581 / 534 |
| 323 | Franklin Gothic ATF | extraschmal / extra condensed / extra étroit | N 100: 081 0584 / 535 |
| 331 | Franklin Gothic ATF | schmal / condensed / étroit | N 100: 081 0583 / 536 |
| 335 | Franklin Gothic ATF | kursiv schmal / condensed italic / italique étroit | N 100: 081 1514 / 537 |
| 343 | Franklin Gothic Wide ATF | | N 100: 081 0585 / 538 |
| 401 | Franklin Gothic ATF | schmal licht / condensed outline / étroit éclairé | N 020: 081 0341 / 539 |
| 293 | Franklin Gothic ITC | Buch / book / romain labeur | N 020: 081 2454 / 1371 |
| 309 | Franklin Gothic ITC | Buch kursiv / book italic / italique romain labeur | N 020: 081 2458 / 1372 |
| 297 | Franklin Gothic ITC | normal / regular / normal | N 020: 081 2455 / 1373 |
| 311 | Franklin Gothic ITC | kursiv / italic / italique | N 020: 081 2459 / 1374 |
| 301 | Franklin Gothic ITC | halbfett / demi / demi-gras | N 020: 081 2456 / 1375 |
| 313 | Franklin Gothic ITC | kursiv halbfett / demi italic / italique demi-gras | N 020: 081 2460 / 1376 |
| 303 | Franklin Gothic ITC | fett / heavy / gras | N 020: 081 2457 / 1377 |
| 313 | Franklin Gothic ITC | kursiv fett / heavy italic / italique gras | N 020: 081 2461 / 1378 |
| 399 | Franklin Gothic ITC | licht / outline / éclairé | N 020: 081 2486 / 1379 |
| 415 | Franklin Gothic ITC | Kontur / contour / contour | N 020: 081 2485 / 1380 |
| 255 | Friz Quadrata ITC | normal / regular / normal | N 020: 081 1810 / 540 |
| 257 | Friz Quadrata ITC | fett / bold / gras | N 020: 081 1815 / 541 |
| 389 | Fupper Fono | | N 010: 081 0008 / 542 |
| 277 | Futura | mager / light / maigre | N 100: 081 0586 / 543 |

27

# SYNOPSIS

## BERTHOLD HEADLINES

| Page | Sample | Style | Code |
|---|---|---|---|
| 283 | *Futura* | schräg mager / light oblique / oblique maigre | N 100: 081 1504 / 544 |
| 277 | Futura | Buchschrift / book / romain labeur | N 100: 081 0617 / 545 |
| 283 | *Futura* | Buchschrift schräg / book oblique / romain labeur oblique | N 100: 081 0621 / 546 |
| 277 | **Futura** | halbfett / medium / demi-gras | N 100: 081 0587 / 547 |
| 283 | *Futura* | schräg halbfett / medium oblique / oblique demi-gras | N 100: 081 0590 / 548 |
| 279 | **Futura** | dreiviertelfett / demi-bold / trois quarts de gras | N 100: 081 0593 / 549 |
| 283 | *Futura* | schräg dreiviertelfett / demi-bold oblique / oblique trois quarts de gras | N 020: 081 0672 / 1278 |
| 279 | **Futura** | kräftig / bold / gras | N 020: 081 0476 / 1329 |
| 281 | **Futura** | fett / bold / gras | N 100: 081 0597 / 550 |
| 285 | **Futura** | schräg fett / bold oblique / oblique gras | N 100: 081 0599 / 551 |
| 281 | **Futura** | extrafett / extra bold / extra gras | N 100: 081 0600 / 552 |
| 285 | **Futura** | schräg extrafett / extra bold oblique / oblique extra gras | N 100: 081 0602 / 553 |
| 285 | Futura | schmalhalbfett / medium condensed / étroit demi-gras | N 100: 081 0603 / 554 |
| 287 | **Futura** | schmalfett / bold condensed / étroit gras | N 100: 081 0606 / 555 |
| 335 | *Futura* | schräg schmalfett / bold condensed oblique / oblique étroit gras | N 100: 081 0609 / 556 |
| 287 | **Futura** | extrafett schmal / extra bold condensed / étroit extra gras | N 100: 081 0611 / 557 |
| 337 | *Futura* | schräg extrafett schmal / extra bold condensed oblique / oblique étroit extra gras | N 100: 081 0616 / 558 |
| 399 | Futura | fett licht / bold outline / gras éclairé | N 020: 081 1972 / 559 |
| 399 | Futura | extrafett licht / extra bold outline / extra gras éclairé | N 020: 081 0851 / 1279 |
| 401 | Futura | extrafett schmal licht / extra bold condensed outline / étroit extra gras éclairé | N 020: 081 1971 / 560 |
| 409 | Futura | extrafett schattiert / extra bold shaded / extra gras ombré | N 020: 081 2233 / 1280 |
| 399 | FUTURA | licht / outline / éclairé | V 000: 081 0626 / 561 |
| 209, 389 | **Futura Black** | | N 100: 081 0623 / 562 |
| 427 | FUTURA BLACK ART DECO | Flipper | VD 018: 081 0274 * / 563 |

28

# SYNOPSIS

## BERTHOLD HEADLINES

| Page | Sample | Style | Code |
|---|---|---|---|
| 427 | FUTURA BLACK ART DECO | Flipper Outline | VD 018: 081 0274 * <br> 563 |
| 427 | FUTURA BLACK ART DECO | Gravur | VD 018: 081 0291 * <br> 565 |
| 429 | FUTURA BLACK ART DECO | Horizont | VD 018: 081 0283 * <br> 566 |
| 427 | FUTURA BLACK ART DECO | Light Inline | VD 018: 081 0291 * <br> 565 |
| 427 | FUTURA BLACK ART DECO | Orginal | VD 018: 081 0260 * <br> 568 |
| 405 | FUTURA BLACK ART DECO | Outline | VD 018: 081 0260 * <br> 568 |
| 429 | FUTURA BLACK ART DECO | Point | VD 018: 081 0283 * <br> 566 |
| 427 | FUTURA BLACK ART DECO | Reflex Duo | VD 018: 081 0297 * <br> 571 |
| 429 | FUTURA BLACK ART DECO | Stripes | VD 018: 081 0288 * <br> 572 |
| 429 | FUTURA BLACK ART DECO | Stripes Diagonal | VD 018: 081 0288 * <br> 572 |
| 427 | FUTURA BLACK ART DECO | Textil | VD 018: 081 0297 * <br> 571 |
| 333 | Futura Display | | N 100: 081 0625 <br> 575 |
| 419 | GALLIA | | V 000: 081 0627 <br> 576 |
| 65 | Ganz grobe Gotisch | | N 000: 081 0628 <br> 577 |
| 77 | Garamond BERTHOLD | normal <br> regular <br> normal | N 020: 081 1742 <br> 1381 |
| 87 | Garamond BERTHOLD | kursiv <br> italic <br> italique | N 020: 081 1787 <br> 1382 |
| 81 | Garamond BERTHOLD | halbfett <br> medium <br> demi-gras | N 020: 081 1756 <br> 1383 |
| 89 | Garamond BERTHOLD | kursiv halbfett <br> medium italic <br> italique demi-gras | N 020: 081 1790 <br> 1330 |
| 83 | Garamond BERTHOLD | fett <br> bold <br> gras | N 020: 081 1773 <br> 1331 |
| 97 | Garamond BERTHOLD | schmal <br> condensed <br> étroit | N 020: 081 1806 <br> 1332 |
| 79 | Garamond ITC | mager <br> light <br> maigre | N 020: 081 2362 <br> 578 |
| 87 | Garamond ITC | kursiv mager <br> light italic <br> italique maigre | N 020: 081 2363 <br> 579 |
| 81 | Garamond ITC | Buch <br> book <br> romain labeur | N 020: 081 2245 <br> 580 |
| 89 | Garamond ITC | Buch kursiv <br> book italic <br> italique romain labeur | N 020: 081 2246 <br> 581 |

# SYNOPSIS

## BERTHOLD HEADLINES

| Page | Typeface | Weight | Code |
|---|---|---|---|
| 83 | **Garamond** ITC | fett / bold / gras | N 020: 081 2364 / 582 |
| 89 | *Garamond* ITC | kursiv fett / bold italic / italique gras | N 020: 081 2380 / 583 |
| 85 | **Garamond** ITC | ultra / ultra / ultra | N 010: 081 2111 / 584 |
| 91 | *Garamond* ITC | kursiv ultra / ultra italic / italique ultra | N 010: 081 2114 / 585 |
| 97 | Garamond ITC | schmalmager / light condensed / étroit maigre | N 020: 081 2365 / 586 |
| 101 | *Garamond* ITC | kursiv schmalmager / light condensed italic / italique étroit maigre | N 020: 081 2366 / 587 |
| 97 | Garamond ITC | Buch schmal / book condensed / étroit romain labeur | N 020: 081 2367 / 588 |
| 101 | *Garamond* ITC | Buch kursiv schmal / book condensed italic / romain labeur italique étroit | N 020: 081 2368 / 589 |
| 99 | **Garamond** ITC | schmalfett / bold condensed / étroit gras | N 020: 081 2369 / 590 |
| 101 | *Garamond* ITC | kursiv schmalfett / bold condensed italic / italique étroit gras | N 020: 081 2370 / 591 |
| 99 | **Garamond** ITC | ultra schmal / ultra condensed / ultra étroit | N 020: 081 2371 / 592 |
| 103 | *Garamond* ITC | ultra schmal kursiv / ultra condensed italic / ultra italique étroit | N 020: 081 2372 / 593 |
| 77 | Garamond STEMPEL | normal / regular / normal | N 100: 081 0630 / 594 |
| 85 | *Garamond* STEMPEL | kursiv / italic / italique | N 100: 081 0634 / 595 |
| 81 | **Garamond** STEMPEL | halbfett / medium / demi-gras | N 100: 081 0636 / 596 |
| 77 | Garamont HAAS | normal / regular / normal | N 100: 081 0652 / 597 |
| 89 | *Garamont* HAAS | kursiv / italic / italique | N 100: 081 0657 / 598 |
| 77 | Garamont AMSTERDAM | normal / regular / normal | N 100: 081 0639 / 599 |
| 85 | *Garamont* AMSTERDAM | kursiv / italic / italique | N 100: 081 0643 / 600 |
| 79 | **Garamont** AMSTERDAM | halbfett / medium / demi-gras | N 100: 081 0647 / 601 |
| 89 | *Garamont* AMSTERDAM | kursiv halbfett / medium italic / italique demi-gras | N 100: 081 0651 / 602 |
| 387 | Geard Graphic | | N 100: 081 0659 / 603 |
| 275 | Genny | | N 100: 081 0660 / 604 |
| 373 | Georges Lemon | | N 100: 081 1502 / 605 |

# SYNOPSIS

## BERTHOLD HEADLINES

| Page | Typeface | Weight (de/en/fr) | Reference |
|---|---|---|---|
| 389 | **Gesh Export 233** | | N 100: 081 1527 / 606 |
| 269 | Gesh Introduction | | N 100: 081 1480 / 607 |
| 137 | **Gesh Ortega Roman 275** | | N 100: 081 1528 / 608 |
| 263 | Gill Sans | mager / light / maigre | N 100: 081 0661 / 609 |
| 273 | *Gill Sans* | kursiv mager / light italic / italique maigre | N 020: 081 2451 / 1384 |
| 263 | Gill Sans | normal / regular / normal | N 100: 081 0662 / 610 |
| 273 | *Gill Sans* | kursiv / italic / italique | N 020: 081 2452 / 1333 |
| 649 | **Gill Sans** | halbfett / bold / demi-gras | N 100: 081 0665 / 611 |
| 273 | ***Gill Sans*** | kursiv halbfett / bold italic / italique demi-gras | N 020: 081 2453 / 1385 |
| 271 | **Gill Sans** | fett / extra bold / gras | N 100: 081 0666 / 612 |
| 275 | ***Gill Sans*** | kursiv ultrafett / ultra bold italic / italique ultra gras | N 100: 081 1429 / 613 |
| 271 | **Gill Kayo** | | N 100: 081 0667 / 614 |
| 275 | **Gill Sans** | eng halbfett / bold extra condensed / extra étroit demi-gras | N 100: 081 1427 / 615 |
| 275 | **Gill Sans** | schmalhalbfett / bold condensed / étroit demi-gras | N 100: 081 0668 / 616 |
| 275 | **Gill Sans** | ultra schmalfett / ultra bold condensed / étroit ultra gras | N 100: 081 1428 / 617 |
| 397 | Gill Sans (outline) | extrafett licht / extra bold outline / extra gras éclairé | N 020: 081 2315 / 618 |
| 397 | Gill Sans (outline) | licht ultrafett / ultra bold outline / éclairé ultra gras | N 100: 081 1543 / 619 |
| 233 | **Girder Heavy** | | N 100: 081 0671 / 620 |
| 393 | G.K.W. COMPUTER | | V 000: 081 0673 / 621 |
| 433 | Globe-S | | N 020: 081 2261 / 622 |
| 415 | **GOLD RUSH** | | V 000: 081 0674 / 623 |
| 167 | Gorilla | | N 100: 081 1789 / 624 |
| 401 | GOTHIC OUTLINE TITLE | | V 000: 081 0675 / 625 |
| 81 | Goudy | halbfett / bold / demi-gras | N 100: 081 0685 / 626 |

31

# SYNOPSIS

## BERTHOLD HEADLINES

| Page | Typeface | Weight | Code |
|---|---|---|---|
| 81 | Goudy | fett / extra bold / gras | N 100: 081 0687 / 627 |
| 101 | **Goudy** | schmal extrafett / heavy faced condensed / étroit extra gras | N 100: 081 0689 / 628 |
| 79 | Goudy Catalogue | normal / regular / normal | N 100: 081 0679 / 629 |
| 177 | *Goudy Catalogue* | kursiv / italic / italique | N 020: 081 0493 / 1334 |
| 417 | Goudy Handtooled | | N 100: 081 0684 / 630 |
| 85 | **Goudy Heavyface** | normal / regular / normal | N 100: 081 1510 / 631 |
| 439 | Goudy Mediäval | | N 100: 081 0688 / 632 |
| 77 | Goudy Old Style | normal / regular / normal | N 100: 081 0678 / 633 |
| 305 | **Granby Elephant** | | N 100: 081 0690 / 634 |
| 409 | GRAPHIQUE | | V 000: 081 0691 / 635 |
| 101 | **Graphis** | extrafett / extra bold / extra gras | N 100: 081 2145 / 636 |
| 269 | **Grizzly** ITC | | N 100: 081 0692 / 637 |
| 301 | **Grotesk** | breitfett / bold extended / large gras | N 100: 081 0706 / 638 |
| 313 | ***Grotesk*** | kursiv fett / bold italic / italique gras | N 100: 081 0704 / 639 |
| 317 | Grotesk | schmal / condensed / étroit | N 100: 081 0701 / 640 |
| 323 | **Grotesk** | schmalfett / bold condensed / étroit gras | N 100: 081 0703 / 641 |
| 293 | Grotesque No. 215 | normal / regular / normal | N 100: 081 0699 / 642 |
| 299 | **Grotesque No. 216** | halbfett / bold / demi-gras | N 100: 081 0700 / 643 |
| 331 | **Grotesque No. 9a** | schmalfett / bold condensed / étroit gras | N 100: 081 0697 / 644 |
| 335 | ***Grotesque No. 9*** | kursiv schmalfett / bold condensed italic / italique étroit gras | N 100: 081 0698 / 645 |
| 331 | **Grotesque No. 9b** | schmalfett / bold condensed / étroit gras | N 100: 081 0696 / 646 |
| 317 | Grotesque No. 7 | eng / condensed / étroit | N 100: 081 0693 / 647 |
| 137 | **Grouch** ITC | | N 100: 081 0708 / 648 |
| 207 | **Haenel-Antiqua** | schmalfett / bold condensed / étroit gras | N 100: 081 0709 / 649 |

# SYNOPSIS

## BERTHOLD HEADLINES

| Page | Typeface | Style (de / en / fr) | Code / No. |
|---|---|---|---|
| 363 | **Handel Gothic** | normal / regular / normal | N 100: 081 1481 — 650 |
| 377 | HARLEKIN | | V 000: 081 0940 — 651 |
| 289 | Helvetica | ultraleicht / ultra light / ultra maigre | N 100: 081 0717 — 652 |
| 307 | *Helvetica* | kursiv ultraleicht / ultra light italic / italique ultra maigre | N 100: 081 0718 — 653 |
| 289 | Helvetica | leicht / light / maigre | N 100: 081 0720 — 654 |
| 307 | *Helvetica* | kursiv leicht / light italic / italique maigre | N 100: 081 0721 — 655 |
| 293 | Helvetica | normal / regular / normal | N 100: 081 0723 — 656 |
| 309 | *Helvetica* | kursiv / italic / italique | N 100: 081 0726 — 657 |
| 297 | **Helvetica** | halbfett / medium / demi-gras | N 010: 081 2301 — 658 |
| 311 | ***Helvetica*** | kursiv halbfett / medium italic / italique demi-gras | N 100: 081 0733 — 659 |
| 303 | **Helvetica** | fett / bold / gras | N 100: 081 0734 — 660 |
| 313 | ***Helvetica*** | kursiv fett / bold italic / italique gras | N 100: 081 0737 — 661 |
| 315 | ***Helvetica Diagonal*** | | N 100: 081 0738 — 662 |
| 327 | Helvetica | schmalmager / light condensed / étroit maigre | N 100: 081 0739 — 663 |
| 321 | **Helvetica** | schmalhalbfett / medium condensed / étroit demi-gras | N 100: 081 0740 — 664 |
| 323 | **Helvetica** | schmalfett / bold condensed / étroit gras | N 100: 081 0742 — 665 |
| 339 | Helvetica | breitmager / light extended / large maigre | N 100: 081 0745 — 666 |
| 341 | **Helvetica** | breithalbfett / medium condensed / large demi-gras | N 100: 081 0747 — 667 |
| 345 | **Helvetica** | breitfett / bold extended / large gras | N 100: 081 0749 — 668 |
| 373 | **Herkules** | | N 100: 081 0751 — 669 |
| 375 | **Herold Reklameschrift** | | N 100: 081 0755 — 670 |
| 405 | Herold Reklameschrift | licht / outline / éclairé | N 020: 081 0042 — 671 |
| 375 | **Herold** | schmal / condensed / étroit | N 100: 081 0752 — 672 |
| 245 | **HIDALGO** | | V 000: 081 0759 — 673 |

# SYNOPSIS

## BERTHOLD HEADLINES

| Page | Typeface | Style | Code |
|---|---|---|---|
| 379 | Hobo | | N 100: 081 0760 / 674 |
| 287 | Hochblock | | N 020: 081 2416 / 1386 |
| 385 | Honda Display ITC | | N 100: 081 0762 / 675 |
| 73 | Horley Old Style | normal / regular / normal | N 020: 081 2406 / 676 |
| 75 | Horley Old Style | kursiv / italic / italique | N 020: 081 2129 / 677 |
| 73 | Horley Old Style | halbfett / bold / demi-gras | N 020: 081 2407 / 678 |
| 453 | Houston | | N 100: 081 1424 / 679 |
| 217 | IBM–Dokument | | N 000: 081 0763 / 680 |
| 325 | Impact | | N 100: 081 0768 / 681 |
| 217 | Impressum | mager / light / maigre | N 100: 081 0769 / 682 |
| 221 | Impressum | kursiv mager / light italic / italique maigre | N 100: 081 0772 / 683 |
| 219 | Impressum | halbfett / medium / demi-gras | N 100: 081 0773 / 684 |
| 125 | Imprimatur | normal / regular / normal | N 100: 081 0774 / 685 |
| 131 | Imprimatur | kursiv / italic / italique | N 100: 081 0776 / 686 |
| 127 | Imprimatur | halbfett / medium / demi-gras | N 100: 081 0777 / 687 |
| 129 | Imprimatur | fett / bold / gras | N 100: 081 0778 / 688 |
| 153 | Imprimatur | schmalfett / bold condensed / étroit gras | N 100: 081 0781 / 689 |
| 441 | Impuls | | N 100: 081 0782 / 690 |
| 323 | Information | schmalfett / extra bold condensed / étroit extra gras | N 100: 081 0786 / 691 |
| 317 | Information | engfett / bold condensed / étroit gras | N 100: 081 0785 / 692 |
| 345 | Information | breitfett / bold extended / large gras | N 100: 081 0790 / 693 |
| 163 | Isbell ITC | Buch / book / romain labeur | N 020: 081 2522 / 1387 |
| 177 | Isbell ITC | Buch kursiv / book italic / italique romain labeur | N 020: 081 2523 / 1388 |
| 165 | Isbell ITC | normal / regular / normal | N 020: 081 2524 / 1389 |

# SYNOPSIS

## BERTHOLD HEADLINES

| Page | Typeface | Weight (de/en/fr) | Code |
|---|---|---|---|
| 179 | *Isbell* ITC | kursiv / italic / italique | N 020: 081 2525 / 1390 |
| 167 | **Isbell** ITC | halbfett / bold / demi-gras | N 020: 081 2526 / 1391 |
| 181 | ***Isbell*** ITC | kursiv halbfett / bold italic / italique demi-gras | N 020: 081 2527 / 1392 |
| 171 | **Isbell** ITC | fett / heavy / gras | N 020: 081 2528 / 1393 |
| 181 | ***Isbell*** ITC | kursiv fett / heavy italic / italique gras | N 020: 081 2529 / 1394 |
| 325 | ISO 3098 (DIN 6776) A | vertikal / vertical / vertical | N 101: 081 1816 / 694 |
| 335 | ISO 3098 (DIN 6776) A | kursiv / italic / italique | N 101: 081 1817 / 695 |
| 335 | ISO 3098 (DIN 6776) B | kursiv / italic / italique | N 101: 081 1819 / 696 |
| 73, 249 | Italia ITC | Buch / book / romain labeur | N 020: 081 2383 / 697 |
| 73, 249 | Italia ITC | normal / medium / normal | N 020: 081 2384 / 698 |
| 75, 249 | **Italia** ITC | halbfett / bold / demi-gras | N 020: 081 2385 / 699 |
| 73 | Italian Old Style | normal / regular / normal | N 020: 081 2408 / 700 |
| 75 | *Italian Old Style* | kursiv / italic / italique | N 020: 081 2409 / 701 |
| 73 | **Italian Old Style** | halbfett / bold / demi-gras | N 020: 081 2410 / 702 |
| 245 | Italienne | breit / extended / large | N 100: 081 1541 / 703 |
| 383 | *Italique de Giraldon* | | N 100: 081 0791 / 704 |
| 441 | Jaguar | | N 100: 081 0793 / 705 |
| 427 | Jalousette | | N 010: 081 2141 / 706 |
| 125 | Janson-Antiqua | normal / regular / normal | N 100: 081 0795 / 707 |
| 139 | *Janson* | kursiv / italic / italique | N 100: 081 0797 / 708 |
| 379 | **Janus** | | N 100: 081 1847 / 709 |
| 411 | Jockey | | N 100: 081 1798 / 710 |
| 367 | JUMBO | normal / regular / normal | V 000: 081 0800 / 711 |
| 369 | *JUMBO* | kursiv / italic / italique | V 000: 081 0801 / 712 |

# SYNOPSIS

## BERTHOLD HEADLINES

| Page | Sample | Weight (de/en/fr) | Code |
|---|---|---|---|
| 289 | Kabel Hairline | | N 100: 081 0802 / 713 |
| 289 | Kabel Hairline | Zierbuchstaben / swash letters / lettres ornées | Z 000: 081 0804 / 714 |
| 263 | Kabel ITC | Buch / book / romain labeur | N 020: 081 2341 / 715 |
| 267 | Kabel ITC | normal / medium / normal | N 020: 081 2342 / 716 |
| 267 | Kabel ITC | halbfett / demi / demi-gras | N 020: 081 2349 / 717 |
| 269 | Kabel ITC | fett / bold / gras | N 020: 081 2343 / 718 |
| 271 | Kabel ITC | ultra / ultra / ultra | N 020: 081 2344 / 719 |
| 397 | Kabel ITC | licht / outline / éclairé | N 020: 081 2345 / 720 |
| 415 | Kabel ITC | Kontur / contour / contour | N 020: 081 2006 / 721 |
| 261 | Kabel STEMPEL | leicht / light / maigre | N 100: 081 0806 / 722 |
| 265 | Kabel STEMPEL | grob / medium / demi-gras | N 100: 081 0812 / 723 |
| 269 | Kabel STEMPEL | fett / heavy / gras | N 100: 081 0816 / 724 |
| 275 | Kabel STEMPEL | schmalhalbfett / medium condensed / étroit demi-gras | N 100: 081 0818 / 725 |
| 397 | Kabel STEMPEL | fett licht / heavy outline / éclairé gras | N 100: 081 0822 / 726 |
| 415 | Kabel STEMPEL | schattiert / shaded / ombré | N 100: 081 0819 / 727 |
| 385 | Klio | | N 100: 081 1449 / 728 |
| 429 | Knirsch | | N 020: 081 0039 / 729 |
| 363 | Komet | | N 020: 081 2277 / 730 |
| 305 | Kompakte Grotesk | | N 100: 081 0823 / 731 |
| 161 | Korinna ITC | normal / regular / normal | N 010: 081 2078 / 732 |
| 161 | Korinna ITC | normal Zierbuchstaben / regular swash letters / normal lettres ornées | Z 000: 081 2093 * / 733 |
| 175 | Korinna ITC | kursiv / italic / italique | N 020: 081 2358 / 734 |
| 165 | Korinna ITC | halbfett / bold / demi-gras | N 010: 081 2083 / 735 |
| 165 | Korinna ITC | halbfett Zierbuchstaben / bold swash letters / demi-gras lettres ornées | Z 000: 081 2093 * / 733 |

36

# SYNOPSIS

## BERTHOLD HEADLINES

| Page | Sample | Style | Code |
|---|---|---|---|
| 179 | *Korinna* ITC | kursiv halbfett / bold italic / italique demi-gras | N 020: 081 2359 / 737 |
| 169 | **Korinna** ITC | fett / extra bold / gras | N 010: 081 2086 / 738 |
| 169 | **Korinna** ITC | fett Zierbuchstaben / extra bold swash letters / gras lettres ornées | Z 000: 081 2093 * / 733 |
| 181 | ***Korinna*** ITC | kursiv fett / extra bold italic / italique gras | N 020: 081 2360 / 740 |
| 171 | **Korinna** ITC | extrafett / heavy / extra gras | N 010: 081 2089 / 741 |
| 171 | **Korinna** ITC | extrafett Zierbuchstaben / heavy swash letters / extra gras lettres ornées | Z 000: 081 2093 * / 733 |
| 181 | ***Korinna*** ITC | kursiv extrafett / heavy italic / italique extra gras | N 020: 081 2361 / 743 |
| 395 | Korinna ITC (outline) | licht / outline / éclairé | N 010: 081 2092 / 744 |
| 395 | Korinna ITC (outline) | licht Zierbuchstaben / outline swash letters / éclairé lettres ornées | Z 000: 081 2093 * / 733 |
| 447 | *Künstlerschreibschrift* | halbfett / medium / demi-gras | N 100: 081 0824 / 746 |
| 449 | *Künstlerschreibschrift* | fett / bold / gras | N 100: 081 0829 / 747 |
| 367 | **Lapidar** | | N 020: 081 1442 / 748 |
| 393 | LARGO | licht / outline / éclairé | V 000: 081 0855 / 749 |
| 249 | **Latin** | fett / bold / gras | N 100: 081 0832 / 750 |
| 247 | Latin | schmalfett / bold condensed / étroit gras | N 100: 081 0833 / 751 |
| 249 | **Latin Wide** | | N 100: 081 0838 / 752 |
| 387 | latue | | N 100: 081 1869 / 753 |
| 133 | Le Cochin | normal / regular / normal | N 100: 081 0841 / 754 |
| 175 | *Le Cochin* | kursiv / italic / italique | N 000: 081 1923 / 755 |
| 91 | Lectura | normal / regular / normal | N 100: 081 0843 / 756 |
| 87 | *Lectura* | kursiv / italic / italique | N 100: 081 0844 / 757 |
| 93 | **Lectura** | halbfett / medium / demi-gras | N 100: 081 0845 / 758 |
| 99 | **Lectura** | schmalfett / bold condensed / étroit gras | N 100: 081 0846 / 759 |
| 427 | LEOPARD | | V 009: 081 0073 / 760 |

37

# SYNOPSIS

## BERTHOLD HEADLINES

| Page | Sample | Style | Code |
|---|---|---|---|
| 431 | LETTRES ORNEES | | V 000: 081 0847 / 761 |
| 423 | LICHTE FETTE GROTESK | | V 000: 081 0852 / 762 |
| 127 | Life | mager / light / maigre | N 100: 081 1566 / 763 |
| 131 | Life | kursiv / italic / italique | N 100: 081 1530 / 764 |
| 127 | Life | fett / bold / gras | N 100: 081 0079 / 765 |
| 325 | Lightline Gothic | | N 000: 081 0860 / 766 |
| 413 | Logotype | schattiert / shaded / ombré | N 020: 081 2127 / 767 |
| 163, 373 | Lo-Type | mager / light / maigre | N 020: 081 2424 / 768 |
| 169, 377 | Lo-Type | normal / regular / normal | N 020: 081 0453 / 1335 |
| 173, 377 | Lo-Type | halbfett / medium / demi-gras | N 020: 081 2425 / 769 |
| 183, 385 | Lo-Type | kursiv halbfett / medium italic / italique demi-gras | N 020: 081 2421 / 1336 |
| 173, 377 | Lo-Type | fett / bold / gras | N 020: 081 2422 / 770 |
| 377 | Lo-Type | schmalhalbfett / bold condensed / étroit demi-gras | N 020: 081 2423 / 771 |
| 113 | LSC Book Roman ITC | normal / regular / normal | N 020: 081 1928 / 772 |
| 121 | LSC Book ITC | kursiv / italic / italique | N 020: 081 1933 / 773 |
| 115 | LSC Book Roman ITC | halbfett / medium / demi-gras | N 020: 081 1939 / 774 |
| 121 | LSC Book ITC | kursiv halbfett / bold italic / italique demi-gras | N 020: 081 1944 / 775 |
| 117 | LSC Book Roman ITC | fett / bold / gras | N 020: 081 1950 / 776 |
| 123 | LSC Book ITC | kursiv fett / x-bold italic / italique gras | N 020: 081 1956 / 777 |
| 133 | LSC Caslon No. 223 ITC | mager / light / maigre | N 100: 081 1620 / 778 |
| 141 | LSC Caslon No. 223 ITC | kursiv mager / light italic / italique maigre | N 100: 081 1625 / 779 |
| 135 | LSC Caslon No. 223 ITC | normal / regular / normal | N 100: 081 1632 / 780 |
| 141 | LSC Caslon No. 223 ITC | kursiv / italic / italique | N 100: 081 1637 / 781 |
| 135 | LSC Caslon No. 223 ITC | fett / bold / gras | N 100: 081 1642 / 782 |

# SYNOPSIS

## BERTHOLD HEADLINES

| Page | Typeface | Style | Code |
|---|---|---|---|
| 141 | *LSC Caslon No. 223* ITC | kursiv fett / bold italic / italique gras | N 100: 081 1648 / 783 |
| 137 | **LSC Caslon No. 223** ITC | extrafett / extra bold / extra gras | N 100: 081 0868 / 784 |
| 141 | ***LSC Caslon No. 223*** ITC | kursiv extrafett / extra bold italic / italique extra gras | N 100: 081 0869 / 785 |
| 207 | **LSC Condensed** ITC | normal / regular / normal | N 100: 081 0515 / 786 |
| 205 | LSC Condensed ITC | schmal / condensed / étroit | N 100: 081 0516 / 787 |
| 707 | LSC Condensed ITC | kursiv schmal / condensed italic / italique étroit | N 100: 081 0518 / 788 |
| 209 | LSC Manhattan ITC | | N 100: 081 0870 / 789 |
| 227 | Lubalin Graph ITC | mager / light / maigre | N 020: 081 1834 / 790 |
| 227 | Lubalin Graph ITC | mager Zierbuchstaben / light swash letters / maigre lettres ornées | Z 000: 081 1929 / 791 |
| 227 | Lubalin Graph ITC | Buch / book / romain labeur | N 020: 081 1835 / 792 |
| 229 | Lubalin Graph ITC | Buch Zierbuchstaben / book swash letters / romain labeur lettres ornées | Z 000: 081 1917 / 793 |
| 231 | Lubalin Graph ITC | normal / regular / normal | N 020: 081 1836 / 794 |
| 231 | Lubalin Graph ITC | normal Zierbuchstaben / regular swash letters / normal lettres ornées | Z 000: 081 1916 / 795 |
| 233 | **Lubalin Graph** ITC | halbfett / medium / demi-gras | N 020: 081 1839 / 796 |
| 233 | **Lubalin Graph** ITC | halbfett Zierbuchstaben / medium swash letters / demi-gras lettres ornées | Z 000: 081 1925 / 797 |
| 235 | **Lubalin Graph** ITC | fett / bold / gras | N 020: 081 1841 / 798 |
| 235 | **Lubalin Graph** ITC | fett Zierbuchstaben / bold swash letters / gras lettres ornées | Z 000: 081 1926 / 799 |
| 165 | Lucian | normal / regular / normal | N 100: 081 0864 / 800 |
| 169 | **Lucian** | halbfett / bold / demi-gras | N 100: 081 0866 / 801 |
| 265 | Lydian | normal / regular / normal | N 100: 081 0871 / 802 |
| 365 | MACHINE ITC | normal / regular / normal | V 000: 081 1964 / 803 |
| 365 | **MACHINE** ITC | halbfett / bold / demi-gras | V 000: 081 1970 / 804 |
| 431 | MADAME | | V 000: 081 1423 / 805 |
| 187 | Madison | mager / regular / normal | N 100: 081 0872 / 806 |

39

# SYNOPSIS

## BERTHOLD HEADLINES

| | | | |
|---|---|---|---|
| 201 | *Madison* | kursiv mager / italic / italique | N 100: 081 0874 / 807 |
| 187 | **Madison** | halbfett / medium / demi-gras | N 100: 081 0875 / 808 |
| 189 | **Madison** | fett / bold / gras | N 100: 081 0876 / 809 |
| 205 | Madison | schmalmager / condensed / étroit maigre | N 100: 081 0877 / 810 |
| 205 | **Madison** | schmalhalbfett / medium condensed / étroit demi-gras | N 100: 081 0878 / 811 |
| 383 | **Manessa** | | N 100: 081 0880 / 812 |
| 65 | 𝔐anuskript-Gotisch | | N 000: 081 0881 / 813 |
| 379 | **Mark Twain** | | N 100: 081 0884 / 814 |
| 227 | Media | mager / light / maigre | N 020: 081 2414 / 815 |
| 227 | Media | normal / regular / normal | N 100: 081 1727 / 816 |
| 231 | Media | halbfett / medium / demi-gras | N 020: 081 2415 / 817 |
| 233 | **Media** | fett / bold / gras | N 100: 081 1732 / 818 |
| 415 | Media Inline | fett / bold / gras | N 100: 081 1886 / 819 |
| 397 | Media Kontur | fett / bold / gras | N 100: 081 1880 / 820 |
| 397 | Media Outline | fett / bold / gras | N 100: 081 1875 / 821 |
| 429 | Media Relief | fett / bold / gras | N 100: 081 0056 / 822 |
| 421 | Media Triline | fett / bold / gras | N 020: 081 2256 / 823 |
| 217 | Melior | normal / regular / normal | N 100: 081 0885 / 824 |
| 221 | *Melior* | kursiv / italic / italique | N 100: 081 0886 / 825 |
| 219 | **Melior** | halbfett / bold / demi-gras | N 100: 081 0888 / 826 |
| 241 | **Melior** | schmalfett / bold condensed / étroit gras | N 100: 081 0889 / 827 |
| 227 | Memphis | zart / extra light / extra maigre | N 020: 081 2181 / 828 |
| 229 | Memphis | mager / light / maigre | N 100: 081 0891 / 829 |
| 231 | **Memphis** | halbfett / medium / demi-gras | N 100: 081 0892 / 830 |

# SYNOPSIS

## BERTHOLD HEADLINES

| Page | Typeface | | Weight | Code |
|---|---|---|---|---|
| 235 | **Memphis** | | fett / bold / gras | N 100: 081 0893 / 831 |
| 293 | Mercator | | normal / regular / normal | N 100: 081 0895 / 832 |
| 301 | **Mercator** | | fett / bold / gras | N 100: 081 0897 / 833 |
| 91 | Méridien | | normal / regular / normal | N 100: 081 0898 / 834 |
| 93 | Méridien | | halbfett / medium / demi-gras | N 100: 081 0899 / 835 |
| 93 | **Méridien** | | fett / bold / gras | N 100: 081 0904 / 836 |
| 171 | **Metropolis** | | fett / bold / gras | N 100: 081 0905 / 837 |
| 423 | MEXICO OLYMPIC | | | V 000: 081 1526 / 838 |
| 207 | *Milanor* | | kursiv / italic / italique | N 100: 081 1544 / 839 |
| 137 | Milano Roman ITC | | | N 100: 081 1710 / 840 |
| 453 | *Mistral* | | | N 100: 081 0907 / 841 |
| 143 | Modern | MONOTYPE | normal / extended / normal | N 020: 081 2235 / 1281 |
| 147 | *Modern* | MONOTYPE | kursiv / extended italic / italique | N 020: 081 2236 / 1337 |
| 145 | **Modern** | MONOTYPE | halbfett / bold / demi-gras | N 020: 081 2238 / 1282 |
| 195 | Modern No. 20 | STEPHENSON BLAKE | normal / regular / normal | N 100: 081 0910 / 842 |
| 201 | *Modern No. 20* | STEPHENSON BLAKE | kursiv / italic / italique | N 100: 081 0912 / 843 |
| 419 | Mona Lisa | | | N 100: 081 0914 / 844 |
| 291 | Monotone Gothic | | | N 100: 081 0918 / 845 |
| 387 | motter alustyle | | | x 000: 081 1545 / 846 |
| 387 | **Motter Ombra** | | | N 100: 081 1519 / 847 |
| 365 | **Motter Tektura** | | halbfett / medium / demi-gras | N 100: 081 1896 / 848 |
| 361 | **Mr. Big** | | | N 100: 081 1476 / 849 |
| 365 | **Murrpoint** | | fett / bold / gras | N 100: 081 1698 / 850 |
| 365 | ***Murrpoint Swing*** | | fett / bold / gras | N 100: 081 1703 / 851 |

# SYNOPSIS

## BERTHOLD HEADLINES

| Page | Typeface | Style (DE / EN / FR) | Code |
|---|---|---|---|
| 365 | Musspoint Swing | fett Zierbuchstaben / bold swash letters / gras lettres ornées | Z 000: 081 1709 / 852 |
| 379 | Neptun | | N 100: 081 0919 / 853 |
| 433 | NEUBAUER BLACK CHIPS | | Vb 018: 081 2346 * / 854 |
| 433 | NEUBAUER WHITE CHIPS | | Vb 018: 081 2346 * / 854 |
| 317 | Neue Aurora-Grotesk | schmalhalbfett / medium condensed / étroit demi-gras | N 000: 081 0920 / 856 |
| 325 | Neue Aurora-Grotesk | schmalfett / bold condensed / étroit gras | N 000: 081 0922 / 857 |
| 289 | Neuzeit-Grotesk | leicht / light / maigre | N 100: 081 0926 / 858 |
| 293 | Neuzeit-Grotesk | mager / regular / normal | N 000: 081 0928 / 859 |
| 297 | Neuzeit-Grotesk | halbfett / medium / demi-gras | N 100: 081 0930 / 860 |
| 301 | Neuzeit-Grotesk | fett / bold / gras | N 100: 081 0931 / 861 |
| 321 | Neuzeit-Grotesk | schmalhalbfett / medium condensed / étroit demi-gras | N 000: 081 0934 / 862 |
| 291 | Neuzeit S | Buch / book / romain labeur | N 000: 081 0924 / 863 |
| 299 | Neuzeit S | kräftig / bold / gras | N 000: 081 0925 / 864 |
| 133 | New Caslon | normal / regular / normal | N 000: 081 0935 / 865 |
| 141 | New Caslon | kursiv / italic / italique | N 100: 081 0936 / 866 |
| 291 | News Gothic | normal / regular / normal | N 100: 081 0938 / 867 |
| 299 | News Gothic | fett / bold / gras | N 000: 081 0939 / 868 |
| 319 | News Gothic | schmal / condensed / étroit | N 100: 081 0941 / 869 |
| 253 | Newtext ITC | mager / light / maigre | N 020: 081 2096 / 870 |
| 253 | Newtext ITC | mager Zierbuchstaben / light swash letters / maigre lettres ornées | Z 000: 081 2108 * / 871 |
| 259 | Newtext ITC | kursiv mager / light italic / italique maigre | N 020: 081 2098 / 872 |
| 259 | Newtext ITC | kursiv mager Zierbuchstaben / light italic swash letters / italique maigre lettres ornées | Z 000: 081 2102 * / 873 |
| 255 | Newtext ITC | Buch / book / romain labeur | N 020: 081 2097 / 874 |
| 255 | Newtext ITC | Buch Zierbuchstaben / book swash letters / romain labeur lettres ornées | Z 000: 081 2108 * / 871 |

# SYNOPSIS

## BERTHOLD HEADLINES

| Page | Sample | Style | Code |
|---|---|---|---|
| 259 | *Newtext* ITC | Buch kursiv / book italic / italique romain labeur | N 020: 081 2099 / 876 |
| 261 | *Newtext* ITC | Buch kursiv Zierbuchstaben / book italic swash letters / italique romain labeur lettres ornées | Z 000: 081 2102 * / 873 |
| 255 | Newtext ITC | normal / regular / normal | N 020: 081 2100 / 878 |
| 255 | Newtext ITC | normal Zierbuchstaben / regular swash letters / normal lettres ornées | Z 000: 081 2108 * / 871 |
| 261 | *Newtext* ITC | kursiv / italic / italique | N 020: 081 2107 / 880 |
| 261 | *Newtext* ITC | kursiv Zierbuchstaben / italic swash letters / italique lettres ornées | Z 000: 081 2102 * / 873 |
| 257 | **Newtext** ITC | halbfett / demi-bold / demi-gras | N 020: 081 2104 / 882 |
| 257 | **Newtext** ITC | halbfett Zierbuchstaben / demi-bold swash letters / demi-gras lettres ornées | Z 000: 081 2108 * / 871 |
| 261 | ***Newtext*** ITC | kursiv halbfett / demi-bold italic / italique demi-gras | N 020: 081 2101 / 884 |
| 261 | ***Newtext*** ITC | kursiv halbfett Zierbuchstaben / demi-bold italic swash letters / italique demi-gras lettres ornées | Z 000: 081 2102 * / 873 |
| 159 | Nicolas Cochin | normal / regular / normal | N 100: 081 0942 / 886 |
| 173 | *Nicolas Cochin* | kursiv / italic / italique | N 100: 081 0943 / 887 |
| 165 | **Nicolas Cochin** | fett / bold / gras | N 100: 081 0944 / 888 |
| 277 | Nobel | normal / regular / normal | N 100: 081 0945 / 889 |
| 281 | **Nobel** | fett / bold / gras | N 100: 081 0949 / 890 |
| 285 | Nobel | schmal / condensed / étroit | N 100: 081 0947 / 891 |
| 197 | **Normande** | normal / regular / normal | N 100: 081 0951 / 892 |
| 203 | ***Normande*** | kursiv / italic / italique | N 100: 081 0953 / 893 |
| 205 | **Normande** | schmal / condensed / étroit | N 100: 081 0957 / 894 |
| 241 | **Nova** | | N 100: 081 0959 / 895 |
| 161 | Novarese ITC | Buch / book / romain labeur | N 020: 081 0792 / 1283 |
| 175 | *Novarese* ITC | Buch kursiv / book italic / italique romain labeur | N 020: 081 0808 / 1284 |
| 161 | Novarese ITC | normal / medium / normal | N 020: 081 0798 / 1285 |
| 177 | *Novarese* ITC | kursiv / medium italic / italique | N 020: 081 0811 / 1286 |

43

# SYNOPSIS

## BERTHOLD HEADLINES

| Page | Typeface | Style | Code |
|---|---|---|---|
| 169 | Novarese ITC | halbfett / bold / demi-gras | N 020: 081 0803 / 1287 |
| 179 | Novarese ITC | kursiv halbfett / bold italic / italique demi-gras | N 020: 081 0817 / 1288 |
| 173 | Novarese ITC | fett / ultra bold | N 020: 081 0805 / 1289 |
| 415 | Nubian | | N 100: 081 0960 / 896 |
| 375 | Ocean Current | | N 100: 081 1477 / 897 |
| 375 | Ocean Current | Zierbuchstaben / swash letters / lettres ornées | Z 000: 081 1478 / 898 |
| 83 | Octavia | halbfett / bold / demi-gras | N 010: 081 2149 / 899 |
| 439 | Okay | | N 100: 081 0962 / 900 |
| 417 | OLD BOWERY | | V 000: 081 0964 / 901 |
| 245 | Old Towne No. 536 | | N 100: 081 0965 / 902 |
| 437 | Ondine | | N 100: 081 0967 / 903 |
| 263 | Optima | normal / regular / normal | N 100: 081 0969 / 904 |
| 273 | Optima | kursiv / italic / italique | N 100: 081 0975 / 905 |
| 265 | Optima | kräftig / medium / fort | N 020: 081 0221 / 1290 |
| 273 | Optima | kursiv kräftig / medium italic / italique | N 020: 081 0235 / 1338 |
| 267 | Optima | halbfett / bold / demi-gras | N 100: 081 0982 / 906 |
| 269 | Optima | fett / extra bold / gras | N 020: 081 0243 / 1339 |
| 159 | Orator | | N 100: 081 0988 / 907 |
| 381 | ORIENTE | | V 000: 081 0991 / 908 |
| 79 | Palatino | normal / regular / normal | N 100: 081 0993 / 909 |
| 87 | Palatino | kursiv / italic / italique | N 020: 081 0520 / 910 |
| 83 | Palatino | halbfett / bold / demi-gras | N 100: 081 0996 / 911 |
| 441 | Palette | | N 100: 081 0997 / 912 |
| 431 | | | N 010: 081 2138 / 913 |

# SYNOPSIS

## BERTHOLD HEADLINES

| Page | Typeface | Weight (de/en/fr) | Code / No. |
|---|---|---|---|
| 265 | Pascal | | N 100: 081 0998 / 914 |
| 211 | Peignot | mager / light / maigre | N 100: 081 1493 / 915 |
| 211 | Peignot | halbfett / medium / demi-gras | N 100: 081 1494 / 916 |
| 211 | Peignot | fett / bold / gras | N 100: 081 1495 / 917 |
| 295 | Permanent | halbfett / medium / demi-gras | N 100: 081 1001 / 918 |
| 341 | Permanent | breithalbfett / medium extended / large demi-gras | N 100: 081 1006 / 919 |
| 319 | Permanent Headline | normal / regular / normal | N 100: 081 0711 / 920 |
| 337 | Permanent Headline | kursiv / italic / italque | N 100: 081 0715 / 921 |
| 401 | Permanent Headline | licht / outline / éclairé | N 100: 081 0716 / 922 |
| 91 | Perpetua | normal / regular / normal | N 020: 081 1983 / 923 |
| 93 | Perpetua | halbfett / bold / demi-gras | N 100: 081 1009 / 924 |
| 95 | Perpetua Black | | N 020: 081 2275 / 925 |
| 405 | Perpetua | schattiert / shaded / ombré | N 020: 081 2276 / 926 |
| 271 | Persona Black | | N 020: 081 2178 / 927 |
| 453 | Piccadilly-Script | | N 100: 081 1010 / 928 |
| 381 | Pierrot | | N 000: 081 1011 / 929 |
| 383 | Pinocchio | | V 000: 081 1013 / 930 |
| 411 | Pioneer ITC | | V 000: 081 1015 / 931 |
| 317 | Placard | halbfett / medium / demi-gras | N 000: 081 1016 / 932 |
| 323 | Placard | fett / bold / gras | N 100: 081 1017 / 933 |
| 321 | Planschrift | normal / regular / normal | N 000: 081 1023 / 934 |
| 307 | Planschrift | kursiv / italic / italique | N 000: 081 1024 / 935 |
| 315 | Planschrift | linkskursiv / reclining / penche á gauche | N 000: 081 1025 / 936 |
| 81 | Plantin | normal / regular / normal | N 020: 081 2126 / 937 |

45

# SYNOPSIS

## BERTHOLD HEADLINES

| Page | Typeface | Style | Code |
|---|---|---|---|
| 89 | *Plantin* | kursiv / italic / italique | N 020: 081 2125 / 938 |
| 81 | **Plantin** | halbfett / bold / demi-gras | N 000: 081 1018 / 939 |
| 121 | ***Plantin*** | kursiv halbfett / bold italic / italique demi-gras | N 100: 081 1020 / 940 |
| 99 | **Plantin** | schmalfett / bold condensed / étroit gras | N 100: 081 1021 / 941 |
| 433 | PLASTICA | | V 000: 081 1026 / 942 |
| 367 | *Plural* | | N 000: 081 2488 / 1395 |
| 367 | *Plural* | Zierbuchstaben / swash letters / lettres ornées | Z 000: 081 2489 / 1396 |
| 361 | Poell Black | | N 100: 081 1484 / 943 |
| 403 | Poell Medium Outline | | N 100: 081 1486 / 944 |
| 403 | Poell Outline | | N 000: 081 1485 / 945 |
| 411 | POELL SHADED | | V 000: 081 1488 / 946 |
| 445 | *Poema* | | N 100: 081 1027 / 947 |
| 437 | **Polka** | normal / regular / normal | N 100: 081 1029 / 948 |
| 437 | **Polka** | halbfett / medium / demi-gras | N 100: 081 1030 / 949 |
| 133 | Poppl-Antiqua | normal / regular / normal | N 000: 081 1032 / 950 |
| 135 | Poppl-Antiqua | halbfett / medium / demi-gras | N 100: 081 1033 / 951 |
| 137 | **Poppl-Antiqua** | fett / bold / gras | N 100: 081 1034 / 952 |
| 155 | **Poppl-Antiqua** | schmalfett / bold condensed / étroit gras | N 100: 081 1039 / 953 |
| 141 | ***Poppl-Antiqua*** | kursiv schmalfett / bold condensed italic / italique étroit gras | N 100: 081 1040 / 954 |
| 141 | ***Poppl-Antiqua*** | kursiv schmalfett Zierbuchstaben / bold condensed italic swash letters / italique étroit gras lettres ornées | Z 000: 081 1779 / 955 |
| 451 | *Poppl-College 1* | normal / regular / normal | N 020: 081 2442 / 1340 |
| 451 | *Poppl-College 2* | normal / regular / normal | N 020: 081 2443 / 1408 |
| 451 | *Poppl-College 1* | halbfett / medium / demi-gras | N 020: 081 2444 / 1341 |
| 451 | *Poppl-College 2* | halbfett / medium / demi-gras | N 020: 081 2445 / 1342 |

# SYNOPSIS

## BERTHOLD HEADLINES

| Page | Typeface | Style | Code |
|---|---|---|---|
| 451 | *Poppl-College 1* | fett / bold / gras | N 020: 081 2446 / 1409 |
| 451 | *Poppl-College 2* | fett / bold / gras | N 020: 081 2447 / 1410 |
| 449 | *Poppl Exquisit* | | N 100: 081 1042 / 956 |
| 449 | *Poppl Exquisit* | Zierbuchstaben / swash letters / lettres ornées | Z 000: 081 1043 / 957 |
| 383 | **Poppl Heavy** | | N 100: 081 1533 / 958 |
| 363 | **Poppl Leporello** | | N 020: 081 2159 / 959 |
| 111 | Poppl-Pontifex | normal / regular / normal | N 020: 081 2494 / 1397 |
| 119 | *Poppl-Pontifex* | kursiv / italic / italique | N 020: 081 2495 / 1398 |
| 115 | **Poppl-Pontifex** | halbfett / medium / demi-gras | N 020: 081 2496 / 1399 |
| 117 | **Poppl-Pontifex** | fett / bold / gras | N 020: 081 2462 / 1343 |
| 153 | **Poppl-Pontifex** | schmalhalbfett / medium condensed / étroit demi-gras | N 020: 081 2463 / 1400 |
| 447 | *Poppl Residenz* | mager / light / maigre | N 020: 081 1943 / 960 |
| 449 | *Poppl Residenz* | normal / regular / normal | N 020: 081 1942 / 961 |
| 379 | **POPPL SALADIN** | normal / regular / normal | V 000: 081 0431 * / 962 |
| 405 | POPPL SALADIN (outline) | licht / outline / éclairé | V 000: 081 0431 * / 962 |
| 453 | Poppl Stretto | | N 100: 081 1044 / 964 |
| 439 | Post-Antiqua | normal / regular / normal | N 100: 081 1046 / 965 |
| 271 | **Post-Marcato** | extrafett / extra bold / extra gras | N 100: 081 1050 / 966 |
| 209 | **Primate** | | N 100: 081 1051 / 967 |
| 159 | **Primus** | | N 100: 081 1056 / 968 |
| 143 | Primus-Antiqua | mager / light / maigre | N 100: 081 1052 / 969 |
| 147 | *Primus* | kursiv mager / light italic / italique maigre | N 100: 081 1054 / 970 |
| 145 | **Primus-Antiqua** | halbfett / medium / demi-gras | N 100: 081 1055 / 971 |
| 245 | **PRO ARTE** | | Sp 000: 081 1063 / 972 |

# SYNOPSIS

## BERTHOLD HEADLINES

| Page | Typeface | Style (de/en/fr) | Code |
|---|---|---|---|
| 417 | PROFIL | | V 000: 081 1068 / 973 |
| 157 | Promotor | | N 100: 081 1073 / 974 |
| 235 | Quadra 57 | | N 100: 081 1754 / 975 |
| 79 | Quadriga-Antiqua | normal / regular / normal | N 020: 081 1991 / 976 |
| 89 | Quadriga | kursiv / italic / italique | N 020: 081 0171 / 977 |
| 83 | Quadriga-Antiqua | halbfett / medium / demi-gras | N 020: 081 1992 / 978 |
| 83 | Quadriga-Antiqua | fett / bold / gras | N 020: 081 1997 / 979 |
| 85 | Quadriga-Antiqua | extrafett / extra bold / extra gras | N 020: 081 1998 / 1291 |
| 253 | Quorum ITC | mager / light / maigre | N 020: 081 2373 / 980 |
| 253 | Quorum ITC | Buch / book / romain labeur | N 020: 081 2374 / 981 |
| 255 | Quorum ITC | normal / medium / normal | N 020: 081 2375 / 982 |
| 257 | Quorum ITC | halbfett / bold / demi-gras | N 020: 081 2376 / 983 |
| 259 | Quorum Black ITC | | N 020: 081 2377 / 984 |
| 343 | Reform-Grotesk | | N 100: 081 1078 / 985 |
| 407 | REGINA | | V 000: 081 1081 / 986 |
| 141 | Renaissance | kursiv fett / bold italic / italique gras | N 100: 081 1082 / 987 |
| 247 | Renaissance | schmal / condensed / étroit | N 100: 081 1083 / 988 |
| 69 | Rhapsodie | | F 006: 081 2186 / 989 |
| 69 | Rhapsodie | Zierbuchstaben / swash letters / lettres ornées | Z 000: 081 2187 / 990 |
| 377 | Roberta | normal / regular / normal | N 100: 081 1085 / 991 |
| 413 | ROBERTA RAISED | schattiert / shaded / ombré | V 000: 081 1086 / 992 |
| 315 | ROC | mager / light / maigre | V 000: 081 1087 / 993 |
| 319 | Roc | normal / regular / normal | N 100: 081 1089 / 994 |
| 229 | Rockwell | mager / light / maigre | N 100: 081 1094 / 995 |

48

# SYNOPSIS

## BERTHOLD HEADLINES

| Page | Typeface | Weight (de/en/fr) | Code |
|---|---|---|---|
| 237 | *Rockwell* | kursiv mager / light italic / italique maigre | N 020: 081 2168 / 996 |
| 237 | *Rockwell* | kursiv / italic / italique | N 020: 081 0517 / 1344 |
| 233 | **Rockwell** | halbfett / bold / demi-gras | N 100: 081 1095 / 997 |
| 237 | ***Rockwell*** | kursiv halbfett / bold italic / italique demi-gras | N 020: 081 0512 / 1345 |
| 235 | **Rockwell** | fett / extra bold / gras | N 100: 081 1097 / 998 |
| 239 | Rockwell | schmal / condensed / étroit | N 020: 081 0526 / 1346 |
| 241 | **Rockwell** | schmalhalbfett / bold condensed / étroit demi-gras | N 020: 081 1571 / 1347 |
| 97 | Romana | mager / light / maigre | N 100: 081 1454 / 999 |
| 99 | **Romana** | halbfett / medium / demi-gras | N 100: 081 1455 / 1000 |
| 99 | **Romana** | ultra / ultra / ultra | N 020: 081 2278 / 1001 |
| 163 | Romic | mager / light / maigre | N 020: 081 2549 / 1401 |
| 165 | Romic | normal / medium / normal | N 020: 081 2550 / 1402 |
| 169 | **Romic** | halbfett / bold / demi-gras | N 020: 081 2551 / 1403 |
| 171 | **Romic** | fett / extra bold / gras | N 020: 081 2552 / 1404 |
| 175 | *Römische Zirkular* | kursiv / italic / italique | N 100: 081 1098 / 1002 |
| 349 | Ronda ITC | mager / light / maigre | N 100: 081 1507 / 1003 |
| 351 | Ronda ITC | normal / regular / normal | N 100: 081 1508 / 1004 |
| 353 | **Ronda ITC** | fett / bold / gras | N 100: 081 1509 / 1005 |
| 413 | SACHER | | V 000: 081 1099 / 1006 |
| 323 | SANS SERIF | schmal / condensed / étroit | V 000: 081 1531 / 1007 |
| 411 | SANS SERIF | schattiert / shaded / ombré | V 000: 081 1100 / 1008 |
| 385 | Santana | | N 100: 081 1457 / 1009 |
| 391 | Sat Modern | | N 100: 081 1101 / 1010 |
| 217 | Schadow-Antiqua | Werk / book / romain labeur | N 000: 081 1115 / 1011 |

49

# SYNOPSIS

## BERTHOLD HEADLINES

| Page | Sample | Weight | Code |
|---|---|---|---|
| 217 | Schadow-Antiqua | mager / light / maigre | N 000: 081 1102 / 1012 |
| 221 | *Schadow* | kursiv / italic / italique | N 000: 081 1105 / 1013 |
| 219 | **Schadow-Antiqua** | halbfett / medium / demi-gras | N 000: 081 1107 / 1014 |
| 219 | **Schadow-Antiqua** | fett / bold / gras | N 000: 081 1114 / 1015 |
| 241 | **Schadow-Antiqua** | schmalfett / bold condensed / étroit gras | N 000: 081 1111 / 1016 |
| 77 | SCHNEIDLER INITIALEN | | V 000: 081 1118 / 1017 |
| 229 | Schreibmaschinenschrift | | N 000: 081 1121 / 1018 |
| 431 | SCHWABING DAY | | Vb 100: 081 1814 * / 1019 |
| 431 | SCHWABING NIGHT | | Vb 100: 081 1814 * / 1019 |
| 417 | SCULPTURA | | V 000: 081 1122 / 1021 |
| 211 | **Semin-Antiqua** | | N 020: 081 2280 / 1022 |
| 73 | Seneca | mager / light / maigre | N 020: 081 2497 / 1348 |
| 73 | Seneca | normal / regular / normal | N 020: 081 2498 / 1349 |
| 75 | *Seneca* | kursiv / italic / italique | N 020: 081 2499 / 1350 |
| 75 | **Seneca** | halbfett / medium / demi-gras | N 020: 081 2500 / 1351 |
| 75 | **Seneca** | fett / bold / gras | N 020: 081 2501 / 1352 |
| 75 | **Seneca** | extrafett / extra bold / extra gras | N 020: 081 2502 / 1353 |
| 253 | Serif Gothic ITC | mager / light / maigre | N 020: 081 2070 / 1023 |
| 253 | Serif Gothic ITC | mager Zierbuchstaben / light swash letters / maigre lettres ornées | Z 000: 081 2071 / 1024 |
| 253 | Serif Gothic ITC | normal / regular / normal | N 100: 081 1512 / 1025 |
| 253 | Serif Gothic ITC | normal Zierbuchstaben / regular swash letters / normal lettres ornées | Z 000: 081 2028 / 1026 |
| 255 | **Serif Gothic** ITC | fett / bold / gras | N 100: 081 1513 / 1027 |
| 255 | **Serif Gothic** ITC | fett Zierbuchstaben / bold swash letters / gras lettres ornées | Z 000: 081 2029 / 1028 |
| 257 | **Serif Gothic** ITC | extrafett / extra bold / extra gras | N 100: 081 1902 / 1029 |

# SYNOPSIS

## BERTHOLD HEADLINES

| Page | Typeface | Style | Code |
|---|---|---|---|
| 257 | Serif Gothic ITC | extrafett Zierbuchstaben / extra bold swash letters / extra gras lettres ornées | Z 000: 081 2030 / 1030 |
| 257 | Serif Gothic ITC | ultrafett / heavy / ultra gras | N 100: 081 1908 / 1031 |
| 257 | Serif Gothic ITC | ultrafett Zierbuchstaben / heavy swash letters / ultra gras lettres ornées | Z 000: 081 2031 / 1032 |
| 259 | Serif Gothic Black ITC | | N 010: 081 2074 / 1033 |
| 259 | Serif Gothic Black ITC | Zierbuchstaben / swash letters / lettres ornées | Z 000: 081 2075 / 1034 |
| 403 | Serif Gothic ITC | licht / outline / éclairé | N 010: 081 2012 / 1035 |
| 403 | Serif Gothic ITC | licht Zierbuchstaben / outline swash letters / éclairé lettres ornées | Z 000: 081 2032 / 1036 |
| 441 | Signal | | N 100: 081 1123 / 1037 |
| 317 | Signum | | N 000: 081 1124 / 1038 |
| 151 | Simone | | N 100: 081 1128 / 1039 |
| 445 | Skizze | | N 100: 081 1129 / 1040 |
| 441 | Slogan | | N 100: 081 1133 / 1041 |
| 143 | Sorbonne | normal / regular / normal | N 020: 081 2324 / 1042 |
| 175 | Sorbonne | kursiv / italic / italique | N 020: 081 2325 / 1043 |
| 167 | Sorbonne | halbfett / medium / demi-gras | N 020: 081 2398 / 1044 |
| 145 | Sorbonne | fett / bold / gras | N 020: 081 2326 / 1045 |
| 151 | Sorbonne | schmalhalbfett / medium condensed / étroit demi-gras | N 020: 081 2325 / 1046 |
| 161 | Souvenir ITC | mager / light / maigre | N 100: 081 0937 / 1047 |
| 175 | Souvenir ITC | kursiv mager / light italic / italique maigre | N 100: 081 1659 / 1048 |
| 165 | Souvenir ITC | normal / medium / normal | N 100: 081 1665 / 1049 |
| 179 | Souvenir ITC | kursiv / medium italic / italique | N 100: 081 1670 / 1050 |
| 167 | Souvenir ITC | halbfett / demi-bold / demi-gras | N 100: 081 1547 / 1051 |
| 181 | Souvenir ITC | kursiv halbfett / demi-bold italic / italique demi-gras | N 100: 081 1681 / 1052 |
| 171 | Souvenir ITC | fett / bold / gras | N 100: 081 1548 / 1053 |

# SYNOPSIS

## BERTHOLD HEADLINES

| Page | Sample | Style | Reference |
|---|---|---|---|
| 181 | *Souvenir* ITC | kursiv fett / bold italic / italique gras | N 100: 081 1693 / 1054 |
| 395 | Souvenir ITC (outline) | fett licht / bold outline / gras éclairé | N 020: 081 2248 / 1055 |
| 359 | **Splash** | | N 020: 081 0266 / 1354 |
| 135 | Statesman | | N 020: 081 0011 / 1056 |
| 331 | **Steile Futura** | fett / bold / gras | N 100: 081 1137 / 1057 |
| 335 | *Steile Futura* | schrägfett / bold oblique / oblique gras | N 100: 081 1141 / 1058 |
| 321 | Steinschrift | | N 000: 081 1144 / 1059 |
| 389 | STENCIL | | V 000: 081 1147 / 1060 |
| 365 | STOP 1 | | V 000: 081 1150 / 1061 |
| 443 | Stop 2 | | N 000: 081 1152 / 1062 |
| 225 | Stymie Hairline | | N 100: 081 0867 / 1063 |
| 229 | Stymie | mager / light / maigre | N 020: 081 1160 / 1292 |
| 237 | *Stymie* | kursiv mager / light italic / italique maigre | N 020: 081 1188 / 1064 |
| 229 | Stymie | normal / medium / normal | N 020: 081 1165 / 1065 |
| 237 | *Stymie* | kursiv / italic / italique | N 020: 081 1191 / 1066 |
| 233 | **Stymie** | halbfett / bold / demi-gras | N 020: 081 1174 / 1067 |
| 233 | *Stymie* | kursiv halbfett / bold italic / italique demi-gras | N 020: 081 1196 / 1068 |
| 235 | **Stymie** | Black / Black / Black | N 020: 081 1179 / 1069 |
| 407 | STYMIE OPEN | | V 000: 081 1156 / 1070 |
| 385 | **Swing** | | N 100: 081 1158 / 1071 |
| 263 | Syntax | normal / regular / normal | N 020: 081 2402 / 1072 |
| 273 | *Syntax* | kursiv / italic / italique | N 020: 081 2403 / 1073 |
| 267 | Syntax | halbfett / medium / demi-gras | N 020: 081 2404 / 1074 |
| 271 | **Syntax** | extrafett / extra bold / extra gras | N 020: 081 2405 / 1075 |

# SYNOPSIS

## BERTHOLD HEADLINES

| Page | Typeface | Weight/Style | Code |
|---|---|---|---|
| 69 | Tannenberg | | N 000: 081 1159 / 1076 |
| 239 | Telegraph | | N 100: 081 1163 / 1077 |
| 281 | Tempo Black | normal / regular / normal | N 100: 081 1521 / 1078 |
| 287 | Tempo Black | schmal / condensed / étroit | N 100: 081 1522 / 1079 |
| 375 | Thalia | | N 100: 081 1471 / 1080 |
| 199 | Thorowgood | normal / roman / normal | N 100: 081 1168 / 1081 |
| 203 | Thorowgood | kursiv / italic / italique | N 100: 081 1169 / 1082 |
| 247 | THUNDERBIRD | normal / regular / normal | V 000: 081 1164 / 1083 |
| 247 | THUNDERBIRD | extraschmal / extra condensed / extra étroit | V 000: 081 1166 / 1084 |
| 133 | Tiffany ITC | mager / light / maigre | N 100: 081 1019 / 1085 |
| 133 | Tiffany ITC | normal / medium / normal | N 100: 081 0999 / 1086 |
| 135 | Tiffany ITC | halbfett / demi-bold / demi-gras | N 100: 081 1005 / 1087 |
| 139 | Tiffany ITC | fett / bold / gras | N 100: 081 1550 / 1088 |
| 437 | Time-Script | mager / light / maigre | N 100: 081 1170 / 1089 |
| 437 | Time-Script | halbfett / medium / demi-gras | N 000: 081 1171 / 1090 |
| 437 | Time-Script | fett / bold / gras | N 000: 081 1172 / 1091 |
| 127 | Times New Roman | | N 100: 081 1175 / 1092 |
| 131 | Times | kursiv / italic / italique | N 100: 081 1178 / 1093 |
| 127 | Times | fett / bold / gras | N 100: 081 1181 / 1094 |
| 127 | Times | fett Zierbuchstaben / bold swash letters / gras lettres ornées | Z 000: 081 1919 / 1095 |
| 131 | Times | kursiv fett / bold italic / italique gras | N 100: 081 1186 / 1096 |
| 129 | Times | extrafett / extra bold / extra gras | N 020: 081 2312 / 1097 |
| 129 | Times Modern | normal / regular / normal | N 020: 081 0591 / 1098 |
| 129 | Times Modern | Zierbuchstaben / swash letters / lettres ornées | Z 000: 081 0596 / 1099 |

53

# SYNOPSIS

## BERTHOLD HEADLINES

| Page | Name | Style | Code |
|---|---|---|---|
| 375 | Tip Top | | N 100: 081 1443 / 1100 |
| 379 | **Titania** | | N 100: 081 1190 / 1101 |
| 137 | Tom's Roman ITC | | N 100: 081 1792 / 1102 |
| 193 | Torino | normal / regular / normal | N 100: 081 1192 / 1103 |
| 199 | *Torino* | kursiv / italic / italique | N 100: 081 1197 / 1104 |
| 391 | Touring | | N 100: 081 1199 / 1105 |
| 163 | Transit | | N 100: 081 1200 / 1106 |
| 423 | Tri-Star | | N 020: 081 0087 / 1107 |
| 379 | Triton | | N 100: 081 1858 / 1108 |
| 381 | **TRIXI** | | V 000: 081 1202 / 1109 |
| 91 | Trump-Mediäval | normal / regular / normal | N 100: 081 1203 / 1110 |
| 95 | *Trump-Mediäval* | kursiv / italic / italique | N 100: 081 1204 / 1111 |
| 93 | **Trump-Mediäval** | halbfett / bold / demi-gras | N 100: 081 1205 / 1112 |
| 95 | **Trump-Mediäval** | fett / extra bold / gras | N 000: 081 1206 / 1113 |
| 97 | ***Trump-Mediäval*** | kursiv fett / extra bold italic / italique gras | N 000: 081 1211 / 1114 |
| 419 | TRUMP-GRAVUR | | N 000: 081 1214 / 1115 |
| 421 | Twice | | N 010: 081 2131 / 1116 |
| 159 | Tyfa-Antiqua | normal / regular / normal | N 100: 081 1219 / 1117 |
| 175 | *Tyfa-Antiqua* | kursiv / italic / italique | N 100: 081 1220 / 1118 |
| 447 | *Typo-Script* | | N 100: 081 1221 / 1119 |
| 197 | **Ultra Bodoni** | normal / regular / normal | N 100: 081 1222 / 1120 |
| 203 | ***Ultra Bodoni*** | kursiv / italic / italique | N 100: 081 1223 / 1121 |
| 245 | UMBRA 27 | | V 000: 081 1225 / 1122 |
| 411 | UNCLE BILL | | V 000: 081 1226 / 1123 |

# SYNOPSIS

## BERTHOLD HEADLINES

| Page | Typeface | German | English | French | Code |
|---|---|---|---|---|---|
| 289 | Univers 45 | mager | light | maigre | N 100: 081 1228 / 1124 |
| 307 | Univers 46 | kursiv mager | light italic | italique maigre | N 100: 081 1234 / 1125 |
| 295 | Univers 55 | normal | medium | normal | N 100: 081 1250 / 1126 |
| 309 | Univers 56 | kursiv | medium italic | italique | N 100: 081 1254 / 1127 |
| 297 | Univers 65 | halbfett | bold | demi-gras | N 100: 081 1276 / 1128 |
| 311 | Univers 66 | kursiv halbfett | bold italic | italique demi-gras | N 100: 081 1283 / 1129 |
| 303 | Univers 75 | fett | extra bold | gras | N 100: 081 1301 / 1130 |
| 313 | Univers 76 | kursiv fett | extra bold italic | italique gras | N 100: 081 1307 / 1131 |
| 305 | Univers 85 | extrafett | ultra bold | extra gras | N 020: 081 2274 / 1132 |
| 315 | Univers 39 | extraschmal ultraleicht | ultra light extra condensed | extra étroit ultra maigre | N 100: 081 1227 / 1133 |
| 317 | Univers 49 | extra schmalmager | extra light condensed | extra étroit maigre | N 100: 081 1243 / 1134 |
| 321 | Univers 59 | extraschmal | extra condensed | extra étroit | N 100: 081 1266 / 1135 |
| 327 | Univers 47 | schmalmager | light condensed | étroit maigre | N 100: 081 1236 / 1136 |
| 333 | Univers 48 | kursiv schmalmager | light condensed italic | italique étroit maigre | N 100: 081 1240 / 1137 |
| 327 | Univers 57 | schmal | medium condensed | étroit | N 100: 081 1258 / 1138 |
| 335 | Univers 58 | kursiv schmal | medium condensed italic | italique étroit | N 100: 081 1261 / 1139 |
| 331 | Univers 67 | schmalhalbfett | bold condensed | étroit demi-gras | N 100: 081 1289 / 1140 |
| 337 | Univers 68 | kursiv schmalhalbfett | bold condensed italic | italique étroit demi-gras | N 100: 081 1295 / 1141 |
| 339 | Univers 53 | breit | medium expanded | large | N 100: 081 1245 / 1142 |
| 341 | Univers 63 | breithalbfett | bold expanded | large demi-gras | N 100: 081 1270 / 1143 |
| 343 | Univers 73 | breitfett | extra bold expanded | large gras | N 100: 081 1297 / 1144 |
| 343 | Univers 83 | breit extrafett | ultra bold expanded | large extra gras | N 100: 081 1311 / 1145 |
| 399 | Univers 65 | halbfett licht | bold outline | demi-gras éclairé | N 020: 081 2279 / 1146 |
| 421 | Uptight ITC | normal | regular | normal | N 100: 081 1786 / 1147 |

55

# SYNOPSIS

## BERTHOLD HEADLINES

| | | | |
|---|---|---|---|
| 421 | Uptight ITC | normal Zierbuchstaben / regular swash letters / normal lettres ornées | Z 000: 081 1788 / 1148 |
| 421 | Uptight Neon ITC | | N 100: 081 1785 / 1149 |
| 359 | V.A.G.-Rundschrift | | N 020: 081 2413 / 1150 |
| 265 | Vega Grotesk | | N 100: 081 1317 / 1151 |
| 91 | Vendôme | normal / regular / normal | N 100: 081 1318 / 1152 |
| 95 | Vendôme | kursiv / italic / italique | N 100: 081 1313 / 1153 |
| 95 | Vendôme | halbfett / medium / demi-gras | N 100: 081 1320 / 1154 |
| 97 | Vendôme | kursiv halbfett / medium italic / italique demi-gras | N 100: 081 1321 / 1155 |
| 95 | Vendôme | fett / extra bold / noir | N 100: 081 1323 / 1156 |
| 97 | Vendôme | schmal / condensed / étroit | N 100: 081 1328 / 1157 |
| 277 | Venus | mager / light / maigre | N 100: 081 1329 / 1158 |
| 283 | Venus | kursiv mager / light italic / italique maigre | N 100: 081 1333 / 1159 |
| 277 | Venus | halbfett / medium / demi-gras | N 100: 081 1334 / 1160 |
| 283 | Venus | kursiv halbfett / medium italic / italique demi-gras | N 100: 081 1337 / 1161 |
| 285 | Venus | linkskursiv / reclining / penché á gauche | N 100: 081 1338 / 1162 |
| 279 | Venus | dreiviertelfett / demi-bold / trois quarts de gras | N 100: 081 1339 / 1163 |
| 313 | Venus | kursiv fett / bold italic / italique gras | N 100: 081 1340 / 1164 |
| 319 | Venus | schmalmager / light condensed / étroit maigre | N 100: 081 1342 / 1165 |
| 321 | Venus | schmalhalbfett / medium condensed / étroit demi-gras | N 000: 081 1346 / 1166 |
| 339 | Venus | breithalbfett / medium extended / large demi-gras | N 100: 081 1347 / 1167 |
| 345 | Venus | breitfett / bold extended / large gras | N 000: 081 1348 / 1168 |
| 231 | VENUS-EGYPTIENNE | halbfett / medium / demi-gras | Sp000: 081 1349 / 1169 |
| 237 | Venus-Egyptienne | kursiv halbfett / medium italic / italique demi-gras | N 000: 081 1350 / 1170 |
| 205 | Vertikal | | N 100: 081 1351 / 1171 |

## SYNOPSIS

### BERTHOLD HEADLINES

| Page | Typeface | Style | Code |
|---|---|---|---|
| 391 | Vienna | | N 100: 081 1354 / 1172 |
| 391 | Vienna | Zierbuchstaben / swash letters / lettres ornées | Z 000: 081 1355 / 1173 |
| 195 | **Viola** | | N 100: 081 1356 / 1174 |
| 429 | Voel Beat | | N 020: 081 2288 / 1175 |
| 387 | Voel Bianca | | N 020: 081 2289 / 1176 |
| 431 | Voel Hars | | N 020: 081 2297 / 1177 |
| 223 | Volta | normal / regular / normal | N 100: 081 1359 / 1178 |
| 225 | **Volta** | halbfett / medium / demi-gras | N 100: 081 1364 / 1179 |
| 223 | *Volta* | kursiv halbfett / medium italic / italique demi-gras | N 100: 081 1369 / 1180 |
| 223 | **Volta** | fett / bold / gras | N 100: 081 1366 / 1181 |
| 195 | Walbaum-Antiqua | normal / regular / normal | N 100: 081 1374 / 1182 |
| 201 | *Walbaum-Antiqua* | kursiv / italic / italique | N 100: 081 1378 / 1183 |
| 197 | **Walbaum-Antiqua** | halbfett / medium / demi-gras | N 100: 081 1380 / 1184 |
| 187 | Walbaum Buch | normal / regular / normal | N 020: 081 1840 / 1355 |
| 191 | *Walbaum Buch* | kursiv / italic / italique | N 020: 081 1871 / 1356 |
| 187 | **Walbaum Buch** | halbfett / medium / demi-gras | N 020: 081 1854 / 1357 |
| 191, 201 | *Walbaum Buch* | kursiv halbfett / medium italic / italique demi-gras | N 020: 081 1885 / 1358 |
| 189, 197 | **Walbaum Buch** | fett / bold / gras | N 020: 081 1868 / 1359 |
| 191, 203 | ***Walbaum Buch*** | kursiv fett / bold italic / italique gras | N 020: 081 1891 / 1360 |
| 67 | Walbaum-Fraktur | | N 020: 081 1381 / 1185 |
| 193 | Walbaum Standard | normal / regular / normal | N 020: 081 0753 / 1186 |
| 199 | *Walbaum Standard* | kursiv / italic / italique | N 020: 081 0761 / 1187 |
| 195 | **Walbaum Standard** | halbfett / medium / demi-gras | N 020: 081 0758 / 1188 |
| 347 | Washington | extramager / extra light / extra maigre | N 100: 081 0887 / 1189 |

# SYNOPSIS

## BERTHOLD HEADLINES

| | | | |
|---|---|---|---|
| 349 | Washington | mager / light / maigre | N 100: 081 1022 / 1190 |
| 351 | Washington | normal / regular / normal | N 100: 081 0971 / 1191 |
| 351 | Washington | halbfett / bold / demi-gras | N 100: 081 0985 / 1192 |
| 353 | Washington Black | | N 100: 081 0890 / 1193 |
| 389 | watzlcross | | x 016: 081 0090 / 1194 |
| 367 | watzlform | full | x 016: 081 2285 / 1195 |
| 405 | watzlform | open | x 016: 081 2286 / 1196 |
| 387 | watzlkrap | | x 016: 081 2227 / 1197 |
| 79 | Weiß-Antiqua | halbfett / medium / demi-gras | N 100: 081 1382 / 1198 |
| 81 | Weiß-Antiqua | fett / bold / gras | N 100: 081 1383 / 1199 |
| 85 | Weiß-Antiqua | extrafett / extra bold / extra gras | N 020: 081 1842 / 1200 |
| 85 | Weiß-Antiqua | ultrafett / ultra bold / ultra gras | N 020: 081 1845 / 1201 |
| 99 | Weiß-Antiqua | schmalfett / extra bold condensed / étroit extra gras | N 020: 081 1843 / 1202 |
| 99 | Weiß-Antiqua | schmal extrafett / extra bold condensed / étroit extra gras | N 020: 081 2204 / 1203 |
| 77 | WEISS-KAPITALE | normal / regular / normal | V 009: 081 2188 / 1204 |
| 81 | WEISS-KAPITALE | kräftig / medium / demi-gras | V 009: 081 2189 / 1205 |
| 65 | Weiß-Rundgotisch 1 | | N 000: 081 1385 / 1206 |
| 67 | Weiß-Rundgotisch 2 | | N 000: 081 1386 / 1207 |
| 393 | Westminster | | N 100: 081 1390 / 1208 |
| 375 | Whelan Antique | | N 100: 081 1391 / 1209 |
| 219 | Whitin Black | normal / regular / normal | N 100: 081 1393 / 1210 |
| 241 | Whitin Black | schmal / condensed / étroit | N 100: 081 1394 / 1211 |
| 367 | Wiegands Adbold | | N 100: 081 1771 / 1212 |
| 367 | Wiegands Adbold | alternative Buchstaben / alternative characters / caractères alternatifs | Z 000: 081 1777 / 1213 |

# SYNOPSIS

## BERTHOLD HEADLINES

| page | typeface | style (de/en/fr) | code |
|---|---|---|---|
| 167 | **Wiegands Baroque** | normal / regular / normal | N 020: 081 2337 — 1214 |
| 179 | *Wiegands Baroque* | kursiv / italic / italique | N 020: 081 2338 — 1215 |
| 101 | *Wiegands Renaissance* | kursiv / italic / italique | N 020: 081 2411 — 1216 |
| 101 | *Wiegands Renaissance* | kursiv Zierbuchstaben / italic swash letters / italique lettres ornées | Z 000: 081 2412 — 1217 |
| 359 | Wiegands Roundhead | | N 100: 081 1765 — 1218 |
| 361 | Wiegands Roundhead | alternative Buchstaben / alternative characters / caractères alternatifs | Z 000: 081 1770 — 1219 |
| 161 | Windsor | mager / light / maigre | N 020: 081 0106 — 1220 |
| 167 | **Windsor** | fett / bold / gras | N 100: 081 1395 — 1221 |
| 151 | **Windsor** | schmalfett / elongated / étroit gras | N 100: 081 1397 — 1222 |
| 395 | Windsor | licht outline / éclairé | N 000: 081 1399 — 1223 |
| 187 | Zapf Book ITC | mager / licht / maigre | N 020: 081 1945 — 1224 |
| 189 | *Zapf Book* ITC | kursiv mager / light italic / italique maigre | N 020: 081 1946 — 1225 |
| 187 | Zapf Book ITC | normal / medium / normal | N 020: 081 1947 — 1226 |
| 191 | *Zapf Book* ITC | kursiv / italic / italique | N 020: 081 1948 — 1227 |
| 189 | **Zapf Book** ITC | halbfett / demi / demi-gras | N 020: 081 2347 — 1228 |
| 191 | ***Zapf Book*** ITC | kursiv halbfett / demi italic / italique demi-gras | N 020: 081 2348 — 1229 |
| 189 | **Zapf Book** ITC | fett / heavy / gras | N 020: 081 2249 — 1230 |
| 191 | ***Zapf Book*** ITC | kursiv fett / heavy italic / italique gras | N 020: 081 2254 — 1231 |
| 103 | *Zapf Chancery* ITC | mager / light / maigre | N 020: 081 1330 — 1293 |
| 103 | *Zapf Chancery* ITC | mager Swash / light swash / maigre lettres ornées | Z 000: 081 1367 — 1294 |
| 105 | *Zapf Chancery* ITC | kursiv mager / light italic / italique maigre | N 020: 081 1358 — 1361 |
| 105 | *Zapf Chancery* ITC | kursiv mager Swash / light italic swash / italique maigre lettres ornées | Z 100: 081 1389 — 1295 |
| 103 | *Zapf Chancery* ITC | normal / medium / normal | N 020: 081 1336 — 1296 |
| 103 | *Zapf Chancery* ITC | normal Swash / normal swash / normal lettres ornées | Z 000: 081 1370 — 1297 |

# SYNOPSIS

## BERTHOLD HEADLINES

| Page | Typeface | Style | Code |
|---|---|---|---|
| 105 | *Zapf Chancery* ITC | kursiv / italic / italique | N 020: 081 1361 / 1362 |
| 105 | *Zapf Chancery* ITC | kursiv Swash / italic swash / italique lettres ornées | Z 000: 081 1392 / 1298 |
| 103 | **Zapf Chancery** ITC | halbfett / demi / demi-gras | N 020: 081 1344 / 1299 |
| 103 | **Zapf Chancery** ITC | halbfett Swash / demi swash / demi gras lettres ornées | Z 000: 081 1375 / 1300 |
| 105 | **Zapf Chancery** ITC | fett / bold / gras | N 020: 081 1353 / 1301 |
| 105 | **Zapf Chancery** ITC | fett Swash / bold swash / gras lettres ornées | Z 000: 081 1384 / 1302 |
| 133 | Zapf International ITC | mager / light / maigre | N 020: 081 2350 / 1232 |
| 119 | *Zapf International* ITC | kursiv mager / light italic / italique maigre | N 020: 081 2351 / 1233 |
| 135 | Zapf International ITC | normal / medium / normal | N 020: 081 2352 / 1234 |
| 119 | *Zapf International* ITC | kursiv / italic / italique | N 020: 081 2353 / 1235 |
| 137 | **Zapf International** ITC | halbfett / demi / demi-gras | N 020: 081 2354 / 1236 |
| 123 | ***Zapf International*** ITC | kursiv halbfett / demi italic / italique demi-gras | N 020: 081 2355 / 1237 |
| 139 | **Zapf International** ITC | fett / heavy / gras | N 020: 081 2356 / 1238 |
| 125 | ***Zapf International*** ITC | kursiv fett / heavy italic / italique gras | N 020: 081 2357 / 1239 |
| 67 | Zentenar-Fraktur | normal / regular / normal | N 000: 081 1400 / 1240 |

**Spezial-Typenplatten**
**Special typeface fount plates**
**Plaquettes spécial**

| Page | Typeface | Code |
|---|---|---|
| 464 | Fancy Label | Sp 013: 081 0002 / 131 |
| 472 | Ornamentic | Sp 000: 081 1554 / 133 |
| 465 | Varia Old Style | Sp 000: 081 0355 / 135 |
| 466 | Zapf Dingbats 100 | Sp 000: 081 2426 / 564 |
| 466 | Zapf Dingbats 200 | Sp 000: 081 2427 / 567 |
| 467 | Zapf Dingbats 300 | Sp 000: 081 2428 / 569 |
| 467 | Zapf Dingbats 199 | Sp 000: 081 2441 / 570 |
| 468 | Sonstige | |

> # SYNOPSIS

## BERTHOLD HEADLINES

**Nichtlateinische Schriften**
**Not Roman type-faces**
**Caractères non-romains**

| Page | Sample | Name | Code |
|---|---|---|---|
| 461 | برتهولد ـ عربى | Berthold Arabisch halbfett / Berthold Arabisch medium / Berthold Arabisch demi-gras | Sp014: 0811421 / 1241 |
| 461 | برتهولد ـ عربى | Berthold Arabisch licht / Berthold Arabisch outline / Berthold Arabisch éclairé | Sp014: 0811422 / 1242 |
| 461 | Ara-Garde | Ara-Garde fett / Ara-Garde bold / Ara-Garde gras | Sp000: 0811612 / 1405 |
| 461 | Mozaïque | Mozaïque mager / Mozaïque light / Mozaïque maigre | Sp000: 0811619 / 1406 |
| 461 | Nile | Nile halbfett / Nile bold / Nile demi-gras | Sp000: 0811613 / 1407 |
| 457 | Αττικα | Attika | Sp011: 0810128 / 1243 |
| 457 | Γρίκ Νρ.5 | Greek No. 5 | Sp011: 0810145 / 1244 |
| 457 | DIN 30640 λεπτή | DIN 30640 mager / DIN 30640 light / DIN 30640 maigre | Sp011: 0810212 / 1245 |
| 457 | DIN 30640 λεπτή πλάγια | DIN 30640 kursiv mager / DIN 30640 light italic / DIN 30640 italique maigre | Sp011: 0810226 / 1246 |
| 457 | DIN 30640 ἡμίμαυρα στενά | DIN 30640 schmalhalbfett / DIN 30640 medium condensed / DIN 30640 étroit demi-gras | Sp011: 0810162 / 1247 |
| 457 | DIN 30640 ἡμίμαυρα στενά πλάγια | DIN 30640 kursiv schmalhalbfett / DIN 30640 medium condensed italic / DIN 30640 italique étroit demi-gras | Sp011: 0810176 / 1248 |
| 457 | Ερακλίτ | Heraklit | Sp011: 0810131 / 1249 |
| 457 | Φαίδων | Phaidon kursiv / Phaidon italic / Phaidon italique | Sp011: 0810159 / 1250 |
| 461 | העכרעיאש | Hadassah normal / Hadassah regular / Hadassah normal | Sp000: 0811418 / 1251 |
| 461 | העכרעיאש | Hadassah fett / Hadassah bold / Hadassah gras | Sp000: 0811419 / 1252 |
| 459 | Акцидэнс Гротэск | Akzidenz-Grotesk normal / Akzidenz-Grotesk regular / Akzidenz-Grotesk normal | Sp000: 0811415 / 1253 |
| 459 | **Акцидэнс Гротэск** | Akzidenz-Grotesk halbfett / Akzidenz-Grotesk medium / Akzidenz-Grotesk demi-gras | Sp000: 0811416 / 1254 |
| 459 | Амтс Антиква | Amts-Antiqua normal / Amts-Antiqua regular / Amts-Antiqua normal | Sp000: 0811412 / 1255 |
| 459 | **Амтс Антиква** | Amts-Antiqua halbfett / Amts-Antiqua medium / Amts-Antiqua demi-gras | Sp000: 0811414 / 1256 |
| 459 | *Амтс Антиква* | Amts-Antiqua kursiv / Amts-Antiqua italic / Amts-Antiqua italique | Sp000: 0811413 / 1257 |
| 72 | Sonderbelegungen | Tschechisch, Türkisch, Jugoslawisch / Isländisch, Polnisch, Slawisch / Anglo-Amerikanisch | |

# BERTHOLD HEADLINES I

# 1-6

*Gebrochene Schriften*
*Black Letters*
*Caractères «allemands» (Gothiques)*

**BERTHOLD HEADLINES I** — Gebrochene Schriften / Black Letters / Caractères «allemands» (Gothiques)

THE QUICK BROWN FOX JUMPS OVER
THE LAZY DOG 1234567890

THE QUICK BROWN FOX JUMPS OVER
THE LAZY DOG 1234567890

QUICK BROWN FOX JUMPS OVER
THE LAZY DOG 1234567890

QUICK BROWN FOX JUMPS OVER
THE LAZY DOG 1234567890

**BERTHOLD HEADLINES I** — Gebrochene Schriften / Black Letters / Caractères «allemands» (Gothiques)

QUICK BROWN FOX JUMPS OVER
THE LAZY DOG 1234567890

**BERTHOLD HEADLINES I** — Gebrochene Schriften / Black Letters / Caractères «allemands» (Gothiques)

THE QUICK BROWN FOX JUMPS OVER
THE LAZY DOG 1234567890

| | Gotisch / Textura / Gothique | **1** |

**Breda-Gotisch**
252

the quick brown fox jumps
over the lazy dog

F 006: 081 2142
H. Berthold AG
H 1–x 0,67–k 1,00–p 0,23

**Fette Gotisch**
508

the quick brown fox jumps
over the lazy dog

N 000: 081 0524
1911
Johannes Wagner
H 1–x 0,69–k 1,00–p 0,25

**Manuskript-Gotisch**
813

the quick brown fox jumps
over the lazy dog

N 000: 081 0881
1900
Fundición Tipográfica Neufville, S.A.
H 1–x 0,70–k 1,00–p 0,27

**Ganz grobe Gotisch**
577

the quick brown fox jumps
over the lazy dog

N 000: 081 0628
F. H. Ernst Schneidler 1930
Fundición Tipográfica Neufville, S.A.
H 1–x 0,72–k 1,00–p 0,18

| | Schwabacher / Schwabacher / Caractère dit de Schwabach | **2** |

**Alte Schwabacher**
42

the quick brown fox jumps
over the lazy dog

N 100: 081 0060
H. Berthold AG
H 1–x 0,69–k 1,00–p 0,28

| | Rundgotisch / Rotunda / Gothic rond | **3** |

**Weiß-Rundgotisch 1**
1206

the quick brown fox jumps
over the lazy dog

N 000: 081 1385
Emil Rudolf Weiß 1937
Fundición Tipográfica Neufville, S.A.
H 1–x 0,75–k 1,08–p 0,31

**BERTHOLD HEADLINES I** — Gebrochene Schriften / Black Letters / Caractères «allemands» (Gothiques)

THE QUICK BROWN FOX JUMPS OVER THE LAZY DOG 1234567890

**BERTHOLD HEADLINES I** — Gebrochene Schriften / Black Letters / Caractères «allemands» (Gothiques)

THE QUICK BROWN FOX JUMPS OVER THE LAZY DOG 1234567890

THE QUICK BROWN FOX JUMPS OVER THE LAZY DOG 1234567890

THE QUICK BROWN FOX JUMPS OVER THE LAZY DOG 1234567890

**BERTHOLD HEADLINES I** — Gebrochene Schriften / Black Letters / Caractères «allemands» (Gothiques)

THE QUICK BROWN FOX JUMPS OVER THE LAZY DOG 1234567890

THE QUICK BROWN FOX JUMPS OVER THE LAZY DOG 1234567890

| | Rundgotisch Rotunda Gothic rond | **3** |

**Weiß-Rundgotisch 2**
1207

the quick brown fox jumps
over the lazy dog

N 000: 081 1386
Emil Rudolf Weiß 1937
Fundición Tipográfica Neufville, S.A.
H 1–x 0,75–k 1,08–p 0,31

| | Fraktur Fraktur Caractère allemand «Fraktur» | **4** |

**Zentenar-Fraktur**
1240
normal
regular
normal

the quick brown fox jumps
over the lazy dog

N 000: 081 1400
F. H. Ernst Schneidler 1937
Fundición Tipográfica Neufville, S.A.
H 1–x 0,75–k 1,05–p 0,29

**Walbaum-Fraktur**
1185

the quick brown fox jumps
over the lazy dog

N 000: 081 1381
J. E. Walbaum 1800
H. Berthold AG
H 1–x 0,75–k 1,01–p 0,23

**Fette Fraktur**
507

the quick brown fox jumps
over the lazy dog

N 000: 081 0523
1875
Johannes Wagner
H 1–x 0,75–k 1,00–p 0,31

| | Kanzlei Chancery Caractère allemand «Kanzlei» | **5** |

**Breite Kanzlei**
253

the quick brown fox jumps
over the lazy dog

N 100: 081 0229
Haas'sche Schriftgießerei AG
H 1–x 0,70–k 1,00–p 0,38

**Fette Kanzlei**
509

the quick brown fox jumps
over the lazy dog

N 000: 081 0527
Haas'sche Schriftgießerei AG
H 1–x 0,77–k 1,00–p 0,23

## BERTHOLD HEADLINES I

Gebrochene Schriften  
Black Letters  
Caractères «allemands» (Gothiques)

THE QUICK BROWN FOX JUMPS OVER THE LAZY DOG 1234567890

QUICK BROWN FOX JUMPS OVER THE LAZY DOG

THE QUICK BROWN FOX JUMPS OVER THE LAZY DOG 1234567890

Sonstige / Others / Autres — 6

**Rhapsodie**
989

the quick brown fox jumps over the lazy dog

F 006: 081 2186
Ilse Schüle 1951
Ludwig & Mayer
H 1–x 0,64–k 1,11–p 0,46

**Rhapsodie**
990
Zierbuchstaben
swash letters
lettres ornées
Z 000: 081 2187
Ilse Schüle 1951
Ludwig & Mayer
H 1–x 0,60–k 1,33–p 0,53

**Tannenberg**
1076

the quick brown fox jumps over the lazy dog

N 000: 081 1159
Erich Meyer 1934
D. Stempel AG
H 1–x 0,72–k 1,00–p 0,25

# BERTHOLD HEADLINES II

# 7-16

*Renaissance-Antiqua*
*Old Style*
*Renaissance-Antiqua (Garaldes, Humanes)*

**BERTHOLD HEADLINES II**  Renaissance-Antiqua
Old Style
Renaissance-Antiqua (Garaldes, Humanes)

THE QUICK BROWN FOX JUMPS OVER THE LAZY DOG 1234567890

THE QUICK BROWN FOX JUMPS OVER THE LAZY DOG 1234567890

THE QUICK BROWN FOX JUMPS OVER THE LAZY DOG 1234567890

THE QUICK BROWN FOX JUMPS OVER THE LAZY DOG 1234567890

THE QUICK BROWN FOX JUMPS OVER THE LAZY DOG 1234567890

THE QUICK BROWN FOX JUMPS OVER THE LAZY DOG 1234567890

THE QUICK BROWN FOX JUMPS OVER THE LAZY DOG 1234567890

QUICK BROWN FOX JUMPS OVER THE LAZY DOG 1234567890

Venezianische Renaissance-Antiqua **7**
Venetian Old Style
Renaissance vénitienne Antiqua

**Seneca**
1348
mager
light
maigre
N 020: 081 2497
Gustav Jaeger 1979
H. Berthold AG
H 1–x 0,64–k 1,03–p 0,38

the quick brown fox jumps
over the lazy dog

**Horley Old Style**
676
normal
regular
normal
N 020: 081 2406
1925
Monotype Corporation Ltd.
H 1–x 0,58–k 1,01–p 0,36

the quick brown fox jumps
over the lazy dog

ITC **Italia**
697
Buch
book
romain labeur
N 020: 081 2383
Colin Brignall 1977
International Typeface Corp.
H 1–x 0,68–k 1,04–p 0,29

the quick brown fox jumps
over the lazy dog

**Italian Old Style**
700
normal
regular
normal
N 020: 081 2408
Frederic W. Goudy 1924
Monotype Corporation Ltd.
H 1–x 0,65–k 1,02–p 0,24

the quick brown fox jumps
over the lazy dog

**Seneca**
1349
normal
regular
normal
N 020: 081 2498
Gustav Jaeger 1977
H. Berthold AG
H 1–x 0,64–k 1,03–p 0,38

the quick brown fox jumps
over the lazy dog

ITC **Italia**
698
normal
medium
normal
N 020: 081 2384
Colin Brignall 1977
International Typeface Corp.
H 1–x 0,68–k 1,03–p 0,31

**the quick brown fox jumps
over the lazy dog**

**Italian Old Style**
702
halbfett
bold
demi-gras
N 020: 081 2410
Frederic W. Goudy 1924
Monotype Corporation Ltd.
H 1–x 0,64–k 1,02–p 0,24

**the quick brown fox jumps
over the lazy dog**

**Horley Old Style**
678
halbfett
bold
demi-gras
N 020: 081 2407
1925
Monotype Corporation Ltd.
H 1–x 0,61–k 1,02–p 0,33

**the quick brown fox jumps
over the lazy dog**

## BERTHOLD HEADLINES II
Renaissance-Antiqua
Old Style
Renaissance-Antiqua (Garaldes, Humanes)

QUICK BROWN FOX JUMPS OVER THE LAZY DOG 1234567890

THE QUICK BROWN FOX JUMPS OVER THE LAZY DOG 1234567890

QUICK BROWN FOX JUMPS OVER THE LAZY DOG 1234567890

QUICK BROWN FOX JUMPS OVER THE LAZY DOG 1234567890

## BERTHOLD HEADLINES II
Renaissance-Antiqua
Old Style
Renaissance-Antiqua (Garaldes, Humanes)

*THE QUICK BROWN FOX JUMPS OVER THE LAZY DOG 1234567890*

*THE QUICK BROWN FOX JUMPS OVER THE LAZY DOG 1234567890*

*THE QUICK BROWN FOX JUMPS OVER THE LAZY DOG 1234567890*

## 7 Venezianische Renaissance-Antiqua / Venetian Old Style / Renaissance vénitienne Antiqua

the quick brown fox jumps over the lazy dog

**Seneca**
1351
halbfett
medium
demi-gras
N 020: 081 2500
Gustav Jaeger 1977
H. Berthold AG
H 1–x 0,64–k 1,00–p 0,36

the quick brown fox jumps over the lazy dog

ITC **Italia**
699
halbfett
bold
demi-gras
N 020: 081 2385
Colin Brignall 1977
International Typeface Corp.
H 1–x 0,68–k 1,03–p 0,30

the quick brown fox jumps over the lazy dog

**Seneca**
1352
fett
bold
gras
N 020: 081 2501
Gustav Jaeger 1977
H. Berthold AG
H 1–x 0,64–k 1,04–p 0,37

the quick brown fox jumps over the lazy dog

**Seneca**
1353
extrafett
extra bold
extra gras
N 020: 081 2502
Gustav Jaeger 1977
H. Berthold AG
H 1–x 0,63–k 1,02–p 0,38

## 8 Venezianische Renaissance-Antiqua, kursive / Venetian Old Style, italic / Renaissance vénitienne Antiqua, italique

*the quick brown fox jumps over the lazy dog*

**Horley Old Style**
677
kursiv
italic
italique
N 020: 081 2129
1925
Monotype Corporation Ltd.
H 1–x 0,58–k 1,03–p 0,35

*the quick brown fox jumps over the lazy dog*

**Italian Old Style**
701
kursiv
italic
italique
N 020: 081 2409
Frederic W. Goudy 1924
Monotype Corporation Ltd.
H 1–x 0,63–k 1,01–p 0,25

*the quick brown fox jumps over the lazy dog*

**Seneca**
1350
kursiv
italic
italique
N 020: 081 2499
Gustav Jaeger 1977
H. Berthold AG
H 1–x 0,64–k 1,03–p 0,38

**BERTHOLD HEADLINES II** — Renaissance-Antiqua / Old Style / Renaissance-Antiqua (Garaldes, Humanes)

THE QUICK BROWN FOX JUMPS OVER
THE LAZY DOG

THE QUICK BROWN FOX JUMPS OVER
THE LAZY DOG 1234567890

THE QUICK BROWN FOX JUMPS OVER
THE LAZY DOG 1234567890

THE QUICK BROWN FOX JUMPS OVER
THE LAZY DOG 1234567890

THE QUICK BROWN FOX JUMPS OVER
THE LAZY DOG 1234567890

THE QUICK BROWN FOX JUMPS OVER
THE LAZY DOG 1234567890

THE QUICK BROWN FOX JUMPS OVER
THE LAZY DOG 1234567890

THE QUICK BROWN FOX JUMPS OVER
THE LAZY DOG 1234567890

Französische Renaissance-Antiqua **9**
French Old Style
Renaissance française Antiqua

**Schneidler-Initialen**
1017

V 000: 081 1118
F. H. Ernst Schneidler 1937
Fundición Tipográfica Neufville, S.A.
H 1–Q 1,19

**Weiß-Kapitale**
1204
normal
regular
normal
V 009: 081 2188
Emil Rudolf Weiß 1931
Fundición Tipográfica Neufville, S.A.
H 1–Q 1,05

the quick brown fox jumps over the lazy dog

**Berling-Antiqua**
160
normal
regular
normal
N 100: 081 0151
Karl Erik Forsberg 1951
Berlingska Stilgjuteri AB
H 1–x 0,63–k 1,13–p 0,37

the quick brown fox jumps over the lazy dog

**Goudy Old Style**
633
normal
regular
normal
N 100: 081 0678
Frederic W. Goudy 1915
American Typefounders
H 1–x 0,58–k 1,07–p 0,26

the quick brown fox jumps over the lazy dog

STEMPEL **Garamond**
594
normal
regular
normal
N 100: 081 0630
1924
D. Stempel AG
H 1–x 0,63–k 1,12–p 0,38

the quick brown fox jumps over the lazy dog

AMSTERDAM **Garamont**
599
normal
regular
normal
N 100: 081 0639
M. F. Benton, T. M. Cleland 1914
Lettergieterij Amsterdam
H 1–x 0,63–k 1,07–p 0,40

the quick brown fox jumps over the lazy dog

HAAS **Garamont**
597
normal
regular
normal
N 100: 081 0652
G. und C. Peignot 1928
Haas'sche Schriftgießerei AG
H 1–x 0,59–k 1,06–p 0,47

the quick brown fox jumps over the lazy dog

BERTHOLD **Garamond**
1381
normal
regular
normal
N 020: 081 1742
Günter Gerhard Lange 1972
H. Berthold AG
H 1–x 0,63–k 1,07–p 0,34

**BERTHOLD HEADLINES II** Renaissance-Antiqua / Old Style / Renaissance-Antiqua (Garaldes, Humanes)

THE QUICK BROWN FOX JUMPS OVER THE LAZY DOG 1234567890

THE QUICK BROWN FOX JUMPS OVER THE LAZY DOG 1234567890

THE QUICK BROWN FOX JUMPS OVER THE LAZY DOG 1234567890

THE QUICK BROWN FOX JUMPS OVER THE LAZY DOG 1234567890

THE QUICK BROWN FOX JUMPS OVER THE LAZY DOG 1234567890

THE QUICK BROWN FOX JUMPS OVER THE LAZY DOG 1234567890

THE QUICK BROWN FOX JUMPS OVER THE LAZY DOG 1234567890

THE QUICK BROWN FOX JUMPS OVER THE LAZY DOG 1234567890

| | Französische Renaissance-Antiqua<br>French Old Style<br>Renaissance française Antiqua | 9 |

the quick brown fox jumps
over the lazy dog

**Palatino**
909
normal
regular
normal
N 100: 081 0993
Hermann Zapf 1950
D. Stempel AG
H 1–x 0,63–k 1,12–p 0,34

the quick brown fox jumps
over the lazy dog

ITC **Garamond**
578
mager
light
maigre
N 020: 081 2362
Tony Stan 1977
International Typeface Corp.
H 1–x 0,71–k 1,13–p 0,37

the quick brown fox jumps
over the lazy dog

**Aldus-Buchschrift**
1303
normal
regular
normal
N 020: 081 0204
Hermann Zapf 1954
D. Stempel AG
H 1–x 0,64–k 1,13–p 0,36

the quick brown fox jumps
over the lazy dog

**Bembo**
143
normal
regular
normal
N 100: 081 0147
1930
Monotype Corporation Ltd.
H 1–x 0,64–k 1,15–p 0,41

the quick brown fox jumps
over the lazy dog

**Goudy Catalogue**
629
normal
regular
normal
N 100: 081 0679
F. W. Goudy, Morris F. Benton 1921
American Typefounders
H 1–x 0,59–k 1,07–p 0,28

the quick brown fox jumps
over the lazy dog

AMSTERDAM **Garamont**
601
halbfett
medium
demi-gras
N 100: 081 0647
M. F. Benton, T. M. Cleland 1931
Lettergieterij Amsterdam
H 1–x 0,63–k 1,07–p 0,40

the quick brown fox jumps
over the lazy dog

**Quadriga-Antiqua**
976
normal
regular
normal
N 020: 081 1991
Manfred Barz 1979
(Johan Michael Smit 1750)
H 1–x 0,64–k 1,05–p 0,40

the quick brown fox jumps
over the lazy dog

**Weiß-Antiqua**
1198
halbfett
medium
demi-gras
N 100: 081 1382
Emil Rudolf Weiß 1931
Fundición Tipográfica Neufville, S.A.
H 1–x 0,62–k 1,06–p 0,31

**BERTHOLD HEADLINES II** Renaissance-Antiqua
Old Style
Renaissance-Antiqua (Garaldes, Humanes)

THE QUICK BROWN FOX JUMPS OVER THE LAZY DOG 1234567890

THE QUICK BROWN FOX JUMPS OVER THE LAZY DOG 1234567890

THE QUICK BROWN FOX JUMPS OVER THE LAZY DOG 1234567890

THE QUICK BROWN FOX JUMPS OVER THE LAZY DOG 1234567890

THE QUICK BROWN FOX JUMPS OVER THE LAZY DOG 1234567890

THE QUICK BROWN FOX JUMPS OVER THE LAZY DOG 1234567890

QUICK BROWN FOX JUMPS OVER THE LAZY DOG 1234567890

THE QUICK BROWN FOX JUMPS OVER THE LAZY DOG 1234567890

Französische Renaissance-Antiqua
French Old Style
Renaissance française Antiqua  **9**

the quick brown fox jumps
over the lazy dog

**Plantin**
937
normal
regular
normal
N 020: 081 2126
F. H. Pierpont 1913
Monotype Corporation Ltd.
H 1–x 0,66–k 1,02–p 0,24

the quick brown fox jumps
over the lazy dog

ITC **Garamond**
580
Buch
book
romain labeur
N 020: 081 2245
Tony Stan 1975
International Typeface Corp.
H 1–x 0,72–k 1,07–p 0,35

the quick brown fox jumps
over the lazy dog

STEMPEL **Garamond**
596
halbfett
medium
demi-gras
N 100: 081 0636
1927
D. Stempel AG
H 1–x 0,65–k 1,11–p 0,36

**Weiß-Kapitale**
1205
kräftig
medium
demi-gras
V 009: 081 2189
Emil Rudolf Weiß 1931
Fundición Tipográfica Neufville, S.A.
H 1–Q 1,08

the quick brown fox jumps
over the lazy dog

**Goudy**
626
halbfett
bold
demi-gras
N 100: 081 0685
Frederic W. Goudy 1926
American Typefounders
H 1–x 0,63–k 1,06–p 0,25

the quick brown fox jumps
over the lazy dog

BERTHOLD **Garamond**
1383
halbfett
medium
demi-gras
N 020: 081 1756
Günter Gerhard Lange 1972
H. Berthold AG
H 1–x 0,63–k 1,07–p 0,34

the quick brown fox jumps
over the lazy dog

**Goudy**
627
fett
extra bold
gras
N 100: 081 0687
Frederic W. Goudy 1926
American Typefounders
H 1–x 0,61–k 1,05–p 0,29

the quick brown fox jumps
over the lazy dog

**Weiß-Antiqua**
1199
fett
bold
gras
N 100: 081 1383
1948
Fundición Tipográfica Neufville, S.A.
H 1–x 0,64–k 1,11–p 0,29

## BERTHOLD HEADLINES II
Renaissance-Antiqua
Old Style
Renaissance-Antiqua (Garaldes, Humanes)

THE QUICK BROWN FOX JUMPS OVER THE LAZY DOG 1234567890

THE QUICK BROWN FOX JUMPS OVER THE LAZY DOG 1234567890

QUICK BROWN FOX JUMPS OVER THE LAZY DOG 1234567890

QUICK BROWN FOX JUMPS OVER THE LAZY DOG 1234567890

THE QUICK BROWN FOX JUMPS OVER THE LAZY DOG 1234567890

THE QUICK BROWN FOX JUMPS OVER THE LAZY DOG 1234567890

THE QUICK BROWN FOX JUMPS OVER THE LAZY DOG 1234567890

QUICK BROWN FOX JUMPS OVER THE LAZY DOG 1234567890

Französische Renaissance-Antiqua
French Old Style
Renaissance française Antiqua  **9**

**Quadriga-Antiqua**
978
halbfett
medium
demi-gras
N 020: 081 1992
Manfred Barz 1979
(Johan Michael Smit 1750)
H 1–x 0,65–k 1,05–p 0,40

the quick brown fox jumps over the lazy dog

**Palatino**
911
halbfett
bold
demi-gras
N 100: 081 0996
Hermann Zapf 1951
D. Stempel AG
H 1–x 0,64–k 1,02–p 0,35

the quick brown fox jumps over the lazy dog

**Octavia**
899
halbfett
bold
demi-gras
N 010: 081 2149
Leslie Usherwood 1973
Typsettra
H 1–x 0,75–k 1,25–p 0,35

the quick brown fox jumps over the lazy dog

**Bembo**
145
halbfett
bold
demi-gras
N 100: 081 0149
1935
Monotype Corporation Ltd.
H 1–x 0,65–k 1,14–p 0,41

the quick brown fox jumps over the lazy dog

**Plantin**
939
halbfett
bold
demi-gras

N 000: 081 1018
Monotype Corporation Ltd.
H 1–x 0,65–k 1,08–p 0,33

the quick brown fox jumps over the lazy dog

BERTHOLD **Garamond**
1331
fett
bold
gras
N 020: 081 1773
Günter Gerhard Lange 1975
H. Berthold AG
H 1–x 0,62–k 1,08–p 0,33

the quick brown fox jumps over the lazy dog

**Quadriga-Antiqua**
979
fett
bold
gras
N 020: 081 1997
Manfred Barz 1979
(Johan Michael Smit 1750)
H 1–x 0,65–k 1,05–p 0,40

the quick brown fox jumps over the lazy dog

ITC **Garamond**
582
fett
bold
gras
N 020: 081 2364
Tony Stan 1977
International Typeface Corp.
H 1–x 0,73–k 1,13–p 0,38

the quick brown fox jumps over the lazy dog

**BERTHOLD HEADLINES II** — Renaissance-Antiqua / Old Style / Renaissance-Antiqua (Garaldes, Humanes)

THE QUICK BROWN FOX JUMPS OVER THE LAZY DOG 1234567890

THE QUICK BROWN FOX JUMPS OVER THE LAZY DOG 1234567890

THE QUICK BROWN FOX JUMPS OVER THE LAZY DOG 1234567890

QUICK BROWN FOX JUMPS OVER THE LAZY DOG 1234567890

QUICK BROWN FOX JUMPS OVER THE LAZY DOG 1234567890

**BERTHOLD HEADLINES II** — Renaissance-Antiqua / Old Style / Renaissance-Antiqua (Garaldes, Humanes)

*THE QUICK BROWN FOX JUMPS OVER THE LAZY DOG 1234567890*

*THE QUICK BROWN FOX JUMPS OVER THE LAZY DOG 1234567890*

## 9 Französische Renaissance-Antiqua / French Old Style / Renaissance française Antiqua

**the quick brown fox jumps over the lazy dog**

Weiß-Antiqua
1200
extrafett
extra bold
extra gras
N 020: 081 1842
Berthold-Schriftenatelier 1976
Fundición Tipográfica Neufville, S.A.
H 1–x 0,64–k 1,03–p 0,29

**the quick brown fox jumps over the lazy dog**

Quadriga-Antiqua
1291
extrafett
extra bold
extra gras
N 020: 081 1998
Manfred Barz 1979
(Johan Michael Smit 1750)
H 1–x 0,65–k 1,05–p 0,40

**the quick brown fox jumps over the lazy dog**

Weiß-Antiqua
1201
ultrafett
ultra bold
ultra gras
N 020: 081 1845
Berthold-Schriftenatelier 1976
Fundición Tipográfica Neufville, S.A.
H 1–x 0,65–k 1,03–p 0,29

**the quick brown fox jumps over the lazy dog**

ITC **Garamond**
584
ultra
ultra
ultra
N 010: 081 2111
Tony Stan 1975
International Typeface Corp.
H 1–x 0,70–k 1,09–p 0,35

**the quick brown fox jumps over the lazy dog**

**Goudy Heavyface**
631
normal
regular
normal
N 100: 081 1510
Frederic W. Goudy 1926
American Typefounders
H 1–x 0,78–k 1,09–p 0,35

## 10 Französische Renaissance-Antiqua, kursive / French Old Style, italic / Renaissance française Antiqua, italique

*the quick brown fox jumps over the lazy dog*

AMSTERDAM **Garamont**
600
kursiv
italic
italique
N 100: 081 0643
M. F. Benton, T. M. Cleland 1918
Lettergieterij Amsterdam
H 1–x 0,64–k 1,10–p 0,42

*the quick brown fox jumps over the lazy dog*

STEMPEL **Garamond**
595
kursiv
italic
italique
N 100: 081 0634
1926
D. Stempel AG
H 1–x 0,66–k 1,10–p 0,38

# BERTHOLD HEADLINES II
Renaissance-Antiqua
Old Style
Renaissance-Antiqua (Garaldes, Humanes)

THE QUICK BROWN FOX JUMPS OVER
THE LAZY DOG 1234567890

THE QUICK BROWN FOX JUMPS OVER
THE LAZY DOG 1234567890

THE QUICK BROWN FOX JUMPS OVER
THE LAZY DOG 1234567890

THE QUICK BROWN FOX JUMPS OVER
THE LAZY DOG 1234567890

THE QUICK BROWN FOX JUMPS OVER
THE LAZY DOG 1234567890

THE QUICK BROWN FOX JUMPS OVER
THE LAZY DOG

THE QUICK BROWN FOX JUMPS OVER
THE LAZY DOG 1234567890

THE QUICK BROWN FOX JUMPS OVER
THE LAZY DOG 1234567890

Französische Renaissance-Antiqua, kursive
French Old Style, italic
Renaissance française Antiqua, italique

**10**

*the quick brown fox jumps over the lazy dog*

**Palatino**
910
kursiv
italic
italique
N 020: 081 0520
Hermann Zapf 1951
D. Stempel AG
H 1–x 0,63–k 1,12–p 0,34

*the quick brown fox jumps over the lazy dog*

BERTHOLD **Garamond**
1382
kursiv
italic
italique
N 020: 081 1787
Günter Gerhard Lange 1972
H. Berthold AG
H 1–x 0,63–k 1,05–p 0,35

*the quick brown fox jumps over the lazy dog*

**Lectura**
794
kursiv
italic
italique
N 100: 081 0844
Dick Dooijes 1969
Lettergieterij Amsterdam
H 1–x 0,72–k 1,16–p 0,34

*the quick brown fox jumps over the lazy dog*

**Aldus-Buchschrift**
1261
kursiv
italic
italique
N 020: 081 0218
Hermann Zapf 1954
D. Stempel AG
H 1–x 0,64–k 1,13–p 0,36

*the quick brown fox jumps over the lazy dog*

**Diethelm**
442
kursiv
italic
italique
N 100: 081 0427
Walter Diethelm 1948
Haas'sche Schriftgießerei AG
H 1–x 0,66–k 1,06–p 0,34

**Diethelm**
443
kursiv Zierbuchstaben
italic swash letters
italique lettres ornées
Z 000: 081 0429
Walter Diethelm 1948
Haas'sche Schriftgießerei AG
H 1–x 0,66–k 1,06–p 0,34

*the quick brown fox jumps over the lazy dog*

ITC **Garamond**
579
kursiv mager
light italic
italique maigre
N 020: 081 2363
Tony Stan 1977
International Typeface Corp.
H 1–x 0,73–k 1,13–p 0,35

*the quick brown fox jumps over the lazy dog*

**Bembo**
144
kursiv
italic
italique
N 100: 081 0148
Alfred Fairbank 1930
(Giovanni Tagliente 1524)
H 1–x 0,65–k 1,16–p 0,42

## BERTHOLD HEADLINES II
Renaissance-Antiqua
Old Style
Renaissance-Antiqua (Garaldes, Humanes)

*THE QUICK BROWN FOX JUMPS OVER THE LAZY DOG 1234567890*

*THE QUICK BROWN FOX JUMPS OVER THE LAZY DOG 1234567890*

*THE QUICK BROWN FOX JUMPS OVER THE LAZY DOG 1234567890*

*THE QUICK BROWN FOX JUMPS OVER THE LAZY DOG 1234567890*

*THE QUICK BROWN FOX JUMPS OVER THE LAZY DOG 1234567890*

*THE QUICK BROWN FOX JUMPS OVER THE LAZY DOG 1234567890*

*QUICK BROWN FOX JUMPS OVER THE LAZY DOG 1234567890*

*QUICK BROWN FOX JUMPS OVER THE LAZY DOG 1234567890*

Französische Renaissance-Antiqua, kursive  
French Old Style, italic  
Renaissance française Antiqua, italique  
**10**

*the quick brown fox jumps over the lazy dog*

HAAS **Garamont**  
598  
kursiv  
italic  
italique  
N 100: 081 0657  
G. und C. Peignot 1928  
Haas'sche Schriftgießerei AG  
H 1–x 0,66–k 1,13–p 0,43

*the quick brown fox jumps over the lazy dog*

**Quadriga**  
977  
kursiv  
italic  
italique  
N 020: 081 0171  
Manfred Barz 1979  
(Johan Michael Smit 1750)  
H 1–x 0,64–k 1,04–p 0,40

*the quick brown fox jumps over the lazy dog*

**Plantin**  
938  
kursiv  
italic  
italique  

N 020: 081 2125  
Monotype Corporation Ltd.  
H 1–x 0,63–k 1,03–p 0,25

*the quick brown fox jumps over the lazy dog*

AMSTERDAM **Garamont**  
602  
kursiv halbfett  
medium italic  
italique demi-gras  
N 100: 081 0651  
M. F. Benton, T. M. Cleland 1931  
Lettergieterij Amsterdam  
H 1–x 0,63–k 1,08 p 0,41

*the quick brown fox jumps over the lazy dog*

ITC **Garamond**  
581  
Buch kursiv  
book italic  
italique romain labeur  
N 020: 081 2246  
Tony Stan 1975  
International Typeface Corp.  
H 1–x 0,73–k 1,05–p 0,35

*the quick brown fox jumps over the lazy dog*

BERTHOLD **Garamond**  
1330  
kursiv halbfett  
medium italic  
italique demi-gras  
N 020: 081 1790  
Günter Gerhard Lange 1972  
H. Berthold AG  
H 1–x 0,63–k 1,04–p 0,33

*the quick brown fox jumps over the lazy dog*

**Bembo**  
146  
kursiv halbfett  
bold italic  
italique demi-gras  
N 100: 081 0150  
1935  
Monotype Corporation Ltd.  
H 1–x 0,66–k 1,15–p 0,42

*the quick brown fox jumps over the lazy dog*

ITC **Garamond**  
583  
kursiv fett  
bold italic  
italique gras  
N 020: 081 2380  
Tony Stan 1977  
International Typeface Corp.  
H 1–x 0,73–k 1,10–p 0,35

**BERTHOLD HEADLINES II** Renaissance-Antiqua / Old Style / Renaissance-Antiqua (Garaldes, Humanes)

*QUICK BROWN FOX JUMPS OVER THE LAZY DOG 1234567890*

**BERTHOLD HEADLINES II** Renaissance-Antiqua / Old Style / Renaissance-Antiqua (Garaldes, Humanes)

THE QUICK BROWN FOX JUMPS OVER THE LAZY DOG 1234567890

THE QUICK BROWN FOX JUMPS OVER THE LAZY DOG 1234567890

THE QUICK BROWN FOX JUMPS OVER THE LAZY DOG 1234567890

THE QUICK BROWN FOX JUMPS OVER THE LAZY DOG 1234567890

THE QUICK BROWN FOX JUMPS OVER THE LAZY DOG 1234567890

THE QUICK BROWN FOX JUMPS OVER THE LAZY DOG 1234567890

| | Französische Renaissance-Antiqua, kursive<br>French Old Style, italic<br>Renaissance française Antiqua, italique | **10** |

*the quick brown fox jumps*
*over the lazy dog*

ITC **Garamond**
585
kursiv ultra
ultra italic
italique ultra
N 010: 081 2114
Tony Stan 1975
International Typeface Corp.
H 1–x 0,73–k 1,09–p 0,33

| | Jüngere Renaissance-Antiqua<br>Old Style (Early Renaissance)<br>Renaissance Antiqua récente | **11** |

the quick brown fox jumps
over the lazy dog

**Diethelm-Antiqua**
441
normal
regular
normal
N 100: 081 0425
Walter Diethelm 1948
Haas'sche Schriftgießerei AG
H 1–x 0,69–k 1,06–p 0,37

the quick brown fox jumps
over the lazy dog

**Trump-Mediäval**
1110
normal
regular
normal
N 100: 081 1203
Georg Trump 1954
D. Stempel AG
H 1–x 0,68–k 1,13–p 0,30

the quick brown fox jumps
over the lazy dog

**Méridien**
834
normal
regular
normal
N 100: 081 0898
Adrian Frutiger 1957
Haas'sche Schriftgießerei AG
H 1–x 0,72–k 1,13–p 0,31

the quick brown fox jumps
over the lazy dog

**Perpetua**
923
normal
regular
normal
N 020: 081 1983
Eric Gill 1927
Monotype Corporation Ltd.
H 1–x 0,62–k 1,10–p 0,42

the quick brown fox jumps
over the lazy dog

**Lectura**
756
normal
regular
normal
N 100: 081 0843
Dick Dooijes 1969
Lettergieterij Amsterdam
H 1–x 0,69–k 1,13–p 0,37

the quick brown fox jumps
over the lazy dog

**Vendôme**
1152
normal
regular
normal
N 100: 081 1318
François Ganeau 1952
Marcel Olive
H 1–x 0,65–k 1,03–p 0,35

**BERTHOLD HEADLINES II** — Renaissance-Antiqua / Old Style / Renaissance-Antiqua (Garaldes, Humanes)

THE QUICK BROWN FOX JUMPS OVER THE LAZY DOG 1234567890

THE QUICK BROWN FOX JUMPS OVER THE LAZY DOG 1234567890

THE QUICK BROWN FOX JUMPS OVER THE LAZY DOG 1234567890

THE QUICK BROWN FOX JUMPS OVER THE LAZY DOG 1234567890

THE QUICK BROWN FOX JUMPS OVER THE LAZY DOG 1234567890

QUICK BROWN FOX JUMPS OVER THE LAZY DOG 1234567890

THE QUICK BROWN FOX JUMPS OVER THE LAZY DOG 1234567890

QUICK BROWN FOX JUMPS OVER THE LAZY DOG 1234567890

Jüngere Renaissance-Antiqua  
Old Style (Early Renaissance)  
Renaissance Antiqua récente  
**11**

**Comenius-Antiqua**  
1313  
normal  
regular  
normal  
N 020: 081 2490  
Hermann Zapf 1976  
H. Berthold AG  
H 1–x 0,68–k 1,06–p 0,38

the quick brown fox jumps over the lazy dog

**Lectura**  
758  
halbfett  
medium  
demi-gras  
N 100: 081 0845  
Dick Dooijes 1969  
Lettergieterij Amsterdam  
H 1–x 0,69–k 1,13–p 0,37

the quick brown fox jumps over the lazy dog

**Trump-Mediäval**  
1112  
halbfett  
bold  
demi-gras  
N 100: 081 1205  
Georg Trump 1958  
D. Stempel AG  
H 1–x 0,68–k 1,13–p 0,30

the quick brown fox jumps over the lazy dog

**Méridien**  
835  
halbfett  
medium  
demi-gras  
N 100: 081 0899  
Adrian Frutiger 1957  
Haas'sche Schriftgießerei AG  
H 1–x 0,72–k 1,13–p 0,31

the quick brown fox jumps over the lazy dog

**Diethelm-Antiqua**  
444  
halbfett  
medium  
demi-gras  
N 100: 081 0426  
Walter Diethelm 1948  
Haas'sche Schriftgießerei AG  
H 1–x 0,69–k 1,06–p 0,34

the quick brown fox jumps over the lazy dog

**Comenius-Antiqua**  
1315  
halbfett  
medium  
demi-gras  
N 020: 081 2492  
Hermann Zapf 1977  
H. Berthold AG  
H 1–x 0,69–k 1,09–p 0,38

the quick brown fox jumps over the lazy dog

**Perpetua**  
924  
halbfett  
bold  
demi-gras  
N 100: 081 1009  
1959  
Monotype Corporation Ltd.  
H 1–x 0,67–k 1,09–p 0,41

the quick brown fox jumps over the lazy dog

**Méridien**  
836  
fett  
bold  
gras  
N 100: 081 0904  
Adrian Frutiger 1957  
Haas'sche Schriftgießerei AG  
H 1–x 0,72–k 1,13–p 0,31

the quick brown fox jumps over the lazy dog

**BERTHOLD HEADLINES II**  Renaissance-Antiqua
Old Style
Renaissance-Antiqua (Garaldes, Humanes)

QUICK BROWN FOX JUMPS OVER
THE LAZY DOG 1234567890

QUICK BROWN FOX JUMPS OVER
THE LAZY DOG 1234567890

QUICK BROWN FOX JUMPS OVER
THE LAZY DOG 1234567890

QUICK BROWN FOX JUMPS OVER
THE LAZY DOG 1234567890

QUICK BROWN FOX JUMPS OVER
THE LAZY DOG 1234567890

**BERTHOLD HEADLINES II**  Renaissance-Antiqua
Old Style
Renaissance-Antiqua (Garaldes, Humanes)

*THE QUICK BROWN FOX JUMPS OVER
THE LAZY DOG 1234567890*

*THE QUICK BROWN FOX JUMPS OVER
THE LAZY DOG 1234567890*

| | Jüngere Renaissance-Antiqua<br>Old Style (Early Renaissance)<br>Renaissance Antiqua récente | **11** |

**Vendôme**
1154
halbfett
medium
demi-gras
N 100: 081 1320
François Ganeau 1952
Marcel Olive
H 1–x 0,65–k 1,05–p 0,33

**the quick brown fox jumps over the lazy dog**

**Trump-Mediäval**
1113
fett
extra bold
gras
N 000: 081 1206
Georg Trump 1958
D. Stempel AG
H 1–x 0,68–k 1,13–p 0,30

**the quick brown fox jumps over the lazy dog**

**Comenius-Antiqua**
1316
fett
bold
gras
N 020: 081 2493
Hermann Zapf 1977
H. Berthold AG
H 1–x 0,73–k 1,09–p 0,38

**the quick brown fox jumps over the lazy dog**

**Perpetua Black**
925

N 020: 081 2275
Monotype Corporation Ltd.
H 1–x 0,66–k 1,02–p 0,41

**the quick brown fox jumps over the lazy dog**

**Vendôme**
1156
fett
extra bold
noir
N 100: 081 1323
François Ganeau 1952
Marcel Olive
H 1–x 0,68–k 1,00–p 0,35

**the quick brown fox jumps over the lazy dog**

| | Jüngere Renaissance-Antiqua, kursive<br>Old Style, italic (Early Renaissance)<br>Renaissance Antiqua récente, italique | **12** |

**Trump-Mediäval**
1111
kursiv
italic
italique
N 100: 081 1204
Georg Trump 1954
D. Stempel AG
H 1–x 0,68–k 1,13–p 0,30

*the quick brown fox jumps over the lazy dog*

**Vendôme**
1153
kursiv
italic
italique
N 100: 081 1313
François Ganeau 1952
Marcel Olive
H 1–x 0,68–k 1,00–p 0,33

*the quick brown fox jumps over the lazy dog*

## BERTHOLD HEADLINES II
Renaissance-Antiqua
Old Style
Renaissance-Antiqua (Garaldes, Humanes)

*THE QUICK BROWN FOX JUMPS OVER THE LAZY DOG 1234567890*

*QUICK BROWN FOX JUMPS OVER THE LAZY DOG 1234567890*

## BERTHOLD HEADLINES II
Renaissance-Antiqua
Old Style
Renaissance-Antiqua (Garaldes, Humanes)

THE QUICK BROWN FOX JUMPS OVER THE LAZY DOG 1234567890

THE QUICK BROWN FOX JUMPS OVER THE LAZY DOG 1234567890

THE QUICK BROWN FOX JUMPS OVER THE LAZY DOG 1234567890

THE QUICK BROWN FOX JUMPS OVER THE LAZY DOG 1234567890

THE QUICK BROWN FOX JUMPS OVER THE LAZY DOG 1234567890

## 12 — Jüngere Renaissance-Antiqua, kursive / Old Style, italic (Early Renaissance) / Renaissance Antiqua récente, italique

*the quick brown fox jumps over the lazy dog*

**Trump-Mediäval**
1114
kursiv fett
extra bold italic
italique gras
N 000: 081 1211
Georg Trump 1962
D. Stempel AG
H 1–x 0,69–k 1,16–p 0,34

*the quick brown fox jumps over the lazy dog*

**Vendôme**
1155
kursiv halbfett
medium italic
italique demi-gras
N 100: 081 1321
François Ganeau 1952
Marcel Olive
H 1–x 0,69–k 1,05–p 0,34

## 13 — Renaissance-Antiqua, schmale / Old Style, condensed / Renaissance Antiqua, étroit

the quick brown fox jumps over the lazy dog

**Vendôme**
1157
schmal
condensed
étroit
N 100: 081 1328
François Ganeau 1952
Marcel Olive
H 1–x 0,68–k 1,04–p 0,32

the quick brown fox jumps over the lazy dog

BERTHOLD **Garamond**
1332
schmal
condensed
étroit
N 020: 081 1806
Günter Gerhard Lange 1975
H. Berthold AG
H 1–x 0,63–k 1,07–p 0,33

the quick brown fox jumps over the lazy dog

ITC **Garamond**
586
schmalmager
light condensed
étroit maigre
N 020: 081 2365
Tony Stan 1977
International Typeface Corp.
H 1–x 0,73–k 1,14–p 0,35

the quick brown fox jumps over the lazy dog

**Romana**
999
mager
light
maigre
N 100: 081 1454
1930
Johannes Wagner
H 1–x 0,69–k 1,01–p 0,34

the quick brown fox jumps over the lazy dog

ITC **Garamond**
588
Buch schmal
book condensed
étroit romain labeur
N 020: 081 2367
Tony Stan 1977
International Typeface Corp.
H 1–x 0,73–k 1,11–p 0,35

## BERTHOLD HEADLINES II
Renaissance-Antiqua
Old Style
Renaissance-Antiqua (Garaldes, Humanes)

THE QUICK BROWN FOX JUMPS OVER
THE LAZY DOG 1234567890

THE QUICK BROWN FOX JUMPS OVER
THE LAZY DOG 1234567890

THE QUICK BROWN FOX JUMPS OVER
THE LAZY DOG 1234567890

THE QUICK BROWN FOX JUMPS OVER
THE LAZY DOG 1234567890

THE QUICK BROWN FOX JUMPS OVER
THE LAZY DOG 1234567890

THE QUICK BROWN FOX JUMPS OVER
THE LAZY DOG 1234567890

THE QUICK BROWN FOX JUMPS OVER
THE LAZY DOG 1234567890

THE QUICK BROWN FOX JUMPS OVER
THE LAZY DOG 1234567890

|  | Renaissance-Antiqua, schmale<br>Old Style, condensed<br>Renaissance Antiqua, étroit | **13** |

**the quick brown fox jumps
over the lazy dog**

**Romana**
1000
halbfett
medium
demi-gras
N 100: 081 1455
1930
Johannes Wagner
H 1–x 0,70–k 1,00–p 0,28

**the quick brown fox jumps
over the lazy dog**

ITC **Garamond**
590
schmalfett
bold condensed
étroit gras
N 020: 081 2369
Tony Stan 1977
International Typeface Corp.
H 1–x 0,72–k 1,11–p 0,37

**the quick brown fox jumps
over the lazy dog**

**Lectura**
759
schmalfett
bold condensed
étroit gras
N 100: 081 0846
Dick Dooijes 1969
Lettergieterij Amsterdam
H 1–x 0,75–k 1,09–p 0,31

**the quick brown fox jumps
over the lazy dog**

**Plantin**
941
schmalfett
bold condensed
étroit gras

N 100: 081 1021
Monotype Corporation Ltd.
H 1–x 0,65–k 1,01–p 0,25

**the quick brown fox jumps
over the lazy dog**

**Weiß-Antiqua**
1202
schmalfett
extra bold condensed
étroit extra gras
N 020: 081 1843
Berthold-Schriftenatelier 1976
Fundición Tipográfica Neufville, S.A.
H 1–x 0,64–k 1,03–p 0,29

**the quick brown fox jumps
over the lazy dog**

**Romana**
1001
ultra
ultra
ultra
N 020: 081 2278
1930
Johannes Wagner
H 1–x 0,70–k 1,01–p 0,30

**the quick brown fox jumps
over the lazy dog**

**Weiß-Antiqua**
1203
schmal extrafett
extra bold condensed
étroit extra gras
N 020: 081 2204
Berthold-Schriftenatelier 1976
Fundición Tipográfica Neufville, S.A.
H 1–x 0,64–k 1,03–p 0,29

**the quick brown fox jumps
over the lazy dog**

ITC **Garamond**
592
ultra schmal
ultra condensed
ultra étroit
N 020: 081 2371
Tony Stan 1977
International Typeface Corp.
H 1–x 0,70–k 1,10–p 0,35

## BERTHOLD HEADLINES II
Renaissance-Antiqua
Old Style
Renaissance-Antiqua (Garaldes, Humanes)

THE QUICK BROWN FOX JUMPS OVER
THE LAZY DOG 1234567890

THE QUICK BROWN FOX JUMPS OVER
THE LAZY DOG 1234567890

## BERTHOLD HEADLINES II
Renaissance-Antiqua
Old Style
Renaissance-Antiqua (Garaldes, Humanes)

THE QUICK BROWN FOX JUMPS OVER
THE LAZY DOG 1234567890

ABCDEFGHJKLMNOPQR
STUEVWY

THE QUICK BROWN FOX JUMPS OVER
THE LAZY DOG 1234567890

THE QUICK BROWN FOX JUMPS OVER
THE LAZY DOG 1234567890

THE QUICK BROWN FOX JUMPS OVER
THE LAZY DOG 1234567890

## 13
Renaissance-Antiqua, schmale
Old Style, condensed
Renaissance Antiqua, étroit

**the quick brown fox jumps over the lazy dog**

**Graphis**
636
extrafett
extra bold
extra gras
N 100: 081 2145
Leslie Usherwood 1971
Typsettra
H 1–x 0,81–k 1,19–p 0,38

**the quick brown fox jumps over the lazy dog**

**Goudy**
628
schmal extrafett
heavy faced condensed
étroit extra gras

N 100: 081 0689
American Typefounders
H 1–x 0,78–k 1,06–p 0,28

## 14
Renaissance-Antiqua, kursiv schmale
Old Style, italic condensed
Renaissance Antiqua, étroit

*the quick brown fox jumps over the lazy dog*

**Wiegands Renaissance**
1216
kursiv
italic
italique
N 020: 081 2411
Jürgen Wiegand 1978
H. Berthold AG
H 1–x 0,69–k 1,03–p 0,26

*the quick brown fox jumps over the lazy dog*

**Wiegands Renaissance**
1217
kursiv Zierbuchstaben
italic swash letters
italique lettres ornées
Z 000: 081 2412
Jürgen Wiegand 1978
H. Berthold AG
B 1–x 0,69–C 1,36–p 0,26

*the quick brown fox jumps over the lazy dog*

ITC **Garamond**
587
kursiv schmalmager
light condensed italic
italique étroit maigre
N 020: 081 2366
Tony Stan 1977
International Typeface Corp.
H 1–x 0,73–k 1,11–p 0,34

*the quick brown fox jumps over the lazy dog*

ITC **Garamond**
589
Buch kursiv schmal
book condensed italic
romain labeur italique étroit
N 020: 081 2368
Tony Stan 1977
International Typeface Corp.
H 1–x 0,72–k 1,05–p 0,35

*the quick brown fox jumps over the lazy dog*

ITC **Garamond**
591
kursiv schmalfett
bold condensed italic
italique étroit gras
N 020: 081 2370
Tony Stan 1977
International Typeface Corp.
H 1–x 0,72–k 1,09–p 0,34

**BERTHOLD HEADLINES II** — Renaissance-Antiqua / Old Style / Renaissance-Antiqua (Garaldes, Humanes)

*THE QUICK BROWN FOX JUMPS OVER THE LAZY DOG 1234567890*

**BERTHOLD HEADLINES II** — Renaissance-Antiqua / Old Style / Renaissance-Antiqua (Garaldes, Humanes)

THE QUICK BROWN FOX JUMPS OVER THE LAZY DOG 1234567890

QUICK BROWN FOX JUMPS OVER THE LAZY DOG 1234567890

THE QUICK BROWN FOX JUMPS OVER THE LAZY DOG 1234567890

QUICK BROWN FOX JUMPS OVER THE LAZY DOG 1234567890

QUICK BROWN FOX JUMPS OVER THE LAZY DOG 1234567890

QUICK BROWN FOX JUMPS OVER THE LAZY DOG 1234567890

| | | 14 |
|---|---|---|
| | Renaissance-Antiqua, kursiv schmale<br>Old Style, italic condensed<br>Renaissance Antiqua, étroit | |

*the quick brown fox jumps over the lazy dog*

ITC **Garamond**
593
ultra schmal kursiv
ultra condensed italic
ultra italique étroit
N 020: 081 2372
Tony Stan 1977
International Typeface Corp.
H 1–x 0,70–k 1,10–p 0,35

| | | 15 |
|---|---|---|
| | Kalligraphische Schriften<br>Calligraphic<br>Caratères calligraphiques | |

the quick brown fox jumps
over the lazy dog

ITC **Zapf Chancery**
1293
mager
light
maigre
N 020: 081 1330
Hermann Zapf 1979
International Typeface Corp.
H 1–x 0,71–k 1,19–p 0,50

the quick brown fox jumps
over the lazy dog

ITC **Zapf Chancery**
1294
mager Swash
light swash
maigre lettres ornées
Z 000: 081 1367
Hermann Zapf 1979
International Typeface Corp.
H 1–x 0,71–k 1,17–p 0,50

the quick brown fox jumps
over the lazy dog

ITC **Zapf Chancery**
1296
normal
medium
normal
N 020: 081 1336
Hermann Zapf 1979
International Typeface Corp.
H 1–x 0,71–k 1,19–p 0,50

the quick brown fox jumps
over the lazy dog

ITC **Zapf Chancery**
1297
normal Swash
medium swash
normal lettres ornées
Z 000: 081 1370
Hermann Zapf 1979
International Typeface Corp.
H 1–x 0,71–k 1,19–p 0,49

the quick brown fox jumps
over the lazy dog

ITC **Zapf Chancery**
1299
halbfett
demi
demi-gras
N 020: 081 1344
Hermann Zapf 1979
International Typeface Corp.
H 1–x 0,73–k 1,20–p 0,50

the quick brown fox jumps
over the lazy dog

ITC **Zapf Chancery**
1300
halbfett Swash
demi swash
demi-gras lettres ornées
Z 000: 081 1375
Hermann Zapf 1979
International Typeface Corp.
H 1–x 0,73–k 1,20–p 0,50

## BERTHOLD HEADLINES II
Renaissance-Antiqua
Old Style
Renaissance-Antiqua (Garaldes, Humanes)

QUICK BROWN FOX JUMPS OVER THE LAZY DOG 1234567890

QUICK BROWN FOX JUMPS OVER THE LAZY DOG 1234567890

## BERTHOLD HEADLINES II
Renaissance-Antiqua
Old Style
Renaissance-Antiqua (Garaldes, Humanes)

THE QUICK BROWN FOX JUMPS OVER THE LAZY DOG 1234567890

ABCDEFGHIJKLMNOPQR STUVWXYZ 1234567890

THE QUICK BROWN FOX JUMPS OVER THE LAZY DOG 1234567890

ABCDEFGHIJKLMNOPQR STUVWXYZ 1234567890

QUICK BROWN FOX JUMPS OVER THE LAZY DOG 1234567890

| | Kalligraphische Schriften<br>Calligraphic<br>Caratères calligraphiques | **15** |

the quick brown fox jumps
over the lazy dog

ITC **Zapf Chancery**
1301
fett
bold
gras
N 020: 081 1353
Hermann Zapf 1979
International Typeface Corp.
H 1–x 0,73–k 1,19–p 0,50

the quick brown fox jumps
over the lazy dog

ITC **Zapf Chancery**
1302
fett Swash
bold swash
gras lettres ornées
Z 000: 081 1384
Hermann Zapf 1979
International Typeface Corp.
H 1–x 0,73–k 1,19–p 0,50

| | Kalligraphische Schriften, kursive<br>Calligraphic, italic<br>Caratères calligraphique, italique | **16** |

the quick brown fox jumps
over the lazy dog

ITC **Zapf Chancery**
1361
kursiv mager
light italic
italique maigre
N 020: 081 1358
Hermann Zapf 1979
International Typeface Corp.
H 1–x 0,69–k 1,19–p 0,50

the quick brown fox jumps
over the lazy dog

ITC **Zapf Chancery**
1295
kursiv mager Swash
light italic swash
italique maigre lettres ornées
Z 000: 081 1389
Hermann Zapf 1979
International Typeface Corp.
H 1–x 0,69–k 1,19–p 0,50

the quick brown fox jumps
over the lazy dog

ITC **Zapf Chancery**
1362
kursiv
italic
italique
N 020: 081 1361
Hermann Zapf 1979
International Typeface Corp.
H 1–x 0,70–k 1,18–p 0,50

the quick brown fox jumps
over the lazy dog

ITC **Zapf Chancery**
1298
kursiv Swash
italic swash
italique lettres ornées
Z 000: 081 1392
Hermann Zapf 1979
International Typeface Corp.
H 1–x 0,70–k 1,18–p 0,50

the quick brown fox jumps
over the lazy dog

**Comenius**
1314
kursiv
italic
italique
N 020: 081 2491
Hermann Zapf 1976
H. Berthold AG
H 1–x 0,68–k 1,09–p 0,37

# BERTHOLD HEADLINES III

# 17-29

*Barock-Antiqua
Transitionals
Latines*

**BERTHOLD HEADLINES III** — Barock-Antiqua / Transitionals / Latines

THE QUICK BROWN FOX JUMPS OVER THE LAZY DOG 1234567890

THE QUICK BROWN FOX JUMPS OVER THE LAZY DOG 1234567890

THE QUICK BROWN FOX JUMPS OVER THE LAZY DOG 1234567890

THE QUICK BROWN FOX JUMPS OVER THE LAZY DOG 1234567890

QUICK BROWN FOX JUMPS OVER THE LAZY DOG 1234567890

QUICK BROWN FOX JUMPS OVER THE LAZY DOG 1234567890

THE QUICK BROWN FOX JUMPS OVER THE LAZY DOG 1234567890

THE QUICK BROWN FOX JUMPS OVER THE LAZY DOG 1234567890

**Englische Antiqua / English Transitional / Anglais Antiqua — 17**

---

the quick brown fox jumps
over the lazy dog

**Columbia**
410

N 100: 081 0380
Walter H. McKay 1955
Lettergieterij Amsterdam
H 1–x 0,59–k 1,03–p 0,35

---

the quick brown fox jumps
over the lazy dog

ITC **Cheltenham**
306
mager
light
maigre
N 020: 081 2429
Tony Stan 1978
International Typeface Corp.
H 1–x 0,68–k 1,01–p 0,30

---

the quick brown fox jumps
over the lazy dog

**Century Old Style**
292
normal
regular
normal
N 020: 081 2336
Morris F. Benton 1906
American Typefounders
H 1–x 0,67–k 1,04–p 0,25

---

the quick brown fox jumps
over the lazy dog

LUDLOW **Bookman**
242
normal
regular
normal
N 100: 081 1597
Ludlow
H 1–x 0,63–k 1,00–p 0,28

---

the quick brown fox jumps
over the lazy dog

**Bookman Meola I**
247
Zierbuchstaben
swash letters
lettres ornées

Z 000: 081 1598
Facsimile Fonts
H 1–x 0,63–k 1,53–p 0,50

---

the quick brown fox jumps
over the lazy dog

**Bookman Meola II**
237
Zierbuchstaben
swash letters
lettres ornées

Z 000: 081 0219
Facsimile Fonts
H 1–x 0,63–k 1,53–p 0,50

---

the quick brown fox jumps
over the lazy dog

**Baskerville Book**
1304
normal
regular
normal
N 020: 081 2474
Günter Gerhard Lange 1980
H. Berthold AG
H 1–x 0,61–k 1,01–p 0,38

---

the quick brown fox jumps
over the lazy dog

BERTHOLD **Baskerville**
120
normal
regular
normal
N 100: 081 0139
1961
H. Berthold AG
H 1–x 0,62–k 1,04–p 0,40

# BERTHOLD HEADLINES III
Barock-Antiqua
Transitionals
Latines

THE QUICK BROWN FOX JUMPS OVER
THE LAZY DOG 1234567890

THE QUICK BROWN FOX JUMPS OVER
THE LAZY DOG 1234567890

THE QUICK BROWN FOX JUMPS OVER
THE LAZY DOG 1234567890

THE QUICK BROWN FOX JUMPS OVER
THE LAZY DOG 1234567890

QUICK BROWN FOX JUMPS OVER
THE LAZY DOG 1234567890

QUICK BROWN FOX JUMPS OVER
THE LAZY DOG 1234567890

THE QUICK BROWN FOX JUMPS OVER
THE LAZY DOG 1234567890

QUICK BROWN FOX JUMPS OVER
THE LAZY DOG

Englische Antiqua
English Transitional
Anglais Antiqua
**17**

**Concorde**
414
normal
regular
normal
N 100: 081 0388
Günter Gerhard Lange 1969
H. Berthold AG
H 1–x 0,70–k 1,08–p 0,32

the quick brown fox jumps over the lazy dog

ITC **Cheltenham**
308
Buch
book
romain labeur
N 020: 081 1960
Tony Stan 1975
International Typeface Corp.
H 1–x 0,68–k 1,00–p 0,28

the quick brown fox jumps over the lazy dog

BERTHOLD **Caslon Buch**
1309
normal
regular
normal
N 020: 081 2481
Günter Gerhard Lange 1977
H. Berthold AG
H 1–x 0,63–k 1,05–p 0,34

the quick brown fox jumps over the lazy dog

**Poppl-Pontifex**
1397
normal
regular
normal
N 020: 081 2494
Friedrich Poppl 1976
H. Berthold AG
H 1–x 0,73–k 1,13–p 0,40

the quick brown fox jumps over the lazy dog

ITC **Bookman**
222
mager
light
maigre
N 020: 081 2306
Ed Benguiat 1975
International Typeface Corp.
H 1–x 0,72–k 1,05–p 0,33

the quick brown fox jumps over the lazy dog

ITC **Bookman**
223
mager Zierbuchstaben
light swash letters
maigre lettres ornées
Z 000: 081 2317
Ed Benguiat 1975
International Typeface Corp.
H 1–x 0,72–k 1,25–p 0,59

The quick brown fox jumps over the lazy dog

LUDLOW **Bookman**
245
fett
bold
gras
N 100: 081 0215
Ludlow
H 1–x 0,66–k 1,00–p 0,22

the quick brown fox jumps over the lazy dog

LUDLOW **Bookman**
246
fett Zierbuchstaben
bold swash letters
gras lettres ornées
Z 000: 081 0217
Ludlow
H 1–x 0,66–k 1,00–p 0,22

the quick brown fox jumps over the lazy dog

## BERTHOLD HEADLINES III
Barock-Antiqua
Transitionals
Latines

THE QUICK BROWN FOX JUMPS OVER
THE LAZY DOG 1234567890

QUICK BROWN FOX JUMPS OVER
THE LAZY DOG 1234567890

QUICK BROWN FOX JUMPS OVER
THE LAZY DOG 1234567890

QUICK BROWN FOX JUMPS OVER
THE LAZY DOG 1234567890

THE QUICK BROWN FOX JUMPS OVER
THE LAZY DOG 1234567890

THE QUICK BROWN FOX JUMPS OVER
THE LAZY DOG 1234567890

THE QUICK BROWN FOX JUMPS OVER
THE LAZY DOG 1234567890

QUICK BROWN FOX JUMPS OVER
THE LAZY DOG 1234567890

Englische Antiqua / English Transitional / Anglais Antiqua — 17

**the quick brown fox jumps over the lazy dog**

ATF **Cheltenham**
300
halbfett
medium
demi-gras
N 100: 081 0292
Morris F. Benton, B. Goodhue 1904
American Typefounders
H 1–x 0,57–k 1,00–p 0,26

**the quick brown fox jumps over the lazy dog**

ITC **Bookman**
226
normal
medium
normal
N 020: 081 2330
Ed Benguiat 1975
International Typeface Corp.
H 1–x 0,75–k 1,03–p 0,32

**The quick brown fox jumps over the lazy dog**

ITC **Bookman**
227
normal Zierbuchstaben
medium swash letters
normal lettres ornées
Z 000: 081 2328
Ed Benguiat 1975
International Typeface Corp.
H 1–x 0,73–k 1,21–p 0,49

the quick brown fox jumps over the lazy dog

LSC **Book Roman**
772
normal
regular
normal
N 020: 081 1928
Herb Lubalin 1970
International Typeface Corp.
H 1–x 0,66–k 1,06–p 0,34

**the quick brown fox jumps over the lazy dog**

STEMPEL **Baskerville**
126
halbfett
medium
demi-gras
N 100: 081 0138
1928
D. Stempel AG
H 1–x 0,63–k 1,03–p 0,31

**the quick brown fox jumps over the lazy dog**

**Caslon Adbold**
276

N 100: 081 1505
H. Berthold AG
H 1–x 0,69–k 1,00–p 0,21

**the quick brown fox jumps over the lazy dog**

BERTHOLD **Baskerville**
122
halbfett
medium
demi-gras
N 100: 081 0143
1965
H. Berthold AG
H 1–x 0,66–k 1,05–p 0,38

**the quick brown fox jumps over the lazy dog**

**Baskerville Book**
1306
halbfett
medium
demi-gras
N 020: 081 2475
Günter Gerhard Lange 1980
H. Berthold AG
H 1–x 0,62–k 1,02–p 0,38

# BERTHOLD HEADLINES III
Barock-Antiqua
Transitionals
Latines

QUICK BROWN FOX JUMPS OVER THE LAZY DOG 1234567890

THE QUICK BROWN FOX JUMPS OVER THE LAZY DOG 1234567890

QUICK BROWN FOX JUMPS OVER THE LAZY DOG 1234567890

QUICK BROWN FOX JUMPS OVER THE LAZY DOG 1234567890

THE QUICK BROWN FOX JUMPS OVER THE LAZY DOG 1234567890

THE QUICK BROWN FOX JUMPS OVER THE LAZY DOG 1234567890

QUICK BROWN FOX JUMPS OVER THE LAZY DOG 1234567890

BROWN FOX JUMPS OVER THE LAZY DOG

Englische Antiqua
English Transitional
Anglais Antiqua
**17**

BERTHOLD **Caslon Buch**
1311
halbfett
medium
demi-gras
N 020: 081 2482
Günter Gerhard Lange 1977
H. Berthold AG
H 1–x 0,63–k 1,05–p 0,33

the quick brown fox jumps over the lazy dog

**Concorde**
416
halbfett
medium
demi-gras
N 100: 081 0390
Günter Gerhard Lange 1969
H. Berthold AG
H 1–x 0,71–k 1,08–p 0,33

the quick brown fox jumps over the lazy dog

ATF **Cheltenham**
304
breithalbfett
bold extended
large demi-gras
N 100: 081 0313
Morris F. Benton, B. Goodhue 1906
American Typefounders
H 1–x 0,66–k 1,00–p 0,28

the quick brown fox jumps over the lazy dog

LSC **Book Roman**
774
halbfett
medium
demi-gras
N 020: 081 1939
Herb Lubalin 1970
International Typeface Corp.
H 1–x 0,63–k 1,03–p 0,37

the quick brown fox jumps over the lazy dog

**Poppl-Pontifex**
1399
halbfett
medium
demi-gras
N 020: 081 2496
Friedrich Poppl 1976
H. Berthold AG
H 1–x 0,73–k 1,13–p 0,39

the quick brown fox jumps over the lazy dog

ITC **Cheltenham**
310
halbfett
bold
demi-gras
N 020: 081 2431
Tony Stan 1978
International Typeface Corp.
H 1–x 0,69–k 1,00–p 0,30

the quick brown fox jumps over the lazy dog

ITC **Bookman**
230
halbfett
demi bold
demi-gras
N 020: 081 2332
Ed Benguiat 1975
International Typeface Corp.
H 1–x 0,73–k 1,06–p 0,32

the quick brown fox jumps over the lazy dog

ITC **Bookman**
231
halbfett Zierbuchstaben
demi-bold swash letters
demi-gras lettres ornées
Z 000: 081 2334
Ed Benguiat 1975
International Typeface Corp.
H 1–x 0,73–k 1,28–p 0,52

The quick brown fox jumps over the lazy dog

## BERTHOLD HEADLINES III
Barock-Antiqua
Transitionals
Latines

**QUICK BROWN FOX JUMPS OVER THE LAZY DOG 1234567890**

**QUICK BROWN FOX JUMPS OVER THE LAZY DOG 1234567890**

QUICK BROWN FOX JUMPS OVER THE LAZY DOG 1234567890

**QUICK BROWN FOX JUMPS OVER THE LAZY DOG 1234567890**

**QUICK BROWN FOX JUMPS OVER THE LAZY DOG 1234567890**

**QUICK BROWN FOX JUMPS OVER THE LAZY DOG 1234567890**

## BERTHOLD HEADLINES III
Barock-Antiqua
Transitionals
Latines

*THE QUICK BROWN FOX JUMPS OVER THE LAZY DOG 1234567890*

| | Englische Antiqua / English Transitional / Anglais Antiqua | **17** |

**the quick brown fox jumps over the lazy dog**

BERTHOLD **Baskerville**
123
fett
bold
gras
N 100: 081 0144
1961
H. Berthold AG
H 1–x 0,62–k 1,04–p 0,40

**the quick brown fox jumps over the lazy dog**

**LSC Book Roman**
776
fett
bold
gras
N 020: 081 1950
Herb Lubalin 1970
International Typeface Corp.
H 1–x 0,63–k 1,03–p 0,37

**the quick brown fox jumps over the lazy dog**

**Poppl-Pontifex**
1343
fett
bold
gras
N 020: 081 2462
Friedrich Poppl 1980
H. Berthold AG
H 1–x 0,72–k 1,12–p 0,36

**the quick brown fox jumps over the lazy dog**

ITC **Bookman**
234
fett
bold
gras
N 020: 081 2308
Ed Benguiat 1975
International Typeface Corp.
H 1–x 0,73–k 1,05–p 0,32

**the quick brown fox jumps over the lazy dog**

ITC **Bookman**
235
fett Zierbuchstaben
bold swash letters
gras lettres ornées
Z 000: 081 2150
Ed Benguiat 1975
International Typeface Corp.
H 1–x 0,72–k 1,25–p 0,59

**the quick brown fox jumps over the lazy dog**

ITC **Cheltenham**
312
ultra
ultra
ultra
N 020: 081 1963
Tony Stan 1975
International Typeface Corp.
H 1–x 0,65–k 1,00–p 0,29

| | Englische Antiqua, kursive / English Transitional, italic / Anglais Antiqua, italique | **18** |

*the quick brown fox jumps over the lazy dog*

ITC **Cheltenham**
307
kursiv mager
light italic
italique maigre
N 020: 081 2430
Tony Stan 1978
International Typeface Corp.
H 1–x 0,68–k 1,00–p 0,28

## BERTHOLD HEADLINES III
Barock-Antiqua
Transitionals
Latines

*THE QUICK BROWN FOX JUMPS OVER THE LAZY DOG 1234567890*

*THE QUICK BROWN FOX JUMPS OVER THE LAZY DOG 1234567890*

*THE QUICK BROWN FOX JUMPS OVER THE LAZY DOG 1234567890*

*THE QUICK BROWN FOX JUMPS OVER THE LAZY DOG 1234567890*

*THE QUICK BROWN FOX JUMPS OVER THE LAZY DOG 1234567890*

*THE QUICK BROWN FOX JUMPS OVER THE LAZY DOG 1234567890*

*THE QUICK BROWN FOX JUMPS OVER THE LAZY DOG 1234567890*

*THE QUICK BROWN FOX JUMPS OVER THE LAZY DOG 1234567890*

Englische Antiqua, kursive
English Transitional, italic
Anglais Antiqua, italique
**18**

*the quick brown fox jumps
over the lazy dog*

**Baskerville Book**
1305
kursiv
italic
italique
N 020: 081 2476
Günter Gerhard Lange 1980
H. Berthold AG
H 1–x 0,62–k 1,01–p 0,39

*the quick brown fox jumps
over the lazy dog*

BERTHOLD **Caslon Buch**
1310
kursiv
italic
italique
N 020: 081 2484
Günter Gerhard Lange 1977
H. Berthold AG
H 1–x 0,63–k 1,06–p 0,41

*the quick brown fox jumps
over the lazy dog*

ITC **Zapf International**
1233
kursiv mager
light italic
italique maigre
N 020: 081 2351
Hermann Zapf 1977
International Typeface Corp.
H 1–x 0,71–k 1,18–p 0,42

*the quick brown fox jumps
over the lazy dog*

LUDLOW **Bookman**
243
kursiv
italic
italique

N 100: 081 0213
Ludlow
H 1–x 0,66–k 1,05–p 0,25

*The quick brown fox jumps
over the lazy dog*

LUDLOW **Bookman**
244
kursiv Zierbuchstaben
italic swash letters
italique lettres ornées

Z 000: 081 0214
Ludlow
H 1–x 0,66–k 1,05–p 0,25

*the quick brown fox jumps
over the lazy dog*

ITC **Cheltenham**
309
Buch kursiv
book italic
italique romain labeur
N 020: 081 1962
Tony Stan 1975
International Typeface Corp.
H 1–x 0,68–k 1,00–p 0,28

*the quick brown fox jumps
over the lazy dog*

ITC **Zapf International**
1235
kursiv
italic
italique
N 020: 081 2353
Hermann Zapf 1977
International Typeface Corp.
H 1–x 0,70–k 1,17–p 0,42

*the quick brown fox jumps
over the lazy dog*

**Poppl-Pontifex**
1398
kursiv
italic
italique
N 020: 081 2495
Friedrich Poppl 1976
H. Berthold AG
H 1–x 0,73–k 1,16–p 0,41

## BERTHOLD HEADLINES III
Barock-Antiqua
Transitionals
Latines

QUICK BROWN FOX JUMPS OVER
THE LAZY DOG 1234567890

QUICK BROWN FOX JUMPS OVER
THE LAZY DOG

THE QUICK BROWN FOX JUMPS OVER
THE LAZY DOG 1234567890

QUICK BROWN FOX JUMPS OVER
THE LAZY DOG 1234567890

THE QUICK BROWN FOX JUMPS OVER
THE LAZY DOG 1234567890

QUICK BROWN FOX JUMPS OVER
THE LAZY DOG 1234567890

QUICK BROWN FOX JUMPS OVER
THE LAZY DOG

QUICK BROWN FOX JUMPS OVER
THE LAZY DOG 1234567890

Englische Antiqua, kursive  
English Transitional, italic  
Anglais Antiqua, italique  
**18**

*the quick brown fox jumps over the lazy dog*

ITC **Bookman**  
224  
kursiv mager  
light italic  
italique maigre  
N 020: 081 2310  
Ed Benguiat 1975  
International Typeface Corp.  
H 1–x 0,72–k 1,04–p 0,33

*the quick brown fox jumps over the lazy dog*

ITC **Bookman**  
225  
kursiv mager Zierbuchstaben  
light italic swash letters  
italique maigre lettres ornées  
Z 000: 081 2151  
Ed Benguiat 1975  
International Typeface Corp.  
H 1–x 0,75–k 1,25–p 0,47

*the quick brown fox jumps over the lazy dog*

ATF **Cheltenham**  
301  
kursiv halbfett  
bold italic  
italique demi-gras  
N 100: 081 0296  
Morris F. Benton, B. Goodhue 1905  
American Typefounders  
H 1–x 0,59–k 1,00–p 0,25

*the quick brown fox jumps over the lazy dog*

**LSC Book**  
773  
kursiv  
italic  
italique  
N 020: 081 1933  
Herb Lubalin 1970  
International Typeface Corp.  
H 1–x 0,67–k 1,03–p 0,39

*the quick brown fox jumps over the lazy dog*

**Plantin**  
940  
kursiv halbfett  
bold italic  
italique demi-gras  
N 100: 081 1020  
Monotype Corporation Ltd.  
H 1–x 0,64–k 1,01–p 0,24

*the quick brown fox jumps over the lazy dog*

ITC **Bookman**  
228  
kursiv  
medium italic  
italique  
N 020: 081 2331  
Ed Benguiat 1975  
International Typeface Corp.  
H 1–x 0,76–k 1,05–p 0,32

*The quick brown fox jumps over the lazy dog*

ITC **Bookman**  
229  
kursiv Zierbuchstaben  
medium italic swash letters  
italique lettres ornées  
Z 000: 081 2329  
Ed Benguiat 1975  
International Typeface Corp.  
H 1–x 0,78–k 1,28–p 0,53

*the quick brown fox jumps over the lazy dog*

**LSC Book**  
775  
kursiv halbfett  
bold italic  
italique demi-gras  
N 020: 081 1944  
Herb Lubalin 1970  
International Typeface Corp.  
H 1–x 0,69–k 1,00–p 0,31

**BERTHOLD HEADLINES III**    Barock-Antiqua / Transitionals / Latines

THE QUICK BROWN FOX JUMPS OVER THE LAZY DOG 1234567890

THE QUICK BROWN FOX JUMPS OVER THE LAZY DOG 1234567890

QUICK BROWN FOX JUMPS OVER THE LAZY DOG 1234567890

QUICK BROWN FOX JUMPS OVER THE LAZY DOG 1234567890

QUICK BROWN FOX JUMPS OVER THE LAZY DOG

QUICK BROWN FOX JUMPS OVER THE LAZY DOG 1234567890

QUICK BROWN FOX JUMPS OVER THE LAZY DOG 1234567890

QUICK BROWN FOX JUMPS OVER THE LAZY DOG

Englische Antiqua, kursive
English Transitional, italic
Anglais Antiqua, italique
**18**

*the quick brown fox jumps over the lazy dog*

**Concorde**
1317
kursiv halbfett
medium italic
italique demi-gras
N 020: 081 0470
Günter Gerhard Lange 1978
H. Berthold AG
H 1–x 0,71–k 1,08–p 0,33

*the quick brown fox jumps over the lazy dog*

ITC **Cheltenham**
311
kursiv halbfett
bold italic
italique demi-gras
N 020: 081 2432
Tony Stan 1978
International Typeface Corp.
H 1–x 0,68–k 1,01–p 0,28

*the quick brown fox jumps over the lazy dog*

ITC **Zapf International**
1237
kursiv halbfett
demi italic
italique demi-gras
N 020: 081 2355
Hermann Zapf 1977
International Typeface Corp.
H 1–x 0,71–k 1,13–p 0,41

*the quick brown fox jumps over the lazy dog*

ITC **Bookman**
232
kursiv halbfett
demi-bold italic
italique demi-gras
N 020: 081 2333
Ed Benguiat 1975
International Typeface Corp.
H 1–x 0,75–k 1,09–p 0,32

*The quick brown fox jumps over the lazy dog*

ITC **Bookman**
233
kursiv halbfett Zierbuchstaben
demi-bold italic swash letters
italique demi-gras lettres ornées
Z 000: 081 2335
Ed Benguiat 1975
International Typeface Corp.
H 1–x 0,75–k 1,25–p 0,56

*the quick brown fox jumps over the lazy dog*

**LSC Book**
777
kursiv fett
x-bold italic
italique gras
N 020: 081 1956
Herb Lubalin 1970
International Typeface Corp.
H 1–x 0,69–k 1,03–p 0,40

*the quick brown fox jumps over the lazy dog*

ITC **Bookman**
236
kursiv fett
bold italic
italique gras
N 020: 081 2309
Ed Benguiat 1975
International Typeface Corp.
H 1–x 0,73–k 1,04–p 0,32

*the quick brown fox jumps over the lazy dog*

ITC **Bookman**
237
kursiv fett Zierbuchstaben
bold italic swash letters
italique gras lettres ornées
Z 000: 081 2153
Ed Benguiat 1975
International Typeface Corp.
H 1–x 0,75–k 1,25–p 0,56

**BERTHOLD HEADLINES III** — Barock-Antiqua / Transitionals / Latines

*QUICK BROWN FOX JUMPS OVER LAZY DOG 1234567890*

*QUICK BROWN FOX JUMPS OVER THE LAZY DOG 1234567890*

**BERTHOLD HEADLINES III** — Barock-Antiqua / Transitionals / Latines

THE QUICK BROWN FOX JUMPS OVER THE LAZY DOG 1234567890

THE QUICK BROWN FOX JUMPS OVER THE LAZY DOG 1234567890

THE QUICK BROWN FOX JUMPS OVER THE LAZY DOG 1234567890

THE QUICK BROWN FOX JUMPS OVER THE LAZY DOG 1234567890

THE QUICK BROWN FOX JUMPS OVER THE LAZY DOG 1234567890

## 18
Englische Antiqua, kursive
English Transitional, italic
Anglais Antiqua, italique

*the quick brown fox jumps over the lazy dog*

ITC **Zapf International**
1239
kursiv fett
heavy italic
italique gras
N 020: 081 2357
Hermann Zapf 1977
International Typeface Corp.
H 1–x 0,70–k 1,11–p 0,42

*the quick brown fox jumps over the lazy dog*

ITC **Cheltenham**
313
kursiv ultra
ultra italic
italique ultra
N 020: 081 1965
Tony Stan 1975
International Typeface Corp.
H 1–x 0,65–k 1,00–p 0,28

## 19
Barock-Antiqua
Transitional
Baroque Antiqua

the quick brown fox jumps over the lazy dog

**Imprimatur**
685
normal
regular
normal
N 100: 081 0774
Konrad F. Bauer, Walter Baum 1952
Fundición Tipográfica Neufville, S.A.
H 1–x 0,63–k 1,06–p 0,25

the quick brown fox jumps over the lazy dog

**Bulmer**
260
normal
regular
normal
N 100: 081 1602
Morris F. Benton 1928
American Typefounders
H 1–x 0,59–k 1,06–p 0,47

the quick brown fox jumps over the lazy dog

**Janson-Antiqua**
707
normal
regular
normal
N 100: 081 0795
1919 (Nicholas Kis 1690)
D. Stempel AG
H 1–x 0,59–k 1,09–p 0,47

the quick brown fox jumps over the lazy dog

STEMPEL **Baskerville**
143
normal
regular
normal
N 100: 081 0134
1924
D. Stempel AG
H 1–x 0,59–k 1,00–p 0,35

the quick brown fox jumps over the lazy dog

**Bell**
141
normal
regular
normal
N 020: 081 2202
Richard Austin 1788
Monotype Corporation Ltd.
H 1–x 0,65–k 1,00–p 0,35

**BERTHOLD HEADLINES III**   Barock-Antiqua / Transitionals / Latines

THE QUICK BROWN FOX JUMPS OVER
THE LAZY DOG 1234567890

THE QUICK BROWN FOX JUMPS OVER
THE LAZY DOG 1234567890

THE QUICK BROWN FOX JUMPS OVER
THE LAZY DOG 1234567890

THE QUICK BROWN FOX JUMPS OVER
THE LAZY DOG 1234567890

THE QUICK BROWN FOX JUMPS OVER
THE LAZY DOG 1234567890

THE QUICK BROWN FOX JUMPS OVER
THE LAZY DOG 1234567890

THE QUICK BROWN FOX JUMPS OVER
THE LAZY DOG 1234567890

THE QUICK BROWN FOX JUMPS OVER
THE LAZY DOG

**Barock-Antiqua / Transitional / Baroque Antiqua** — 19

**Times New Roman**
1092

the quick brown fox jumps
over the lazy dog

N 100: 081 1175
Stanley Morison 1932
Monotype Corporation Ltd.
H 1–x 0,69–k 1,03–p 0,23

**Life**
763
mager
light
maigre

the quick brown fox jumps
over the lazy dog

N 100: 081 1566
F. Simoncini, W. Bilz 1965
Ludwig & Mayer
H 1–x 0,66–k 1,00–p 0,29

**Baskerville Old Face**
127

the quick brown fox jumps
over the lazy dog

N 100: 081 1583
I. Moore 1768
Stephenson Blake & Company Ltd.
H 1–x 0,61–k 1,03–p 0,26

**Imprimatur**
687
halbfett
medium
demi-gras

the quick brown fox jumps
over the lazy dog

N 100: 081 0777
Konrad F. Bauer, Walter Baum 1952
Fundición Tipográfica Neufville, S.A.
H 1–x 0,63–k 1,06–p 0,25

ATF **Caslon**
275
halbfett
bold
demi-gras

the quick brown fox jumps
over the lazy dog

N 100: 081 1605
American Typefounders
H 1–x 0,69–k 1,03–p 0,21

**Life**
800
fett
bold
gras

the quick brown fox jumps
over the lazy dog

N 100: 081 0079
W. Bilz, F. Simoncini 1965
Ludwig & Mayer
H 1–x 0,67–k 1,02–p 0,29

**Times**
1094
fett
bold
gras

the quick brown fox jumps
over the lazy dog

N 100: 081 1181
Stanley Morison 1932
Stephenson Blake & Company Ltd.
H 1–x 0,68–k 1,00–p 0,23

**Times**
1095
fett Zierbuchstaben
bold swash letters
gras lettres ornées

the quick brown fox jumps
over the lazy dog

Z 000: 081 1919
Monotype Corporation Ltd.
H 1–x 0,69–k 1,55–p 0,51

## BERTHOLD HEADLINES III
Barock-Antiqua
Transitionals
Latines

THE QUICK BROWN FOX JUMPS OVER
THE LAZY DOG 1234567890

AABCDEFGHIKLMNNPQRR
STUVWWXYYZ

THE QUICK BROWN FOX JUMPS OVER
THE LAZY DOG 1234567890

QUICK BROWN FOX JUMPS OVER
THE LAZY DOG 1234567890

## BERTHOLD HEADLINES III
Barock-Antiqua
Transitionals
Latines

*THE QUICK BROWN FOX JUMPS OVER
THE LAZY DOG 1234567890*

*THE QUICK BROWN FOX JUMPS OVER
THE LAZY DOG 1234567890*

*THE QUICK BROWN FOX JUMPS OVER
THE LAZY DOG 1234567890*

## 19 Barock-Antiqua / Transitional / Baroque Antiqua

the quick brown fox jumps over the lazy dog

**Times Modern**
1098
normal
regular
normal
N 020: 081 0591
Monotype Corporation Ltd.
H 1–x 0,70–k 1,02–p 0,27

the quick brown fox jumps over the lazy dog

**Times Modern**
1099
Zierbuchstaben
swash letters
lettres ornées
Z 000: 081 0596
Monotype Corporation Ltd.
H 1–x 0,70–T 1,31–p 0,27

the quick brown fox jumps over the lazy dog

**Imprimatur**
688
fett
bold
gras
N 100: 081 0778
Konrad F. Bauer, Walter Baum 1954
Fundición Tipográfica Neufville, S.A.
H 1–x 0,63–k 1,06–p 0,27

the quick brown fox jumps over the lazy dog

**Times**
1097
extrafett
extra bold
extra gras
N 020: 081 2312
Monotype Corporation Ltd.
H 1–x 0,72–k 1,05–p 0,26

## 20 Barock-Antiqua, kursive / Transitional, italic / Baroque Antiqua, italique

*the quick brown fox jumps over the lazy dog*

STEMPEL **Baskerville**
125
kursiv
italic
italique
N 000: 081 0136
1926
D. Stempel AG
H 1–x 0,63–k 1,03–p 0,25

*the quick brown fox jumps over the lazy dog*

BERTHOLD **Baskerville**
121
kursiv
italic
italique
N 100: 081 0141
1961
H. Berthold AG
H 1–x 0,64–k 1,05–p 0,38

*the quick brown fox jumps over the lazy dog*

**Bell**
142
kursiv
medium italic
italique
N 020: 081 2203
Richard Austin 1788
Monotype Corporation Ltd.
H 1–x 0,63–k 1,04–p 0,42

# BERTHOLD HEADLINES III
Barock-Antiqua
Transitionals
Latines

THE QUICK BROWN FOX JUMPS OVER
THE LAZY DOG 1234567890

THE QUICK BROWN FOX JUMPS OVER
THE LAZY DOG 1234567890

THE QUICK BROWN FOX JUMPS OVER
THE LAZY DOG 1234567890

THE QUICK BROWN FOX JUMPS OVER
THE LAZY DOG 1234567890

THE QUICK BROWN FOX JUMPS OVER
THE LAZY DOG 1234567890

THE QUICK BROWN FOX JUMPS OVER
THE LAZY DOG 1234567890

THE QUICK BROWN FOX JUMPS OVER
THE LAZY DOG 1234567890

**Barock-Antiqua, kursive / Transitional, italic / Baroque Antiqua, italique — 20**

*the quick brown fox jumps over the lazy dog*

**Imprimatur**
686
kursiv
italic
italique
N 100: 081 0776
Konrad F. Bauer, Walter Baum 1954
Fundición Tipográfica Neufville, S.A.
H 1–x 0,66–k 1,09–p 0,25

*the quick brown fox jumps over the lazy dog*

**Century Old Style**
293
kursiv
italic
italique
N 020: 081 2296
Morris F. Benton 1906
American Typefounders
H 1–x 0,66–k 1,01–p 0,25

*the quick brown fox jumps over the lazy dog*

**Life**
764
kursiv
italic
italique
N 100: 081 1530
W. Bilz, F. Simoncini 1965
Ludwig & Mayer
H 1–x 0,67–k 1,01–p 0,28

*the quick brown fox jumps over the lazy dog*

**Times**
1093
kursiv
italic
italique
N 100: 081 1178
Stanley Morison 1932
Monotype Corporation Ltd.
H 1–x 0,65–k 1,00–p 0,25

*the quick brown fox jumps over the lazy dog*

**Concorde Nova**
1322
kursiv
italic
italique
N 020: 081 1725
Günter Gerhard Lange 1975
H. Berthold AG
H 1–x 0,68–k 1,07–p 0,32

*the quick brown fox jumps over the lazy dog*

**Concorde**
415
kursiv
italic
italique
N 100: 081 0389
Günter Gerhard Lange 1969
H. Berthold AG
H 1–x 0,71–k 1,08–p 0,33

***the quick brown fox jumps over the lazy dog***

**Times**
1119
kursiv fett
bold italic
italique gras

N 100: 081 1186
Monotype Corporation Ltd.
H 1–x 0,68–k 1,03–p 0,25

**BERTHOLD HEADLINES III** Barock-Antiqua / Transitionals / Latines

THE QUICK BROWN FOX JUMPS OVER THE LAZY DOG 1234567890

THE QUICK BROWN FOX JUMPS OVER THE LAZY DOG 1234567890

THE QUICK BROWN FOX JUMPS OVER THE LAZY DOG 1234567890

THE QUICK BROWN FOX JUMPS OVER THE LAZY DOG 1234567890

THE QUICK BROWN FOX JUMPS OVER THE LAZY DOG 1234567890

QUICK BROWN FOX JUMPS OVER THE LAZY DOG 1234567890

QUICK BROWN FOX JUMPS OVER THE LAZY DOG 1234567890

THE QUICK BROWN FOX JUMPS OVER THE LAZY DOG 1234567890

| | Holländische Antiqua / Dutch Transitional / Hollandais Antiqua | **21** |

the quick brown fox jumps over the lazy dog

ITC **Tiffany**
1085
mager
light
maigre
N 100: 081 1019
Ed Benguiat 1974
International Typeface Corp.
H 1–x 0,64–k 1,02–p 0,29

the quick brown fox jumps over the lazy dog

HAAS **Caslon 471**
271
normal
regular
normal
N 100: 081 0242
1940
Haas'sche Schriftgießerei AG
H 1–x 0,63–k 1,00–p 0,34

the quick brown fox jumps over the lazy dog

**Le Cochin**
754
normal
regular
normal
N 100: 081 0841
1932
Ludwig & Mayer
H 1–x 0,56–k 1,03–p 0,28

the quick brown fox jumps over the lazy dog

**Poppl-Antiqua**
950
normal
regular
normal
N 000: 081 1032
Friedrich Poppl 1967
H. Berthold AG
H 1–x 0,69–k 1,09–p 0,37

the quick brown fox jumps over the lazy dog

**LSC Caslon No. 223**
778
mager
light
maigre
N 100: 081 1620
Herb Lubalin 1970
International Typeface Corp.
H 1–x 0,63–k 1,03–p 0,12

the quick brown fox jumps over the lazy dog

ITC **Tiffany**
1086
normal
medium
normal
N 100: 081 0999
Ed Benguiat 1974
International Typeface Corp.
H 1–x 0,64–k 1,03–p 0,31

the quick brown fox jumps over the lazy dog

ITC **Zapf International**
1232
mager
light
maigre
N 020: 081 2350
Hermann Zapf 1977
International Typeface Corp.
H 1–x 0,71–k 1,15–p 0,41

the quick brown fox jumps over the lazy dog

**New Caslon**
865
normal
regular
normal
N 000: 081 0935
American Typefounders
H 1–x 0,63–k 1,00–p 0,18

**BERTHOLD HEADLINES III** — Barock-Antiqua / Transitionals / Latines

THE QUICK BROWN FOX JUMPS OVER THE LAZY DOG 1234567890

THE QUICK BROWN FOX JUMPS OVER THE LAZY DOG 1234567890

THE QUICK BROWN FOX JUMPS OVER THE LAZY DOG 1234567890

THE QUICK BROWN FOX JUMPS OVER THE LAZY DOG 1234567890

THE QUICK BROWN FOX JUMPS OVER THE LAZY DOG 1234567890

THE QUICK BROWN FOX JUMPS OVER THE LAZY DOG 1234567890

QUICK BROWN FOX JUMPS OVER THE LAZY DOG 1234567890

QUICK BROWN FOX JUMPS OVER THE LAZY DOG 1234567890

Holländische Antiqua
Dutch Transitional
Hollandais Antiqua
**21**

the quick brown fox jumps over the lazy dog

ITC **Zapf International**
1234
normal
medium
normal
N 020: 081 2352
Hermann Zapf 1977
International Typeface Corp.
H 1–x 0,71–k 1,14–p 0,42

the quick brown fox jumps over the lazy dog

**Poppl-Antiqua**
989
halbfett
medium
demi-gras
N 100: 081 1033
Friedrich Poppl 1967
H. Berthold AG
H 1–x 0,69–k 1,09–p 0,34

the quick brown fox jumps over the lazy dog

**LSC Caslon No. 233**
780
normal
regular
normal
N 100: 081 1632
Herb Lubalin 1970
International Typeface Corp.
H 1–x 0,63–k 1,00–p 0,12

the quick brown fox jumps over the lazy dog

**Statesman**
1056


N 020: 081 0011
Leslie Usherwood 1973
Typsettra
H 1–x 0,72–k 1,19–p 0,34

the quick brown fox jumps over the lazy dog

**Elzévir**
474
halbfett
medium
demi-gras
N 100: 081 0475
1900
Haas'sche Schriftgießerei AG
H 1–x 0,69–k 1,03–p 0,28

the quick brown fox jumps over the lazy dog

**LSC Caslon No. 223**
782
fett
bold
gras
N 100: 081 1642
Herb Lubalin 1970
International Typeface Corp.
H 1–x 0,63–k 1,03–p 0,12

the quick brown fox jumps over the lazy dog

ITC **Tiffany**
1087
halbfett
demi-bold
demi-gras
N 100: 081 1005
Ed Benguiat 1974
International Typeface Corp.
H 1–x 0,64–k 1,04–p 0,31

the quick brown fox jumps over the lazy dog

**Caslon Old Face**
278
fett
heavy
gras
N 100: 081 0253
1925
American Typefounders
H 1–x 0,59–k 1,03–p 0,25

**BERTHOLD HEADLINES III** — Barock-Antiqua / Transitionals / Latines

THE QUICK BROWN FOX JUMPS OVER THE LAZY DOG 1234567890

THE QUICK BROWN FOX JUMPS OVER THE LAZY DOG 1234567890

THE QUICK BROWN FOX JUMPS OVER THE LAZY DOG 1234567890

THE QUICK BROWN FOX JUMPS OVER THE LAZY DOG 1234567890

QUICK BROWN FOX JUMPS OVER THE LAZY DOG 1234567890

QUICK BROWN FOX JUMPS OVER THE LAZY DOG 1234567890

QUICK BROWN FOX JUMPS OVER THE LAZY DOG 1234567890

QUICK BROWN FOX JUMPS OVER THE LAZY DOG 1234567890

| | Holländische Antiqua / Dutch Transitional / Hollandais Antiqua | **21** |

**ITC Milano Roman**
840

the quick brown fox jumps over the lazy dog

N 100: 081 1710
Ronne Bonder, Tom Carnase 1970
International Typeface Corp.
H 1−x 0,69−k 1,00−p 0,25

**Gesh Ortega Roman 275**
608

the quick brown fox jumps over the lazy dog

N 100: 081 1528
Gerhard Schwekendick 1972
H. Berthold AG
H 1−x 0,78−k 1,09−p 0,41

ITC **Tom's Roman**
1102

the quick brown fox jumps over the lazy dog

N 100: 081 1792
Ronne Bonder, Tom Carnase 1970
International Typeface Corp.
H 1−x 0,69−k 1,00−p 0,34

**LSC Caslon No. 223**
784
extrafett
extra bold
extra gras
N 100: 081 0868
Herb Lubalin 1970
International Typeface Corp.
H 1−x 0,63−k 1,03−p 0,15

the quick brown fox jumps over the lazy dog

ITC **Zapf International**
1236
halbfett
demi
demi-gras
N 020: 081 2354
Hermann Zapf 1977
International Typeface Corp.
H 1−x 0,71−k 1,13−p 0,42

the quick brown fox jumps over the lazy dog

**Poppl-Antiqua**
952
fett
bold
gras
N 100: 081 1034
Friedrich Poppl 1968
H. Berthold AG
H 1−x 0,69−k 1,09−p 0,37

the quick brown fox jumps over the lazy dog

ITC **Grouch**
648

the quick brown fox jumps over the lazy dog

N 100: 081 0708
Ronne Bonder, Tom Carnase 1970
International Typeface Corp.
H 1−x 0,70−k 1,00−p 0,36

**Domino**
452

the quick brown fox jumps over the lazy dog

N 100: 081 1744
Alfred Riedel 1954
Ludwig & Mayer
H 1−x 0,69−k 1,00−p 0,28

## BERTHOLD HEADLINES III
Barock-Antiqua / Transitionals / Latines

BROWN FOX JUMPS OVER
THE LAZY DOG 1234567890

QUICK BROWN FOX JUMPS OVER
THE LAZY DOG 1234567890

## BERTHOLD HEADLINES III
Barock-Antiqua / Transitionals / Latines

THE QUICK BROWN FOX JUMPS OVER
THE LAZY DOG 1234567890

QUICK BROWN FOX JUMPS OVER
THE LAZY DOG

THE QUICK BROWN FOX JUMPS OVER
THE LAZY DOG 1234567890

THE QUICK BROWN FOX JUMPS OVER
THE LAZY DOG 1234567890

THE QUICK BROWN FOX JUMPS OVER
THE LAZY DOG 1234567890

## 21 Holländische Antiqua / Dutch Transitional / Hollandais Antiqua

**the quick brown fox jumps over the lazy dog**

ITC **Zapf International**
1238
fett
heavy
gras
N 020: 081 2356
Hermann Zapf 1977
International Typeface Corp.
H 1–x 0,73–k 1,13–p 0,41

**the quick brown fox jumps over the lazy dog**

ITC **Tiffany**
1088
fett
bold
gras
N 100: 081 1550
Ed Benguiat 1974
International Typeface Corp.
H 1–x 0,63–k 1,01–p 0,29

## 22 Holländische Antiqua, kursive / Dutch Transitional, italic / Hollandais Antiqua, italique

*the quick brown fox jumps over the lazy dog*

ATF **Caslon 540**
273
kursiv
italic
italique
N 000: 081 0246
American Typefounders
H 1–x 0,63–k 1,00–p 0,25

*the quick brown fox jumps over the lazy dog*

ATF **Caslon 540**
274
kursiv Zierbuchstaben
italic swash letters
italique lettres ornées
Z 000: 081 0248
American Typefounders
H 1–x 0,63–k 1,13–p 0,56

*the quick brown fox jumps over the lazy dog*

**Bulmer**
261
kursiv
italic
italique
N 100: 081 0236
Morris F. Benton 1928
American Typefounders
H 1–x 0,63–k 1,09–p 0,43

*the quick brown fox jumps over the lazy dog*

**Janson**
708
kursiv
italic
italique
N 100: 081 0797
1919
D. Stempel AG
H 1–x 0,66–k 1,06–p 0,43

*the quick brown fox jumps over the lazy dog*

HAAS **Caslon 471**
272
kursiv
italic
italique
N 100: 081 0244
1940
Haas'sche Schriftgießerei AG
H 1–x 0,66–k 1,03–p 0,28

**BERTHOLD HEADLINES III** — Barock-Antiqua / Transitionals / Latines

THE QUICK BROWN FOX JUMPS OVER THE LAZY DOG 1234567890

THE QUICK BROWN FOX JUMPS OVER THE LAZY DOG 1234567890

THE QUICK BROWN FOX JUMPS OVER THE LAZY DOG 1234567890

THE QUICK BROWN FOX JUMPS OVER THE LAZY DOG 1234567890

THE QUICK BROWN FOX JUMPS OVER THE LAZY DOG 1234567890

THE QUICK BROWN FOX JUMPS OVER THE LAZY DOG 1234567890

THE QUICK BROWN FOX JUMPS OVER THE LAZY DOG 1234567890

QUICK BROWN FOX JUMPS OVER THE LAZY DOG 1234567890

Holländische Antiqua, kursive
Dutch Transitional, italic
Hollandais Antiqua, italique

**22**

*the quick brown fox jumps*
*over the lazy dog*

**New Caslon**
866
kursiv
italic
italique

N 100: 081 0936
American Typefounders
H 1–x 0,63–k 1,00–p 0,15

*the quick brown fox jumps*
*over the lazy dog*

**LSC Caslon No. 223**
779
kursiv mager
light italic
italique maigre
N 100: 081 1625
Herb Lubalin 1970
International Typeface Corp.
H 1–x 0,63–k 1,06–p 0,18

*the quick brown fox jumps*
*over the lazy dog*

**Renaissance**
987
kursiv fett
bold italic
italique gras

N 100: 081 1082
Haas'sche Schriftgießerei AG
H 1–x 0,66–k 1,03–p 0,34

*the quick brown fox jumps*
*over the lazy dog*

**LSC Caslon No. 223**
781
kursiv
italic
italique
N 100: 081 1637
Herb Lubalin 1970
International Typeface Corp.
H 1–x 0,66–k 1,09–p 0,15

*the quick brown fox jumps*
*over the lazy dog*

**LSC Caslon No. 223**
783
kursiv fett
bold italic
italique gras
N 100: 081 1648
Herb Lubalin 1970
International Typeface Corp.
H 1–x 0,66–k 1,03–p 0,15

*the quick brown fox jumps*
*over the lazy dog*

**LSC Caslon No. 223**
785
kursiv extrafett
extra bold italic
italique extra gras
N 100: 081 0869
Herb Lubalin 1970
International Typeface Corp.
H 1–x 0,66–k 1,03–p 0,15

*the quick brown fox jumps*
*over the lazy dog*

**Poppl-Antiqua**
954
kursiv schmalfett
bold condensed italic
italique étroit gras
N 100: 081 1040
Friedrich Poppl 1971
H. Berthold AG
H 1–x 0,75–k 1,06–p 0,31

*the quick brown fox jumps*
*over the lazy dog*

**Poppl-Antiqua**
955
kursiv schmalfett Zierbuchstaben
bold condensed italic swash letters
italique étroit gras lettres ornées
Z 000: 081 1779
Friedrich Poppl 1971
H. Berthold AG
H 1–x 0,75–k 1,06–p 0,31

**BERTHOLD HEADLINES III** Barock-Antiqua / Transitionals / Latines

THE QUICK BROWN FOX JUMPS OVER THE LAZY DOG 1234567890

THE QUICK BROWN FOX JUMPS OVER THE LAZY DOG 1234567890

QUICK BROWN FOX JUMPS OVER THE LAZY DOG 1234567890

THE QUICK BROWN FOX JUMPS OVER THE LAZY DOG 1234567890

THE QUICK BROWN FOX JUMPS OVER THE LAZY DOG 1234567890

THE QUICK BROWN FOX JUMPS OVER THE LAZY DOG 1234567890

THE QUICK BROWN FOX JUMPS OVER THE LAZY DOG 1234567890

THE QUICK BROWN FOX JUMPS OVER THE LAZY DOG 1234567890

**Jüngere Barock-Antiqua** **23**
Early Transitional
Baroque Antiqua récent

the quick brown fox jumps
over the lazy dog

**Century Schoolbook**
294
normal
regular
normal
N 100: 081 0277
Morris F. Benton 1915
American Typefounders
H 1-x 0,64-k 1,01-p 0,26

the quick brown fox jumps
over the lazy dog

ATF **Century**
282
normal
expanded
normal
N 100: 081 0270
Morris F. Benton 1900
American Typefounders
H 1-x 0,65-k 1,02-p 0,22

the quick brown fox jumps
over the lazy dog

**Primus-Antiqua**
969
mager
light
maigre
N 100: 081 1052
1950
VEB Typoart
H 1-x 0,68-k 1,04-p 0,32

the quick brown fox jumps
over the lazy dog

**Sorbonne**
1042
normal
regular
normal
N 020: 081 2324
1905
H. Berthold AG
H 1-x 0,63-k 1,00-p 0,30

the quick brown fox jumps
over the lazy dog

MONOTYPE **Modern**
1281
normal
extended
normal
N 020: 081 2235
Monotype Corporation Ltd.
H 1-x 0,64-k 1,02-p 0,35

the quick brown fox jumps
over the lazy dog

ITC **Century**
287
Buch
book
romain labeur
N 020: 081 2007
Tony Stan 1975
International Typeface Corp.
H 1-x 0,70-k 1,00-p 0,25

**the quick brown fox jumps**
**over the lazy dog**

**Century Schoolbook**
296
halbfett
bold
demi-gras
N 100: 081 0279
Morris F. Benton 1923
American Typefounders
H 1-x 0,65-k 1,00-p 0,22

**the quick brown fox jumps**
**over the lazy dog**

ATF **Century**
284
halbfett
bold
demi-gras
N 100: 081 0258
Morris F. Benton 1905
American Typefounders
H 1-x 0,66-k 1,01-p 0,22

**BERTHOLD HEADLINES III**  Barock-Antiqua / Transitionals / Latines

THE QUICK BROWN FOX JUMPS OVER THE LAZY DOG 1234567890

THE QUICK BROWN FOX JUMPS OVER THE LAZY DOG 1234567890

THE QUICK BROWN FOX JUMPS OVER THE LAZY DOG 1234567890

QUICK BROWN FOX JUMPS OVER THE LAZY DOG 1234567890

QUICK BROWN FOX JUMPS OVER THE LAZY DOG 1234567890

**BERTHOLD HEADLINES III**  Barock-Antiqua / Transitionals / Latines

*THE QUICK BROWN FOX JUMPS OVER THE LAZY DOG 1234567890*

*THE QUICK BROWN FOX JUMPS OVER THE LAZY DOG 1234567890*

| | Jüngere Barock-Antiqua
Early Transitional
Baroque Antiqua récent | **23** |

ITC **Caslon Headline**
277

**the quick brown fox jumps
over the lazy dog**

N 100: 081 1791
Ronne Bonder, Tom Carnase 1970
International Typeface Corp.
H 1–x 0,66–k 1,00–p 0,28

**Sorbonne**
1045
fett
bold
gras

**the quick brown fox jumps
over the lazy dog**

N 020: 081 2326
1908
H. Berthold AG
H 1–x 0,63–k 1,00–p 0,26

MONOTYPE **Modern**
1282
halbfett
bold
demi-gras

**the quick brown fox jumps
over the lazy dog**

N 020: 081 2238
Monotype Corporation Ltd.
H 1–x 0,64–k 1,03–p 0,35

**Primus-Antiqua**
971
halbfett
medium
demi-gras

**the quick brown fox jumps
over the lazy dog**

N 100: 081 1055
1950
VEB Typoart
H 1–x 0,68–k 1,03–p 0,28

ITC **Century**
289
ultra
ultra
ultra

**the quick brown fox jumps
over the lazy dog**

N 020: 081 2242
Tony Stan 1975
International Typeface Corp.
H 1–x 0,68–k 1,00–p 0,28

| | Jüngere Barock-Antiqua, kursive
Early Transitional, italic
Baroque Antiqua, italique | **24** |

ITC **Century**
288
Buch kursiv
book italic
italique romain labeur

*the quick brown fox jumps
over the lazy dog*

N 020: 081 2008
Tony Stan 1975
International Typeface Corp.
H 1–x 0,70–k 1,00–p 0,26

ATF **Century Schoolbook**
295
kursiv
italic
italique

*the quick brown fox jumps
over the lazy dog*

N 100: 081 0278
Morris F. Benton 1919
American Typefounders
H 1–x 0,63–k 1,00–p 0,27

**BERTHOLD HEADLINES III**  Barock-Antiqua
Transitionals
Latines

*THE QUICK BROWN FOX JUMPS OVER THE LAZY DOG 1234567890*

*THE QUICK BROWN FOX JUMPS OVER THE LAZY DOG 1234567890*

*THE QUICK BROWN FOX JUMPS OVER THE LAZY DOG 1234567890*

*THE QUICK BROWN FOX JUMPS OVER THE LAZY DOG 1234567890*

*THE QUICK BROWN FOX JUMPS OVER THE LAZY DOG 1234567890*

*QUICK BROWN FOX JUMPS OVER THE DOG 1234567890*

**QUICK BROWN FOX JUMPS OVER THE DOG 1234567890**

Jüngere Barock-Antiqua, kursive
Early Transitional, italic
Baroque Antiqua, italique

**24**

*the quick brown fox jumps
over the lazy dog*

ATF **Century**
283
kursiv expanded
italique
N 100: 081 0272
Morris F. Benton 1900
American Typefounders
H 1–x 0,66–k 1,03–p 0,24

*the quick brown fox jumps
over the lazy dog*

MONOTYPE **Modern**
1337
kursiv extended
italique
N 020: 081 2236
Monotype Corporation Ltd.
H 1–x 0,63–k 1,01–p 0,32

*the quick brown fox jumps
over the lazy dog*

**Primus**
970
kursiv mager
light italic
italique maigre
N 100: 081 1054
1950
VEB Typoart
H 1–x 0,67–k 1,00–p 0,32

*the quick brown fox jumps
over the lazy dog*

**Druckhaus**
454
kursiv
italic
italique
N 000: 081 0437
1919
Johannes Wagner
H 1–x 0,72–k 1,00–p 0,28

*the quick brown fox jumps
over the lazy dog*

ATF **Century**
285
kursiv halbfett
bold italic
italique demi-gras
N 100: 081 0259
Morris F. Benton 1905
American Typefounders
H 1–x 0,66–k 1,00–p 0,22

*the quick brown fox jumps
over the lazy dog*

**Craw Modern**
431
kursiv
italic
italique
N 100: 081 0416
Freeman Craw 1966
American Typefounders
H 1–x 0,75–k 1,00–p 0,28

***the quick brown fox jumps
over the lazy dog***

ITC **Century**
297
kursiv ultra
ultra italic
italique ultra
N 020: 081 2243
Tony Stan 1975
International Typeface Corp.
H 1–x 0,68–k 1,01–p 0,32

147

**BERTHOLD HEADLINES III**  Barock-Antiqua / Transitionals / Latines

THE QUICK BROWN FOX JUMPS OVER
THE LAZY DOG 1234567890

THE QUICK BROWN FOX JUMPS OVER
THE LAZY DOG 1234567890

THE QUICK BROWN FOX JUMPS OVER
THE LAZY DOG 1234567890

THE QUICK BROWN FOX JUMPS OVER
THE LAZY DOG 1234567890

THE QUICK BROWN FOX JUMPS OVER
THE LAZY DOG 1234567890

THE QUICK BROWN FOX JUMPS OVER
THE LAZY DOG 1234567890

THE QUICK BROWN FOX JUMPS OVER
THE LAZY DOG 1234567890

THE QUICK BROWN FOX JUMPS OVER
THE LAZY DOG 1234567890

Barock-Antiqua, schmale
Transitional, condensed
Baroque Antiqua, étroit
**25**

**Cheltenham Old Style**
317
schmal
condensed
étroit
N 100: 081 0318
Morris F. Benton, B. Goodhue
American Typefounders
H 1–x 0,53–k 1,00–p 0,28

the quick brown fox jumps
over the lazy dog

**Century Nova**
291

N 100: 081 0269
Charles E. Hughes 1966
American Typefounders
H 1–x 0,66–k 1,00–p 0,24

the quick brown fox jumps
over the lazy dog

ITC **Cheltenham**
314
schmalmager
light condensed
étroit maigre
N 020: 081 2433
Tony Stan 1978
International Typeface Corp.
H 1–x 0,69–k 1,00–p 0,28

the quick brown fox jumps
over the lazy dog

ITC **Benguiat**
153
Buch schmal
book condensed
étroit romain labeur
N 020: 081 1951
Ed Benguiat 1979
International Typeface Corp.
H 1–x 0,75–k 1,04–p 0,33

the quick brown fox jumps
over the lazy dog

ITC **Cheltenham**
316
Buch schmal
book condensed
romain labeur étroit
N 020: 081 2435
Tony Stan 1978
International Typeface Corp.
H 1–x 0,69–k 1,00–p 0,28

the quick brown fox jumps
over the lazy dog

**Concorde**
1318
schmal
condensed
étroit
N 020: 081 1126
Günter Gerhard Lange 1973
H. Berthold AG
H 1–x 0,69–k 1,09–p 0,31

the quick brown fox jumps
over the lazy dog

**Concorde Nova**
1321
normal
regular
normal
N 020: 081 1708
Günter Gerhard Lange 1975
H. Berthold AG
H 1–x 0,69–k 1,08–p 0,30

the quick brown fox jumps
over the lazy dog

ITC **Benguiat**
155
schmal
medium condensed
étroit
N 020: 081 1953
Ed Benguiat 1979
International Typeface Corp.
H 1–x 0,75–k 1,04–p 0,31

the quick brown fox jumps
over the lazy dog

**BERTHOLD HEADLINES III** Barock-Antiqua / Transitionals / Latines

THE QUICK BROWN FOX JUMPS OVER
THE LAZY DOG 1234567890

THE QUICK BROWN FOX JUMPS OVER
THE LAZY DOG 1234567890

THE QUICK BROWN FOX JUMPS OVER
THE LAZY DOG 1234567890

THE QUICK BROWN FOX JUMPS OVER
THE LAZY DOG 1234567890

THE QUICK BROWN FOX JUMPS OVER
THE LAZY DOG 1234567890

THE QUICK BROWN FOX JUMPS OVER
THE LAZY DOG 1234567890

THE QUICK BROWN FOX JUMPS OVER
THE LAZY DOG 1234567890

THE QUICK BROWN FOX JUMPS OVER
THE LAZY DOG 1234567890

Barock-Antiqua, schmale
Transitional, condensed
Baroque Antiqua, étroit
**25**

the quick brown fox jumps
over the lazy dog

ATF **Century**
286
schmalhalbfett
bold condensed
étroit demi-gras
N 100: 081 0264
Morris F. Benton 1909
American Typefounders
H 1–x 0,66–k 1,00–p 0,22

the quick brown fox jumps
over the lazy dog

ATF **Caslon**
279
schmalhalbfett
bold condensed
étroit demi-gras

N 100: 081 0250
American Typefounders
H 1–x 0,66–k 1,00–p 0,24

the quick brown fox jumps
over the lazy dog

**Simone**
1039

N 100: 081 1128
Karl-Heinz Domning 1974
H. Berthold AG
H 1–x 0,72–k 1,03–p 0,31

the quick brown fox jumps
over the lazy dog

ATF **Cheltenham**
310
eng halbfett
bold extra condensed
extra étroit demi-gras
N 100: 081 0308
Morris F. Benton 1904-1911
American Typefounders
H 1–x 0,61–k 1,01–p 0,22

the quick brown fox jumps
over the lazy dog

**Windsor**
1222
schmalfett
elongated
étroit gras
N 100: 081 1397
1905
Stephenson Blake & Company Ltd.
H 1–x 0,66–k 1,00–p 0,23

the quick brown fox jumps
over the lazy dog

ATF **Cheltenham**
303
schmalhalbfett
bold condensed
étroit demi-gras
N 100: 081 0303
Morris F. Benton 1904-1911
American Typefounders
H 1–x 0,57–k 1,00–p 0,25

the quick brown fox jumps
over the lazy dog

**Sorbonne**
1046
schmalhalbfett
medium condensed
étroit demi-gras
N 020: 081 2325
1908
H. Berthold AG
H 1–x 0,63–k 1,00–p 0,26

the quick brown fox jumps
over the lazy dog

ATF **Clearface**
400
schmalfett
heavy condensed
étroit gras
N 100: 081 0379
Morris F. Benton
American Typefounders
H 1–x 0,69–k 1,03–p 0,25

**BERTHOLD HEADLINES III** — Barock-Antiqua / Transitionals / Latines

THE QUICK BROWN FOX JUMPS OVER
THE LAZY DOG 1234567890

THE QUICK BROWN FOX JUMPS OVER
THE LAZY DOG 1234567890

THE QUICK BROWN FOX JUMPS OVER
THE LAZY DOG 1234567890

THE QUICK BROWN FOX JUMPS OVER
THE LAZY DOG 1234567890

THE QUICK BROWN FOX JUMPS OVER
THE LAZY DOG 1234567890

THE QUICK BROWN FOX JUMPS OVER
THE LAZY DOG 1234567890

THE QUICK BROWN FOX JUMPS OVER
THE LAZY DOG 1234567890

THE QUICK BROWN FOX JUMPS OVER
THE LAZY DOG 1234567890

Barock-Antiqua, schmale
Transitional, condensed
Baroque Antiqua, étroit
**25**

ITC **Bernase Roman**
161

the quick brown fox jumps
over the lazy dog

N 100: 081 0152
Ronne Bonder, Tom Carnase 1970
International Typeface Corp.
H 1–x 0,63–k 1,00–p 0,21

**Poppl-Pontifex**
1400
schmalhalbfett
medium condensed
étroit demi-gras

the quick brown fox jumps
over the lazy dog

N 020: 081 2463
Friedrich Poppl 1981
H. Berthold AG
H 1–x 0,71–k 1,15–p 0,38

**Imprimatur**
728
schmalfett
bold condensed
étroit gras

the quick brown fox jumps
over the lazy dog

N 100: 081 0781
Konrad F. Bauer, Walter Baum 1955
Fundición Tipográfica Neufville, S.A.
H 1–x 0,72–k 1,03–p 0,31

ITC **Cheltenham**
318
schmalhalbfett
bold condensed
étroit demi-gras

the quick brown fox jumps
over the lazy dog

N 020: 081 2439
Tony Stan 1978
International Typeface Corp.
H 1–x 0,69–k 1,00–p 0,31

**Concorde**
1319
schmalhalbfett
medium condensed
étroit demi-gras

the quick brown fox jumps
over the lazy dog

N 020: 081 0543
Günter Gerhard Lange 1969
H. Berthold AG
H 1–x 0,68–k 1,08–p 0,31

**Concorde Nova**
1323
halbfett
medium
demi-gras

the quick brown fox jumps
over the lazy dog

N 020: 081 1711
Günter Gerhard Lange 1975
H. Berthold AG
H 1–x 0,68–k 1,09–p 0,32

ITC **Benguiat**
157
schmalhalbfett
bold condensed
étroit demi-gras

the quick brown fox jumps
over the lazy dog

N 020: 081 1954
Ed Benguiat 1979
International Typeface Corp.
H 1–x 0,75–k 1,02–p 0,33

**Concorde**
1320
schmalfett
bold condensed
étroit gras

the quick brown fox jumps
over the lazy dog

N 020: 081 1739
Günter Gerhard Lange 1972
H. Berthold AG
H 1–x 0,69–k 1,09–p 0,31

## BERTHOLD HEADLINES III
Barock-Antiqua / Transitionals / Latines

**THE QUICK BROWN FOX JUMPS OVER THE LAZY DOG 1234567890**

**THE QUICK BROWN FOX JUMPS OVER THE LAZY DOG 1234567890**

## BERTHOLD HEADLINES III
Barock-Antiqua / Transitionals / Latines

*THE QUICK BROWN FOX JUMPS OVER THE LAZY DOG 1234567890*

*THE QUICK BROWN FOX JUMPS OVER THE LAZY DOG 1234567890*

*THE QUICK BROWN FOX JUMPS OVER THE LAZY DOG 1234567890*

*THE QUICK BROWN FOX JUMPS OVER THE LAZY DOG 1234567890*

*THE QUICK BROWN FOX JUMPS OVER THE LAZY DOG 1234567890*

| | Barock-Antiqua, schmale / Transitional, condensed / Baroque Antiqua, étroit | **25** |

**the quick brown fox jumps over the lazy dog**

Poppl-Antiqua
953
schmalfett
bold condensed
étroit gras
N 100: 081 1039
Friedrich Poppl 1970
H. Berthold AG
H 1–x 0,72–k 1,13–p 0,34

**the quick brown fox jumps over the lazy dog**

ITC **Cheltenham**
320
ultra schmal
ultra condensed
ultra étroit
N 020: 081 2437
Tony Stan 1978
International Typeface Corp.
H 1–x 0,66–k 0,99–p 0,28

| | Barock-Antiqua, kursiv schmale / Transitional, condensed italic / Baroque Antiqua, italique étroit | **26** |

*the quick brown fox jumps over the lazy dog*

ITC **Cheltenham**
315
kursiv schmalmager
light condensed italic
italique étroit maigre
N 020: 081 2434
Tony Stan 1978
International Typeface Corp.
H 1–x 0,68–k 1,00–p 0,26

*the quick brown fox jumps over the lazy dog*

**Concorde Nova**
1322
kursiv
italic
italique
N 020: 081 1725
Günter Gerhard Lange 1975
H. Berthold AG
H 1–x 0,68–k 1,07–p 0,32

*the quick brown fox jumps over the lazy dog*

ITC **Cheltenham**
317
Buch kursiv schmal
book condensed italic
italique romain labeur étroit
N 020: 081 2436
Tony Stan 1978
International Typeface Corp.
H 1–x 0,68–k 1,00–p 0,28

*the quick brown fox jumps over the lazy dog*

ITC **Benguiat**
154
Buch kursiv schmal
book condensed italic
italique romain labeur étroit
N 020: 081 1955
Ed Benguiat 1979
International Typeface Corp.
H 1–x 0,73–k 1,02–p 0,33

*the quick brown fox jumps over the lazy dog*

ITC **Benguiat**
156
kursiv schmal
medium condensed italic
italique étroit
N 020: 081 1957
Ed Benguiat 1979
International Typeface Corp.
H 1–x 0,75–k 1,04–p 0,33

## BERTHOLD HEADLINES III
Barock-Antiqua / Transitionals / Latines

*THE QUICK BROWN FOX JUMPS OVER THE LAZY DOG 1234567890*

***THE QUICK BROWN FOX JUMPS OVER THE LAZY DOG 1234567890***

***THE QUICK BROWN FOX JUMPS OVER THE LAZY DOG 1234567890***

## BERTHOLD HEADLINES III
Barock-Antiqua / Transitionals / Latines

QUICK BROWN FOX JUMPS OVER THE LAZY DOG 1234567890

QUICK BROWN FOX JUMPS OVER THE LAZY DOG 1234567890

BROWN FOX JUMPS OVER THE LAZY DOG 1234567890

BROWN FOX JUMPS OVER THE LAZY DOG 1234567890

**26** Barock-Antiqua, kursiv schmale / Transitional, condensed italic / Baroque Antiqua, italique étroit

*the quick brown fox jumps over the lazy dog*

ITC **Cheltenham**
319
kursiv schmalhalbfett
bold condensed italic
italique étroit demi-gras
N 020: 081 2440
Tony Stan 1978
International Typeface Corp.
H 1–x 0,68–k 1,01–p 0,29

*the quick brown fox jumps over the lazy dog*

ITC **Benguiat**
158
kursiv schmalhalbfett
bold condensed italic
italique étroit demi-gras
N 020: 081 1958
Ed Benguiat 1979
International Typeface Corp.
H 1–x 0,75–k 1,03–p 0,37

*the quick brown fox jumps over the lazy dog*

ITC **Cheltenham**
321
ultra schmal kursiv
ultra condensed italic
ultra italique étroit
N 020: 081 2438
Tony Stan 1978
International Typeface Corp.
H 1–x 0,65–k 1,01–p 0,28

**27** Barock-Antiqua, breite / Transitional, extended / Baroque Antiqua, large

the quick brown fox jumps over the lazy dog

**Americana**
45
normal
regular
normal
N 100: 081 0063
Richard Isbell 1965
American Typefounders
H 1–x 0,81–k 1,16–p 0,35

the quick brown fox jumps over the lazy dog

**Promotor**
974

N 100: 081 1073
Leonard H. D. Smit 1960
Lettergieterij Amsterdam
H 1–x 0,66–k 1,00–p 0,37

QUICK BROWN FOX JUMPS OVER THE LAZY DOG

**Engravers Roman**
477
normal
regular
normal
V 000: 081 0479
American Typefounders
H 1–Q 1,00

the quick brown fox jumps over the lazy dog

**Craw Modern**
430
normal
regular
normal
N 100: 081 0412
Freeman Craw 1966
American Typefounders
H 1–x 0,72–k 1,00–p 0,34

**BERTHOLD HEADLINES III** — Barock-Antiqua Transitionals Latines

QUICK BROWN FOX JUMPS OVER THE LAZY DOG 1234567890

BROWN FOX JUMPS OVER THE LAZY DOG 1234567890

THE QUICK BROWN FOX 1234567890

**BERTHOLD HEADLINES III** — Barock-Antiqua Transitionals Latines

THE QUICK BROWN FOX JUMPS OVER THE LAZY DOG 1234567890

THE QUICK BROWN FOX JUMPS OVER THE LAZY DOG 1234567890

THE QUICK BROWN FOX JUMPS OVER THE LAZY DOG 1234567890

THE QUICK BROWN FOX JUMPS OVER THE LAZY DOG 1234567890

## 27 Barock-Antiqua, breite / Transitional, extended / Baroque Antiqua, large

**Americana**
46
halbfett
bold
demi-gras
N 100: 081 1564
Richard Isbell 1965
American Typefounders
H 1–x 0,81–k 1,16–p 0,35

the quick brown fox jumps over the lazy dog

**Orator**
907

N 100: 081 0988
Leonard H. D. Smit 1962
Lettergieterij Amsterdam
H 1–x 0,66–k 1,03–p 0,40

the quick brown fox jumps over the lazy dog

**Primus**
968

N 100: 081 1056
Friedrich Berthold 1962
H. Berthold AG
H 1–x 0,69–k 1,00–p 0,37

the quick brown fox jumps over

## 28 Sonstige / Others / Autres

**Diotima**
451

N 100: 081 0434
Gudrun Zapf-von Hesse 1953
D. Stempel AG
H 1–x 0,66–k 1,16–p 0,31

the quick brown fox jumps over the lazy dog

**Nicolas Cochin**
886
normal
regular
normal
N 100: 081 0942
1929
Ludwig & Mayer
H 1–x 0,41–k 1,06–p 0,43

the quick brown fox jumps over the lazy dog

**Bernhard Modern**
168
normal
regular
normal
N 020: 081 1832
Lucian Bernhard 1937
American Typefounders
H 1–x 0,50–k 1,20–p 0,30

the quick brown fox jumps over the lazy dog

**Tyfa-Antiqua**
1117
normal
regular
normal
N 100: 081 1219
Josef Tyfa 1959
Czech Art
H 1–x 0,72–k 1,19–p 0,37

the quick brown fox jumps over the lazy dog

**BERTHOLD HEADLINES III**    Barock-Antiqua / Transitionals / Latines

THE QUICK BROWN FOX JUMPS OVER THE LAZY DOG 1234567890

THE QUICK BROWN FOX JUMPS OVER THE LAZY DOG 1234567890

THE QUICK BROWN FOX JUMPS OVER THE LAZY DOG 1234567890

THE QUICK BROWN FOX JUMPS OVER THE LAZY DOG 1234567890

THE QUICK BROWN FOX JUMPS OVER THE LAZY DOG 1234567890

THE QUICK BROWN FOX JUMPS OVER THE LAZY DOG 1234567890

THE QUICK BROWN FOX JUMPS OVER THE LAZY DOG

THE QUICK BROWN FOX JUMPS OVER THE LAZY DOG 1234567890

the quick brown fox jumps over the lazy dog

**ITC Novarese**
1283
Buch
book
romain labeur
N 020: 081 0792
Aldo Novarese 1980
International Typeface Corp.
H 1–x 0,73–k 1,13–p 0,28

the quick brown fox jumps over the lazy dog

**Windsor**
1220
mager
light
maigre
N 020: 081 0106
1905
Stephenson Blake & Company Ltd.
H 1–x 0,61–k 1,00–p 0,22

the quick brown fox jumps over the lazy dog

**ITC Souvenir**
1047
mager
light
maigre
N 100: 081 0937
Ed Benguiat 1970
International Typeface Corp.
H 1–x 0,64–k 1,03–p 0,27

the quick brown fox jumps over the lazy dog

**Cooper Old Style**
424
normal
regular
normal
N 100: 081 0409
Oswald B. Cooper 1919-1924
American Typefounders
H 1–x 0,56–k 1,00–p 0,84

the quick brown fox jumps over the lazy dog

**ITC Clearface**
401
normal
regular
normal
N 020: 081 2210
Vic Caruso 1979
(Morris F. Benton 1907-1911)
H 1–x 0,68–k 1,08–p 0,25

the quick brown fox jumps over the lazy dog

**ITC Korinna**
732
normal
regular
normal
N 010: 081 2078
Ed Benguiat, Vic Caruso 1974
(H. Berthold AG 1904)
H 1–x 0,67–k 1,00–p 0,30

the quick brown fox jumps over the lazy dog

**ITC Korinna**
733
normal Zierbuchstaben
regular swash letters
normal lettres ornées
Z 000: 081 2093 ✱
Ed Benguiat, Vic Caruso 1974
(H. Berthold AG 1904)
H 1–x 0,67–k 1,00–p 0,30

the quick brown fox jumps over the lazy dog

**ITC Novarese**
1285
normal
medium
normal
N 020: 081 0798
Aldo Novarese 1980
International Typeface Corp.
H 1–x 0,73–k 1,13–p 0,28

**BERTHOLD HEADLINES III** — Barock-Antiqua / Transitionals / Latines

THE QUICK BROWN FOX JUMPS OVER
THE LAZY DOG 1234567890

THE QUICK BROWN FOX JUMPS OVER
THE LAZY DOG 1234567890

THE QUICK BROWN FOX JUMPS OVER
THE LAZY DOG 1234567890

THE QUICK BROWN FOX JUMPS OVER
THE LAZY DOG 1234567890

THE QUICK BROWN FOX JUMPS OVER
THE LAZY DOG 1234567890

THE QUICK BROWN FOX JUMPS OVER
THE LAZY DOG 1234567890

THE QUICK BROWN FOX JUMPS OVER
THE LAZY DOG 1234567890

THE QUICK BROWN FOX JUMPS OVER
THE LAZY DOG 1234567890

the quick brown fox jumps
over the lazy dog

**Transit**
1106

N 100: 081 1200
Georg Salden 1973
H. Berthold AG
H 1–x 0,66–k 1,06–p 0,37

the quick brown fox jumps
over the lazy dog

**Blackfriars**
192
normal
regular
normal

N 100: 081 1466
Photoscript Ltd.
H 1–x 0,69–k 1,03–p 0,24

the quick brown fox jumps
over the lazy dog

ATF **Clearface**
397
halbfett
bold
demi-gras
N 100: 081 0371
Morris F. Benton 1907
American Typefounders
H 1–x 0,65–k 1,03–p 0,24

the quick brown fox jumps
over the lazy dog

ITC **Clearface**
402
halbfett
bold
demi-gras
N 020: 081 2211
Vic Caruso 1979
(Morris F. Benton 1907–1911)
H 1–x 0,65–k 1,03–p 0,24

the quick brown fox jumps
over the lazy dog

**Lo-Type**
768
mager
light
maigre
N 020: 081 2424
Erik Spiekermann 1980
(Louis Oppenheim 1924)
H 1–x 0,64–k 1,01–p 0,28

the quick brown fox jumps
over the lazy dog

ITC **Isbell**
1387
Buch
book
romain labeur
N 020: 081 2522
Richard Isbell, Jerry Campbell 1981
International Typeface Corp.
H 1–x 0,75–k 1,00–p 0,28

the quick brown fox jumps
over the lazy dog

**Romic**
1401
mager
light
maigre
N 020: 081 2549
Colin Brignall 1979
TSI Typographic Systems Int. Ltd.
H 1–x 0,72–k 1,00–p 0,23

the quick brown fox jumps
over the lazy dog

**Bernhard Modern**
170
fett
bold
gras
N 020: 081 1838
Lucian Bernhard 1930
American Typefounders
H 1–x 0,50–k 1,19–p 0,29

# BERTHOLD HEADLINES III
Barock-Antiqua
Transitionals
Latines

THE QUICK BROWN FOX JUMPS OVER THE LAZY DOG 1234567890

QUICK BROWN FOX JUMPS OVER THE LAZY DOG 1234567890

QUICK BROWN FOX JUMPS OVER THE LAZY DOG 1234567890

THE QUICK BROWN FOX JUMPS OVER THE LAZY DOG 1234567890

THE QUICK BROWN FOX JUMPS OVER THE LAZY DOG

THE QUICK BROWN FOX JUMPS OVER THE LAZY DOG 1234567890

THE QUICK BROWN FOX JUMPS OVER THE LAZY DOG 1234567890

THE QUICK BROWN FOX JUMPS OVER THE LAZY DOG 1234567890

**the quick brown fox jumps over the lazy dog**

ITC **Benguiat**
147
Buch
Book
romain labeur
N 020: 081 2392
Ed Benguiat 1978
International Typeface Corp.
H 1–x 0,74–k 1,04–p 0,31

the quick brown fox jumps over the lazy dog

**Nicolas Cochin**
888
fett
bold
gras
N 100: 081 0944
1929
Ludwig & Mayer
H 1–x 0,47–k 1,06–p 0,42

the quick brown fox jumps over the lazy dog

**Lucian**
800
normal
regular
normal
N 100: 081 0864
Lucian Bernhard 1925
Fundición Tipográfica Neufville, S.A.
H 1–x 0,47–k 1,09–p 0,37

**the quick brown fox jumps over the lazy dog**

ITC **Korinna**
735
halbfett
bold
demi-gras
N 010: 081 2083
Ed Benguiat, Vic Caruso 1974
(H. Berthold AG 1904)
H 1–x 0,69–k 1,00–p 0,30

**the quick brown fox jumps over the lazy dog**

ITC **Korinna**
736
halbfett Zierbuchstaben
bold swash letters
demi-gras lettres ornées
Z 000: 081 2093 ✳
Ed Benguiat, Vic Caruso
(H. Berthold AG 1904)
H 1–x 0,69–k 1,00–p 0,30

**the quick brown fox jumps over the lazy dog**

ITC **Souvenir**
1049
normal
medium
normal
N 100: 081 1665
Ed Benguiat 1970
International Typeface Corp.
H 1–x 0,64–k 1,04–p 0,27

**the quick brown fox jumps over the lazy dog**

**Romic**
1402
normal
medium
normal
N 020: 081 2550
Colin Brignall 1979
TSI Typographic Systems Int. Ltd.
H 1–x 0,73–k 1,00–p 0,25

**the quick brown fox jumps over the lazy dog**

ITC **Isbell**
1389
normal
medium
normal
N 020: 081 2524
Richard Isbell, Jerry Campbell 1981
International Typeface Corp.
H 1–x 0,75–k 1,00–p 0,28

# BERTHOLD HEADLINES III
Barock-Antiqua
Transitionals
Latines

THE QUICK BROWN FOX JUMPS OVER THE LAZY DOG 1234567890

THE QUICK BROWN FOX JUMPS OVER THE LAZY DOG 1234567890

THE QUICK BROWN FOX JUMPS OVER THE LAZY DOG 1234567890

THE QUICK BROWN FOX JUMPS OVER THE LAZY DOG 1234567890

QUICK BROWN FOX JUMPS OVER THE LAZY DOG 1234567890

THE QUICK BROWN FOX JUMPS OVER THE LAZY DOG 1234567890

THE QUICK BROWN FOX JUMPS OVER THE LAZY DOG 1234567890

THE QUICK BROWN FOX JUMPS OVER THE LAZY DOG 1234567890

## 28 Sonstige / Others / Autres

**Wiegands Baroque**
1214
normal
regular
normal

N 020: 081 2337
Jürgen Wiegand 1977
H 1–x 0,69–k 1,03–p 0,28

the quick brown fox jumps over the lazy dog

**Sorbonne**
1044
halbfett
medium
demi-gras
N 020: 081 2398
1906
H. Berthold AG
H 1–x 0,63–k 1,00–p 0,30

the quick brown fox jumps over the lazy dog

ITC **Benguiat**
149
normal
medium
normal
N 020: 081 2393
Ed Benguiat 1978
International Typeface Corp.
H 1–x 0,75–k 1,04–p 0,31

the quick brown fox jumps over the lazy dog

ITC **Isbell**
1391
halbfett
bold
demi-gras
N 020: 081 2526
Richard Isbell, Jerry Campbell 1981
International Typeface Corp.
H 1–x 0,75–k 1,00–p 0,28

the quick brown fox jumps over the lazy dog

**Windsor**
1221
fett
bold
gras
N 100: 081 1395
1905
Stephenson Blake & Company Ltd.
H 1–x 0,67–k 1,00–p 0,23

the quick brown fox jumps over the lazy dog

ITC **Souvenir**
1051
halbfett
demi-bold
demi-gras
N 100: 081 1547
Ed Benguiat 1970
International Typeface Corp.
H 1–x 0,65–k 1,01–p 0,27

the quick brown fox jumps over the lazy dog

ITC **Gorilla**
624

N 100: 081 1789
Ronne Bonder, Tom Carnase 1970
International Typeface Corp.
H 1–x 0,69–k 1,00–p 0,28

the quick brown fox jumps over the lazy dog

ATF **Clearface**
398
fett
heavy
gras
N 100: 081 0376
Morris F. Benton 1911
American Typefounders
H 1–x 0,66–k 1,01–p 0,24

the quick brown fox jumps over the lazy dog

**BERTHOLD HEADLINES III** Barock-Antiqua / Transitionals / Latines

THE QUICK BROWN FOX JUMPS OVER THE LAZY DOG 1234567890

THE QUICK BROWN FOX JUMPS OVER THE LAZY DOG 1234567890

QUICK BROWN FOX JUMPS OVER THE LAZY DOG 1234567890

QUICK BROWN FOX JUMPS OVER THE LAZY DOG 1234567890

THE QUICK BROWN FOX JUMPS OVER THE LAZY DOG

THE QUICK BROWN FOX JUMPS OVER THE LAZY DOG 1234567890

THE QUICK BROWN FOX JUMPS OVER THE LAZY DOG 1234567890

THE QUICK BROWN FOX JUMPS OVER THE LAZY DOG 1234567890

## Sonstige / Others / Autres — 28

**the quick brown fox jumps over the lazy dog**

ITC **Clearface**
404
fett
heavy
gras
N 020: 081 2212
Vic Caruso 1979
(Morris F. Benton 1907–1911)
H 1–x 0,66–k 1,01–p 0,24

---

**the quick brown fox jumps over the lazy dog**

ITC **Novarese**
1287
halbfett
bold
demi-gras
N 020: 081 0803
Aldo Novarese 1980
International Typeface Corp.
H 1–x 0,73–k 1,13–p 0,28

---

**the quick brown fox jumps over the lazy dog**

**Lucian**
801
halbfett
bold
demi-gras
N 100: 081 0866
1925
Fundición Tipográfica Neufville, S.A.
H 1–x 0,50–k 1,13–p 0,38

---

**the quick brown fox jumps over the lazy dog**

ITC **Korinna**
738
fett
extra bold
gras
N 010: 081 2086
Ed Benguiat, Vic Caruso 1974
H 1–x 0,70–k 1,00–p 0,30

---

**the quick brown fox jumps over the lazy dog**

ITC **Korinna**
739
fett Zierbuchstaben
extra bold swash letters
gras lettres ornées
Z 000: 081 2093 ✱
Ed Benguiat, Vic Caruso 1974
H 1–x 0,70–k 1,00–p 0,30

---

**the quick brown fox jumps over the lazy dog**

**Bernhard**
162
fett
bold
gras
N 100: 081 1584
Lucian Bernhard 1912
Fundición Tipográfica Neufville, S.A.
H 1–x 0,66–k 1,00–p 0,25

---

**the quick brown fox jumps over the lazy dog**

**Lo-Type**
1335
normal
regular
normal
N 020: 081 0453
Erik Spiekermann 1980
(Louis Oppenheim 1914)
H 1–x 0,68–k 1,00–p 0,24

---

**the quick brown fox jumps over the lazy dog**

**Romic**
1403
halbfett
bold
demi-gras
N 020: 081 2551
Colin Brignall 1979
TSI Typographic Systems Int. Ltd.
H 1–x 0,72–k 1,00–p 0,25

**BERTHOLD HEADLINES III** Barock-Antiqua / Transitionals / Latines

BROWN FOX JUMPS OVER
THE LAZY DOG 1234567890

QUICK BROWN FOX JUMPS OVER
THE LAZY DOG 1234567890

THE QUICK BROWN FOX JUMPS OVER
THE LAZY DOG 1234567890

QUICK BROWN FOX JUMPS OVER
THE LAZY DOG 1234567890

THE QUICK BROWN FOX JUMPS OVER
THE LAZY DOG 1234567890

QUICK BROWN FOX JUMPS OVER
THE LAZY DOG 1234567890

QUICK BROWN FOX JUMPS OVER
THE LAZY DOG 1234567890

QUICK BROWN FOX JUMPS OVER
THE LAZY DOG

## 28 Sonstige / Others / Autres

the quick brown fox jumps over the lazy dog

**Metropolis**
837
fett
bold
gras
N 100: 081 0905
W. Schwerdtner 1928
D. Stempel AG
H 1–x 0,50–k 1,00–p 0,28

the quick brown fox jumps over the lazy dog

ITC **Isbell**
1393
fett
heavy
gras
N 020: 081 2528
Richard Isbell, Jerry Campbell 1981
International Typeface Corp.
H 1–x 0,75–k 1,00–p 0,28

the quick brown fox jumps over the lazy dog

**Romic**
1404
fett
extra bold
gras
N 020: 081 2552
Colin Brignall 1979
TSI Typographic Systems Int. Ltd.
H 1–x 0,72–k 1,02–p 0,25

the quick brown fox jumps over the lazy dog

ITC **Benguiat**
151
halbfett
bold
demi-gras
N 020: 081 2394
Ed Benguiat 1978
International Typeface Corp.
H 1–x 0,75–k 1,02–p 0,33

the quick brown fox jumps over the lazy dog

ITC **Clearface**
1273
extrafett
black
extra gras
N 020: 081 2213
Vic Caruso 1979
International Typeface Corp.
H 1–x 0,68–k 1,07–p 0,23

the quick brown fox jumps over the lazy dog

ITC **Souvenir**
1053
fett
bold
gras
N 100: 081 1548
Ed Benguiat 1970
International Typeface Corp.
H 1–x 0,65–k 1,03–p 0,24

the quick brown fox jumps over the lazy dog

ITC **Korinna**
741
extrafett
heavy
extra gras
N 010: 081 2089
Ed Benguiat, Vic Caruso 1974
International Typeface Corp.
H 1–x 0,68–k 1,00–p 0,31

the quick brown fox jumps over the lazy dog

ITC **Korinna**
742
extrafett Zierbuchstaben
heavy swash letters
extra gras lettres ornées
Z 000: 081 2093 *
Ed Benguiat, Vic Caruso 1974
International Typeface Corp.
H 1–x 0,68–k 1,00–p 0,31

## BERTHOLD HEADLINES III
Barock-Antiqua
Transitionals
Latines

THE QUICK BROWN FOX JUMPS OVER THE LAZY DOG 1234567890

QUICK BROWN FOX JUMPS OVER THE LAZY DOG 1234567890

THE QUICK BROWN FOX JUMPS OVER THE LAZY DOG 1234567890

QUICK BROWN FOX JUMPS OVER THE LAZY DOG 1234567890

QUICK BROWN FOX JUMPS OVER THE LAZY DOG 1234567890

## BERTHOLD HEADLINES III
Barock-Antiqua
Transitionals
Latines

THE QUICK BROWN FOX JUMPS OVER THE LAZY DOG 1234567890

THE QUICK BROWN FOX JUMPS OVER THE LAZY DOG 1234567890

## 28 Sonstige / Others / Autres

**the quick brown fox jumps over the lazy dog**

Cooper Black
422
schmal
condensed
étroit
N 100: 081 0403
Oswald B. Cooper 1921
American Typefounders
H 1–x 0,72–k 1,00–p 0,26

**the quick brown fox jumps over the lazy dog**

Cooper Black
419
normal
regular
normal
N 010: 081 2304
Oswald B. Cooper 1921
American Typefounders
H 1–x 0,70–k 1,00–p 0,26

**the quick brown fox jumps over the lazy dog**

Lo-Type
769
halbfett
medium
demi-gras
N 020: 081 2425
Erik Spiekermann 1980
(Louis Oppenheim 1924)
H 1–x 0,77–k 1,00–p 0,16

**the quick brown fox jumps over the lazy dog**

ITC **Novarese**
1289
fett
ultra
gras
N 020: 081 0805
Aldo Novarese 1980
International Typeface Corp.
H 1–x 0,73–k 1,13–p 0,28

**the quick brown fox jumps over the lazy dog**

Lo-Type
770
fett
bold
gras
N 020: 081 2422
Erik Spiekermann 1980
(Louis Oppenheim 1914)
H 1–x 0,75–k 1,00–p 0,15

## 29 Sonstige, kursive / Others, italic / Autres, italique

*the quick brown fox jumps over the lazy dog*

**Bernhard Modern**
169
kursiv
italic
italique
N 020: 081 1915
Lucian Bernhard
American Typefounders
H 1–x 0,50–k 1,20–p 0,30

*the quick brown fox jumps over the lazy dog*

**Nicolas Cochin**
887
kursiv
italic
italique
N 100: 081 0943
1929
Ludwig & Mayer
H 1–x 0,44–k 1,06–p 0,37

# BERTHOLD HEADLINES III
Barock-Antiqua
Transitionals
Latines

*THE QUICK BROWN FOX JUMPS OVER THE LAZY DOG 1234567890*

THE QUICK BROWN FOX JUMPS OVER THE LAZY DOG 1234567890

THE QUICK BROWN FOX JUMPS OVER THE LAZY DOG 1234567890

*THE QUICK BROWN FOX JUMPS OVER THE LAZY DOG 1234567890*

**THE QUICK BROWN FOX JUMPS OVER THE LAZY DOG**

THE QUICK BROWN FOX JUMPS OVER THE LAZY DOG 1234567890

THE QUICK BROWN FOX JUMPS OVER THE LAZY DOG 1234567890

*THE QUICK BROWN FOX JUMPS OVER THE LAZY DOG 1234567890*

## 29 Sonstige, kursive / Others, italic / Autres, italique

*the quick brown fox jumps over the lazy dog*

**Römische Zirkular**
1002
kursiv
italic
italique
N 100: 081 1098
Haas'sche Schriftgießerei AG
H 1–x 0,55–k 1,82–p 0,24

*the quick brown fox jumps over the lazy dog*

**Cooper Old Style**
425
kursiv
italic
italique
N 100: 081 0410
Oswald B. Cooper 1919–1924
American Typefounders
H 1–x 0,63–k 1,03–p 0,21

*the quick brown fox jumps over the lazy dog*

ITC **Novarese**
1284
Buch kursiv
book italic
italique romain labeur
N 020: 081 0808
Aldo Novarese 1980
International Typeface Corp.
H 1–x 0,73–k 1,17–p 0,37

*the quick brown fox jumps over the lazy dog*

ITC **Korinna**
734
kursiv
italic
italique
N 020: 081 2358
Ed Benguiat 1977
International Typeface Corp.
H 1–x 0,70–k 1,04–p 0,33

*the quick brown fox jumps over the lazy dog*

**Le Cochin**
755
kursiv
italic
italique
N 000: 081 1923
1932
Ludwig & Mayer
H 1–x 0,56–k 1,00–p 0,38

*the quick brown fox jumps over the lazy dog*

ITC **Souvenir**
1048
kursiv mager
light italic
italique maigre
N 100: 081 1659
Ed Benguiat 1970
International Typeface Corp.
H 1–x 0,64–k 1,02–p 0,26

*the quick brown fox jumps over the lazy dog*

**Tyfa-Antiqua**
1138
kursiv
italic
italique
N 100: 081 1220
Josef Tyfa 1959
Czech Art
H 1–x 0,75–k 1,19–p 0,38

*the quick brown fox jumps over the lazy dog*

**Sorbonne**
1043
kursiv
italic
italique
N 020: 081 2325
1906
H. Berthold AG
H 1–x 0,60–k 1,00–p 0,31

# BERTHOLD HEADLINES III
Barock-Antiqua
Transitionals
Latines

THE QUICK BROWN FOX JUMPS OVER THE LAZY DOG 1234567890

THE QUICK BROWN FOX JUMPS OVER THE LAZY DOG 1234567890

THE QUICK BROWN FOX JUMPS OVER THE LAZY DOG 1234567890

THE QUICK BROWN FOX JUMPS OVER THE LAZY DOG 1234567890

THE QUICK BROWN FOX JUMPS OVER THE LAZY DOG 1234567890

THE QUICK BROWN FOX JUMPS OVER THE LAZY DOG 1234567890

THE QUICK BROWN FOX JUMPS OVER THE LAZY DOG 1234567890

THE QUICK BROWN FOX JUMPS OVER THE LAZY DOG 1234567890

| | Sonstige, kursive / Others, italic / Autres, italique | **29** |

*the quick brown fox jumps over the lazy dog*

**Bernhard Modern**
171
kursiv fett
bold italic
italique gras
N 020: 081 1844
Lucian Bernhard 1938
American Typefounders
H 1–x 0,50–k 1,18–p 0,29

*the quick brown fox jumps over the lazy dog*

**Blackfriars**
195
kursiv
italic
italique
N 100: 081 1467
Photoscript Ltd.
H 1–x 0,69–k 1,00–p 0,25

*the quick brown fox jumps over the lazy dog*

ITC **Clearface**
1271
kursiv
italic
italique
N 020: 081 2214
Vic Caruso 1979
(Morris F. Benton 1907–1911)
H 1–x 0,68–k 1,08–p 0,26

*the quick brown fox jumps over the lazy dog*

ITC **Novarese**
1286
kursiv
medium italic
italique
N 020: 081 0811
Aldo Novarese 1980
International Typeface Corp.
H 1–x 0,73–k 1,15–p 0,29

*the quick brown fox jumps over the lazy dog*

ITC **Clearface**
403
kursiv halbfett
bold italic
italique demi-gras
N 020: 081 2215
Vic Caruso 1979
(Morris F. Benton 1907–1911)
H 1–x 0,68–k 1,09–p 0,28

*the quick brown fox jumps over the lazy dog*

**Goudy Catalogue**
1334
kursiv
italic
italique
N 020: 081 0493
1921
American Typefounders
H 1–x 0,60–k 1,07–p 0,28

*the quick brown fox jumps over the lazy dog*

ITC **Isbell**
1388
Buch kursiv
book italic
italique romain labeur
N 020: 081 2523
Richard Isbell, Jerry Campbell 1981
International Typeface Corp.
H 1–x 0,74–k 1,00–p 0,29

*the quick brown fox jumps over the lazy dog*

ITC **Benguiat**
148
Buch kursiv
book italic
italique romain labeur
N 020: 081 2395
Ed Benguiat 1978
International Typeface Corp.
H 1–x 0,75–k 1,03–p 0,31

**BERTHOLD HEADLINES III**    Barock-Antiqua / Transitionals / Latines

*THE QUICK BROWN FOX JUMPS OVER THE LAZY DOG 1234567890*

*THE QUICK BROWN FOX JUMPS OVER THE LAZY DOG 1234567890*

*THE QUICK BROWN FOX JUMPS OVER THE LAZY DOG 1234567890*

*THE QUICK BROWN FOX JUMPS OVER THE LAZY DOG 1234567890*

*THE QUICK BROWN FOX JUMPS OVER THE LAZY DOG 1234567890*

*THE QUICK BROWN FOX JUMPS OVER THE LAZY DOG 1234567890*

*THE QUICK BROWN FOX JUMPS OVER THE LAZY DOG 1234567890*

*THE QUICK BROWN FOX JUMPS OVER THE LAZY DOG 1234567890*

## 29 Sonstige, kursive / Others, italic / Autres, italique

*the quick brown fox jumps over the lazy dog*

ITC **Korinna**
737
kursiv halbfett
bold italic
italique demi-gras
N 020: 081 2359
Ed Benguiat 1977
International Typeface Corp.
H 1–x 0,72–k 1,00–p 0,31

*the quick brown fox jumps over the lazy dog*

**Wiegands Baroque**
1215
kursiv
italic
italique
N 020: 081 2338
Jürgen Wiegand 1977
H. Berthold AG
H 1–x 0,69–k 1,00–p 0,28

*the quick brown fox jumps over the lazy dog*

ITC **Souvenir**
1050
kursiv
medium italic
italique
N 100: 081 1670
Ed Benguiat 1970
International Typeface Corp.
H 1–x 0,65–k 1,01–p 0,26

*the quick brown fox jumps over the lazy dog*

ITC **Benguiat**
150
kursiv
italic
italique
N 020: 081 2396
Ed Benguiat 1978
International Typeface Corp.
H 1–x 0,75–k 1,04–p 0,34

*the quick brown fox jumps over the lazy dog*

ITC **Isbell**
1390
kursiv
italic
italique
N 020: 081 2525
Richard Isbell, Jerry Campbell 1981
International Typeface Corp.
H 1–x 0,75–k 1,00–p 0,28

*the quick brown fox jumps over the lazy dog*

ITC **Clearface**
1272
kursiv fett
heavy italic
italique gras
N 020: 081 2219
Vic Caruso 1979
(Morris F. Benton 1911)
H 1–x 0,68–k 1,08–p 0,28

*the quick brown fox jumps over the lazy dog*

ATF **Clearface**
399
kursiv fett
heavy italic
italique gras
N 100: 081 0377
Morris F. Benton 1911
American Typefounders
H 1–x 0,69–k 1,03–p 0,25

*the quick brown fox jumps over the lazy dog*

ITC **Novarese**
1288
kursiv halbfett
bold italic
italique demi-gras
N 020: 081 0817
Aldo Novarese 1980
International Typeface Corp.
H 1–x 0,73–k 1,14–p 0,33

# BERTHOLD HEADLINES III
Barock-Antiqua
Transitionals
Latines

*QUICK BROWN FOX JUMPS OVER THE LAZY DOG 1234567890*

*THE QUICK BROWN FOX JUMPS OVER THE LAZY DOG 1234567890*

*THE QUICK BROWN FOX JUMPS OVER THE LAZY DOG 1234567890*

*THE QUICK BROWN FOX JUMPS OVER THE LAZY DOG 1234567890*

*QUICK BROWN FOX JUMPS OVER THE LAZY DOG 1234567890*

*QUICK BROWN FOX JUMPS OVER THE LAZY DOG 1234567890*

*QUICK BROWN FOX JUMPS OVER THE LAZY DOG 1234567890*

*QUICK BROWN FOX JUMPS OVER THE LAZY DOG 1234567890*

## 29 Sonstige, kursiv / Others, italic / Autres, italique

*the quick brown fox jumps over the lazy dog*

ITC **Korinna**
740
kursiv fett
extra bold italic
italique gras
N 020: 081 2360
Ed Benguiat 1977
International Typeface Corp.
H 1–x 0,72–k 1,00–p 0,28

*the quick brown fox jumps over the lazy dog*

ITC **Souvenir**
1052
kursiv halbfett
demi-bold italic
italique demi-gras
N 100: 081 1681
Ed Benguiat 1970
International Typeface Corp.
H 1–x 0,64–k 1,00–p 0,25

*the quick brown fox jumps over the lazy dog*

ITC **Isbell**
1392
kursiv halbfett
bold italic
italique demi-gras
N 020: 081 2527
Richard Isbell, Jerry Campbell 1981
International Typeface Corp.
H 1–x 0,74–k 1,04–p 0,28

*the quick brown fox jumps over the lazy dog*

ITC **Clearface**
1274
kursiv extrafett
black italic
italique extra gras
N 020: 081 2220
Vic Caruso 1979
(Morris F. Benton 1907–1911)
H 1–x 0,68–k 1,07–p 0,27

*the quick brown fox jumps over the lazy dog*

ITC **Isbell**
1394
kursiv fett
heavy italic
italique gras
N 020: 081 2529
Richard Isbell, Jerry Campbell 1981
International Typeface Corp.
H 1–x 0,75–k 1,00–p 0,28

*the quick brown fox jumps over the lazy dog*

ITC **Souvenir**
1054
kursiv fett
bold italic
italique gras
N 100: 081 1693
Ed Benguiat 1970
International Typeface Corp.
H 1–x 0,66–k 1,02–p 0,27

*the quick brown fox jumps over the lazy dog*

ITC **Benguiat**
152
kursiv halbfett
bold italic
italique demi-gras
N 020: 081 2397
Ed Benguiat 1978
International Typeface Corp.
H 1–x 0,75–k 1,04–p 0,35

*the quick brown fox jumps over the lazy dog*

ITC **Korinna**
743
kursiv extrafett
heavy italic
italique extra gras
N 020: 081 2361
Ed Benguiat 1977
International Typeface Corp.
H 1–x 0,69–k 1,02–p 0,32

# BERTHOLD HEADLINES III
Barock-Antiqua
Transitionals
Latines

ABCDEFGHIJKLMNOPQRS
TUVWXYZ 1234567890

QUICK BROWN FOX JUMPS OVER
THE LAZY DOG 1234567890

Sonstige, kursive
Others, italic
Autres, italique
**29**

*the quick brown fox jumps over the lazy dog*

**Lo-Type**
1336
kursiv halbfett
medium italic
italique demi-gras
N 020: 081 2421
Erik Spiekermann 1980
(Louis Oppenheim 1913–1914)
H 1–x 0,67–k 1,00–p 0,21

*the quick brown fox jumps over the lazy dog*

**Cooper Black**
419
kursiv
italic
italique
N 100: 081 0398
Oswald B. Cooper 1921
American Typefounders
H 1–x 0,71–k 1,00–p 0,26

# BERTHOLD HEADLINES IV

**30-37**

*Klassizistische Antiqua*
*Modern*
*Antiqua classique (Didones)*

**BERTHOLD HEADLINES IV**  Klassizistische Antiqua / Modern / Antiqua classique (Didones)

THE QUICK BROWN FOX JUMPS OVER
THE LAZY DOG 1234567890

THE QUICK BROWN FOX JUMPS OVER
THE LAZY DOG 1234567890

THE QUICK BROWN FOX JUMPS OVER
THE LAZY DOG 1234567890

THE QUICK BROWN FOX JUMPS OVER
THE LAZY DOG 1234567890

QUICK BROWN FOX JUMPS OVER
THE LAZY DOG 1234567890

THE QUICK BROWN FOX JUMPS OVER
THE LAZY DOG 1234567890

THE QUICK BROWN FOX JUMPS OVER
THE LAZY DOG 1234567890

QUICK BROWN FOX JUMPS OVER
THE LAZY DOG 1234567890

Neoklassizistische Antiqua  
Neo-Classicist  
Antiqua néo-classique  
**30**

the quick brown fox jumps
over the lazy dog

**Augustea**
78
normal
regular
normal
N 100: 081 0099
1905
H. Berthold AG
H 1–x 0,67–k 1,00–p 0,28

the quick brown fox jumps
over the lazy dog

**Madison**
806
mager
regular
normal
N 100: 081 0872
Heinrich Hoffmeister 1909
D. Stempel AG
H 1–x 0,70–k 1,01–p 0,30

the quick brown fox jumps
over the lazy dog

ITC **Zapf Book**
1224
mager
light
maigre
N 020: 081 1945
Hermann Zapf 1976
International Typeface Corp.
H 1–x 0,72–k 1,10–p 0,39

the quick brown fox jumps
over the lazy dog

**Walbaum Buch**
1355
normal
regular
normal
N 020: 081 1840
Günter Gerhard Lange 1975
H. Berthold AG
H 1–x 0,68–k 1,00–p 0,31

the quick brown fox jumps
over the lazy dog

ITC **Zapf Book**
1226
normal
regular
normal
N 020: 081 1947
Hermann Zapf 1976
International Typeface Corp.
H 1–x 0,72–k 1,10–p 0,39

the quick brown fox jumps
over the lazy dog

**Madison**
808
halbfett
medium
demi-gras
N 100: 081 0875
Heinrich Hoffmeister 1909
D. Stempel AG
H 1–x 0,70–k 1,02–p 0,30

the quick brown fox jumps
over the lazy dog

**Augustea**
80
halbfett
medium
demi-gras
N 100: 081 0101
1906
H. Berthold AG
H 1–x 0,67–k 1,01–p 0,31

the quick brown fox jumps
over the lazy dog

**Walbaum Buch**
1357
halbfett
medium
demi-gras
N 020: 081 1854
Günter Gerhard Lange 1975
H. Berthold AG
H 1–x 0,69–k 1,01–p 0,31

**BERTHOLD HEADLINES IV** — Klassizistische Antiqua / Modern / Antiqua classique (Didones)

# QUICK BROWN FOX JUMPS OVER THE LAZY DOG 1234567890

## THE QUICK BROWN FOX JUMPS OVER THE LAZY DOG 1234567890

## QUICK BROWN FOX JUMPS OVER THE LAZY DOG 1234567890

## BROWN FOX JUMPS OVER THE LAZY DOG 1234567890

## BROWN FOX JUMPS OVER THE LAZY DOG 1234567890

**BERTHOLD HEADLINES IV** — Klassizistische Antiqua / Modern / Antiqua classique (Didones)

*THE QUICK BROWN FOX JUMPS OVER THE LAZY DOG 1234567890*

*THE QUICK BROWN FOX JUMPS OVER THE LAZY DOG 1234567890*

| | Neoklassizistische Antiqua / Neo-Classicist / Antiqua néo-classique | **30** |

**the quick brown fox jumps over the lazy dog**

ITC **Zapf Book**
1228
halbfett
demi
demi-gras
N 020: 081 2347
Hermann Zapf 1976
International Typeface Corp.
H 1–x 0,73–k 1,13–p 0,38

**the quick brown fox jumps over the lazy dog**

**Augustea**
81
fett
bold
gras
N 100: 081 0102
1912
H. Berthold AG
H 1–x 0,67–k 1,00–p 0,28

**the quick brown fox jumps over the lazy dog**

**Walbaum Buch**
1359
fett
bold
gras
N 020: 081 1868
Günter Gerhard Lange 1976
H. Berthold AG
H 1–x 0,68–k 1,01–p 0,31

**the quick brown fox jumps over the lazy dog**

**Madison**
809
fett
bold
gras
N 100: 081 0876
Heinrich Hoffmeister 1919
D. Stempel AG
H 1–x 0,70–k 1,00–p 0,30

**the quick brown fox jumps over the lazy dog**

ITC **Zapf Book**
1230
fett
heavy
gras
N 020: 081 2249
Hermann Zapf 1976
International Typeface Corp.
H 1–x 0,72–k 1,13–p 0,38

| | Neoklassizistische Antiqua, kursive / Neo-Classicist, italic / Antiqua néo-classique, italique | **31** |

*the quick brown fox jumps over the lazy dog*

ITC **Zapf Book**
1225
kursiv mager
light italic
italique maigre
N 020: 081 1946
Hermann Zapf 1976
International Typeface Corp.
H 1–x 0,71–k 1,13–p 0,40

*the quick brown fox jumps over the lazy dog*

**Augustea**
79
kursiv
italic
italique
N 100: 081 1573
1906
H. Berthold AG
H 1–x 0,67–k 0,99–p 0,30

## BERTHOLD HEADLINES IV
Klassizistische Antiqua
Modern
Antiqua classique (Didones)

*THE QUICK BROWN FOX JUMPS OVER THE LAZY DOG 1234567890*

*QUICK BROWN FOX JUMPS OVER THE LAZY DOG 1234567890*

*QUICK BROWN FOX JUMPS OVER THE LAZY DOG 1234567890*

*THE QUICK BROWN FOX JUMPS OVER THE LAZY DOG 1234567890*

*QUICK BROWN FOX JUMPS OVER THE LAZY DOG 1234567890*

*QUICK BROWN FOX JUMPS OVER THE LAZY DOG 1234567890*

*THE QUICK BROWN FOX JUMPS OVER THE DOG 1234567890*

| | Neoklassizistische Antiqua, kursive |
| --- | --- |
| | Neo-Classicist, italic **31** |
| | Antiqua néo-classique, italique |

*the quick brown fox jumps over the lazy dog*

**Walbaum Buch**
1356
kursiv
italic
italique
N 020: 081 1871
Günter Gerhard Lange 1976
H. Berthold AG
H 1–x 0,68–k 1,00–p 0,31

*the quick brown fox jumps over the lazy dog*

ITC **Zapf Book**
1227
kursiv
italic
italique
N 020: 081 1948
Hermann Zapf 1976
International Typeface Corp.
H 1–x 0,71–k 1,13–p 0,39

***the quick brown fox jumps over the lazy dog***

**Walbaum Buch**
1358
kursiv halbfett
medium italic
italique demi-gras
N 020: 081 1885
Günter Gerhard Lange 1976
H. Berthold AG
H 1–x 0,68–k 1,01–p 0,31

***the quick brown fox jumps over the lazy dog***

**Augustea**
82
kursiv fett
bold italic
italique gras
N 100: 081 0103
1926
H. Berthold AG
H 1–x 0,67–k 1,00–p 0,28

***the quick brown fox jumps over the lazy dog***

ITC **Zapf Book**
1229
kursiv halbfett
demi italic
italique demi-gras
N 020: 081 2348
Hermann Zapf 1976
International Typeface Corp.
H 1–x 0,68–k 1,06–p 0,39

***the quick brown fox jumps over the lazy dog***

**Walbaum Buch**
1360
kursiv fett
bold italic
italique gras
N 020: 081 1891
Günter Gerhard Lange 1976
H. Berthold AG
H 1–x 0,68–k 1,01–p 0,31

***the quick brown fox jumps over the lazy dog***

ITC **Zapf Book**
1231
kursiv fett
heavy italic
italique gras
N 020: 081 2254
Hermann Zapf 1976
H. Berthold AG
H 1–x 0,70–k 1,04–p 0,37

# BERTHOLD HEADLINES IV
Klassizistische Antiqua
Modern
Antiqua classique (Didones)

THE QUICK BROWN FOX JUMPS OVER
THE LAZY DOG 1234567890

THE QUICK BROWN FOX JUMPS OVER
THE LAZY DOG 1234567890

THE QUICK BROWN FOX JUMPS OVER
THE LAZY DOG 1234567890

THE QUICK BROWN FOX JUMPS OVER
THE LAZY DOG 1234567890

THE QUICK BROWN FOX JUMPS OVER
THE LAZY DOG 1234567890

THE QUICK BROWN FOX JUMPS OVER
THE LAZY DOG 1234567890

THE QUICK BROWN FOX JUMPS OVER
THE LAZY DOG 1234567890

THE QUICK BROWN FOX JUMPS OVER
THE LAZY DOG 1234567890

Klassizistische Antiqua
Modern Face
Antiqua classique
**32**

the quick brown fox jumps
over the lazy dog

**Torino**
1103
normal
regular
normal
N 100: 081 1192
1908
Societa Nebiolo S. p. A.
H 1–x 0,66–k 1,00–p 0,31

the quick brown fox jumps
over the lazy dog

ITC **Fenice**
1364
mager
light
maigre
N 020: 081 2530
Aldo Novarese 1980
International Typeface Corp.
H 1–x 0,73–k 1,00–p 0,25

the quick brown fox jumps
over the lazy dog

**Couture Antiqua**
427

N 100: 081 1749
Karl-Heinz Domning 1974
H. Berthold AG
H 1–x 0,75–k 1,03–p 0,28

the quick brown fox jumps
over the lazy dog

**Firmin Didot**
511
normal
regular
normal
N 100: 081 0528
1927
Ludwig & Mayer
H 1–x 0,59–k 1,03–p 0,41

the quick brown fox jumps
over the lazy dog

**Walbaum Standard**
1186
normal
regular
normal
N 020: 081 0753
Günter Gerhard Lange 1976
(J. E. Walbaum 1800)
H 1–x 0,61–k 1,00–p 0,41

the quick brown fox jumps
over the lazy dog

ITC **Fenice**
503
normal
regular
normal
N 020: 081 2251
Aldo Novarese 1980
H. Berthold AG 1977
H 1–x 0,73–k 1,01–p 0,26

NEUFVILLE **Bodoni-Versal**
218
Versal
title
initiales
V 000: 081 0207
1926
Fundición Tipográfica Neufville, S.A.
H 1–x Q 1,34

the quick brown fox jumps
over the lazy dog

AMSTERDAM **Bodoni-Antiqua**
214
normal
regular
normal

N 100: 081 0191
Lettergieterij Amsterdam
H 1–x 0,59–k 1,03–p 0,41

193

**BERTHOLD HEADLINES IV**  Klassizistische Antiqua / Modern / Antiqua classique (Didones)

THE QUICK BROWN FOX JUMPS OVER
THE LAZY DOG 1234567890

THE QUICK BROWN FOX JUMPS OVER
THE LAZY DOG 1234567890

THE QUICK BROWN FOX JUMPS OVER
THE LAZY DOG 1234567890

THE QUICK BROWN FOX JUMPS OVER
THE LAZY DOG 1234567890

THE QUICK BROWN FOX JUMPS OVER
THE LAZY DOG 1234567890

THE QUICK BROWN FOX JUMPS OVER
THE LAZY DOG 1234567890

THE QUICK BROWN FOX JUMPS OVER
THE LAZY DOG 1234567890

THE QUICK BROWN FOX JUMPS OVER
THE LAZY DOG 1234567890

| | Klassizistische Antiqua  Modern Face  Antiqua classique **32** |
|---|---|
| the quick brown fox jumps over the lazy dog | BERTHOLD **Bodoni-Antiqua**  207  normal  regular  normal  N 100: 081 0175  1930  H. Berthold AG  H 1–x 0,58–k 1,00–p 0,40 |
| the quick brown fox jumps over the lazy dog | **Walbaum-Antiqua**  1182  normal  regular  normal  N 100: 081 0175  1804  H. Berthold AG  H 1–x 0,69–k 1,00–p 0,25 |
| the quick brown fox jumps over the lazy dog | STEPHENSON BLAKE **Modern No. 20**  842  normal  regular  normal  N 100: 081 0910  1905  Stephenson Blake & Company Ltd.  H 1–x 0,66–k 1,03–p 0,34 |
| the quick brown fox jumps over the lazy dog | **Viola**  1174    N 100: 081 1356  Karl-Heinz Domning 1973  H. Berthold AG  H 1–x 0,66–k 1,09–p 0,44 |
| the quick brown fox jumps over the lazy dog | ITC **Didi**  440    N 100: 081 1549  Ronne Bonder, Tom Carnase 1970  International Typeface Corp.  H 1–x 0,69–k 1,00–p 0,34 |
| the quick brown fox jumps over the lazy dog | **Walbaum Standard**  1188  halbfett  medium  demi-gras  N 100: 081 0758  Günter Gerhard Lange 1979  H. Berthold AG  H 1–x 0,61–k 1,00–p 0,42 |
| the quick brown fox jumps over the lazy dog | HAAS **Bodoni-Antiqua**  212  halbfett  medium  demi-gras  N 100: 081 0200  Haas'sche Schriftgießerei AG  H 1–x 0,63–k 1,09–p 0,43 |
| the quick brown fox jumps over the lazy dog | BERTHOLD **Bodoni-Antiqua**  209  halbfett  medium  demi-gras  N 100: 081 0182  1930  H. Berthold AG  H 1–x 0,59–k 1,01–p 0,41 |

## BERTHOLD HEADLINES IV
Klassizistische Antiqua
Modern
Antiqua classique (Didones)

THE QUICK BROWN FOX JUMPS OVER
THE LAZY DOG 1234567890

THE QUICK BROWN FOX JUMPS OVER
THE LAZY DOG 1234567890

THE QUICK BROWN FOX JUMPS OVER
THE LAZY DOG 1234567890

THE QUICK BROWN FOX JUMPS OVER
THE LAZY DOG 1234567890

QUICK BROWN FOX JUMPS OVER
THE LAZY DOG 1234567890

QUICK BROWN FOX JUMPS OVER
THE LAZY DOG 1234567890

QUICK BROWN FOX JUMPS OVER
THE LAZY DOG 1234567890

QUICK BROWN FOX JUMPS OVER
THE LAZY DOG 1234567890

| | Klassizistische Antiqua / Modern Face / Antiqua classique | **32** |

**Antiqua**
57
halbfett
medium
demi-gras

the quick brown fox jumps over the lazy dog

N 100: 081 0710
H. Berthold AG
H 1–x 0,66–k 1,00–p 0,40

**Firmin Didot**
512
fett
bold
gras

the quick brown fox jumps over the lazy dog

N 100: 081 0529
1927
Ludwig & Mayer
H 1–x 0,63–k 1,03–p 0,37

**Walbaum-Antiqua**
1184
halbfett
medium
demi-gras

the quick brown fox jumps over the lazy dog

N 100: 081 1380
Monotype 1933
H. Berthold AG
H 1–x 0,69–k 1,00–p 0,31

ITC **Fenice**
505
fett
bold
gras

the quick brown fox jumps over the lazy dog

N 020: 081 2252
Aldo Novarese 1980
(H. Berthold AG 1977)
H 1–x 0,73–k 1,01–p 0,25

**Walbaum Buch**
1359
fett
bold
gras

the quick brown fox jumps over the lazy dog

N 020: 081 1868
Günter Gerhard Lange 1976
H. Berthold AG
H 1–x 0,68–k 1,01–p 0,31

AMSTERDAM **Bodoni-Antiqua**
216
fett
bold
gras

the quick brown fox jumps over the lazy dog

N 100: 081 0197
Lettergieterij Amsterdam
H 1–x 0,63–k 1,00–p 0,40

**Ultra Bodoni**
1120
normal
regular
normal

the quick brown fox jumps over the lazy dog

N 100: 081 1222
Morris F. Benton 1928
American Typefounders
H 1–x 0,69–k 1,00–p 0,31

**Normande**
892
normal
regular
normal

the quick brown fox jumps over the lazy dog

N 100: 081 0951
1860
H. Berthold AG
H 1–x 0,72–k 1,00–p 0,34

**BERTHOLD HEADLINES IV**  Klassizistische Antiqua / Modern / Antiqua classique (Didones)

# THE QUICK BROWN FOX JUMPS OVER THE LAZY DOG 1234567890

# QUICK BROWN FOX JUMPS OVER THE LAZY DOG 1234567890

# QUICK BROWN FOX JUMPS OVER THE LAZY DOG 1234567890

**BERTHOLD HEADLINES IV**  Klassizistische Antiqua / Modern / Antiqua classique (Didones)

*THE QUICK BROWN FOX JUMPS OVER THE LAZY DOG 1234567890*

*THE QUICK BROWN FOX JUMPS OVER THE LAZY DOG 1234567890*

*THE QUICK BROWN FOX JUMPS OVER THE LAZY DOG 1234567890*

*THE QUICK BROWN FOX JUMPS OVER THE LAZY DOG 1234567890*

| | Klassizistische Antiqua<br>Modern Face<br>Antiqua classique | **32** |

**the quick brown fox jumps
over the lazy dog**

ITC **Fenice**
1367
ultra
ultra
ultra
N 020: 081 2533
Aldo Novarese 1980
International Typeface Corp.
H 1–x 0,73–k 1,00–p 0,27

**Fette Antiqua**
506

**the quick brown fox jumps
over the lazy dog**

N 100: 081 0519
1913
Johannes Wagner
H 1–x 0,69–k 1,00–p 0,31

**Thorowgood**
1081
normal
regular
normal

**the quick brown fox jumps
over the lazy dog**

N 100: 081 1168
1836
Stephenson Blake & Company Ltd.
H 1–x 0,75–k 1,00–p 0,25

| | Klassizistische Antiqua, kursive<br>Modern Face, italic<br>Antiqua classique, italique | **33** |

**Torino**
1104
kursiv
italic
italique

*the quick brown fox jumps
over the lazy dog*

N 100: 081 1197
1908
Societa Nebiolo S.p.A.
H 1–x 0,69–k 1,00–p 0,31

ITC **Fenice**
1365
kursiv mager
light italic
italique maigre

*the quick brown fox jumps
over the lazy dog*

N 020: 081 2531
Aldo Novarese 1980
International Typeface Corp.
H 1–x 0,73–k 1,00–p 0,25

**Walbaum Standard**
1187
kursiv
italic
italique

*the quick brown fox jumps
over the lazy dog*

N 020: 081 0761
Günter Gerhard Lange 1976
(J. E. Walbaum 1800)
H 1–x 0,61–k 1,01–p 0,42

ITC **Fenice**
504
kursiv
italic
italique

*the quick brown fox jumps
over the lazy dog*

N 020: 081 2258
Aldo Novarese 1980
(H. Berthold AG 1977)
H 1–x 0,73–k 1,00–p 0,25

**BERTHOLD HEADLINES IV** — Klassizistische Antiqua / Modern / Antiqua classique (Didones)

*THE QUICK BROWN FOX JUMPS OVER THE LAZY DOG 1234567890*

*THE QUICK BROWN FOX JUMPS OVER THE LAZY DOG 1234567890*

*THE QUICK BROWN FOX JUMPS OVER THE LAZY DOG 1234567890*

*THE QUICK BROWN FOX JUMPS OVER THE LAZY DOG 1234567890*

*THE QUICK BROWN FOX JUMPS OVER THE LAZY DOG 1234567890*

*THE QUICK BROWN FOX JUMPS OVER THE LAZY DOG 1234567890*

*THE QUICK BROWN FOX JUMPS OVER THE LAZY DOG 1234567890*

*QUICK BROWN FOX JUMPS OVER THE LAZY DOG 1234567890*

| | Klassizistische Antiqua, kursive<br>Modern Face, italic<br>Antiqua classique, italique | **33** |

*the quick brown fox jumps over the lazy dog*

BERTHOLD **Bodoni**
208
kursiv
italic
italique
N 100: 081 0178
1930
H. Berthold AG
H 1–x 0,58–k 1,01–p 0,41

*the quick brown fox jumps over the lazy dog*

AMSTERDAM **Bodoni**
215
kursiv
italic
italique

N 100: 081 0194
Lettergieterij Amsterdam
H 1–x 0,59–k 1,00–p 0,38

*the quick brown fox jumps over the lazy dog*

**Madison**
807
kursiv mager
italic
italique
N 100: 081 0874
1965
D. Stempel AG
H 1–x 0,70–k 1,00–p 0,30

*the quick brown fox jumps over the lazy dog*

**Walbaum-Antiqua**
1183
kursiv
italic
italique
N 100: 081 1378
1804
H. Berthold AG
H 1–x 0,69–k 1,00–p 0,28

*the quick brown fox jumps over the lazy dog*

STEPHENSON BLAKE **Modern No. 20**
843
kursiv
italic
italique

N 100: 081 0912
Stephenson Blake & Company Ltd.
H 1–x 0,69–k 1,03–p 0,28

*the quick brown fox jumps over the lazy dog*

HAAS **Bodoni**
213
kursiv halbfett
medium italic
italique demi-gras

N 000: 081 1595
Haas'sche Schriftgießerei AG
H 1–x 0,66–k 1,09–p 0,43

*the quick brown fox jumps over the lazy dog*

**Amsterdam 698**
54



N 100: 081 0065
Lettergieterij Amsterdam
H 1–x 0,66–k 1,00–p 0,34

*the quick brown fox jumps over the lazy dog*

**Walbaum Buch**
1358
kursiv halbfett
medium italic
italique demi-gras
N 020: 081 1885
Günter Gerhard Lange 1976
H. Berthold AG
H 1–x 0,68–k 1,01–p 0,31

# BERTHOLD HEADLINES IV
Klassizistische Antiqua
Modern
Antiqua classique (Didones)

THE QUICK BROWN FOX JUMPS OVER
THE LAZY DOG 1234567890

THE QUICK BROWN FOX JUMPS OVER
THE LAZY DOG 1234567890

QUICK BROWN FOX JUMPS OVER
THE LAZY DOG 1234567890

QUICK BROWN FOX JUMPS OVER
THE LAZY DOG 1234567890

BROWN FOX JUMPS OVER
THE LAZY DOG 1234567890

QUICK BROWN FOX JUMPS OVER
THE LAZY DOG 1234567890

THE QUICK BROWN FOX JUMPS OVER
THE LAZY DOG 1234567890

BROWN FOX JUMPS OVER
THE LAZY DOG 1234567890

Klassizistische Antiqua, kursive
Modern Face, italic
Antiqua classique, italique
**33**

*the quick brown fox jumps over the lazy dog*

BERTHOLD **Bodoni**
210
kursiv halbfett
medium italic
italique demi-gras
N 100: 081 1591
1930
H. Berthold AG
H 1–x 0,60–k 1,01–p 0,40

*the quick brown fox jumps over the lazy dog*

ITC **Fenice**
1366
kursiv fett
bold italic
italique gras
N 020: 081 2532
Aldo Novarese 1980
International Typeface Corp.
H 1–x 0,73–k 1,00–p 0,25

*the quick brown fox jumps over the lazy dog*

**Walbaum Buch**
1360
kursiv fett
bold italic
italique gras
N 020: 081 1891
Günter Gerhard Lange 1976
H. Berthold AG
H 1–x 0,68–k 1,01–p 0,31

*the quick brown fox jumps over the lazy dog*

AMSTERDAM **Bodoni**
217
kursiv fett
bold italic
italique gras

N 100: 081 0193
Lettergieterij Amsterdam
H 1–x 0,63–k 1,00–p 0,37

*the quick brown fox jumps over the lazy dog*

**Normande**
893
kursiv
italic
italique
N 100: 081 0953
1860
H. Berthold AG
H 1–x 0,69–k 1,00–p 0,37

*the quick brown fox jumps over the the lazy dog*

**Ultra Bodoni**
1121
kursiv
italic
italique
N 100: 081 1223
Morris F. Benton 1930
American Typefounders
H 1–x 0,69–k 1,00–p 0,34

*the quick brown fox jumps over the lazy dog*

ITC **Fenice**
1368
kursiv ultra
ultra italic
italique ultra
N 020: 081 2534
Aldo Novarese 1980
International Typeface Corp.
H 1–x 0,73–k 1,00–p 0,27

*the quick brown fox jumps over the lazy dog*

**Thorowgood**
1082
kursiv
italic
italique
N 100: 081 1169
1836
Stephenson Blake & Company Ltd.
H 1–x 0,72–k 1,00–p 0,25

# BERTHOLD HEADLINES IV
Klassizistische Antiqua
Modern
Antiqua classique (Didones)

THE QUICK BROWN FOX JUMPS OVER
THE LAZY DOG 1234567890

THE QUICK BROWN FOX JUMPS OVER
THE LAZY DOG 1234567890

THE QUICK BROWN FOX JUMPS OVER
THE LAZY DOG 1234567890

THE QUICK BROWN FOX JUMPS OVER
THE LAZY DOG 1234567890

THE QUICK BROWN FOX JUMPS OVER
THE LAZY DOG 1234567890

THE QUICK BROWN FOX JUMPS OVER
THE LAZY DOG 1234567890

THE QUICK BROWN FOX JUMPS OVER
THE LAZY DOG 1234567890

THE QUICK BROWN FOX JUMPS OVER
THE LAZY DOG 1234567890

Klassizistische Antiqua, schmale
Modern Face, condensed
Antiqua classique, étroit
**34**

**Vertikal**
1171

the quick brown fox jumps
over the lazy dog

N 100: 081 1351
1955
Haas'sche Schriftgießerei AG
H 1–x 0,75–k 1,00–p 0,25

**Amati**
43

the quick brown fox jumps
over the lazy dog

N 000: 081 0061
Georg Trump 1952
Johannes Wagner
H 1–x 0,72–k 1,00–p 0,19

LSC **Condensed**
787
schmal
condensed
étroit
N 100: 081 0516
Herb Lubalin 1970
International Typeface Corp.
H 1–x 0,72–k 1,00–p 0,25

the quick brown fox jumps
over the lazy dog

**Arsis**
76
normal
regular
normal
N 100: 081 0097
Gerry Powell
Lettergieterij Amsterdam
H 1–x 0,72–k 1,03–p 0,28

the quick brown fox jumps
over the lazy dog

**Madison**
810
schmalmager
condensed
étroit
N 100: 081 0877
Heinrich Hoffmeister 1919
D. Stempel AG
H 1–x 0,70–k 1,02–p 0,30

the quick brown fox jumps
over the lazy dog

**Normande**
894
schmal
condensed
étroit
N 100: 081 0957
1952
H. Berthold AG
H 1–x 0,78–k 1,00–p 0,22

the quick brown fox jumps
over the lazy dog

**Elongated Roman**
471

V 000: 081 1525
Stephenson Blake & Company Ltd.
H 1–Q 1,25

**Madison**
811
schmalhalbfett
medium condensed
étroit demi-gras
N 100: 081 0878
Heinrich Hoffmeister 1922
D. Stempel AG
H 1–x 0,70–k 1,02–p 0,29

the quick brown fox jumps
over the lazy dog

**BERTHOLD HEADLINES IV** Klassizistische Antiqua / Modern / Antiqua classique (Didones)

THE QUICK BROWN FOX JUMPS OVER
THE LAZY DOG 1234567890

THE QUICK BROWN FOX JUMPS OVER
THE LAZY DOG 1234567890

THE QUICK BROWN FOX JUMPS OVER
THE LAZY DOG 1234567890

THE QUICK BROWN FOX JUMPS OVER
THE LAZY DOG 1234567890

**BERTHOLD HEADLINES IV** Klassizistische Antiqua / Modern / Antiqua classique (Didones)

*THE QUICK BROWN FOX JUMPS OVER*
*THE LAZY DOG 1234567890*

*THE QUICK BROWN FOX JUMPS OVER*
*THE LAZY DOG 1234567890*

*THE QUICK BROWN FOX JUMPS OVER*
*THE LAZY DOG 1234567890*

| | **34** |
|---|---|
| | Klassizistische Antiqua, schmale |
| | Modern Face, condensed |
| | Antiqua classique, étroit |

BERTHOLD **Bodoni-Antiqua**
211
schmalfett
bold condensed
étroit gras
N 100: 081 0187
1930
H. Berthold AG
H 1–x 0,68–k 1,01–p 0,37

the quick brown fox jumps over the lazy dog

**Editorial Tondo**
457

N 100: 081 0444
Aldo Novarese 1972
H. Berthold AG
H 1–x 0,75–k 1,00–p 0,22

the quick brown fox jumps over the lazy dog

**Haenel-Antiqua**
649
schmalfett
bold condensed
étroit gras

N 100: 081 0709
H. Berthold AG
H 1–x 0,72–k 1,00–p 0,28

the quick brown fox jumps over the lazy dog

**LSC Condensed**
786
normal
regular
normal
N 100: 081 0515
Herb Lubalin 1970
International Typeface Corp.
H 1–x 0,72–k 1,00–p 0,34

the quick brown fox jumps over the lazy dog

---

| | **35** |
|---|---|
| | Klassizistische Antiqua, kursiv schmale |
| | Modern Face, condensed italic |
| | Antiqua classique, italique étroit |

**Arsis**
77
kursiv
italic
italique
N 100: 081 0098
Gerry Powell
Lettergieterij Amsterdam
H 1–x 0,72–k 1,00–p 0,25

*the quick brown fox jumps over the lazy dog*

**LSC Condensed**
788
kursiv schmal
condensed italic
italique étroit

N 100: 081 0518
International Typeface Corp.
H 1–x 0,75–k 1,00–p 0,25

*the quick brown fox jumps over the lazy dog*

**Milanor**
839
kursiv
italic
italique
N 100: 081 1544
Karl-Heinz Domning 1972
H. Berthold AG
H 1–x 0,78–k 1,03–p 0,31

*the quick brown fox jumps over the lazy dog*

**BERTHOLD HEADLINES IV** — Klassizistische Antiqua / Modern / Antiqua classique (Didones)

*THE QUICK BROWN FOX JUMPS OVER THE LAZY DOG 1234567890*

---

**BERTHOLD HEADLINES IV** — Klassizistische Antiqua / Modern / Antiqua classique (Didones)

THE QUICK BROWN FOX JUMPS OVER THE LAZY DOG 1234567890

QUICK BROWN FOX JUMPS OVER THE LAZY DOG 1234567890

QUICK BROWN FOX JUMPS OVER THE LAZY DOG 1234567890

THE QUICK BROWN FOX JUMPS OVER THE LAZY DOG 1234567890

THE QUICK BROWN FOX JUMPS OVER THE LAZY DOG 1234567890

THE QUICK BROWN FOX JUMPS OVER THE LAZY DOG 1234567890

| | Klassizistische Antiqua, kursiv schmale  Modern Face, condensed italic  Antiqua classique, italique étroit | **35** |

*the quick brown fox jumps over the lazy dog*

**Editorial**
473
kursiv
italic
italique
N 100: 081 0446
Aldo Novarese 1972
H. Berthold AG
H 1–x 0,75–k 1,03–p 0,25

| | Sonstige  Others  Autres | **36** |

**LSC Manhattan**
789

the quick brown fox jumps over the lazy dog

N 100: 081 0870
Herb Lubalin 1970
International Typeface Corp.
H 1–x 0,69–k 1,00–p 0,34

**Clyde**
409

V 000: 081 1491
H. Berthold AG
H 1–Q 1,03

**Broadway**
257
normal
regular
normal
N 100: 081 0233
Morris F. Benton 1929
American Typefounders
H 1–x 0,81–k 1,03–p 0,03

the quick brown fox jumps over the lazy dog

**Britannic**
255
fett
bold
gras
N 100: 081 0231
1901
Stephenson Blake & Company Ltd.
H 1–x 0,75–k 1,00–p 0,25

the quick brown fox jumps over the lazy dog

**Primate**
967

the quick brown fox jumps over the lazy dog

N 100: 081 1051
Aldo Novarese 1972
H. Berthold AG
H 1–x 0,72–k 1,00–p 0,25

**Futura Black**
562

the quick brown fox jumps over the lazy dog

N 100: 081 0623
Paul Renner 1929
Fundición Tipográfica Neufville, S.A.
H 1–Q 1,29

**BERTHOLD HEADLINES IV** — Klassizistische Antiqua / Modern / Antiqua classique (Didones)

THE QUICK BROWN FOX JUMPS OVER
THE LAZY DOG 1234567890

THE QUICK BROWN FOX JUMPS OVER
THE LAZY DOG 1234567890

THE QUICK BROWN FOX JUMPS OVER
THE LAZY DOG 1234567890

THE QUICK BROWN FOX JUMPS OVER
THE LAZY DOG 1234567890

THE QUICK BROWN FOX JUMPS OVER
THE LAZY DOG 1234567890

BROWN FOX JUMPS OVER
THE LAZY DOG 1234567890

**BERTHOLD HEADLINES IV** — Klassizistische Antiqua / Modern / Antiqua classique (Didones)

BROWN FOX JUMPS OVER
THE LAZY DOG 1234567890

## 36 Sonstige / Others / Autres

THE QUICK BROWN FOX JUMPS
OVER THE LAZY DOG

**Peignot**
915
mager
light
maigre
N 100: 081 1493
A. M. Cassandre 1937
Haas'sche Schriftgießerei AG
H 1–x 0,66–k 1,13–p 0,31

THE QUICK BROWN FOX JUMPS
OVER THE LAZY DOG

**Peignot**
916
halbfett
medium
demi-gras
N 100: 081 1494
A. M. Cassandre 1937
Haas'sche Schriftgießerei AG
H 1–x 0,66–k 1,13–p 0,31

THE QUICK BROWN FOX JUMPS
OVER THE LAZY DOG

**Peignot**
917
fett
bold
gras
N 100: 081 1495
A. M. Cassandre 1937
Haas'sche Schriftgießerei AG
H 1–x 0,66–k 1,08–p 0,31

the quick brown fox jumps
over the lazy dog

**Britannic**
254
normal
regular
normal
N 100: 081 0230
Stephenson Blake & Company Ltd.
H 1–x 0,75–k 1,00–p 0,25

the quick brown fox jumps
over the lazy dog

ITC **Firenze**
510
N 020: 081 1961
Herb Lubalin 1970
International Typeface Corp.
H 1–x 0,72–k 1,00–p 0,31

the quick brown fox jumps
over the lazy dog

**Semin-Antiqua**
1022
N 020: 081 2280
Gustav Jaeger 1976
H. Berthold AG
H 1–x 0,81–k 1,00–p 0,38

## 37 Sonstige, kursiv / Others, italic / Autres, italique

the quick brown fox jumps
over the lazy dog

**Abold**
1
kursiv
italic
italique
N 100: 081 1453
Thomas Abold 1972
H. Berthold AG
H 1–x 0,69–k 1,25–p 0,62

211

## BERTHOLD HEADLINES IV
Klassizistische Antiqua
Modern
Antiqua classique (Didones)

# THE QUICK BROWN FOX JUMPS OVER THE LAZY DOG 1234567890

Sonstige, kursive
Others, italic
Autres, italique
**37**

*the quick brown fox jumps over the lazy dog*

**Britannic**
256
kursiv fett
bold italic
italique gras
N 100: 081 0232
1905
Stephenson Blake & Company Ltd.
H 1–x 0,75–k 1,00–p 0,25

# BERTHOLD HEADLINES V

**38-48**

*Serifenbetonte Linear-Antiqua*
*Slab Serifs (Square Serifs)*
*Linéar Antiqua avec empattements (Mécanes)*

**BERTHOLD HEADLINES V**  Serifenbetonte Linear-Antiqua
Slab Serifs (Square Serifs)
Linéar Antiqua avec empattements (Mécanes)

THE QUICK BROWN FOX JUMPS OVER THE LAZY DOG 1234567890

QUICK BROWN FOX JUMPS OVER THE LAZY DOG 1234567890

THE QUICK BROWN FOX JUMPS OVER THE LAZY DOG 1234567890

THE QUICK BROWN FOX JUMPS OVER THE LAZY DOG 1234567890

THE QUICK BROWN FOX JUMPS OVER THE LAZY DOG 1234567890

THE QUICK BROWN FOX JUMPS OVER THE LAZY DOG 1234567890

THE QUICK BROWN FOX JUMPS OVER THE LAZY DOG 1234567890

THE QUICK BROWN FOX JUMPS OVER THE LAZY DOG 1234567890

Serifenbetonte Antiqua  
Legibility Faces  
Antiqua de transition  
**38**

the quick brown fox jumps over the lazy dog

**Schadow-Antiqua**
1011
Werk
book
romain labeur
N 000: 081 1115
Georg Trump 1942
Johannes Wagner
H 1–x 0,69–k 1,00–p 0,31

the quick brown fox jumps over the lazy dog

**IBM Dokument**
680

N 000: 081 0763
1960
D. Stempel AG
H 1–x 0,69–k 1,06–p 0,40

the quick brown fox jumps over the lazy dog

**Impressum**
682
mager
light
maigre
N 100: 081 0769
Konrad F. Bauer, Walter Baum 1963
Fundición Tipográfica Neufville, S.A.
H 1–x 0,69–k 1,02–p 0,26

the quick brown fox jumps over the lazy dog

**Schadow-Antiqua**
1062
mager
light
maigre
N 000: 081 1102
Georg Trump 1937
Johannes Wagner
H 1–x 0,70–k 1,00–p 0,30

the quick brown fox jumps over the lazy dog

**Candida**
267
normal
regular
normal
N 100: 081 0238
Jakob Erbar 1936
Ludwig & Mayer
H 1–x 0,69–k 1,00–p 0,32

the quick brown fox jumps over the lazy dog

**Dominante**
1325
normal
regular
normal
N 020: 081 2448
Johannes Schweitzer 1959
Ludwig & Mayer
H 1–x 0,73–k 1,03–p 0,27

the quick brown fox jumps over the lazy dog

**Melior**
824
normal
regular
normal
N 100: 081 0885
Hermann Zapf 1952
D. Stempel AG
H 1–x 0,68–k 1,08–p 0,29

the quick brown fox jumps over the lazy dog

**Druckhaus-Antiqua**
453
normal
regular
normal
N 100: 081 0435
1919
Johannes Wagner
H 1–x 0,69–k 1,00–p 0,31

**BERTHOLD HEADLINES V**
Serifenbetonte Linear-Antiqua
Slab Serifs (Square Serifs)
Linéar Antiqua avec empattements (Mécanes)

QUICK BROWN FOX JUMPS OVER
THE LAZY DOG 1234567890

THE QUICK BROWN FOX JUMPS OVER
THE LAZY DOG 1234567890

THE QUICK BROWN FOX JUMPS OVER
THE LAZY DOG 1234567890

QUICK BROWN FOX JUMPS OVER
THE LAZY DOG 1234567890

THE QUICK BROWN FOX JUMPS OVER
THE LAZY DOG 1234567890

THE QUICK BROWN FOX JUMPS OVER
THE LAZY DOG 1234567890

THE QUICK BROWN FOX JUMPS OVER
THE LAZY DOG 1234567890

QUICK BROWN FOX JUMPS OVER
THE LAZY DOG 1234567890

**Serifenbetonte Antiqua / Legibility Faces / Antiqua de transition — 38**

the quick brown fox jumps over the lazy dog

**Impressum**
684
halbfett
medium
demi-gras
N 100: 081 0773
Konrad F. Bauer, Walter Baum 1964
Fundición Tipográfica Neufville, S.A.
H 1–x 0,69–k 1,03–p 0,26

the quick brown fox jumps over the lazy dog

**Melior**
826
halbfett
bold
demi-gras
N 100: 081 0888
Hermann Zapf 1952
D. Stempel AG
H 1–x 0,68–k 1,07–p 0,28

the quick brown fox jumps over the lazy dog

**Schadow-Antiqua**
1014
halbfett
medium
demi-gras
N 000: 081 1107
Georg Trump 1938
Johannes Wagner
H 1–x 0,72–k 1,00–p 0,28

the quick brown fox jumps over the lazy dog

**Candida**
219
halbfett
medium
demi-gras
N 100: 081 0240
Jakob Erbar 1937
Ludwig & Mayer
H 1–x 0,72–k 1,00–p 0,30

the quick brown fox jumps over the lazy dog

**Dominante**
1327
fett
bold
gras
N 020: 081 2449
Johannes Schweitzer 1959
Ludwig & Mayer
H 1–x 0,74–k 1,03–p 0,28

the quick brown fox jumps over the lazy dog

**Druckhaus-Antiqua**
455
halbfett
medium
demi-gras
N 000: 081 0438
1919
Johannes Wagner
H 1–x 0,69–k 1,00–p 0,25

the quick brown fox jumps over the lazy dog

**Schadow-Antiqua**
1015
fett
bold
gras
N 000: 081 1114
Georg Trump 1952
Johannes Wagner
H 1–x 0,73–k 1,00–p 0,30

the quick brown fox jumps over the lazy dog

**Whitin Black**
1210
normal
regular
normal
N 100: 081 1393
Morris F. Benton 1904
American Typefounders
H 1–x 0,75–k 1,03–p 0,25

**BERTHOLD HEADLINES V**  
Serifenbetonte Linear-Antiqua  
Slab Serifs (Square Serifs)  
Linéar Antiqua avec empattements (Mécanes)

# QUICK BROWN FOX JUMPS OVER THE LAZY DOG 1234567890

**BERTHOLD HEADLINES V**  
Serifenbetonte Linear-Antiqua  
Slab Serifs (Square Serifs)  
Linéar Antiqua avec empattements (Mécanes)

*THE QUICK BROWN FOX JUMPS OVER THE LAZY DOG 1234567890*

*THE QUICK BROWN FOX JUMPS OVER THE LAZY DOG 1234567890*

*THE QUICK BROWN FOX JUMPS OVER THE LAZY DOG 1234567890*

*THE QUICK BROWN FOX JUMPS OVER THE LAZY DOG 1234567890*

*THE QUICK BROWN FOX JUMPS OVER THE LAZY DOG 1234567890*

*THE QUICK BROWN FOX JUMPS OVER THE LAZY DOG 1234567890*

| | Serifenbetonte Antiqua  
Legibility Faces  
Antiqua de transition | **38** |

**the quick brown fox jumps over the lazy dog**

Antiqua 505
59
fett
bold
gras
N 100: 081 0076
Arno Drescher 1956
Johannes Wagner
H 1–x 0,69–k 1,00–p 0,25

| | Serifenbetonte Antiqua, kursive  
Legibility Faces, italic  
Antiqua de transition, italique | **39** |

*the quick brown fox jumps over the lazy dog*

Schadow
1013
kursiv
italic
italique
N 000: 081 1105
Georg Trump 1942
Johannes Wagner
H 1–x 0,69–k 1,00–p 0,34

*the quick brown fox jumps over the lazy dog*

Dominante
1326
kursiv
italic
italique
N 020: 081 2450
Johannes Schweitzer 1959
Ludwig & Mayer
H 1–x 0,73–k 1,02–p 0,27

*the quick brown fox jumps over the lazy dog*

Melior
825
kursiv
italic
italique
N 100: 081 0886
Hermann Zapf 1952
D. Stempel AG
H 1–x 0,68–k 1,08–p 0,28

*the quick brown fox jumps over the lazy dog*

Egizio
460
kursiv
italic
italique
N 100: 081 0448
Aldo Novarese 1955-1958
Societa Nebiolo S.p.A.
H 1–x 0,63–k 1,98–p 0,29

*the quick brown fox jumps over the lazy dog*

Impressum
683
kursiv mager
light italic
italique maigre
N 100: 081 0772
Konrad F. Bauer, Walter Baum 1964
Fundición Tipográfica Neufville, S.A.
H 1–x 0,69–k 1,02–p 0,27

*the quick brown fox jumps over the lazy dog*

Candida
268
kursiv
italic
italique
N 100: 081 0239
Jakob Erbar 1937
Ludwig & Mayer
H 1–x 0,69–k 1,00–p 0,31

## BERTHOLD HEADLINES V
Serifenbetonte Linear-Antiqua
Slab Serifs (Square Serifs)
Linéar Antiqua avec empattements (Mécanes)

*QUICK BROWN FOX JUMPS OVER THE LAZY DOG 1234567890*

*QUICK BROWN FOX JUMPS OVER THE LAZY DOG 1234567890*

## BERTHOLD HEADLINES V
Serifenbetonte Linear-Antiqua
Slab Serifs (Square Serifs)
Linéar Antiqua avec empattements (Mécanes)

QUICK BROWN FOX JUMPS OVER THE LAZY DOG 1234567890

QUICK BROWN FOX JUMPS OVER THE LAZY DOG 1234567890

QUICK BROWN FOX JUMPS OVER THE LAZY DOG 1234567890

QUICK BROWN FOX JUMPS OVER THE LAZY DOG 1234567890

QUICK BROWN FOX JUMPS OVER THE LAZY DOG 1234567890

## 39
Serifenbetonte Antiqua, kursive
Legibility Faces, italic
Antiqua de transition, italique

*the quick brown fox jumps over the lazy dog*

**Volta**
1180
kursiv halbfett
medium italic
italique demi-gras
N 100: 081 1366
Konrad F. Bauer, Walter Baum 1957
Fundición Tipográfica Neufville, S.A.
H 1–x 0,69–k 1,00–p 0,28

*the quick brown fox jumps over the lazy dog*

**Egizio**
462
kursiv fett
bold italic
italique gras
N 100: 081 0451
Aldo Novarese 1955-1958
Societa Nebiolo S.p.A.
H 1–x 0,64–k 1,00–p 0,28

## 40
Clarendon
Clarendon
Clarendon

the quick brown fox jumps over the lazy dog

**Egizio**
459
normal
regular
normal
N 100: 081 0447
Aldo Novarese 1955-1958
Societa Nebiolo S.p.A.
H 1–x 0,64–k 1,00–p 0,31

the quick brown fox jumps over the lazy dog

**Volta**
1178
normal
regular
normal
N 100: 081 1359
Konrad F. Bauer, Walter Baum 1956
Fundición Tipográfica Neufville, S.A.
H 1–x 0,69–k 1,00–p 0,34

the quick brown fox jumps over the lazy dog

**Craw Clarendon**
428
Buch
book
romain labeur
N 100: 081 0417
Freeman Craw 1957
American Typefounders
H 1–x 0,69–k 1,00–p 0,37

the quick brown fox jumps over the lazy dog

**Clarendon**
390
mager
light
maigre
N 100: 081 0359
1962
D. Stempel AG
H 1–x 0,70–k 1,00–p 0,30

the quick brown fox jumps over the lazy dog

**Clarendon**
391
kräftig
medium
normal
N 100: 081 0363
Hermann Eidenbenz 1953
Haas'sche Schriftgießerei AG
H 1–x 0,69–k 1,00–p 0,32

## BERTHOLD HEADLINES V
Serifenbetonte Linear-Antiqua
Slab Serifs (Square Serifs)
Linéar Antiqua avec empattements (Mécanes)

BROWN FOX JUMPS OVER
THE LAZY DOG 1234567890

QUICK BROWN FOX JUMPS OVER
THE LAZY DOG 1234567890

QUICK BROWN FOX JUMPS OVER
THE LAZY DOG 1234567890

QUICK BROWN FOX JUMPS OVER
THE LAZY DOG 1234567890

BROWN FOX JUMPS OVER
THE LAZY DOG 1234567890

## BERTHOLD HEADLINES V
Serifenbetonte Linear-Antiqua
Slab Serifs (Square Serifs)
Linéar Antiqua avec empattements (Mécanes)

THE QUICK BROWN FOX JUMPS OVER
THE LAZY DOG 1234567890

THE QUICK BROWN FOX JUMPS OVER
THE LAZY DOG 1234567890

## 40 Clarendon / Clarendon / Clarendon

the quick brown fox jumps over the lazy dog

**Volta**
1179
halbfett
medium
demi-gras
N 100: 081 1364
Konrad F. Bauer, Walter Baum 1956
Fundición Tipográfica Neufville, S.A.
H 1–x 0,72–k 1,00–p 0,40

the quick brown fox jumps over the lazy dog

**Clarendon**
392
halbfett
medium
demi-gras
N 100: 081 0363
1962/63
D. Stempel AG
H 1–x 0,72–k 1,00–p 0,30

the quick brown fox jumps over the lazy dog

**Egizio**
461
fett
bold
gras
N 100: 081 0449
Aldo Novarese 1955-1958
Societa Nebiolo S.p.A.
H 1–x 0,64–k 1,00–p 0,26

the quick brown fox jumps over the lazy dog

**Clarendon**
393
fett
bold
gras
N 100: 081 0366
Hermann Eidenbenz 1953
Haas'sche Schriftgießerei AG
H 1–x 0,69–k 1,00–p 0,31

quick brown fox jumps over the lazy dog

**Volta**
1181
fett
bold
gras
N 100: 081 1369
Konrad F. Bauer, Walter Baum 1956
Fundición Tipográfica Neufville, S.A.
H 1–x 0,72–k 1,00–p 0,34

## 41 Egyptienne / Egyptian / Egyptienne

the quick brown fox jumps over the lazy dog

ITC **Stymie Hairline**
1063

N 100: 081 0867
Ronne Bonder, Tom Carnase 1970
International Typeface Corp.
H 1–x 0,59–k 1,00–p 0,25

the quick brown fox jumps over the lazy dog

**Beton Hairline**
184

N 100: 081 1511
Berthold-Schriftenatelier
Fundición Tipográfica Neufville, S.A.
H 1–x 0,56–k 1,00–p 0,25

## BERTHOLD HEADLINES V

Serifenbetonte Linear-Antiqua
Slab Serifs (Square Serifs)
Linéar Antiqua avec empattements (Mécanes)

THE QUICK BROWN FOX JUMPS OVER
THE LAZY DOG 1234567890

THE QUICK BROWN FOX JUMPS OVER
THE LAZY DOG

THE QUICK BROWN FOX JUMPS OVER
THE LAZY DOG 1234567890

THE QUICK BROWN FOX JUMPS OVER
THE LAZY DOG 1234567890

THE QUICK BROWN FOX JUMPS OVER
THE LAZY DOG 1234567890

THE QUICK BROWN FOX JUMPS OVER
THE LAZY DOG 1234567890

THE QUICK BROWN FOX JUMPS OVER
THE LAZY DOG 1234567890

THE QUICK BROWN FOX JUMPS OVER
THE LAZY DOG 1234567890

Egyptienne / Egyptian / Egyptienne 41

the quick brown fox jumps
over the lazy dog

ITC **Lubalin Graph**
790
mager
light
maigre
N 020: 081 1834
Lubalin, Dispigna, Sundwall 1979
International Typeface Corp.
H 1–x 0,73–k 1,00–p 0,28

the quick brown fox jumps
over the lazy dog

ITC **Lubalin Graph**
791
mager Zierbuchstaben
light swash letters
maigre lettres ornées
Z 000: 081 1929
Lubalin, Dispigna, Sundwall 1974
International Typeface Corp.
H 1–x 0,73–k 1,00–p 0,28

the quick brown fox jumps
over the lazy dog

**Beton**
183
mager
light
maigre
N 100: 081 0160
Heinrich Jost 1931
Fundición Tipográfica Neufville, S.A.
H 1–x 0,56–k 1,00–p 0,28

the quick brown fox jumps
over the lazy dog

**Media**
815
mager
light
maigre
N 020: 081 2414
Jürgen Riebling 1978
H. Berthold AG
H 1–x 0,74–k 1,00–p 0,25

the quick brown fox jumps
over the lazy dog

ITC **American Typewriter**
47
mager
light
maigre
N 020: 081 2305
Joel Kaden, Tony Stan 1974
International Typeface Corp.
H 1–x 0,73–k 1,00–p 0,28

the quick brown fox jumps
over the lazy dog

**Memphis**
828
zart
extra light
extra maigre
N 020: 081 2181
Rudolf Wolf 1930
D. Stempel AG
H 1–x 0,63–k 1,00–p 0,23

the quick brown fox jumps
over the lazy dog

**Media**
816
normal
regular
normal
N 100: 081 1727
Jürgen Riebling 1976
H. Berthold AG
H 1–x 0,75–k 1,00–p 0,25

the quick brown fox jumps
over the lazy dog

ITC **Lubalin Graph**
792
Buch
book
romain labeur
N 020: 081 1835
Lubalin, Dispigna, Sundwall 1974
International Typeface Corp.
H 1–x 0,73–k 1,00–p 0,24

**BERTHOLD HEADLINES V** — Serifenbetonte Linear-Antiqua / Slab Serifs (Square Serifs) / Linéar Antiqua avec empattements (Mécanes)

THE QUICK BROWN FOX JUMPS OVER THE LAZY DOG

THE QUICK BROWN FOX JUMPS OVER THE LAZY DOG 1234567890

THE QUICK BROWN FOX JUMPS OVER THE LAZY DOG 1234567890

THE QUICK BROWN FOX JUMPS OVER THE LAZY DOG 1234567890

THE QUICK BROWN FOX JUMPS OVER THE LAZY DOG 1234567890

THE QUICK BROWN FOX JUMPS OVER THE LAZY DOG 1234567890

THE QUICK BROWN FOX JUMPS OVER THE LAZY DOG 1234567890

THE QUICK BROWN FOX JUMPS OVER THE LAZY DOG 1234567890

Egyptienne / Egyptian / Egyptienne — 41

the quick brown fox jumps
over the lazy dog

ITC **Lubalin Graph**
793
Buch Zierbuchstaben
book swash letters
romain labeur lettres ornées
Z 000: 081 1917
Lubalin, Dispigna, Sundwall 1974
International Typeface Corp.
H 1–x 0,73–k 1,00–p 0,24

the quick brown fox jumps
over the lazy dog

**Stymie**
1292
mager
light
maigre
N 020: 081 1160
Morris F. Benton 1931
American Typefounders
H 1–x 0,61–k 1,00–p 0,25

the quick brown fox jumps
over the lazy dog

**Rockwell**
995
mager
light
maigre
N 100: 081 1094
1934
Monotype Corporation Ltd.
H 1–x 0,70–k 1,00–p 0,30

the quick brown fox jumps
over the lazy dog

**City**
379
mager
light
maigre
N 100: 081 0356
Georg Trump 1937
H. Berthold AG
H 1–x 0,64–k 1,00–p 0,26

the quick brown fox jumps
over the lazy dog

**Beton**
184
halbfett
demi-bold
demi-gras
N 100: 081 1793
Heinrich Jost
Fundición Tipográfica Neufville, S.A.
H 1–x 0,59–k 1,00–p 0,29

the quick brown fox jumps
over the lazy dog

**Schreibmaschinenschrift**
1018
N 000: 081 1121
1969
H. Berthold AG
H 1–x 0,72–k 1,00–p 0,28

the quick brown fox jumps
over the lazy dog

**Memphis**
829
mager
light
maigre
N 100: 081 0891
Rudolf Wolf 1932
D. Stempel AG
H 1–x 0,63–k 1,00–p 0,20

the quick brown fox jumps
over the lazy dog

**Stymie**
1065
normal
medium
normal
N 020: 081 1165
Morris F. Benton 1931
American Typefounders
H 1–x 0,61–k 1,01–p 0,25

**BERTHOLD HEADLINES V**    Serifenbetonte Linear-Antiqua / Slab Serifs (Square Serifs) / Linéar Antiqua avec empattements (Mécanes)

THE QUICK BROWN FOX JUMPS OVER THE LAZY DOG 1234567890

THE QUICK BROWN FOX JUMPS OVER THE LAZY DOG 1234567890

THE QUICK BROWN FOX JUMPS OVER THE LAZY DOG

THE QUICK BROWN FOX JUMPS OVER THE LAZY DOG 1234567890

THE QUICK BROWN FOX JUMPS OVER THE LAZY DOG 1234567890

THE QUICK BROWN FOX JUMPS OVER THE LAZY DOG

THE QUICK BROWN FOX JUMPS OVER THE LAZY DOG 1234567890

THE QUICK BROWN FOX JUMPS OVER THE LAZY DOG 1234567890

| | Egyptienne / Egyptian / Egyptienne **41** |
|---|---|

the quick brown fox jumps over the lazy dog

ITC **American Typewriter**
48
normal
medium
normal
N 020: 081 1151
Joel Kaden, Tony Stan 1974
International Typeface Corp.
H 1–x 0,73–k 1,00–p 0,26

the quick brown fox jumps over the lazy dog

**Antiqua 505**
58
normal
regular
normal
N 100: 081 0074
Arno Drescher 1955
Johannes Wagner GmbH
H 1–x 0,66–k 1,00–p 0,28

**Venus-Egyptienne**
1169
halbfett
medium
demi-gras

Sp 000: 081 1349
Fundición Tipográfica Neufville, S.A.
H 1–Q 1,09

the quick brown fox jumps over the lazy dog

**Media**
817
halbfett
medium
demi-gras
N 020: 081 2415
Jürgen Riebling
H. Berthold AG
H 1–x 0,76–k 1,00–p 0,25

the quick brown fox jumps over the lazy dog

ITC **Lubalin Graph**
794
normal
regular
normal
N 020: 081 1836
Lubalin, Dispigna, Sundwall 1974
International Typeface Corp.
H 1–x 0,76–k 1,00–p 0,25

the quick brown fox jumps over the lazy dog

ITC **Lubalin Graph**
795
normal Zierbuchstaben
regular swash letters
normal lettres ornées
Z 000: 081 1916
Lubalin, Dispigna, Sundwall 1974
International Typeface Corp.
H 1–x 0,76–k 1,00–p 0,25

the quick brown fox jumps over the lazy dog

**City**
388
halbfett
medium
demi-gras
N 100: 081 0357
Georg Trump 1930
H. Berthold AG
H 1–x 0,66–k 1,00–p 0,27

the quick brown fox jumps over the lazy dog

**Memphis**
830
halbfett
medium
demi-gras
N 100: 081 0892
Rudolf Wolf 1929
D. Stempel AG
H 1–x 0,63–k 1,00–p 0,16

## BERTHOLD HEADLINES V
Serifenbetonte Linear-Antiqua
Slab Serifs (Square Serifs)
Linéar Antiqua avec empattements (Mécanes)

THE QUICK BROWN FOX JUMPS OVER THE LAZY DOG 1234567890

QUICK BROWN FOX JUMPS OVER THE LAZY DOG 1234567890

THE QUICK BROWN FOX JUMPS OVER THE LAZY DOG 1234567890

THE QUICK BROWN FOX JUMPS OVER THE LAZY DOG 1234567890

THE QUICK BROWN FOX JUMPS OVER THE LAZY DOG 1234567890

THE QUICK BROWN FOX JUMPS OVER THE LAZY DOG

THE QUICK BROWN FOX JUMPS OVER THE LAZY DOG 1234567890

QUICK BROWN FOX JUMPS OVER THE LAZY DOG 1234567890

Egyptienne / Egyptian / Egyptienne  **41**

**Stymie**
1067
halbfett
bold
demi-gras
N 020: 081 1174
Morris F. Benton 1931
American Typefounders
H 1–x 0,60–k 1,00–p 0,26

the quick brown fox jumps over the lazy dog

**Girder Heavy**
620



N 100: 081 0671
H. Berthold AG
H 1–x 0,59–k 1,00–p 0,28

the quick brown fox jumps over the lazy dog

**Beton**
185
fett
bold
gras
N 100: 081 0161
Heinrich Jost 1931
Fundición Tipográfica Neufville, S.A.
H 1–x 0,63–k 1,00–p 0,26

the quick brown fox jumps over the lazy dog

**Media**
818
fett
bold
gras
N 100: 081 1732
Jürgen Riebling 1976
H. Berthold AG
H 1–x 0,75–k 1,00–p 0,31

the quick brown fox jumps over the lazy dog

ITC **Lubalin Graph**
796
halbfett
medium
demi-gras
N 020: 081 1839
Lubalin, Dispigna, Sundwall 1974
International Typeface Corp.
H 1–x 0,76–k 1,00–p 0,24

the quick brown fox jumps over the lazy dog

ITC **Lubalin Graph**
797
halbfett Zierbuchstaben
medium swash letters
demi-gras lettres ornées
Z 000: 081 1925
Lubalin, Dispigna, Sundwall 1974
International Typeface Corp.
H 1–x 0,76–k 1,00–p 0,24

the quick brown fox jumps over the lazy dog

**Rockwell**
997
halbfett
bold
demi-gras
N 100: 081 1095
1934
Monotype Corporation Ltd.
H 1–x 0,71–k 1,00–p 0,29

the quick brown fox jumps over the lazy dog

ITC **American Typewriter**
49
fett
bold
demi-gras
N 020: 081 1157
Joel Kaden, Tony Stan 1974
International Typeface Corp.
H 1–x 0,75–k 1,00–p 0,25

the quick brown fox jumps over the lazy dog

## BERTHOLD HEADLINES V

Serifenbetonte Linear-Antiqua
Slab Serifs (Square Serifs)
Linéar Antiqua avec empattements (Mécanes)

THE QUICK BROWN FOX JUMPS OVER THE LAZY DOG 1234567890

THE QUICK BROWN FOX JUMPS OVER THE LAZY DOG

THE QUICK BROWN FOX JUMPS OVER THE LAZY DOG 1234567890

QUICK BROWN FOX JUMPS OVER THE LAZY DOG 1234567890

THE QUICK BROWN FOX JUMPS OVER THE LAZY DOG 1234567890

QUICK BROWN FOX JUMPS OVER THE LAZY DOG 1234567890

QUICK BROWN FOX JUMPS OVER THE LAZY DOG 1234567890

QUICK BROWN FOX JUMPS OVER THE LAZY DOG 1234567890

| | Egyptienne / Egyptian / Egyptienne | **41** |

**the quick brown fox jumps over the lazy dog**

ITC **Lubalin Graph**
798
fett
bold
gras
N 020: 081 1841
Lubalin, Dispigna, Sundwall 1974
International Typeface Corp.
H 1–x 0,76–k 1,00–p 0,25

*the quick brown fox jumps over the lazy dog*

ITC **Lubalin Graph**
799
fett Zierbuchstaben
bold swash letters
gras lettres ornées
Z 000: 081 1926
Lubalin. Dispigna, Sundwall 1974
International Typeface Corp.
H 1–x 0,76–k 1,00–p 0,25

**the quick brown fox jumps over the lazy dog**

**City**
389
fett
bold
gras
N 100: 081 0358
Georg Trump 1930
H. Berthold AG
H 1–x 0,67–k 1,00–p 0,28

**the quick brown fox jumps over the lazy dog**

**Memphis**
831
fett
bold
gras
N 100: 081 0893
Rudolf Wolf 1933
D. Stempel AG
H 1–x 0,68–k 1,00–p 0,25

**the quick brown fox jumps over the lazy dog**

**Beton**
186
extrafett
extra bold
extra gras
N 100: 081 0163
Heinrich Jost 1930
Fundición Tipográfica Neufville, S.A.
H 1–x 0,66–k 1,00–p 0,28

**the quick brown fox jumps over the lazy dog**

**Stymie**
1069
Black
Black
Black
N 020: 081 1179
Morris F. Benton 1931
American Typefounders
H 1–x 0,69–k 1,01–p 0,28

**the quick brown fox jumps over the lazy dog**

**Rockwell**
998
fett
extra bold
gras
N 100: 081 1097
1934
Monotype Corporation Ltd.
H 1–x 0,70–k 1,00–p 0,30

**the quick brown fox jumps over the lazy dog**

**Quadra 57**
975

N 100: 081 1754
Karl-Heinz Domning 1974
H. Berthold AG
H 1–x 0,75–k 1,00–p 0,25

**BERTHOLD HEADLINES V**  
Serifenbetonte Linear-Antiqua  
Slab Serifs (Square Serifs)  
Linéar Antiqua avec empattements (Mécanes)

*THE QUICK BROWN FOX JUMPS OVER THE LAZY DOG 1234567890*

*THE QUICK BROWN FOX JUMPS OVER THE LAZY DOG 1234567890*

*THE QUICK BROWN FOX JUMPS OVER THE LAZY DOG*

*THE QUICK BROWN FOX JUMPS OVER THE LAZY DOG 1234567890*

***THE QUICK BROWN FOX JUMPS OVER THE LAZY DOG 1234567890***

*THE QUICK FOX BROWN JUMPS OVER THE LAZY DOG 1234567890*

***THE QUICK BROWN FOX JUMPS OVER THE LAZY DOG 1234567890***

Egyptienne, kursive
Egyptian, italic
Egyptienne, italique
**42**

*the quick brown fox jumps over the lazy dog*

**Stymie**
1064
kursiv mager
light italic
italique maigre
N 020: 081 1188
Morris F. Benton 1931
American Typefounders
H 1–x 0,61–k 1,00–p 0,25

*the quick brown fox jumps over the lazy dog*

**Rockwell**
996
kursiv mager
light italic
italique maigre
N 020: 081 2168
1934
Monotype Corporation Ltd.
H 1–x 0,71–k 1,00–p 0,31

*the quick brown fox jumps over the lazy dog*

**Venus-Egyptienne**
1170
kursiv halbfett
medium italic
italique demi-gras

N 000: 081 1350
Fundición Tipográfica Neufville, S.A.
H 1–x 0,66–k 1,00–p 0,24

*the quick brown fox jumps over the lazy dog*

**Stymie**
1066
kursiv
italic
italique
N 020: 081 1191
Morris F. Benton 1931
American Typefounders
H 1–x 0,61–k 1,02–p 0,25

*the quick brown fox jumps over the lazy dog*

**Stymie**
1068
kursiv halbfett
bold italic
italique demi-gras
N 020: 081 1196
Morris F. Benton 1931
American Typefounders
H 1–x 0,60–k 1,00–p 0,25

*the quick brown fox jumps over the lazy dog*

**Rockwell**
1344
kursiv
italic
italique
N 020: 081 0517
1934
Monotype Corporation Ltd.
H 1–x 0,70–k 1,00–p 0,30

***the quick brown fox jumps over the lazy dog***

**Rockwell**
1345
kursiv halbfett
bold italic
italique demi-gras
N 020: 081 0512
1934
Monotype Corporation Ltd.
H 1–x 0,70–k 1,00–p 0,30

## BERTHOLD HEADLINES V

Serifenbetonte Linear-Antiqua
Slab Serifs (Square Serifs)
Linéar Antiqua avec empattements (Mécanes)

THE QUICK BROWN FOX JUMPS OVER
THE LAZY DOG 1234567890

THE QUICK BROWN FOX JUMPS OVER
THE LAZY DOG 1234567890

THE QUICK BROWN FOX JUMPS OVER
THE LAZY DOG 1234567890

THE QUICK BROWN FOX JUMPS OVER
THE LAZY DOG 1234567890

THE QUICK BROWN FOX JUMPS OVER
THE LAZY DOG 1234567890

THE QUICK BROWN FOX JUMPS OVER
THE LAZY DOG 1234567890

THE QUICK BROWN FOX JUMPS OVER
THE LAZY DOG 1234567890

THE QUICK BROWN FOX JUMPS OVER
THE LAZY DOG 1234567890

Serifenbetonte Linear-Antiqua, schmale
Slab Serifs, condensed
Linéar Antique avec empattements, étroit

**43**

the quick brown fox jumps
over the lazy dog

ITC **American Typewriter**
50
schmalmager
light condensed
étroit maigre
N 020: 081 2231
Joel Kaden, Tony Stan 1974
International Typeface Corp.
H 1–x 0,70–k 1,00–p 0,27

the quick brown fox jumps
over the lazy dog

**Alexandria**
39

N 100: 081 0058
Haas'sche Schriftgießerei AG
H 1–x 0,66–k 1,00–p 0,31

the quick brown fox jumps
over the lazy dog

**Egizio**
463
schmal
condensed
étroit
N 100: 081 0456
Aldo Novarese 1955-1958
Societa Nebiolo S.p.A.
H 1–x 0,66–k 1,00–p 0,32

the quick brown fox jumps
over the lazy dog

**Clarendon**
394
schmalmager
light condensed
étroit maigre
N 100: 081 0368
1966
D. Stempel AG
H 1–x 0,73–k 1,00–p 0,27

the quick brown fox jumps
over the lazy dog

ITC **American Typewriter**
51
schmal
medium condensed
étroit
N 020: 081 2234
Joel Kaden, Tony Stan 1974
International Typeface Corp.
H 1–x 0,74–k 1,00–p 0,23

the quick brown fox jumps
over the lazy dog

**Telegraph**
1077

N 100: 081 1163
Karl-Heinz Domning 1971
H. Berthold AG
H 1–x 0,78–k 1,00–p 0,22

the quick brown fox jumps
over the lazy dog

**Rockwell**
1346
schmal
condensed
étroit
N 020: 081 0526
1934
Monotype Corporation Ltd.
H 1–x 0,69–k 1,00–p 0,24

the quick brown fox jumps
over the lazy dog

**Egyptienne**
464
schmalhalbfett
medium condensed
étroite demi-grasse

N 100: 081 1517
Lettergieterij Amsterdam
H 1–x 0,75–k 1,03–p 0,25

## BERTHOLD HEADLINES V

Serifenbetonte Linear-Antiqua
Slab Serifs (Square Serifs)
Linéar Antiqua avec empattements (Mécanes)

THE QUICK BROWN FOX JUMPS OVER
THE LAZY DOG 1234567890

THE QUICK BROWN FOX JUMPS OVER
THE LAZY DOG 1234567890

THE QUICK BROWN FOX JUMPS OVER
THE LAZY DOG 1234567890

THE QUICK BROWN FOX JUMPS OVER
THE LAZY DOG 1234567890

THE QUICK BROWN FOX JUMPS OVER
THE LAZY DOG 1234567890

THE QUICK BROWN FOX JUMPS OVER
THE LAZY DOG 1234567890

THE QUICK BROWN FOX JUMPS OVER
THE LAZY DOG 1234567890

THE QUICK BROWN FOX JUMPS OVER
THE LAZY DOG 1234567890

| | |
|---|---|
| | Serifenbetonte Linear-Antiqua, schmale **43**<br>Slab Serifs, condensed<br>Linéar Antique avec empattements, étroit |

**the quick brown fox jumps
over the lazy dog**

Schadow-Antiqua
1016
schmalfett
bold condensed
étroit gras
N 000: 081 1111
Georg Trump 1945
Johannes Wagner
H 1–x 0,73–k 1,00–p 0,28

**the quick brown fox jumps
over the lazy dog**

Clarendon
395
schmalfett
bold condensed
étroit gras
N 100: 081 0370
D. Stempel AG
H 1–x 0,78–k 1,03–p 0,25

**the quick brown fox jumps
over the lazy dog**

Rockwell
1347
schmalhalbfett
bold condensed
étroit demi-gras
N 020: 081 1571
1934
Monotype Corporation Ltd.
H 1–x 0,70–k 1,00–p 0,30

**the quick brown fox jumps
over the lazy dog**

Melior
827
schmalfett
bold condensed
étroit gras
N 100: 081 0889
Hermann Zapf 1953
D. Stempel AG
H 1–x 0,78–k 1,00–p 0,25

**the quick brown fox jumps
over the lazy dog**

Nova
895

N 100: 081 0959
Photoscript Ltd.
H 1–x 0,75–k 1,03–p 0,25

**the quick brown fox jumps
over the lazy dog**

ITC **American Typewriter**
52
schmalfett
bold condensed
étroit gras
N 020: 081 2237
Joel Kaden, Tony Stan 1974
International Typeface Corp.
H 1–x 0,74–k 1,00–p 0,27

**the quick brown fox jumps
over the lazy dog**

**Whitin Black**
1211
schmal
condensed
étroit
N 100: 081 1394
Morris F. Benton 1904
American Typefounders
H 1–x 0,75–k 1,00–p 0,22

**the quick brown fox jumps
over the lazy dog**

**Egyptienne**
465
schmalfett
bold condensed
étroite grasse
N 100: 081 0457
19. Jh.
Lettergieterij Amsterdam
H 1–x 0,73–k 1,00–p 0,20

**BERTHOLD HEADLINES V** — Serifenbetonte Linear-Antiqua / Slab Serifs (Square Serifs) / Linéar Antiqua avec empattements (Mécanes)

THE QUICK BROWN FOX JUMPS OVER THE LAZY DOG 1234567890

**BERTHOLD HEADLINES V** — Serifenbetonte Linear-Antiqua / Slab Serifs (Square Serifs) / Linéar Antiqua avec empattements (Mécanes)

OVER THE LAZY DOG 1234567890

FOX JUMPS OVER THE LAZY DOG 1234567890

BROWN FOX JUMPS OVER THE LAZY DOG 1234567890

**BERTHOLD HEADLINES V** — Serifenbetonte Linear-Antiqua / Slab Serifs (Square Serifs) / Linéar Antiqua avec empattements (Mécanes)

THE QUICK BROWN FOX JUMPS OVER THE LAZY DOG 1234567890

THE QUICK BROWN FOX JUMPS OVER THE LAZY DOG 1234567890

**43** Serifenbetonte Linear-Antiqua, schmale / Slab Serifs, condensed / Linéar Antique avec empattements, étroit

the quick brown fox jumps over the lazy dog

**Beton**
187
schmalfett
bold condensed
étroit gras
N 100: 081 1587
Heinrich Jost 1936
Fundición Tipográfica Neufville, S.A.
H 1–x 0,75–k 1,03–p 0,28

**44** Serifenbetonte Linear-Antiqua, breite / Slab Serifs, extended / Linéar Antique avec empattements, large

brown fox jumps over the lazy dog

**Egyptienne**
466
breithalbfett
medium extended
large demi-grasse

N 100: 081 1518
Lettergieterij Amsterdam
H 1–x 0,75–k 1,00–p 0,28

brown fox jumps over the lazy dog

**Clarendon**
396
breitfett
bold extended
large gras
N 100: 081 1737
1964
D. Stempel AG
H 1–x 0,72–k 1,00–p 0,37

quick brown fox jumps over the lazy dog

**Egyptienne**
467
breitfett
bold extended
large grasse

N 100: 081 0461
Lettergieterij Amsterdam
H 1–x 0,75–k 1,00–p 0,22

**45** Italienne / Italienne / Italienne

the quick brown fox jumps over the lazy dog

**Datonga**
435

N 100: 081 1760
Karl-Heinz Domning 1974
H. Berthold AG
H 1–x 0,75–k 1,00–p 0,25

the quick brown fox jumps over the lazy dog

**Circo**
385

N 100: 081 0351
Jan Solpera 1971
H. Berthold AG
H 1–x 0,75–k 1,00–p 0,38

243

# BERTHOLD HEADLINES V

Serifenbetonte Linear-Antiqua
Slab Serifs (Square Serifs)
Linéar Antiqua avec empattements (Mécanes)

THE QUICK BROWN FOX JUMPS OVER
THE LAZY DOG 1234567890

THE QUICK BROWN FOX JUMPS OVER
THE LAZY DOG 1234567890

THE QUICK BROWN FOX JUMPS OVER
THE LAZY DOG 1234567890

THE QUICK BROWN FOX JUMPS OVER
THE LAZY DOG 1234567890

*THE QUICK BROWN FOX JUMPS OVER*
*THE LAZY DOG 1234567890*

THE QUICK BROWN FOX JUMPS OVER
THE LAZY DOG 1234567890

BROWN FOX JUMPS
OVER DOG 1234567890

Italienne  
Italienne  
Italienne  
**45**

**Old Towne No. 536**
902

the quick brown fox jumps
over the lazy dog

N 100: 081 0965
American Typefounders
H 1–x 0,81–k 1,00–p 0,22

**Hidalgo**
673

V 000: 081 0759
Stefan Schlesinger 1939
Lettergieterij Amsterdam
H 1–Q 1,09

**Pro Arte**
972

Sp 000: 081 1063
Max Miedinger 1954
Haas'sche Schriftgießerei AG
H 1–Q 1,16

**Churchward Maricia**
375
normal
regular
normal
N 100: 081 0334
Joseph Churchward 1972
H. Berthold AG
H 1–x 0,69–k 1,00–p 0,37

the quick brown fox jumps
over the lazy dog

**Churchward Maricia**
376
kursiv
italic
italique
N 100: 081 1447
Joseph Churchward 1972
H. Berthold AG
H 1–x 0,69–k 1,00–p 0,37

the quick brown fox jumps
over the lazy dog

**Umbra 27**
1122

V 000: 081 1225
Karl-Heinz Domning 1972
H. Berthold AG
H 1–Q 1,0

**Italienne**
703
breit
extended
large

quick brown fox jumps
over the lazy dog

N 100: 081 1541
H. Berthold AG
H 1–x 0,69–k 1,00–p 0,34

**BERTHOLD HEADLINES V** — Serifenbetonte Linear-Antiqua / Slab Serifs (Square Serifs) / Linéar Antiqua avec empattements (Mécanes)

THE QUICK BROWN FOX JUMPS OVER
THE LAZY DOG 1234567890

THE QUICK BROWN FOX JUMPS OVER
THE LAZY DOG 1234567890

*THE QUICK BROWN FOX JUMPS OVER*
*THE LAZY DOG 1234567890*

OVER THE LAZY
DOG 1234567890

**BERTHOLD HEADLINES V** — Serifenbetonte Linear-Antiqua / Slab Serifs (Square Serifs) / Linéar Antiqua avec empattements (Mécanes)

THE QUICK BROWN FOX JUMPS OVER
THE LAZY DOG 1234567890

THE QUICK BROWN FOX JUMPS OVER
THE LAZY DOG 1234567890

THE QUICK BROWN FOX JUMPS OVER
THE LAZY DOG 1234567890

## 46
Tuscan
Tuscan
Tuscan

**Thunderbird**
1084
extraschmal
extra condensed
extra étroit

V 000: 081 1166
American Typefounders
H 1–Q 1,16

the quick brown fox jumps
over the lazy dog

**Churchward Tua**
383
normal
regular
normal
N 100: 081 0332
Joseph Churchward 1972
H. Berthold AG
H 1–x 0,69–k 1,00–p 0,37

the quick brown fox jumps
over the lazy dog

**Churchward Tua**
384
kursiv
italic
italique
N 000: 081 1469
Joseph Churchward 1972
H. Berthold AG
H 1–x 0,69–k 1,00–p 0,37

**Thunderbird**
1083
normal
regular
normal

V 000: 081 1164
American Typefounders
H 1–Q 1,31

## 47
Latin
Latin
Latin

**Renaissance**
988
schmal
condensed
étroit

the quick brown fox jumps
over the lazy dog

N 100: 081 1083
Haas'sche Schriftgießerei AG
H 1–x 0,75–k 1,00–p 0,25

**Diador**
439

the quick brown fox jumps
over the lazy dog

N 100: 081 0424
Karl-Heinz Domning 1971
H. Berthold AG
H 1–x 0,75–k 1,06–p 0,31

**Latin**
751
schmalfett
bold condensed
étroit gras

the quick brown fox jumps
over the lazy dog

N 100: 081 0833
Stephenson Blake & Company Ltd.
H 1–x 0,69–k 1,00–p 0,31

**BERTHOLD HEADLINES V**  
Serifenbetonte Linear-Antiqua  
Slab Serifs (Square Serifs)  
Linéar Antiqua avec empattements (Mécanes)

QUICK BROWN FOX JUMPS OVER THE LAZY DOG 1234567890

QUICK BROWN FOX JUMPS 1234567890

**BERTHOLD HEADLINES V**  
Serifenbetonte Linear-Antiqua  
Slab Serifs (Square Serifs)  
Linéar Antiqua avec empattements (Mécanes)

THE QUICK BROWN FOX JUMPS OVER THE LAZY DOG 1234567890

THE QUICK BROWN FOX JUMPS OVER THE LAZY DOG 1234567890

THE QUICK BROWN FOX JUMPS OVER THE LAZY DOG 1234567890

## 47 Latin / Latin / Latin

**the quick brown fox jumps over the lazy dog**

**Latin**
750
fett
bold
gras

N 100: 081 0832
Stephenson Blake & Company Ltd.
H 1–x 0,75–k 1,00–p 0,25

**quick brown fox jumps over dog**

**Latin Wide**
752

N 100: 081 0838
Stephenson Blake & Company Ltd.
H 1–x 0,72–k 1,03–p 0,34

## 48 Sonstige / Others / Autres

the quick brown fox jumps over the lazy dog

ITC **Italia**
697
Buch
book
romain labeur
N 020: 081 2383
Colin Brignall 1977
International Typeface Corp.
H 1–x 0,68–k 1,04–p 0,29

the quick brown fox jumps over the lazy dog

ITC **Italia**
698
normal
medium
normal
N 020: 081 2384
Colin Brignall 1977
International Typeface Corp.
H 1–x 0,68–k 1,03–p 0,31

**the quick brown fox jumps over the lazy dog**

ITC **Italia**
699
halbfett
bold
demi-gras
N 020: 081 2385
Colin Brignall 1977
International Typeface Corp.
H 1–x 0,68–k 1,03–p 0,30

# BERTHOLD HEADLINES VI

**49-70**

*Serifenlose Linear-Antiqua*
*Sans Serifs (Grotesques)*
*Linéar Antiqua sans empattements (Linéales)*

## BERTHOLD HEADLINES VI
Serifenlose Linear-Antiqua
Sans Serifs (Grotesques)
Linéar Antiqua sans empattements (Linéales)

THE QUICK BROWN FOX JUMPS OVER
THE LAZY DOG 1234567890

THE QUICK BROWN FOX JUMPS OVER
THE LAZY DOG

THE QUICK BROWN FOX JUMPS OVER
THE LAZY DOG 1234567890

QUICK BROWN FOX JUMPS OVER
THE LAZY DOG 1234567890

QUICK BROWN FOX JUMPS OVER
THE LAZY DOG

THE QUICK BROWN FOX JUMPS OVER
THE LAZY DOG 1234567890

THE QUICK BROWN FOX JUMPS OVER
THE LAZY DOG

THE QUICK BROWN FOX JUMPS OVER
THE LAZY DOG 1234567890

the quick brown fox jumps over the lazy dog

ITC **Serif Gothic**
1023
mager
light
maigre
N 020: 081 2070
Herb Lubalin, Antonio Dispigna 1974
International Typeface Corp.
H 1–x 0,68–k 1,00–p 0,32

the quick brown fox jumps over the lazy dog

ITC **Serif Gothic**
1024
mager Zierbuchstaben
light swash letters
maigre lettres ornées
Z 000: 081 2071
Herb Lubalin, Antonio Dispigna 1974
International Typeface Corp.
H 1–x 0,68–k 1,00–p 0,35

the quick brown fox jumps over the lazy dog

ITC **Quorum**
980
mager
light
maigre
N 020: 081 2373
Ray Baker 1977
International Typeface Corp.
H 1–x 0,75–k 1,02–p 0,30

the quick brown fox jumps over the lazy dog

ITC **Newtext**
870
mager
light
maigre
N 020: 081 2096
Ray Baker 1974
International Typeface Corp.
H 1–x 0,70–k 1,00–p 0,22

the quick brown fox jumps over the lazy dog

ITC **Newtext**
871
mager Zierbuchstaben
light swash letters
maigre lettres ornées
Z 000: 081 2108 *
Ray Baker 1974
International Typeface Corp.
H 1–x 0,70–k 1,00–p 0,22

the quick brown fox jumps over the lazy dog

ITC **Serif Gothic**
1025
normal
regular
normal
N 100: 081 1512
Herb Lubalin, Antonio Dispigna 1974
International Typeface Corp.
H 1–x 0,68–k 1,00–p 0,31

the quick brown fox jumps over the lazy dog

ITC **Serif Gothic**
1026
normal Zierbuchstaben
regular swash letters
normal lettres ornées
Z 000: 081 2028
Herb Lubalin, Antonio Dispigna 1974
International Typeface Corp.
H 1–x 0,68–k 1,00–p 0,34

the quick brown fox jumps over the lazy dog

ITC **Quorum**
981
Buch
book
romain labeur
N 020: 081 2374
Ray Baker 1977
International Typeface Corp.
H 1–x 0,75–k 1,01–p 0,29

**BERTHOLD HEADLINES VI**  
Serifenlose Linear-Antiqua  
Sans Serifs (Grotesques)  
Linéar Antiqua sans empattements (Linéales)

QUICK BROWN FOX JUMPS OVER
THE LAZY DOG 1234567890

QUICK BROWN FOX JUMPS OVER
THE LAZY DOG

THE QUICK BROWN FOX JUMPS OVER
THE LAZY DOG 1234567890

THE QUICK BROWN FOX JUMPS OVER
THE LAZY DOG 1234567890

THE QUICK BROWN FOX JUMPS OVER
THE LAZY DOG 1234567890

THE QUICK BROWN FOX JUMPS OVER
THE LAZY DOG

QUICK BROWN FOX JUMPS OVER
THE LAZY DOG 1234567890

QUICK BROWN FOX JUMPS OVER
THE LAZY DOG

the quick brown fox jumps over the lazy dog

ITC **Newtext**
874
Buch
book
romain labeur
N 020: 081 2097
Ray Baker 1974
International Typeface Corp.
H 1–x 0,70–k 1,00–p 0,21

the quick brown fox jumps over the lazy dog

ITC **Newtext**
875
Buch Zierbuchstaben
book swash letters
romain labeur lettres ornées
Z 000: 081 2108 *
Ray Baker 1974
International Typeface Corp.
H 1–x 0,70–k 1,00p 0,21

the quick brown fox jumps over the lazy dog

ITC **Quorum**
982
normal
regular
normal
N 020: 081 2375
Ray Baker 1977
International Typeface Corp.
H 1–x 0,75–k 1,01–p 0,30

the quick brown fox jumps over the lazy dog

ITC **Friz Quadrata**
540
normal
regular
normal
N 020: 081 1810
Ernst Friz 1973 (1965)
International Typeface Corp.
H 1–x 0,69–k 1,03–p 0,31

the quick brown fox jumps over the lazy dog

ITC **Serif Gothic**
1027
fett
bold
gras
N 100: 081 1513
Herb Lubalin, Antonio Dispigna 1974
International Typeface Corp.
H 1–x 0,68–k 1,00–p 0,31

the quick brown fox jumps over the lazy dog

ITC **Serif Gothic**
1028
fett Zierbuchstaben
bold swash letters
gras lettres ornées
Z 000: 081 2029
Herb Lubalin, Antonio Dispigna 1974
International Typeface Corp.
H 1–x 0,68–k 1,00–p 0,34

the quick brown fox jumps over the lazy dog

ITC **Newtext**
878
normal
regular
normal
N 020: 081 2100
Ray Baker 1974
International Typeface Corp.
H 1–x 0,70–k 1,00–p 0,21

the quick brown fox jumps over the lazy dog

ITC **Newtext**
879
normal Zierbuchstaben
regular swash letters
normal lettres ornées
Z 000: 081 2108 *
Ray Baker 1974
International Typeface Corp.
H 1–x 0,70–k 1,00–p 0,21

**BERTHOLD HEADLINES VI** — Serifenlose Linear-Antiqua / Sans Serifs (Grotesques) / Linéar Antiqua sans empattements (Linéales)

THE QUICK BROWN FOX JUMPS OVER THE LAZY DOG 1234567890

THE QUICK BROWN FOX JUMPS OVER THE LAZY DOG

THE QUICK BROWN FOX JUMPS OVER THE LAZY DOG 1234567890

QUICK BROWN FOX JUMPS OVER THE LAZY DOG 1234567890

QUICK BROWN FOX JUMPS OVER THE LAZY DOG

THE QUICK BROWN FOX JUMPS OVER THE LAZY DOG 1234567890

THE QUICK BROWN FOX JUMPS OVER THE LAZY DOG

THE QUICK BROWN FOX JUMPS OVER THE LAZY DOG 1234567890

Serifs / Serifs / Serifs — 49

the quick brown fox jumps over the lazy dog

ITC **Serif Gothic**
1029
extrafett
extra bold
extra gras
N 100: 081 1902
Herb Lubalin, Antonio Dispigna 1974
International Typeface Corp.
H 1–x 0,69–k 1,00–p 0,32

the quick brown fox jumps over the lazy dog

ITC **Serif Gothic**
1030
extrafett Zierbuchstaben
extra bold swash letters
extra gras lettres ornées
Z 000: 081 2030
Herb Lubalin, Antonio Dispigna 1974
International Typeface Corp.
H 1–x 0,69–k 1,00–p 0,35

the quick brown fox jumps over the lazy dog

ITC **Quorum**
983
halbfett
bold
demi-gras
N 020: 081 2376
Ray Baker 1977
International Typeface Corp.
H 1–x 0,75–k 1,02–p 0,29

the quick brown fox jumps over the lazy dog

ITC **Newtext**
882
halbfett
demi-bold
demi-gras
N 020: 081 2104
Ray Baker 1974
International Typeface Corp.
H 1–x 0,70–k 1,00–p 0,21

the quick brown fox jumps over the lazy dog

ITC **Newtext**
883
halbfett Zierbuchstaben
demi-bold swash letters
demi-gras lettres ornées
Z 000: 081 2108 ✱
Ray Baker 1974
International Typeface Corp.
H 1–x 0,70–k 1,00–p 0,21

the quick brown fox jumps over the lazy dog

ITC **Serif Gothic**
1031
ultrafett
heavy
ultra gras
N 100: 081 1908
Herb Lubalin, Antonio Dispigna 1974
International Typeface Corp.
H 1–x 0,70–k 1,00–p 0,30

the quick brown fox jumps over the lazy dog

ITC **Serif Gothic**
1032
ultrafett Zierbuchstaben
heavy swash letters
ultra gras lettres ornées
Z 000: 081 2031
Herb Lubalin, Antonio Dispigna 1974
International Typeface Corp.
H 1–x 0,70–k 1,00–p 0,33

the quick brown fox jumps over the lazy dog

ITC **Friz Quadrata**
541
fett
bold
gras
N 020: 081 1815
Vic Caruso 1973
International Typeface Corp.
H 1–x 0,70–k 1,03–p 0,30

**BERTHOLD HEADLINES VI** — Serifenlose Linear-Antiqua / Sans Serifs (Grotesques) / Linéar Antiqua sans empattements (Linéales)

# THE QUICK BROWN FOX JUMPS OVER THE LAZY DOG 1234567890

# THE QUICK BROWN FOX JUMPS OVER THE LAZY DOG 1234567890

# THE QUICK BROWN FOX JUMPS OVER THE LAZY DOG

# THE QUICK BROWN FOX JUMPS OVER THE LAZY DOG 1234567890

**BERTHOLD HEADLINES VI** — Serifenlose Linear-Antiqua / Sans Serifs (Grotesques) / Linéar Antiqua sans empattements (Linéales)

# QUICK BROWN FOX JUMPS OVER THE LAZY DOG 1234567890

# QUICK BROWN FOX JUMPS OVER THE LAZY DOG

# QUICK BROWN FOX JUMPS OVER THE LAZY DOG 1234567890

## Serifs / Serifs / Serifs — 49

**the quick brown fox jumps over the lazy dog**

ITC **Quorum Black**
984
N 020: 081 2377
Ray Baker 1977
International Typeface Corp.
H 1–x 0,75–k 1,03–p 0,29

**the quick brown fox jumps over the lazy dog**

ITC **Serif Gothic Black**
1033
N 010: 081 2074
Herb Lubalin, Antonio Dispigna 1974
International Typeface Corp.
H 1–x 0,71–k 1,00–p 0,29

**the quick brown fox jumps over the lazy dog**

ITC **Serif Gothic Black**
1034
Zierbuchstaben
swash letters
lettres ornées
Z 000: 081 2075
Herb Lubalin, Antonio Dispigna 1974
International Typeface Corp.
H 1–x 0,21–k 1,00–p 0,32

**the quick brown fox jumps over the lazy dog**

**Flange**
513
fett
bold
gras
N 020: 081 0025
Leslie Usherwood
Typsettra
H 1–x 0,85–k 1,11–p 0,27

## Serifs, kursive / Serifs, italic / Serifs, italique — 50

*the quick brown fox jumps over the lazy dog*

ITC **Newtext**
872
kursiv mager
light italic
italique maigre
N 020: 081 2098
Ray Baker 1974
International Typeface Corp.
H 1–x 0,70–k 1,00–p 0,23

*the quick brown fox jumps over the lazy dog*

ITC **Newtext**
873
kursiv mager Zierbuchstaben
light italic swash letters
italique maigre lettres ornées
Z 000: 081 2102 ✻
Ray Baker 1974
International Typeface Corp.
H 1–x 0,70–k 1,00–p 0,23

*the quick brown fox jumps over the lazy dog*

ITC **Newtext**
876
Buch kursiv
book italic
italique romain labeur
N 020: 081 2099
Ray Baker 1974
International Typeface Corp.
H 1–x 0,70–k 1,00–p 0,23

**BERTHOLD HEADLINES VI** — Serifenlose Linear-Antiqua / Sans Serifs (Grotesques) / Linéar Antiqua sans empattements (Linéales)

QUICK BROWN FOX JUMPS OVER THE LAZY DOG

QUICK BROWN FOX JUMPS OVER THE LAZY DOG 1234567890

QUICK BROWN FOX JUMPS OVER THE LAZY DOG

QUICK BROWN FOX JUMPS OVER THE LAZY DOG 1234567890

QUICK BROWN FOX JUMPS OVER THE LAZY DOG

**BERTHOLD HEADLINES VI** — Serifenlose Linear-Antiqua / Sans Serifs (Grotesques) / Linéar Antiqua sans empattements (Linéales)

THE QUICK BROWN FOX JUMPS OVER THE LAZY DOG 1234567890

THE QUICK BROWN FOX JUMPS OVER THE LAZY DOG 1234567890

## 50 Serifs, kursive / Serifs, italic / Serifs, italique

*the quick brown fox jumps over the lazy dog*

ITC **Newtext**
877
Buch kursiv Zierbuchstaben
book italic swash letters
italique romain labeur lettres ornées
Z 000: 081 2102 ✻
Ray Baker 1974
International Typeface Corp.
H 1–x 0,70–k 1,00–p 0,23

*the quick brown fox jumps over the lazy dog*

ITC **Newtext**
880
kursiv
italic
italique
N 020: 081 2107
Ray Baker 1974
International Typeface Corp.
H 1–x 0,70–k 1,00–p 0,23

*the quick brown fox jumps over the lazy dog*

ITC **Newtext**
881
kursiv Zierbuchstaben
italic swash letters
italique lettres ornées
Z 000: 081 2102 ✻
Ray Baker 1974
International Typeface Corp.
H 1–x 0,70–k 1,00–p 0,23

*the quick brown fox jumps over the lazy dog*

ITC **Newtext**
884
kursiv halbfett
demi-bold italic
italique demi-gras
N 020: 081 2101
Ray Baker 1974
International Typeface Corp.
H 1–x 0,70–k 1,00–p 0,21

*the quick brown fox jumps over the lazy dog*

ITC **Newtext**
885
kursiv halbfett Zierbuchstaben
demi-bold italic swash letters
italique demi-gras lettres ornées
Z 000: 081 2102 ✻
Ray Baker 1974
International Typeface Corp.
H 1–x 0,70–k 1,00–p 0,21

## 51 Lapidar / Lapidar / Lapidaire

the quick brown fox jumps over the lazy dog

ITC **Eras**
479
mager
light
maigre
N 020: 081 1930
Albert Boton 1976 (Boton, Hollenstein 1968)
International Typeface Corp.
H 1–x 0,74–k 1,00–p 0,33

the quick brown fox jumps over the lazy dog

STEMPEL **Kabel**
722
leicht
light
maigre
N 100: 081 0806
Rudolf Koch 1927
D. Stempel AG
H 1–x 0,51–k 1,00–p 0,21

**BERTHOLD HEADLINES VI**    Serifenlose Linear-Antiqua
Sans Serifs (Grotesques)
Linéar Antiqua sans empattements (Linéales)

THE QUICK BROWN FOX JUMPS OVER
THE LAZY DOG 1234567890

THE QUICK BROWN FOX JUMPS OVER
THE LAZY DOG 1234567890

THE QUICK BROWN FOX JUMPS OVER
THE LAZY DOG 1234567890

THE QUICK BROWN FOX JUMPS OVER
THE LAZY DOG 1234567890

THE QUICK BROWN FOX JUMPS OVER
THE LAZY DOG 1234567890

THE QUICK BROWN FOX JUMPS OVER
THE LAZY DOG 1234567890

THE QUICK BROWN FOX JUMPS OVER
THE LAZY DOG 1234567890

THE QUICK BROWN FOX JUMPS OVER
THE LAZY DOG 1234567890

Lapidar
Lapidar
Lapidaire
**51**

the quick brown fox jumps
over the lazy dog

**Gill Sans**
609
mager
light
maigre
N 100: 081 0661
Eric Gill 1928-1930
Monotype Corporation Ltd.
H 1–x 0,66–k 1,00–p 0,35

the quick brown fox jumps
over the lazy dog

ORIGINAL HOLLENSTEIN **Eras**
478

N 100: 081 0482
A. Hollenstein, Albert Boton 1968
H. Berthold AG
H 1–x 0,74–k 1,00–p 0,32

the quick brown fox jumps
over the lazy dog

ITC **Eras**
480
Buch
book
romain labeur
N 020: 081 1931
Albert Boton 1976
International Typeface Corp.
H 1–x 0,74–k 1,00–p 0,33

the quick brown fox jumps
over the lazy dog

ITC **Kabel**
715
Buch
book
romain labeur
N 020: 081 2341
Photo-Lettering Inc. 1976
(Rudolf Koch 1927-1930)
H 1–x 0,72–k 1,03–p 0,28

the quick brown fox jumps
over the lazy dog

**Optima**
904
normal
regular
normal
N 100: 081 0969
Hermann Zapf 1958
D. Stempel AG
H 1–x 0,68–k 1,09–p 0,40

the quick brown fox jumps
over the lazy dog

**Bernhard Gothic**
164
mager
light
maigre
N 100: 081 1794
Lucian Bernhard 1930
American Typefounders
H 1–x 0,55–k 1,02–p 0,28

the quick brown fox jumps
over the lazy dog

**Syntax**
1072
normal
regular
normal
N 020: 081 2402
Hans Eduard Meyer 1968
D. Stempel AG
H 1–x 0,72–k 1,08–p 0,33

the quick brown fox jumps
over the lazy dog

**Gill Sans**
610
normal
regular
normal
N 100: 081 0662
Eric Gill 1928-1930
Monotype Corporation Ltd.
H 1–x 0,65–k 1,00–p 0,37

## BERTHOLD HEADLINES VI
Serifenlose Linear-Antiqua
Sans Serifs (Grotesques)
Linéar Antiqua sans empattements (Linéales)

THE QUICK BROWN FOX JUMPS OVER
THE LAZY DOG 1234567890

THE QUICK BROWN FOX JUMPS OVER
THE LAZY DOG 1234567890

THE QUICK BROWN FOX JUMPS OVER
THE LAZY DOG 1234567890

THE QUICK BROWN FOX JUMPS OVER
THE LAZY DOG 1234567890

THE QUICK BROWN FOX JUMPS OVER
THE LAZY DOG 1234567890

THE QUICK BROWN FOX JUMPS OVER
THE LAZY DOG 1234567890

THE QUICK BROWN FOX JUMPS OVER
THE LAZY DOG 1234567890

THE QUICK BROWN FOX JUMPS OVER
THE LAZY DOG 1234567890

| | Lapidar / Lapidar / Lapidaire | **51** |

**ITC Eras**
481
normal
medium
normal
N 020: 081 1932
Albert Boton 1976
International Typeface Corp.
H 1–x 0,74–k 1,00–p 0,32

the quick brown fox jumps
over the lazy dog

**Pascal**
914

N 100: 081 0998
José Mendoza y Almeida 1960
Lettergieterij Amsterdam
H 1–x 0,72–k 1,06–p 0,28

the quick brown fox jumps
over the lazy dog

**Vega-Grotesk**
1151

N 100: 081 1317
1965
Czech Art
H 1–x 0,75–k 1,09–p 0,34

the quick brown fox jumps
over the lazy dog

**Bernhard Gothic**
165
halbfett
medium
demi-gras
N 100: 081 1520
Lucian Bernhard 1929
American Typefounders
H 1–x 0,56–k 1,03–p 0,28

the quick brown fox jumps
over the lazy dog

**Optima**
1290
kräftig
medium
fort
N 020: 081 0221
Hermann Zapf 1968
D. Stempel AG
H 1–x 0,71–k 1,08–p 0,38

the quick brown fox jumps
over the lazy dog

**Lydian**
802
normal
regular
normal
N 100: 081 0871
Warren Chappell 1938
American Typefounders
H 1–x 0,66–k 1,00–p 0,34

the quick brown fox jumps
over the lazy dog

**Clearface Gothic**
406
normal
regular
normal
N 020: 081 2281
Morris F. Benton 1908
American Typefounders
H 1–x 0,70–k 1,00–p 0,26

the quick brown fox jumps
over the lazy dog

**STEMPEL Kabel**
723
grob
medium
demi-gras
N 100: 081 0812
Rudolf Koch 1928
D. Stempel AG
H 1–x 0,54–k 1,00–p 0,23

the quick brown fox jumps
over the lazy dog

**BERTHOLD HEADLINES VI** — Serifenlose Linear-Antiqua / Sans Serifs (Grotesques) / Linéar Antiqua sans empattements (Linéales)

THE QUICK BROWN FOX JUMPS OVER
THE LAZY DOG 1234567890

THE QUICK BROWN FOX JUMPS OVER
THE LAZY DOG 1234567890

THE QUICK BROWN FOX JUMPS OVER
THE LAZY DOG 1234567890

THE QUICK BROWN FOX JUMPS OVER
THE LAZY DOG 1234567890

THE QUICK BROWN FOX JUMPS OVER
THE LAZY DOG 1234567890

THE QUICK BROWN FOX JUMPS OVER
THE LAZY DOG 1234567890

THE QUICK BROWN FOX JUMPS OVER
THE LAZY DOG 1234567890

THE QUICK BROWN FOX JUMPS OVER
THE LAZY DOG 1234567890

| | Lapidar / Lapidar / Lapidaire **51** |

**the quick brown fox jumps
over the lazy dog**

ITC **Kabel**
716
normal
medium
normal
N 020: 081 2342
Photo-Lettering Inc. 1976
International Typeface Corp.
H 1–x 0,75–k 1,03–p 0,26

**the quick brown fox jumps
over the lazy dog**

**Gesh Introduction**
607

N 100: 081 1480
Gerhard Schwekendick 1972
H. Berthold AG
H 1–x 0,72–k 1,00–p 0,40

**the quick brown fox jumps
over the lazy dog**

**Syntax**
1074
halbfett
medium
demi-gras
N 020: 081 2404
Hans Eduard Meyer 1969
D. Stempel AG
H 1–x 0,73–k 1,08–p 0,33

**the quick brown fox jumps
over the lazy dog**

ITC **Kabel**
717
halbfett
demi
demi-gras
N 020: 081 2349
Photo-Lettering Inc. 1976
(Rudolf Koch 1927–1930)
H 1–x 0,75–k 1,01–p 0,25

**the quick brown fox jumps
over the lazy dog**

**Gill Sans**
611
halbfett
bold
demi-gras
N 100: 081 0665
Eric Gill 1928-1930
Monotype Corporation Ltd.
H 1–x 0,65–k 1,00–p 0,37

**the quick brown fox jumps
over the lazy dog**

ITC **Eras**
482
halbfett
demi-bold
demi-gras
N 020: 081 1934
Albert Boton 1976
International Typeface Corp.
H 1–x 0,74–k 1,00–p 0,33

**the quick brown fox jumps
over the lazy dog**

**Optima**
906
halbfett
bold
demi-gras
N 100: 081 0982
Hermann Zapf 1958
D. Stempel AG
H 1–x 0,70–k 1,10–p 0,38

**the quick brown fox jumps
over the lazy dog**

**Bernhard Gothic**
166
fett
heavy
gras
N 100: 081 1795
Lucian Bernhard 1930
American Typefounders
H 1–x 0,59–k 1,06–p 0,29

**BERTHOLD HEADLINES VI**  Serifenlose Linear-Antiqua
Sans Serifs (Grotesques)
Linéar Antiqua sans empattements (Linéales)

THE QUICK BROWN FOX JUMPS OVER
THE LAZY DOG 1234567890

THE QUICK BROWN FOX JUMPS OVER
THE LAZY DOG 1234567890

THE QUICK BROWN FOX JUMPS OVER
THE LAZY DOG 1234567890

THE QUICK BROWN FOX JUMPS OVER
THE LAZY DOG 1234567890

THE QUICK BROWN FOX JUMPS OVER
THE LAZY DOG 1234567890

THE QUICK BROWN FOX JUMPS OVER
THE LAZY DOG 1234567890

QUICK BROWN FOX JUMPS OVER
THE LAZY DOG 1234567890

THE QUICK BROWN FOX JUMPS OVER
THE LAZY DOG 1234567890

Lapidar  
Lapidar  
Lapidaire  **51**

the quick brown fox jumps  
over the lazy dog

**ITC Kabel**  
718  
fett  
bold  
gras  
N 020: 081 2343  
Photo-Lettering Inc. 1976  
(Rudolf Koch 1927–1930)  
H 1–x 0,75–k 1,01–p 0,26

the quick brown fox jumps  
over the lazy dog

**Clearface Gothic**  
407  
fett  
heavy  
gras  
N 020: 081 2282  
Morris F. Benton 1908  
American Typefounders  
H 1–x 0,70–k 1,00–p 0,27

the quick brown fox jumps  
over the lazy dog

**Optima**  
1339  
fett  
extra bold  
gras  
N 020: 081 0243  
Hermann Zapf 1967  
D. Stempel AG  
H 1–x 0,70–k 1,06–p 0,38

the quick brown fox jumps  
over the lazy dog

**ITC Grizzly**  
637  
N 100: 081 0692  
Ronne Bonder, Tom Carnase 1970  
International Typeface Corp.  
H 1–x 0,63–k 1,00–p 0,40

the quick brown fox jumps  
over the lazy dog

**Bernhard Gothic**  
167  
extrafett  
extra heavy  
extra gras  
N 100: 081 0155  
Lucian Bernhard 1931  
American Typefounders  
H 1–x 0,58–k 1,04–p 0,28

the quick brown fox jumps  
over the lazy dog

**Clearface Gothic**  
408  
extrafett  
ultra bold  
extra gras  
N 020: 081 2255  
Morris F. Benton 1908  
American Typefounders  
H 1–x 0,71–k 1,00–p 0,28

the quick brown fox jumps  
over the lazy dog

**ITC Eras**  
483  
fett  
bold  
gras  
N 020: 081 1935  
Albert Boton 1976  
International Typeface Corp.  
H 1–x 0,74–k 1,00–p 0,33

the quick brown fox jumps  
over the lazy dog

**STEMPEL Kabel**  
724  
fett  
heavy  
gras  
N 100: 081 0816  
Rudolf Koch 1930  
D. Stempel AG  
H 1–x 0,72–k 1,00–p 0,23

**BERTHOLD HEADLINES VI** — Serifenlose Linear-Antiqua / Sans Serifs (Grotesques) / Linéar Antiqua sans empattements (Linéales)

THE QUICK BROWN FOX JUMPS OVER
THE LAZY DOG 1234567890

THE QUICK BROWN FOX JUMPS OVER
THE LAZY DOG 1234567890

QUICK BROWN FOX JUMPS OVER
THE LAZY DOG 1234567890

QUICK BROWN FOX JUMPS OVER
THE LAZY DOG 1234567890

THE QUICK BROWN FOX JUMPS OVER
THE LAZY DOG 1234567890

QUICK BROWN FOX JUMPS OVER
THE LAZY DOG 1234567890

QUICK BROWN FOX JUMPS OVER
THE LAZY DOG 1234567890

THE QUICK BROWN FOX JUMPS OVER
THE LAZY DOG 1234567890

| | Lapidar Lapidar Lapidaire **51** |

**the quick brown fox jumps over the lazy dog**

ITC **Kabel**
719
ultra
ultra
ultra
N 020: 081 2344
Photo-Lettering Inc. 1976
(Rudolf Koch 1927-1930)
H 1–x 0,75–k 1,04–p 0,23

**the quick brown fox jumps over the lazy dog**

**Gill Sans**
612
fett
extra bold
gras
N 100: 081 0666
Eric Gill 1928-1930
Monotype Corporation Ltd.
H 1–x 0,78–k 1,00–p 0,36

**the quick brown fox jumps over the lazy dog**

**Syntax**
1075
extrafett
extra bold
extra gras
N 020: 081 2405
Hans Eduard Meyer 1970
D. Stempel AG
H 1–x 0,74–k 1,10–p 0,38

**the quick brown fox jumps over the lazy dog**

ITC **Eras**
484
ultra
ultra
ultra
N 020: 081 1936
Albert Boton 1976
International Typeface Corp.
H 1–x 0,75–k 1,00–p 0,35

**the quick brown fox jumps over the lazy dog**

**Post-Marcato**
966
extrafett
extra bold
extra gras
N 100: 081 1050
Herbert Post 1959
H. Berthold AG
H 1–x 0,81–k 1,00–p 0,16

**the quick brown fox jumps over the lazy dog**

**Persona Black**
927

N 020: 081 2178
Günter Jäntsch 1975
H. Berthold AG
H 1–x 0,81–k 1,00–p 0,19

**the quick brown fox jumps over the lazy dog**

**Gill Kayo**
614

N 100: 081 0667
Monotype Corporation Ltd.
H 1–x 0,80–k 1,00–p 0,24

**the quick brown fox jumps over the lazy dog**

**Black Body**
190

N 100: 081 0166
Peter Steiner 1973
H. Berthold AG
H 1–x 0,88–k 1,09–p 0,18

**BERTHOLD HEADLINES VI** Serifenlose Linear-Antiqua / Sans Serifs (Grotesques) / Linéar Antiqua sans empattements (Linéales)

# THE QUICK BROWN JUMPS OVER THE LAZY DOG

**BERTHOLD HEADLINES VI** Serifenlose Linear-Antiqua / Sans Serifs (Grotesques) / Linéar Antiqua sans empattements (Linéales)

THE QUICK BROWN FOX JUMPS OVER
THE LAZY DOG 1234567890

THE QUICK BROWN FOX JUMPS OVER
THE LAZY DOG 1234567890

THE QUICK BROWN FOX JUMPS OVER
THE LAZY DOG 1234567890

THE QUICK BROWN FOX JUMPS OVER
THE LAZY DOG 1234567890

THE QUICK BROWN FOX JUMPS OVER
THE LAZY DOG 1234567890

**THE QUICK BROWN FOX JUMPS OVER
THE LAZY DOG 1234567890**

## 51
Lapidar / Lapidar / Lapidaire

**the quick brown fox jumps over the lazy dog**

**Black Body**
191
Zierbuchstaben
swash letters
lettres ornées
Z 000: 081 0167
Peter Steiner 1973
H. Berthold AG
H 1–x 0,88–k 1,09–p 0,18

## 52
Lapidar, kursive / Lapidar, italic / Lapidaire, italique

*the quick brown fox jumps over the lazy dog*

**Gill Sans**
1384
kursiv mager
light italic
italique maigre
N 020: 081 2451
Eric Gill 1928-1930
Monotype Corporation Ltd.
H 1–x 0,66–k 1,00–p 0,33

*the quick brown fox jumps over the lazy dog*

**Optima**
905
kursiv
italic
italique
N 100: 081 0975
Hermann Zapf 1958
D. Stempel AG
H 1–x 0,68–k 1,09–p 0,39

*the quick brown fox jumps over the lazy dog*

**Syntax**
1073
kursiv
italic
italique
N 020: 081 2403
Hans Eduard Meyer 1972
D. Stempel AG
H 1–x 0,72–k 1,07–p 0,33

*the quick brown fox jumps over the lazy dog*

**Optima**
1338
kursiv kräftig
medium italic
italique
N 020: 081 0235
Hermann Zapf 1969
D. Stempel AG
H 1–x 0,70–k 1,06–p 0,38

*the quick brown fox jumps over the lazy dog*

**Gill Sans**
1333
kursiv
italic
italique
N 020: 081 2452
Eric Gill 1928-1930
Monotype Corporation Ltd.
H 1–x 0,65–k 1,00–p 0,37

*the quick brown fox jumps over the lazy dog*

**Gill Sans**
1385
kursiv halbfett
bold italic
italique demi-gras
N 020: 081 2453
Eric Gill 1928-1930
Monotype Corporation Ltd.
H 1–x 0,65–k 1,00–p 0,35

**BERTHOLD HEADLINES VI** — Serifenlose Linear-Antiqua / Sans Serifs (Grotesques) / Linéar Antiqua sans empattements (Linéales)

THE QUICK BROWN FOX JUMPS OVER
THE LAZY DOG 1234567890

**BERTHOLD HEADLINES VI** — Serifenlose Linear-Antiqua / Sans Serifs (Grotesques) / Linéar Antiqua sans empattements (Linéales)

THE QUICK BROWN FOX JUMPS OVER
THE LAZY DOG 1234567890

THE QUICK BROWN FOX JUMPS OVER
THE LAZY DOG 1234567890

THE QUICK BROWN FOX JUMPS OVER
THE LAZY DOG 1234567890

THE QUICK BROWN FOX JUMPS OVER
THE LAZY DOG 1234567890

**BERTHOLD HEADLINES VI** — Serifenlose Linear-Antiqua / Sans Serifs (Grotesques) / Linéar Antiqua sans empattements (Linéales)

THE QUICK BROWN FOX JUMPS OVER
THE LAZY DOG 1234567890

| | Lapidar, kursive / Lapidar, italic / Lapidaire, italique | **52** |

*the quick brown fox jumps over the lazy dog*

**Gill Sans**
613
kursiv ultrafett
ultra bold italic
italique ultra gras

N 100: 081 1429
Monotype Corporation Ltd.
H 1–x 0,81–k 1,00–p 0,22

| | Lapidar, schmale / Lapidar, condensed / Lapidaire, étroit | **53** |

the quick brown fox jumps
over the lazy dog

**Gill Sans**
615
eng halbfett
bold extra condensed
extra étroit demi-gras
N 100: 081 1427
Eric Gill 1928-1930
Monotype Corporation Ltd.
H 1–x 0,78–k 1,00–p 0,16

the quick brown fox jumps
over the lazy dog

STEMPEL **Kabel**
725
schmalhalbfett
medium condensed
étroit demi-gras
N 100: 081 0818
Rudolf Koch 1928
D. Stempel AG
H 1–x 0,72–k 1,00–p 0,19

the quick brown fox jumps
over the lazy dog

**Gill Sans**
616
schmalhalbfett
bold condensed
étroit demi-gras
N 100: 081 0668
Eric Gill 1928-1930
Monotype Corporation Ltd.
H 1–x 0,68–k 1,03–p 0,35

the quick brown fox jumps
over the lazy dog

**Gill Sans**
617
ultra schmalfett
ultra bold condensed
étroit ultra gras

N 100: 081 1428
Monotype Corporation Ltd.
H 1–x 0,80–k 1,00–p 0,22

| | Ältere Grotesk / Grotesque / Grotesque ancien | **54** |

the quick brown fox jumps
over the lazy dog

**Genny**
604

N 100: 081 0660
H. Berthold AG
H 1–x 0,56–k 1,00–p 0,38

## BERTHOLD HEADLINES VI

Serifenlose Linear-Antiqua
Sans Serifs (Grotesques)
Linéar Antiqua sans empattements (Linéales)

THE QUICK BROWN FOX JUMPS OVER
THE LAZY DOG 1234567890

THE QUICK BROWN FOX JUMPS OVER
THE LAZY DOG 1234567890

THE QUICK BROWN FOX JUMPS OVER
THE LAZY DOG 1234567890

THE QUICK BROWN FOX JUMPS OVER
THE LAZY DOG 1234567890

THE QUICK BROWN FOX JUMPS OVER
THE LAZY DOG 1234567890

THE QUICK BROWN FOX JUMPS OVER
THE LAZY DOG 1234567890

THE QUICK BROWN FOX JUMPS OVER
THE LAZY DOG 1234567890

THE QUICK BROWN FOX JUMPS OVER
THE LAZY DOG 1234567890

| | Ältere Grotesk / Grotesque / Grotesque ancien | **54** |

the quick brown fox jumps  
over the lazy dog

**Aurora-Grotesk**  
84  
mager  
light  
maigre  
N 100: 081 1574  
1912  
Johannes Wagner  
H 1–x 0,63–k 1,00–p 0,31

the quick brown fox jumps  
over the lazy dog

**Venus**  
1158  
mager  
light  
maigre  
N 100: 081 1329  
1907  
Fundición Tipográfica Neufville, S.A.  
H 1–x 0,67–k 1,00–p 0,29

the quick brown fox jumps  
over the lazy dog

**Futura**  
543  
mager  
light  
maigre  
N 100: 081 0586  
Paul Renner 1928  
Fundición Tipográfica Neufville, S.A.  
H 1–x 0,62–k 1,06–p 0,30

the quick brown fox jumps  
over the lazy dog

**Futura**  
545  
Buchschrift  
book  
romain labeur  
N 100: 081 0617  
Paul Renner 1932  
Fundición Tipográfica Neufville, S.A.  
H 1–x 0,62–k 1,06–p 0,29

the quick brown fox jumps  
over the lazy dog

**Erbar-Werkschrift**  
487  

N 100: 081 0483  
Jakob Erbar 1960  
Ludwig & Mayer  
H 1–x 0,63–k 1,00–p 0,28

the quick brown fox jumps  
over the lazy dog

**Venus**  
1160  
halbfett  
medium  
demi-gras  
N 100: 081 1334  
1907  
Fundición Tipográfica Neufville, S.A.  
H 1–x 0,66–k 1,00–p 0,31

the quick brown fox jumps  
over the lazy dog

**Futura**  
578  
halbfett  
medium  
demi-gras  
N 100: 081 0587  
Paul Renner 1928  
Fundición Tipográfica Neufville, S.A.  
H 1–x 0,62–k 1,05–p 0,33

the quick brown fox jumps  
over the lazy dog

**Nobel**  
889  
normal  
regular  
normal  
N 100: 081 0945  
S. H. de Roos 1929-1931  
Lettergieterij Amsterdam  
H 1–x 0,56–k 1,00–p 0,25

## BERTHOLD HEADLINES VI
Serifenlose Linear-Antiqua
Sans Serifs (Grotesques)
Linéar Antiqua sans empattements (Linéales)

THE QUICK BROWN FOX JUMPS OVER THE LAZY DOG 1234567890

THE QUICK BROWN FOX JUMPS OVER THE LAZY DOG 1234567890

THE QUICK BROWN FOX JUMPS OVER THE LAZY DOG 1234567890

THE QUICK BROWN FOX JUMPS OVER THE LAZY DOG 1234567890

THE QUICK BROWN FOX JUMPS OVER THE LAZY DOG 1234567890

THE QUICK BROWN FOX JUMPS OVER THE LAZY DOG 1234567890

THE QUICK BROWN FOX JUMPS OVER THE LAZY DOG 1234567890

THE QUICK BROWN FOX JUMPS OVER THE LAZY DOG 1234567890

| | |
|---|---|
| | Ältere Grotesk **54**<br>Grotesque<br>Grotesque ancien |

the quick brown fox jumps
over the lazy dog

**Berthold-Grotesk**
174
normal
regular
normal
N 100: 081 0156
1928
H. Berthold AG
H 1–x 0,56–k 1,00–p 0,25

the quick brown fox jumps
over the lazy dog

**Venus**
1163
dreiviertelfett
demi-bold
trois quarts de gras
N 100: 081 1339
1911
Fundición Tipográfica Neufville, S.A.
H 1–x 0,69–k 1,00–p 0,22

the quick brown fox jumps
over the lazy dog

**Erbar-Grotesk**
488
halbfett
medium
demi-gras
N 100: 081 0488
Jakob Erbar 1929
Ludwig & Mayer
H 1–x 0,59–k 1,00–p 0,32

the quick brown fox jumps
over the lazy dog

**Aurora-Grotesk**
87
dreiviertelfett
demi-bold
trois quarts de gras
N 000: 081 0113
1912
Johannes Wagner
H 1–x 0,68–k 1,00–p 0,20

the quick brown fox jumps
over the lazy dog

**Futura**
549
dreiviertelfett
demi-bold
trois quarts de gras
N 100: 081 0593
Paul Renner 1930
Fundición Tipográfica Neufville, S.A.
H 1–x 0,62–k 1,05–p 0,28

the quick brown fox jumps
over the lazy dog

**Berliner Grotesk**
159
halbfett
medium
demi-gras
N 020: 081 2419
Erik Spiekermann 1979
(Berthold-Hausschnitt 1913)
H 1–x 0,75–k 1,00–p 0,17

the quick brown fox jumps
over the lazy dog

**Futura**
1329
kräftig
bold
gras
N 020: 081 0476
Paul Renner 1954
Fundición Tipográfica Neufville, S.A.
H 1–x 0,64–k 1,05–p 0,33

the quick brown fox jumps
over the lazy dog

**Berthold-Grotesk**
175
fett
bold
gras
N 100: 081 1586
1929
H. Berthold AG
H 1–x 0,59–k 1,00–p 0,28

## BERTHOLD HEADLINES VI
Serifenlose Linear-Antiqua
Sans Serifs (Grotesques)
Linéar Antiqua sans empattements (Linéales)

THE QUICK BROWN FOX JUMPS OVER
THE LAZY DOG 1234567890

THE QUICK BROWN FOX JUMPS OVER
THE LAZY DOG 1234567890

THE QUICK BROWN FOX JUMPS OVER
THE LAZY DOG 1234567890

THE QUICK BROWN FOX JUMPS OVER
THE LAZY DOG 1234567890

THE QUICK BROWN FOX JUMPS OVER
THE LAZY DOG 1234567890

THE QUICK BROWN FOX JUMPS OVER
THE LAZY DOG 1234567890

THE QUICK BROWN FOX JUMPS OVER
THE LAZY DOG 1234567890

| | Ältere Grotesk |
| --- | --- |
| | Grotesque |
| | Grotesque ancien **54** |

**the quick brown fox jumps over the lazy dog**

    **Nobel**
    890
    fett
    bold
    gras
    N 100: 081 0949
    S. H. de Roos 1929-1931
    Lettergieterij Amsterdam
    H 1–x 0,56–k 1,03–p 0,32

**the quick brown fox jumps over the lazy dog**

    **Erbar-Grotesk**
    489
    fett
    bold
    gras
    N 100: 081 0491
    Jakob Erbar 1926
    Ludwig & Mayer
    H 1–x 0,63–k 1,00–p 0,31

**the quick brown fox jumps over the lazy dog**

    **Futura**
    581
    fett
    bold
    gras
    N 100: 081 0597
    Paul Renner 1928
    Fundición Tipográfica Neufville, S.A.
    H 1–x 0,68–k 1,06–p 0,29

**the quick brown fox jumps over the lazy dog**

    **Aurora-Grotesk**
    88
    fett
    bold
    gras
    N 000: 081 0115
    1912
    Johannes Wagner
    H 1–x 0,72–k 1,00–p 0,19

**the quick brown fox jumps over the lazy dog**

    **Flyer**
    514
    fett
    bold
    gras
    N 020: 081 0324
    H 1–x 0,69–k 1,00–p 0,25

**the quick brown fox jumps over the lazy dog**

    **Tempo Black**
    1078
    normal
    regular
    normal
    N 100: 081 1521
    R. H. Middleton 1930
    Ludlow Typograph Co.
    H 1–x 0,63–k 1,00–p 0,21

**the quick brown fox jumps over the lazy dog**

    **Futura**
    552
    extrafett
    extra bold
    extra gras
    N 100: 081 0600
    Berthold-Schriftenatelier
    Fundición Tipográfica Neufville, S.A.
    H 1–x 0,70–k 1,06–p 0,29

## BERTHOLD HEADLINES VI

Serifenlose Linear-Antiqua
Sans Serifs (Grotesques)
Linéar Antiqua sans empattements (Linéales)

*THE QUICK BROWN FOX JUMPS OVER
THE LAZY DOG 1234567890*

*THE QUICK BROWN FOX JUMPS OVER
THE LAZY DOG 1234567890*

THE QUICK BROWN FOX JUMPS OVER
THE LAZY DOG 1234567890

THE QUICK BROWN FOX JUMPS OVER
THE LAZY DOG 1234567890

THE QUICK BROWN FOX JUMPS OVER
THE LAZY DOG 1234567890

*THE QUICK BROWN FOX JUMPS OVER
THE LAZY DOG 1234567890*

**THE QUICK BROWN FOX JUMPS OVER
THE LAZY DOG 1234567890**

**THE QUICK BROWN FOX JUMPS OVER
THE LAZY DOG 1234567890**

## 55 Ältere Grotesk, kursive / Grotesque, italic / Grotesque ancien, italique

*the quick brown fox jumps over the lazy dog*

**Aurora-Grotesk**
85
kursiv mager
light italic
italique maigre
N 100: 081 0109
1912
Johannes Wagner
H 1–x 0,66–k 1,00–p 0,28

*the quick brown fox jumps over the lazy dog*

**Venus**
1159
kursiv mager
light italic
italique maigre
N 100: 081 1333
1910
Fundición Tipográfica Neufville, S.A.
H 1–x 0,69–k 1,03–p 0,25

*the quick brown fox jumps over the lazy dog*

**Futura**
544
schräg mager
light oblique
oblique maigre
N 100: 081 1504
Paul Renner 1930
Fundición Tipográfica Neufville, S.A.
H 1–x 0,61–k 1,06–p 0,32

*the quick brown fox jumps over the lazy dog*

**Futura**
546
Buchschrift schräg
book oblique
romain labeur oblique
N 100: 081 0621
Paul Renner 1939
Fundición Tipográfica Neufville, S.A.
H 1–x 0,62–k 1,05–p 0,29

*the quick brown fox jumps over the lazy dog*

**Futura**
548
schräg halbfett
medium oblique
oblique demi-gras
N 100: 081 0590
Paul Renner 1930
Fundición Tipográfica Neufville, S.A.
H 1–x 0,62–k 1,06–p 0,35

*the quick brown fox jumps over the lazy dog*

**Venus**
1161
kursiv halbfett
medium italic
italique demi-gras
N 100: 081 1337
1910
Fundición Tipográfica Neufville, S.A.
H 1–x 0,68–k 1,00–p 0,29

***the quick brown fox jumps over the lazy dog***

**Aurora-Grotesk**
89
kursiv fett
bold italic
italique gras
N 100: 081 0118
1912
Johannes Wagner
H 1–x 0,66–k 1,00–p 0,28

***the quick brown fox jumps over the lazy dog***

**Futura**
1278
schräg dreiviertelfett
demi-bold oblique
oblique trois quarts de gras
N 020: 081 0672
Paul Renner 1930
Fundición Tipográfica Neufville, S.A.
H 1–x 0,62–k 1,00–p 0,28

## BERTHOLD HEADLINES VI
Serifenlose Linear-Antiqua
Sans Serifs (Grotesques)
Linéar Antiqua sans empattements (Linéales)

*THE QUICK BROWN FOX JUMPS OVER THE LAZY DOG 1234567890*

**THE QUICK BROWN FOX JUMPS OVER THE LAZY DOG 1234567890**

**THE QUICK BROWN FOX JUMPS OVER THE LAZY DOG 1234567890**

THE QUICK BROWN FOX JUMPS OVER THE LAZY DOG

## BERTHOLD HEADLINES VI
Serifenlose Linear-Antiqua
Sans Serifs (Grotesques)
Linéar Antiqua sans empattements (Linéales)

THE QUICK BROWN FOX JUMPS OVER THE LAZY DOG 1234567890

THE QUICK BROWN FOX JUMPS OVER THE LAZY DOG 1234567890

THE QUICK BROWN FOX JUMPS OVER THE LAZY DOG 1234567890

| | Ältere Grotesk, kursive / Grotesque, italic / Grotesque ancien, italique | **55** |

*the quick brown fox jumps over the lazy dog*

**Block**
1308
kursiv
italic
italique
N 020: 081 2418
H. Hoffmann 1927
H. Berthold AG
H 1–x 0,71–k 1,00–p 0,14

*the quick brown fox jumps over the lazy dog*

**Futura**
551
schräg fett
bold oblique
oblique gras
N 100: 081 0599
Paul Renner 1937
Fundición Tipográfica Neufville, S.A.
H 1–x 0,68–k 1,06–p 0,34

*the quick brown fox jumps over the lazy dog*

**Futura**
553
schräg extrafett
extra bold oblique
oblique extra gras
N 100: 081 0602
Berthold-Schriftenatelier
Fundición Tipográfica Neufville, S.A.
H 1–x 0,69–k 1,09–p 0,31

the quick brown fox jumps over the lazy dog

**Venus**
1162
linkskursiv
reclining
penché à gauche
N 100: 081 1338
Fundición Tipográfica Neufville, S.A.
H 1–x 0,72–k 1,00–p 0,28

| | Ältere Grotesk, schmale / Grotesque, condensed / Grotesque ancien, étroit | **56** |

the quick brown fox jumps over the lazy dog

**Futura**
554
schmalhalbfett
medium condensed
étroit demi-gras
N 100: 081 0603
Paul Renner 1928
Fundición Tipográfica Neufville, S.A.
H 1–x 0,68–k 1,06–p 0,28

the quick brown fox jumps over the lazy dog

**Nobel**
891
schmal
condensed
étroit
N 100: 081 0947
S. H. de Roos 1929-1931
Lettergieterij Amsterdam
H 1–x 0,56–k 1,00–p 0,25

the quick brown fox jumps over the lazy dog

**Berthold-Grotesk**
176
schmal
condensed
étroit
N 100: 081 0157
1935
H. Berthold AG
H 1–x 0,56–k 1,00–p 0,25

## BERTHOLD HEADLINES VI

Serifenlose Linear-Antiqua
Sans Serifs (Grotesques)
Linéar Antiqua sans empattements (Linéales)

THE QUICK BROWN FOX JUMPS OVER
THE LAZY DOG 1234567890

THE QUICK BROWN FOX JUMPS OVER
THE LAZY DOG 1234567890

THE QUICK BROWN FOX JUMPS OVER
THE LAZY DOG 1234567890

THE QUICK BROWN FOX JUMPS OVER
THE LAZY DOG 1234567890

THE QUICK BROWN FOX JUMPS OVER
THE LAZY DOG 1234567890

THE QUICK BROWN FOX JUMPS OVER
THE LAZY DOG 1234567890

THE QUICK BROWN FOX JUMPS OVER
THE LAZY DOG 1234567890

Ältere Grotesk, schmale
Grotesque, condensed
Grotesque ancien, étroit
**56**

**Erbar-Grotesk**
490
schmalhalbfett
medium condensed
étroit demi-gras
N 100: 081 0492
Jakob Erbar 1929
Ludwig & Mayer
H 1–x 0,69–k 1,00–p 0,19

**the quick brown fox jumps over the lazy dog**

**Berthold-Grotesk**
177
schmalfett
bold condensed
étroit gras
N 100: 081 0158
1935
H. Berthold AG
H 1–x 0,56–k 1,00–p 0,25

**the quick brown fox jumps over the lazy dog**

**Futura**
555
schmalfett
bold condensed
étroit demi-gras
N 100: 081 0606
Paul Renner 1930
Fundición Tipográfica Neufville, S.A.
H 1–x 0,68–k 1,05–p 0,31

**the quick brown fox jumps over the lazy dog**

**Hochblock**
1386

N 020: 081 2416
1926
H. Berthold AG
H 1–x 0,46–k 1,00–p 0,10

**the quick brown fox jumps over the lazy dog**

**Tempo Black**
1101
schmal
condensed
étroit
N 100: 081 1522
R. H. Middleton 1930
Ludlow Typograph Co.
H 1–x 0,63–k 1,00–p 0,25

**the quick brown fox jumps over the lazy dog**

**Futura**
557
extrafett schmal
extra bold condensed
étroit extra gras
N 100: 081 0611
Berthold-Schriftenatelier
Fundición Tipográfica Neufville, S.A.
H 1–x 0,70–k 1,07–p 0,32

**the quick brown fox jumps over the lazy dog**

**Flyer**
515
schmalfett
bold condensed
étroit gras

N 020: 081 2009
H 1–x 0,68–k 1,00–p 0,23

**the quick brown fox jumps over the lazy dog**

## BERTHOLD HEADLINES VI
'Serifenlose Linear-Antiqua
Sans Serifs (Grotesques)
Linéar Antiqua sans empattements (Linéales)

THE QUICK BROWN FOX JUMPS OVER
THE LAZY DOG 1234567890

THE QUICK BROWN FOX JUMPS OVER
THE LAZY DOG 1234567890

THE QUICK BROWN FOX JUMPS OVER
THE LAZY DOG 1234567890

THE QUICK BROWN FOX JUMPS OVER
THE LAZY DOG 1234567890

THE QUICK BROWN FOX JUMPS OVER
THE LAZY DOG

THE QUICK BROWN FOX JUMPS OVER
THE LAZY DOG 1234567890

THE QUICK BROWN FOX JUMPS OVER
THE LAZY DOG 1234567890

THE QUICK BROWN FOX JUMPS OVER
THE LAZY DOG 1234567890

| | Jüngere Grotesk / Late Grotesque / Grotesque moderne **57** |

**Kabel Hairline**
713

the quick brown fox jumps
over the lazy dog

N 100: 081 0802
H. Berthold AG
H 1–x 0,66–k 1,00–p 0,25

**Kabel Hairline**
714
Zierbuchstaben
swash letters
lettres ornées

the quick brown fox jumps
over the lazy dog

Z 000: 081 0804
H. Berthold AG
H 1–x 0,66–k 1,13–p 0,47

**Helvetica**
652
ultraleicht
ultra light
ultra maigre

the quick brown fox jumps
over the lazy dog

N 100: 081 0717
1970
Haas'sche Schriftgießerei AG
H 1–x 0,71–k 1,00–p 0,24

ITC **Avant Garde Gothic**
96
mager
extra light
maigre

the quick brown fox jumps
over the lazy dog

N 100: 081 1578
Herb Lubalin, Tom Carnase 1970
International Typeface Corp.
H 1–x 0,72–k 1,00–p 0,28

ITC **Avant Garde Gothic**
97
mager Zierbuchstaben
extra light swash letters
maigre lettres ornées

the quick brown fox jumps
over the lazy dog

Z 000: 081 1579
Herb Lubalin, Tom Carnase 1970
International Typeface Corp.
H 1–x 0,72–k 1,00–p 0,28

**Univers 45**
1124
mager
light
maigre

the quick brown fox jumps
over the lazy dog

N 100: 081 1228
Adrian Frutiger 1957
Haas'sche Schriftgießerei AG
H 1–x 0,70–k 1,00–p 0,25

**Neuzeit-Grotesk**
858
leicht
light
maigre

the quick brown fox jumps
over the lazy dog

N 100: 081 0926
Wilhelm Pischner 1932
D. Stempel AG
H 1–x 0,69–k 1,00–p 0,34

**Helvetica**
654
leicht
light
maigre

the quick brown fox jumps
over the lazy dog

N 100: 081 0720
1966/67
D. Stempel AG
H 1–x 0,73–k 1,00–p 0,26

**BERTHOLD HEADLINES VI**  
Serifenlose Linear-Antiqua  
Sans Serifs (Grotesques)  
Linéar Antiqua sans empâttements (Linéales)

THE QUICK BROWN FOX JUMPS OVER
THE LAZY DOG 1234567890

THE QUICK BROWN FOX JUMPS OVER
THE LAZY DOG 1234567890

THE QUICK BROWN FOX JUMPS OVER
THE LAZY DOG 1234567890

THE QUICK BROWN FOX JUMPS OVER
THE LAZY DOG 1234567890

THE QUICK BROWN FOX JUMPS OVER
THE LAZY DOG 1234567890

THE QUICK BROWN FOX JUMPS OVER
THE LAZY DOG

THE QUICK BROWN FOX JUMPS OVER
THE LAZY DOG 1234567890

THE QUICK BROWN FOX JUMPS OVER
THE LAZY DOG 1234567890

Jüngere Grotesk  
Late Grotesque  
Grotesque moderne  
**57**

the quick brown fox jumps  
over the lazy dog

**Akzidenz-Grotesk**  
5  
mager  
light  
maigre  
N 100: 081 0004  
1902  
H. Berthold AG  
H 1–x 0,68–k 1,00–p 0,36

the quick brown fox jumps  
over the lazy dog

**Antique Olive**  
60  
mager  
light  
maigre  
N 010: 081 2121  
Roger Excoffon 1969  
Marcel Olive  
H 1–x 0,77–k 1,03–p 0,19

the quick brown fox jumps  
over the lazy dog

**News Gothic**  
867  
normal  
regular  
normal  
N 100: 081 0938  
Morris F. Benton 1909  
American Typefounders  
H 1–x 0,71–k 1,00–p 0,23

the quick brown fox jumps  
over the lazy dog

**Folio**  
516  
mager  
light  
maigre  
N 100: 081 0530  
K. F. Bauer, W. Baum 1957  
Fundición Tipográfica Neufville, S.A.  
H 1–x 0,65–k 1,00–p 0,30

the quick brown fox jumps  
over the lazy dog

ITC **Avant Garde Gothic**  
99  
Buch  
book  
romain labeur  
N 010: 081 2118  
Herb Lubalin, Tom Carnase 1970  
International Typeface Corp.  
H 1–x 0,73–k 1,00–p 0,25

the quick brown fox jumps  
over the lazy dog

ITC **Avant Garde Gothic**  
100  
Buch Zierbuchstaben  
book swash letters  
romain labeur lettres ornées  
Z 000: 081 0503  
Herb Lubalin, Tom Carnase 1970  
International Typeface Corp.  
H 1–x 0,73–k 1,00–p 0,25

the quick brown fox jumps  
over the lazy dog

**Neuzeit S**  
863  
Buch  
book  
romain labeur  
N 000: 081 0924  
1965/66  
D. Stempel AG  
H 1–x 0,67–k 1,00–p 0,32

the quick brown fox jumps  
over the lazy dog

**Monotone Gothic**  
845  

N 100: 081 0918  
Morris F. Benton 1908  
American Typefounders  
H 1–x 0,69–k 1,00–p 0,28

## BERTHOLD HEADLINES VI

Serifenlose Linear-Antiqua
Sans Serifs (Grotesques)
Linéar Antiqua sans empattements (Linéales)

THE QUICK BROWN FOX JUMPS OVER
THE LAZY DOG 1234567890

THE QUICK BROWN FOX JUMPS OVER
THE LAZY DOG 1234567890

THE QUICK BROWN FOX JUMPS OVER
THE LAZY DOG 1234567890

THE QUICK BROWN FOX JUMPS OVER
THE LAZY DOG 1234567890

THE QUICK BROWN FOX JUMPS OVER
THE LAZY DOG 1234567890

THE QUICK BROWN FOX JUMPS OVER
THE LAZY DOG 1234567890

THE QUICK BROWN FOX JUMPS OVER
THE LAZY DOG 1234567890

THE QUICK BROWN FOX JUMPS OVER
THE LAZY DOG 1234567890

Jüngere Grotesk
Late Grotesque
Grotesque moderne

**57**

**Eurostile**
495
normal
regular
normal
N 100: 081 0496
Aldo Novarese 1962
Societa Nebiolo S.p.A.
H 1–x 0,71–k 1,00–p 0,30

the quick brown fox jumps
over the lazy dog

**Mercator**
832
normal
regular
normal
N 100: 081 0895
Dick Dooijes 1958
Lettergieterij Amsterdam
H 1–x 0,69–k 1,00–p 0,25

the quick brown fox jumps
over the lazy dog

**Akzidenz-Grotesk**
6
normal
regular
normal
N 100: 081 0001
1898
H. Berthold AG
H 1–x 0,67–k 1,00–p 0,28

the quick brown fox jumps
over the lazy dog

ITC **Franklin Gothic**
1371
Buch
book
romain labeur
N 020: 081 2454
Vic Caruso 1980
International Typeface Corp.
H 1–x 0,75–k 1,00–p 0,25

the quick brown fox jumps
over the lazy dog

**Helvetica**
656
normal
regular
normal
N 100: 081 0723
Max Miedinger 1958
Haas'sche Schriftgießerei AG
H 1–x 0,73–k 1,00–p 0,23

the quick brown fox jumps
over the lazy dog

**Churchward Tranquillity**
379
normal
medium
normal
N 100: 081 1468
Joseph Churchward 1972
H. Berthold AG
H 1–x 0,72–k 1,00–p 0,28

the quick brown fox jumps
over the lazy dog

**Grotesque No. 215**
642
normal
regular
normal
N 100: 081 0699
1926
Monotype Corporation Ltd.
H 1–x 0,69–k 1,00–p 0,25

the quick brown fox jumps
over the lazy dog

**Neuzeit-Grotesk**
859
mager
regular
normal
N 000: 081 0928
Wilhelm Pischner 1928
D. Stempel AG
H 1–x 0,69–k 1,00–p 0,32

the quick brown fox jumps
over the lazy dog

## BERTHOLD HEADLINES VI
Serifenlose Linear-Antiqua
Sans Serifs (Grotesques)
Linéar Antiqua sans empattements (Linéales)

THE QUICK BROWN FOX JUMPS OVER
THE LAZY DOG 1234567890

THE QUICK BROWN FOX JUMPS OVER
THE LAZY DOG 1234567890

THE QUICK BROWN FOX JUMPS OVER
THE LAZY DOG 1234567890

THE QUICK BROWN FOX JUMPS OVER
THE LAZY DOG 1234567890

THE QUICK BROWN FOX JUMPS OVER
THE LAZY DOG

THE QUICK BROWN FOX JUMPS OVER
THE LAZY DOG 1234567890

THE QUICK BROWN FOX JUMPS OVER
THE LAZY DOG 1234567890

THE QUICK BROWN FOX JUMPS OVER
THE LAZY DOG 1234567890

## Jüngere Grotesk / Late Grotesque / Grotesque moderne — 57

the quick brown fox jumps over the lazy dog

**Aurora-Grotesk**
86
halbfett
medium
demi-gras
N 100: 081 0110
1912
Johannes Wagner
H 1–x 0,69–k 1,00–p 0,25

the quick brown fox jumps over the lazy dog

**Univers 55**
1126
normal
medium
normal
N 100: 081 1250
Adrian Frutiger 1957
Haas'sche Schriftgießerei AG
H 1–x 0,69–k 1,00–p 0,27

the quick brown fox jumps over the lazy dog

**Akzidenz-Grotesk Buch**
25
normal
regular
normal
N 100: 081 0052
Günter Gerhard Lange 1969
H. Berthold AG
H 1–x 0,73–k 1,00–p 0,27

the quick brown fox jumps over the lazy dog

ITC **Avant Garde Gothic**
102
normal
medium
normal
N 100: 081 1581
Herb Lubalin, Tom Carnase 1970
International Typeface Corp.
H 1–x 0,76–k 1,00–p 0,24

the quick brown fox jumps over the lazy dog

ITC **Avant Garde Gothic**
103
normal Zierbuchstaben
medium swash letters
normal lettres ornées
Z 000: 081 1582
Herb Lubalin, Tom Carnase 1970
International Typeface Corp.
H 1–x 0,76–k 1,00–p 0,24

the quick brown fox jumps over the lazy dog

**Antique Olive**
61
normal
regular
normale
N 100: 081 0080
Roger Excoffon 1963
Marcel Olive
H 1–x 0,84–k 1,04–p 0,20

the quick brown fox jumps over the lazy dog

**DIN 1451-Mittelschrift Teil 2**
1369
fett
bold
gras
N 020: 081 2548
1981
H. Berthold AG
H 1–x 0,72–k 1,00–p 0,29

the quick brown fox jumps over the lazy dog

**Permanent**
918
halbfett
medium
demi-gras
N 100: 081 1001
Karlgeorg Hoefer 1962
Ludwig & Mayer
H 1–x 0,69–k 1,00–p 0,28

**BERTHOLD HEADLINES VI**  
Serifenlose Linear-Antiqua  
Sans Serifs (Grotesques)  
Linéar Antiqua sans empattements (Linéales)

THE QUICK BROWN FOX JUMPS OVER THE LAZY DOG 1234567890

THE QUICK BROWN FOX JUMPS OVER THE LAZY DOG 1234567890

THE QUICK BROWN FOX JUMPS OVER THE LAZY DOG 1234567890

THE QUICK BROWN FOX JUMPS OVER THE LAZY DOG 1234567890

THE QUICK BROWN FOX JUMPS OVER THE LAZY DOG 1234567890

THE QUICK BROWN FOX JUMPS OVER THE LAZY DOG 1234567890

THE QUICK BROWN FOX JUMPS OVER THE LAZY DOG 1234567890

THE QUICK BROWN FOX JUMPS OVER THE LAZY DOG 1234567890

## 57 Jüngere Grotesk / Late Grotesque / Grotesque moderne

the quick brown fox jumps over the lazy dog

**Folio**
518
halbfett
medium
demi-gras
N 100: 081 0537
K. F. Bauer, W. Baum 1957
Fundición Tipográfica Neufville, S.A.
H 1–x 0,65–k 1,00–p 0,30

the quick brown fox jumps over the lazy dog

**Churchward Tranquillity**
381
halbfett
demi-bold
demi-gras
N 100: 081 0348
Joseph Churchward 1972
H. Berthold AG
H 1–x 0,72–k 1,00–p 0,31

the quick brown fox jumps over the lazy dog

ITC **Franklin Gothic**
1373
normal
regular
normal
N 020: 081 2455
Vic Caruso 1980
International Typeface Corp.
H 1–x 0,74–k 1,00–p 0,26

the quick brown fox jumps over the lazy dog

**Akzidenz-Grotesk**
8
halbfett
medium
demi-gras
N 100: 081 1553
1909
H. Berthold AG
H 1–x 0,71–k 1,00–p 0,23

the quick brown fox jumps over the lazy dog

**Helvetica**
658
halbfett
medium
demi-gras
N 010: 081 2301
Max Miedinger 1957
Haas'sche Schriftgießerei AG
H 1–x 0,72–k 1,00–p 0,23

the quick brown fox jumps over the lazy dog

**Univers 65**
1128
halbfett
bold
demi-gras
N 100: 081 1276
Adrian Frutiger 1957
Haas'sche Schriftgießerei AG
H 1–x 0,72–k 1,00–p 0,27

the quick brown fox jumps over the lazy dog

**Neuzeit-Grotesk**
860
halbfett
medium
demi-gras
N 100: 081 0930
Wilhelm Pischner 1928/30
D. Stempel AG
H 1–x 0,69–k 1,00–p 0,34

the quick brown fox jumps over the lazy dog

**DIN-Mittelschrift**
1324

N 100: 081 0432
H. Berthold AG
H 1–x 0,71–k 1,00–p 0,22

**BERTHOLD HEADLINES VI** — Serifenlose Linear-Antiqua / Sans Serifs (Grotesques) / Linéar Antiqua sans empattements (Linéales)

THE QUICK BROWN FOX JUMPS OVER
THE LAZY DOG 1234567890

THE QUICK BROWN FOX JUMPS OVER
THE LAZY DOG

THE QUICK BROWN FOX JUMPS OVER
THE LAZY DOG 1234567890

THE QUICK BROWN FOX JUMPS OVER
THE LAZY DOG 1234567890

THE QUICK BROWN FOX JUMPS OVER
THE LAZY DOG 1234567890

THE QUICK BROWN FOX JUMPS OVER
THE LAZY DOG 1234567890

THE QUICK BROWN FOX JUMPS OVER
THE LAZY DOG 1234567890

THE QUICK BROWN FOX JUMPS OVER
THE LAZY DOG 1234567890

Jüngere Grotesk
Late Grotesque
Grotesque moderne
**57**

the quick brown fox jumps over the lazy dog

ITC **Avant Garde Gothic**
105
halbfett
demi bold
demi-gras
N 100: 081 1610
Herb Lubalin, Tom Carnase 1970
International Typeface Corp.
H 1–x 0,76–k 1,00–p 0,24

the quick brown fox jumps over the lazy dog

ITC **Avant Garde Gothic**
106
halbfett Zierbuchstaben
demi-bold swash letters
demi-gras lettres ornées
Z 000: 081 1611
Herb Lubalin, Tom Carnase 1970
International Typeface Corp.
H 1–x 0,76–k 1,00–p 0,24

the quick brown fox jumps over the lazy dog

**Airport**
3



N 100: 081 1470
Crosby/Fletcher/Forbes
H 1–x 0,78–k 1,00–p 0,22

the quick brown fox jumps over the lazy dog

**News Gothic**
868
fett
bold
gras
N 000: 081 0939
John L. Renshaw 1958
American Typefounders
H 1–x 0,71–k 1,00–p 0,24

the quick brown fox jumps over the lazy dog

**Neuzeit S**
864
kräftig
bold
gras
N 000: 081 0925
1965/66
D. Stempel AG
H 1–x 0,68–k 1,00–p 0,29

the quick brown fox jumps over the lazy dog

**Grotesque No. 216**
643
halbfett
bold
demi-gras
N 100: 081 0700
1926
Monotype Corporation Ltd.
H 1–x 0,69–k 1,00–p 0,25

the quick brown fox jumps over the lazy dog

**Akzidenz-Grotesk Buch**
27
halbfett
medium
demi-gras
N 100: 081 0054
Günter Gerhard Lange 1969
H. Berthold AG
H 1–x 0,73–k 1,00–p 0,23

the quick brown fox jumps over the lazy dog

**Antique Olive**
63
halbfett
medium
demi-grasse
N 100: 081 0082
Roger Excoffon 1964
Marcel Olive
H 1–x 0,84–k 1,04–p 0,21

## BERTHOLD HEADLINES VI
Serifenlose Linear-Antiqua
Sans Serifs (Grotesques)
Linéar Antiqua sans empattements (Linéales)

THE QUICK BROWN FOX JUMPS OVER
THE LAZY DOG 1234567890

THE QUICK BROWN FOX JUMPS OVER
THE LAZY DOG 1234567890

THE QUICK BROWN FOX JUMPS OVER
THE LAZY DOG 1234567890

THE QUICK BROWN FOX JUMPS OVER
THE LAZY DOG 1234567890

THE QUICK BROWN FOX JUMPS OVER
THE LAZY DOG 1234567890

THE QUICK BROWN FOX JUMPS OVER
THE LAZY DOG 1234567890

THE QUICK BROWN FOX JUMPS OVER
THE LAZY DOG 1234567890

THE QUICK BROWN FOX JUMPS OVER
THE LAZY DOG 1234567890

Jüngere Grotesk
Late Grotesque
Grotesque moderne
**57**

**the quick brown fox jumps over the lazy dog**

**Mercator**
833
fett
bold
gras
N 100: 081 0897
Dick Dooijes 1958
Lettergieterij Amsterdam
H 1–x 0,69–k 1,00–p 0,25

**the quick brown fox jumps over the lazy dog**

ITC **Franklin Gothic**
1375
halbfett
demi
demi-gras
N 020: 081 2456
Vic Caruso 1980
International Typeface Corp.
H 1–x 0,74–k 1,00–p 0,26

**the quick brown fox jumps over the lazy dog**

**Akzidenz-Grotesk**
10
fett
bold
gras
N 100: 081 0015
1909
H. Berthold AG
H 1–x 0,74–k 1,00–p 0,26

**the quick brown fox jumps over the lazy dog**

**Neuzeit Grotesk**
861
fett
bold
gras
N 100: 081 0931
Wilhelm Pischner 1928
D. Stempel AG
H 1–x 0,70–k 1,00–p 0,30

**the quick brown fox jumps over the lazy dog**

**Block**
202
normal
regular
normal
N 100: 081 0169
H. Hoffmann 1908
H. Berthold AG
H 1–x 0,71–k 1,00–p 0,15

**the quick brown fox jumps over the lazy dog**

ATF **Franklin Gothic**
533
normal
regular
normal
N 100: 081 0580
Morris F. Benton 1904
American Typefounders
H 1–x 0,71–k 1,00–p 0,21

**the quick brown fox jumps over the lazy dog**

**Eurostile**
496
fett
bold
gras
N 100: 081 0501
Aldo Novarese 1962
Societa Nebiolo S.p.A.
H 1–x 0,71–k 1,00–p 0,30

**the quick brown fox jumps over the lazy dog**

**Grotesk**
638
breitfett
bold extended
large gras

N 100: 081 0706
Lettergieterij Amsterdam
H 1–x 0,69–k 1,00–p 0,25

## BERTHOLD HEADLINES VI
Serifenlose Linear-Antiqua
Sans Serifs (Grotesques)
Linéar Antiqua sans empattements (Linéales)

THE QUICK BROWN FOX JUMPS OVER THE LAZY DOG 1234567890

QUICK BROWN FOX JUMPS OVER THE LAZY DOG 1234567890

THE QUICK BROWN FOX JUMPS OVER THE LAZY DOG 1234567890

THE QUICK BROWN FOX JUMPS OVER THE LAZY DOG

THE QUICK BROWN FOX JUMPS OVER THE LAZY DOG 1234567890

THE QUICK BROWN FOX JUMPS OVER THE LAZY DOG 1234567890

QUICK BROWN FOX JUMPS OVER THE LAZY DOG 1234567890

THE QUICK BROWN FOX JUMPS OVER THE LAZY DOG 1234567890

Jüngere Grotesk
Late Grotesque
Grotesque moderne
**57**

**the quick brown fox jumps over the lazy dog**

Univers 75
1130
fett
extra bold
gras
N 100: 081 1301
Adrian Frutiger 1957
Haas'sche Schriftgießerei AG
H 1–x 0,70–k 1,00–p 0,26

**the quick brown fox jumps over the lazy dog**

Folio
519
fett
bold
gras
N 100: 081 0540
K. F. Bauer, W. Baum 1959
Fundición Tipográfica Neufville, S.A.
H 1–x 0,66–k 1,00–p 0,28

**the quick brown fox jumps over the lazy dog**

ITC **Avant Garde Gothic**
108
fett
bold
gras
N 100: 081 0132
Herb Lubalin, Tom Carnase 1970
International Typeface Corp.
H 1–x 0,76–k 1,00–p 0,24

**the quick brown fox jumps over the lazy dog**

ITC **Avant Garde Gothic**
109
fett Zierbuchstaben
bold swash letters
gras lettres ornées
Z 000: 081 0133
Herb Lubalin, Tom Carnase 1970
International Typeface Corp.
H 1–x 0,76–k 1,00–p 0,24

**the quick brown fox jumps over the lazy dog**

Helvetica
660
fett
bold
gras
N 100: 081 0734
Max Miedinger 1959
Haas'sche Schriftgießerei AG
H 1–x 0,72–k 1,00–p 0,23

**the quick brown fox jumps over the lazy dog**

Antique Olive
64
fett
bold
grasse
N 100: 081 0083
Roger Excoffon 1965
Marcel Olive
H 1–x 0,84–k 1,04–p 0,20

**the quick brown fox jumps over the lazy dog**

Akzidenz-Grotesk
12
super
super
super
N 100: 081 0018
Günter Gerhard Lange 1968
H. Berthold AG
H 1–x 0,73–k 1,00–p 0,27

**the quick brown fox jumps over the lazy dog**

ITC **Franklin Gothic**
1377
fett
heavy
gras
N 020: 081 2457
Vic Caruso 1980
International Typeface Corp.
H 1–x 0,75–k 1,00–p 0,24

## BERTHOLD HEADLINES VI
Serifenlose Linear-Antiqua
Sans Serifs (Grotesques)
Linéar Antiqua sans empattements (Linéales)

THE QUICK BROWN FOX JUMPS OVER THE LAZY DOG 1234567890

THE QUICK BROWN FOX JUMPS OVER THE LAZY DOG 1234567890

THE QUICK BROWN FOX JUMPS OVER THE LAZY DOG 1234567890

QUICK BROWN FOX JUMPS OVER THE LAZY DOG 1234567890

THE QUICK BROWN FOX JUMPS OVER THE LAZY DOG 1234567890

THE QUICK BROWN FOX JUMPS OVER THE LAZY DOG 1234567890

THE QUICK BROWN FOX JUMPS OVER THE LAZY DOG 1234567890

THE QUICK BROWN FOX JUMPS OUER THE LAZY DOG 1234567890

## 57 Jüngere Grotesk / Late Grotesque / Grotesque moderne

the quick brown fox jumps over the lazy dog

**Etrusco 403-30**
493
fett
extra bold
gras
N 100: 081 1430
vor 1920
Societa Nebiolo S.p.A.
H 1–x 0,69–k 1,00–p 0,31

the quick brown fox jumps over the lazy dog

**Kompakte Grotesk**
731

N 100: 081 0823
Haas'sche Schriftgießerei AG
H 1–x 0,72–k 1,00–p 0,28

the quick brown fox jumps over the lazy dog

**Granby Elephant**
634

N 100: 081 0690
Photoscript Ltd.
H 1–x 0,78–k 1,00–p 0,25

the quick brown fox jumps over the lazy dog

**Univers 85**
1132
extrafett
ultra bold
extra gras
N 020: 081 2274
Adrian Frutiger 1957
Haas'sche Schriftgießerei AG
H 1–x 0,70–k 1,00–p 0,26

the quick brown fox jumps over the lazy dog

**Folio**
520
extrafett
extra bold
extra gras
N 100: 081 0568
K. F. Bauer, W. Baum 1959
Fundición Tipográfica Neufville, S.A.
H 1–x 0,78–k 1,00–p 0,28

the quick brown fox jumps over the lazy dog

**Block**
203
schwer
heavy
lourd
N 100: 081 1444
H. Hoffmann 1919
H. Berthold AG
H 1–x 0,80–k 1,00–p 0,13

the quick brown fox jumps over the lazy dog

**Antique Olive**
65
kompakt
compact
compacte
N 100: 081 0092
Roger Excoffon 1962
Marcel Olive
H 1–x 0,84–k 1,04–p 0,20

the quick brown fox jumps over the lazy dog

**Churchward 69**
332
extrafett
extra bold
extra gras
N 100: 081 0329
Joseph Churchward 1969
H. Berthold AG
H 1–x 0,75–k 1,00–p 0,31

**BERTHOLD HEADLINES VI**  Serifenlose Linear-Antiqua
Sans Serifs (Grotesques)
Linéar Antiqua sans empattements (Linéales)

# QUICK BROWN FOX JUMPS OVER THE LAZY DOG 1234567890

**BERTHOLD HEADLINES VI**  Serifenlose Linear-Antiqua
Sans Serifs (Grotesques)
Linéar Antiqua sans empattements (Linéales)

THE QUICK BROWN FOX JUMPS OVER THE LAZY DOG 1234567890

THE QUICK BROWN FOX JUMPS OVER THE LAZY DOG 1234567890

THE QUICK BROWN FOX JUMPS OVER THE LAZY DOG 1234567890

THE QUICK BROWN FOX JUMPS OVER THE LAZY DOG 1234567890

THE QUICK BROWN FOX JUMPS OVER THE LAZY DOG 1234567890

THE QUICK BROWN FOX JUMPS OVER THE LAZY DOG 1234567890

## 57 Jüngere Grotesk / Late Grotesque / Grotesque moderne

the quick brown fox jumps
over the lazy dog

**Churchward 69**
334
ultrafett
ultra bold
ultra gras
N 100: 081 1437
Joseph Churchward 1969
H. Berthold AG
H 1–x 0,78–k 1,00–p 0,31

## 58 Jüngere Grotesk, kursive / Late Grotesque, italic / Grotesque moderne, italique

the quick brown fox jumps
over the lazy dog

**Helvetica**
653
kursiv ultraleicht
ultra light italic
italique ultra maigre
N 100: 081 0718
Haas'sche Schriftgießerei AG
H 1–x 0,72–k 1,00–p 0,25

the quick brown fox jumps
over the lazy dog

ITC **Avant Garde Gothic**
98
schräg mager
extra light oblique
oblique maigre
N 020: 081 2386
Gschwind, Gürtler, Mengelt 1977
International Typeface Corp.
H 1–x 0,72–k 1,00–p 0,28

the quick brown fox jumps
over the lazy dog

**Univers 46**
1125
kursiv mager
light italic
italique maigre
N 100: 081 1234
Adrian Frutiger 1957
Haas'sche Schriftgießerei AG
H 1–x 0,70–k 1,00–p 0,25

the quick brown fox jumps
over the lazy dog

**Helvetica**
655
kursiv leicht
light italic
italique maigre
N 100: 081 0721
1967/68
D. Stempel AG
H 1–x 0,74–k 1,00–p 0,27

the quick brown fox jumps
over the lazy dog

ITC **Avant Garde Gothic**
101
Buch schräg
book oblique
romain labeur oblique
N 020: 081 2387
Gschwind, Gürtler, Mengelt 1977
International Typeface Corp.
H 1–x 0,74–k 1,00–p 0,26

the quick brown fox jumps
over the lazy dog

**Planschrift**
935
kursiv
italic
italique
N 000: 081 1024
H. Berthold AG
H 1–x 0,69–k 1,00–p 0,37

**BERTHOLD HEADLINES VI**
Serifenlose Linear-Antiqua
Sans Serifs (Grotesques)
Linéar Antiqua sans empattements (Linéales)

THE QUICK BROWN FOX JUMPS OVER
THE LAZY DOG 1234567890

THE QUICK BROWN FOX JUMPS OVER
THE LAZY DOG 1234567890

THE QUICK BROWN FOX JUMPS OVER
THE LAZY DOG 1234567890

THE QUICK BROWN FOX JUMPS OVER
THE LAZY DOG 1234567890

THE QUICK BROWN FOX JUMPS OVER
THE LAZY DOG 1234567890

THE QUICK BROWN FOX JUMPS OVER
THE LAZY DOG 1234567890

THE QUICK BROWN FOX JUMPS OVER
THE LAZY DOG 1234567890

THE QUICK BROWN FOX JUMPS OVER
THE LAZY DOG 1234567890

## 58 Jüngere Grotesk, kursive / Late Grotesque, italic / Grotesque moderne, italique

*the quick brown fox jumps over the lazy dog*

**Folio**
517
kursiv mager
light italic
italique maigre
N 100: 081 0533
K. F. Bauer, W. Baum 1959
Fundición Tipográfica Neufville, S.A.
H 1–x 0,65–k 1,00–p 0,30

*the quick brown fox jumps over the lazy dog*

**Akzidenz-Grotesk**
7
kursiv
italic
italique
N 100: 081 0007
Günter Gerhard Lange 1967
H. Berthold AG
H 1–x 0,67–k 1,00–p 0,30

*the quick brown fox jumps over the lazy dog*

ITC **Franklin Gothic**
1372
Buch kursiv
book italic
italique romain labeur
N 020: 081 2458
Vic Caruso 1980
International Typeface Corp.
H 1–x 0,74–k 1,00–p 0,25

*the quick brown fox jumps over the lazy dog*

**Akzidenz-Grotesk Buch**
26
kursiv
italic
italique
N 100: 081 0053
Günter Gerhard Lange 1969
H. Berthold AG
H 1–x 0,73–k 1,00–p 0,27

*the quick brown fox jumps over the lazy dog*

**Churchward Tranquillity**
380
kursiv
medium italic
italique
N 100: 081 0346
Joseph Churchward 1972
H. Berthold AG
H 1–x 0,72–k 1,00–p 0,28

*the quick brown fox jumps over the lazy dog*

**Univers 56**
1127
kursiv
medium italic
italique
N 100: 081 1254
Adrian Frutiger 1957
Haas'sche Schriftgießerei AG
H 1–x 0,69–k 1,00–p 0,28

*the quick brown fox jumps over the lazy dog*

**Helvetica**
657
kursiv
italic
italique
N 100: 081 0726
Max Miedinger 1961
Haas'sche Schriftgießerei AG
H 1–x 0,74–k 1,00–p 0,26

*the quick brown fox jumps over the lazy dog*

ITC **Avant Garde Gothic**
104
schräg normal
medium oblique
oblique normal

N 020: 081 2388
Gschwind, Gürtler, Mengelt 1977
H 1–x 0,76–k 1,00–p 0,25

## BERTHOLD HEADLINES VI
Serifenlose Linear-Antiqua
Sans Serifs (Grotesques)
Linéar Antiqua sans empattements (Linéales)

THE QUICK BROWN FOX JUMPS OVER
THE LAZY DOG 1234567890

THE QUICK BROWN FOX JUMPS OVER
THE LAZY DOG 1234567890

THE QUICK BROWN FOX JUMPS OVER
THE LAZY DOG 1234567890

THE QUICK BROWN FOX JUMPS OVER
THE LAZY DOG 1234567890

THE QUICK BROWN FOX JUMPS OVER
THE LAZY DOG 1234567890

THE QUICK BROWN FOX JUMPS OVER
THE LAZY DOG 1234567890

THE QUICK BROWN FOX JUMPS OVER
THE LAZY DOG 1234567890

THE QUICK BROWN FOX JUMPS OVER
THE LAZY DOG 1234567890

Jüngere Grotesk, kursive
Late Grotesque, italic
Grotesque moderne, italique

**58**

*the quick brown fox jumps over the lazy dog*

**Antique Olive**
62
kursiv
italic
italique
N 100: 081 1567
Roger Excoffon 1966
Marcel Olive
H 1–x 0,84–k 1,03–p 0,20

*the quick brown fox jumps over the lazy dog*

ITC **Franklin Gothic**
1374
kursiv
italic
italique
N 020: 081 2459
Vic Caruso 1980
International Typeface Corp.
H 1–x 0,74–k 1,00–p 0,26

*the quick brown fox jumps over the lazy dog*

**Akzidenz-Grotesk**
9
kursiv halbfett
medium italic
italique demi-gras
N 100: 081 0014
Günter Gerhard Lange 1963
H. Berthold AG
H 1–x 0,70–k 1,00–p 0,25

*the quick brown fox jumps over the lazy dog*

**Churchward Tranquillity**
382
kursiv halbfett
demi-bold italic
italique demi-gras
N 100: 081 0349
Joseph Churchward 1972
H. Berthold AG
H 1–x 0,69–k 1,00–p 0,26

*the quick brown fox jumps over the lazy dog*

**Univers 66**
1129
kursiv halbfett
bold italic
italique demi-gras
N 100: 081 1283
Adrian Frutiger 1957
Haas'sche Schriftgießerei AG
H 1–x 0,69–k 1,00–p 0,27

*the quick brown fox jumps over the lazy dog*

ITC **Avant Garde Gothic**
107
schräg halbfett
demi oblique
oblique demi-gras
N 020: 081 2389
Gschwind, Gürtler, Mengelt 1977
International Typeface Corp.
H 1–x 0,76–k 1,00–p 0,25

*the quick brown fox jumps over the lazy dog*

**Helvetica**
659
kursiv halbfett
medium italic
italique demi-gras
N 100: 081 0733
1969
Haas'sche Schriftgießerei AG
H 1–x 0,72–k 1,00–p 0,28

*the quick brown fox jumps over the lazy dog*

**Akzidenz-Grotesk**
11
kursiv fett
bold italic
italique gras
N 100: 081 0017
Günter Gerhard Lange 1968
H. Berthold AG
H 1–x 0,72–k 1,00–p 0,25

**BERTHOLD HEADLINES VI** — Serifenlose Linear-Antiqua / Sans Serifs (Grotesques) / Linéar Antiqua sans empattements (Linéales)

*THE QUICK BROWN FOX JUMPS OVER THE LAZY DOG 1234567890*

*THE QUICK BROWN FOX JUMPS OVER THE LAZY DOG 1234567890*

*THE QUICK BROWN FOX JUMPS OVER THE LAZY DOG 1234567890*

*THE QUICK BROWN FOX JUMPS OVER THE LAZY DOG 1234567890*

*THE QUICK BROWN FOX JUMPS OVER THE LAZY DOG 1234567890*

*THE QUICK BROWN FOX JUMPS OVER THE LAZY DOG 1234567890*

*THE QUICK BROWN FOX JUMPS OVER THE LAZY DOG 1234567890*

*QUICK BROWN FOX JUMPS OVER THE LAZY DOG 1234567890*

Jüngere Grotesk, kursive
Late Grotesque, italic
Grotesque moderne, italique
**58**

*the quick brown fox jumps over the lazy dog*

**Venus**
1164
kursiv fett
bold italic
italique gras
N 100: 081 1340
1913
Fundición Tipográfica Neufville, S.A.
H 1–x 0,72–k 1,00–p 0,22

*the quick brown fox jumps over the lazy dog*

ITC **Franklin Gothic**
1376
kursiv halbfett
demi italic
italique demi-gras
N 020: 081 2460
Vic Caruso 1980
International Typeface Corp.
H 1–x 0,74–k 1,00–p 0,25

*the quick brown fox jumps over the lazy dog*

ITC **Avant Garde Gothic**
110
schräg fett
bold oblique
oblique gras
N 020: 081 2390
Gschwind, Gürtler, Mengelt 1977
International Typeface Corp.
H 1–x 0,76–k 1,01–p 0,25

*the quick brown fox jumps over the lazy dog*

ATF **Franklin Gothic**
534
kursiv
italic
italique
N 100: 081 0581
Morris F. Benton 1913
American Typefounders
H 1–x 0,70–k 1,00–p 0,25

*the quick brown fox jumps over the lazy dog*

**Univers 76**
1131
kursiv fett
extra bold italic
italique gras
N 100: 081 1307
Adrian Frutiger 1957
Haas'sche Schriftgießerei AG
H 1–x 0,69–k 1,00–p 0,26

*the quick brown fox jumps over the lazy dog*

ITC **Franklin Gothic**
1378
kursiv fett
heavy italic
italique gras
N 020: 081 2461
Vic Caruso 1980
International Typeface Corp.
H 1–x 0,74–k 1,00–p 0,24

*the quick brown fox jumps over the lazy dog*

**Helvetica**
661
kursiv fett
bold italic
italique gras
N 100: 081 0737
1967
Haas'sche Schriftgießerei AG
H 1–x 0,71–k 1,00–p 0,25

*the quick brown fox jumps over the lazy dog*

**Grotesk**
639
kursiv fett
bold italic
italique gras

N 100: 081 0704
Lettergieterij Amsterdam
H 1–x 0,72–k 1,00–p 0,28

## BERTHOLD HEADLINES VI
Serifenlose Linear-Antiqua
Sans Serifs (Grotesques)
Linéar Antiqua sans empattements (Linéales)

QUICK BROWN FOX JUMPS OVER
THE LAZY DOG 1234567890

QUICK BROWN FOX JUMPS
OVER THE DOG 1234567890

THE QUICK BROWN FOX JUMPS OVER
THE LAZY DOG 1234567890

QUICK BROWN FOX JUMPS
OVER THE DOG 1234567890

THE QUICK BROWN FOX JUMPS OVER
THE LAZY DOG 1234567890

## BERTHOLD HEADLINES VI
Serifenlose Linear-Antiqua
Sans Serifs (Grotesques)
Linéar Antiqua sans empattements (Linéales)

THE QUICK BROWN FOX JUMPS OVER
THE LAZY DOG 1234567890

THE QUICK BROWN FOX JUMPS OVER
THE LAZY DOG 1234567890

## 58
Jüngere Grotesk, kursive
Late Grotesque, italic
Grotesque moderne, italique

**Etrusco 403-35**
494
kursiv fett
extra bold italic
italique gras
N 100: 081 1431
vor 1920
Societa Nebiolo S.p.A.
H 1–x 0,72–k 1,00–p 0,28

*the quick brown fox jumps over the lazy dog*

**Helvetica Diagonal**
662

*the quick brown fox jumps over the lazy dog*

N 100: 081 0738
Haas'sche Schriftgießerei AG
H 1–x 0,72–k 1,00–p 0,31

**Churchward 69**
333
kursiv extrafett
extra bold italic
italique extra gras
N 100: 081 1446
Joseph Churchward 1969
H. Berthold AG
H 1–x 0,75–k 1,00–p 0,31

*the quick brown fox jumps over the lazy dog*

**Churchward 69**
335
kursiv ultrafett
ultra bold italic
italique ultra gras
N 100: 081 1438
Joseph Churchward 1969
H. Berthold AG
H 1–x 0,81–k 1,00–p 0,34

*quick brown fox jumps over the lazy dog*

**Planschrift**
936
linkskursiv
reclining
penché à gauche

the quick brown fox jumps
over the lazy dog

N 000: 081 1025
H. Berthold AG
H 1–x 0,69–k 1,00–p 0,37

## 59
Jüngere Grotesk, enge
Late Grotesque, narrow
Grotesque moderne, très étroit

**Univers 39**
1133
extraschmal ultraleicht
ultra light extra consensed
extra étroit ultra maigre
N 100: 081 1227
Adrian Frutiger 1957
Haas'sche Schriftgießerei AG
H 1–x 0,70–k 1,02–p 0,26

the quick brown fox jumps
over the lazy dog

**Roc**
993
mager
light
maigre
V 000: 081 1087
A. Hollenstein
H. Berthold AG
H 1–Q 1,00

## BERTHOLD HEADLINES VI
Serifenlose Linear-Antiqua
Sans Serifs (Grotesques)
Linéar Antiqua sans empattements (Linéales)

THE QUICK BROWN FOX JUMPS OVER
THE LAZY DOG 1234567890

THE QUICK BROWN FOX JUMPS OVER
THE LAZY DOG 1234567890

THE QUICK BROWN FOX JUMPS OVER
THE LAZY DOG 1234567890

THE QUICK BROWN FOX JUMPS OVER
THE LAZY DOG 1234567890

THE QUICK BROWN FOX JUMPS OVER
THE LAZY DOG 1234567890

THE QUICK BROWN FOX JUMPS OVER
THE LAZY DOG 1234567890

THE QUICK BROWN FOX JUMPS OVER
THE LAZY DOG 1234567890

THE QUICK BROWN FOX JUMPS OVER
THE LAZY DOG 1234567890

## 59 Jüngere Grotesk, enge / Late Grotesque, narrow / Grotesque moderne, très étroit

**Signum**
1038

the quick brown fox jumps
over the lazy dog

N 000: 081 1124
Georg Trump 1955
Johannes Wagner
H 1–x 0,72–k 1,00–p 0,25

**Univers 49**
1134
extra schmalmager
extra light condensed
extra étroit maigre

the quick brown fox jumps
over the lazy dog

N 100: 081 1243
Adrian Frutiger 1957
Haas'sche Schriftgießerei AG
H 1–x 0,69–k 1,00–p 0,26

**Grotesk**
640
schmal
condensed
étroit

the quick brown fox jumps
over the lazy dog

N 100: 081 0701
Lettergieterij Amsterdam
H 1–x 0,76–k 1,00–p 0,18

**Grotesque No. 7**
647
eng
condensed
étroit

the quick brown fox jumps
over the lazy dog

N 100: 081 0693
Stephenson Blake & Company Ltd.
H 1–x 0,74–k 1,00–p 0,29

**Neue Aurora-Grotesk**
856
schmalhalbfett
medium condensed
étroit demi-gras

the quick brown fox jumps
over the lazy dog

N 000: 081 0920
1964
Johannes Wagner
H 1–x 0,88–k 1,00–p 0,09

**Placard**
932
halbfett
medium
demi-gras

the quick brown fox jumps
over the lazy dog

N 000: 081 1016
1958
Monotype Corporation Ltd.
H 1–x 0,81–k 1,00–p 0,10

**Aurora-Grotesk**
90
schmalhalbfett
medium condensed
étroit demi-gras

the quick brown fox jumps
over the lazy dog

N 000: 081 0120
1912
Johannes Wagner
H 1–x 0,88–k 1,00–p 0,09

**Information**
692
engfett
bold condensed
étroit gras

the quick brown fox jumps
over the lazy dog

N 100: 081 0785
1919
D. Stempel AG
H 1–x 0,78–k 1,00–p 0,16

## BERTHOLD HEADLINES VI
Serifenlose Linear-Antiqua
Sans Serifs (Grotesques)
Linéar Antiqua sans empattements (Linéales)

THE QUICK BROWN FOX JUMPS OVER
THE LAZY DOG 1234567890

THE QUICK BROWN FOX JUMPS OVER
THE LAZY DOG 1234567890

THE QUICK BROWN FOX JUMPS OVER
THE LAZY DOG 1234567890

THE QUICK BROWN FOX JUMPS OVER
THE LAZY DOG 1234567890

## BERTHOLD HEADLINES VI
Serifenlose Linear-Antiqua
Sans Serifs (Grotesques)
Linéar Antiqua sans empattements (Linéales)

THE QUICK BROWN FOX JUMPS OVER
THE LAZY DOG 1234567890

THE QUICK BROWN FOX JUMPS OVER
THE LAZY DOG 1234567890

THE QUICK BROWN FOX JUMPS OVER
THE LAZY DOG 1234567890

## 59 — Jüngere Grotesk, enge / Late Grotesque, narrow / Grotesque moderne, très étroit

**the quick brown fox jumps over the lazy dog**

Roc
994
normal
regular
normal
N 100: 081 1089
A. Hollenstein
H. Berthold AG
H 1–x 0,78–k 1,00–p 0,22

**the quick brown fox jumps over the lazy dog**

Folio
521
engfett
bold extra condensed
extra étroit gras
N 100: 081 0558
K. F. Bauer, W. Baum 1966
Fundición Tipográfica Neufville, S.A.
H 1–x 0,72–k 1,00–p 0,28

**the quick brown fox jumps over the lazy dog**

Churchward 69
336
schmalhalbfett
elongated
étroit demi-gras
N 100: 081 0330
Joseph Churchward 1969
H. Berthold AG
H 1–x 0,72–k 1,00–p 0,19

**the quick brown fox jumps over the lazy dog**

Permanent Headline
920
normal
regular
normal
N 100: 081 0711
1967
Ludwig & Mayer
H 1–x 0,81–k 1,00–p 0,00

## 60 — Jüngere Grotesk, engschmale / Late Grotesque, narrow condensed / Grotesque moderne, étroit

the quick brown fox jumps over the lazy dog

Venus
1165
schmalmager
light condensed
étroit maigre
N 100: 081 1342
1912
Fundición Tipográfica Neufville, S.A.
H 1–x 0,72–k 1,00–p 0,19

the quick brown fox jumps over the lazy dog

Akzidenz-Grotesk
13
schmalmager
light condensed
étroit maigre
N 100: 081 0023
1953
H. Berthold AG
H 1–x 0,71–k 1,00–p 0,23

the quick brown fox jumps over the lazy dog

News Gothic
869
schmal
condensed
étroit
N 100: 081 0941
Morris F. Benton 1909
American Typefounders
H 1–x 0,72–k 1,00–p 0,25

## BERTHOLD HEADLINES VI

Serifenlose Linear-Antiqua
Sans Serifs (Grotesques)
Linéar Antiqua sans empattements (Linéales)

THE QUICK BROWN FOX JUMPS OVER
THE LAZY DOG 1234567890

THE QUICK BROWN FOX JUMPS OVER
THE LAZY DOG 1234567890

THE QUICK BROWN FOX JUMPS OVER
THE LAZY DOG 1234567890

THE QUICK BROWN FOX JUMPS OVER
THE LAZY DOG 1234567890

THE QUICK BROWN FOX JUMPS OVER
THE LAZY DOG 1234567890

THE QUICK BROWN FOX JUMPS OVER
THE LAZY DOG 1234567890

THE QUICK BROWN FOX JUMPS OVER
THE LAZY DOG 1234567890

THE QUICK BROWN FOX JUMPS OVER
THE LAZY DOG 1234567890

Jüngere Grotesk, engschmale
Late Grotesque, narrow condensed
Grotesque moderne, étroit
**60**

**Planschrift**
934
normal
regular
normal

N 000: 081 1023
H. Berthold AG
H 1−x 0,72−k 1,00−p 0,28

the quick brown fox jumps
over the lazy dog

---

**Akzidenz-Grotesk**
14
eng
condensed
étroit
N 100: 081 0022
1912
H. Berthold AG
H 1−x 0,71−k 1,00−p 0,23

the quick brown fox jumps
over the lazy dog

---

**Venus**
1166
schmalhalbfett
medium condensed
étroit demi-gras
N 000: 081 1346
1913
Fundición Tipográfica Neufville, S.A.
H 1−x 0,72−k 1,00−p 0,22

the quick brown fox jumps
over the lazy dog

---

**Akzidenz-Grotesk**
15
schmalhalbfett
medium condensed
étoit demi-gras
N 100: 081 0024
1896
H. Berthold AG
H 1−x 0,75−k 1,00−p 0,20

the quick brown fox jumps
over the lazy dog

---

**Neuzeit-Grotesk**
862
schmalhalbfett
medium condensed
étroit demi-gras
N 000: 081 0934
Wilhelm Pischner 1938/39
D. Stempel AG
H 1−x 0,72−k 1,00−p 0,25

the quick brown fox jumps
over the lazy dog

---

**Univers 59**
1135
extraschmal
extra condensed
extra étroit
N 100: 081 1266
Adrian Frutiger 1957
Haas'sche Schriftgießerei AG
H 1−x 0,69−k 1,00−p 0,26

the quick brown fox jumps
over the lazy dog

---

**Steinschrift**
1059

N 000: 081 1144
1912
Johannes Wagner
H 1−x 0,69−k 1,00−p 0,31

the quick brown fox jumps
over the lazy dog

---

**Helvetica**
664
schmalhalbfett
medium condensed
étroit demi-gras
N 100: 081 0740
1940
Haas'sche Schriftgießerei AG
H 1−x 0,75−k 1,00−p 0,25

the quick brown fox jumps
over the lazy dog

## BERTHOLD HEADLINES VI
Serifenlose Linear-Antiqua
Sans Serifs (Grotesques)
Linéar Antiqua sans empattements (Linéales)

**THE QUICK BROWN FOX JUMPS OVER THE LAZY DOG 1234567890**

**THE QUICK BROWN FOX JUMPS OVER THE LAZY DOG 1234567890**

**THE QUICK BROWN FOX JUMPS OVER THE LAZY DOG 1234567890**

**THE QUICK BROWN FOX JUMPS OVER THE LAZY DOG 1234567890**

**THE QUICK BROWN FOX JUMPS OVER THE LAZY DOG 1234567890**

**THE QUICK BROWN FOX JUMPS OVER THE LAZY DOG 1234567890**

**THE QUICK BROWN FOX JUMPS OVER THE LAZY DOG 1234567890**

**THE QUICK BROWN FOX JUMPS OVER THE LAZY DOG 1234567890**

## 60
Jüngere Grotesk, engschmale  
Late Grotesque, narrow condensed  
Grotesque moderne, étroit

**the quick brown fox jumps over the lazy dog**

**Grotesk**
641
schmalfett
bold condensed
étroit gras
N 100: 081 0703
Lettergieterij Amsterdam
H 1–x 0,72–k 1,00–p 0,22

**Sans Serif**
1007
schmal
condensed
étroit
V 000: 081 1531
Thorowgood 1839
Stephenson Blake & Company Ltd.
H 1–Q 1,25

**the quick brown fox jumps over the lazy dog**

ATF **Franklin Gothic**
535
extraschmal
extra condensed
extra étroit
N 100: 081 0584
Morris F. Benton 1906
American Typefounders
H 1–x 0,71–k 1,00–p 0,21

**the quick brown fox jumps over the lazy dog**

**Placard**
933
fett
bold
gras
N 100: 081 1017
1958
Monotype Corporation Ltd.
H 1–x 0,81–k 1,00–p 0,19

**the quick brown fox jumps over the lazy dog**

**Folio**
524
schmalfett
bold condensed
étroit gras
N 100: 081 0552
K. F. Bauer, W. Baum 1956
Fundición Tipográfica Neufville, S.A.
H 1–x 0,72–k 1,00–p 0,25

**the quick brown fox jumps over the lazy dog**

**Information**
691
schmalfett
extra bold condensed
étroit gras
N 100: 081 0786
1919
D. Stempel AG
H 1–x 0,75–k 1,00–p 0,19

**the quick brown fox jumps over the lazy dog**

**Helvetica**
665
schmalfett
bold condensed
étroit gras
N 100: 081 0742
1946
Haas'sche Schriftgießerei AG
H 1–x 0,76–k 1,00–p 0,21

**the quick brown fox jumps over the lazy dog**

**Anzeigen-Grotesk**
71

N 100: 081 0093
Haas'sche Schriftgießerei AG
H 1–x 0,86–k 1,00–p 0,11

**BERTHOLD HEADLINES VI** — Serifenlose Linear-Antiqua / Sans Serifs (Grotesques) / Linéar Antiqua sans empattements (Linéales)

THE QUICK BROWN FOX JUMPS OVER
THE LAZY DOG 1234567890

THE QUICK BROWN FOX JUMPS OVER
THE LAZY DOG 1234567890

THE QUICK BROWN FOX JUMPS OVER
THE LAZY DOG 1234567890

THE QUICK BROWN FOX JUMPS OVER
THE LAZY DOG 1234567890

THE QUICK BROWN FOX JUMPS OVER
THE LAZY DOG 1234567890

**BERTHOLD HEADLINES VI** — Serifenlose Linear-Antiqua / Sans Serifs (Grotesques) / Linéar Antiqua sans empattements (Linéales)

THE QUICK BROWN FOX JUMPS OVER
THE LAZY DOG 1234567890

THE QUICK BROWN FOX JUMPS OVER
THE LAZY DOG 1234567890

## 60 Jüngere Grotesk, engschmale / Late Grotesque, narrow condensed / Grotesque moderne, étroit

**Aurora-Grotesk**
91
schmalfett
bold condensed
étroit gras
N 000: 081 0121
1912
Johannes Wagner
H 1–x 0,86–k 1,00–p 0,09

the quick brown fox jumps
over the lazy dog

**Neue Aurora-Grotesk**
857
schmalfett
bold condensed
étroit gras
N 000: 081 0922
1964
Johannes Wagner
H 1–x 0,88–k 1,00–p 0,09

the quick brown fox jumps
over the lazy dog

**Impact**
681

N 100: 081 0768
Geoffrey Lee 1965
Lettergieterij Amsterdam
H 1–x 0,81–k 1,00–p 0,13

the quick brown fox jumps
over the lazy dog

**Block**
204
eng
extra condensed
extra étroit
N 100: 081 0170
H. Hoffmann 1926
H. Berthold AG
H 1–x 0,78–k 1,00–p 0,11

the quick brown fox jumps
over the lazy dog

**Churchward 69**
338
schmalfett
bold condensed
étroit gras
N 100: 081 0327
Joseph Churchward 1969
H. Berthold AG
H 1–x 0,72–k 1,00–p 0,28

the quick brown fox jumps
over the lazy dog

## 61 Jüngere Grotesk, schmale / Late Grotesque, medium condensed / Grotesque moderne, demi-étroit

**Lightline Gothic**
802

N 000: 081 0860
Morris F. Benton 1908
American Typefounders
H 1–x 0,68–k 1,00–p 0,27

the quick brown fox jumps
over the lazy dog

**ISO 3098 (DIN 6776) A**
694
vertikal
vertical
vertical
N 101: 081 1816
1981
H. Berthold AG
H 1–x 0,74–k 1,00–p 0,28

the quick brown fox jumps
over the lazy dog

**BERTHOLD HEADLINES VI**  Serifenlose Linear-Antiqua
Sans Serifs (Grotesques)
Linéar Antiqua sans empattements (Linéales)

THE QUICK BROWN FOX JUMPS OVER
THE LAZY DOG 1234567890

THE QUICK BROWN FOX JUMPS OVER
THE LAZY DOG 1234567890

THE QUICK BROWN FOX JUMPS OVER
THE LAZY DOG 1234567890

THE QUICK BROWN FOX JUMPS OVER
THE LAZY DOG 1234567890

THE QUICK BROWN FOX JUMPS OVER
THE LAZY DOG

THE QUICK BROWN FOX JUMPS OVER
THE LAZY DOG 1234567890

THE QUICK BROWN FOX JUMPS OVER
THE LAZY DOG 1234567890

THE QUICK BROWN FOX JUMPS OVER
THE LAZY DOG 1234567890

**Jüngere Grotesk, schmale**
**Late Grotesque, medium condensed**
**Grotesque moderne, demi-étroit**

# 61

the quick brown fox jumps
over the lazy dog

**Univers 47**
1136
schmalmager
light condensed
étroit maigre
N 100: 081 1236
Adrian Frutiger
Haas'sche Schriftgießerei AG
H 1–x 0,70–k 1,00–p 0,25

the quick brown fox jumps
over the lazy dog

**Digi-Grotesk Serie S**
445
schmal
condensed
étroit
N 100: 081 1450
1968
Dr.-Ing. Rudolf Hell GmbH
H 1–x 0,67–k 1,00–p 0,33

the quick brown fox jumps
over the lazy dog

**Folio**
522
schmalmager
light condensed
étroit maigre
N 100: 081 0544
K. F. Bauer, W. Baum 1962
Fundición Tipográfica Neufville, S.A.
H 1–x 0,72–k 1,00–p 0,25

the quick brown fox jumps
over the lazy dog

ITC **Avant Garde Gothic**
111
Buch schmal
book condensed
étroit romain labeur
N 100: 081 1606
Ed Benguiat 1974
International Typeface Corp.
H 1–x 0,76–k 1,00–p 0,28

the quick brown fox jumps
over the lazy dog

ITC **Avant Garde Gothic**
112
Buch schmal Zierbuchstaben
book condensed swash letters
étroit romain labeur lettres ornées
Z 000: 081 1607
Ed Benguiat 1974
International Typeface Corp.
H 1–x 0,76–k 1,00–p 0,28

the quick brown fox jumps
over the lazy dog

**Helvetica**
663
schmalmager
light condensed
étroit maigre
N 100: 081 0739
1963
D. Stempel AG
H 1–x 0,74–k 1,00–p 0,25

the quick brown fox jumps
over the lazy dog

**Univers 57**
1138
schmal
medium condensed
étroit
N 100: 081 1258
Adrian Frutiger 1957
Haas'sche Schriftgießerei AG
H 1–x 0,69–k 1,00–p 0,25

the quick brown fox jumps
over the lazy dog

ITC **Avant Garde Gothic**
113
schmal
medium condensed
étroit
N 100: 081 1608
Ed Benguiat 1974
International Typeface Corp.
H 1–x 0,78–k 1,00–p 0,28

# BERTHOLD HEADLINES VI

Serifenlose Linear-Antiqua
Sans Serifs (Grotesques)
Linéar Antiqua sans empattements (Linéales)

THE QUICK BROWN FOX JUMPS OVER
THE LAZY DOG

THE QUICK BROWN FOX JUMPS OVER
THE LAZY DOG 1234567890

THE QUICK BROWN FOX JUMPS OVER
THE LAZY DOG 1234567890

THE QUICK BROWN FOX JUMPS OVER
THE LAZY DOG 1234567890

THE QUICK BROWN FOX JUMPS OVER
THE LAZY DOG 1234567890

THE QUICK BROWN FOX JUMPS OVER
THE LAZY DOG 1234567890

THE QUICK BROWN FOX JUMPS OVER
THE LAZY DOG

THE QUICK BROWN FOX JUMPS OVER
THE LAZY DOG 1234567890

Jüngere Grotesk, schmale
Late Grotesque, medium condensed
Grotesque moderne, demi-étroit  **61**

the quick brown fox jumps
over the lazy dog

**ITC Avant Garde Gothic**
114
schmal Zierbuchstaben
medium condensed swash letters
étroit lettres ornées
Z 100: 081 1609
Ed Benguiat 1974
International Typeface Corp.
H 1–x 0,78–k 1,00–p 0,28

the quick brown fox jumps
over the lazy dog

**Alternate Gothic No. 3**
41
normal
regular
normal
N 100: 081 0059
Morris F. Benton 1903
American Typefounders
H 1–x 0,76–k 1,00–p 0,24

the quick brown fox jumps
over the lazy dog

**Antique Olive**
66
schmal
condensed
étroite
N 100: 081 1569
Roger Excoffon 1967
Marcel Olive
H 1–x 0,84–k 1,04–p 0,20

the quick brown fox jumps
over the lazy dog

**Folio**
523
schmalhalbfett
medium condensed
étroit demi-gras
N 100: 081 0549
K. F. Bauer, W. Baum 1962
Fundición Tipográfica Neufville, S.A.
H 1–x 0,72–k 1,00–p 0,28

the quick brown fox jumps
over the lazy dog

**DIN 1451-Engschrift Teil 2**
1370
fett
bold
gras
N 020: 081 2547
1981
H. Berthold AG
H 1–x 0,72–k 1,00–p 0,29

the quick brown fox jumps
over the lazy dog

**ITC Avant Garde Gothic**
115
schmalhalbfett
demi-bold condensed
étroit demi-gras
N 010: 081 2053
Ed Benguiat 1974
International Typeface Corp.
H 1–x 0,79–k 1,00–p 0,20

the quick brown fox jumps
over the lazy dog

**ITC Avant Garde Gothic**
116
schmalhalbfett Zierbuchstaben
demi-bold condensed swash letters
étroit demi-gras lettres ornées
Z 000: 081 2056
Ed Benguiat 1974
International Typeface Corp.
H 1–x 0,79–k 1,00–p 0,20

the quick brown fox jumps
over the lazy dog

**Akzidenz-Grotesk**
16
schmalfett
bold condensed
étroit gras
N 100: 081 1556
1896
H. Berthold AG
H 1–x 0,73–k 1,00–p 0,25

**BERTHOLD HEADLINES VI** — Serifenlose Linear-Antiqua / Sans Serifs (Grotesques) / Linéar Antiqua sans empattements (Linéales)

THE QUICK BROWN FOX JUMPS OVER
THE LAZY DOG 1234567890

THE QUICK BROWN FOX JUMPS OVER
THE LAZY DOG 1234567890

THE QUICK BROWN FOX JUMPS OVER
THE LAZY DOG 1234567890

THE QUICK BROWN FOX JUMPS OVER
THE LAZY DOG 1234567890

THE QUICK BROWN FOX JUMPS OVER
THE LAZY DOG 1234567890

THE QUICK BROWN FOX JUMPS OVER
THE LAZY DOG

THE QUICK BROWN FOX JUMPS OVER
THE LAZY DOG 1234567890

THE QUICK BROWN FOX JUMPS OVER
THE LAZY DOG 1234567890

## 61
Jüngere Grotesk, schmale
Late Grotesque, medium condensed
Grotesque moderne, demi-étroit

**the quick brown fox jumps over the lazy dog**

**Univers 67**
1140
schmalhalbfett
bold condensed
étroit demi-gras
N 100: 081 1289
Adrian Frutiger 1957
Haas'sche Schriftgießerei AG
H 1–x 0,69–k 1,00–p 0,25

**the quick brown fox jumps over the lazy dog**

**Steile Futura**
1057
fett
bold
gras
N 100: 081 1137
Paul Renner 1953
Fundición Tipográfica Neufville, S.A.
H 1–x 0,69–k 1,00–p 0,26

**the quick brown fox jumps over the lazy dog**

**Digi-Grotesk Serie S**
446
schmal kräftig
bold condensed
étroit gras
N 100: 081 1452
1968
Dr.-Ing. Rudolf Hell GmbH
H 1–x 0,67–k 1,00–p 0,29

**the quick brown fox jumps over the lazy dog**

ATF **Franklin Gothic**
536
schmal
condensed
étroit
N 100: 081 0583
Morris F. Benton 1906
American Typefounders
H 1–x 0,71–k 1,00–p 0,20

**the quick brown fox jumps over the lazy dog**

ITC **Avant Garde Gothic**
117
schmalfett
bold condensed
étroit gras
N 010: 081 2059
Ed Benguiat 1974
International Typeface Corp.
H 1–x 0,79–k 1,00–p 0,21

**the quick brown fox jumps over the lazy dog**

ITC **Avant Garde Gothic**
118
schmalfett Zierbuchstaben
bold condensed swash letters
étroit gras lettres ornées
Z 000: 081 2062
Ed Benguiat 1974
International Typeface Corp.
H 1–x 0,79–k 1,00–p 0,21

**the quick brown fox jumps over the lazy dog**

**Grotesque No. 9b**
646
schmalfett
bold condensed
étroit gras

N 100: 081 0696
Monotype Corporation Ltd.
H 1–x 0,74–k 1,00–p 0,23

**the quick brown fox jumps over the lazy dog**

**Grotesque No. 9a**
644
schmalfett
bold condensed
étroit gras

N 100: 081 0697
Monotype Corporation Ltd.
H 1–x 0,74–k 1,00–p 0,26

## BERTHOLD HEADLINES VI
Serifenlose Linear-Antiqua
Sans Serifs (Grotesques)
Linéar Antiqua sans empattements (Linéales)

THE QUICK BROWN FOX JUMPS OVER
THE LAZY DOG 1234567890

THE QUICK BROWN FOX JUMPS OVER
THE LAZY DOG 1234567890

THE QUICK BROWN FOX JUMPS OVER
THE LAZY DOG 1234567890

THE QUICK BROWN FOX JUMPS OVER
THE LAZY DOG 1234567890

THE QUICK BROWN FOX JUMPS OVER
THE LAZY DOG 1234567890

THE QUICK BROWN FOX JUMPS OVER
THE LAZY DOG 1234567890

## BERTHOLD HEADLINES VI
Serifenlose Linear-Antiqua
Sans Serifs (Grotesques)
Linéar Antiqua sans empattements (Linéales)

*THE QUICK BROWN FOX JUMPS OVER*
*THE LAZY DOG 1234567890*

**61** Jüngere Grotesk, schmale
Late Grotesque, medium condensed
Grotesque moderne, demi-étroit

**Eurostile**
497
schmalfett
bold condensed
étroit gras
N 100: 081 0513
Aldo Novarese 1962
Societa Nebiolo S.p.A.
H 1–x 0,71–k 1,00–p 0,25

# the quick brown fox jumps over the lazy dog

**Akzidenz-Grotesk**
17
extra
extra bold condensed
étroit extra gras
N 100: 081 0029
Günter Gerhard Lange 1958
H. Berthold AG
H 1–x 0,75–k 1,00–p 0,27

# the quick brown fox jumps over the lazy dog

**Antique Olive**
67
schmalfett
bold condensed
étroite grasse
N 100: 081 0085
Roger Excoffon 1968
Marcel Olive
H 1–x 0,84–k 1,04–p 0,20

# the quick brown fox jumps over the lazy dog

**Block**
205
schmal
condensed
étroit
N 100: 081 0174
H. Hoffmann 1922
H. Berthold AG
H 1–x 0,78–k 1,00–p 0,12

# the quick brown fox jumps over the lazy dog

**Akzidenz-Grotesk**
19
extrafett
extra bold
extra gras
N 100: 081 0031
Günter Gerhard Lange 1966
H. Berthold AG
H 1–x 0,75–k 1,00–p 0,24

# the quick brown fox jumps over the lazy dog

**Futura Display**
575

N 100: 081 0625
Paul Renner 1932
H. Berthold AG
H 1–x 0,78–k 1,00–p 0,28

# the quick brown fox jumps over the lazy dog

**62** Jüngere Grotesk, kursiv schmale
Late Grotesque, condensed italic
Grotesque moderne, italique étroit

**Univers 48**
1137
kursiv schmalmager
light condensed italic
italique étroit maigre
N 100: 081 1240
Adrian Frutiger 1957
Haas'sche Schriftgießerei AG
H 1–x 0,70–k 1,00–p 0,27

*the quick brown fox jumps over the lazy dog*

## BERTHOLD HEADLINES VI
Serifenlose Linear-Antiqua
Sans Serifs (Grotesques)
Linéar Antiqua sans empattements (Linéales)

*THE QUICK BROWN FOX JUMPS OVER*
*THE LAZY DOG 1234567890*

*THE QUICK BROWN FOX JUMPS OVER*
*THE LAZY DOG 1234567890*

*THE QUICK BROWN FOX JUMPS OVER*
*THE LAZY DOG 1234567890*

*THE QUICK BROWN FOX JUMPS OVER*
*THE LAZY DOG 1234567890*

*THE QUICK BROWN FOX JUMPS OVER*
*THE LAZY DOG 1234567890*

*THE QUICK BROWN FOX JUMPS OVER*
*THE LAZY DOG 1234567890*

*THE QUICK BROWN FOX JUMPS OVER*
*THE LAZY DOG 1234567890*

*THE QUICK BROWN FOX JUMPS OVER*
*THE LAZY DOG 1234567890*

Jüngere Grotesk, kursiv schmale  
Late Grotesque, condensed italic  
Grotesque moderne, italique étroit  
**62**

*the quick brown fox jumps over the lazy dog*

**ISO 3098 (DIN 6776) A**  
695  
kursiv  
italic  
italique  
N 101: 081 1817  
1981  
H. Berthold AG  
H 1–x 0,74–k 1,00–p 0,28

*the quick brown fox jumps over the lazy dog*

**ISO 3098 (DIN 6776) B**  
696  
kursiv  
italic  
italique  
N 101: 081 1819  
1981  
H. Berthold AG  
H 1–x 0,72–k 1,00–p 0,32

*the quick brown fox jumps over the lazy dog*

**Univers 58**  
1139  
kursiv schmal  
medium condensed italic  
italique étroit  
N 100: 081 1261  
Adrian Frutiger 1957  
Haas'sche Schriftgießerei AG  
H 1–x 0,69–k 1,00–p 0,26

***the quick brown fox jumps over the lazy dog***

**Steile Futura**  
1058  
schrägfett  
bold oblique  
oblique gras  
N 100: 081 1141  
Paul Renner 1954  
Fundición Tipográfica Neufville, S.A.  
H 1–x 0,69–k 1,00–p 0,28

***the quick brown fox jumps over the lazy dog***

**ATF Franklin Gothic**  
537  
kursiv schmal  
condensed italic  
italique étroit  
N 100: 081 1514  
Morris F. Benton  
American Typefounders  
H 1–x 0,69–k 1,00–p 0,25

***the quick brown fox jumps over the lazy dog***

**Grotesque No. 9**  
645  
kursiv schmalfett  
bold condensed italic  
italique étroit gras  

N 100: 081 0698  
Monotype Corporation Ltd.  
H 1–x 0,69–k 1,00–p 0,25

***the quick brown fox jumps over the lazy dog***

**Futura**  
556  
schräg schmalfett  
bold condensed oblique  
oblique étroit gras  
N 100: 081 0609  
Berthold-Schriftenatelier  
Fundición Tipográfica Neufville, S.A.  
H 1–x 0,72–k 1,06–p 0,22

***the quick brown fox jumps over the lazy dog***

**Folio**  
525  
kursiv schmalfett  
bold condensed italic  
italique étroit gras  
N 100: 081 0555  
K. F. Bauer, W. Baum 1964  
Fundición Tipográfica Neufville, S.A.  
H 1–x 0,72–k 1,00–p 0,28

**BERTHOLD HEADLINES VI**  
Serifenlose Linear-Antiqua  
Sans Serifs (Grotesques)  
Linéar Antiqua sans empattements (Linéales)

THE QUICK BROWN FOX JUMPS OVER
THE LAZY DOG 1234567890

THE QUICK BROWN FOX JUMPS OVER
THE LAZY DOG 1234567890

THE QUICK BROWN FOX JUMPS OVER
THE LAZY DOG 1234567890

THE QUICK BROWN FOX JUMPS OVER
THE LAZY DOG 1234567890

THE QUICK BROWN FOX JUMPS OVER
THE LAZY DOG 1234567890

THE QUICK BROWN FOX JUMPS OVER
THE LAZY DOG 1234567890

**BERTHOLD HEADLINES VI**  
Serifenlose Linear-Antiqua  
Sans Serifs (Grotesques)  
Linéar Antiqua sans empattements (Linéales)

QUICK BROWN FOX JUMPS OVER
THE LAZY DOG 1234567890

**62** Jüngere Grotesk, kursiv schmale / Late Grotesque, condensed italic / Grotesque moderne, italique étroit

*the quick brown fox jumps over the lazy dog*

**Permanent Headline**
921
kursiv
italic
italique
N 100: 081 0715
1969
Ludwig & Mayer
H 1–x 0,81–k 1,00–p 0,16

*the quick brown fox jumps over the lazy dog*

**Churchward 69**
337
kursiv schmalhalbfett
elongated italic
italique demi-gras
N 100: 081 0331
Joseph Churchward 1969
H. Berthold AG
H 1–x 0,69–k 1,00–p 0,20

*the quick brown fox jumps over the lazy dog*

**Churchward 69**
339
kursiv schmalfett
bold condensed italic
italique étroit gras
N 100: 081 0328
Joseph Churchward 1969
H. Berthold AG
H 1–x 0,72–k 1,00–p 0,25

*the quick brown fox jumps over the lazy dog*

**Univers 68**
1141
kursiv schmalhalbfett
bold condensed italic
italique étroit demi-gras
N 100: 081 1295
Adrian Frutiger 1957
Haas'sche Schriftgießerei AG
H 1–x 0,70–k 1,00–p 0,25

*the quick brown fox jumps over the lazy dog*

**Akzidenz-Grotesk**
18
kursiv extra
extra bold condensed italic
italique étroit extra gras
N 100: 081 1557
Günter Gerhard Lange 1968
H. Berthold AG
H 1–x 0,76–k 1,00–p 0,28

*the quick brown fox jumps over the lazy dog*

**Futura**
558
schräg extrafett schmal
extra bold condensed oblique
oblique étroit extra gras
N 100: 081 0616
Berthold-Schriftenatelier
Fundición Tipográfica Neufville, S.A.
H 1–x 0,72–k 1,09–p 0,22

**63** Jüngere Grotesk, breite / Late Grotesque, extended / Grotesque moderne, large

the quick brown fox jumps over the lazy dog

**Aurora-Grotesk**
92
breitmager
light extended
large maigre
N 000: 081 0122
1912
Johannes Wagner
H 1–x 0,69–k 1,00–p 0,28

337

## BERTHOLD HEADLINES VI
Serifenlose Linear-Antiqua
Sans Serifs (Grotesques)
Linéar Antiqua sans empattements (Linéales)

QUICK BROWN FOX JUMPS OVER THE LAZY DOG 1234567890

BROWN FOX JUMPS OVER THE LAZY DOG 1234567890

QUICK BROWN FOX JUMPS OVER THE LAZY DOG 1234567890

QUICK BROWN FOX JUMPS OVER THE LAZY DOG 1234567890

THE QUICK BROWN FOX JUMPS OVER THE LAZY DOG 1234567890

QUICK BROWN FOX JUMPS OVER THE LAZY DOG 1234567890

QUICK BROWN FOX JUMPS OVER THE LAZY DOG 1234567890

BROWN FOX JUMPS OVER THE LAZY DOG 1234567890

**Jüngere Grotesk, breite** **63**
**Late Grotesque, extended**
**Grotesque moderne, large**

the quick brown fox jumps over the lazy dog

Akzidenz-Grotesk
20
breitmager
light extended
large maigre
N 100: 081 0037
1911
H. Berthold AG
H 1–x 0,70–k 1,00–p 0,26

the quick brown fox jumps over the lazy dog

Eurostile
498
breit
extended
large
N 100: 081 0505
Aldo Novarese 1962
Societa Nebiolo S.p.A.
H 1–x 0,70–k 1,00–p 0,31

the quick brown fox jumps over the lazy dog

Univers 53
1142
breit
medium expanded
large
N 100: 081 1245
Adrian Frutiger 1957
Haas'sche Schriftgießerei AG
H 1–x 0,69–k, 1,00–p 0,26

the quick brown fox jumps over the lazy dog

Venus
1167
breithalbfett
medium extended
large demi-gras

N 100: 081 1347
Fundición Tipográfica Neufville, S.A.
H 1–x 0,69–k 1,00–p 0,28

the quick brown fox jumps over the lazy dog

Brasilia
250
normal
medium
demi-gras
N 100: 081 0225
Albert Hollenstein
H. Berthold AG
H 1–x 0,72–k 1,00–p 0,33

the quick brown fox jumps over the lazy dog

Akzidenz-Grotesk
21
breit
extended
large
N 100: 081 0038
1909
H. Berthold AG
H 1–x 0,69–k 1,00–p 0,28

the quick brown fox jumps over the lazy dog

Helvetica
666
breitmager
light extended
large maigre
N 100: 081 0745
1963
D. Stempel AG
H 1–x 0,74–k 1,00–p 0,25

the quick brown fox jumps over the lazy dog

Aurora-Grotesk
93
breithalbfett
medium extended
large demi-gras
N 100: 081 0124
1912
Johannes Wagner
H 1–x 0,73–k 1,00–p 0,27

## BERTHOLD HEADLINES VI
Serifenlose Linear-Antiqua
Sans Serifs (Grotesques)
Linéar Antiqua sans empattements (Linéales)

QUICK BROWN FOX JUMPS OVER THE LAZY DOG 1234567890

QUICK BROWN FOX JUMPS OVER THE LAZY DOG 1234567890

QUICK BROWN FOX JUMPS OVER THE LAZY DOG 1234567890

QUICK BROWN FOX JUMPS OVER THE LAZY DOG 1234567890

QUICK BROWN FOX JUMPS OVER THE LAZY DOG 1234567890

QUICK BROWN FOX JUMPS OVER THE LAZY DOG 1234567890

QUICK BROWN FOX JUMPS OVER THE LAZY DOG 1234567890

QUICK BROWN FOX JUMPS OVER THE LAZY DOG 1234567890

| | Jüngere Grotesk, breite  
Late Grotesque, extended  
Grotesque moderne, large | **63** |

### the quick brown fox jumps over the lazy dog

**Univers 63**  
1143  
breithalbfett  
bold expanded  
large demi-gras  
N 100: 081 1270  
Adrian Frutiger 1957  
Haas'sche Schriftgießerei AG  
H 1–x 0,70–k 1,00–p 0,25

### the quick brown fox jumps over the lazy dog

**Folio**  
526  
breithalbfett  
medium extended  
large demi-gras  
N 100: 081 0559  
K. F. Bauer, W. Baum 1959  
Fundición Tipográfica Neufville, S.A.  
H 1–x 0,74–k 1,00–p 0,29

### the quick brown fox jumps over the lazy dog

**Permanent**  
919  
breithalbfett  
medium extended  
large demi-gras  
N 100: 081 1006  
Karlgeorg Hoefer 1963  
Ludwig & Mayer  
H 1–x 0,74–k 1,00–p 0,29

### the quick brown fox jumps over the lazy dog

**DIN-Breitschrift**  
450  

N 000: 081 0433  
H. Berthold AG  
H 1–x 0,72–k 1,00–p 0,34

### the quick brown fox jumps over the lazy dog

**Brasilia**  
251  
halbfett  
bold  
demi-gras  
N 100: 081 0228  
Albert Hollenstein  
H. Berthold AG  
H 1–x 0,69–k 1,00–p 0,34

### the quick brown fox jumps over the lazy dog

**Antique Olive**  
68  
breit  
extended  
large  
N 100: 081 0088  
Roger Excoffon 1968  
Marcel Olive  
H 1–x 0,84–k 1,04–p 0,20

### the quick brown fox jumps over the lazy dog

**Helvetica**  
667  
breithalbfett  
medium extended  
large demi-gras  
N 100: 081 0747  
1961  
D. Stempel AG  
H 1–x 0,74–k 1,00–p 0,27

### the quick brown fox jumps over the lazy dog

**Akzidenz-Grotesk**  
22  
breithalbfett  
medium extended  
large demi-gras  
N 100: 081 1559  
1961  
H. Berthold AG  
H 1–x 0,72–k 1,00–p 0,28

## BERTHOLD HEADLINES VI

Serifenlose Linear-Antiqua
Sans Serifs (Grotesques)
Linéar Antiqua sans empattements (Linéales)

QUICK BROWN FOX JUMPS OVER
THE LAZY DOG 1234567890

BROWN FOX JUMPS OVER
THE LAZY DOG 1234567890

FOX JUMPS OVER THE
LAZY DOG 1234567890

QUICK BROWN FOX JUMPS OVER
THE LAZY DOG 1234567890

BROWN FOX JUMPS OVER
THE LAZY DOG 1234567890

QUICK BROWN FOX JUMPS OVER
THE LAZY DOG 1234567890

BROWN FOX JUMPS OVER
THE LAZY DOG 1234567890

BROWN FOX JUMPS OVER
THE LAZY DOG 1234567890

Jüngere Grotesk, breite  
Late Grotesque, extended  
Grotesque moderne, large  
**63**

**Univers 73**  
1144  
breitfett  
extra bold expanded  
large gras  
N 100: 081 1297  
Adrian Frutiger 1957  
Haas'sche Schriftgießerei AG  
H 1–x 0,70–k 1,00–p 0,25

the quick brown fox jumps over the lazy dog

**Eurostile**  
499  
breitfett  
bold extended  
large gras  
N 100: 081 0508  
Aldo Novarese 1962  
Societa Nebiolo S.p.A.  
H 1–x 0,70–k 1,00–p 0,32

the quick brown fox jumps over the lazy dog

**Reform-Grotesk**  
985  
N 100: 081 1078  
1909/19  
D. Stempel AG  
H 1–x 0,72–k 1,00–p 0,28

the quick brown fox jumps over the lazy dog

ATF **Franklin Gothic Wide**  
538  
N 100: 081 0585  
Morris F. Benton  
American Typefounders  
H 1–x 0,72–k 1,00–p 0,22

the quick brown fox jumps over the lazy dog

**Folio**  
528  
breitfett  
bold extended  
large gras  
N 100: 081 0564  
K. F. Bauer, W. Baum 1963  
H 1–x 0,72–k 1,00–p 0,28

the quick brown fox jumps over the lazy dog

**Univers 83**  
1145  
breit extrafett  
ultra bold expanded  
large extra gras  
N 100: 081 1311  
Adrian Frutiger 1957  
Haas'sche Schriftgießerei AG  
H 1–x 0,69–k 1,00–p 0,26

the quick brown fox jumps over the lazy dog

**Akzidenz-Grotesk**  
23  
breitfett  
bold extended  
large gras  
N 100: 081 0043  
1957  
H. Berthold AG  
H 1–x 0,75–k 1,00–p 0,27

the quick brown fox jumps over the lazy dog

**Annonce**  
55  
fett  
bold  
gras  
N 100: 081 0068  
Lettergieterij Amsterdam  
H 1–x 0,75–k 1,00–p 0,22

the quick brown fox jumps over the lazy dog

## BERTHOLD HEADLINES VI
Serifenlose Linear-Antiqua
Sans Serifs (Grotesques)
Linéar Antiqua sans empattements (Linéales)

**FOX JUMPS OVER THE LAZY DOG 1234567890**

**BROWN FOX JUMPS OVER THE LAZY DOG 1234567890**

**BROWN FOX JUMPS OVER THE LAZY DOG 1234567890**

**FOX JUMPS OVER THE LAZY DOG 1234567890**

**BROWN FOX JUMPS OVER THE LAZY DOG 1234567890**

## BERTHOLD HEADLINES VI
Serifenlose Linear-Antiqua
Sans Serifs (Grotesques)
Linéar Antiqua sans empattements (Linéales)

*QUICK BROWN FOX JUMPS OVER THE LAZY DOG 1234567890*

***QUICK BROWN FOX JUMPS OVER THE LAZY DOG 1234567890***

## 63

Jüngere Grotesk, breite  
Late Grotesque, extended  
Grotesque moderne, large

**the quick brown fox jumps over the lazy dog**

**Aurora-Grotesk**  
94  
breitfett  
bold extended  
large gras  
N 100: 081 0126  
1912  
Johannes Wagner  
H 1–x 0,77–k 1,00–p 0,20

**the quick brown fox jumps over the lazy dog**

**Venus**  
1168  
breitfett  
bold extended  
large gras  
N 000: 081 1348  
1927  
Fundición Tipográfica Neufville, S.A.  
H 1–x 0,75–k 1,00–p 0,22

**quick brown fox jumps over the lazy dog**

**Helvetica**  
668  
breitfett  
bold extended  
large gras  
N 100: 081 0749  
Haas'sche Schriftgießerei AG  
H 1–x 0,77–k 1,00–p 0,24

**quick brown fox jumps over the lazy dog**

**Information**  
693  
breitfett  
bold extended  
large gras  
N 100: 081 0790  
Karl Friedrich Sallwey 1958  
D. Stempel AG  
H 1–x 0,72–k 1,00–p 0,25

**quick brown fox jumps over the lazy dog**

**Antique Olive Nord**  
69  
normal  
regular  
normale  
N 100: 081 0089  
Roger Excoffon 1960  
Marcel Olive  
H 1–x 0,84–k 1,04–p 0,20

## 64

Jüngere Grotesk, kursiv breite  
Late Grotesque, extended italic  
Grotesque moderne, italique large

*the quick brown fox jumps over the lazy dog*

**Folio**  
527  
kursiv breithalbfett  
medium extended italic  
italique large demi-gras  
N 100: 081 0562  
K. F. Bauer, W. Baum 1959  
Fundición Tipográfica Neufville, S.A.  
H 1–x 0,74–k 1,00–p 0,29

*the quick brown fox jumps over the lazy dog*

**Akzidenz-Grotesk**  
24  
kursiv breitfett  
bold extended italic  
italique large gras  
N 100: 081 0048  
Günter Gerhard Lange 1968  
H. Berthold AG  
H 1–x 0,75–k 1,00–p 0,25

**BERTHOLD HEADLINES VI**   Serifenlose Linear-Antiqua
Sans Serifs (Grotesques)
Linéar Antiqua sans empattements (Linéales)

# BROWN FOX JUMPS OVER THE LAZY DOG 1234567890

**BERTHOLD HEADLINES VI**   Serifenlose Linear-Antiqua
Sans Serifs (Grotesques)
Linéar Antiqua sans empattements (Linéales)

THE QUICK BROWN FOX JUMPS OVER
THE LAZY DOG 1234567890

THE QUICK BROWN FOX JUMPS OVER
THE LAZY DOG 1234567890

THE QUICK BROWN FOX JUMPS OVER
THE LAZY DOG 1234567890

THE QUICK BROWN FOX JUMPS OVER
THE LAZY DOG 1234567890

THE QUICK BROWN FOX JUMPS OVER
THE LAZY DOG 1234567890

THE QUICK BROWN FOX JUMPS OVER
THE LAZY DOG 1234567890

## 64
Jüngere Grotesk, kursiv breite  
Late Grotesque, extended italic  
Grotesque moderne, italique large

*the quick brown fox jumps over the lazy dog*

**Antique Olive Nord**
70
kursiv
italic
italique
N 100: 081 1570
Roger Excoffon 1961
Marcel Olive
H 1–x 0,84–k 1,04–p 0,20

## 65
Circle  
Geometric Sans Serif  
Circle

the quick brown fox jumps over the lazy dog

**Circulus**
286
N 100: 081 1462
Michael Neugebauer 1972
H. Berthold AG
H 1–x 0,75–k 1,00–p 0,25

ITC **Busorama**
262
mager
light
maigre
N 000: 081 1497
Herb Lubalin 1970
International Typeface Corp.
H 1–Q 1,22

the quick brown fox jumps over the lazy dog

**Washington**
1183
extramager
extra light
extra maigre
N 100: 081 0887
Russell Bean 1970
Type Designers International
H 1–x 0,50–k 1,00–p 0,34

the quick brown fox jumps over the lazy dog

**Churchward Design 70**
340
ultraleicht
hairline
ultra maigre
N 100: 081 0337
Joseph Churchward 1970
H. Berthold AG
H 1–x 0,72–k 1,00–p 0,28

the quick brown fox jumps over the lazy dog

**Churchward Design 70**
342
leicht
light
extra maigre
N 100: 081 0338
Joseph Churchward 1970
H. Berthold AG
H 1–x 0,72–k 1,00–p 0,28

the quick brown fox jumps over the lazy dog

ITC **Bauhaus**
128
mager
light
maigre
N 020: 081 1830
Ed Benguiat, Vic Caruso 1975
(Herbert Bayer 1925)
H 1–x 0,66–k 1,00–p 0,33

**BERTHOLD HEADLINES VI**  
Serifenlose Linear-Antiqua  
Sans Serifs (Grotesques)  
Linéar Antiqua sans empattements (Linéales)

THE QUICK BROWN FOX JUMPS OVER
THE LAZY DOG

THE QUICK BROWN FOX JUMPS OVER
THE LAZY DOG 1234567890

THE QUICK BROWN FOX JUMPS OVER
THE LAZY DOG 1234567890

THE QUICK BROWN FOX JUMPS OVER
THE LAZY DOG 1234567890

THE QUICK BROWN FOX JUMPS OVER
THE LAZY DOG 1234567890

THE QUICK BROWN FOX JUMPS OVER
THE LAZY DOG 1234567890

THE QUICK BROWN FOX JUMPS OVER
THE LAZY DOG 1234567890

THE QUICK BROWN FOX JUMPS OVER
THE LAZY DOG

| | Circle / Geometric Sans Serif / Circle | **65** |

the quick brown fox jumps over the lazy dog

ITC **Bauhaus**
129
mager Zierbuchstaben
light swash letters
maigre lettres ornées
Z 000: 081 1913 *
Ed Benguiat, Vic Caruso 1975
International Typeface Corp.
H 1–x 0,66–k 1,00–p 0,33

the quick brown fox jumps over the lazy dog

**Washington**
1190
mager
light
maigre
N 100: 081 1022
Russell Bean 1970
Type Designers International
H 1–x 0,50–k 1,00–p 0,34

ITC **Busorama**
263
halbfett
medium
demi-gras
V 000: 081 1498
Herb Lubalin 1970
International Typeface Corp.
H 1–Q 1,06

the quick brown fox jumps over the lazy dog

**Churchward Design 70**
344
mager
regular
maigre
N 100: 081 1458
Joseph Churchward 1970
H. Berthold AG
H 1–x 0,72–k 1,00–p 0,28

the quick brown fox jumps over the lazy dog

ITC **Ronda**
1003
mager
light
maigre
N 100: 081 1507
Herb Lubalin 1970
International Typeface Corp.
H 1–x 0,66–k 1,00–p 0,34

ITC **Busorama**
264
fett
bold
gras
V 000: 081 1499
Herb Lubalin 1970
International Typeface Corp.
H 1–Q 1,19

the quick brown fox jumps over the lazy dog

ITC **Bauhaus**
130
normal
regular
normal
N 020: 081 1813
Ed Benguiat, Vic Caruso 1975
(Herbert Bayer 1925)
H 1–x 0,69–k 1,00–p 0,31

the quick brown fox jumps over the lazy dog

ITC **Bauhaus**
131
normal Zierbuchstaben
regular swash letters
normal lettres ornées
Z 000: 081 1913 *
Ed Benguiat, Vic Caruso 1975
International Typeface Corp.
H 1–x 0,69–k 1,00–p 0,31

**BERTHOLD HEADLINES VI** — Serifenlose Linear-Antiqua / Sans Serifs (Grotesques) / Linéar Antiqua sans empattements (Linéales)

THE QUICK BROWN FOX JUMPS OVER
THE LAZY DOG 1234567890

THE QUICK BROWN FOX JUMPS OVER
THE LAZY DOG 1234567890

THE QUICK BROWN FOX JUMPS OVER
THE LAZY DOG 1234567890

THE QUICK BROWN FOX JUMPS OVER
THE LAZY DOG 1234567890

THE QUICK BROWN FOX JUMPS OVER
THE LAZY DOG

THE QUICK BROWN FOX JUMPS OVER
THE LAZY DOG 1234567890

THE QUICK BROWN FOX JUMPS OVER
THE LAZY DOG 1234567890

THE QUICK BROWN FOX JUMPS OVER
THE LAZY DOG 1234567890

| | Circle<br>Geometric Sans Serif<br>Circle | **65** |

the quick brown fox jumps
over the lazy dog

**Washington**
1191
normal
regular
normal
N 100: 081 0971
Russell Bean 1970
Type Designers International
H 1–x 0,50–k 1,00–p 0,34

the quick brown fox jumps
over the lazy dog

**Churchward Design 70**
345
normal
medium
normal
N 100: 081 0339
Joseph Churchward 1970
H. Berthold AG
H 1–x 0,72–k 1,00–p 0,28

the quick brown fox jumps
over the lazy dog

ITC **Ronda**
1004
normal
regular
normal
N 100: 081 1508
Herb Lubalin 1970
International Typeface Corp.
H 1–x 0,66–k 1,00–p 0,34

the quick brown fox jumps
over the lazy dog

**Blippo**
196
halbfett
bold
demi-gras

N 100: 081 1432
Facsimile Fonts
H 1–x 0,74–k 1,00–p 0,26

the quick brown fox jumps
over the lazy dog

**Blippo**
197
halbfett Zierbuchstaben
bold swash letters
demi-gras lettres ornées

Z 000: 081 2036
Facsimile Fonts
H 1–x 0,74–k 1,00–p 0,26

the quick brown fox jumps
over the lazy dog

**Washington**
1192
halbfett
bold
demi-gras
N 100: 081 0985
Russell Bean 1970
Type Designers International
H 1–x 0,50–k 1,00–p 0,34

the quick brown fox jumps
over the lazy dog

**Churchward Design 70**
347
halbfett
demi-gras
demi-gras
N 100: 081 0340
Joseph Churchward 1970
H. Berthold AG
H 1–x 0,72–k 1,00–p 0,28

the quick brown fox jumps
over the lazy dog

ITC **Bauhaus**
132
halbfett
medium
demi-gras
N 020: 081 1833
Ed Benguiat, Vic Caruso 1975
(Herbert Bayer 1925)
H 1–x 0,69–k 1,00–p 0,30

**BERTHOLD HEADLINES VI** — Serifenlose Linear-Antiqua / Sans Serifs (Grotesques) / Linéar Antiqua sans empattements (Linéales)

THE QUICK BROWN FOX JUMPS OVER THE LAZY DOG

THE QUICK BROWN FOX JUMPS OVER THE LAZY DOG 1234567890

THE QUICK BROWN FOX JUMPS OVER THE LAZY DOG 1234567890

THE QUICK BROWN FOX JUMPS OVER THE LAZY DOG

THE QUICK BROWN FOX JUMPS OVER THE LAZY DOG 1234567890

THE QUICK BROWN FOX JUMPS OVER THE LAZY DOG 1234567890

THE QUICK BROWN FOX JUMPS OVER THE LAZY DOG 1234567890

THE QUICK BROWN FOX JUMPS OVER THE LAZY DOG 1234567890

Circle  
Geometric Sans Serif  
Circle **65**

the quick brown fox jumps
over the lazy dog

ITC **Bauhaus**  
133  
halbfett Zierbuchstaben  
medium swash letters  
demi-gras lettres ornées  
Z 000: 081 1913 ✽  
Ed Benguiat, Vic Caruso 1975  
International Typeface Corp.  
H 1–x 0,69–k 1,00–p 0,30

the quick brown fox jumps
over the lazy dog

ITC **Ronda**  
1005  
fett  
bold  
gras  
N 100: 081 1509  
Herb Lubalin 1970  
International Typeface Corp.  
H 1–x 0,66–k 1,00–p 0,34

the quick brown fox jumps
over the lazy dog

ITC **Bauhaus**  
134  
fett  
bold  
gras  
N 020: 081 1837  
Ed Benguiat, Vic Caruso 1975  
(Herbert Bayer 1925)  
H 1–x 0,70–k 1,00–p 0,29

the quick brown fox jumps
over the lazy dog

ITC **Bauhaus**  
135  
fett Zierbuchstaben  
bold swash letters  
gras lettres ornées  
Z 000: 081 1913 ✽  
Ed Benguiat, Vic Caruso 1975  
International Typeface Corp.  
H 1–x 0,70–k 1,00–p 0,29

the quick brown fox jumps
over the lazy dog

**Washington Black**  
1193  

N 100: 081 0890  
Russell Bean 1970  
Type Designers International  
H 1–x 0,50–k 1,00–p 0,38

the quick brown fox jumps
over the lazy dog

**Churchward Design 70**  
349  
fett  
bold  
gras  
N 100: 081 0342  
Joseph Churchward 1970  
H. Berthold AG  
H 1–x 0,72–k 1,00–p 0,31

the quick brown fox jumps
over the lazy dog

**Blippo Black**  
198  

N 100: 081 1435  
Facsimile Fonts  
H 1–x 0,73–k 1,00–p 0,36

the quick brown fox jumps
over the lazy dog

**Blippo Black**  
199  
Zierbuchstaben  
swash letters  
lettres ornées  
Z 000: 081 1920  
Facsimile Fonts  
H 1–x 0,73–k 1,00–p 0,36

## BERTHOLD HEADLINES VI
Serifenlose Linear-Antiqua
Sans Serifs (Grotesques)
Linéar Antiqua sans empattements (Linéales)

THE QUICK BROWN FOX JUMPS OVER THE LAZY DOG 1234567890

THE QUICK BROWN FOX JUMPS OVER THE LAZY DOG

THE QUICK BROWN FOX JUMPS OVER THE LAZY DOG 1234567890

THE QUICK BROWN FOX JUMPS OVER THE LAZY DOG

THE QUICK BROWN FOX JUMPS OVER THE LAZY DOG 1234567890

## BERTHOLD HEADLINES VI
Serifenlose Linear-Antiqua
Sans Serifs (Grotesques)
Linéar Antiqua sans empattements (Linéales)

THE QUICK BROWN FOX JUMPS OVER THE LAZY DOG 1234567890

THE QUICK BROWN FOX JUMPS OVER THE LAZY DOG 1234567890

## 65 Circle / Geometric Sans Serif / Circle

**Embrionic**
475

the quick brown fox jumps over the lazy dog

N 100: 081 0477
Ilja Feldstein
Graphic Systems Ltd.
H 1–x 0,72–k 1,00–p 0,31

**Embrionic**
476
Zierbuchstaben
swash letters
lettres ornées
Z 000: 081 0478
Ilja Feldstein 1972
Graphic Systems Ltd.
M 1,56

the quick brown fox jumps over the lazy dog

ITC **Bauhaus**
136
extrafett
extra bold
extra gras
N 020: 081 1826
Ed Benguiat, Vic Caruso 1975
(Herbert Bayer 1925)
H 1–x 0,72–k 1,00–p 0,31

the quick brown fox jumps over the lazy dog

ITC **Bauhaus**
137
extrafett Zierbuchstaben
extra bold swash letters
extra gras lettres ornées
Z 000: 081 1913
Ed Benguiat, Vic Caruso 1975
International Typeface Corp.
H 1–x 0,72–k 1,00–p 0,31

the quick brown fox jumps over the lazy dog

**Churchward Design 70**
351
extrafett
ultra bold
extra gras
N 100: 081 0343
Joseph Churchward 1970
H. Berthold AG
H 1–x 0,78–k 1,00–p 0,40

## 66 Circle, kursive / Geometric Sans Serif, italic / Circle, italique

**Churchward Design 70**
341
kursiv ultraleicht
hairline italic
italique ultra maigre
N 100: 081 1516
Joseph Churchward 1970
H. Berthold AG
H 1–x 0,72–k 1,00–p 0,31

the quick brown fox jumps over the lazy dog

**Churchward Design 70**
343
kursiv mager
light italic
italique maigre
N 100: 081 1441
Joseph Churchward 1970
H. Berthold AG
H 1–x 0,72–k 1,00–p 0,31

the quick brown fox jumps over the lazy dog

## BERTHOLD HEADLINES VI
Serifenlose Linear-Antiqua
Sans Serifs (Grotesques)
Linéar Antiqua sans empattements (Linéales)

THE QUICK BROWN FOX JUMPS OVER
THE LAZY DOG 1234567890

THE QUICK BROWN FOX JUMPS OVER
THE LAZY DOG 1234567890

THE QUICK BROWN FOX JUMPS OVER
THE LAZY DOG 1234567890

THE QUICK BROWN FOX JUMPS OVER
THE LAZY DOG 1234567890

## BERTHOLD HEADLINES VI
Serifenlose Linear-Antiqua
Sans Serifs (Grotesques)
Linéar Antiqua sans empattements (Linéales)

THE QUICK BROWN FOX JUMPS OVER
THE LAZY DOG 1234567890

THE QUICK BROWN FOX JUMPS OVER
THE LAZY DOG 1234567890

THE QUICK BROWN FOX JUMPS OVER
THE LAZY DOG 1234567890

## 66 — Circle, kursive / Geometric Sans Serif, italic / Circle, italique

*the quick brown fox jumps over the lazy dog*

**Churchward Design 70**
346
kursiv
medium
italique
N 100: 081 1440
Joseph Churchward 1970
H. Berthold AG
H 1–x 0,72–k 1,00–p 0,31

*the quick brown fox jumps over the lazy dog*

**Churchward Design 70**
348
kursiv halbfett
demi-bold italic
italique demi-gras
N 100: 081 1459
Joseph Churchward 1970
H. Berthold AG
H 1–x 0,72–k 1,00–p 0,31

*the quick brown fox jumps over the lazy dog*

**Churchward Design 70**
350
kursiv fett
bold italic
italique gras
N 100: 081 1460
Joseph Churchward 1970
H. Berthold AG
H 1–x 0,72–k 1,00–p 0,31

*the quick brown fox jumps over the lazy dog*

**Churchward Design 70**
352
kursiv extrafett
ultra bold italic
italique extra gras
N 100: 081 0344
Joseph Churchward 1970
H. Berthold AG
H 1–x 0,76–k 1,00–p 0,40

## 67 — Gerundete Grotesk / Rounded / Rounded

the quick brown fox jumps over the lazy dog

ITC **Benguiat Gothic**
1263
Buch
book
romain labeur
N 020: 081 0333
Ed Benguiat 1979
International Typeface Corp.
H 1–x 0,73–k 0,98–p 0,28

the quick brown fox jumps over the lazy dog

ITC **Benguiat Gothic**
1265
normal
regular
normal
N 020: 081 0347
Ed Benguiat 1979
International Typeface Corp.
H 1–x 0,74–k 0,98–p 0,31

the quick brown fox jumps over the lazy dog

**Berliner Grotesk**
1270
mager
light
maigre
N 020: 081 2420
Erik Spiekermann 1979
(Berthold 1913)
H 1–x 0,75–k 1,01–p 0,16

**BERTHOLD HEADLINES VI** — Serifenlose Linear-Antiqua / Sans Serifs (Grotesques) / Linéar Antiqua sans empattements (Linéales)

THE QUICK BROWN FOX JUMPS OVER
THE LAZY DOG 1234567890

THE QUICK BROWN FOX JUMPS OVER
THE LAZY DOG 1234567890

THE QUICK BROWN FOX JUMPS OVER
THE LAZY DOG 1234567890

THE QUICK BROWN FOX JUMPS OVER
THE LAZY DOG 1234567890

THE QUICK BROWN FOX JUMPS OVER
THE LAZY DOG 1234567890

THE QUICK BROWN FOX JUMPS OVER
THE LAZY DOG 1234567890

THE QUICK BROWN FOX JUMPS OVER
THE LAZY DOG 1234567890

THE QUICK BROWN FOX JUMPS OVER
THE LAZY DOG 1234567890

| | Gerundete Grotesk / Rounded / Rounded | 67 |

**the quick brown fox jumps over the lazy dog**

ITC **Benguiat Gothic**
1267
halbfett
bold
demi-gras
N 020: 081 0350
Ed Benguiat 1979
International Typeface Corp.
H 1–x 0,75–k 1,04–p 0,31

**the quick brown fox jumps over the lazy dog**

**AG Buch Rounded**
30
halbfett
medium
demi-gras
N 020: 081 1973
Günter Gerhard Lange 1976
H. Berthold AG
H 1–x 0,73–k 1,01–p 0,23

**the quick brown fox jumps over the lazy dog**

**Splash**
1354

N 020: 081 0266
Claude-Eric Stern 1980
H. Berthold AG
H 1–x 0,74–k 1,01–p 0,29

**the quick brown fox jumps over the lazy dog**

**V.A.G.-Rundschrift**
1150

N 020: 081 2413
1979
H. Berthold AG
H 1–x 0,75–k 1,09–p 0,31

**the quick brown fox jumps over the lazy dog**

ITC **Benguiat Gothic**
1269
fett
heavy
gras
N 020: 081 0364
Ed Benguiat 1979
International Typeface Corp.
H 1–x 0,75–k 1,01–p 0,31

**the quick brown fox jumps over the lazy dog**

**AG Buch Rounded**
31
fett
bold
gras
N 020: 081 0484
Günter Gerhard Lange 1976
H. Berthold AG
H 1–x 0,73–k 1,00–p 0,26

**the quick brown fox jumps over the lazy dog**

**AG Buch Rounded**
32
schmalfett
bold condensed
étroit gras
N 020: 081 1974
Günter Gerhard Lange 1976
H. Berthold AG
H 1–x 0,73–k 1,01–p 0,26

**the quick brown fox jumps over the lazy dog**

**Wiegands Roundhead**
1218

N 100: 081 1765
Jürgen Wiegand 1974
H. Berthold AG
H 1–x 0,69–k 1,00–p 0,31

**BERTHOLD HEADLINES VI** — Serifenlose Linear-Antiqua / Sans Serifs (Grotesques) / Linéar Antiqua sans empattements (Linéales)

THE QUICK BROWN FOX JUMPS OVER THE LAZY DOG

THE QUICK BROWN FOX JUMPS OVER THE LAZY DOG 1234567890

THE QUICK BROWN FOX JUMPS OVER THE LAZY DOG 1234567890

THE QUICK BROWN FOX JUMPS OVER THE LAZY DOG 1234567890

**BERTHOLD HEADLINES VI** — Serifenlose Linear-Antiqua / Sans Serifs (Grotesques) / Linéar Antiqua sans empattements (Linéales)

THE QUICK BROWN FOX JUMPS OVER THE LAZY DOG 1234567890

THE QUICK BROWN FOX JUMPS OVER THE LAZY DOG 1234567890

THE QUICK BROWN FOX JUMPS OVER THE LAZY DOG 1234567890

## 67 Gerundete Grotesk / Rounded / Rounded

the quick brown fox jumps over the lazy dog

**Wiegands Roundhead**
1219
alternative Buchstaben
alternative characters
caractères alternatifs
Z 000: 081 1770
Jürgen Wiegand 1974
H. Berthold AG
H 1–x 0,69–k 1,00–p 0,31

the quick brown fox jumps over the lazy dog

**Poell Black**
943

N 100: 081 1484
Erwin Poell 1972
H. Berthold AG
H 1–x 0,66–k 1,00–p 0,34

the quick brown fox jumps over the lazy dog

**Churchward Marianna**
371
normal
regular
normal
N 100: 081 0323
Joseph Churchward 1970
H. Berthold AG
H 1–x 0,74–k 1,03–p 0,36

the quick brown fox jumps over the lazy dog

**Mr. Big**
849

N 100: 081 1476
Jürgen Riebling 1972
H. Berthold AG
H 1–x 0,78–k 1,13–p 0,19

## 68 Gerundete Grotesk, kursive / Rounded, italic / Rounded, italique

*the quick brown fox jumps over the lazy dog*

ITC **Benguiat Gothic**
1264
Buch kursiv
book italic
romain labeur italique
N 020: 081 0369
Ed Benguiat 1979
International Typeface Corp.
H 1–x 0,75–k 1,00–p 0,28

*the quick brown fox jumps over the lazy dog*

ITC **Benguiat Gothic**
1266
kursiv
medium italic
italique
N 020: 081 0372
Ed Benguiat 1979
International Typeface Corp.
H 1–x 0,75–k 1,00–p 0,30

ITC **Benguiat Gothic**
1268
kursiv halbfett
bold italic
italique demi-gras
N 020: 081 0378
Ed Benguiat 1979
International Typeface Corp.
H 1–x 0,72–k 1,00–p 0,29

## BERTHOLD HEADLINES VI
Serifenlose Linear-Antiqua
Sans Serifs (Grotesques)
Linéar Antiqua sans empattements (Linéales)

THE QUICK BROWN FOX JUMPS OVER
THE LAZY DOG 1234567890

THE QUICK BROWN FOX JUMPS OVER
THE LAZY DOG 1234567890

## BERTHOLD HEADLINES VI
Serifenlose Linear-Antiqua
Sans Serifs (Grotesques)
Linéar Antiqua sans empattements (Linéales)

THE QUICK BROWN FOX JUMPS OVER
THE LAZY DOG 1234567890

THE QUICK BROWN FOX JUMPS OVER
THE LAZY DOG 1234567890

THE QUICK BROWN FOX JUMPS OVER
THE LAZY DOG 1234567890

BROWN FOX JUMPS OVER
THE LAZY DOG 1234567890

THE QUICK
THE LAZY D

## 68 Gerundete Grotesk, kursive / Rounded, italic / Rounded, italique

*the quick brown fox jumps over the lazy dog*

ITC **Benguiat Gothic**
1363
kursiv fett
heavy italic
italique gras
N 020: 081 0381
Ed Benguiat 1979
International Typeface Corp.
H 1–x 0,76–k 1,02–p 0,30

*the quick brown fox jumps over the lazy dog*

**Churchward Marianna**
372
kursiv
italic
italique
N 100: 081 0325
Joseph Churchward 1970
H. Berthold AG
H 1–x 0,75–k 1,00–p 0,34

## 69 Sonstige / Others / Autres

the quick brown fox jumps over the lazy dog

**Alpine**
40

N 100: 081 1463
Peter Steiner 1972
H. Berthold AG
H 1–x 0,73–k 1,06–p 0,30

the quick brown fox jumps over the lazy dog

**Handel-Gothic**
650
normal
regular
normal

N 100: 081 1481
Facsimile Fonts
H 1–x 0,74–k 1,00–p 0,26

the quick brown fox jumps over the lazy dog

**Ad Lib**
2

N 100: 081 0000
Freeman Craw 1961
American Typefounders
H 1–x 0,69–k 1,00–p 0,34

the quick brown fox jumps over the lazy dog

**Komet**
730

N 020: 081 2277
Gustav Jaeger 1976
H. Berthold AG
H 1–x 0,78–k 1,09–p 0,44

the quick brown fox jumps over the lazy dog

**Poppl Leporello**
959

N 020: 081 2159
Friedrich Poppl 1977
H. Berthold AG
H 1–x 0,76–k 1,00–p 0,30

# BERTHOLD HEADLINES VI

Serifenlose Linear-Antiqua
Sans Serifs (Grotesques)
Linéar Antiqua sans empattements (Linéales)

THE QUICK BROWN FOX JUMPS OVER THE LAZY DOG 1234567890

THE QUICK BROWN FOX JUMPS OVER THE LAZY DOG 1234567890

THE QUICK BROWN FOX JUMPS OVER THE LAZY DOG 1234567890

QUICK BROWN FOX JUMPS OVER THE LAZY DOG 1234567890

QUICK BROWN FOX JUMPS OVER THE LAZY DOG 1234567890

THE QUICK BROWN FOX JUMPS OVER THE LAZY DOG 1234567890

QUICK BROWN FOX JUMPS OVER THE LAZY DOG 1234567890

QUICK BROWN FOX JUMPS OVER THE LAZY DOG

| | Sonstige **69** |
| --- | --- |
| | Others |
| | Autres |

**Stop 1**
1061

V 000: 081 1150
Aldo Novarese 1971
Societa Nebiolo S.p.A.
H 1–Q 1,0

ITC **Machine**
803
normal
regular
normal
V 000: 081 1964
Ronne Bonder, Tom Carnase 1970
International Typeface Corp.
H 1–Q 1,0

ITC **Machine**
804
halbfett
bold
demi-gras
V 000: 081 1970
Ronne Bonder, Tom Carnase 1970
International Typeface Corp.
H 1–Q 1,0

**the quick brown fox jumps over the lazy dog**

Motter **Tektura**
848
halbfett
medium
demi-gras
N 100: 081 1896
Vorarlberger Grafik 1975
H. Berthold AG
H 1–x 0,78–k 1,00–p 0,22

**the quick brown fox jumps over the lazy dog**

ITC **Bolt**
221
fett
bold
gras
N 100: 081 0220
Ronne Bonder, Tom Carnase 1970
International Typeface Corp.
H 1–x 0,74–k 1,00–p 0,32

**the quick brown fox jumps over the lazy dog**

**Murrpoint**
850
fett
bold
gras
N 100: 081 1698
Günther Murr 1975
H. Berthold AG
H 1–x 0,74–k 1,00–p 0,30

**the quick brown fox jumps over the lazy dog**

**Murrpoint Swing**
851
fett
bold
gras
N 100: 081 1703
Günther Murr 1975
H. Berthold AG
H 1–x 0,74–k 1,25–p 0,45

**the quick brown fox jumps over the lazy dog**

**Murrpoint Swing**
852
fett Zierbuchstaben
bold swash letters
gras lettres ornées
Z 000: 081 1709
Günther Murr 1975
H. Berthold AG
H 1–x 0,74–k 1,13–p 0,51

## BERTHOLD HEADLINES VI
Serifenlose Linear-Antiqua
Sans Serifs (Grotesques)
Linéar Antiqua sans empattements (Linéales)

THE QUICK BROWN FOX JUMPS OVER
THE LAZY DOG 1234567890

THE QUICK BROWN FOX JUMPS OVER
THE LAZY DOG 1234567890

BROWN FOX JUMPS OVER
THE LAZY DOG 123456789

## BERTHOLD HEADLINES VI
Serifenlose Linear-Antiqua
Sans Serifs (Grotesques)
Linéar Antiqua sans empattements (Linéales)

THE QUICK BROWN FOX JUMPS OVER
THE LAZY DOG 1234567890

THE QUICK BROWN FOX JUMPS OVER
THE LAZY DOG 1234567890

THE QUICK BROWN FOX JUMPS OVER
THE LAZY DOG 1234567890

## 69 Sonstige / Others / Autres

**Wiegands Adbold** 1212

the quick brown fox jumps over the lazy dog

N 100: 081 1771
Jürgen Wiegand 1974
H. Berthold AG
H 1–x 0,69–k 1,00–p 0,34

**Wiegand Adbold** 1213
alternative Buchstaben
alternative characters
caractères alternatifs

the quick brown fox jumps over the lazy dog

Z 000: 081 1777
Jürgen Wiegand 1974
H. Berthold AG
H 1–x 0,69–k 1,00–p 0,34

**Jumbo** 711
normal
regular
normal

V 000: 081 0800
Gustav Jaeger 1973
H. Berthold AG
H 1–Q 1,0

**Watzlform** 1195
full
full
full

quick brown fox jumps over the lazy dog 1234567890

X 016: 081 2285
Peter Watzl 1977
H. Berthold AG
H 1–x 0,87–k 1,00–p 0,16

## 70 Sonstige, kursive / Others, italic / Autres, italique

**Lapidar** 748

the quick brown fox jumps over the lazy dog

N 020: 081 1442
Aldo Novarese 1977
H. Berthold AG
H 1–x 0,78–1,02–p 0,20

**Plural** 1395

the quick brown fox jumps over the lazy dog

N 000: 081 2488
Günter Jäntsch 1981
H. Berthold AG
H 1 (K 1,04)–x 0,69 (u 0,72)–k 1,03–p 0,34

**Plural** 1396
Zierbuchstaben
swash letters
lettres ornées

the quick brown fox jumps over the lazy dog

Z 000: 081 2489
Günter Jäntsch 1981
H. Berthold AG
H 1 (V 1,37)–x 0,69 (r 1,16)–k 1,03–p 0,34

## BERTHOLD HEADLINES VI
Serifenlose Linear-Antiqua
Sans Serifs (Grotesques)
Linéar Antiqua sans empattements (Linéales)

# BROWN FOX JUMPS OVER THE LAZY DOG 123456789

Sonstige, kursive
Others, italic
Autres, italique
**70**

**Jumbo**
712
kursiv
italic
italique
V 000: 081 0801
Gustav Jaeger 1973
H. Berthold AG
H 1–Q 1,0

# BERTHOLD HEADLINES VII

## 71-82

*Antiqua-Varianten*
*Decoratives*
*Variantes*

## BERTHOLD HEADLINES VII
Antiqua-Varianten
Decoratives
Variantes

THE QUICK BROWN FOX JUMPS OVER
THE LAZY DOG 1234567890

---

THE QUICK BROWN FOX JUMPS OVER
THE LAZY DOG 1234567890

---

THE QUICK BROWN FOX JUMPS OVER
THE LAZY DOG 1234567890

---

THE QUICK BROWN FOX JUMPS OVER
THE LAZY DOG 1234567890

---

THE QUICK BROWN FOX JUMPS OVER
THE LAZY DOG 1234567890

---

THE QUICK BROWN FOX JUMPS OVER
THE LAZY DOG 1234567890

---

THE QUICK BROWN FOX JUMPS OVER
THE LAZY DOG 1234567890

---

THE QUICK BROWN FOX JUMPS OVER
THE LAZY DOG 1234567890

Jugendstil / Art Nouveau / Art Nouveau **71**

**Charlemagne**
298

V 000: 081 0285
Eleisha Pechey 1886
Photoscript Ltd.
H 1–Q 1,20

the quick brown fox jumps over the lazy dog

**Lo-Type**
768
mager
light
maigre
N 020: 081 2424
Erik Spiekermann 1980
(Louis Oppenheim 1924)
H 1–x 0,64–k 1,01–p 0,28

the quick brown fox jumps over the lazy dog

**Etienne Modern**
491
normal
regular
normal
N 100: 081 0494
Haas'sche Schriftgießerei AG
H 1–x 0,66–k 1,00–p 0,28

the quick brown fox jumps over the lazy dog

**Georges Lemon**
605

N 100: 081 1502
H. Berthold AG
H 1–x 0,63–k 1,06–p 0,31

the quick brown fox jumps over the lazy dog

**Charleston**
299

N 100: 081 0286
Hace Frey 1967
Ludwig & Mayer
H 1–x 0,67–k 1,00–p 0,30

the quick brown fox jumps over the lazy dog

**Eckmann**
456

N 000: 081 0441
Otto Eckmann 1900
D. Stempel AG
H 1–x 0,69–k 1,00–p 0,28

the quick brown fox jumps over the lazy dog

**Arnold Böcklin**
75

N 100: 081 1031
H. Berthold AG
H 1–x 0,74–k 1,00–p 0,23

the quick brown fox jumps over the lazy dog

**Herkules**
669

N 100: 081 0751
1899
Haas'sche Schriftgießerei AG
H 1–x 0,78–k 1,00–p 0,19

## BERTHOLD HEADLINES VII
Antiqua-Varianten
Decoratives
Variantes

THE QUICK BROWN FOX JUMPS OVER
THE LAZY DOG 1234567890

THE QUICK BROWN FOX JUMPS OVER
THE LAZY DOG 1234567890

THE QUICK BROWN FOX JUMPS OVER
THE LAZY DOG 1234567890

THE QUICK BROWN FOX JUMPS OVER
THE LAZY DOG 1234567890

THE QUICK BROWN FOX JUMPS OVER
THE LAZY DOG 1234567890

THE QUICK BROWN FOX JUMPS OVER
THE LAZY DOG 1234567890

THE QUICK BROWN FOX JUMPS OVER
THE LAZY DOG 1234567890

THE QUICK BROWN FOX JUMPS OVER
THE LAZY DOG 1234567890

Jugendstil
Art Nouveau
Art Nouveau
**71**

**Herold**
672
schmal
condensed
étroit

the quick brown fox jumps
over the lazy dog

N 100: 081 0752
H. Hoffmann 1904
H. Berthold AG
H 1–x 0,81–k 1,00–p 0,13

**Whelan-Antiqua**
1209

the quick brown fox jumps
over the lazy dog

N 100: 081 1391
Rubens ca. 1890
Photoscript Ltd.
H 1–x 0,81–k 1,00–p 0,13

**Ocean Current**
897

the quick brown fox jumps
over the lazy dog

N 100: 081 1477
Karl-Heinz Domning 1972
H. Berthold AG
H 1–x 0,66–k 1,03–p 0,28

**Ocean Current**
898
Zierbuchstaben
swash letters
lettres ornées

the quick brown fox jumps
over the lazy dog

Z 000: 081 1478
Karl-Heinz Domning 1972
H. Berthold AG
H 1–x 0,66–k 1,03–p 0,28

**Etienne**
492
schmalfett
bold condensed
étroit gras

the quick brown fox jumps
over the lazy dog

N 100: 081 0495
Haas'sche Schriftgießerei AG
H 1–x 0,76–k 1,00–p 0,21

**Herold Reklameschrift**
670

the quick brown fox jumps
over the lazy dog

N 100: 081 0755
H. Hoffmann 1901
H. Berthold AG
H 1–x 0,84–k 1,00–p 0,11

**Thalia**
1080

the quick brown fox jumps
over the lazy dog

N 100: 081 1471
H. Berthold AG
H 1–x 0,59–k 0,81–p 0,22

**Tip Top**
1100

the quick brown fox jumps
over the lazy dog

N 100: 081 1443
H. Berthold AG
H 1–x 0,78–k 1,00–p 0,13

## BERTHOLD HEADLINES VII
Antiqua-Varianten / Decoratives / Variantes

THE QUICK BROWN FOX JUMPS OVER
THE LAZY DOG 1234567890

THE QUICK BROWN FOX JUMPS OVER
THE LAZY DOG 1234567890

THE QUICK BROWN FOX JUMPS OVER
THE LAZY DOG 1234567890

THE QUICK BROWN FOX JUMPS OVER
THE LAZY DOG 1234567890

THE QUICK BROWN FOX JUMPS OVER
THE LAZY DOG 1234567890

QUICK BROWN FOX JUMPS OVER
THE LAZY DOG 1234567890

## BERTHOLD HEADLINES VII
Antiqua-Varianten / Decoratives / Variantes

THE QUICK BROWN FOX JUMPS OVER
THE LAZY DOG 1234567890

## 71 Jugendstil / Art Nouveau / Art Nouveau

**Roberta**
991
normal
regular
normal

the quick brown fox jumps over the lazy dog

N 100: 081 1085
Facsimile Fonts
H 1-x 0,74-k 1,00-p 0,29

**Bernhard**
163
schmalfett
bold condensed
étroit gras

the quick brown fox jumps over the lazy dog

N 100: 081 0153
Lucian Bernhard 1912
Fundición Tipográfica Neufville, S.A.
H 1-x 0,81-k 1,00-p 0,19

**Lo-Type**
771
schmalhalbfett
bold condensed
étroit demi-gras

the quick brown fox jumps over the lazy dog

N 020: 081 2423
Erik Spiekermann 1980
(Louis Oppenheim 1913-1914)
H 1-x 0,85-k 1,00-p 0,18

**Lo-Type**
1335
normal
regular
normal

the quick brown fox jumps over the lazy dog

N 020: 081 0453
Erik Spiekermann 1980
(Louis Oppenheim 1914)
H 1-x 0,68-k 1,00-p 0,24

**Lo-Type**
769
halbfett
medium
demi-gras

the quick brown fox jumps over the lazy dog

N 020: 081 2425
Erik Spiekermann 1980
(Louis Oppenheim 1924)
H 1-x 0,77-k 1,00-p 0,16

**Lo-Type**
770
fett
bold
gras

the quick brown fox jumps over the lazy dog

N 020: 081 2422
Erik Spiekermann 1980
(Louis Oppenheim 1914)
H 1-x 0,75-k 1,00-p 0,15

## 72 Fancy / Fancy / Fancy

**Harlekin**
651

V 000: 081 0940
Klaus Meier 1974
H. Berthold AG
H 1-Q 1,19

## BERTHOLD HEADLINES VII
Antiqua-Varianten
Decoratives
Variantes

THE QUICK BROWN FOX JUMPS OVER
THE LAZY DOG 1234567890

THE QUICK BROWN FOX JUMPS OVER
THE LAZY DOG 1234567890

THE QUICK BROWN FOX JUMPS OVER
THE LAZY DOG 1234567890

THE QUICK BROWN FOX JUMPS OVER
THE LAZY DOG 1234567890

THE QUICK BROWN FOX JUMPS OVER
THE LAZY DOG 1234567890

THE QUICK BROWN FOX JUMPS OVER
THE LAZY DOG 1234567890

THE QUICK BROWN FOX JUMPS OVER
THE LAZY DOG 1234567890

THE QUICK BROWN FOX JUMPS OVER
THE LAZY DOG 1234567890

Fancy
Fancy
Fancy
**72**

**Boutique**
249

the quick brown fox jumps
over the lazy dog

N 100: 081 1600
1900
Haas'sche Schriftgießerei AG
H 1–x 0,71–k 1,04–p 0,22

**Hobo**
674

the quick brown fox jumps
over the lazy dog

N 100: 081 0760
Morris F. Benton 1910
American Typefounders
H 1–x 0,78–k 1,03–p 0,00

**Neptun**

the quick brown fox jumps
over the lazy dog

N 100: 081 0919
H. Berthold AG
H 1–x 0,66–k 1,03–p 0,34

**Titania**
1101

the quick brown fox jumps
over the lazy dog

N 100: 081 1190
1908
Haas'sche Schriftgießerei AG
H 1–x 0,75–k 1,00–p 0,22

**Poppl Saladin**
962
normal
regular
normal
V 000: 081 0431 *
Friedrich Poppl 1979
H. Berthold AG
L 1–Q 1,32

**Mark Twain**
814

the quick brown fox jumps
over the lazy dog

N 100: 081 0884
Gustav Jaeger 1973
H. Berthold AG
H 1–x 0,72–k 0,97–p 0,28

**Janus**
709

the quick brown fox jumps
over the lazy dog

N 100: 081 1847
Ivan Boldizar 1975
H. Berthold AG
H 1–x 0,72–k 1,09–p 0,37

**Triton**
1108

the quick brown fox jumps
over the lazy dog

N 100: 081 1858
Ivan Boldizar 1975
H. Berthold AG
H 1–x 0,78–k 1,09–p 0,35

379

## BERTHOLD HEADLINES VII
Antiqua-Varianten / Decoratives / Variantes

THE QUICK BROWN FOX JUMPS OVER THE LAZY DOG 1234567890

THE QUICK BROWN FOX JUMPS OVER THE LAZY DOG 1234567890

THE QUICK BROWN FOX JUMPS OVER THE LAZY DOG 1234567890

THE QUICK BROWN FOX JUMPS OVER THE LAZY DOG 1234567890

THE QUICK BROWN FOX JUMPS OVER THE LAZY DOG 1234567890

THE QUICK BROWN FOX JUMPS OVER THE LAZY DOG 1234567890

THE QUICK BROWN FOX JUMPS OVER THE LAZY DOG 1234567890

QUICK BROWN FOX JUMPS OVER THE LAZY DOG 1234567890

Fancy
Fancy
Fancy
**72**

**De Vinne Ornamented**
437
normal
regular
normal

the quick brown fox jumps
over the lazy dog

N 100: 081 0421
Photoscript Ltd.
H 1–x 0,69–k 1,06–p 0,37

**Oriente**
908

V 000: 081 0991
Reiner Laich 1971
H. Berthold AG
H 1–Q 1,13

**Fortunata**
530

the quick brown fox jumps
over the lazy dog

N 100: 081 0573
Karlo Wagner 1971
H. Berthold AG
H 1–x 0,63–k 1,00–p 0,28

**Boldiz**
220

the quick brown fox jumps
over the lazy dog

N 100: 081 1852
Ivan Boldizar 1975
H. Berthold AG
H 1–x 0,76–k 1,09–p 0,33

**Trixi**
1109

V 000: 081 1202
J. Seifert, K. Wegner 1970
H. Berthold AG
H 1–Q 1,00

**Black Wings**
195

the quick brown fox jumps
over the lazy dog

N 020: 081 2283
Otmar F. Adler 1976
H. Berthold AG
H 1–x 0,63–k 1,06–p 0,37

**Churchward Blackbeauty 72**
366
normal
regular
normal

the quick brown fox jumps
over the lazy dog

N 100: 081 1472
Joseph Churchward 1972
H. Berthold AG
H 1–x 0,74–k 1,03–p 0,34

**Pierrot**
929

the quick brown fox jumps
over the lazy dog

N 000: 081 1011
Günter Jäntsch 1973
H. Berthold AG
H 1–x 0,72–k 1,00–p 0,41

## BERTHOLD HEADLINES VII — Antiqua-Varianten / Decoratives / Variantes

THE QUICK BROWN FOX JUMPS OVER THE LAZY DOG 1234567890

QUICK BROWN FOX JUMPS OVER THE LAZY DOG 1234567890

THE QUICK BROWN FOX JUMPS OVER THE LAZY DOG 1234567890

## BERTHOLD HEADLINES VII — Antiqua-Varianten / Decoratives / Variantes

THE QUICK BROWN FOX JUMPS OVER THE LAZY DOG 1234567890

THE QUICK BROWN FOX JUMPS OVER THE LAZY DOG 1234567890

QUICK BROWN FOX JUMPS OVER THE LAZY DOG 1234567890

THE QUICK BROWN FOX JUMPS OVER THE LAZY DOG 1234567890

| | Fancy<br>Fancy<br>Fancy | **72** |

**Poppl Heavy**
958

the quick brown fox jumps
over the lazy dog

N 100: 081 1533
Friedrich Poppl 1971
H. Berthold AG
H 1–x 0,78–k 1,09–p 0,35

**Manessa**
812

the quick brown fox jumps
over the lazy dog

N 100: 081 0880
Georg Wilkens 1971
H. Berthold AG
H 1–x 0,56–k 1,00–p 0,35

**Pinocchio**
930

V 000: 081 1013
Gustav Jaeger 1973
H. Berthold AG
H 1–Q 1,00

| | Fancy, kursive<br>Fancy, italic<br>Fancy, italique | **73** |

**Italique de Giraldon**
704

the quick brown fox jumps
over the lazy dog

N 100: 081 0791
H. Berthold AG
H 1–x 0,63–k 1,00–p 0,31

**Bohn-Script**
219

the quick brown fox jumps
over the lazy dog

N 100: 081 0211
Hans Bohn 1974
H. Berthold AG
H 1–x 0,72–k 1,00–p 0,28

**Calligraphia**
266

the quick brown fox jumps
over the lazy dog

N 100: 081 1524
H. Berthold AG
H 1–x 0,63–k 1,00–p 0,37

**De Vinne Ornamented**
438
kursiv
italic
italique

the quick brown fox jumps
over the lazy dog

N 100: 081 0423
Photoscript Ltd.
H 1–x 0,69–k 1,00–p 0,31

## BERTHOLD HEADLINES VII — Antiqua-Varianten / Decoratives / Variantes

ABCDEFGHIJKLMNOPQRS
TUVWXYZ 1234567890

QUICK BROWN FOX JUMPS
OVER THE LAZY DOG 1234567890

THE QUICK BROWN FOX JUMPS OVER
THE LAZY DOG 1234567890

## BERTHOLD HEADLINES VII — Antiqua-Varianten / Decoratives / Variantes

THE QUICK BROWN FOX JUMPS OVER
THE LAZY DOG 1234567890

THE QUICK BROWN FOX JUMPS OVER
THE LAZY DOG 1234567890

THE QUICK BROWN FOX JUMPS OVER
THE LAZY DOG 1234567890

THE QUICK BROWN FOX JUMPS OVER
THE LAZY DOG 1234567890

| | Fancy, kursive / Fancy, italic / Fancy, italique | **73** |

*the quick brown fox jumps over the lazy dog*

**Lo-Type**
1336
kursiv halbfett
medium italic
italique demi-gras
N 020: 081 2421
Erik Spiekermann 1980
(Louis Oppenheim 1913-1914)
H 1–x 0,67–k 1,00–p 0,21

*the quick brown fox jumps over the lazy dog*

**Elvira**
473
kursiv fett
bold italic
italique gras
N 000: 081 0474
1926
Johannes Wagner
H 1–x 0,66–k 1,00–p 0,18

*the quick brown fox jumps over the lazy dog*

**Swing**
1071

N 100: 081 1158
Peter Steiner 1974
H. Berthold AG
H 1–x 0,74–k 1,00–p 0,32

| | Pop / Pop / Pop | **74** |

the quick brown fox jumps over the lazy dog

**Klio**
728

N 100: 081 1449
Ursula Hofelich 1972
H. Berthold AG
H 1–x 0,78–k 1,00–p 0,22

the quick brown fox jumps over the lazy dog

**Santana**
1009

N 100: 081 1457
A. M. Barth, H. Reichel 1972
H. Berthold AG
H 1–x 0,72–k 1,00–p 0,28

the quick brown fox jumps over the lazy dog

**Beat Star**
140

N 100: 081 1540
Karl-Heinz Domning 1972
H. Berthold AG
H 1–x 0,78–k 1,06–p 0,31

the quick brown fox jumps over the lazy dog

ITC **Honda Display**
675

N 100: 081 0762
Ronne Bonder, Tom Carnase 1970
International Typeface Corp.
H 1–x 0,69–k 1,00–p 0,34

## BERTHOLD HEADLINES VII
Antiqua-Varianten
Decoratives
Variantes

THE QUICK BROWN FOX JUMPS OVER
THE LAZY DOG 1234567890

QUICK BROWN FOX JUMPS OVER
THE LAZY DOG 1234567890

QUICK BROWN FOX JUMPS OVER
THE LAZY DOG 1234567890

THE QUICK BROWN FOX JUMPS OVER
THE LAZY DOG 1234567890

THE QUICK BROWN FOX JUMPS OVER
THE LAZY DOG 1234567890

QUICK BROWN FOX JUMPS OVER
THE LAZY DOG 1234567890

Pop  
Pop  
Pop **74**

**Fanfare**  
501  
schmal  
condensed  
étroit  
N 100: 081 1436  
Louis Oppenheim 1927  
H. Berthold AG  
H 1–x 0,78–k 1,00–p 0,10

the quick brown fox jumps  
over the lazy dog

**Motter Alustyle**  
846

the quick brown fox jumps  
over the lazy dog 1234567890

X 000: 081 1545  
Vorarlberger Grafik 1972  
H. Berthold AG  
x 0,69–k 1,00–p 0,31

**Watzlsnap**  
1197

the quick brown fox jumps  
over the lazy dog 1234567890

X 016: 081 2227  
Peter Watzl 1976  
H. Berthold AG  
x 0,74–k 1,00–p 0,26

**Motter Ombra**  
847

the quick brown fox jumps  
over the lazy dog 1234567890

N 100: 081 1519  
Vorarlberger Grafik 1972  
H. Berthold AG  
H 1–x 0,75–k 1,00–p 0,25

**Voel Bianca**  
1176

the quick brown fox jumps  
over the lazy dog

N 020: 081 2289  
Ernst Völker 1978  
H. Berthold AG  
H 1–x 0,78–k 1,00–p 0,27

**Bulk**  
259

the quick brown fox jumps  
over the lazy dog

N 100: 081 1863  
Klaus Berthelmann 1975  
H. Berthold AG  
H 1–x 0,76–k 1,00–p 0,27

**Geard Graphic**  
603

the quick brown fox jumps  
over the lazy dog

N 100: 081 0659  
M. N. Geard 1974  
H. Berthold AG  
H 1–x 0,72–k 0,97–p 0,16

**Latus**  
753

the quick brown fox jumps  
over the lazy dog

N 100: 081 1869  
Willy Wirtz 1975  
H. Berthold AG  
H 1–x 0,78–k 1,00–p 0,10

## BERTHOLD HEADLINES VII
Antiqua-Varianten / Decoratives / Variantes

QUICK BROWN FOX JUMPS OVER THE LAZY DOG 1234567890

## BERTHOLD HEADLINES VII
Antiqua-Varianten / Decoratives / Variantes

THE QUICK BROWN FOX JUMPS OVER THE LAZY DOG 1234567890

THE QUICK BROWN FOX JUMPS OVER THE LAZY DOG 1234567890

THE QUICK BROWN FOX JUMPS OVER THE LAZY DOG 1234567890

THE QUICK BROWN FOX JUMPS OVER THE LAZY DOG 1234567890

## Pop Pop Pop 74

**Furrer Fono**
542

the quick brown fox jumps
over the lazy dog

N 010: 081 0008
F. Furrer 1975
H. Berthold AG
H 1–x 0,78–k 1,00–p 0,25

## Stencil Stencil Stencil 75

**Stencil**
1060

V 000: 081 1147
R. H. Middleton, Gerry Powell 1938
American Typefounders
H 1–Q 1,05

**Gesh Export 233**
606

the quick brown fox jumps
over the lazy dog

N 100: 081 1527
Gerhard Schwekendick 1972
H. Berthold AG
H 1–x 0,78–k 1,06–p 0,31

**Futura Black**
562

the quick brown fox jumps
over the lazy dog

N 100: 081 0623
Paul Renner 1929
Fundición Tipográfica Neufville, S.A.
H 1–x 0,72–k 1,00–p 0,28

**Dalmock**
432

the quick brown fox jumps
over the lazy dog

N 020: 081 0140
Gerd-Dieter Popielaty 1976
H. Berthold AG
H 1–x 0,78–k 1,00–p 0,22

**Watzlcross**
1194

the quick brown fox jumps
over the lazy dog 1234567890

X 016: 081 0090
Peter Watzl 1976
H. Berthold AG
x 0,81–k 1,00–p 0,19

**Fat Watzlline**
502

the quick brown fox jumps
over the lazy dog 1234567890

X 016: 081 2225
Peter Watzl 1976
H. Berthold AG
x 0,66–k 1,00–p 0,34

## BERTHOLD HEADLINES VII
Antiqua-Varianten
Decoratives
Variantes

THE QUICK BROWN FOX JUMPS OVER
THE LAZY DOG 1234567890

THE QUICK BROWN FOX JUMPS OVER
THE LAZY DOG 1234567890

THE QUICK BROWN FOX JUMPS OVER
THE LAZY DOG 1234567890

QUICK BROWN FOX JUMPS OVER
THE LAZY DOG 1234567890

QUICK BROWN FOX JUMPS OVER
THE LAZY DOG

QUICK BROWN FOX JUMPS OVER
THE LAZY DOG 1234567890

FOX JUMPS OVER THE
LAZY DOG 1234567890

THE QUICK BROWN FOX JUMPS OVER
THE LAZY DOG 1234567890

Computer
Computer
Computer
**76**

the quick brown fox jumps
over the lazy dog

**Chin Century 2000 Nr. 1**
326
normal
regular
normal

N 100: 081 1536
Photoscript Ltd.
H 1–x 0,69–k 1,00–p 0,22

the quick brown fox jumps
over the lazy dog

**Chin Century 2000 Nr. 2**
327
halbfett
medium
demi-gras

N 100: 081 1538
Photoscript Ltd.
H 1–x 0,72–k 1,00–p 0,28

*the quick brown fox jumps
over the lazy dog*

**Chin Century 2000 Nr. 3**
328
kursiv halbfett
medium italic
italique demi-gras

N 100: 081 1539
Photoscript Ltd.
H 1–x 0,72–k 1,00–p 0,19

the quick brown fox jumps
over the lazy dog

**Vienna**
1172

N 100: 081 1354
Joh. Pfeil 1973
H. Berthold AG
H 1–x 0,78–k 1,00–p 0,19

the quick brown fox jumps
over the lazy dog

**Vienna**
1173
Zierbuchstaben
swash letters
lettres ornées
Z 000: 081 1355
Joh. Pfeil 1973
H. Berthold AG
H 1–x 0,78–k 1,00–p 0,22

the quick brown fox jumps
over the lazy dog

**Touring**
1105

N 100: 081 1199
Joh. Pfeil 1973
H. Berthold AG
H 1–x 0,72–k 1,00–p 0,28

the quick brown fox jumps
over the lazy dog

**Sar Modern**
1010

N 100: 081 1101
Stan Rosenblum 1971
H. Berthold AG
H 1–x 0,66–k 1,00–p 0,31

the quick brown fox jumps
over the lazy dog

**Amelia**
44

N 100: 081 1464
1967
Visual Graphics Corporation
H 1–x 0,69–k 1,00–p 0,21

**BERTHOLD HEADLINES VII** — Antiqua-Varianten / Decoratives / Variantes

THE QUICK BROWN FOX JUMPS OVER
THE LAZY DOG 1234567890

THE QUICK BROWN FOX JUMPS OVER
THE LAZY DOG 1234567890

**BERTHOLD HEADLINES VII** — Antiqua-Varianten / Decoratives / Variantes

THE QUICK BROWN FOX JUMPS OVER
THE LAZY DOG 1234567890

THE QUICK BROWN FOX JUMPS OVER
THE LAZY DOG 1234567890

QUICK BROWN FOX JUMPS OVER
THE LAZY DOG 1234567890

THE QUICK BROWN FOX JUMPS OVER
THE LAZY DOG 1234567890

THE QUICK BROWN FOX JUMPS OVER
THE LAZY DOG 1234567890

| | Computer Computer Computer | **76** |

**Westminster**
1208

# the quick brown fox jumps over the lazy dog

N 100: 081 1390
Leo Maggs 1973
H. Berthold AG
H 1–x 0,69–k 1,03–p 0,41

**G. K. W. Computer**
621

V 000: 081 0673
G. K. W. G. Kuhle Werbung 1974
H. Berthold AG
H 1–Q 1,0

| | Outline Outline Outline | **77** |

**Contura**
418

# the quick brown fox jumps over the lazy dog

N 100: 081 0392
Dick Dooijes 1966
Lettergieterij Amsterdam
H 1–x 0,69–k 1,06–p 0,40

**Columna Open**
411

V 000: 081 0384
Max Caflisch 1952
Fundición Tipográfica Neufville, S.A.
H 1–Q 1,25

**Largo**
749

V 000: 081 0855
H. Wagner 1950
Ludwig & Mayer
H 1–Q 1,15

ITC **Clearface**
1312
licht
outline
éclairé
N 020: 081 2221
Vic Caruso 1979
(Morris Fuller Benton 1907-1911)
H 1–x 0,69–k 1,07–p 0,22

# the quick brown fox jumps over the lazy dog

ITC **Cheltenham**
322
licht
outline
éclairé
N 020: 081 1994
Tony Stan 1978
International Typeface Corp.
H 1–x 0,69–k 1,09–p 0,27

# the quick brown fox jumps over the lazy dog

**BERTHOLD HEADLINES VII** Antiqua-Varianten / Decoratives / Variantes

THE QUICK BROWN FOX JUMPS OVER THE LAZY DOG 1234567890

QUICK BROWN FOX JUMPS OVER THE LAZY DOG 1234567890

QUICK BROWN FOX JUMPS OVER THE LAZY DOG 1234567890

QUICK BROWN FOX JUMPS OVER THE LAZY DOG 1234567890

QUICK BROWN FOX JUMPS OVER THE LAZY DOG 1234567890

BROWN FOX JUMPS OVER THE LAZY DOG 1234567890

THE QUICK BROWN FOX JUMPS OVER THE LAZY DOG 1234567890

THE QUICK BROWN FOX JUMPS OVER THE LAZY DOG

Outline Outline Outline **77**

the quick brown fox jumps over the lazy dog

ATF **Cheltenham**
305
licht halbfett
bold open
demi-gras éclairé
N 100: 081 0298
Morris F. Benton, B. Goodhue 1908
American Typefounders
H 1–x 0,60–k 1,00–p 0,24

the quick brown fox jumps over the lazy dog

**Windsor**
1223
licht
outline
éclairé
N 000: 081 1399
Eleisha Pechey 1910
Stephenson Blake & Company Ltd.
H 1–x 0,69–k 1,00–p 0,25

the quick brown fox jumps over the lazy dog

**Cooper Black**
423
licht
outline
éclairé
N 100: 081 0404
Oswald B. Cooper 1924
American Typefounders
H 1–x 0,73–k 1,00–p 0,26

the quick brown fox jumps over the lazy dog

ITC **Souvenir**
1055
fett licht
bold outline
gras éclairé
N 020: 081 2248
Ed Benguiat 1970
International Typeface Corp.
H 1–x 0,66–k 1,03–p 0,28

the quick brown fox jumps over the lazy dog

ITC **Bookman**
238
licht
outline
éclairé
N 020: 081 2340
Ed Benguiat 1975
International Typeface Corp.
H 1–x 0,77–k 1,09–p 0,39

The quick brown fox jumps over the lazy dog

ITC **Bookman**
239
licht Zierbuchstaben
outline swash letters
éclairé lettres ornées
Z 000: 081 2157
Ed Benguiat 1975
International Typeface Corp.
H 1–x 0,77–k 1,20–p 0,63

the quick brown fox jumps over the lazy dog

ITC **Korinna**
744
licht
outline
éclairé
N 010: 081 2092
Ed Benguiat, Vic Caruso 1974
International Typeface Corp.
H 1–x 0,73–k 1,00–p 0,28

the quick brown fox jumps over the lazy dog

ITC **Korinna**
745
licht Zierbuchstaben
outline swash letters
éclairé lettres ornées
Z 000: 081 2093 *
Ed Benguiat, Vic Caruso 1974
International Typeface Corp.
H 1–x 0,73–k 1,00–p 0,28

## BERTHOLD HEADLINES VII
Antiqua-Varianten
Decoratives
Variantes

BROWN FOX JUMPS OVER
THE LAZY DOG 1234567890

QUICK BROWN FOX JUMPS OVER
THE LAZY DOG 1234567890

THE QUICK BROWN FOX JUMPS OVER
THE LAZY DOG 1234567890

THE QUICK BROWN FOX JUMPS OVER
THE LAZY DOG 1234567890

THE QUICK BROWN FOX JUMPS OVER
THE LAZY DOG 1234567890

THE QUICK BROWN FOX JUMPS OVER
THE LAZY DOG 1234567890

QUICK BROWN FOX JUMPS OVER
THE LAZY DOG 1234567890

THE QUICK BROWN FOX JUMPS OVER
THE LAZY DOG 1234567890

Outline Outline Outline 77

the quick brown fox jumps over the lazy dog

**Craw Clarendon**
429
licht
outline
éclairé
N 100: 081 1489
Freeman Craw
American Typefounders
H 1–x 0,72–k 1,00–p 0,31

the quick brown fox jumps over the lazy dog

ITC **American Typewriter**
53
fett licht
bold outline
gras éclairé
N 020: 081 1846
Tony Stan, Joel Kaden 1974
International Typeface Corp.
H 1–x 0,74–k 1,03–p 0,34

the quick brown fox jumps over the lazy dog

**Media Kontur**
820
fett
bold
gras
N 100: 081 1880
Jürgen Riebling 1976
H. Berthold AG
H 1–x 0,76–k 1,00–p 0,27

the quick brown fox jumps over the lazy dog

**Media Outline**
821
fett
bold
gras
N 100: 081 1875
Jürgen Riebling 1976
H. Berthold AG
H 1–x 0,76–k 1,00–p 0,27

the quick brown fox jumps over the lazy dog

ITC **Kabel**
720
licht
outline
éclairé
N 020: 081 2345
Photo-Lettering Inc. 1976
(Rudolf Koch 1927-1930)
H 1–x 0,76–k 1,06–p 0,30

the quick brown fox jumps over the lazy dog

STEMPEL **Kabel**
726
fett licht
heavy outline
gras éclairé
N 100: 081 0822
1929
D. Stempel AG
H 1–x 0,72–k 1,00–p 0,20

the quick brown fox jumps over the lazy dog

**Gill Sans**
619
licht ultrafett
ultra bold outline
ultra gras éclairé
N 100: 081 1543
Monotype Corporation Ltd.
H 1–x 0,81–k 1,00–p 0,22

the quick brown fox jumps over the lazy dog

**Gill Sans**
618
extrafett licht
extra bold outline
extra gras éclairé
N 020: 081 2315
Monotype Corporation Ltd.
H 1–x 0,78–k 1,03–p 0,35

# BERTHOLD HEADLINES VII
Antiqua-Varianten
Decoratives
Variantes

THE QUICK BROWN FOX JUMPS OVER LAZY DOG 1234567890

THE QUICK BROWN FOX JUMPS OVER THE LAZY DOG 1234567890

THE QUICK BROWN FOX JUMPS OVER THE LAZY DOG 1234567890

THE QUICK BROWN FOX JUMPS OVER THE LAZY DOG 1234567890

THE QUICK BROWN FOX JUMPS OVER THE LAZY DOG 1234567890

THE QUICK BROWN FOX JUMPS OVER THE LAZY DOG 1234567890

THE QUICK BROWN FOX JUMPS OVER THE LAZY DOG 1234567890

THE QUICK BROWN FOX JUMPS OVER THE LAZY DOG 1234567890

| | Outline Outline Outline **77** |

**the quick brown fox jumps over the lazy dog**

ITC **Eras**
485
licht
outline
éclairé
N 020: 081 2400
Albert Boton 1976
International Typeface Corp.
H 1–x 0,73–k 1,00–p 0,31

the quick brown fox jumps over the lazy dog

ITC **Franklin Gothic**
1379
licht
outline
éclairé
N 020: 081 2486
Vic Caruso 1980
International Typeface Corp.
H 1–x 0,75–k 1,00–p 0,26

the quick brown fox jumps over the lazy dog

**AG Buch Outline**
29
halbfett
medium
demi-gras
N 020: 081 1811
Günter Gerhard Lange 1977
H. Berthold AG
H 1–x 0,74 k 1,00–p 0,22

the quick brown fox jumps over the lazy dog

**Futura**
559
fett licht
bold outline
gras éclairé
N 020: 081 1972
Berthold-Schriftenatelier 1976
Fundición Tipográfica Neufville, S.A.
H 1–x 0,68–k 1,05–p 0,30

the quick brown fox jumps over the lazy dog

**Univers 65**
1146
halbfett licht
bold outline
demi-gras éclairé
N 020: 081 2279
Adrian Frutiger
Fundición Tipográfica Neufville, S.A.
H 1–x 0,69–k 1,00–p 0,25

the quick brown fox jumps over the lazy dog

**Futura**
1279
extrafett licht
extra bold outline
extra gras éclairé
N 020: 081 0851
Berthold-Schriftenatelier 1980
Fundición Tipográfica Neufville, S.A.
H 1–x 0,70–k 1,06–p 0,29

the quick brown fox jumps over the lazy dog

**AG Buch Outline**
1260
fett
bold
gras
N 020: 081 2230
Günter Gerhard Lange 1977
H. Berthold AG
H 1–x 0,73–k 1,00–p 0,25

**Futura**
561
licht
outline
éclairé
V 000: 081 0626
Paul Renner 1932
Fundición Tipográfica Neufville, S.A.
H 1–Q 1,05

399

## BERTHOLD HEADLINES VII
Antiqua-Varianten / Decoratives / Variantes

THE QUICK BROWN FOX JUMPS OVER
THE LAZY DOG  1234567890

THE QUICK BROWN FOX JUMPS OVER
THE LAZY DOG  1234567890

THE QUICK BROWN FOX JUMPS OVER
THE LAZY DOG  1234567890

THE QUICK BROWN FOX JUMPS OVER
THE LAZY DOG  1234567890

THE QUICK BROWN FOX JUMPS OVER
THE LAZY DOG  1234567890

THE QUICK BROWN FOX JUMPS OVER
THE LAZY DOG 1234567890

THE QUICK BROWN FOX JUMPS OVER
THE LAZY DOG 1234567890

THE QUICK BROWN FOX JUMPS OVER
THE LAZY DOG  1234567890

Outline Outline Outline **77**

the quick brown fox jumps over the lazy dog

**Permanent Headline**
922
licht
outline
éclairé
N 100: 081 0716
1968
Ludwig & Mayer
H 1–x 0,81–k 1,00–p 0,00

the quick brown fox jumps over the lazy dog

**Futura**
560
extrafett schmal licht
extra bold condensed outline
étroit extra gras éclairé
N 020: 081 1971
Berthold-Schriftenatelier 1976
Fundición Tipográfica Neufville, S.A.
H 1–x 0,70–k 1,07–p 0,33

**Gothic Outline Title**
625

V 000: 081 0675
Whedon Davis 1965
American Typefounders
H 1–Q 1,28

the quick brown fox jumps over the lazy dog

ATF **Franklin Gothic**
539
schmal licht
condensed outline
étroit éclairé

N 020: 081 0341
American Typefounders
H 1–x 0,72–k 1,00–p 0,22

the quick brown fox jumps over the lazy dog

**AG Buch Rounded**
34
schmalfett licht
bold condensed outline
étroit gras éclairé
N 020: 081 2379
Günter Gerhard Lange 1979
H. Berthold AG
H 1–x 0,74–k 1,01–p 0,25

the quick brown fox jumps over the lazy dog

**AG Buch Rounded**
1259
halbfett licht
medium outline
demi-gras éclairé
N 020: 081 2232
Günter Gerhard Lange 1980
H. Berthold AG
H 1–x 0,73–k 1,01–p 0,23

the quick brown fox jumps over the lazy dog

**AG Buch Rounded**
33
fett licht
bold outline
gras éclairé
N 020: 081 2378
Günter Gerhard Lange 1977
H. Berthold AG
H 1–x 0,74–k 1,01–p 0,24

the quick brown fox jumps over the lazy dog

ITC **Bauhaus**
138
extrafett licht
extra bold outline
extra gras éclairé
N 020: 081 1827
Ed Benguiat, Vic Caruso 1975
International Typeface Corp.
H 1–x 0,72–k 1,00–p 0,31

# BERTHOLD HEADLINES VII
Antiqua-Varianten / Decoratives / Variantes

THE QUICK BROWN FOX JUMPS OVER
THE LAZY DOG

BROWN FOX JUMPS OVER
THE LAZY DOG 123456789

THE QUICK BROWN FOX JUMPS OVER
THE LAZY DOG 1234567890

THE QUICK BROWN FOX JUMPS OVER
THE LAZY DOG 1234567890

THE QUICK BROWN FOX JUMPS OVER
THE LAZY DOG 1234567890

THE QUICK BROWN FOX JUMPS OVER
THE LAZY DOG 1234567890

THE QUICK BROWN FOX JUMPS OVER
THE LAZY DOG 1234567890

THE QUICK BROWN FOX JUMPS OVER
THE LAZY DOG

Outline / Outline / Outline **77**

the quick brown fox jumps over the lazy dog

ITC **Bauhaus**
139
extrafett licht Zierbuchstaben
extra bold outline swash letters
extra gras éclairé lettres ornées
Z 000: 081 1913 *
Ed Benguiat, Vic Caruso 1975
International Typeface Corp.
H 1–x 0,72–k 1,00–p 0,31

the quick brown fox jumps over the lazy dog

**Annonce**
56
fett licht
bold outline
gras éclairé
N 000: 081 0070
B. Th. P. Verkaart 1967
H. Berthold AG
H 1–x 0,74–k 1,00–p 0,23

the quick brown fox jumps over the lazy dog

**Blippo Black**
200
licht
outline
éclairé

N 100: 081 1433
Facsimile Fonts
H 1–x 0,74–k 1,00–p 0,32

the quick brown fox jumps over the lazy dog

**Blippo Black**
201
licht Zierbuchstaben
outline swash letters
éclairé lettres ornées

Z 000: 081 1922
Facsimile Fonts
H 1–x 0,74–k 1,00–p 0,32

the quick brown fox jumps over the lazy dog

**Poell Outline**
945

N 000: 081 1485
Erwin Poell 1972
H. Berthold AG
H 1–x 0,69–k 1,00–p 0,31

the quick brown fox jumps over the lazy dog

**Poell Medium Outline**
944

N 100: 081 1486
Erwin Poell 1972
H. Berthold AG
H 1–x 0,69–k 1,00–p 0,31

the quick brown fox jumps over the lazy dog

ITC **Serif Gothic**
1035
licht
outline
éclairé
N 010: 081 2012
Herb Lubalin, Antonio Dispigna 1974
International Typeface Corp.
H 1–x 0,71–k 1,00–p 0,30

the quick brown fox jumps over the lazy dog

ITC **Serif Gothic**
1036
licht Zierbuchstaben
outline swash letters
éclairé lettres ornées
Z 000: 081 2032
Herb Lubalin, Antonio Dispigna 1974
International Typeface Corp.
H 1–x 0,71–k 1,00–p 0,33

403

## BERTHOLD HEADLINES VII
Antiqua-Varianten / Decoratives / Variantes

THE QUICK BROWN FOX JUMPS OVER
THE LAZY DOG 1234567890

QUICK BROWN FOX JUMPS OVER
THE LAZY DOG 1234567890

THE QUICK BROWN FOX JUMPS OVER
THE LAZY DOG 1234567890

THE QUICK BROWN FOX JUMPS OVER
THE LAZY DOG 1234567890

THE QUICK BROWN FOX JUMPS OVER
THE LAZY DOG 1234567890

## BERTHOLD HEADLINES VII
Antiqua-Varianten / Decoratives / Variantes

THE QUICK BROWN FOX JUMPS OVER
THE LAZY DOG 1234567890

## 77 Outline / Outline / Outline

the quick brown fox jumps over the lazy dog

**Herold Reklameschrift**
671
licht
outline
éclairé
N 020: 081 0042
1904
H. Berthold AG
H 1–x 0,84–k 1,03–p 0,13

**Alexandra**
38

V 000: 081 1483
H. Berthold AG
E 1–U 1,60

**Poppl Saladin**
963
licht
outline
éclairé
VD 000: 081 0431 *
Friedrich Poppl 1979
H. Berthold AG
L 1–Q 1,34

the quick brown fox jumps over the lazy dog

**Churchward Blackbeauty 72**
367
licht
outline
éclairé
N 100: 081 1474
Joseph Churchward 1972
H. Berthold AG
H 1–x 0,74–k 1,00–p 0,26

**Futura Black Art Deco**
569
Outline

VD 018: 081 0260 *
Berthold-Schriftenatelier 1976
Fundición Tipográfica Neufville, S.A.
H 1–Q 1,32

quick brown fox jumps over the lazy dog 1234567890

**Watzlform**
1196
Open

X 016: 081 2286
Peter Watzl 1977
H. Berthold AG
H 1–x 0,86–k 1,00–p 0,14

## 78 Shaded / Shaded / Shaded

the quick brown fox jumps over the lazy dog

**Perpetua**
926
schattiert
shaded
ombré

N 020: 081 2276
Monotype Corporation Ltd.
H 1–x 0,69–k 1,08–p 0,77

# BERTHOLD HEADLINES VII
Antiqua-Varianten / Decoratives / Variantes

THE QUICK BROWN FOX JUMPS OVER
THE LAZY DOG 1234567890

THE QUICK BROWN FOX JUMPS OVER
THE LAZY DOG 1234567890

THE QUICK BROWN FOX JUMPS OVER
THE LAZY DOG 1234567890

THE QUICK BROWN FOX JUMPS OVER
THE LAZY DOG 1234567890

THE QUICK BROWN FOX JUMPS OVER
THE LAZY DOG 1234567890

THE QUICK BROWN FOX JUMPS OVER
THE LAZY DOG 1234567890

THE QUICK BROWN FOX JUMPS OVER
THE LAZY DOG 1234567890

THE QUICK BROWN FOX JUMPS OVER
THE LAZY DOG 1234567890

Shaded
Shaded
Shaded
**78**

the quick brown fox jumps
over the lazy dog

ITC **Clearface**
405
licht schattiert
outline shadow
éclairé ombré
N 020: 081 2223
Vic Caruso 1979
International Typeface Corp.
H 1–x 0,71–k 1,08–p 0,23

the quick brown fox jumps
over the lazy dog

ITC **Cheltenham**
323
licht schattiert
outline shaded
éclairé ombré
N 020: 081 1995
Tony Stan 1978
International Typeface Corp.
H 1–x 0,69–k 1,00–p 0,27

**Elongated Roman**
472
schattiert
shaded
ombré
V 000: 081 1796
1940
Stephenson Blake & Company Ltd.
H 1–Q 1,14

**Regina**
986

V 000: 081 1081
1954
H. Berthold AG
H 1–Q 1,17

**Forum II**
532

Sp 000: 081 0577
Georg Trump 1952
Johannes Wagner
H 1–Q 1,16

**Forum I**
531
mit Griechisch
with greek
avec grecque
Sp 000: 081 0575
Georg Trump 1948
Johannes Wagner
H 1–Q 1,20

**Beton Open**
188

V 100: 081 1500
Heinrich Jost 1930
Fundición Tipográfica Neufville, S.A.
H 1–Q 1,10

**Stymie Open**
1070

V 000: 081 1156
American Typefounders
H 1–Q 1,10

**BERTHOLD HEADLINES VII** — Antiqua-Varianten / Decoratives / Variantes

# OVER THE LAZY DOG 123456789

THE QUICK BROWN FOX JUMPS OVER
THE LAZY DOG 1234567890

THE QUICK BROWN FOX JUMPS OVER
THE LAZY DOG 1234567890

THE QUICK BROWN FOX JUMPS OVER
THE LAZY DOG 1234567890

QUICK BROWN FOX JUMPS OVER
THE LAZY DOG 1234567890

THE QUICK BROWN FOX JUMPS OVER
THE LAZY DOG 1234567890

THE QUICK BROWN FOX JUMPS OVER
THE LAZY DOG 1234567890

THE QUICK BROWN FOX JUMPS OVER
THE LAZY DOG

Shaded
Shaded
Shaded
**78**

fox jumps over the lazy dog

**Egyptienne**
468
breit schattiert
expanded shaded
large ombrée

N 100: 081 0465
Stephenson Blake & Company Ltd.
H 1–x 0,72–k 1,03–p 0,28

the quick brown fox jumps over the lazy dog

**Churchward Maricia**
377
schattiert
shaded
ombré
N 100: 081 1534
Joseph Churchward 1972
H. Berthold AG
H 1–x 0,73–k 1,00–p 0,47

the quick brown fox jumps over the lazy dog

**Churchward Maricia**
378
kursiv schattiert
italic shaded
italique ombré
N 100: 081 1535
Joseph Churchward 1972
H. Berthold AG
H 1–x 0,73–k 1,00–p 0,47

the quick brown fox jumps over the lazy dog

**AG Buch White**
35
halbfett schattiert
medium shaded
demi-gras ombré
N 020: 081 1812
Günter Gerhard Lange 1977
H. Berthold AG
H 1–x 0,74–k 1,00–p 0,33

the quick brown fox jumps over the lazy dog

**Futura**
1280
extrafett schattiert
extra bold shaded
extra gras ombré
N 020: 081 2233
Berthold-Schriftenatelier 1980
Fundición Tipográfica Neufville, S.A.
H 1–x 0,70–k 1,06–p 0,29

the quick brown fox jumps over the lazy dog

**Churchward Design 70**
354
Deep Shadow normal
Deep Shadow regular
Deep Shadow normal
N 100: 081 1716
Joseph Churchward 1970
H. Berthold AG
H 1–x 0,69–k 1,00–p 0,61

the quick brown fox jumps over the lazy dog

**Churchward Design 70**
-355
Deep Shadow kursiv
Deep Shadow italic
Deep Shadow italique
N 100: 081 1721
Joseph Churchward 1970
H. Berthold AG
H 1–x 0,69–k 1,00–p 0,61

**Graphique**
635

V 000: 081 0691
Hermann Eidenbenz 1945
Haas'sche Schriftgießerei AG
H 1–Q 1,00

409

## BERTHOLD HEADLINES VII
Antiqua-Varianten / Decoratives / Variantes

THE QUICK BROWN FOX JUMPS OVER
THE LAZY DOG 1234567890

THE QUICK BROWN FOX JUMPS OVER
THE LAZY DOG 1234567890

THE QUICK BROWN FOX JUMPS OVER
THE LAZY DOG 1234567890

THE QUICK BROWN FOX JUMPS OVER
THE LAZY DOG 1234567890

THE QUICK BROWN FOX JUMPS OVER
THE LAZY DOG 1234567890

THE QUICK BROWN FOX JUMPS OVER
THE LAZY DOG 1234567890

THE QUICK BROWN FOX JUMPS OVER
THE LAZY DOG 1234567890

THE QUICK BROWN FOX JUMPS OVER
THE LAZY DOG 1234567890

| | Shaded Shaded Shaded **78** |

**Sans Serif**
1008
schattiert
shaded
ombré

V 000: 081 1100
Stephenson Blake & Company Ltd.
H 1–Q 1,33

ITC **Pioneer**
931

V 000: 081 1015
Ronne Bonder, Tom Carnase 1970
International Typeface Corp.
H 1–Q 1,32

**Poell Shaded**
946

V 000: 081 1488
Erwin Poell 1972
H. Berthold AG
H 1–Q 1,23

**Uncle Bill**
1123

V 000: 081 1226
Facsimile Fonts
H 1–Q 1,14

the quick brown fox jumps over the lazy dog

**Jockey**
710

N 100: 081 1798
Peter Steiner 1975
H. Berthold AG
H 1–x 0,81–k 1,00–p 0,54

the quick brown fox jumps over the lazy dog

**Churchward Marianna**
373
schattiert
shaded
ombré
N 100: 081 1461
Joseph Churchward 1970
H. Berthold AG
H 1–x 0,73–k 1,00–p 0,40

the quick brown fox jumps over the lazy dog

**Churchward Marianna**
374
kursiv schattiert
italic shaded
italique ombré
N 100: 081 0326
Joseph Churchward 1970
H. Berthold AG
H 1–x 0,73–k 1,00–p 0,40

the quick brown fox jumps over the lazy dog

**Churchward Blackbeauty 72**
368
schattiert
shaded
ombré
N 100: 081 1475
Joseph Churchward 1972
H. Berthold AG
H 1–x 0,78–k 1,03–p 0,44

## BERTHOLD HEADLINES VII — Antiqua-Varianten / Decoratives / Variantes

THE QUICK BROWN FOX JUMPS OVER
THE LAZY DOG 1234567890

THE QUICK BROWN FOX JUMPS OVER
THE LAZY DOG 1234567890

THE QUICK BROWN FOX JUMPS OVER
THE LAZY DOG 1234567890

## BERTHOLD HEADLINES VII — Antiqua-Varianten / Decoratives / Variantes

THE QUICK BROWN FOX JUMPS OVER
THE LAZY DOG 1234567890

THE QUICK BROWN FOX JUMPS OVER
THE LAZY DOG 1234567890

QUICK BROWN FOX JUMPS OVER
THE LAZY DOG 1234567890

AABBCCDEFGHIJJKLMNOPQ
RSTUVWXYZ 1234567890

## 78 Shaded / Shaded / Shaded

the quick brown fox jumps over the lazy dog

**Logotype**
767
schattiert
shaded
ombré
N 020: 081 2127
Helmut Langer 1975
H. Berthold AG
H 1–x 0,60–k 1,00–p 0,50

**Sacher**
1006

V 000: 081 1099
Gustav Jaeger 1973
H. Berthold AG
H 1–Q 1,13

**Roberta Raised**
992
schattiert
shaded
ombré

V 000: 081 1086
Facsimile Fonts
H 1–Q 1,58

## 79 Kontur / Contour / Contour

the quick brown fox jumps over the lazy dog

ITC **Cheltenham**
324
Kontur
contour
contour
N 020: 081 1996
Tony Stan 1978
International Typeface Corp.
H 1–x 0,72–k 1,03–p 0,26

the quick brown fox jumps over the lazy dog

ITC **Clearface**
1275
Kontur
contour
contour
N 020: 081 0224
Vic Caruso 1979
International Typeface Corp.
H 1–x 0,70–k 1,08–p 0,26

the quick brown fox jumps over the lazy dog

ITC **Bookman**
240
Kontur
contour
contour
N 020: 081 2339
Ed Benguiat 1975
H. Berthold AG
H 1–x 0,78–k 1,10–p 0,30

the quick brown fox jumps over the lazy dog

ITC **Bookman**
241
Kontur Zierbuchstaben
contour swash letters
contour lettres ornées
Z 000: 081 2156
Ed Benguiat 1975
H. Berthold AG
H 1–x 0,77–V 1,36–p 0,51

413

**BERTHOLD HEADLINES VII**  Antiqua-Varianten / Decoratives / Variantes

THE QUICK BROWN FOX JUMPS OVER THE LAZY DOG 1234567890

BROWN FOX JUMPS OVER THE LAZY DOG 1234567890

BROWN FOX JUMPS OVER THE LAZY DOG 1234567890

THE QUICK BROWN FOX JUMPS OVER THE LAZY DOG 1234567890

THE QUICK BROWN FOX JUMPS OVER THE LAZY DOG 1234567890

QUICK BROWN FOX JUMPS OVER THE LAZY DOG 1234567890

THE QUICK BROWN FOX JUMPS OVER THE LAZY DOG

THE QUICK BROWN FOX JUMPS OVER THE LAZY DOG 1234567890

Kontur
Contour
Contour
**79**

the quick brown fox jumps over the lazy dog

**Media Inline**
819
fett
bold
gras
N 100: 081 1886
Jürgen Riebling 1976
H. Berthold AG
H 1–x 0,75–k 1,00–p 0,28

the quick brown fox jumps over the lazy dog

**Nubian**
896

N 100: 081 0960
H. Berthold AG
H 1–x 0,70–k 1,02–p 0,42

**Gold Rush**
623

V 000: 081 0674
1885
American Typefounders
H 1–Q 1,12

the quick brown fox jumps over the lazy dog

STEMPEL **Kabel**
727
schattiert
shaded
ombré
N 100: 081 0819
1930
D. Stempel AG
H 1–x 0,53–k 0,97–p 0,25

the quick brown fox jumps over the lazy dog

ITC **Kabel**
721
Kontur
contour
contour
N 020: 081 2006
Photo-Lettering Inc. 1976
(Rudolf Koch 1927-1930)
E 1–x 0,79–k 1,06–p 0,24

the quick brown fox jumps over the lazy dog

ITC **Eras**
486
Kontur
contour
contour
N 020: 081 2401
Albert Boton 1976
International Typeface Corp.
H 1–x 0,80–k 1,06–p 0,32

the quick brown fox jumps over the lazy dog

**AG Buch Inline**
28
halbfett schattiert
medium shaded
demi-gras ombré
N 020: 081 1813
Günter Gerhard Lange 1977
H. Berthold AG
H 1–x 0,73–k 1,00–p 0,32

the quick brown fox jumps over the lazy dog

ITC **Franklin Gothic**
1380
Kontur
contour
contour
N 020: 081 2485
Vic Caruso 1980
International Typeface Corp.
H 1–x 0,75–k 1,00–p 0,24

415

## BERTHOLD HEADLINES VII
Antiqua-Varianten / Decoratives / Variantes

QUICK BROWN FOX JUMPS OVER
THE LAZY DOG 1234567890

THE QUICK BROWN FOX JUMPS OVER
THE LAZY DOG 1234567890

THE QUICK BROWN FOX JUMPS OVER
THE LAZY DOG 1234567890

BROWN FOX JUMPS OVER
THE LAZY DOG 1234567890

## BERTHOLD HEADLINES VII
Antiqua-Varianten / Decoratives / Variantes

QUICK BROWN FOX JUMPS OVER
THE LAZY DOG 1234567890

THE QUICK BROWN FOX JUMPS OVER
THE LAZY DOG 1234567890

THE QUICK BROWN FOX JUMPS OVER
THE LAZY DOG 1234567890

| | Kontur / Contour / Contour | **79** |

**Comstock**
413

**the quick brown fox jumps over the lazy dog**

N 100: 081 0387
1880
Fundición Tipográfica Neufville, S.A.
H 1–x 0,72–k 1,00–p 0,25

**Old Bowery**
901

V 000: 081 0964
H. Berthold AG
H 1–Q 1,30

**Sculptura**
1021

V 000: 081 1122
Walter Diethelm 1957
Haas'sche Schriftgießerei AG
H 1–Q 1,20

**Profil**
973

V 000: 081 1068
Eugen Lenz, Max Lenz 1947
Haas'sche Schriftgießerei AG
H 1–Q 1,46

| | Gravur / Engraved / Gravure | **80** |

**Caslon Open Face**
280

the quick brown fox jumps
over the lazy dog

N 100: 081 0251
Monotype Corporation Ltd.
H 1–x 0,43–k 1,03–p 0,28

**Goudy Handtooled**
630

the quick brown fox jumps
over the lazy dog

N 100: 081 0684
Morris F. Benton 1912
American Typefounders
H 1–x 0,63–k 1,06–p 0,21

**Augustea**
83
licht
outline
éclairé
V 000: 081 0105
A. Butti, Aldo Novarese 1951
Societa Nebiolo S.p.A.
H 1–Q 1,05

417

# BERTHOLD HEADLINES VII
Antiqua-Varianten
Decoratives
Variantes

THE QUICK BROWN FOX JUMPS OVER THE LAZY DOG 1234567890

QUICK BROWN FOX JUMPS OVER THE LAZY DOG 1234567890

THE QUICK BROWN FOX JUMPS OVER THE LAZY DOG 1234567890

THE QUICK BROWN FOX JUMPS OVER THE LAZY DOG 1234567890

THE QUICK BROWN FOX JUMPS OVER THE LAZY DOG 1234567890

QUICK BROWN FOX JUMPS OVER THE LAZY DOG 1234567890

QUICK BROWN FOX JUMPS OVER THE LAZY DOG 1234567890

Gravur
Engraved
Gravure
**80**

**Castor**
281

V 100: 081 0254
Albert Auspurg 1924
Haas'sche Schriftgießerei AG
H 1–Q 1,25

**Trump Gravur**
1115

N 000: 081 1214
Georg Trump 1960
D. Stempel AG
H 1–Q 1,32

**Mona Lisa**
844

the quick brown fox jumps
over the lazy dog

N 100: 081 0914
Albert Auspurg 1930
Ludwig & Mayer
H 1–x 0,38–k 1,00 p 0,18

ATF **Bodoni-Antiqua**
206
licht
outline
éclairé
N 100: 081 0210
Morris F. Benton 1928
American Typefounders
H 1–x 0,60–k 1,00–p 0,43

the quick brown fox jumps
over the lazy dog

**Chisel**
329

the quick brown fox jumps
over the lazy dog

N 100: 081 0319
Robert Harling 1939
Stephenson Blake & Company Ltd.
H 1–x 0,72–k 1,00–p 0,28

**Chrystal**
331

V 000: 081 0322
Haas'sche Schriftgießerei AG
H 1–Q 1,10

**Gallia**
576

V 000: 081 0627
W. A. Parker 1927
American Typefounders
H 1–Q 1,15

## BERTHOLD HEADLINES VII
Antiqua-Varianten
Decoratives
Variantes

THE QUICK BROWN FOX JUMPS OVER
THE LAZY DOG 1234567890

THE QUICK BROWN FOX JUMPS OVER
THE LAZY DOG 1234567890

THE QUICK BROWN FOX JUMPS OVER
THE LAZY DOG 1234567890

THE QUICK BROWN FOX JUMPS OVER
THE LAZY DOG 1234567890

THE QUICK BROWN FOX JUMPS OVER
THE LAZY DOG

THE QUICK BROWN FOX JUMPS OVER
THE LAZY DOG 1234567890

THE QUICK BROWN FOX JUMPS OVER
THE LAZY DOG 1234567890

Double- und Multilines  
Double and Multilines  
Double-lines et multilines

**Media Triline**
823
fett
bold
gras
N 020: 081 2256
Jürgen Riebling 1978
H. Berthold AG
H 1–x 0,78–k 1,00–p 0,27

the quick brown fox jumps over the lazy dog

**Churchward Design 70**
363
No-End
No-End
No-End
N 100: 081 1445
Joseph Churchward 1970
H. Berthold AG
H 1–x 0,72–k 1,03–p 0,31

the quick brown fox jumps over the lazy dog

**Twice**
1116

N 010: 081 2131
Michael Neugebauer 1972
H. Berthold AG
H 1–x 0,75–k 1,00–p 0,25

the quick brown fox jumps over the lazy dog

ITC **Uptight**
1147
normal
regular
normal
N 100: 081 1786
Jack Deskin 1970
International Typeface Corp.
H 1–x 0,81–k 1,00–p 0,23

the quick brown fox jumps over the lazy dog

ITC **Uptight**
1148
normal Zierbuchstaben
regular swash letters
normal lettres ornées
Z 000: 081 1788
Jack Deskin 1970
International Typeface Corp.
H 1–x 0,81–k 1,00–p 0,23

the quick brown fox jumps over the lazy dog

ITC **Uptight Neon**
1149

N 100: 081 1785
Jack Deskin 1970
International Typeface Corp.
H 1–x 0,81–k 1,00–p 0,23

the quick brown fox jumps over the lazy dog

**Dektiv Double**
436

N 010: 081 2124
Peter Steiner 1975
H. Berthold AG
H 1–x 0,78–k 1,00–p 0,22

the quick brown fox jumps over the lazy dog

**Austrian Watzlline**
95

X 016: 081 2226
Peter Watzl 1976
H. Berthold AG
H 1–x 0,66–k 1,00–p 0,34

the quick brown fox jumps over the lazy dog

**BERTHOLD HEADLINES VII**  Antiqua-Varianten / Decoratives / Variantes

THE QUICK BROWN FOX JUMPS OVER
THE LAZY DOG 1234567890

THE QUICK BROWN FOX JUMPS OVER
THE LAZY DOG 1234567890

THE QUICK BROWN FOX JUMPS OVER
THE LAZY DOG 1234567890

THE QUICK BROWN FOX JUMPS OVER
THE LAZY DOG 1234567890

THE QUICK BROWN FOX JUMPS OVER
THE LAZY DOG 1234567890

THE QUICK BROWN FOX JUMPS OVER
THE LAZY DOG 1234567890

THE QUICK BROWN FOX JUMPS OVER
THE LAZY DOG 1234567890

Double- und Multilines
Double and Multilines
Double-lines et multilines
**81**

**Lichte Fette Grotesk**
762

V 000: 081 0852
1925
Ludwig & Mayer
H 1–Q 1,03

**Mexico Olympic**
828

V 000: 081 1526
Photoscript Ltd.
H 1–Q 1,13

**Tri-Star**
1107

the quick brown fox jumps
over the lazy dog

N 020: 081 0087
Georg Wilkens 1976
H. Berthold AG
H 1–x 0,80–k 1,00–p 0,38

**Churchward Design 70**
358
Lines Deep Shadow normal
Lines Deep Shadow regular
Lines Deep Shadow normal
N 100: 081 2016
Joseph Churchward 1970
H. Berthold AG
H 1–x 0,70–k 1,00–p 0,60

the quick brown fox jumps
over the lazy dog

**Churchward Design 70**
359
Lines Deep Shadow kursiv
Lines Deep Shadow italic
Lines Deep Shadow italique
N 100: 081 2023
Joseph Churchward 1970
H. Berthold AG
H 1–x 0,70–k 1,00–p 0,60

the quick brown fox jumps
over the lazy dog

**Churchward Design 70**
357
Lines
Lines
Lines
N 100: 081 1784
Joseph Churchward 1970
H. Berthold AG
H 1–x 0,69–k 1,03–p 0,34

the quick brown fox jumps
over the lazy dog

ITC **Aki Lines**
4

V 009: 081 1797
Akihiko Seki 1970
International Typeface Corp.
H 1–Q 1,00

## BERTHOLD HEADLINES VII
Antiqua-Varianten / Decoratives / Variantes

THE QUICK BROWN FOX JUMPS OVER THE LAZY DOG 1234567890

THE QUICK BROWN FOX JUMPS OVER THE LAZY DOG 1234567890

THE QUICK BROWN FOX JUMPS OVER THE LAZY DOG 1234567890

THE QUICK BROWN FOX JUMPS OVER THE LAZY DOG 1234567890

THE QUICK BROWN FOX JUMPS OVER THE LAZY DOG 1234567890

THE QUICK BROWN FOX JUMPS OVER THE LAZY DOG 1234567890

THE QUICK BROWN FOX JUMPS OVER THE LAZY DOG 1234567890

THE QUICK BROWN FOX JUMPS OVER THE LAZY DOG 1234567890

Ornamented und 3D
Ornamented and 3D
Ornamented et 3D
**82**

**Churchward Design 70**
361
Modern normal
Modern regular
Modern normal
N 100: 081 0968
Joseph Churchward 1970
H. Berthold AG
H 1–x 0,72–k 1,00–p 0,41

the quick brown fox jumps over the lazy dog

**Churchward Design 70**
362
Modern kursiv
Modern italic
Modern italique
N 100: 081 0906
Joseph Churchward 1970
H. Berthold AG
H 1–x 0,72–k 1,00–p 0,41

the quick brown fox jumps over the lazy dog

**Black Line**
194

V 000: 081 1588
Wolf Magin 1976
H. Berthold AG
H 1–Q 1,00

**Churchward Design 70**
364
Sparkly normal
Sparkly regular
Sparkly normal
N 100: 081 0954
Joseph Churchward 1970
H. Berthold AG
H 1–x 0,72–k 1,00–p 0,41

the quick brown fox jumps over the lazy dog

**Churchward Design 70**
365
Sparkly kursiv
Sparkly italic
Sparkly italique
N 100: 081 0923
Joseph Churchward 1970
H. Berthold AG
H 1–x 0,72–k 1,00–p 0,41

the quick brown fox jumps over the lazy dog

**Churchward Design 70**
356
Double
Double
Double
N 100: 081 1542
Joseph Churchward 1970
H. Berthold AG
H 1–x 0,72–k 1,00–p 0,31

the quick brown fox jumps over the lazy dog

**Churchward Design 70**
353
Chisel
Chisel
Chisel
N 100: 081 0345
Joseph Churchward 1970
H. Berthold AG
H 1–x 0,72–k 1,00–p 0,31

the quick brown fox jumps over the lazy dog

**Churchward Design 70**
360
Metalic
Metalic
Metalic
N 100: 081 1036
Joseph Churchward 1970
H. Berthold AG
H 1–x 0,78–k 1,00–p 0,50

the quick brown fox jumps over the lazy dog

**BERTHOLD HEADLINES VII** — Antiqua-Varianten / Decoratives / Variantes

THE QUICK BROWN FOX JUMPS OVER THE LAZY DOG 1234567890

THE QUICK BROWN FOX JUMPS OVER THE LAZY DOG 1234567890

THE QUICK BROWN FOX JUMPS OVER THE LAZY DOG 1234567890

THE QUICK BROWN FOX JUMPS OVER THE LAZY DOG 1234567890

THE QUICK BROWN FOX JUMPS OVER THE LAZY DOG 1234567890

THE QUICK BROWN FOX JUMPS OVER THE LAZY DOG 1234567890

THE QUICK BROWN FOX JUMPS OVER THE LAZY DOG 1234567890

THE QUICK BROWN FOX JUMPS OVER THE LAZY DOG 1234567890

Ornamented und 3 D  
Ornamented and 3 D  
Ornamented et 3 D  
**82**

**Leopard**
760

V 009: 081 0073
Christof Gassner 1976
H. Berthold AG
H 1–Q 1,05

**Futura Black Art Deco**
568
Original
Original
Original
VD 018: 081 0260 ✳
Paul Renner 1929
Fundición Tipográfica Neufville, S.A.
H 1–Q 1,30

**Futura Black Art Deco**
571
Reflex Duo
Reflex Duo
Reflex Duo
VD 018: 081 0297 ✳
Berthold-Schriftenatelier 1976
Fundición Tipográfica Neufville, S.A.
H 1–Q 1,30

**Futura Black Art Deco**
563
Flipper
Flipper
Flipper
VD 018: 081 0274 ✳
Berthold-Schriftenatelier 1976
Fundición Tipográfica Neufville, S.A.
H 1–Q 1,30

**Futura Black Art Deco**
574
Textil
Textil
Textil
VD 018: 081 0297 ✳
Berthold-Schriftenatelier 1976
Fundición Tipográfica Neufville, S.A.
H 1–Q 1,30

**Futura Black Art Deco**
564
Flipper Outline
Flipper Outline
Flipper Outline
VD 018: 081 0274 ✳
Berthold-Schriftenatelier 1976
Fundición Tipográfica Neufville, S.A.
H 1–Q 1,30

**Futura Black Art Deco**
565
Gravur
Gravur
Gravur
VD 018: 081 0291 ✳
Berthold-Schriftenatelier 1976
Fundición Tipográfica Neufville, S.A.
H 1–Q 1,30

**Futura Black Art Deco**
567
Light Inline
Light Inline
Light Inline
VD 018: 081 0291 ✳
Berthold-Schriftenatelier 1976
Fundición Tipográfica Neufville, S.A.
H 1–Q 1,30

## BERTHOLD HEADLINES VII
Antiqua-Varianten / Decoratives / Variantes

THE QUICK BROWN FOX JUMPS OVER THE LAZY DOG 1234567890

THE QUICK BROWN FOX JUMPS OVER THE LAZY DOG 1234567890

THE QUICK BROWN FOX JUMPS OVER THE LAZY DOG 1234567890

THE QUICK BROWN FOX JUMPS OVER THE LAZY DOG 1234567890

QUICK BROWN FOX JUMPS OVER THE LAZY DOG 1234567890

THE QUICK BROWN FOX JUMPS OVER THE LAZY DOG 1234567890

QUICK BROWN FOX JUMPS OVER THE LAZY DOG 1234567890

QUICK BROWN FOX JUMPS OVER THE LAZY DOG 1234567890

Ornamented und 3D  
Ornamented and 3D  
Ornamented et 3D **82**

**Futura Black Art Deco**
570
Point
Point
Point
VD 018: 081 0283 ✻
Berthold-Schriftenatelier 1976
Fundición Tipográfica Neufville, S.A.
H 1–Q 1,30

**Futura Black Art Deco**
566
Horizont
Horizont
Horizont
VD 018: 081 0283 ✻
Berthold-Schriftenatelier 1976
Fundición Tipográfica Neufville, S.A.
H 1–Q 1,30

**Futura Black Art Deco**
572
Stripes
Stripes
Stripes
VD 018: 081 0288 ✻
Berthold-Schriftenatelier 1976
Fundición Tipográfica Neufville, S.A.
H 1–Q 1,30

**Futura Black Art Deco**
573
Stripes Diagonal
Stripes Diagonal
Stripes Diagonal
VD 018: 081 0288 ✻
Berthold-Schriftenatelier 1976
Fundición Tipográfica Neufville, S.A.
H 1–Q 1,30

**Jalousette**
706

the quick brown fox jumps
over the lazy dog

N 010: 081 2141
Eberhard Belser 1975
H. Berthold AG
H 1–x 0,73–k 1,03–p 0,30

**Media Relief**
822
fett
bold
gras

the quick brown fox jumps
over the lazy dog

N 100: 081 0056
Jürgen Riebling 1976
H. Berthold AG
H 1–x 0,75–k 1,00–p 0,28

**Voel Beat**
1175

the quick brown fox jumps
over the lazy dog

N 020: 081 2288
Ernst Völker 1978
H. Berthold AG
H 1–x 0,81–k 1,00–p 0,21

**Knirsch**
729

the quick brown fox jumps
over the lazy dog

N 020: 081 0039
Christof Gassner 1976
H. Berthold AG
H 1–x 0,76–k 1,00–p 0,24

## BERTHOLD HEADLINES VII
Antiqua-Varianten / Decoratives / Variantes

THE QUICK BROWN FOX JUMPS OVER THE LAZY DOG 1234567890

THE QUICK BROWN FOX JUMPS OVER THE LAZY DOG 1234567890

QUICK BROWN FOX JUMPS OVER THE LAZY DOG

QUICK BROWN FOX JUMPS OVER THE LAZY DOG 1234567890

QUICK BROWN FOX JUMPS OVER THE LAZY DOG 1234567890

THE QUICK BROWN FOX JUMPS OVER THE LAZY DOG 1234567890

THE QUICK BROWN FOX JUMPS OVER THE LAZY DOG 1234567890

THE QUICK BROWN FOX JUMPS OVER THE LAZY DOG 1234567890

| | Ornamented und 3D Ornamented and 3D Ornamented et 3D | **82** |

**Paperline**
913

*the quick brown fox jumps over the lazy dog*

N 010: 081 2138
Eberhard Belser 1975
H. Berthold AG
H 1–x 0,78–k 1,00–p 0,22

**Buxom**
265

V 000: 081 0237
Facsimile Fonts
H 1–Q 1,37

**Egyptienne Filetée**
469

Sp 000: 081 0468
Haas'sche Schriftgießerei AG
H 1–Q 1,25

**Madame**
805

V 000: 081 1423
H. Berthold AG
H 1–Q 1,20

**Lettres Ornées**
761

V 000: 081 0847
Gillé 1820
Haas'sche Schriftgießerei AG
H 1–Q 1,20

**Voel Kars**
1177

the quick brown fox jumps over the lazy dog

N 020: 081 2297
Ernst Völker 1978
H. Berthold AG
H 1–x 0,71–k 1,00–p 0,30

**Schwabing Day**
1019

VD 018: 081 1814 *
Gert Blass 1979
H. Berthold AG
H 1–Q 1,00

**Schwabing Night**
1020

VD 018: 081 1814 *
Gert Blass 1979
H. Berthold AG
H 1–Q 1,00

## BERTHOLD HEADLINES VII
Antiqua-Varianten / Decoratives / Variantes

THE QUICK BROWN FOX JUMPS OVER
THE LAZY DOG 1234567890

THE QUICK BROWN FOX JUMPS OVER
THE LAZY DOG 1234567890

THE QUICK BROWN FOX JUMPS OVER
THE LAZY DOG 1234567890

THE QUICK BROWN FOX JUMPS OVER
THE LAZY DOG 1234567890

Ornamented und 3D
Ornamented and 3D
Ornamented et 3D

## 82

**Plastica**
942

V 000: 081 1026
1926
H. Berthold AG
H 1–Q 1,15

**Neubauer White Chips**
855

VD 018: 081 2346 ✱
Klaus Neubauer 1977
H. Berthold AG
H 1–Q 1,00

**Neubauer Black Chips**
854

VD 018: 081 2346 ✱
Klaus Neubauer 1977
H. Berthold AG
H 1–Q 1,00

**Globe 6**
622

the quick brown fox jumps
over the lazy dog

N 020: 081 2261
Bogdan Zochowski 1979
H. Berthold AG
H 1–x 0,86–k 1,04–p 0,16

# BERTHOLD HEADLINES VIII

**83-88**

*Schreibschriften
Scripts
Scriptes, Manuaires*

## BERTHOLD HEADLINES VIII
Schreibschriften / Scripts / Scriptes, Manuaires

THE QUICK BROWN FOX JUMPS OVER
THE LAZY DOG 1234567890

QUICK BROWN FOX JUMPS OVER
THE LAZY DOG 1234567890

QUICK BROWN FOX JUMPS OVER
THE LAZY DOG 1234567890

THE QUICK BROWN FOX JUMPS OVER
THE LAZY DOG 1234567890

THE QUICK BROWN FOX JUMPS OVER
THE LAZY DOG 1234567890

THE QUICK BROWN FOX JUMPS OVER
THE LAZY DOG 1234567890

THE QUICK BROWN FOX JUMPS OVER
THE LAZY DOG 1234567890

THE QUICK BROWN FOX JUMPS OVER
THE LAZY DOG 1234567890

| | Handschriftliche Antiqua Informal Caractère d'écriture à la main Antiqua | **83** |

the quick brown fox jumps
over the lazy dog

**Time-Script**
1089
mager
light
maigre
N 100: 081 1170
Georg Trump 1956
D. Stempel AG
H 1–x 0,67–k 1,13–p 0,36

the quick brown fox jumps
over the lazy dog

**Time-Script**
1090
halbfett
medium
demi-gras
N 000: 081 1171
Georg Trump 1957
D. Stempel AG
H 1–x 0,67–k 1,13–p 0,28

the quick brown fox jumps
over the lazy dog

**Time-Script**
1091
fett
bold
gras
N 000: 081 1172
Georg Trump 1957
Johannes Wagner
H 1–x 0,67–k 1,13–p 0,28

the quick brown fox jumps
over the lazy dog

**Ondine**
903

N 100: 081 0967
Adrian Frutiger 1954
Haas'sche Schriftgießerei AG
H 1–x 0,69–k 1,13–p 0,37

the quick brown fox jumps
over the lazy dog

**Polka**
948
normal
regular
normal
N 100: 081 1029
Peter Dom 1950
American Typefounders
H 1–x 0,63–k 1,00–p 0,34

the quick brown fox jumps
over the lazy dog

**Polka**
949
halbfett
medium
demi-gras
N 100: 081 1030
Peter Dom 1950
American Typefounders
H 1–x 0,66–k 1,00–p 0,31

the quick brown fox jumps
over the lazy dog

**Churchward Brush**
369
normal
regular
normal
N 100: 081 0335
Joseph Churchward 1970
H. Berthold AG
H 1–x 0,75–k 1,00–p 0,30

**Carolus**
270

V 000: 081 0241
Karl Erik Forsberg 1954
Berlingska Stilgjuteri AB
H 1–Q 1,32

## BERTHOLD HEADLINES VIII
Schreibschriften / Scripts / Scriptes, Manuaires

THE QUICK BROWN FOX JUMPS OVER
THE LAZY DOG 1234567890

The QUICK BROWN FOX JUMPS OVER
The LAZY DOG 1234567890

## BERTHOLD HEADLINES VIII
Schreibschriften / Scripts / Scriptes, Manuaires

THE QUICK BROWN FOX JUMPS OVER
THE LAZY DOG 1234567890

THE QUICK BROWN FOX JUMPS OVER
THE LAZY DOG 1234567890

THE QUICK BROWN FOX JUMPS OVER
THE LAZY DOG 1234567890

QUICK BROWN FOX JUMPS OVER
THE LAZY DOG 1234567890

| | Handschriftliche Antiqua  Informal  Caractère d'écriture à la main Antiqua | **83** |

**Post-Antiqua**
965
normal
regular
normal
N 100: 081 1046
Herbert Post 1939
H. Berthold AG
H 1–x 0,66–k 1,06–p 0,28

the quick brown fox jumps
over the lazy dog

**Goudy Mediäval**
632



N 100: 081 0688
American Typefounders
H 1–x 0,63–k 1,13–p 0,56

the quick brown fox jumps
over the lazy dog

| | Handschriftliche Antiqua, kursive  Informal, italic  Caractère d'écriture à la main Antiqua, italique | **84** |

**Okay**
900

*the quick brown fox jumps*
*over the lazy dog*

N 100: 081 0962
H. Berthold AG
H 1–x 0,76–k 1,00–p 0,30

**Churchward Brush**
370
kursiv
italic
italique
N 100: 081 0336
Joseph Churchward 1970
H. Berthold AG
H 1–x 0,75–k 1,00–p 0,30

*the quick brown fox jumps*
*over the lazy dog*

**Daphne**
433

the quick brown fox jumps
over the lazy dog

N 100: 081 0418
Georg Salden 1970
H. Berthold AG
H 1–x 0,78–k 1,00–p 0,28

**Daphne**
434
Zierbuchstaben
swash letters
lettres ornées
Z 000: 081 0420
Georg Salden 1970
H. Berthold AG
H 1–x 0,78–k 1,32–p 0,40

the quick brown fox jumps
over the lazy dog

## BERTHOLD HEADLINES VIII
Schreibschriften / Scripts / Scriptes, Manuaires

ABCDEFGHIJKLMNOPQR
STUVWXYZ 1234567890

ABCDEFGHIJKLMNOPQR
STUVWXYZ 1234567890

ABCDEFGHIJKLMNOPQR
STUVWXYZ 1234567890

ABCDEFGHIJKLMNOPQR
STUVWXYZ 1234567890

ABCDEFGHIJKLMNOPQR
STUVWXYZ 1234567890

ABCDEFGHIJKLMNOPQRSTUVWXYZ
1234567890

ABCDEFGHIJKLMNOPQR
STUVWXYZ 1234567890

THE QUICK BROWN FOX JUMPS OVER
THE LAZY DOG 1234567890

## Pinselschriften / Brush Scripts / Caractères à pinceau — 85

**Jaguar**
705

*the quick brown fox jumps over the lazy dog*

N 100: 081 0793
Georg Trump 1965
D. Stempel AG
H 1–x 0,60–k 1,07–p 0,20

**Express**
500

*the quick brown fox jumps over the lazy dog*

N 100: 081 0514
Walter Höhnisch 1957
Ludwig & Mayer
H 1–x 0,59–k 1,94–p 0,19

**Slogan**
1041

*the quick brown fox jumps over the lazy dog*

N 100: 081 1133
Helmut Matheis 1959
Ludwig & Mayer
H 1–x 0,41–k 1,00–p 0,42

**Champion**
297

*the quick brown fox jumps over the lazy dog*

N 100: 081 0280
Günter Gerhard Lange 1957
H. Berthold AG
H 1–x 0,57–k 1,00–p 0,28

**Palette**
912

*the quick brown fox jumps over the lazy dog*

N 100: 081 0997
Martin Wilke 1950
H. Berthold AG
H 1–x 0,57–k 1,01–p 0,40

**Signal**
1037

*the quick brown fox jumps over the lazy dog*

N 100: 081 1123
Walter Wege 1931
H. Berthold AG
H 1–x 0,63–k 1,00–p 0,31

**Impuls**
690

*the quick brown fox jumps over the lazy dog*

N 100: 081 0782
Paul Zimmermann 1945
Johannes Wagner
H 1–x 0,59–k 1,01–p 0,28

**Bison**
189

*the quick brown fox jumps over the lazy dog*

N 100: 081 0164
Julius Kirn 1938
D. Stempel AG
H 1–x 0,63–k 1,00–p 0,28

## BERTHOLD HEADLINES VIII
Schreibschriften / Scripts / Scriptes, Manuaires

THE QUICK BROWN FOX JUMPS OVER
THE LAZY DOG 1234567890

THE QUICK BROWN FOX JUMPS OVER
THE LAZY DOG 1234567890

THE QUICK BROWN FOX JUMPS OVER
THE LAZY DOG 1234567890

THE QUICK BROWN FOX JUMPS OVER
THE LAZY DOG 1234567890

## BERTHOLD HEADLINES VIII
Schreibschriften / Scripts / Scriptes, Manuaires

ABCDEFGHIJKLMNOPQR
STUVWXYZ 1234567890

ABCDEFGHIJKLMNOPQR
STUVWXYZ 1234567890

ABCDEFGHIJKLMNOPQR
STUVWXYZ 1234567890

## 85 Pinselschriften / Brush Scripts / Caractères à pinceau

*the quick brown fox jumps over the lazy dog*

**Choc** 330
N 100: 081 0320
Roger Excoffon 1955
Marcel Olive
H 1–x 0,63–k 1,06–p 0,34

*the quick brown fox jumps over the lazy dog*

**Contact** 417
N 100: 081 0391
Helmut Matheis 1963
Ludwig & Mayer
H 1–x 0,74–k 1,06–p 0,23

**the quick brown fox jumps over the lazy dog**

**Batik** 1262
N 020: 081 0770
Margott Schilling 1980
H. Berthold AG
H 1–x 0,67–k 1,00–p 0,24

the quick brown fox jumps over the lazy dog

**Stop 2** 1062
N 000: 081 1152
Walter Höhnisch 1939
Ludwig & Mayer
H 1–x 0,69–k 1,00–p 0,31

## 86 Federschriften / Formal Pen / Caractères à plume

*the quick brown fox jumps over the lazy dog*

**Bernhard Schönschrift** 172
zart
light
maigre
N 020: 081 2182
Lucian Bernhard 1925
Fundición Tipográfica Neufville, S.A.
H 1–x 0,28–k 1,03–p 0,19

*the quick brown fox jumps over the lazy dog*

**Bernhard Schönschrift** 173
kräftig
regular
normal
N 020: 081 2185
Lucian Bernhard 1928
Fundición Tipográfica Neufville, S.A.
H 1–x 0,30–k 1,86–p 0,19

*the quick brown fox jumps over the lazy dog*

**Coronet** 426
N 100: 081 0411
R. H. Middleton 1937
Ludlow Typograph Co.
H 1–x 0,31–k 1,00–p 0,35

## BERTHOLD HEADLINES VIII
Schreibschriften / Scripts / Scriptes, Manuaires

ABCDEFGHIJKLMNOPQR
STUVWXYZ 1234567890

ABCDEFGHIJKLMNOPQR
STUVWXYZ 1234567890

ABCDEFGHIJKLMNOPQR
STUVWXYZ 1234567890

ABCDEFGHIJKLMNOPQR
STUVWXYZ 1234567890

ABCDEFGHIJKLMNOPQR
STUVWXYZ 1234567890

ABCDEFGHIJKLMNOPQR
STUVWXYZ 1234567890

## BERTHOLD HEADLINES VIII
Schreibschriften / Scripts / Scriptes, Manuaires

ABCDEFGHIJKLMNOPQRS
STUVWXYZ 1234567890

## Federschriften / Formal Pen / Caractères à plume — 86

**Arabella** 72

*the quick brown fox jumps over the lazy dog*

N 100: 081 0094
Arno Drescher 1936
Johannes Wagner
H 1–x 0,31–k 1,00–p 0,32

**Skizze** 1040

*the quick brown fox jumps over the lazy dog*

N 100: 081 1129
Walter Höhnisch 1935
Ludwig & Mayer
H 1–x 0,50–k 1,07–p 0,25

**El Greco** 470

*the quick brown fox jumps over the lazy dog*

N 100: 081 0473
Günter Gerhard Lange 1964
H. Berthold AG
H 1–x 0,53–k 1,07–p 0,40

**Arabella Favorit** 73

*the quick brown fox jumps over the lazy dog*

N 100: 081 1572
Arno Drescher 1939
Johannes Wagner
H 1–x 0,38–k 1,00–p 0,25

**Forelle Auszeichnung** 445

*the quick brown fox jumps over the lazy dog*

N 100: 081 0571
Erich Mollowitz 1936
Johannes Wagner
H 1–x 0,33–k 1,07–p 0,23

**Poema** 947

*the quick brown fox jumps over the lazy dog*

N 100: 081 1027
H. Berthold AG
H 1–x 0,54–k 1,00–p 0,28

## Kurrent / Current / Kurrent — 87

**Aja** 1258

*the quick brown fox jumps over the lazy dog*

N 020: 081 0767
Gustav Jaeger 1980
H. Berthold AG
H 1–x 0,62–k 1,02–p 0,38

# BERTHOLD HEADLINES VIII
Schreibschriften / Scripts / Scriptes, Manuaires

ABCDEFGHIJKLMNOPQR
STUVWXYZ 1234567890

ABCDEFGHIJKLMNOPQuR
SStTUVWXYZ

ABCDEFGHIJKLMNOPQR
STUVWXYZ 1234567890

ABCDEFGHIJKLMNOPQRS
TUVWXYZ 1234567890

ABCDEFGHIJKLMNOPQR
STUVWXYZ 1234567890

ABCDEFGHIJKLMNOPQR
STUVWXYZ 1234567890

ABCDEFGHIJKLMNOPQR
STUVWXYZ 1234567890

ABCDEFGHIJKLMNOPQR
STUVWXYZ 1234567890

Kurrent
Current
Kurrent
**87**

*the quick brown fox jumps over the lazy dog*

**Berthold-Script**
178
normal
regular
normal
N 020: 081 1940
Günter Gerhard Lange 1977
H. Berthold AG
H 1–x 0,50–k 1,12–p 0,57

*the quick brown fox jumps over the lazy dog*

**Berthold-Script**
179
normal Zierbuchstaben
regular swash letters
normal lettres ornées
Z 000: 081 2391
Günter Gerhard Lange 1977
H. Berthold AG
T 1–x 0,52–f 1,18–p 0,54

*the quick brown fox jumps over the lazy dog*

**Künstlerschreibschrift**
746
halbfett
medium
demi-gras
N 100: 081 0824
1903
D. Stempel AG
H 1–x 0,31–k 0,84–p 0,35

*the quick brown fox jumps over the lazy dog*

**Englische Schreibschrift**
1276
normal
regular
normal
N 020: 081 1686
1970
H. Berthold AG
H 1–x 0,46–k 1,00–p 0,38

*the quick brown fox jumps over the lazy dog*

**Typo Script**
1119

N 100: 081 1221
Morris F. Benton
American Typefounders
H 1–x 0,38–k 1,00–p 0,47

*the quick brown fox jumps over the lazy dog*

**Poppl Residenz**
960
mager
light
maigre
N 020: 081 1943
Friedrich Poppl 1977
H. Berthold AG
H 1–x 0,50–k 1,16–p 0,38

*the quick brown fox jumps over the lazy dog*

**Ariston**
74
normal
regular
normal
N 100: 081 0096
Martin Wilke 1932
H. Berthold AG
H 1–x 0,55–k 1,01–p 0,29

*the quick brown fox jumps over the lazy dog*

**Berthold-Script**
180
halbfett
medium
demi-gras
N 020: 081 1941
Günter Gerhard Lange 1977
H. Berthold AG
H 1–x 0,50–k 1,12–p 0,57

## BERTHOLD HEADLINES VIII
Schreibschriften / Scripts / Scriptes, Manuaires

ABCDEFGHIJKLMNOPQQu
RSTUVWXYZ

ABCDEFGHIJKLMNOPQR
STUVWXYZ 1234567890

ABCDEFGHIJKLMNOPQRS
TUVWXYZ 1234567890

ABCDEFGHIJKLMNOPQR
STUVWXYZ 1234567890

CELMNQuSTVWXZ
1234567890

ABCDEFGHIJKLMNOPQR
STUVWXYZ 1234567890

ABCDEFGHIJKLMNOPQR
STUVWXYZ 1234567890

ABCDEFGHIJKLMNOPQR
STUVWXYZ 1234567890

| | Kurrent / Current / Kurrent | **87** |

*the quick brown fox jumps over the lazy dog*

**Berthold-Script**
181
halbfett Zierbuchstaben
medium swash letters
demi-gras lettres ornées
Z 000: 081 2399
Günter Gerhard Lange 1977
H. Berthold AG
T 1–x 0,52–f 1,21–p 0,52

*the quick brown fox jumps over the lazy dog*

**Bank Script**
119

N 100: 081 1492
James West
American Typefounders
H 1–x 0,44–k 1,06–p 0,56

*the quick brown fox jumps over the lazy dog*

**Englische Schreibschrift**
1328
halbfett
medium
demi-gras
N 020: 081 1689
1972
H. Berthold AG
H 1–x 0,46–k 0,99–p 0,38

*the quick brown fox jumps over the lazy dog*

**Poppl Exquisit**
956

N 100: 081 1042
Friedrich Poppl 1970
H. Berthold AG
H 1–x 0,58–k 1,13–p 0,38

*the quick brown fox jumps over the lazy dog*

**Poppl Exquisit**
957
Zierbuchstaben
swash letters
lettres ornées
Z 000: 081 1043
Friedrich Poppl 1970
H. Berthold AG
H 1–x 0,58–k 1,13–p 0,38

*the quick brown fox jumps over the lazy dog*

**Poppl Residenz**
961
normal
regular
normal
N 020: 081 1942
Friedrich Poppl 1977
H. Berthold AG
H 1–x 0,50–k 1,18–p 0,38

*the quick brown fox jumps over the lazy dog*

**Commercial Script**
412

N 100: 081 1503
Morris F. Benton 1908
American Typefounders
H 1–x 0,50–k 1,00–p 0,50

*the quick brown fox jumps over the lazy dog*

**Künstlerschreibschrift**
747
fett
bold
gras
N 100: 081 0829
Hans Bohn 1958
D. Stempel AG
H 1–x 0,50–k 1,00–p 0,38

## BERTHOLD HEADLINES VIII — Schreibschriften / Scripts / Scriptes, Manuaires

ABCDEFGHIJKLMNOPQRS
TUVWXYZ 1234567890

## BERTHOLD HEADLINES VIII — Schreibschriften / Scripts / Scriptes, Manuaires

THE QUICK BROWN FOX JUMPS OVER
THE LAZY DOG 1234567890

ABCDEFGHIJKLMNOPQRS
TUVWXYZ 1234567890

THE QUICK BROWN FOX JUMPS OVER
THE LAZY DOG 1234567890

ABCDEFGHIJKLMNOPQRS
TUVWXYZ 1234567890

THE QUICK BROWN FOX JUMPS OVER
THE LAZY DOG 1234567890

ABCDEFGHIJKLMNOPQRS
TUVWXYZ 1234567890

| | Kurrent / Current / Kurrent **87** |
|---|---|
| *the quick brown fox jumps over the lazy dog* | **Englische Schreibschrift**<br>1277<br>fett<br>bold<br>gras<br>N 020: 081 1692<br>1972<br>H. Berthold AG<br>H 1–x 0,46–k 0,99–p 0,40 |

| | Handschriften / Free Style / Caractères d'écriture à la main **88** |
|---|---|
| *the quick brown fox jumps over the lazy dog* | **Poppl-College 1**<br>1340<br>normal<br>regular<br>normal<br>N 020: 081 2442<br>Friedrich Poppl 1981<br>H. Berthold AG<br>H 1–x 0,69–k 1,06–p 0,34 |
| *the quick brown fox jumps over the lazy dog* | **Poppl-College 2**<br>1408<br>normal<br>regular<br>normal<br>N 020: 081 2443<br>Friedrich Poppl 1981<br>H. Berthold AG<br>H 1–x 0,69–k 1,06–p 0,34 |
| ***the quick brown fox jumps over the lazy dog*** | **Poppl-College 1**<br>1341<br>halbfett<br>medium<br>demi-gras<br>N 020: 081 2444<br>Friedrich Poppl 1981<br>H. Berthold AG<br>H 1–x 0,71–k 1,05–p 0,33 |
| ***the quick brown fox jumps over the lazy dog*** | **Poppl-College 2**<br>1342<br>halbfett<br>medium<br>demi-gras<br>N 020: 081 2445<br>Friedrich Poppl 1981<br>H. Berthold AG<br>H 1–x 0,71–k 1,05–p 0,33 |
| ***the quick brown fox jumps over the lazy dog*** | **Poppl-College 1**<br>1409<br>fett<br>bold<br>gras<br>N 020: 081 2446<br>Friedrich Poppl 1981<br>H. Berthold AG<br>H 1–x 0,75–k 1,06–p 0,29 |
| ***the quick brown fox jumps over the lazy dog*** | **Poppl-College 2**<br>1410<br>fett<br>bold<br>gras<br>N 020: 081 2447<br>Friedrich Poppl 1981<br>H. Berthold AG<br>H 1–x 0,75–k 1,06–p 0,29 |

# BERTHOLD HEADLINES VIII

Schreibschriften  
Scripts  
Scriptes, Manuaires

THE QUICK BROWN FOX JUMPS OVER
THE LAZY DOG 1234567890

THE QUICK BROWN FOX JUMPS OVER
THE LAZY DOG 1234567890

THE QUICK BROWN FOX JUMPS OVER
THE LAZY DOG 1234567890

QUICK BROWN FOX JUMPS OVER
THE LAZY DOG 1234567890

QUICK BROWN FOX JUMPS OVER
THE LAZY DOG 1234567890

Handschriften
Free Style
Caractères d'écriture à la main

**88**

**Houston**
679

*the quick brown fox jumps over the lazy dog*

N 100: 081 1424
H. Berthold AG
H 1–x 0,53–k 0,94–p 0,38

**Poppl Stretto**
964

*the quick brown fox jumps over the lazy dog*

N 100: 081 1044
Friedrich Poppl 1969
H. Berthold AG
H 1–x 0,75–k 1,12–p 0,38

**Mistral**
841

*the quick brown fox jumps over the lazy dog*

N 100: 081 0907
Roger Excoffon 1953
Marcel Olive
H 1–x 0,53–k 0,94–p 0,47

**Picadilly-Script**
928

*the quick brown fox jumps over the lazy dog*

N 100: 081 1010
Martin Wilke 1968
H. Berthold AG
H 1–x 0,50–k 1,00–p 0,38

**Brush**
258

*the quick brown fox jumps over the lazy dog*

N 100: 081 0234
Robert E. Smith 1972
American Typefounders
H 1–x 0,60–k 1,07–p 0,40

# BERTHOLD HEADLINES IX

**89-92**

*Nichtlateinische Schriften*
*Non Latins*
*Caractères Non-Romains*

# BERTHOLD HEADLINES IX
Nichtlateinische Schriften / Non Latins / Caractères non-romains

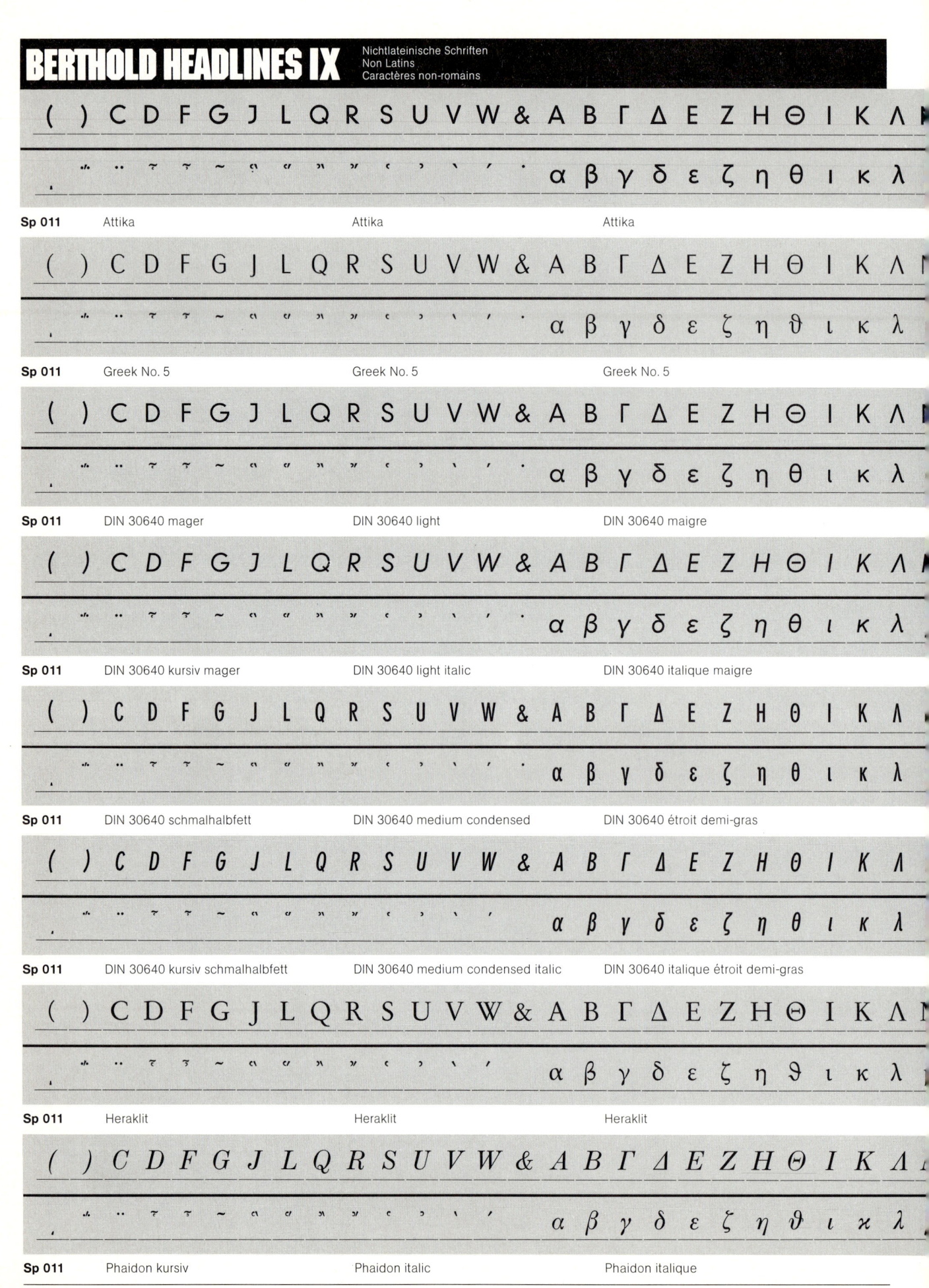

( ) C D F G J L Q R S U V W & A B Γ Δ E Z H Θ I K Λ
α β γ δ ε ζ η θ ι κ λ

**Sp 011**  Attika    Attika    Attika

( ) C D F G J L Q R S U V W & A B Γ Δ E Z H Θ I K Λ
α β γ δ ε ζ η θ ι κ λ

**Sp 011**  Greek No. 5    Greek No. 5    Greek No. 5

( ) C D F G J L Q R S U V W & A B Γ Δ E Z H Θ I K Λ
α β γ δ ε ζ η θ ι κ λ

**Sp 011**  DIN 30640 mager    DIN 30640 light    DIN 30640 maigre

( ) C D F G J L Q R S U V W & A B Γ Δ E Z H Θ I K Λ
α β γ δ ε ζ η θ ι κ λ

**Sp 011**  DIN 30640 kursiv mager    DIN 30640 light italic    DIN 30640 italique maigre

( ) C D F G J L Q R S U V W & A B Γ Δ E Z H Θ I K Λ
α β γ δ ε ζ η θ ι κ λ

**Sp 011**  DIN 30640 schmalhalbfett    DIN 30640 medium condensed    DIN 30640 étroit demi-gras

( ) C D F G J L Q R S U V W & A B Γ Δ E Z H Θ I K Λ
α β γ δ ε ζ η θ ι κ λ

**Sp 011**  DIN 30640 kursiv schmalhalbfett    DIN 30640 medium condensed italic    DIN 30640 italique étroit demi-gras

( ) C D F G J L Q R S U V W & A B Γ Δ E Z H Θ I K Λ
α β γ δ ε ζ η θ ι κ λ

**Sp 011**  Heraklit    Heraklit    Heraklit

( ) C D F G J L Q R S U V W & A B Γ Δ E Z H Θ I K Λ
α β γ δ ε ζ η θ ι κ λ

**Sp 011**  Phaidon kursiv    Phaidon italic    Phaidon italique

Griechisch / Greek / Grec — 89

Ν Ξ Ο Π Ρ Σ Τ Υ Φ Χ Ψ Ω / – 1 2 3 4 5 6 7 8 9 0 % +
ν ξ ο π ρ σ τ υ φ χ ψ ω ς – , . ; : ! ? ' « »

1243     Attika 081 0128

Ν Ξ Ο Π Ρ Σ Τ Υ Φ Χ Ψ Ω / – 1 2 3 4 5 6 7 8 9 0 % +
ν ξ ο π ρ σ τ υ φ χ ψ ω ς – , . ; : ! ? ' « »

1244     Greek No. 5 081 0145

Ν Ξ Ο Π Ρ Σ Τ Υ Φ Χ Ψ Ω / – 1 2 3 4 5 6 7 8 9 0 % +
ν ξ ο π ρ σ τ υ φ χ ψ ω ς – , . ; : ! ? ' « »

1245     DIN 30640 mager 081 0212

Ν Ξ Ο Π Ρ Σ Τ Υ Φ Χ Ψ Ω / – 1 2 3 4 5 6 7 8 9 0 % +
ν ξ ο π ρ σ τ υ φ χ ψ ω ς – , . ; : ! ? ' « »

1246     DIN 30640 kursiv mager 081 0226

Ν Ξ Ο Π Ρ Σ Τ Υ Φ Χ Ψ Ω / – 1 2 3 4 5 6 7 8 9 0 % +
ν ξ ο π ρ σ τ υ φ χ ψ ω ς – , . ; : ! ? ' « »

1247     DIN30640 schmalhalbfett 081 0162

Ν Ξ Ο Π Ρ Σ Τ Υ Φ Χ Ψ Ω / – 1 2 3 4 5 6 7 8 9 0 % +
ν ξ ο π ρ σ τ υ φ χ ψ ω ς – , . ; : ! ? ' « »

1248     DIN 30640 kursiv schmalhalbfett 081 0176

Ν Ξ Ο Π Ρ Σ Τ Υ Φ Χ Ψ Ω / – 1 2 3 4 5 6 7 8 9 0 % +
ν ξ ο π ρ σ τ υ φ χ ψ ω ς – , . ; : ! ? ' « »

1249     Heraklit 081 0131

Ν Ξ Ο Π Ρ Σ Τ Υ Φ Χ Ψ Ω / – 1 2 3 4 5 6 7 8 9 0 % +
ν ξ ο π ϱ σ τ υ φ χ ψ ω ς – , . ; : ! ? ' « »

1250     Phaidon kursiv 081 0159

# BERTHOLD HEADLINES IX
Nichtlateinische Schriften
Non Latins
Caractères non-romains

% № § » « : . , - / А Б В Г Д Е Ё Ж З И Й К Л М Н О
1 2 3 4 5 6 7 8 9 0 а б в г д е ё ж з и й к л м н о

**Sp 000** Akzidenz-Grotesk normal · Akzidenz-Grotesk regular · Akzidenz-Grotesk normal

% № § » « : . , - / А Б В Г Д Е Ё Ж З И Й К Л М Н О
1 2 3 4 5 6 7 8 9 0 а б в г д е ё ж з и й к л м н о

**Sp 000** Akzidenz-Grotesk halbfett · Akzidenz-Grotesk medium · Akzidenz-Grotesk demi-gras

% № § » « : . , - ё А Б В Г Д Е Ж З И Й К Л М Н О П
1 2 3 4 5 6 7 8 9 0 а б в г д е ж з и й к л м н о п

**Sp 000** Amts-Antiqua normal · Amts-Antiqua regular · Amts-Antiqua normal

% № § » « : . , - ё А Б В Г Д Е Ж З И Й К Л М Н О П
1 2 3 4 5 6 7 8 9 0 а б в г д е ж з и й к л м н о п

**Sp 000** Amts-Antiqua halbfett · Amts-Antiqua medium · Amts-Antiqua demi-gras

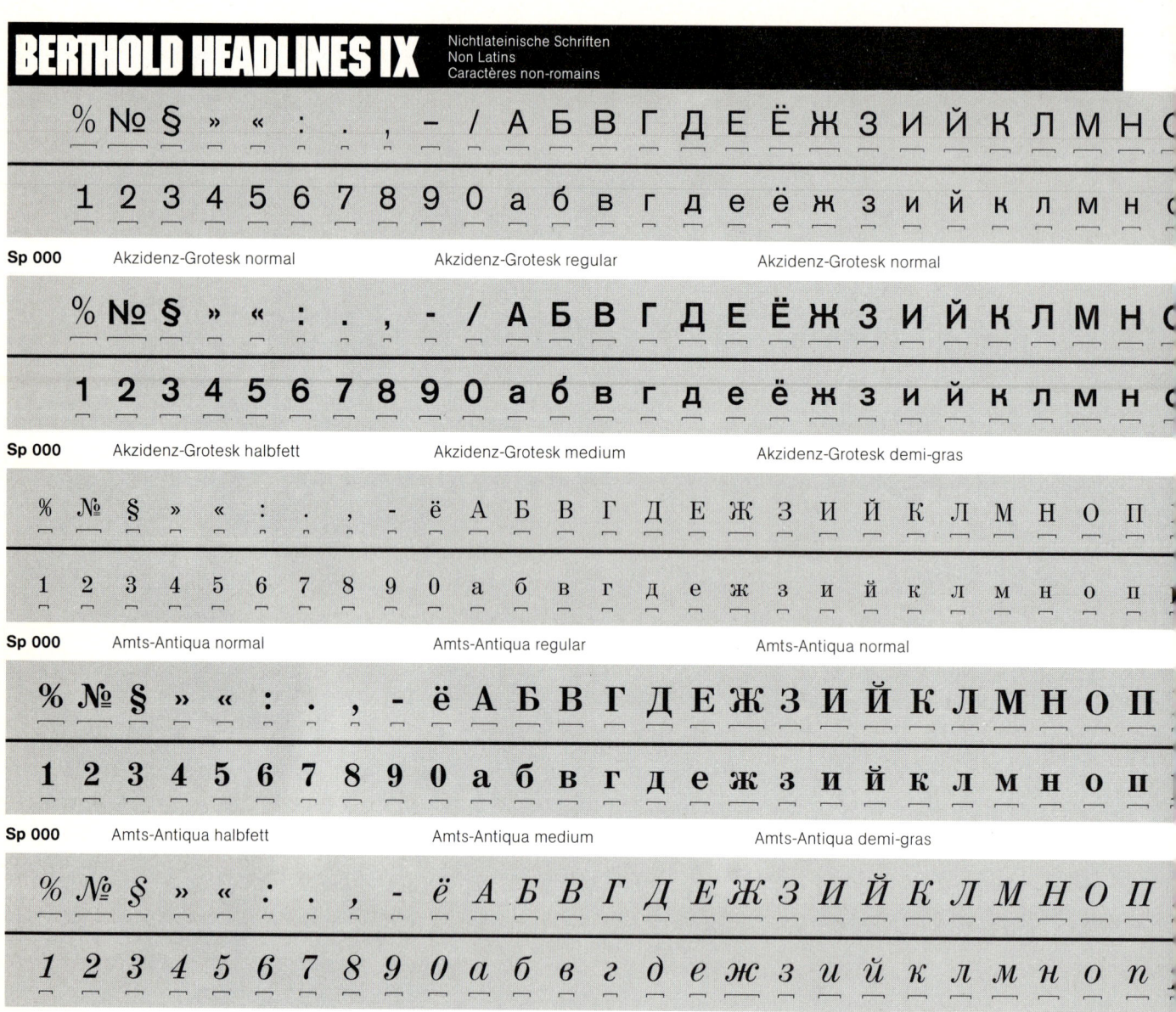

% № § » « : . , - ё А Б В Г Д Е Ж З И Й К Л М Н О П
1 2 3 4 5 6 7 8 9 0 а б в г д е ж з и й к л м н о п

**Sp 000** Amts-Antiqua kursiv · Amts-Antiqua italic · Amts-Antiqua italique

## Kyrillisch / Cyrillic / Cyrillique 90

Р С Т У Ф Х Ц Ч Ш Щ Ъ Ы Ь Э Ю Я ? ! ' *
р с т у ф х ц ч ш щ ъ ы ь э ю я ( ) „ "

1253    Akzidenz-Grotesk normal 081 1415

**Р С Т У Ф Х Ц Ч Ш Щ Ъ Ы Ь Э Ю Я ? ! ' ***
**р с т у ф х ц ч ш щ ъ ы ь э ю я ( ) „ "**

1254    Akzidenz-Grotesk halbfett 081 1416

Т У Ф Х Ц Ч Ш Щ Ъ Ы Ь Э Ю Я Ђ Ј Љ Њ Ћ Џ Ж ? ! ' *
т у ф х ц ч ш щ ъ ы ь э ю я ђ ј љ њ ћ џ ж ( ) „ "

1255    Amts-Antiqua normal 081 1412

**Т У Ф Х Ц Ч Ш Щ Ъ Ы Ь Э Ю Я Ђ Ј Љ Њ Ћ Џ Ж ? ! ' ***
**т у ф х ц ч ш щ ъ ы ь э ю я ђ ј љ њ ћ џ ж ( ) „ "**

1256    Amts-Antiqua halbfett 081 1414

*Т У Ф Х Ц Ч Ш Щ Ъ Ы Ь Э Ю Я Ђ Ј Љ Њ Ћ Џ Ж ? ! ' **
*т у ф х ц ч ш щ ъ ы ь э ю я ђ ј љ њ ћ џ ж ( ) „ "*

1257    Amts-Antiqua kursiv 081 1413

# BERTHOLD HEADLINES IX
Nichtlateinische Schriften
Non Latins
Caractères non-romains

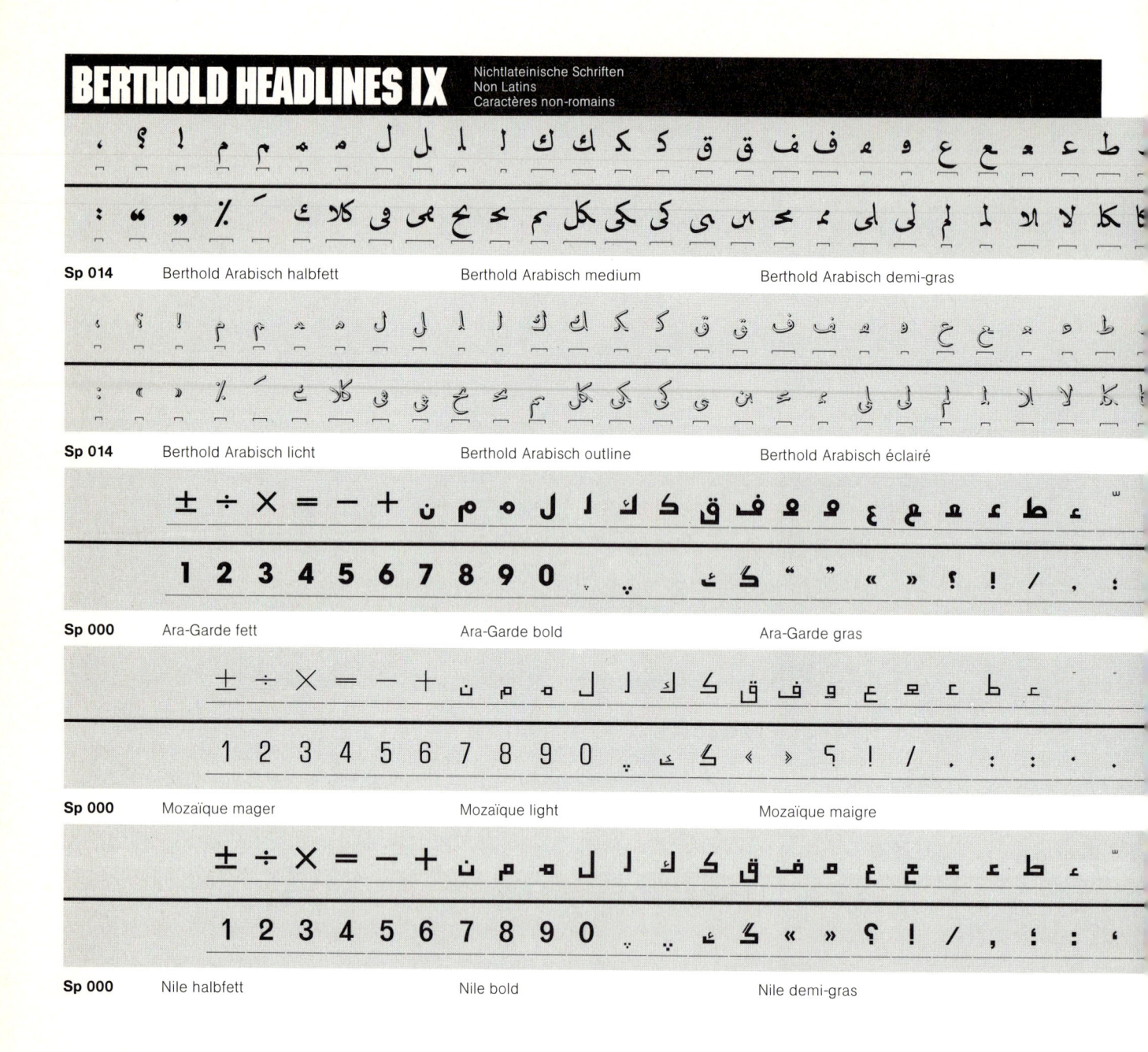

**Sp 014**    Berthold Arabisch halbfett      Berthold Arabisch medium      Berthold Arabisch demi-gras

**Sp 014**    Berthold Arabisch licht      Berthold Arabisch outline      Berthold Arabisch éclairé

**Sp 000**    Ara-Garde fett      Ara-Garde bold      Ara-Garde gras

**Sp 000**    Mozaïque mager      Mozaïque light      Mozaïque maigre

**Sp 000**    Nile halbfett      Nile bold      Nile demi-gras

# BERTHOLD HEADLINES IX
Nichtlateinische Schriften
Non Latins
Caractères non-romains

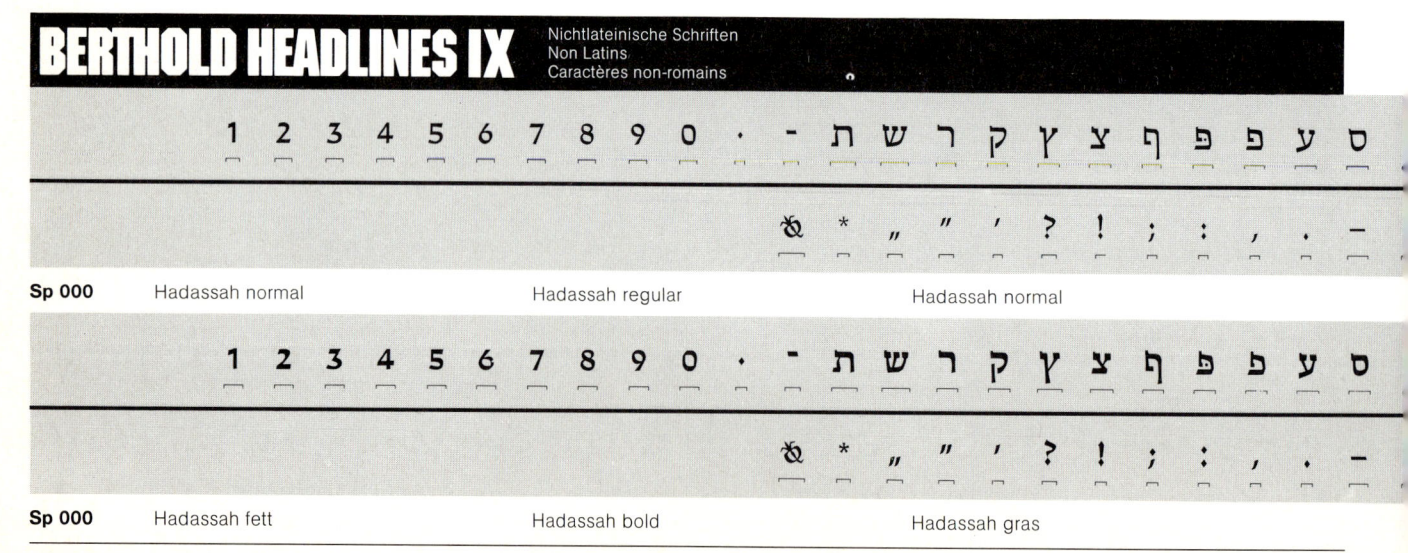

**Sp 000**    Hadassah normal      Hadassah regular      Hadassah normal

**Sp 000**    Hadassah fett      Hadassah bold      Hadassah gras

# 91 Arabisch / Arabic / Arabe

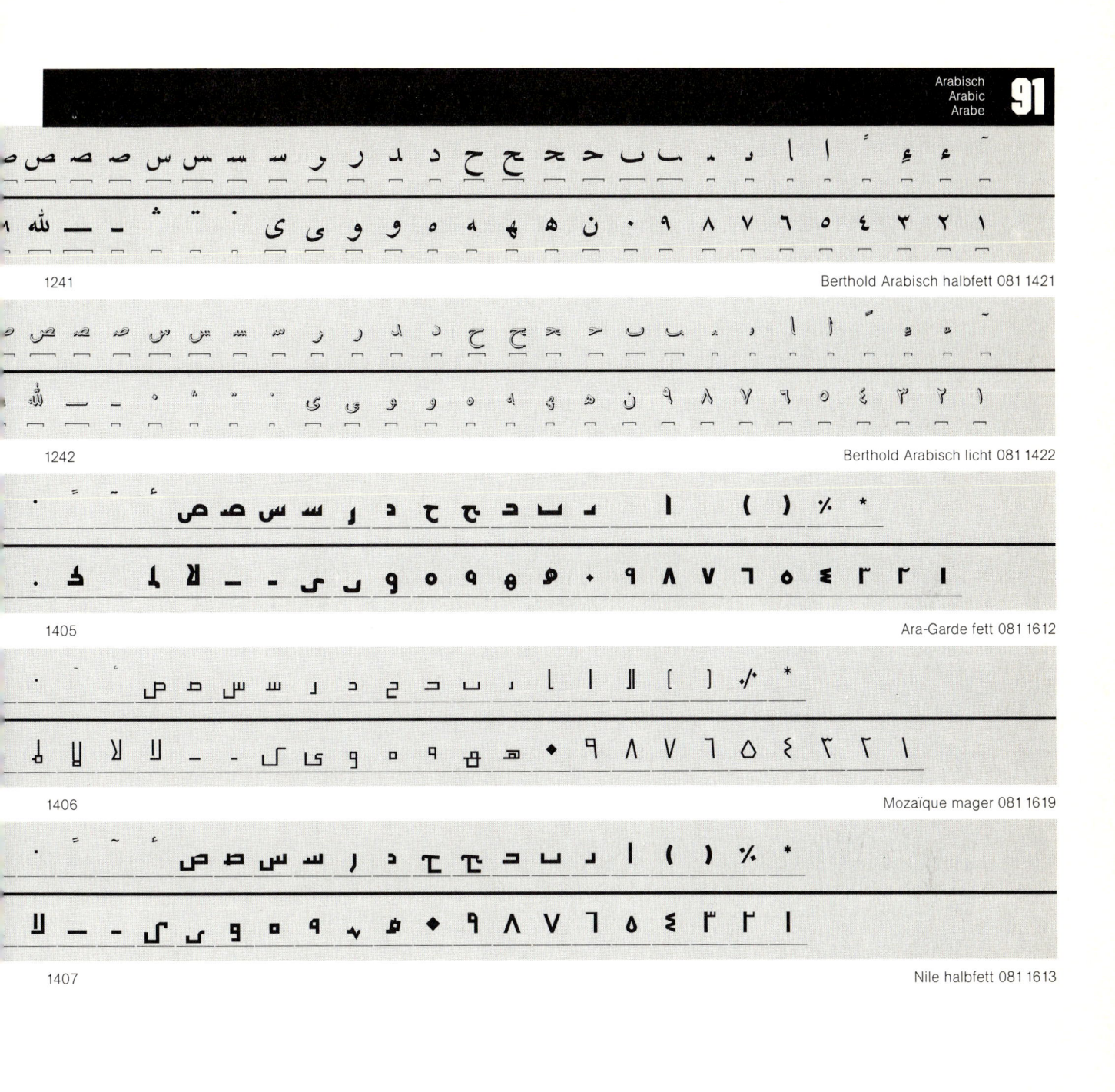

1241 Berthold Arabisch halbfett 081 1421

1242 Berthold Arabisch licht 081 1422

1405 Ara-Garde fett 081 1612

1406 Mozaïque mager 081 1619

1407 Nile halbfett 081 1613

# 92 Hebräisch / Hebrew / Hébreux

1251 Hadassah normal 081 1418

1252 Hadassah fett 081 1419

# BERTHOLD HEADLINES

# BERTHOLD HEADLINES

*Sonderbelegungen und Layouts*
*Specials and Layouts*
*Plaquettes Spéciales et Schémas de Disposition*

# FANCY LABEL

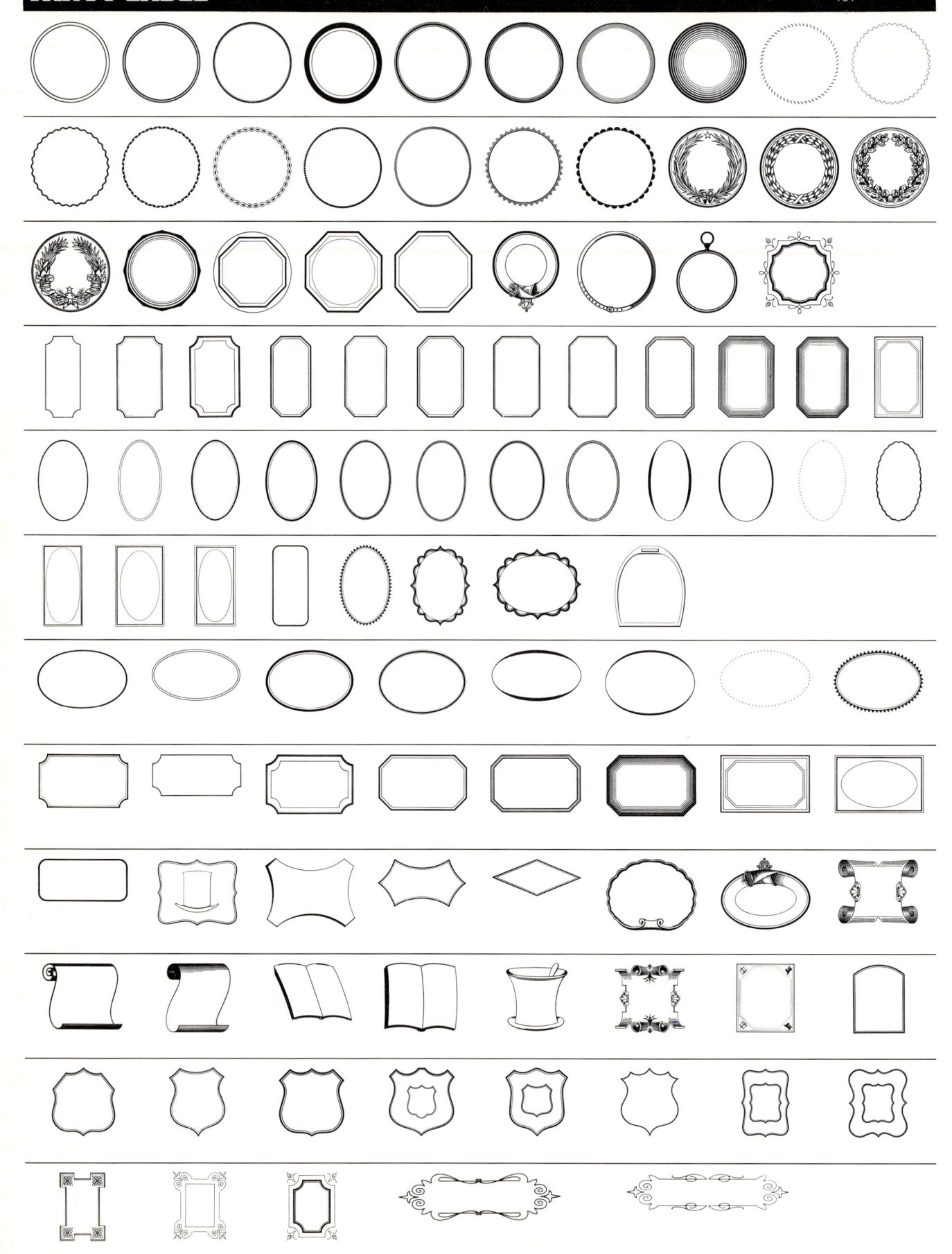

Sp013: 081 0002
131

# VARIA OLD STYLE

# ZAPF DINGBATS 100+200

100: Sp000: 081 2426
200: Sp000: 081 2427
564, 567

```
300: Sp000: 081 2428
199: Sp000: 081 2441
569, 570
```

# ZAPF DINGBATS 300+199

467

# LAYOUTS

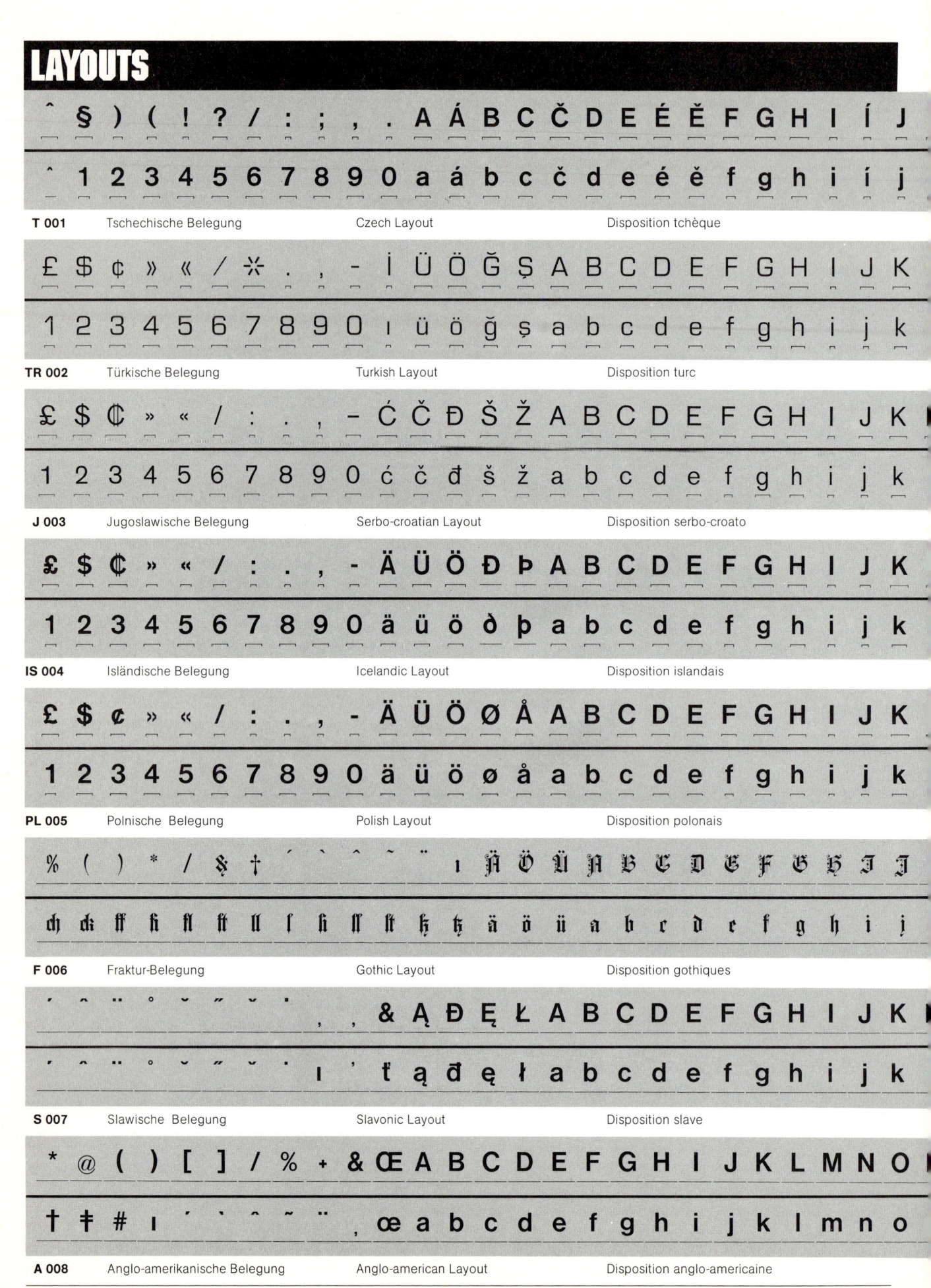

^ § ) ( ! ? / : ; , . A Á B C Č D E É Ě F G H I Í J
^ 1 2 3 4 5 6 7 8 9 0 a á b c č d e é ě f g h i í j

**T 001**    Tschechische Belegung    Czech Layout    Disposition tchèque

£ $ ¢ » « / ⁂ . , - İ Ü Ö Ğ Ş A B C D E F G H I J K
1 2 3 4 5 6 7 8 9 0 ı ü ö ğ ş a b c d e f g h i j k

**TR 002**    Türkische Belegung    Turkish Layout    Disposition turc

£ $ ₡ » « / : . , - Ć Č Đ Š Ž A B C D E F G H I J K
1 2 3 4 5 6 7 8 9 0 ć č đ š ž a b c d e f g h i j k

**J 003**    Jugoslawische Belegung    Serbo-croatian Layout    Disposition serbo-croato

£ $ ₡ » « / : . , - Ä Ü Ö Ð Þ A B C D E F G H I J K
1 2 3 4 5 6 7 8 9 0 ä ü ö ð þ a b c d e f g h i j k

**IS 004**    Isländische Belegung    Icelandic Layout    Disposition islandais

£ $ ¢ » « / : . , - Ä Ü Ö Ø Å A B C D E F G H I J K
1 2 3 4 5 6 7 8 9 0 ä ü ö ø å a b c d e f g h i j k

**PL 005**    Polnische Belegung    Polish Layout    Disposition polonais

% ( ) * / § † ´ ` ^ ~ ¨ ı Ä Ö Ü A B C D E F G H I J
ch ck ff fi fl ft ll ſ ſi ſſ ſt ß tz ä ö ü a b c d e f g h i j

**F 006**    Fraktur-Belegung    Gothic Layout    Disposition gothiques

´ ¨ ° ˇ ˝ ˘ , , & Ą Đ Ę Ł A B C D E F G H I J K
´ ¨ ° ˇ ˝ ˘ , ' ı ' ť ą đ ę ł a b c d e f g h i j k

**S 007**    Slawische Belegung    Slavonic Layout    Disposition slave

* @ ( ) [ ] / % + & Œ A B C D E F G H I J K L M N O
† ‡ # ı ´ ` ^ ~ , œ a b c d e f g h i j k l m n o

**A 008**    Anglo-amerikanische Belegung    Anglo-american Layout    Disposition anglo-americaine

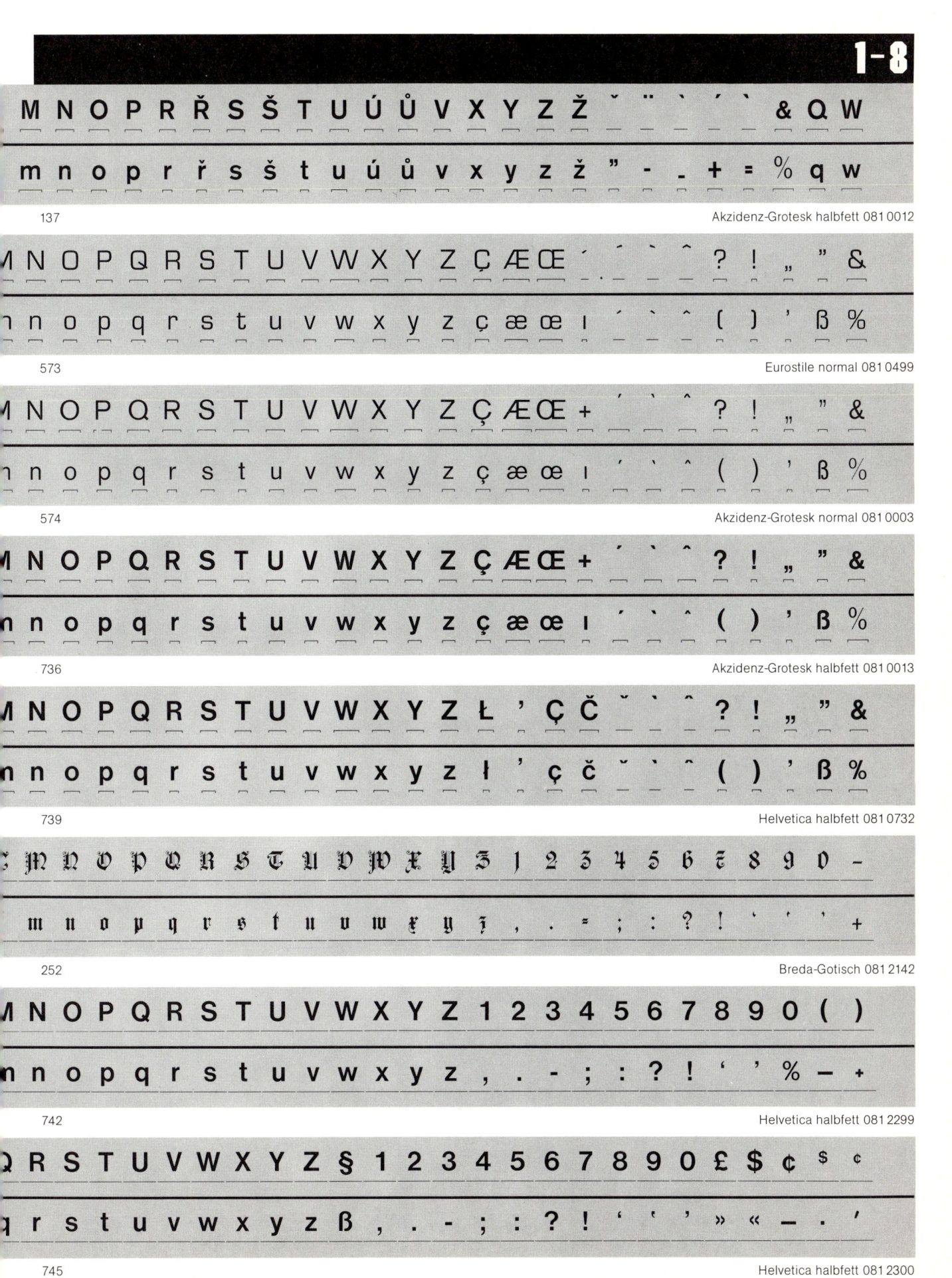

# 1-8

| M N O P R Ř S Š T U Ú Ů V X Y Z Ž ˇ ¨ ` ´ ` | & Q W |
| m n o p r ř s š t u ú ů v x y z ž " - . + = | % q w |

137      Akzidenz-Grotesk halbfett 081 0012

M N O P Q R S T U V W X Y Z Ç Æ Œ ´ ` ˆ ? ! „ " &
m n o p q r s t u v w x y z ç æ œ ı ´ ` ˆ ( ) ' ß %

573      Eurostile normal 081 0499

M N O P Q R S T U V W X Y Z Ç Æ Œ + ´ ` ˆ ? ! „ " &
m n o p q r s t u v w x y z ç æ œ ı ´ ` ˆ ( ) ' ß %

574      Akzidenz-Grotesk normal 081 0003

M N O P Q R S T U V W X Y Z Ç Æ Œ + ´ ` ˆ ? ! „ " &
m n o p q r s t u v w x y z ç æ œ ı ´ ` ˆ ( ) ' ß %

736      Akzidenz-Grotesk halbfett 081 0013

M N O P Q R S T U V W X Y Z Ł ' Ç Č ˇ ` ˆ ? ! „ " &
m n o p q r s t u v w x y z ł ' ç č ˇ ` ˆ ( ) ' ß %

739      Helvetica halbfett 081 0732

M N O P Q R S T U V W X Y Z J 1 2 3 4 5 6 7 8 9 0 -
m n o p q r s t u v w x y z , . - ; : ? ! ' ' ' +

252      Breda-Gotisch 081 2142

M N O P Q R S T U V W X Y Z 1 2 3 4 5 6 7 8 9 0 ( )
m n o p q r s t u v w x y z , . - ; : ? ! ' ' % - +

742      Helvetica halbfett 081 2299

Q R S T U V W X Y Z § 1 2 3 4 5 6 7 8 9 0 £ $ ¢ $ ¢
q r s t u v w x y z ß , . - ; : ? ! ' ' ' » « - . '

745      Helvetica halbfett 081 2300

# LAYOUTS

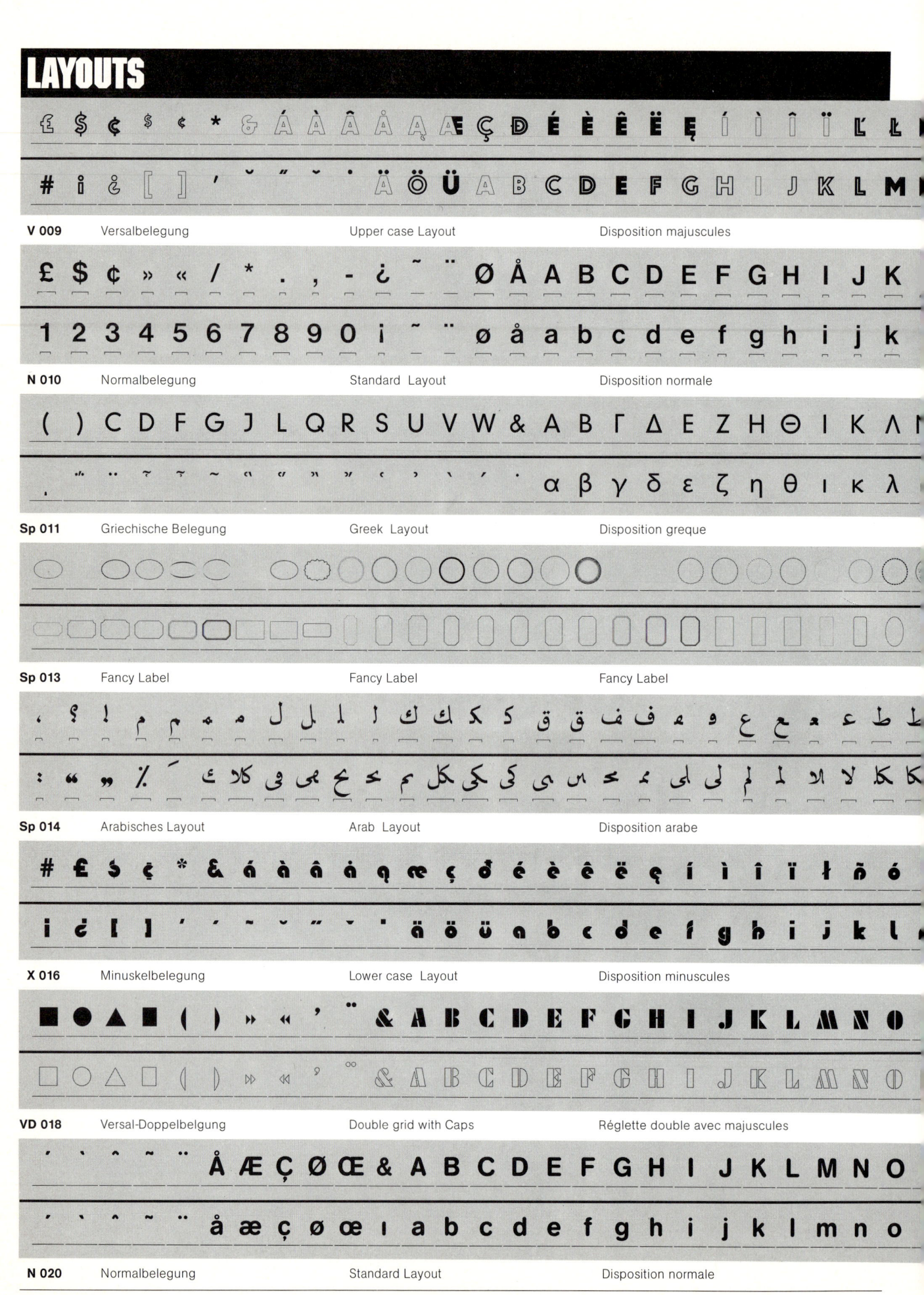

£ $ ¢ ¢ ¢ * & Á À Â Å Ą Æ Ç Đ É È Ê Ë Ę Í Ì Î Ï Ľ Ł

# ¡ ¿ [ ] ' ˇ ˝ · Ä Ö Ü A B C D E F G H I J K L M

**V 009**    Versalbelegung     Upper case Layout     Disposition majuscules

£ $ ¢ » « / * . , - ¿ ˜ ¨ Ø Å A B C D E F G H I J K

1 2 3 4 5 6 7 8 9 0 ¡ ˜ ¨ ø å a b c d e f g h i j k

**N 010**    Normalbelegung     Standard Layout     Disposition normale

( ) C D F G J L Q R S U V W & A B Γ Δ E Z H Θ I K Λ

. ·· ·· ¯ ˜ « » ‹ › ' ' · α β γ δ ε ζ η θ ι κ λ

**Sp 011**    Griechische Belegung     Greek Layout     Disposition greque

**Sp 013**    Fancy Label     Fancy Label     Fancy Label

**Sp 014**    Arabisches Layout     Arab Layout     Disposition arabe

# £ $ ¢ * & á à â ą ǫ æ ç đ é è ê ë ę í ì î ï ł ñ ó

¡ ¿ [ ] ' ˇ ˝ · ä ö ü a b c d e f g h i j k l

**X 016**    Minuskelbelegung     Lower case Layout     Disposition minuscules

■ ● ▲ ( ) » « ' ¨ & A B C D E F G H I J K L M N O

□ ○ △ ( ) » « ° ∞ & A B C D E F G H I J K L M N O

**VD 018**    Versal-Doppelbelgung     Double grid with Caps     Réglette double avec majuscules

´ ` ˆ ¨ Å Æ Ç Ø Œ & A B C D E F G H I J K L M N O

´ ` ˆ ¨ å æ ç ø œ & a b c d e f g h i j k l m n o

**N 020**    Normalbelegung     Standard Layout     Disposition normale

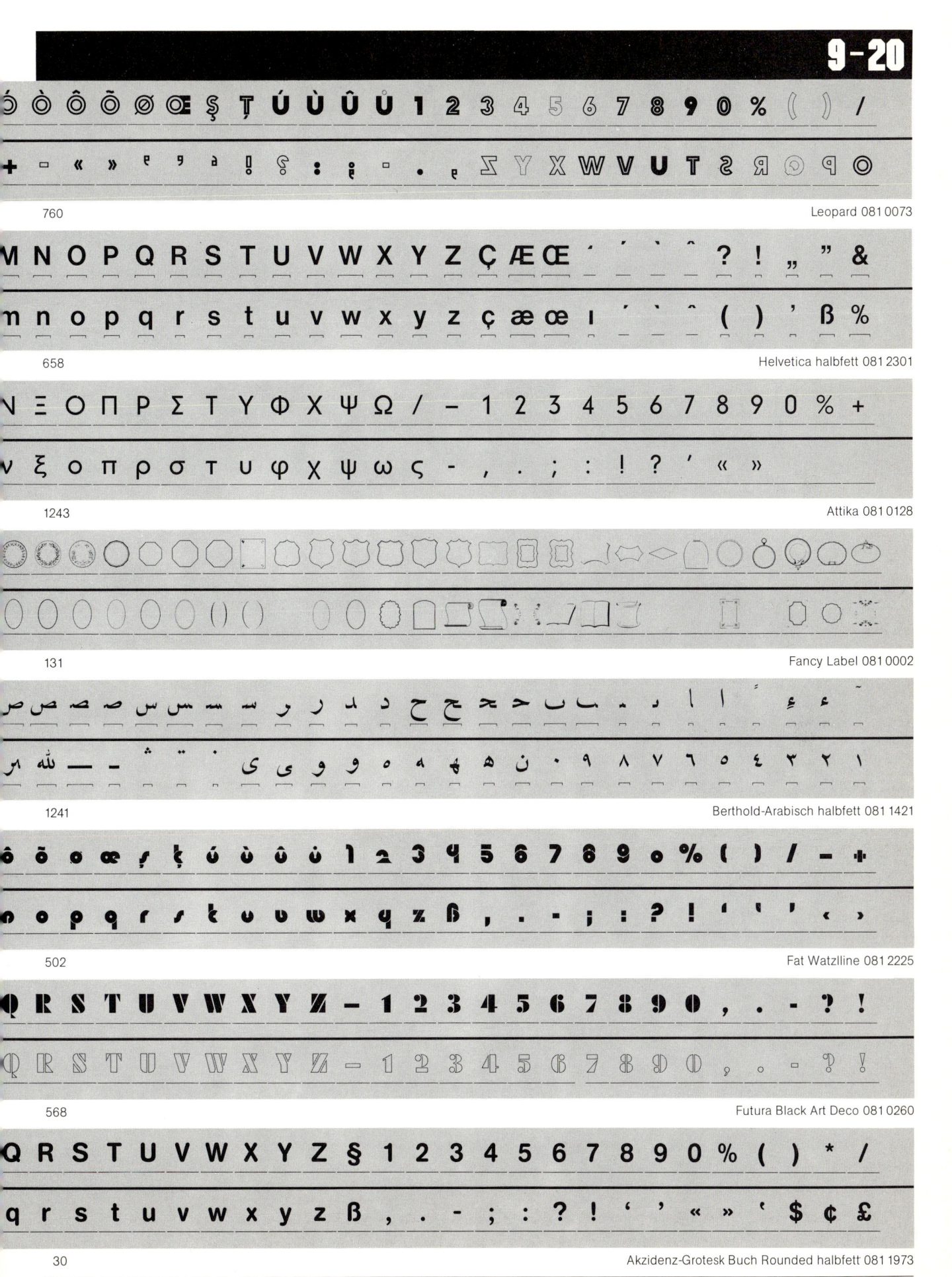

# 9-20

760 — Leopard 081 0073

M N O P Q R S T U V W X Y Z Ç Æ Œ ´ ` ˆ ? ! „ " &

m n o p q r s t u v w x y z ç æ œ ı ´ ` ˆ ( ) ' ß %

658 — Helvetica halbfett 081 2301

Ν Ξ Ο Π Σ Τ Υ Φ Χ Ψ Ω / − 1 2 3 4 5 6 7 8 9 0 % +

ν ξ ο π σ τ υ φ χ ψ ω ς - , . ; : ! ? ' « »

1243 — Attika 081 0128

131 — Fancy Label 081 0002

1241 — Berthold-Arabisch halbfett 081 1421

502 — Fat Watzlline 081 2225

Q R S T U V W X Y Z - 1 2 3 4 5 6 7 8 9 0 , . - ? !

Q R S T U V W X Y Z - 1 2 3 4 5 6 7 8 9 0 , . - ? !

568 — Futura Black Art Deco 081 0260

Q R S T U V W X Y Z § 1 2 3 4 5 6 7 8 9 0 % ( ) * /

q r s t u v w x y z ß , . - ; : ? ! ' ' « » ' $ ¢ £

30 — Akzidenz-Grotesk Buch Rounded halbfett 081 1973

471

# LAYOUTS

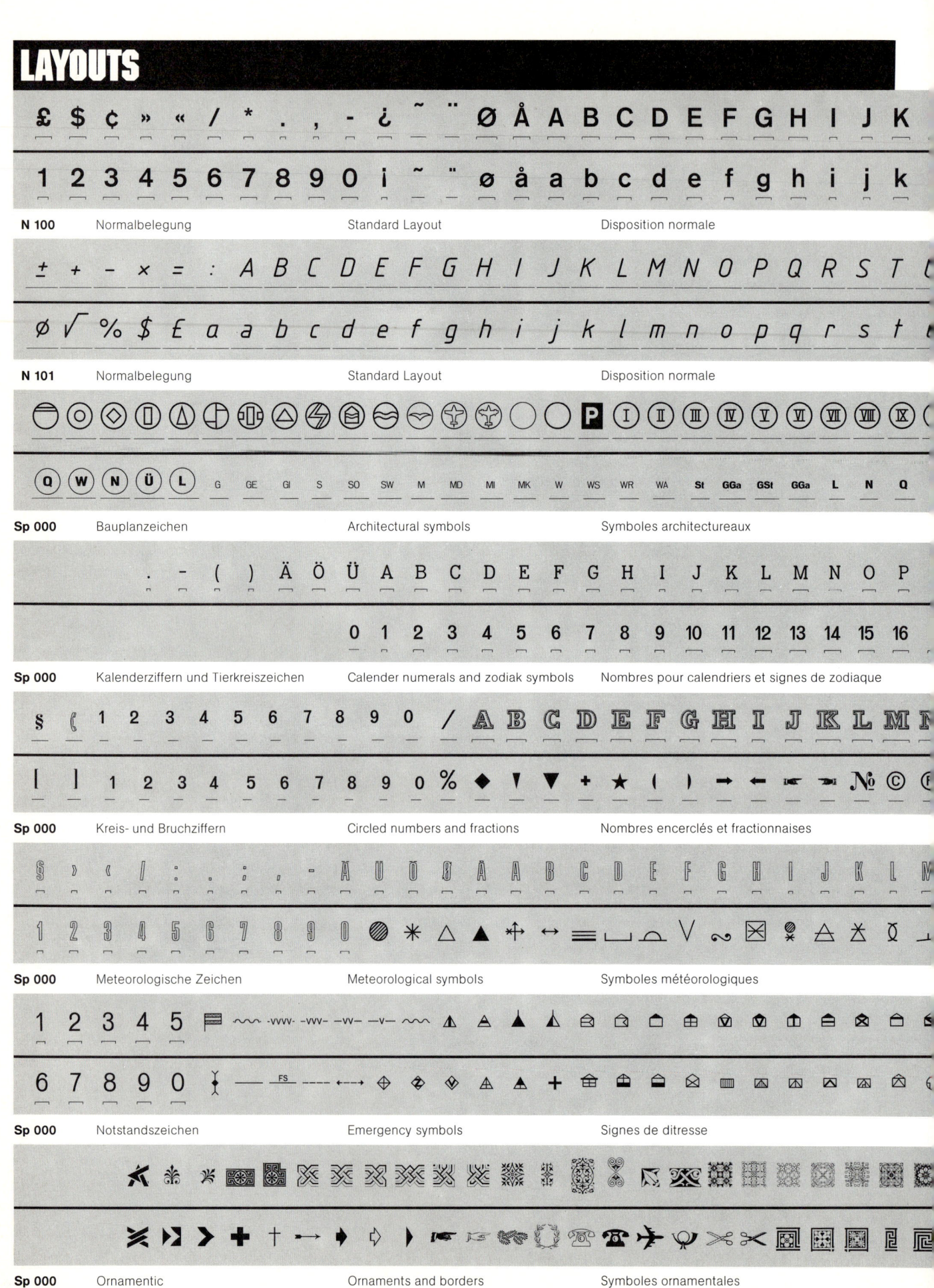

£ $ ¢ » « / * . , - ¿ ~ ¨ Ø Å A B C D E F G H I J K

1 2 3 4 5 6 7 8 9 0 ¡ ~ ¨ ø å a b c d e f g h i j k

**N 100**    Normalbelegung    Standard Layout    Disposition normale

± + - × = : A B C D E F G H I J K L M N O P Q R S T

ø √ % $ £ a a b c d e f g h i j k l m n o p q r s t

**N 101**    Normalbelegung    Standard Layout    Disposition normale

**Sp 000**    Bauplanzeichen    Architectural symbols    Symboles architectureaux

. - ( ) Ä Ö Ü A B C D E F G H I J K L M N O P

0 1 2 3 4 5 6 7 8 9 10 11 12 13 14 15 16

**Sp 000**    Kalenderziffern und Tierkreiszeichen    Calender numerals and zodiak symbols    Nombres pour calendriers et signes de zodiaque

§ ( 1 2 3 4 5 6 7 8 9 0 / A B C D E F G H I J K L M

| | 1 2 3 4 5 6 7 8 9 0 % ◆ ▼ + ★ ( ) → ← № © 

**Sp 000**    Kreis- und Bruchziffern    Circled numbers and fractions    Nombres encerclés et fractionnaises

**Sp 000**    Meteorologische Zeichen    Meteorological symbols    Symboles météorologiques

**Sp 000**    Notstandszeichen    Emergency symbols    Signes de ditresse

**Sp 000**    Ornamentic    Ornaments and borders    Symboles ornamentales

# 100-000

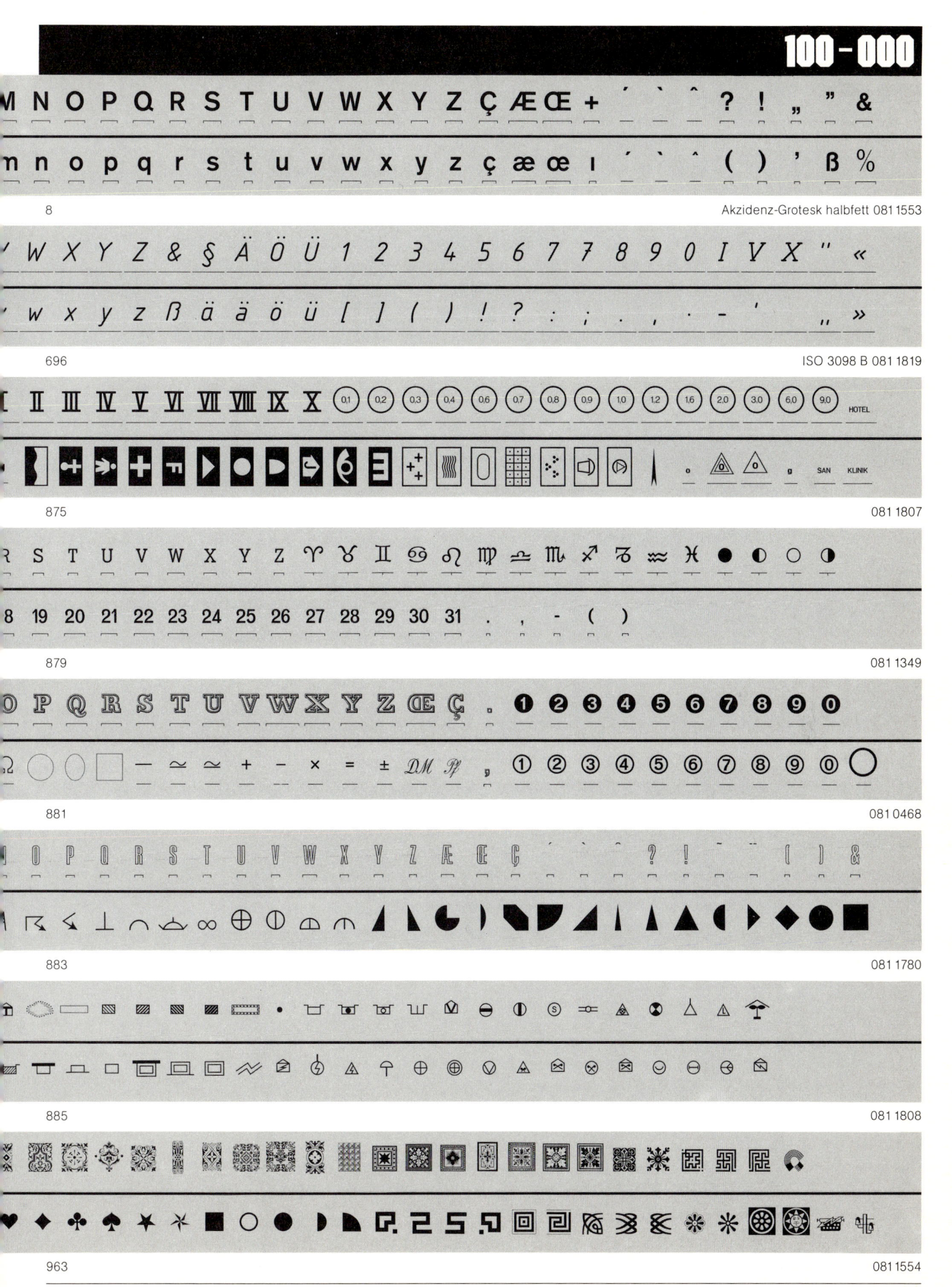

M N O P Q R S T U V W X Y Z Ç Æ Œ + ´ ` ^ ? ! „ " &

m n o p q r s t u v w x y z ç æ œ ı ´ ` ^ ( ) ' ß %

8     Akzidenz-Grotesk halbfett 081 1553

*V W X Y Z & § Ä Ö Ü 1 2 3 4 5 6 7 8 9 0 I V X " «*

*w x y z ß ä ä ö ü [ ] ( ) ! ? : ; . , . - ' „ »*

696     ISO 3098 B 081 1819

875     081 1807

R S T U V W X Y Z ♈ ♉ ♊ ♋ ♌ ♍ ♎ ♏ ♐ ♑ ♒ ♓ ● ◐ ○ ◑

8 19 20 21 22 23 24 25 26 27 28 29 30 31 . , - ( )

879     081 1349

O P Q R S T U V W X Y Z Æ Ç . ❶ ❷ ❸ ❹ ❺ ❻ ❼ ❽ ❾ ❿

○ ○ □ — ≃ ≈ + − × = ± *DM ₰* , ① ② ③ ④ ⑤ ⑥ ⑦ ⑧ ⑨ ⑩ ○

881     081 0468

N O P Q R S T U V W X Y Z Æ Ç    ? ! [ ] &

883     081 1780

885     081 1808

963     081 1554

473

# LAYOUTS

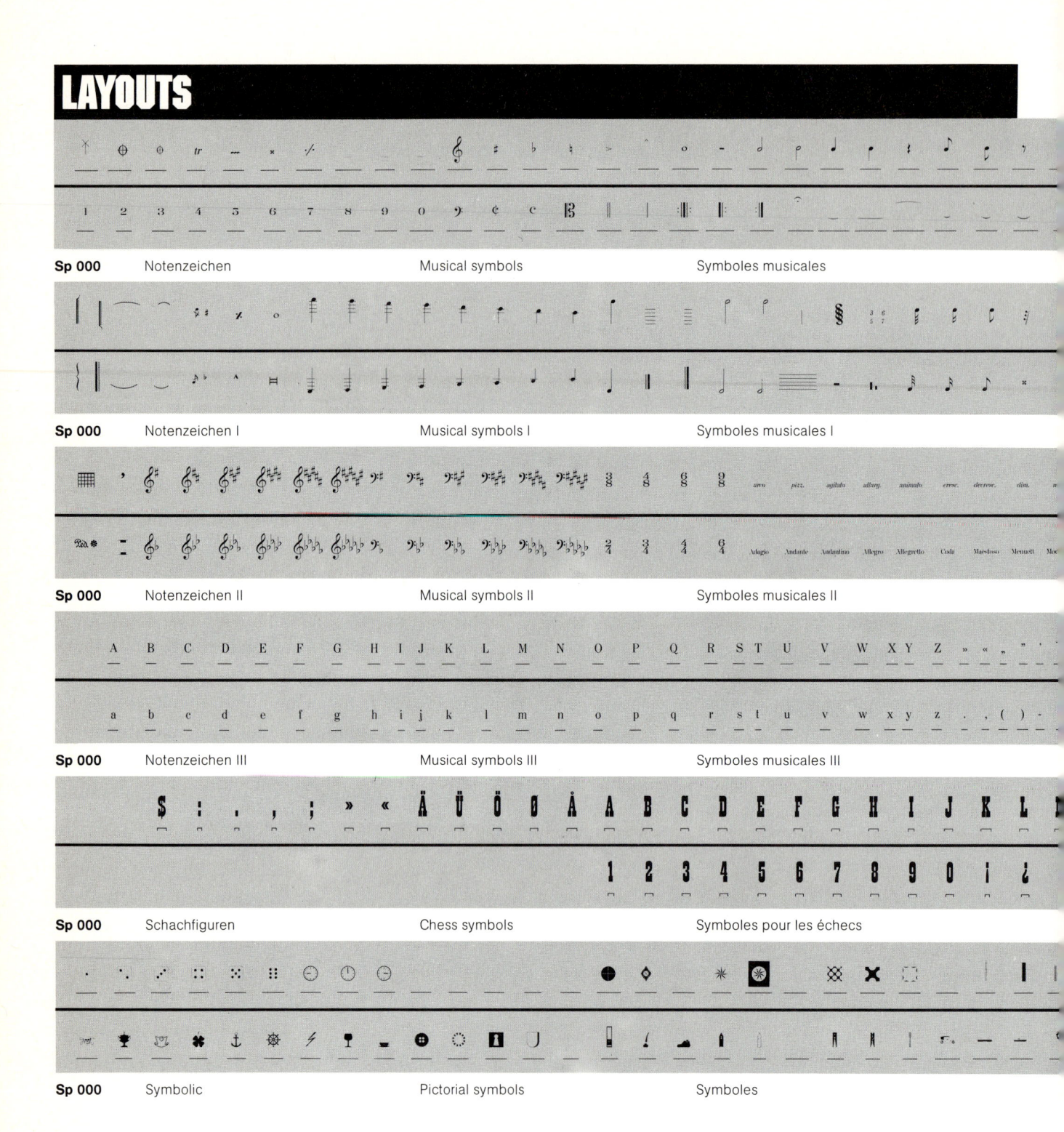

**Sp 000**     Notenzeichen     Musical symbols     Symboles musicales

**Sp 000**     Notenzeichen I     Musical symbols I     Symboles musicales I

**Sp 000**     Notenzeichen II     Musical symbols II     Symboles musicales II

**Sp 000**     Notenzeichen III     Musical symbols III     Symboles musicales III

**Sp 000**     Schachfiguren     Chess symbols     Symboles pour les échecs

**Sp 000**     Symbolic     Pictorial symbols     Symboles

000-000

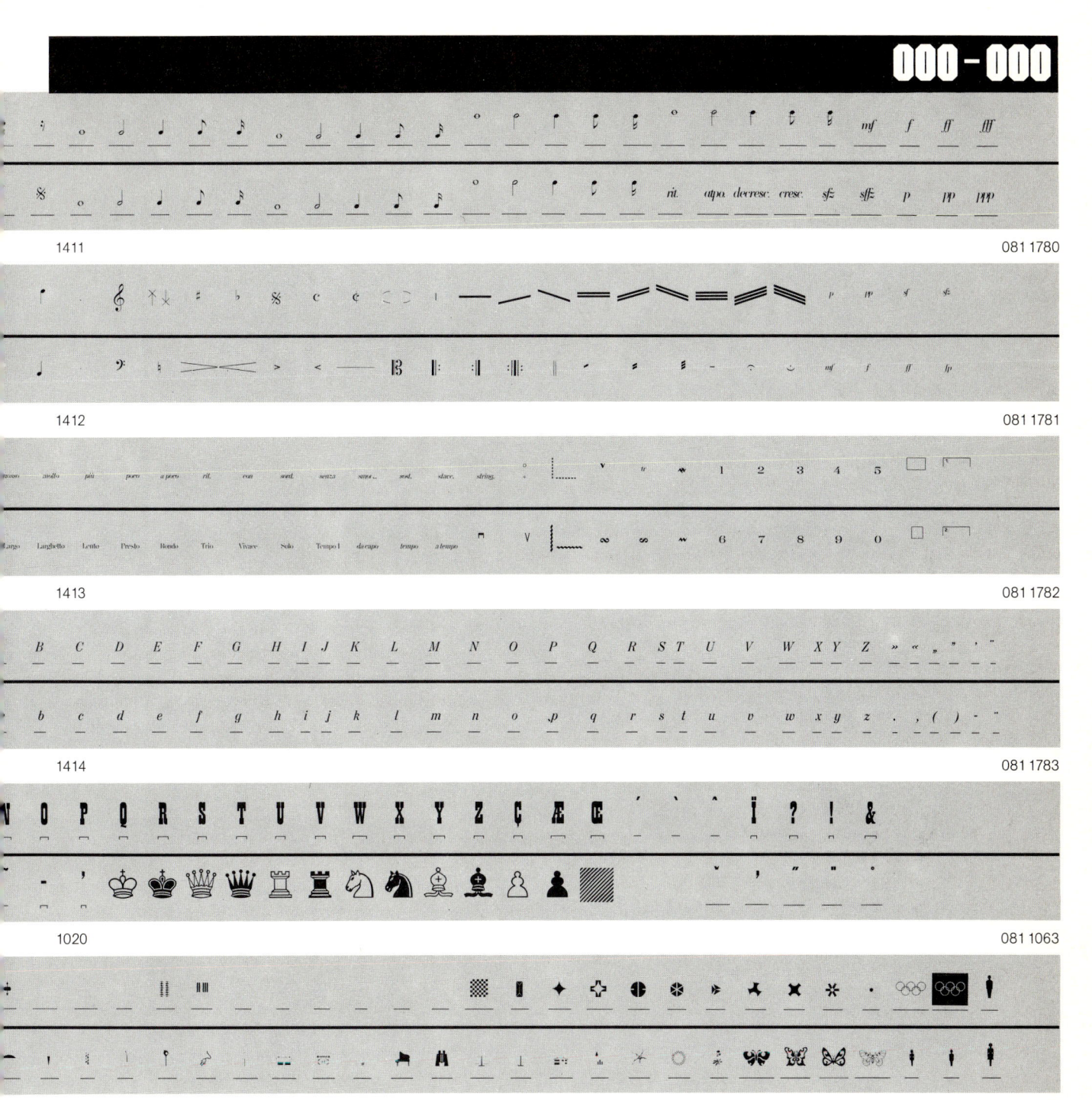

1411 081 1780

1412 081 1781

1413 081 1782

1414 081 1783

1020 081 1063

855 081 1778

475

# BERTHOLD HEADLINES

# BERTHOLD HEADLINES

*Zierbuchstaben*
*Swash Letters*
*Lettres Ornées*

# SWASH

A A CA EA FA GA KA LA LA RA HT TH NT UT
e ff fi fl ffi ffl t v

**Z 000**  Avant Garde Gothic mager    Avant Garde Gothic extra light    Avant Garde Gothic maigre

A A CA © EA FA R GA HT KA LA LL M
c e ff fi fl ffi ffl t

**Z 000**  Avant Garde Gothic Buch    Avant Garde Gothic book    Avant Garde Gothic romain labeur

A A CA EA FA GA KA LA LA RA HT TH NT
c e ff fi fl ffi ffl t

**Z 000**  Avant Garde Gothic normal    Avant Garde Gothic medium    Avant Garde Gothic normal

A A CA © EA FA R GA HT KA LA LL M M
c ç e ¼ ½ / - † # § ( )

**Z 000**  Avant Garde Gothic halbfett    Avant Garde Gothic demi-bold    Avant Garde Gothic demi-gras

A CA EA FA GA KA LA RA TH HT NT UT LL
e fi ff fl ffi ffl v

**Z 000**  Avant Garde Gothic fett    Avant Garde Gothic bold    Avant Garde Gothic gras

A A CA EA FA R GA HT KA LA LL M M
e – / # † ( ) ° ;

**Z 000**  Avant Garde Gothic Buch schmal    Avant Garde Gothic book condensed    Avant Garde Gothic étroit romain labeur

A A CA EA FA R GA HT KA LA LL M N
e – / # † ( ) ° ;

**Z 000**  Avant Garde Gothic schmal    Avant Garde Gothic medium condensed    Avant Garde Gothic étroit

A A CA © EA FA R GA HT KA LA LL M
c e t v v w y : ; ( ) °

**Z 000**  Avant Garde Gothic schmalhalbfett    Avant Garde Gothic demi-bold condensed    Avant Garde Gothic étroit demi-gras

# A–A

97  Avant Garde Gothic mager 081 1579

100  Avant Garde Gothic Buch 081 0503

103  Avant Garde Gothic normal 081 1582

106  Avant Garde Gothic halbfett 081 1611

109  Avant Garde Gothic fett 081 0133

112  Avant Garde Gothic Buch schmal 081 1607

114  Avant Garde Gothic schmal 081 1609

116  Avant Garde Gothic schmalhalbfett 081 2056

# SWASH

| | | |
|---|---|---|
| A A C4 © EA FA FR GA HT K4 LA LL M | | |
| ( e t v v w w y : ; ( ) ° | | |
| **Z 000** Avant Garde Gothic schmalfett | Avant Garde Gothic bold condensed | Avant Garde Gothic étroit gras |
| m n ʃ ӿ & $ | m n ʃ ӿ & $ | m n ʃ ӿ & $ |
| e r ʃ ӿ y | e r ʃ ӿ y | e r ʃ ӿ y |
| **Z 000** Bauhaus-Serie | Bauhaus-Serie | Bauhaus-Serie |
| A A AA ÆB ÆF AH ÆK ÆP ÆR M SS TT fi | A A AA ÆB ÆF AH ÆK | |
| A A AA ÆB ÆF AH ÆK ÆP ÆR M SS TT fi | A A AA ÆB ÆF AH ÆK | |
| **Z 000** Benguiat-Serie | Benguiat-Serie | Benguiat-Serie |
| AB AG AG AG Corp Corp C Dr Dr Dr Fa Fa KG KG KG Ltd Prof Prof Sir A B C D E F F G | | |
| L DM No No Nr Stck Std Tel The The the of von & @ & b ch ck ʃ ʃ ff ll l gg h | | |
| **Z 000** Berthold-Script normal | Berthold-Script regular | Berthold-Serie normal |
| AB AG AG AG Corp Corp C Dr Dr Dr Fa Fa KG KG KG Ltd Prof Prof Sir A B C D E F F G | | |
| L DM No No Nr Stck Std Tel The The the of von & @ & b ch ck ʃ ʃ ff ll l gg h | | |
| **Z 000** Berthold-Script halbfett | Berthold-Script medium | Berthold-Script demi-gras |
| | | Ä |
| | | a ä c c F h |
| **Z 000** Black Body | Black Body | Black Body |
| | | |
| | | a b c d e f g h |
| **Z 000** Blippo halbfett | Blippo bold | Blippo demi-gras |
| | | : : ? A B C D E F G H I |
| | | 1 2 3 4 5 6 7 8 9 0 a b c d e f g h i |
| **Z 000** Blippo Black | Blippo Black | Blippo Black |

480

# A-B

N NT R RA SS § ST TH U V W W

118  Avant Garde Gothic schmalfett 081 2062

m n ſ x & $   m n ſ x & $   m n ſ x & $
e r ſ x y   e r ſ x y   e r ſ x y

129  Bauhaus-Serie 081 1913

P Æ M SS TT fi   A A AA Æ Æ A IK Æ P Æ M SS TT fi
P Æ M SS TT fi   A A AA Æ Æ A IK Æ P Æ M SS TT fi

1307  Benguiat-Serie 081 1577

179  Berthold-Script normal 081 2391

181  Berthold-Script halbfett 081 2399

M ö s ü
n n ö r ü

191  Black Body 081 0167

s & G
k p q r s t y

196  Blippo halbfett 081 2036

K L M N O P Q R ſ T U V W X Y Z &
k l m n o p q r ſ t u v w x y z ß

199  Blippo Black 081 1920

481

# SWASH

ABCDEFGHIJK
1234567890abcdefghijk

**Z 000**    Blippo Black licht      Blippo Black outline      Blippo Black éclairé

& A B C D E F G H I J K L M N O P Q R
æ b d e f fi k m n o œ p q r t u v w y

**Z 000**    Bookman mager      Bookman light      Bookman maigre

A A B B C D E F G H I J J K L M N O P Q R R
e fi fi h h k m n o p q t - *

**Z 000**    Bookman kursiv mager      Bookman light italic      Bookman italique maigre

& A A B B C D E F G H I J J K L M N O P Q R R
æ b d e f fi k m n o œ p q r t u v w

**Z 000**    Bookman normal      Bookman medium      Bookman normal

A A B B C D E F G H I J J K L M N O P Q R R
e fi fi h h k m n o p q t

**Z 000**    Bookman kursiv      Bookman medium italic      Bookman italique

& A A B B C D E F G H I J J K L M N O P Q R R
æ b d e f fi k m n o œ p q r t u v w

**Z 000**    Bookman halbfett      Bookman demi-bold      Bookman demi-gras

& A A B B C D E F G H I J J K L M N O P Q R R
e fi fi h h k m n o p q t - .

**Z 000**    Bookman kursiv halbfett      Bookman demi-bold italic      Bookman italique demi-gras

& A A B B C D E F G H I J J K L M N O P Q R R
æ b d e f fi k m n o œ p q r t u v w

**Z 000**    Bookman fett      Bookman bold      Bookman gras

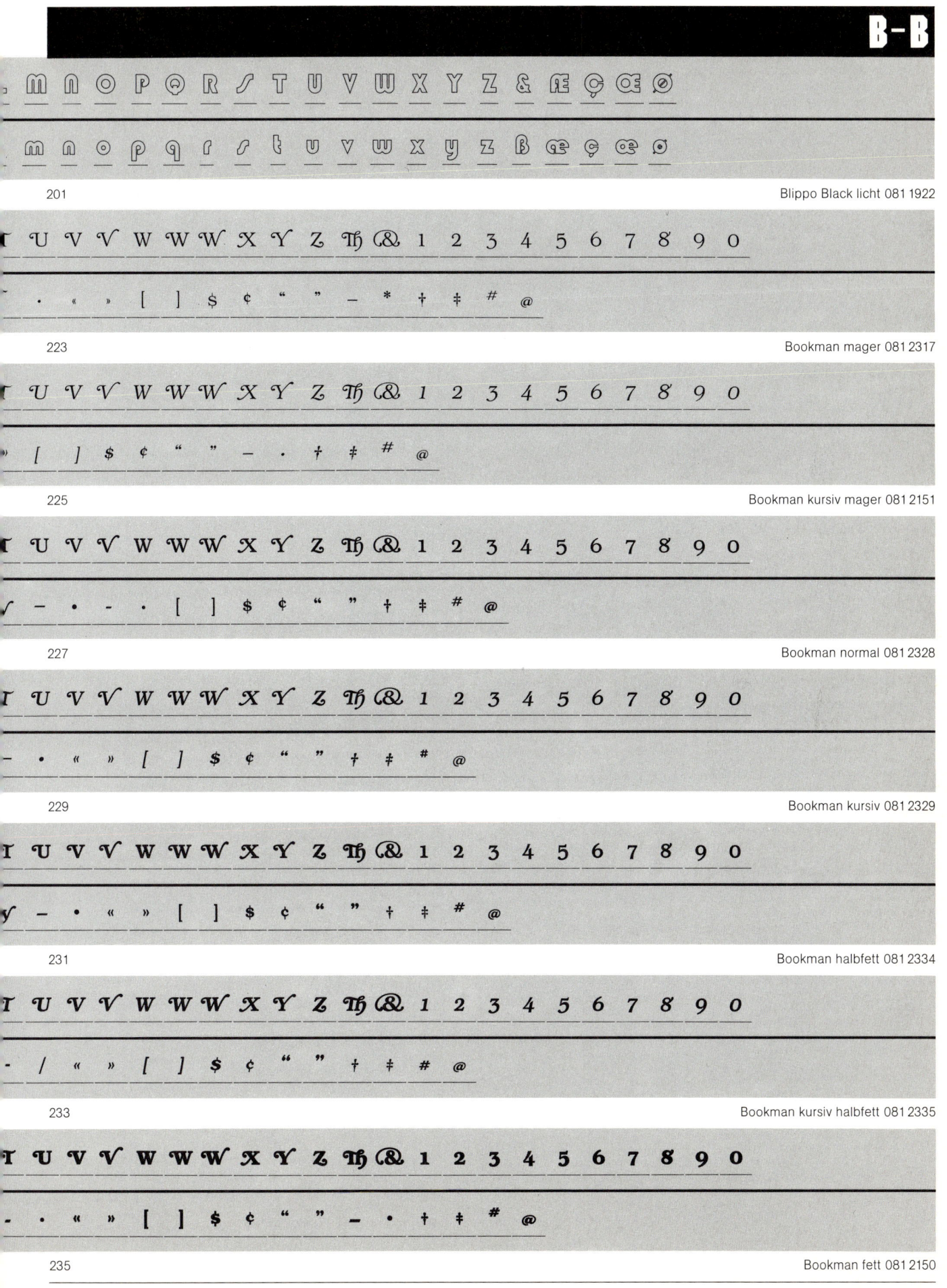

201     Blippo Black licht 081 1922

223     Bookman mager 081 2317

225     Bookman kursiv mager 081 2151

227     Bookman normal 081 2328

229     Bookman kursiv 081 2329

231     Bookman halbfett 081 2334

233     Bookman kursiv halbfett 081 2335

235     Bookman fett 081 2150

# SWASH

| Z 000 | Bookman kursiv fett | Bookman bold italic | Bookman italique gras |
|---|---|---|---|
| Z 000 | Bookman licht | Bookman outline | Bookman éclairé |
| Z 000 | Bookman Kontur | Bookman contour | Bookman contour |
| Z 000 | Bookman LUDLOW kursiv | Bookman italic | Bookman italique |
| Z 000 | Bookman LUDLOW fett | Bookman bold | Bookman gras |
| Z 000 | Bookman Meola I | Bookman Meola I | Bookman Meola I |
| Z 000 | Bookman Meola II | Bookman Meola II | Bookman Meola II |
| Z 000 | Caslon 540 kursiv | Caslon 540 italic | Caslon 540 italique |

# B-C

237 Bookman kursiv fett 081 2153

239 Bookman licht 081 2157

241 Bookman Kontur 081 2156

244 Bookman LUDLOW kursiv 081 0214

246 Bookman LUDLOW fett 081 0217

247 Bookman Meola I 081 1598

248 Bookman Meola II 081 0219

274 Caslon 540 kursiv 081 0248

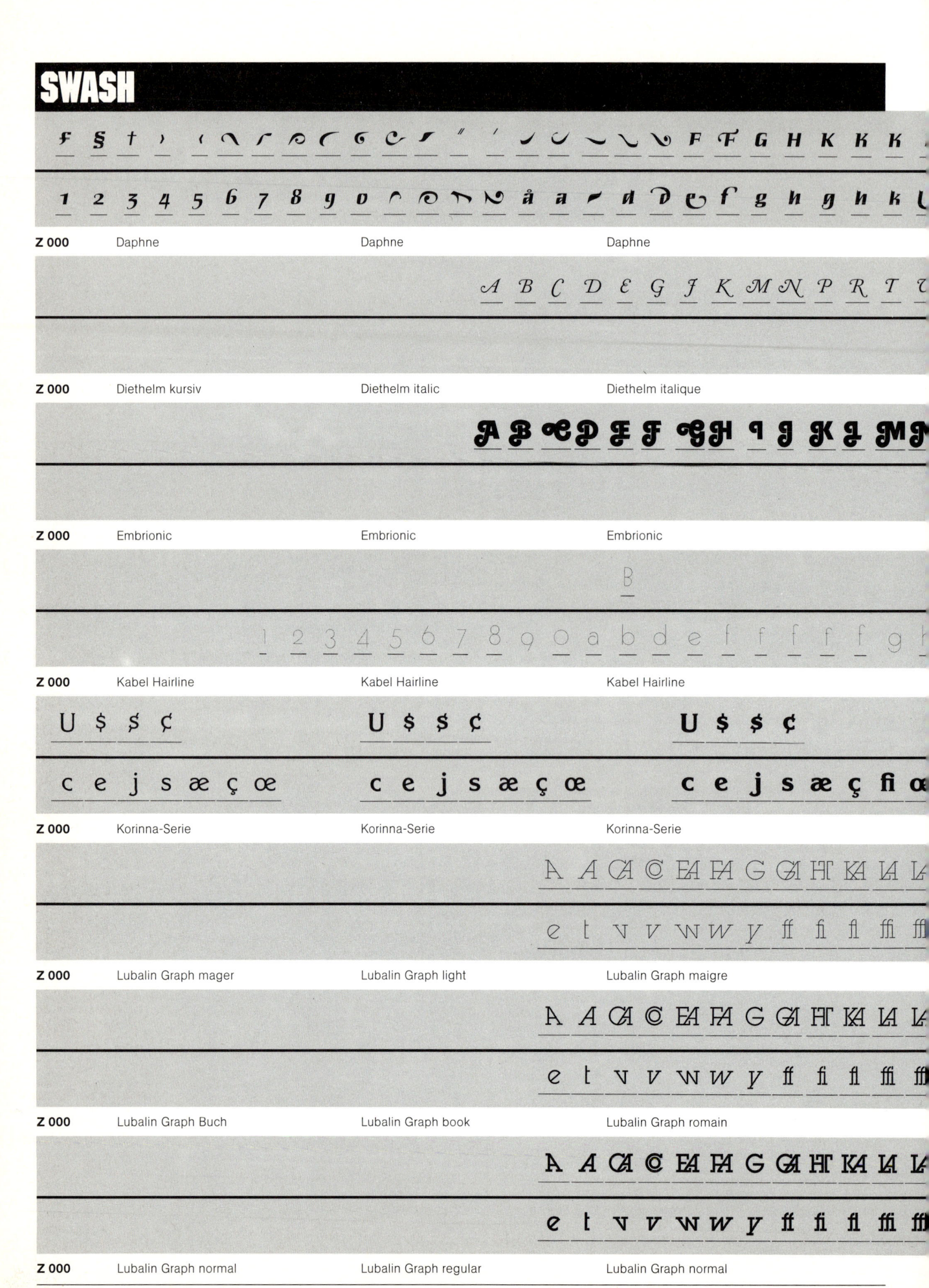

# SWASH

Z 000 — Daphne — Daphne — Daphne

Z 000 — Diethelm kursiv — Diethelm italic — Diethelm italique

Z 000 — Embrionic — Embrionic — Embrionic

Z 000 — Kabel Hairline — Kabel Hairline — Kabel Hairline

Z 000 — Korinna-Serie — Korinna-Serie — Korinna-Serie

Z 000 — Lubalin Graph mager — Lubalin Graph light — Lubalin Graph maigre

Z 000 — Lubalin Graph Buch — Lubalin Graph book — Lubalin Graph romain

Z 000 — Lubalin Graph normal — Lubalin Graph regular — Lubalin Graph normal

# D-L

N P O R T U V W X Y Z Æ ' ˘ ˇ ˆ ˙ ˝ ` ´ ¸ &
˛ ˜ ¯ ˚ ŕ ů ñ y̌ ç ẑ ź ż ö ð đ ı † ‡ [ ] к ß %

434      Daphne 081 0420

443      Diethelm kursiv 081 0429

p e R S T u v w x y z ( )

476      Embrionic 081 0478

J    M   Q    W    ? & &
j j k k k l   p q r s t u w y y

714      Kabel Hairline 081 0804

U $ ¢     U $ ¢
c e j s æ ç fi œ     c e j s æ ç œ

733      Korinna-Serie 081 2093

M N R A S S T Th U V W

791      Lubalin Graph mager 081 1929

M N R A S S T Th U V W

793      Lubalin Graph Buch 081 1917

M N R A S S T Th U V W

795      Lubalin Graph normal 081 1916

# SWASH

| Z 000 | Lubalin Graph halbfett | Lubalin Graph medium | Lubalin Graph demi-gras |
|---|---|---|---|
| Z 000 | Lubalin Graph fett | Lubalin Graph bold | Lubalin Graph gras |
| Z 000 | Murrpoint Swing fett | Murrpoint Swing bold | Murrpoint Swing gras |
| Z 000 | Newtext-Serie I | Newtext-Serie I | Newtext-Serie I |
| Z 000 | Newtext-Serie II | Newtext-Serie II | Newtext-Serie II |
| Z 000 | Ocean Current | Ocean Current | Ocean Current |
| Z 000 | Poppl-Antiqua kursiv schmalfett | Poppl-Antiqua bold condensed italic | Poppl-Antiqua italique étroit gras |
| Z 000 | Poppl Exquisit | Poppl Exquisit | Poppl Exquisit |

## L-P

M M N T R A S S ST TH U V V W W
797  Lubalin Graph halbfett 081 1925

ST TH V V W W
799  Lubalin Graph fett 081 1926

m m m n n n n p q r s u u y z
852  Murrpoint Swing fett 081 1709

a e m n w tf ¶    a e m n w tf ¶
g j p q y y y ff ft    a g j p q y y y œ ff ft
871  Newtext-Serie I 081 2108

a e m n w tf ¶    a e m n T w tf ¶
a g j p q y y y œ ff ft    a g j p q y y y œ ff ft
873  Newtext-Serie II 081 2102

L ʾ ʿ ʾ ʾ ʿ ʾ ʾ ʾ    Z Ç Æ Œ + ´ ` ˆ ? ! „ " &
m n o p q r s t u v w x y z ç æ œ † ´ ` ˆ ( ) ' ß %
898  Ocean Current 081 1478

M M N N P Q R R S   T T U V W X X Y Z Æ
l m  n   p   s ß t  u        y z
955  Poppl-Antiqua kursiv schmalfett 081 1779

V W X Z . . §
d g h k k l ſ s ß v w z
957  Poppl Exquisit 081 1043

# SWASH

| | | | |
|---|---|---|---|
| | | | ABCDEFGHIJKLMNO |
| Z 000 | Rhapsodie | Rhapsodie | Rhapsodie |
| | | | E L ÆŒ ( ) 8 0 |
| | | | a e f k r s t z |
| Z 000 | Serif Gothic mager | Serif Gothic light | Serif Gothic maigre |
| | | | E L ÆŒ ( ) 8 0 |
| | | | a e f k r s t z |
| Z 000 | Serif Gothic normal | Serif Gothic regular | Serif Gothic normal |
| | | | E L ÆŒ ( ) [ ] 8 0 |
| | | | a e f k r s t z œ ff |
| Z 000 | Serif Gothic fett | Serif Gothic bold | Serif Gothic gras |
| | | | A E L M N V W Æ Œ ( |
| | | | a e f k r s t v w z |
| Z 000 | Serif Gothic extrafett | Serif Gothic extra bold | Serif Gothic extra gras |
| | | | A E L M N V W Æ Œ ( |
| | | | a e f k r s t v w z |
| Z 000 | Serif Gothic ultrafett | Serif Gothic heavy | Serif Gothic ultra gras |
| | | | E L ÆŒ ( ) 8 0 |
| | | | a e f k r s t z |
| Z 000 | Serif Gothic Black | Serif Gothic Black | Serif Gothic Black |
| | | | A E L M N V W Æ Œ ( |
| | | | a e f k r s t v w z |
| Z 000 | Serif Gothic licht | Serif Gothic outline | Serif Gothic éclairé |

# R-S

P Q R S T U V W X Y Z

990     Rhapsodie 081 2187

œ ff fi fl ffi ffl œ

1024     Serif Gothic mager 081 2071

œ ff fi fl ffi ffl œ

1026     Serif Gothic normal 081 2028

fi fl ffi ffl œ

1028     Serif Gothic fett 081 2029

) 1 4 8 0

œ æ æ ff fi fl ffi ffl œ

1030     Serif Gothic extrafett 081 2030

) 1 4 8 0

œ æ æ ff fi fl ffi ffl œ

1032     Serif Gothic ultrafett 081 2031

æ æ œ ff fi fl ffi ffl œ

1034     Serif Gothic Black 081 2075

) 1 4 8 0

æ æ œ ff fi fl ffi ffl œ

1036     Serif Gothic licht 081 2032

491

# SWASH

A A A B C D E F G H I J K K K K L L M M
a a a a b b d d d d f f fi fl fy g h h h h k k m

**Z 000** Times Modern — Times Modern — Times Modern

**Z 000** Uptight normal — Uptight regular — Uptight normal

**Z 000** Vienna — Vienna — Vienna

**Z 000** Wiegands Adbold — Wiegands Adbold — Wiegands Adbold

**Z 000** Wiegands Renaissance kursiv — Wiegands Renaissance italic — Wiegands Renaissance italique

**Z 000** Wiegands Roundhead — Wiegands Roundhead — Wiegands Roundhead

**Z 000** Zapf Chancery mager — Zapf Chancery light — Zapf Chancery maigre

**Z 000** Zapf Chancery kursiv mager — Zapf Chancery light italic — Zapf Chancery italique maigre

# T-Z

NNN.PQRRRSTUVWWXYYZ.

m m n n n. o p p r s t t u u u u v w y y

1099     Times Modern 081 0596

P R S S S U W X Y    Ç Ç ¨ ˝ &

s s s    W X y Z ç ¸ [ ]

1148     Uptight normal 081 1788

] Q Q R \ \ W Y Y Z &

▲ @ r t t w y y z ◇

1173     Vienna 081 1355

M M N R R U W W    Æ S

m   n r    u w w y    [ ]

1213     Wiegands Adbold 081 1777

N O P Q R S T U U V W Y

n o r s t u v w

1217     Wiegands Renaissance 081 2412

G M N R U W S

m n r    [ ]

1219     Wiegands Roundhead 081 1770

Q R S T U V W X Y Z § 1 2 3 4 5 6 7 8 9 0 ® ( ) y Y

q r s t u v w x y z ß , . - ; : ? ! ſt th of › ‹ $ ¢ £

1294     Zapf Chancery mager 081 1367

Q R S T U V W X Y Z § 1 2 3 4 5 6 7 8 9 0 ® ( ) y Y

q r s t u v w x y z ß , . - ; : ? ! ſt th of › ‹ $ ¢ £

1295     Zapf Chancery kursiv mager 081 1389

# SWASH

| Z 000 | Zapf Chancery normal | Zapf Chancery normal | Zapf Chancery normal |

| Z 000 | Zapf Chancery kursiv | Zapf Chancery italic | Zapf Chancery italique |

| Z 000 | Zapf Chancery halbfett | Zapf Chancery demi | Zapf Chancery demi-gras |

| Z 000 | Zapf Chancery fett | Zapf Chancery bold | Zapf Chancery gras |

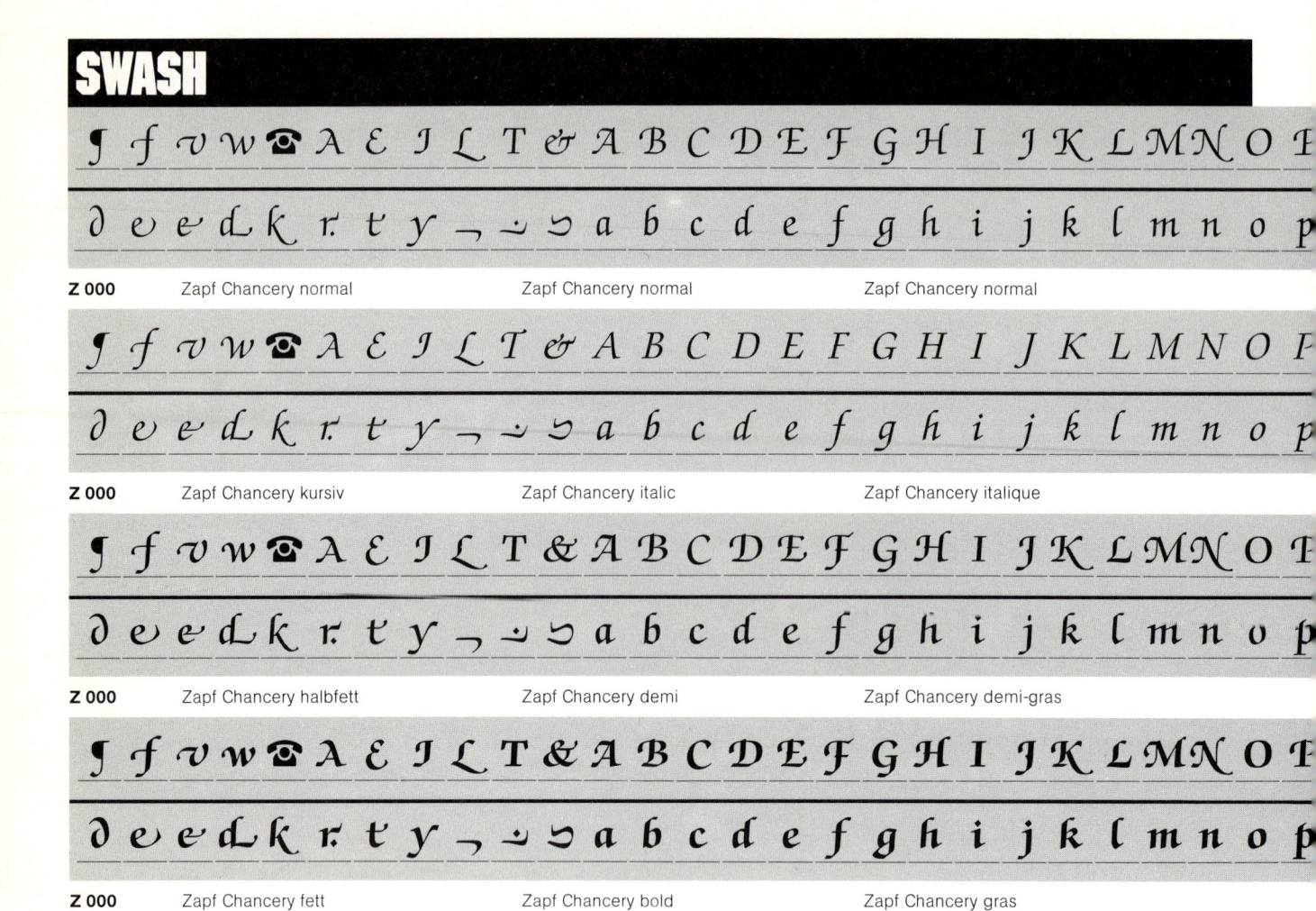

# Z-Z

QRSTUVWXYZ § 1 2 3 4 5 6 7 8 9 0 ® ( ) Y Y
q r s t u v w x y z ß , . - ; : ? ! st th of › ‹ $ ¢ £

1297            Zapf Chancery normal 081 1370

QRSTUVWXYZ § 1 2 3 4 5 6 7 8 9 0 ® ( ) Y Y
q r s t u v w x y z ß , . - ; : ? ! st th of › ‹ $ ¢ £

1298            Zapf Chancery kursiv 081 1392

**QRSTUVWXYZ § 1 2 3 4 5 6 7 8 9 0 ® ( ) Y Y**
**q r s t u v w x y z ß , . - ; : ? ! st th of › ‹ $ ¢ £**

1300            Zapf Chancery halbfett 081 1375

**QRSTUVWXYZ § 1 2 3 4 5 6 7 8 9 0 ® ( ) Y Y**
**q r s t u v w x y z ß , . - ; : ? ! st th of › ‹ $ ¢ £**

1302            Zapf Chancery fett 081 1384

# T 001
Tschechoslowakische Belegung
Czech layout
Disposition tchèque

| | | |
|---|---|---|
| T 001: 081 0005 Akzidenz-Grotesk mager | T 001: 081 0521 Fette Antiqua | T 001: 081 1699 Murrpoint fett |
| T 001: 081 0012 Akzidenz-Grotesk halbfett | T 001: 081 2044 Fette Fraktur | T 001: 081 1704 Murrpoint Swing fett |
| T 001: 081 0019 Akzidenz-Grotesk super | T 001: 081 0525 Fette Gotisch | T 001: 081 0921 Neue Aurora-Grotesk schmalhalbfett |
| T 001: 081 1558 Akzidenz-Grotesk breit | T 001: 081 0535 Folio kursiv mager | |
| T 001: 081 0057 Aldus Buchschrift kursiv | T 001: 081 0538 Folio halbfett | T 001: 081 0950 Nobel fett |
| T 001: 081 2040 Amati | T 001: 081 0541 Folio fett | T 001: 081 0952 Normande normal |
| T 001: 081 0069 Annonce fett | T 001: 081 0556 Folio kursiv schmalfett | T 001: 081 0958 Normande schmal |
| T 001: 081 0075 Antiqua 505 normal | T 001: 081 0561 Folio breithalbfett | T 001: 081 0961 Nubian |
| T 001: 081 0086 Antique Olive schmalfett | T 001: 081 0563 Folio kursiv breithalbfett | T 001: 081 0966 Old Towne No. 536 |
| T 001: 081 2039 Arabella Favorit | T 001: 081 0572 Forelle Auszeichnung | T 001: 081 0970 Optima normal |
| T 001: 081 2041 Arsis normal | T 001: 081 0578 Forum II | T 001: 081 0976 Optima kursiv |
| T 001: 081 0104 Augustea kursiv fett | T 001: 081 0618 Futura Buchschrift | T 001: 081 0983 Optima halbfett |
| T 001: 081 2042 Augustea licht | T 001: 081 0594 Futura dreiviertelfett | T 001: 081 0989 Orator |
| T 001: 081 0107 Aurora-Grotesk mager | T 001: 081 0598 Futura fett | T 001: 081 0995 Palatino normal |
| T 001: 081 0111 Aurora-Grotesk halbfett | T 001: 081 0631 Garamond (STEMPEL) normal | T 001: 081 1012 Pierrot |
| T 001: 081 1575 Aurora-Grotesk dreiviertelfett | T 001: 081 0635 Garamond (STEMPEL) kursiv | T 001: 081 1057 Primus |
| T 001: 081 0119 Aurora-Grotesk kursiv fett | T 001: 081 0637 Garamond (STEMPEL) halbfett | T 001: 081 1079 Reform-Grotesk |
| T 001: 081 0125 Aurora-Grotesk breithalbfett | T 001: 081 0658 Garamont (HAAS) kursiv | T 001: 081 1090 Roc normal |
| T 001: 081 0130 Baskerville (BERTHOLD) normal | T 001: 081 0640 Garamont (AMSTERDAM) normal | T 001: 081 1104 Schadow-Antiqua mager |
| T 001: 081 0129 Baskerville (STEMPEL) kursiv | T 001: 081 0644 Garamont (AMSTERDAM) kursiv | T 001: 081 1106 Schadow-Antiqua kursiv |
| T 001: 081 1821 Bernhard Gothic mager | T 001: 081 0664 Gill Sans normal | T 001: 081 1108 Schadow-Antiqua halbfett |
| T 001: 081 1590 Bodoni-Antiqua (BERTHOLD) normal | T 001: 081 0702 Grotesk schmal | T 001: 081 1903 Serif Gothic extrafett |
| T 001: 081 0183 Bodoni-Antiqua (BERTHOLD) halbfett | T 001: 081 0724 Helvetica normal | T 001: 081 1909 Serif Gothic ultrafett |
| | T 001: 081 0728 Helvetica kursiv | T 001: 081 1130 Skizze |
| T 001: 081 0205 Bodoni (HAAS) kursiv halbfett | T 001: 081 0731 Helvetica halbfett | T 001: 081 1135 Slogan |
| T 001: 081 0192 Bodoni-Antiqua (AMSTERDAM) normal | T 001: 081 0741 Helvetica schmalhalbfett | T 001: 081 1654 Souvenir mager |
| | T 001: 081 0750 Helvetica breitfett | T 001: 081 1660 Souvenir kursiv mager |
| T 001: 081 1853 Boldiz | T 001: 081 0756 Herold Reklameschrift | T 001: 081 1666 Souvenir normal |
| T 001: 081 1864 Bulk | T 001: 081 0754 Herold schmal | T 001: 081 1671 Souvenir kursiv |
| T 001: 081 0247 Caslon 540 (ATF) kursiv | T 001: 081 0771 Impressum mager | T 001: 081 1677 Souvenir halbfett |
| T 001: 081 0245 Caslon 471 (HAAS) kursiv | T 001: 081 0783 Impuls | T 001: 081 1682 Souvenir kursiv halbfett |
| T 001: 081 0273 Century (ATF) kursiv | T 001: 081 0794 Jaguar | T 001: 081 1687 Souvenir fett |
| T 001: 081 0265 Century (LINOTYPE) schmalhalbfett | T 001: 081 0796 Janson-Antiqua | T 001: 081 1694 Souvenir kursiv fett |
| | T 001: 081 0799 Janson kursiv | T 001: 081 1145 Steinschrift |
| T 001: 081 0287 Charleston | T 001: 081 1848 Janus | T 001: 081 1153 Stop 2 |
| T 001: 081 0309 Cheltenham eng halbfett | T 001: 081 1892 Jockey | T 001: 081 1161 Tannenberg |
| T 001: 081 2043 Chisel | T 001: 081 0821 Kabel schattiert | T 001: 081 1176 Times New Roman |
| T 001: 081 1717 Churchward Deep Shadow normal | T 001: 081 0830 Künstlerschreibschrift fett | T 001: 081 1183 Times fett |
| T 001: 081 1722 Churchward Deep Shadow kursiv | T 001: 081 0840 Latin Wide | T 001: 081 1187 Times kursiv fett |
| T 001: 081 2018 Churchward Design 70 Lines Deep Shadow normal | T 001: 081 1870 Latus | T 001: 081 1859 Triton |
| | T 001: 081 0849 Lettres Ornées | T 001: 081 1208 Trump-Mediäval fett |
| T 001: 081 2024 Churchward Design 70 Lines Deep Shadow kursiv | T 001: 081 0853 Lichte Fette Grotesk | T 001: 081 2033 Tyfa-Antiqua normal |
| | T 001: 081 1621 LSC Caslon No. 223 mager | T 001: 081 1244 Univers 49 |
| T 001: 081 0360 Clarendon mager | T 001: 081 1626 LSC Caslon No. 223 kursiv mager | T 001: 081 1267 Univers 59 |
| T 001: 081 0365 Clarendon kräftig | T 001: 081 1633 LSC Caslon No. 223 normal | T 001: 081 1259 Univers 57 |
| T 001: 081 1738 Clarendon breitfett | T 001: 081 1638 LSC Caslon No. 223 kursiv | T 001: 081 1290 Univers 67 |
| T 001: 081 0382 Columbia | T 001: 081 1643 LSC Caslon No. 223 fett | T 001: 081 1296 Univers 68 |
| T 001: 081 0394 Cooper Black normal | T 001: 081 1649 LSC Caslon No. 223 kursiv fett | T 001: 081 1271 Univers 63 |
| T 001: 081 0406 Cooper Black licht | T 001: 081 1728 Media normal | T 001: 081 1302 Univers 75 |
| T 001: 081 1750 Couture Antiqua | T 001: 081 1733 Media fett | T 001: 081 1357 Viola |
| T 001: 081 0413 Craw Modern normal | T 001: 081 1887 Media Inline fett | T 001: 081 1360 Volta normal |
| T 001: 081 1761 Datonga | T 001: 081 1881 Media Kontur fett | T 001: 081 1368 Volta kursiv halbfett |
| T 001: 081 1745 Domino | T 001: 081 1876 Media Outline fett | T 001: 081 1376 Walbaum-Antiqua normal |
| T 001: 081 0450 Egizio fett | T 001: 081 1712 Milano Roman | T 001: 081 1379 Walbaum kursiv |
| T 001: 081 0458 Egyptienne schmalfett | T 001: 081 0908 Mistral | T 001: 081 1387 Weiß Rundgotisch 1 |
| T 001: 081 0466 Egyptienne breit schattiert | T 001: 081 0911 Modern No. 20 normal | T 001: 081 1388 Weiß Rundgotisch 2 |
| T 001: 081 0502 Eurostile fett | T 001: 081 0913 Modern No. 20 kursiv | T 001: 081 1772 Wiegands Adbold |
| T 001: 081 0510 Eurostile breitfett | T 001: 081 0916 Mona Lisa | T 001: 081 1766 Wiegands Roundhead |
| | T 001: 081 1897 Motter Tektura halbfett | T 001: 081 1396 Windsor fett |

# TR 002
Türkische Belegung
Turkish Layout
Disposition turc

| | | |
|---|---|---|
| TR 002: 081 0020 Akzidenz-Grotesk super | TR 002: 081 0613 Futura extrafett schmal | TR 002: 081 1910 Serif Gothic ultrafett |
| TR 002: 081 0108 Aurora-Grotesk mager | TR 002: 081 0633 Garamond (STEMPEL) normal | TR 002: 081 1655 Souvenir mager |
| TR 002: 081 1822 Bernhard Gothic mager | TR 002: 081 0654 Garamont (HAAS) normal | TR 002: 081 1662 Souvenir kursiv mager |
| TR 002: 081 0186 Bodoni (BERTHOLD) kursiv halbfett | TR 002: 081 0649 Garamont (AMSTERDAM) halbfett | TR 002: 081 1667 Souvenir normal |
| | TR 002: 081 0707 Grotesk breitfett | TR 002: 081 1672 Souvenir kursiv |
| TR 002: 081 0189 Bodoni-Antiqua (BERTHOLD) schmalfett | TR 002: 081 0748 Helvetica breithalbfett | TR 002: 081 1678 Souvenir halbfett |
| | TR 002: 081 0765 IBM Dokument | TR 002: 081 1683 Souvenir kursiv halbfett |
| TR 002: 081 0202 Bodoni-Antiqua (DEBERNY & PEIGNOT) halbfett | TR 002: 081 1849 Janus | TR 002: 081 1688 Souvenir fett |
| | TR 002: 081 1893 Jockey | TR 002: 081 1142 Steile Futura schrägfett |
| TR 002: 081 1855 Boldiz | TR 002: 081 0827 Künstlerschreibschrift halbfett | TR 002: 081 1860 Triton |
| TR 002: 081 1865 Bulk | TR 002: 081 0862 Lightline Gothic | TR 002: 081 1252 Univers 55 |
| TR 002: 081 1718 Churchward Design 70 Deep Shadow normal | TR 002: 081 1622 LSC Caslon No. 223 mager | TR 002: 081 1264 Univers 58 |
| | TR 002: 081 1628 LSC Caslon No. 223 kursiv mager | TR 002: 081 1291 Univers 67 |
| TR 002: 081 1723 Churchward Design 7o Deep Shadow kursiv | TR 002: 081 1634 LSC Caslon No. 223 normal | TR 002: 081 1343 Venus schmalmager |
| | TR 002: 081 1639 LSC Caslon No. 223 kursiv | TR 002: 081 1774 Wiegands Adbold |
| TR 002: 081 2019 Churchward Design 70 Lines Deep Shadow normal | TR 002: 081 1645 LSC Caslon No. 223 fett | TR 002: 081 1767 Wiegands Roundhead |
| | TR 002: 081 1650 LSC Caslon No. 223 kursiv fett | |
| TR 002: 081 2025 Churchward Desing 70 Lines Deep Shadow kursiv | TR 002: 081 1729 Media normal | |
| | TR 002: 081 1734 Media fett | |
| TR 002: 081 1740 Clarendon breitfett | TR 002: 081 1888 Media Inline fett | |
| TR 002: 081 0396 Cooper Black normal | TR 002: 081 1882 Media Kontur fett | |
| TR 002: 081 1751 Couture Antiqua | TR 002: 081 1877 Media Outline fett | |
| TR 002: 081 1762 Datonga | TR 002: 081 1713 Milano Roman | |
| TR 002: 081 1746 Domino | TR 002: 081 0909 Mistral | |
| TR 002: 081 0499 Eurostile normal | TR 002: 081 0917 Mona Lisa | |
| TR 002: 081 0507 Eurostile breit | TR 002: 081 1898 Motter Tektura halbfett | |
| TR 002: 081 0576 Forum I | TR 002: 081 1700 Murrpoint fett | |
| TR 002: 081 0619 Futura Buchschnitt | TR 002: 081 1705 Murrpoint Swing fett | |
| TR 002: 081 0589 Futura halbfett | TR 002: 081 1048 Post-Antiqua normal | |
| TR 002: 081 0592 Futura schräg halbfett | TR 002: 081 1905 Serif Gothic extrafett | |
| TR 002: 081 0604 Futura schmalhalbfett | | |

## J 003 — Jugoslawische Belegung / Serbo-croatian layout / Disposition serbo-croato

| | | |
|---|---|---|
| J 003: 081 0003 Akzidenz-Grotesk normal | J 003: 081 0460 Egyptienne schmalfett | J 003: 081 1008 Permanent breithalbfett |
| J 003: 081 0010 Akzidenz-Grotesk kursiv | J 003: 081 0490 Erbar-Grotesk halbfett | J 003: 081 0714 Permanent Headline normal |
| J 003: 081 0021 Akzidenz-Grotesk super | J 003: 081 0570 Folio extrafett | J 003: 081 1088 Roc mager |
| J 003: 081 0040 Akzidenz-Grotesk breit | J 003: 081 0536 Folio kursiv mager | J 003: 081 1092 Roc normal |
| J 003: 081 0046 Akzidenz-Grotesk breitfett | J 003: 081 0554 Folio schmalfett | J 003: 081 1906 Serif Gothic extrafett |
| J 003: 081 0072 Annonce licht fett | J 003: 081 0567 Folio breitfett | J 003: 081 1911 Serif Gothic ultrafett |
| J 003: 081 0077 Antiqua 505 fett | J 003: 081 0605 Futura schmalhalbfett | J 003: 081 1132 Skizze |
| J 003: 081 0084 Antique Olive fett | J 003: 081 0766 IBM-Dokument | J 003: 081 1656 Souvenir mager |
| J 003: 081 0091 Antique Olive Nord kursiv | J 003: 081 0780 Imprimatur fett | J 003: 081 1663 Souvenir kursiv mager |
| J 003: 081 0112 Aurora Grotesk halbfett | J 003: 081 0788 Information schmalfett | J 003: 081 1668 Souvenir normal |
| J 003: 081 0117 Aurora Grotesk fett | J 003: 081 1850 Janus | J 003: 081 1673 Souvenir kursiv |
| J 003: 081 1824 Bernhard Gothic mager | J 003: 081 1894 Jockey | J 003: 081 1679 Souvenir halbfett |
| J 003: 081 0165 Bison | J 003: 081 1873 Latus | J 003: 081 1684 Souvenir kursiv halbfett |
| J 003: 081 0181 Bodoni (BERTHOLD) kursiv | J 003: 081 1623 LSC Caslon No. 223 mager | J 003: 081 1690 Souvenir fett |
| J 003: 081 0206 Bodoni (HAAS) kursiv halbfett | J 003: 081 1629 LSC Caslon No. 223 kursiv mager | J 003: 081 1177 Times New Roman |
| J 003: 081 0209 Bodoni-Antiqua (NEUFVILLE) Versal | J 003: 081 1635 LSC Caslon No. 223 normal | J 003: 081 1180 Times kursiv |
| J 003: 081 0198 Bodoni fett | J 003: 081 1640 LSC Caslon No. 223 kursiv | J 003: 081 1184 Times fett |
| J 003: 081 1856 Boldiz | J 003: 081 1646 LSC Caslon No. 223 fett | J 003: 081 1189 Times kursiv fett |
| J 003: 081 1866 Bulk | J 003: 081 1651 LSC Caslon No. 223 kursiv fett | J 003: 081 1194 Torino normal |
| J 003: 081 0271 Century (ATF) expanded | J 003: 081 1730 Media normal | J 003: 081 1861 Triton |
| J 003: 081 1724 Churchward Design 70 Deep Shadow kursiv | J 003: 081 1735 Media fett | J 003: 081 1213 Trump-Mediäval kursiv fett |
| | J 003: 081 1889 Media Inline fett | J 003: 081 1304 Univers 75 |
| J 003: 081 2021 Churchward Design 70 Lines Deep Shadow normal | J 003: 081 1883 Media Kontur fett | J 003: 081 1257 Univers 56 |
| | J 003: 081 1878 Media Outline.fett | J 003: 081 1287 Univers 66 |
| J 003: 081 2026 Churchward Design 7o Lines Deep Shadow kursiv | J 003: 081 1714 Milano Roman | J 003: 081 1239 Univers 47 |
| | J 003: 081 1900 Motter Tektura halbfett | J 003: 081 1292 Univers 67 |
| J 003: 081 0354 Circo | J 003: 081 1701 Murrpoint fett | J 003: 081 1249 Univers 53 |
| J 003: 081 1741 Clarendon breitfett | J 003: 081 1706 Murrpoint Swing fett | J 003: 081 1300 Univers 73 |
| J 003: 081 0402 Cooper Black kursiv | J 003: 081 0933 Neuzeit-Grotesk fett | J 003: 081 1326 Vendôme fett |
| J 003: 081 0408 Cooper Black licht | J 003: 081 0948 Nobel schmal | J 003: 081 1377 Walbaum-Antiqua normal |
| J 003: 081 1752 Couture Antiqua | J 003: 081 0956 Normande kursiv | J 003: 081 1768 Wiegands Roundhead |
| J 003: 081 1763 Datonga | J 003: 081 0986 Optima halbfett | |
| J 003: 081 1747 Domino | J 003: 081 1004 Permanent halbfett | |

## IS 004 — Isländische Belegung / Icelandic layout / Disposition islandais

| | | |
|---|---|---|
| IS 004: 081 0006 Akzidenz-Grotesk mager | IS 004: 081 0472 Egyptienne Filetée | IS 004: 081 1136 Slogan |
| IS 004: 081 0013 Akzidenz-Grotesk halbfett | IS 004: 081 0511 Eurostile breitfett | IS 004: 081 1146 Steinschrift |
| IS 004: 081 0041 Akzidenz-Grotesk breit | IS 004: 081 0831 Künstlerschreibschrift fett | IS 004: 081 1162 Tannenberg |
| IS 004: 081 1560 Akzidenz-Grotesk breitfett | IS 004: 081 0974 Optima normal | IS 004: 081 1185 Times fett |
| IS 004: 081 0067 Amsterdam 698 | IS 004: 081 0981 Optima kursiv | IS 004: 081 1195 Torino normal |
| IS 004: 081 1565 Annonce licht fett | IS 004: 081 0987 Optima halbfett | IS 004: 081 1209 Trump-Mediäval fett |
| IS 004: 081 0203 Bodoni-Antiqua (HAAS) halbfett | IS 004: 081 1077 Promotor | IS 004: 081 1281 Univers 65 |
| IS 004: 081 0227 Brasilia normal | IS 004: 081 1091 Roc normal | IS 004: 081 1275 Univers 63 |
| IS 004: 081 0284 Champion | IS 004: 081 1127 Signum | IS 004: 081 1363 Volta normal |

## P 005 — Polnische Belegung / Polish layout / Disposition polonais

| | | |
|---|---|---|
| P 005: 081 0032 Akzidenz-Grotesk extrafett | P 005: 081 0645 Garamont (AMSTERDAM) kursiv | P 005: 081 1715 Media Milano Roman |
| P 005: 081 1825 Bernhard Gothic mager | P 005: 081 0725 Helvetica normal | P 005: 081 1901 Motter Tektura halbfett |
| P 005: 081 0177 Bodoni-Antiqua (BERTHOLD) normal | P 005: 081 0732 Helvetica halbfett | P 005: 081 1702 Murrpoint fett |
| P 005: 081 0184 Bodoni-Antiqua (BERTHOLD) halbfett | P 005: 081 0743 Helvetica schmalfett | P 005: 081 1707 Murrpoint Swing fett |
| | P 005: 081 1851 Janus | P 005: 081 1907 Serif Gothic extrafett |
| P 005: 081 1857 Boldiz | P 005: 081 1895 Jockey | P 005: 081 1912 Serif Gothic ultrafett |
| P 005: 081 1867 Bulk | P 005: 081 1874 Latus | P 005: 081 1657 Souvenir mager |
| P 005: 081 1726 Churchward Design 70 Deep Shadow kursiv | P 005: 081 1624 LSC Caslon No. 223 mager | P 005: 081 1664 Souvenir kursiv mager |
| | P 005: 081 1631 LSC Caslon No. 223 kursiv mager | P 005: 081 1669 Souvenir normal |
| P 005: 081 2022 Churchward Design 70 Lines Deep Shadow normal | P 005: 081 1636 LSC Caslon No. 223 normal | P 005: 081 1674 Souvenir kursiv |
| | P 005: 081 1641 LSC Caslon No. 223 kursiv | P 005: 081 1680 Souvenir halbfett |
| P 005: 081 2027 Churchward Design 70 Lines Deep Shadow kursiv | P 005: 081 1647 LSC Caslon No. 223 fett | P 005: 081 1685 Souvenir kursiv halbfett |
| | P 005: 081 1652 LSC Caslon No. 223 kursiv fett | P 005: 081 1691 Souvenir fett |
| P 005: 081 1743 Clarendon breitfett | P 005: 081 1731 Media normal | P 005: 081 1697 Souvenir kursiv fett |
| P 005: 081 1753 Couture Antiqua | P 005: 081 1736 Media fett | P 005: 081 1862 Triton |
| P 005: 081 1764 Datonga | P 005: 081 1890 Media Inline fett | P 005: 081 1282 Univers 65 |
| P 005: 081 1748 Domino | P 005: 081 1884 Media Kontur fett | P 005: 081 1293 Univers 67 |
| P 005: 081 0642 Garamont (AMSTERDAM) normal | P 005: 081 1879 Media Outline fett | P 005: 081 1769 Wiegands Roundhead |

## S 007 — Slawische Belegung / Slavonic layout / Disposition slave

| | | |
|---|---|---|
| S 007: 081 2119 Antique Olive mager | S 007: 081 2293 Futura fett | S 007: 081 2087 Korinna extrafett |
| S 007: 081 2191 Antique Olive normal | S 007: 081 2294 Futura extrafett | S 007: 081 2090 Korinna licht |
| S 007: 081 2290 Antique Olive fett | S 007: 081 0610 Futura extrafett schmal | S 007: 081 2147 Octavia halbfett |
| S 007: 081 2316 Antique Olive Nord normal | S 007: 081 2109 Garamond (ITC) ultra | S 007: 081 2136 Paperline |
| S 007: 081 2116 Avant Garde Gothic Buch | S 007: 081 2112 Garamond (ITC) kursiv ultra | S 007: 081 2072 Serif Gothic Black |
| S 007: 081 2192 Avant Garde Gothic normal | S 007: 081 2321 Garamont (AMSTERDAM) normal | S 007: 081 2021 Serif Gothic licht |
| S 007: 081 2050 Avant Garde Gothic schmalhalbfett | S 007: 081 2322 Garamont (AMSTERDAM) kursiv | S 007: 081 1978 Times New Roman |
| | S 007: 081 2314 Garamont (AMSTERDAM) halbfett | S 007: 081 1182 Times fett |
| S 007: 081 2057 Avant Garde Gothic schmalfett | S 007: 081 1979 Gill Sans fett | S 007: 081 2128 Twice |
| S 007: 081 2382 Baskerville kursiv | S 007: 081 0669 Gill Kayo | S 007: 081 2201 Univers 45 |
| S 007: 081 2323 Bodoni-Antiqua normal | S 007: 081 2143 Graphis extrafett | S 007: 081 2154 Univers 55 |
| S 007: 081 2195 Clarendon mager | S 007: 081 2292 Helvetica fett | S 007: 081 0252 Univers 65 |
| S 007: 081 2196 Clarendon fett | S 007: 081 2320 Helvetica normal | S 007: 081 0255 Univers 66 |
| S 007: 081 2197 Concorde normal | S 007: 081 2299 Helvetica halbfett | S 007: 081 0257 Univers 75 |
| S 007: 081 2198 Concorde kursiv | S 007: 081 0722 Helvetica fett | S 007: 081 0256 Univers 67 |
| S 007: 081 2199 Concorde halbfett | S 007: 081 2139 Jalousette | S 007: 081 2313 Univers 83 |
| S 007: 081 2302 Cooper Black normal | S 007: 081 1975 Kabel fett | |
| S 007: 081 2200 Cooper Black licht | S 007: 081 2076 Korinna normal | |
| S 007: 081 2122 Dektiv Double | S 007: 081 2080 Korinna halbfett | |
| S 007: 081 0310 Futura Buchschrift | S 007: 081 2084 Korinna fett | |

# A 008

Anglo-Amerikanische Belegung
Anglo-american layout
Disposition anglo-américaine

| | | |
|---|---|---|
| A 008: 081 2120  Antique Olive mager | A 008: 081 2113  Garamond (ITC) kursiv ultra | A 008: 081 2088  Korinna extrafett |
| A 008: 081 2117  Avant Garde Gothic Buch | A 008: 081 2144  Graphic extrafett | A 008: 081 2091  Korinna licht |
| A 008: 081 2052  Avant Garde Gothic schmalhalbfett | A 008: 081 2300  Helvetica halbfett | A 008: 081 2148  Octavia halbfett |
| A 008: 081 2058  Avant Garde Gothic schmalfett | A 008: 081 2140  Jalousette | A 008: 081 2137  Paperline |
| A 008: 081 2303  Cooper Black normal | A 008: 081 2077  Korinna normal | A 008: 081 2073  Serif Gothic Black |
| A 008: 081 2123  Dektiv Double | A 008: 081 2081  Korinna halbfett | A 008: 081 2011  Serif Gothic licht |
| A 008: 081 2110  Garamond (ITC) ultra | A 008: 081 2085  Korinna fett | A 008: 081 2130  Twice |

**BERTHOLD HEADLINES**

# BERTHOLD HEADLINES

«Berthold Fototypes E3,
Berthold Headlines»
wurde in einer Erstauflage von
8000 Exemplaren gedruckt.
Dieses Buch hat die Nummer:

3481 ✻

# NACHTRAGSDIENST E 3

Diese Karte berechtigt den Einsender, den Berthold-Nachtragsdienst kostenlos in Anspruch zu nehmen.

Aus: «Berthold Fototypes E3, Berthold Headlines», 1. Auflage 1982

3481 ✻

☐ Nehmen Sie mich in den Berthold-Nachtragsdienst auf

Ich bestelle gegen Rechnung:

☐ Exemplare E3, à 68 DM
(Bestellnummer 649 5 398)

☐ Größenmaß(e) à 10 DM
(Bestellnummer 272 0134)

☐ Zeilenmaß(e) à 18 DM
(Bestellnummer 272 0130)

Datum und Unterschrift                                      Rechnungsnummer

---

«Berthold Fototypes E3,
Berthold Headlines»
was printed as a first edition
of 8000.
This book bears the number:

3481 ✻

# UP-DATING SERVICE E 3

This card entitles the sender to take advantage of the Berthold up-dating service free-of-charge.

From: «Berthold Fototypes E3, Berthold Headlines», 1st edition 1982

3481 ✻

☐ Please include me in the Berthold-up-dating service

I would like to order on receipt:

☐ copies of E3, at 68 DM each
(order no. 649 5 398)

☐ type- and rule-size gauge(s) at
10 DM each (order no. 272 0134)

☐ leading gauge(s) at 18 DM each
(order no. 272 0130)

Date and signature                                      Total amount to be paid

---

«Berthold Fototypes E3,
Berthold Headlines»
a été imprimée
à 8000 exemplaires pour sa
première édition.
Ce volume porte le numéro:

3481 ✻

# SERVICE D'ENVOI E 3

Cette carte donne droit
à l'envoi gratuit de toutes les
feuilles additionelles.

De: «Berthold Fototypes E3, Berthold Headlines», 1re édition 1982

3481 ✻

☐ Veuillez me faire les envois des feuilles additionnelles

Je commande avec facturation:

☐ Exemplaires E3, à DM 68
(Nr. de commande 649 5 398)

☐ Indicateur(s) des hauteurs d'œil à
DM 10 (Nr. de comm. 272 0134)

☐ Indicateur(s) d'interlignage à
DM 18 (Nr. de comm. 272 0130)

Date et signature                                      Montant de la facture

Absender:

H. Berthold AG
Teltowkanalstraße 1–4
Abt. Öffentlichkeitsarbeit Schrift
D–1000 Berlin 46

Sender:

H. Berthold AG
Teltowkanalstraße 1–4
Abt. Öffentlichkeitsarbeit Schrift
D–1000 Berlin 46

Envoyer:

H. Berthold AG
Teltowkanalstraße 1–4
Abt. Öffentlichkeitsarbeit Schrift
D–1000 Berlin 46